Lecture Notes in Computer Scie

Commenced Publication in 1973
Founding and Former Series Editors:
Gerhard Goos, Juris Hartmanis, and Jan van Leeuwen

Alberto Apostolico Massimo Melucci (Eds.)

String Processing and Information Retrieval

11th International Conference, SPIRE 2004
Padova, Italy, October 5-8, 2004
Proceedings

Springer

Volume Editors

Alberto Apostolico
Purdue University, Department of Computer Sciences
250 N. University Street, West Lafayette, IN, 47907-2066, USA
E-mail: axa@cs.purdue.edu

Alberto Apostolico
Massimo Melucci
University of Padova, Department of Information Engineering
Via Gradenigo 6a, 35131 Padova, Italy
E-mail: {axa,melo}@dei.unipd.it

Library of Congress Control Number: 2004112520

CR Subject Classification (1998): H.3, H.2.8, I.2, E.1, E.5, F.2.2

ISSN 0302-9743
ISBN 3-540-23210-9 Springer Berlin Heidelberg New York

Springer is a part of Springer Science+Business Media

springeronline.com

Printed in Germany

Typesetting: Camera-ready by author, data conversion by Olgun Computergrafik
Printed on acid-free paper SPIN: 11325949 06/3142 5 4 3 2 1 0

Foreword

The papers contained in this volume were presented at the 11th Conference on String Processing and Information Retrieval (SPIRE), held Oct. 5–8, 2004 at the Department of Information Engineering of the University of Padova, Italy. They were selected from 123 papers submitted in response to the call for papers. In addition, there were invited lectures by C.J. van Rijsbergen (University of Glasgow, UK) and Setsuo Arikawa (Kyushu University, Japan). In view of the large number of good-quality submissions, some were accepted this year also as short abstracts. These also appear in the proceedings.

Papers solicited for SPIRE 2004 were meant to constitute original contributions to areas such as string pattern searching, matching and discovery; data compression; text and data mining; machine learning; tasks, methods, algorithms, media, and evaluation in information retrieval; digital libraries; and applications to and interactions with domains such as genome analysis, speech and natural language processing, Web links and communities, and multilingual data.

SPIRE has its origins in the South American Workshop on String Processing which was first held in 1993. Starting in 1998, the focus of the symposium was broadened to include the area of information retrieval due to the common emphasis on information processing. The first 10 meetings were held in Belo Horizonte (Brazil, 1993), Valparaiso (Chile, 1995), Recife (Brazil, 1996), Valparaiso (Chile, 1997), Santa Cruz (Bolivia, 1998), Cancun (Mexico, 1999), A Coruña (Spain, 2000), Laguna San Rafael (Chile, 2001), Lisbon (Portugal, 2002), and Manaus (Brazil, 2003).

SPIRE 2004 was held as part of Dialogues 2004, a concerted series of conferences and satellite meetings fostering exchange and integration in the modeling, design and implementation of advanced tools for the representation, encoding, storage, search, retrieval and discovery of information and knowledge. In Dialogues 2004, the companion conferences for SPIRE were the 15th International Conference on Algorithmic Learning Theory and the 7th International Conference on Discovery Science.

The Program Committee consisted of: Rakesh Agrawal, *IBM Almaden, USA*, Maristella Agosti, *Univ. of Padova, Italy*, Amihood Amir, *Bar-Ilan Univ., Israel and Georgia Tech, USA*, Alberto Apostolico, *Univ. of Padova, Italy and Purdue Univ., USA (Chair)*, Ricardo Baeza-Yates, *Univ. of Chile, Chile*, Krishna Bharat, *Google Inc., USA*, Andrei Broder, *IBM T.J. Watson Research Center, Hawthorne, USA*, Maxime Crochemore, *Univ. of Marne la Vallée, France*, Bruce Croft, *Univ. of Massachusetts Amherst, USA*, Pablo de la Fuente, *Univ. of Valladolid, Spain*, Edleno S. de Moura, *Univ. Federal of Amazonas, Brazil*, Edward Fox, *Virginia Tech., USA*, Norbert Fuhr, *Univ. of Duisburg, Germany*, Raffaele Giancarlo, *Univ. of Palermo, Italy*, Roberto Grossi, *Univ. of Pisa, Italy*, Costas Iliopoulos, *King's College London, UK*, Gad M. Landau, *Univ. of Haifa, Israel*, Joao Meidanis, *Univ. of Campinas, Brazil*, Massimo Melucci, *Univ.*

of Padova, Italy (Chair), Alistair Moffat, *Univ. of Melbourne, Australia*, Mario A. Nascimento, *Univ. of Alberta, Canada*, Arlindo L. Oliveira, *Instituto Superior Técnico/INESC-ID, Portugal*, Laxmi Parida, *IBM T.J. Watson Research Center, Yorktown, USA*, Kunsoo Park, *Seoul National Univ., South Korea*, Berthier Ribeiro-Neto, *Univ. Federal of Minas Gerais, Brazil*, Stephen Robertson, *Microsoft Research, UK*, Marie-France Sagot, *INRIA Rhônes-Alpes, France*, Fabrizio Sebastiani, *ISTI CNR, Italy*, Ayumi Shinohara, *Kyushu Univ., Japan*, Alan Smeaton, *Dublin City Univ., Ireland*, James Storer, *Brandeis Univ., USA*, Wojciech Szpankowski, *Purdue Univ., USA*, Esko Ukkonen, *Univ. of Helsinki, Finland*, Keith van Rijsbergen, *Univ. of Glasgow, UK*, Jeffrey S. Vitter, *Purdue Univ., USA*, Hugh E. Williams, *RMIT Univ., Australia*, Nivio Ziviani, *Univ. Federal of Minas Gerais, Brazil*.

The following external reviewers helped with the selection of papers: Eduardo Abinader, *Federal Univ. of Amazonas, Brazil*, Halil Ali, *RMIT Univ., Australia*, Charles Ornelas Almeida, *Federal Univ. of Minas Gerais, Brazil*, Shlomo Argamon, *Illinois Institute of Technology*, Hagay Aronowitz, *Bar-Ilan University*, Michela Bacchin, *Univ. of Padova, Italy*, Claudine Santos Badue, *Federal Univ. of Minas Gerais, Brazil*, Bodo Billerbeck, *RMIT Univ., Australia*, Fabiano Cupertino Botelho, *Federal Univ. of Minas Gerais, Brazil*, Pável Calado, *Federal Univ. of Minas Gerais, Brazil*, Alexandra Carvalho, *Instituto Superior Técnico/INESC-ID, Portugal*, Tom Conway, *Inquirion Pty. Ltd., Australia*, Ido Dagan, *Bar-Ilan University*, Ilmerio Reis da Silva, *Federal Univ. of Uberlandia, Brazil*, Giorgio Maria Di Nunzio, *Univ. of Padova, Italy*, Paolo Ferragina, *Universita di Pisa*, Nicola Ferro, *Univ. of Padova, Italy*, Gudrun Fischer, *Univ. of Duisburg-Essen, Germany*, Bruno Maciel Fonseca, *Federal Univ. of Minas Gerais, Brazil*, Leszek Gasieniec, *University of Liverpool*, Gosta Grahne, *Concordia Univ., Canada*, Danny Hermelin, *Univ. of Haifa, Israel*, Heikki Hyyrö, *PRESTO, JST, Japan*, Juha Kärkkäinen, *Univ. of Helsinki, Finland*, Carmel Kent, *Univ. of Haifa, Israel*, Dong Kyue Kim, *Pusan National Univ., South Korea*, Sung-Ryul Kim, *Konkuk Univ., South Korea*, Tomi Klein, *Bar-Ilan University*, Anisio Mendes Lacerda, *Federal Univ. of Minas Gerais, Brazil*, Alberto Lavelli, *ITC-IRST, Italy*, Kjell Lemström, *Univ. of Helsinki, Finland*, Veli Mäkinen, *Univ. of Helsinki, Finland*, Henrik Nottelmann, *Univ. of Duisburg-Essen*, Nicola Orio, *Univ. of Padova*, Kimmo Palin, *Univ. of Helsinki, Finland*, Heejin Park, *Hanyang Univ., South Korea*, Alvaro Rodrigues Pereira Junior, *Federal Univ. of Minas Gerais, Brazil*, Marco Antônio Pinheiro de Cristo, *Federal Univ. of Minas Gerais, Brazil*, Cinzia Pizzi, *Univ. of Padova, Italy*, Luca Pretto, *Univ. of Padova, Italy*, Thierson Couto Rosa, *Federal Univ. of Minas Gerais, Brazil*, Luís Russo, *Instituto Superior Técnico/INESC-ID, Portugal*, Falk Scholer, *RMIT Univ., Australia*, Shinichi Shimozono, *Kyushu Institute of Technology, Japan*, Dekel Tsur, *CRI Univ. of Haifa, Israel*, Bruno Augusto Vivas e Possas, *Federal Univ. of Minas Gerais, Brazil*, Oren Weimann, *Univ. of Haifa, Israel*, Jianfei Zhu, *Concordia Univ., Canada*, Michal Ziv-Ukelson, *Technion Haifa, Israel*.

SPIRE 2004 was held in cooperation with the ACM Special Interest Group in Information Retrieval (ACM SIGIR), and was sponsored by the Department of Information Engineering of the University of Padova, the Institute of High Performance Computing and Networking (ICAR) of the National Research Council (CNR), the Italian Association for Informatics and Automatic Computation (AICA), and Elsevier.

We thank Valerio Pulese and Angela Visco for their support in the organization of SPIRE.

Padova, October 2004

Alberto Apostolico
Massimo Melucci

In Cooperation with

Special Interest Group in Information Retrieval (SIGIR)

Sponsoring Institutions

Table of Contents

Efficient One Dimensional Real Scaled Matching

Amihood Amir[1,⋆], Ayelet Butman[2], Moshe Lewenstein[3], Ely Porat[3], and Dekel Tsur[4]

[1] Bar-Ilan University and Georgia Tech.
amir@cs.biu.ac.il
[2] Holon Academic Institute of Technology
butmosh@zahav.net.il
[3] Bar-Ilan University
{moshe,poratelY}@cs.biu.ac.il
[4] University of Haifa
dekelts@cs.haifa.ac.il

Abstract. *Real Scaled Matching* refers to the problem of finding all locations in the text where the pattern, proportionally enlarged according to an *arbitrary real-sized* scale, appears. Real scaled matching is an important problem that was originally inspired by Computer Vision.
In this paper, we present a new, more precise and realistic, definition for one dimensional real scaled matching, and an efficient algorithm for solving this problem. For a text of length n and a pattern of length m, the algorithm runs in time $O(n \log m + \sqrt{n}m^{3/2}\sqrt{\log m})$.

1 Introduction

The original classical string matching problem [10, 13] was motivated by text searching. Wide advances in technology, e.g. computer vision, multimedia libraries, and web searches in heterogeneous data, have given rise to much study in the field of pattern matching.

Landau and Vishkin [15] examined issues arising from the digitization process. Once the image is digitized, one wants to search it for various data. A whole body of literature examines the problem of seeking an object in an image.

In reality one seldom expects to find an exact match of the object being sought, henceforth referred to as the *pattern*. Rather, it is interesting to find all text locations that "approximately" match the pattern. The types of differences that make up these "approximations" are:

1. *Local Errors* – introduced by differences in the digitization process, noise, and occlusion (the pattern partly obscured by another object).
2. *Scale* – size difference between the image in the pattern and the text.
3. *Rotation* – angle differences between the pattern and text images.

⋆ Partially supported by ISF grant 282/01. Part of this work was done when the author was at Georgia Tech, College of Computing and supported by NSF grant CCR–01–04494.

A. Apostolico and M. Melucci (Eds.): SPIRE 2004, LNCS 3246, pp. 1–9, 2004.

Some early attempts to handle local errors were made in [14]. These results were improved in [8]. The algorithms in [8] heavily depend on the fact that the pattern is a rectangle. In reality this is hardly ever the case. In [6], Amir and Farach show how to deal with local errors in non-rectangular patterns.

The rotation problem is to find all rotated occurrences of a pattern in an image. Fredriksson and Ukkonen [12], made the first step by giving a reasonable definition of rotation in discrete images and introduce a filter for seeking a rotated pattern. Amir et al. [2] presented an $O(n^2m^3)$ time algorithm. This was improved to $O(n^2m^2)$ in [7].

For scaling it was shown [9, 5] that all occurrences of a given rectangular pattern in a text can be found in all discrete scales in linear time. By discrete scales we mean natural numbers, i.e. the pattern scaled to sizes $1, 2, 3, \ldots$.

The first result handling real scales was given in [3]. In this paper, a linear time algorithm was given for one-dimensional real scaled matching. In [4], the problem of two-dimensional real scaled matching was defined, and an efficient algorithm was presented for this problem.

The definition of one-dimensional scaling in [3] has the following drawback: For a pattern P of length m and a scale r, the pattern P scaled by r can have a length which is far from mr. In this paper, we give a more natural definition for scaling, which has the property that the length of P scaled by r is mr rounded to the nearest integer. This definition is derived from the definition of two-dimensional scaling which was given in [4]. We give an efficient algorithm for the scaled matching problem under the new definition of scaling: For a text T of length n and a pattern P of length m, the algorithm finds in T all occurrences of P scaled to any real value in time $O(n \log m + \sqrt{nm}^{3/2}\sqrt{\log m})$.

Roadmap: In section 2 we give the necessary preliminaries and definitions of the problem. In section 3 we present a simple algorithm that straightforwardly finds the scaled matches of the pattern in the text. In section 4 we present our main result, namely, the efficient algorithm for real scaled matching.

2 Scaled Matching Definition

Let T and P be two strings over some finite alphabet Σ. Let n and m be the lengths of T and P, respectively.

Definition 1. *A* pixel *is an interval $(i-1, i]$ on the real line $\mathbb{R}$, where i is an integer. The* center *of a pixel $(i-1, i]$ is its geometric center point, namely the point $i - 0.5$.*

Definition 2. *Let $r \in \mathbb{R}$, $r > 1$. The r-ary* pixel array *for P consists of m intervals of length r, which are called* r-intervals. *The i-th r-interval is $((i-1)r, ir]$. Each interval is identified with the value from Σ: The i-th interval is identified with the i-th letter of P. For each pixel center that is inside some r-interval, we assign the letter that corresponds to that interval. The string obtained by concatenating all the letters assign to the pixel centers from left to right is denoted by P^r, and called P* scaled *to r.*

The *scaled matching problem* is to find all the locations in the text T in which there is an occurrence of P scaled to some $r \geq 1$.

Example 1. Let $P = aabccc$ then $P^{\frac{3}{2}} = aaabbcccc$, and let $T = aabdaaaabb$ $ccccb$. There is an occurrence of P scaled to $\frac{3}{2}$ at text location 6.

Let $x \in \mathbb{R}$. $\|x\|$ denotes the *rounding* of x, i.e.

$$\|x\| = \begin{cases} \lfloor x \rfloor & \text{if the fraction part of } x \text{ is less than } .5 \\ \lceil x \rceil & \text{otherwise.} \end{cases}$$

We need the following technical claim.

Claim. Let k, k', and l be some positive integers.

1. $\{r | \; \|rk\| = l\} = [\frac{l-0.5}{k}, \frac{l+0.5}{k})$.
2. $\{r | \; \|r(k+k')\| - \|rk'\| = l\} \subseteq (\frac{l-1}{k}, \frac{l+1}{k})$.

Proof. The first part follows immediately from the definition of rounding. To prove the second part, note that $x - 0.5 < \|x\| \leq x + 0.5$, so

$$\|r(k+k')\| - \|rk'\| < r(k+k') + 0.5 - (rk' - 0.5) = rk + 1$$

and

$$\|r(k+k')\| - \|rk'\| > r(k+k') - 0.5 - (rk' + 0.5) = rk - 1.$$

Hence, the r's that satisfy $\|r(k+k')\| - \|rk'\| = l$ are those that satisfy $rk - 1 < l < rk + 1$, which implies $\frac{l-1}{k} < r < \frac{l+1}{k}$. □

3 A Local Verification Algorithm

One possible straightforward approach to solving the scaled matching problem is to verify for each location of the text whether the scaled occurrence definition holds at that location. However, even this verification needs some clarification. To simplify, we define below the symbol form and the run-lengths of the symbols separately. This will give a handle on the verification process. An additional benefit is that this representation also compresses the text and pattern and hence will lead to faster algorithms.

Definition 3. *Let $S = \sigma_1\sigma_2\cdots\sigma_n$ be a string over some alphabet Σ. The* run-length representation *of string S is the string $S' = \sigma_1'^{r_1}\sigma_2'^{r_2}\cdots\sigma_k'^{r_k}$ such that: (1) $\sigma_i' \neq \sigma_{i+1}'$ for $1 \leq i < k$; and (2) S can be described as concatenation of the symbol σ_1' repeated r_1 times, the symbol σ_2' repeated r_2 times, ..., and the symbol σ_k' repeated r_k times. We denote by $S^{\Sigma} = \sigma_1'\sigma_2'\cdots\sigma_k'$, the* symbol part *of S', and by $c(S) = r_1r_2\cdots r_k$, the* run-length part *of S' ($c(S)$ is a string over the alphabet of natural numbers).*

The locator function between S and S' is $\mathrm{loc}_S(i) = j$, where j is the index for which $\sum_{l=1}^{j-1} r_l < i \leq \sum_{l=1}^{j} r_l$.

The center *of S, denoted C_S, is the substring of S that contains all the letters of S except the first r_1 letters and the last r_k letters.*

Example 2. Let $S = aaaaaabbcccaabbbddddd$ then $S' = a^6b^2c^3a^2b^3d^5$, $S^\Sigma = abcabd$ and $c(S) = 623235$. The locator function is $\text{loc}_S(1) = 1, \text{loc}_S(2) = 1, \ldots, \text{loc}_S(6) = 1, \text{loc}_S(7) = 2, \ldots, \text{loc}_S(21) = 6$. The center of S is $bbcccaabbb$.

3.1 Reformulating the Definition

Scaled matching requires finding all scaled occurrences of P in T. To achieve this goal we will use P' and T'. There are two requirements for a scaled occurrence of P at a given location of T. The first is that P^Σ matches a substring of T^Σ beginning at location $\text{loc}_T(i)$ of T. This can be verified in linear time with any classical pattern matching algorithm, e.g. [13]. The second requirement is that there is a scale r for which P scales properly to match at the appropriate location in T. For this we will use $c(P)$ and $c(T)$. Since the first requirement is easy to verify, from here on we will focus on the second requirement.

Denote $m' = |c(P)|$ and $n' = |c(T)|$. We also denote $c(P) = p_1, \ldots, p_{m'}$ and $c(T) = t_1, \ldots, t_{n'}$. We assume that $m' \geq 3$ and $n' \geq 3$ otherwise the problem is easily solvable in linear time. When a scaled match occurs at location i of T the location in the compressed text that corresponds to it is $j = \text{loc}_T(i)$. However, only part of the full length of t_j may need to match the scaled pattern. More precisely, a length $\hat{t}_i = \sum_{l=1}^{j} t_l + 1 - i$ piece of t_j needs to match the scaled pattern. The full set of desired scaling requirements follows.

Scaling requirements at text location i, where $\text{loc}_T(i) = j$

$$\begin{aligned}
\|p_1 \cdot r\| &= \hat{t}_i \\
\|(p_1 + p_2) \cdot r\| &= \hat{t}_i + t_{j+1} \\
&\vdots \\
\|(p_1 + \cdots + p_k) \cdot r\| &= \hat{t}_i + t_{j+1} + \cdots + t_{j+k-1} \\
&\vdots \\
\|(p_1 + \cdots + p_{m'-1}) \cdot r\| &= \hat{t}_i + t_{j+1} + \cdots + t_{j+m'-2} \\
\|m \cdot r\| &\leq \hat{t}_i + t_{j+1} + \cdots + t_{j+m'-1}
\end{aligned}$$

The following claim follows from the discussion above and its correctness follows directly from the definition.

Claim. Let P be a pattern and T a text. There is a scaled occurrence of P at location i of T iff P^Σ matches at location $\text{loc}_T(i)$ of T^Σ and the scaling requirements for location i are satisfied.

3.2 The Algorithm

The importance of verifying the scaling requirements efficiently follows from Claim 3.1. The claim below shows that this can be done efficiently.

Claim. Let i be a location of T. The scaling requirements for i can be verified in $O(m')$ time.

Proof. The scaling requirements are verified by finding the set of all scales r that satisfy requirements. By Claim 2, for each of the first $m'-1$ scaling requirements, the set of all r's that satisfy the requirement is an interval of length 1. Moreover, the last scaling requirement demands that $r \in [1, (\hat{t}_i + t_{j+1} + \cdots t_{j+m^{\square}-1} + 0.5)/m)$. The intersection of these intervals is set of all r's for which P^r appears in location i. This intersection can be found in $O(m')$ time. □

The following straightforward algorithm can now be devised: The algorithm checks the scaling requirement for every location i of T.

Running Time: There are $n-m+1$ locations in T. For each location the existence of a scaled match can be checked in $O(m')$ time by Claim 3.2. So the overall time of the algorithm is $O(nm')$.

4 A Dictionary Based Solution

A different approach for solving the scaled matching problem is to create a dictionary containing the run length part of P scaled at all possible scales. Substrings of the compressed text can then be checked for existence in the dictionary. The problem with this solution is that there may be many scales and hence many different strings in the dictionary. In fact, the dictionary to be created could be as large as, or larger than, the running time of the naive algorithm. To circumvent this problem we will keep in the dictionary only scaled instances of the pattern with a scale at most α, where the value of α will be determined later. Checking for occurrences of the pattern with a scale larger than α will be performed using the algorithm from the previous section.

To bound the number of strings in the dictionary, we use the following lemma, which is a special case of Lemma 1 in [4].

Lemma 1. *Let pattern P be scaled to size $l \geq m$. Then there are $k \leq m'$ intervals, $[a_1, a_2), [a_2, a_3), \ldots, [a_k, a_{k+1})$, where $a_1 < a_2 < \cdots < a_{k+1}$ for which the following hold:*

1. *$P^{r_1} = P^{r_2}$ if r_1 and r_2 are in the same interval.*
2. *$P^{r_1} \neq P^{r_2}$ if r_1 and r_2 are in different intervals.*
3. *P^r has length l if and only if $r \in [a_1, a_{k+1})$.*

Proof. By Claim 2, if the length of P^r is l, then r belongs to the interval $I = [\frac{l-0.5}{m}, \frac{l+0.5}{m})$. Consider the r-ary pixel array for P when the value of r goes from $r = \frac{l-0.5}{m}$ to $r = \frac{l+0.5}{m}$. Consider some value of r in which a new scaled pattern is reached, namely $P^r \neq P^{r-\epsilon}$ for every $\epsilon > 0$. By definition, this happens when the right endpoint of some r-interval coincides with some pixel center. The right endpoint of the rightmost r-interval moves a distance of exactly 1 when r goes over I, and each other endpoint moves a distance smaller than 1. In particular, each endpoint coincides with a pixel center at most one time. □

4.1 Building the Dictionary

Let $\mathcal{P}$ be a set containing $c(C_{P^r})$ for every scaled pattern P^r with $r \leq \alpha$. By Lemma 1, the number strings in $\mathcal{P}$ is $O(\alpha m m')$. For each $P' \in \mathcal{P}$, let $R_{P'}$ be the set of all values of r such that $c(C_{P^r}) = P'$. Each set $R_{P'}$ is a union of intervals, and let $|R_{P'}|$ denote the number the intervals in $R_{P'}$.

Example 3. Let $P = abcd$ and $\alpha = 2$. Then,

$$c(P^r) = \begin{cases} 1111 & \text{for } r \in [1, 1.125) \\ 1112 & \text{for } r \in [1.125, 7/6) \\ 1121 & \text{for } r \in [7/6, 1.25) \\ 1211 & \text{for } r \in [1.25, 1.375) \\ 1212 & \text{for } r \in [1.375, 1.5) \\ 2121 & \text{for } r \in [1.5, 1.625) \\ 2122 & \text{for } r \in [1.625, 1.75) \\ 2212 & \text{for } r \in [1.75, 11/6) \\ 2221 & \text{for } r \in [11/6, 1.875) \\ 2222 & \text{for } r \in [1.875, 2] \end{cases}$$

Thus, $\mathcal{P} = \{11, 12, 21, 22\}$, $R_{11} = [1, 7/6)$, $R_{12} = [7/6, 1.25) \cup [1.5, 1.75)$, $R_{21} = [1.25, 1.5) \cup [1.75, 11/6)$, and $R_{22} = [11/6, 2]$.

Lemma 2. *For every $P' \in \mathcal{P}$, $|R_{P'}| = O(m)$.*

Proof. Let l be the sum of the characters of P', and let a be the number of characters in C_P, namely $a = p_2 + \cdots + p_{m'-1}$. If $r \in R_{P'}$, then $\|r(p_1 + a)\| - \|rp_1\| = l$. By Claim 2 we obtain that $r \in (\frac{l-1}{a}, \frac{l+1}{a})$. For $r \in (\frac{l-1}{a}, \frac{l+1}{a})$, the length of P^r is in the interval $[\ \|\frac{l-1}{a}m\|, \|\frac{l+1}{a}m\|\ ]$. From Lemma 1, it follows that $|R_{P'}| = O(m' \cdot m/a)$. We have assume that $m' \geq 3$, so $a \geq m' - 2 \geq \frac{1}{3}m'$. Hence, $|R_{P'}| = O(m)$. □

We now describe how to build the dictionary. Instead of storing in the dictionary the actual strings of $\mathcal{P}$, we will assign a unique name for every string in $\mathcal{P}$ using the fingerprinting algorithm of Amir et al. [1], and we will store only these names.

The first step is generating all the scaled patterns P^r for $r \leq \alpha$ in an increasing order of r. This is done by finding all the different values of r in which the right endpoint of some r-interval coincides with a pixel center. These values can be easily found for each r-interval, and then sorted using bin sorting. Denote the sorted list by L.

Afterward, build an array $A[1..m' - 2]$ that contains the run length part of C_P. For simplicity, assume that $m' - 2$ is a power of 2 (otherwise, we can append zeros to the end of A until the size of A is a power of 2). Now, compute a name for A by giving a name for every sub-array of A of the form $A[j2^i + 1..(j+1)2^i]$. The name given to a sub-array $A[j..j]$ is equal to its content. The name given to a sub-array $A' = A[j2^i + 1..(j+1)2^i]$ depends on the names given to the two sub-arrays $A[2j2^{i-1} + 1..(2j+1)2^{i-1}]$ and $A[(2j+1)2^{i-1} + 1..(2j+2)2^{i-1}]$. If the names of these sub-arrays are a and b, respectively, then check whether the pair of names (a, b) was encountered before. If it was, then the name of A' is the name that was assigned to the pair (a, b). Otherwise, assign a new name to the pair (a, b) and also assign this name to A'.

After naming A, traverse L, and for each value r in L, update A so it will contain the run length part of C_{P^r}. After each time a value in A is changed, update the names of the $\log(m'-2)+1$ sub-arrays of A that contain the position of A in which the change occurred.

During the computation of the names we also compute the sets $R_{P'}$ for all $P' \in \mathcal{P}$.

Running Time: We store the pairs of names in an $L \times L$ table, where $L = O(\alpha m m')$ is an upper bound on the number of distinct names. Thus, the initial naming of A takes $O(m')$ time, and each update takes $O(\log m')$ time. Therefore, the time for computing all the names is $O(\alpha m m' \log m')$. Using the approach of [11], the space can be reduced to $O(L)$.

4.2 Scanning the Text

The first step is naming every substring of $c(T)$ of length 2^i for $i = 0, \ldots, \log(m'-2)$. The name of a substring of length 1 is equal to its content. The name of a substring T' of length 2^i $(i > 0)$ is computed from the names of the two substrings of length 2^{i-1} whose concatenation forms T'. The naming is done using the same $L \times L$ array that was used for the naming of A, so the names in this stage are consistent with the names in the dictionary building stage. In other words, a substring of T that is equal to a string P' from $\mathcal{P}$, will get the same name as P'.

Now, for every location i of T, compute the range of scales r that satisfy the first and last two scaling requirements. If this range is empty, proceed to the next i. Otherwise, suppose that this interval is $[r_1, r_2)$. If $r_2 > \alpha$, check all the other scaling requirements. If $r_2 \leq \alpha$, check whether the name of the substring of $c(T)$ of length $m' - 2$ that begins at $\mathrm{loc}_T(i) + 1$ is equal to the name of a string $P' \in \mathcal{P}$. If there is such a string P', compute $[r_1, r_2) \cap R_{P'}$, and report a match if the intersection is not empty.

Running Time: Computing the names takes $O(n' \log m')$ time. By storing each set $R_{P'}$ using a balanced binary search tree, we can compute the intersection $[r_1, r_2) \cap R_{P'}$ in time $O(\log |R_{P'}|) = O(\log m)$ (the equality follows from Lemma 2). Therefore, the time complexity of this stage is $O(n \log m + lm')$, where l is the number of locations in which all the scaling requirements are checked. Let S_j be the set of all such locations i with $\mathrm{loc}_T(i) = j$, and let S be the set of all indices j for which S_j is not empty. Clearly, $l = \sum_{j \in S} |S_j|$. The following lemmas give an upper bound on l.

Lemma 3. *For every j, $|S_j| = O(1 + p_1/m')$.*

Proof. Fix a value for j. Let $a = p_2 + \cdots + p_{m-1}$ and $l = t_{j+1} + \cdots + t_{j+m^{\square}-2}$. Suppose that $i \in S_j$. As the first and second last scaling requirements are satisfied, we have that $\|r(p_1 + a)\| - \|rp_1\| = (\hat{t}_i + l) - \hat{t}_i = l$. By Claim 2, $r \in (\frac{l-1}{a}, \frac{l+1}{a})$, so $rp_1 \in (\frac{l-1}{a}p_1, \frac{l+1}{a}p_1)$. Since $i = t_1 + \cdots + t_j + 1 - \hat{t}_i = t_1 + \cdots + t_j + 1 - \|rp_1\|$ and this is true for every $i \in S_j$, it follows that

$$|S_j| \leq \left| \left\{ \|x\| \,\middle|\, x \in \left(\frac{l-1}{a} p_1, \frac{l+1}{a} p_1 \right) \right\} \right| \leq 2 + \frac{2p_1}{a} \leq 2 + \frac{6p_1}{m'},$$

where the last inequality follows from the fact that $m' \geq 3$. □

Lemma 4. $|S| = O(\frac{n}{\alpha p_1})$.

Proof. Suppose that $j \in S$, and let i be some element in S_j. Let $[r_1, r_2)$ be the scales interval computed for location i using the first and last two scaling requirements. By the definition of the algorithm, $r_2 > \alpha$. The interval of r's that satisfy the first scaling requirement is $[\frac{\hat{t}_i - 0.5}{p_1}, \frac{\hat{t}_i + 0.5}{p_1})$, so we obtain that $\frac{\hat{t}_i + 0.5}{p_1} \geq r_2 > \alpha$. Thus, $p_j \geq \hat{t}_i > \alpha p_1 - 0.5$. Since this is true for every $j \in S$, it follows that $|S| \leq \frac{n}{\alpha p_1 - 0.5}$. □

By Lemmas 3 and 4, $l = O(\frac{n}{\alpha p_1}(1 + \frac{p_1}{m^{\square}})) = O(\frac{n}{\alpha})$. Therefore, the total time complexity of the algorithm is $O(\alpha m m' \log m' + n \log m + nm'/\alpha)$. This expression is minimized by choosing $\alpha = \sqrt{n/(m \log m')}$. We obtain the following theorem:

Theorem 1. *The scaled matching problem can be solved in* $O(n \log m + \sqrt{nm}m'\sqrt{\log m'})$ *time.*

References

1. A. Amir, A. Apostolico, G. M. Landau, and G. Satta. Efficient text fingerprinting via Parikh mapping. *J. of Discrete Algorithms*, 1(5–6):409–421, 2003.
2. A. Amir, A. Butman, A. Crochemore, G. M. Landau, and M. Schaps. Two-dimensional pattern matching with rotations. In *Proc. 14th Annual Symposium on Combinatorial Pattern Matching (CPM '03)*, pages 17–31, 2003.
3. A. Amir, A. Butman, and M. Lewenstein. Real scaled matching. *Information Processing Letters*, 70(4):185–190, 1999.
4. A. Amir, A. Butman, M. Lewenstein, and E. Porat. Real two dimensional scaled matching. In *Proc. 8th Workshop on Algorithms and Data Structures (WADS '03)*, pages 353–364, 2003.
5. A. Amir and G. Calinescu. Alphabet independent and dictionary scaled matching. In *Proc. 7th Annual Symposium on Combinatorial Pattern Matching (CPM 96)*, LNCS 1075, pages 320–334. Springer-Verlag, 1996.
6. A. Amir and M. Farach. Efficient 2-dimensional approximate matching of half-rectangular figures. *Information and Computation*, 118(1):1–11, April 1995.
7. A. Amir, O. Kapah, and D. Tsur. Faster two dimensional pattern matching with rotations. In *Proc. 15th Annual Symposium on Combinatorial Pattern Matching (CPM '04)*, pages 409–419, 2004.

8. A. Amir and G. Landau. Fast parallel and serial multidimensional approximate array matching. *Theoretical Computer Science*, 81:97–115, 1991.
9. A. Amir, G. M. Landau, and U. Vishkin. Efficient pattern matching with scaling. *Journal of Algorithms*, 13(1):2–32, 1992.
10. R. S. Boyer and J. S. Moore. A fast string searching algorithm. *Comm. ACM*, 20:762–772, 1977.
11. G. Didier, T. Schmidt, J. Stoye, and D. Tsur. Character sets of strings. Submitted, 2004.
12. K. Fredriksson and E. Ukkonen. A rotation invariant filter for two-dimensional string matching. In *Proc. 9th Annual Symposium on Combinatorial Pattern Matching (CPM 98)*, LNCS 1448, pages 118–125. Springer, 1998.
13. D. E. Knuth, J. H. Morris, and V. R. Pratt. Fast pattern matching in strings. *SIAM J. Comp.*, 6:323–350, 1977.
14. K. Krithivansan and R. Sitalakshmi. Efficient two dimensional pattern matching in the presence of errors. *Information Sciences*, 13:169–184, 1987.
15. G. M. Landau and U. Vishkin. Pattern matching in a digitized image. *Algorithmica*, 12(3/4):375–408, 1994.

Linear Time Algorithm for the Longest Common Repeat Problem*

Inbok Lee[1], Costas S. Iliopoulos[2], and Kunsoo Park[1]

[1] School of Computer Science and Engineering
Seoul National University
Seoul, Korea
{iblee,kpark}@theory.snu.ac.kr

[2] Department of Computer Science
King's College London
London, UK
csi@dcs.kcl.ac.uk

Abstract. Given a set of strings $U = \{T_1, T_2, \ldots, T_\ell\}$, the longest common repeat problem is to find the longest common substring that appears at least twice in each string of U. We also consider reversed and reverse-complemented repeats as well as normal repeats. We present a linear time algorithm for the longest common repeat problem.

1 Introduction

Repetitive or periodic strings have a great importance in a variety of applications including computational molecular biology, data mining, data compression, and computer-assisted music analysis. For example, it is assumed that repetitive substrings in a biological sequence have important meanings and functions [1]. Finding common substrings in a set of strings is also important. For example, motifs or short strings common to protein sequences are assumed to represent a specific property of the sequences [3].

In this paper we want to find common repetitive substrings in a set of strings. We especially focus on finding the longest common repeat in a set since the number of the common repeats in a set can be quite large. We also consider reversed and reverse-complemented strings in finding repeats. Formally we define our problem as follows.

Let T be a string over an alphabet Σ. We assume $\Sigma = \{A, C, G, T\}$ or $\Sigma = \{A, C, G, U\}$ since a major application of the problem is computational molecular biology. $T[i]$ denotes the i-th character of T. $T[i..j]$ is the substring $T[i]T[i+1]\cdots T[j]$ of T. T^R denotes the *reverse string* of T where $|T^R| = |T|$ and $T^R[i] = T[|T|-i+1]$ for $1 \leq i \leq |T|$. T^{RC} denotes the *reverse-complemented string* of T where $|T^{RC}| = |T|$ and, $T^{RC}[i]$ and $T[|T|-i+1]$ form a Watson-Crick pair ($A \equiv (T$ or $U)$ and $C \equiv G$) for $1 \leq i \leq |T|$.

A *repeat* of T is a substring of T which appears at least twice in T. There are three kinds of repeats.

* Work supported by IMT 2000 Project AB02.

A. Apostolico and M. Melucci (Eds.): SPIRE 2004, LNCS 3246, pp. 10–17, 2004.

- **Normal repeat:** A string p is called a *normal repeat* of T if $p = T[i..i+|p|-1]$ and $p = T[i'..i'+|p|-1]$ for $i \neq i'$.
- **Reversed repeat:** A string p is called a *reversed repeat* of T if $p = T[i..i+|p|-1]$ and $p^R = T[i'..i'+|p|-1]$.
- **Reverse-complemented repeat:** A string p is called a *reverse-complemented repeat* if $p = T[i..i+|p|-1]$ and $p^{RC} = T[i'..i'+|p|-1]$.

There are two reasons why we consider reversed and reverse-complemented repeats: (i) We don't know the directions of the strings in advance. (ii) In some situations, reversed and reverse-complemented repeats play an important role. For example, RNA secondary structures are determined by reverse-complemented repeats.

The longest common repeat problem can be defined as follows.

Problem 1. Given a set of strings $U = \{T_1, T_2, \ldots, T_\ell\}$, **the (k, ℓ) longest common repeat problem** is to find the longest repeat (normal, reversed or reverse-complemented) which are common to k strings in U for $1 \leq k \leq \ell$.

For finding the longest normal repeat in a text T, Karp, Miller, and Rosenberg first proposed $O(|T| \log |T|)$ time algorithm [8]. However, it is an easy application of the suffix tree [10, 13, 4] to find it in $O(|T|)$ time.

For approximate normal repeats, Landau and Schmidt gave an $O(k|T| \log k \log |T|)$ time algorithm for finding approximate squares where the allowed edit distance is at most k [9]. Schmidt also gave an $O(|T|^2 \log |T|)$ time algorithm for finding approximate tandem or non-tandem repeats [12].

The longest common repeat problem resembles the longest common substring problem. The difference is that the common substring should appear at least twice in each sequence in the longest common repeat problem. For the longest common substring problem with a set of strings $\{T_1, T_2, \ldots, T_\ell\}$, Hui showed an $O(\sum_{i=1}^{\ell} |T_i|)$ time algorithm [7]. As far as we know, our algorithm is the first one that solves the longest common repeat problem.

2 Preliminaries

A *generalized suffix tree* stores all the suffixes of a set of strings just like a suffix tree stores all the suffixes of a string. It is easy to extend the suffix tree construction algorithm [13] to building a generalized suffix tree [5, page 116]. Figure 1 is an example of the generalized suffix tree for $T_1 = AACTG$ and $T_2 = ACTGCTG$. Each leaf node has an ID representing the original string where the suffix came. Identical suffixes of two or more strings are considered as different ones. In this example, T_1 and T_2 share three identical suffixes CTG, TG, and G. Each of these suffixes has two leaves with different IDs.

From now on, let $ST(T)$ denote the suffix tree of T and $GST(T_1..T_\ell)$ denote the generalized suffix tree of $T_1, T_2, \ldots, T_\ell$. Let $L(v)$ denote the string obtained by concatenating the edge labels on the path from the root to a node v in a suffix tree or a generalized suffix tree.

We define *corresponding nodes* between $ST(T_i)$ and $GST(T_1..T_\ell)$ $(1 \leq i \leq \ell)$.

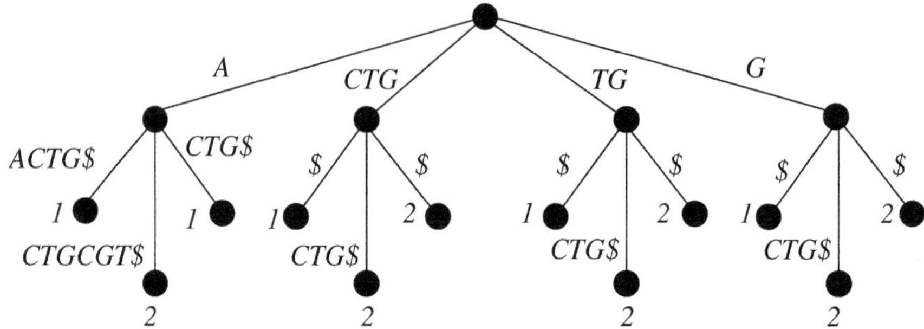

Fig. 1. The generalized suffix tree for $T_1 = AACTG$ and $T_2 = ACTGCTG$.

Definition 1. *The* corresponding node *of an internal node* v *in* $ST(T_i)$ $(1 \leq i \leq \ell)$ *is a node* v' *in* $GST(T_1..T_\ell)$ *such that* $L(v) = L(v')$.

It is trivial to show that each internal node v in $ST(T_i)$ has a corresponding node v' in $GST(T_1..T_\ell)$ since $GST(T_1..T_\ell)$ stores all the suffixes of the strings.

We define repeats with some properties. A *maximal repeat* is a repeat that cannot be extended to the left or right. For example, in $T = \overline{A\underline{AG}}TGTG\overline{A\underline{AG}}$, AG is a repeat, but not a maximal one. We can get a maximal repeat AAG by adding the immediate left character A. It is obvious that a repeat is either maximal or a substring of another maximal one. A *supermaximal repeat* is a maximal repeat that never occurs as a substring of any other maximal repeat. For example, in $T = C\underline{AA}CG\underline{AA}\overline{G\underline{AA}G}$, AA is a maximal repeat since it appears three times in T and CAA and AAC appear only once in T. But it is not a supermaximal repeat because another maximal repeat $G\underline{AA}G$ contains AA. In this example, $GAAG$ is a supermaximal repeat of T. Figure 2 shows a general relation between a maximal repeat and a supermaximal repeat.

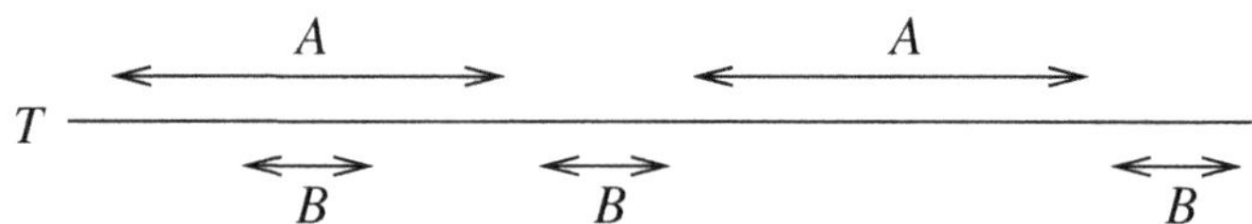

Fig. 2. A is a supermaximal repeat and B is a maximal repeat, but not a supermaximal one.

Lemma 1. *A repeat is either supermaximal or a substring of another supermaximal one.*

Proof. We have only to show that a repeat which is maximal but not supermaximal is a substring of another supermaximal one. It follows from the definition of supermaximal repeats.

For an internal node v in $ST(T)$, $L(v)$ is a supermaximal repeat of T if and only if all of v's children are leaves and each leaf has a distinct character immediately to the left of the suffix corresponding to it [5, pages 143–148]. Hence the number of supermaximal repeats of T is $O(|T|)$, and they can be found in $O(|T|)$ time.

3 Algorithm

Our algorithm for the longest common repeat problem is based on the following property.

Fact 1 *Given a set of strings $U = \{T_1, T_2, \ldots, T_\ell\}$, the longest common repeat of U is the longest string which is a substring of a supermaximal repeat of each string in U.*

The outline of our algorithm for the longest common repeat problem is as follows.

- **Step 1:** Create a new string T_i' for each $1 \le i \le \ell$ to consider reversed and reverse-complemented repeats.
- **Step 2:** Build $ST(T_i')$ for each $1 \le i \le \ell$. Also, build $GST(T_1'..T_\ell')$.
- **Step 3:** Find supermaximal repeats of T_i' for each i in $GST(T_1'..T_\ell')$.
- **Step 4:** Modify $GST(T_1'..T_\ell')$ and build the generalized suffix tree of the supermaximal repeats.
- **Step 5:** Find the longest common repeat among the supermaximal repeats using the generalized suffix tree made in Step 4.

The hard part of the algorithm is Step 4, which changes $GST(T_1'..T_\ell')$ into the generalized suffix tree of the supermaximal repeats in linear time.

Step 1: We first modify each string in U to consider the reversed and reverse-complemented repeats. For each $i = 1, 2, \ldots, \ell$, we create a new string $T_i' = T_i\%T_i^R\#T_i^{RC}$, where % and # are special characters which are not in Σ. Normal repeats of T_i' include normal, reversed, and reverse-complemented repeats of T_i.

Step 2: We build the suffix trees and the generalized suffix tree. For each $i = 1, 2, \ldots, \ell$, we build $ST(T_i')$ with a modification. When we create an internal node v, we store an additional information (j, j') at v. It means that v is the lowest common ancestor (LCA) of two leaves representing $T_i'[j..|T_i'|]$ and $T_i'[j'..|T_i'|]$, respectively. If there are more than two leaves in the subtree rooted at v, arbitrary two leaves can be chosen. See Figure 3. (We can store (3,1) instead of (3,2) at the second internal node.) This modification does not change the time and space complexities. We also build $GST(T_1'..T_\ell')$. This procedure runs in $O(\sum_{i=1}^{\ell} |T_i'|)$ time and space.

Step 3: We find supermaximal repeats of each string in U. For each $i = 1, 2, \ldots, \ell$, we find supermaximal repeats of T_i' using $ST(T_i')$ [5, pages 143–148].

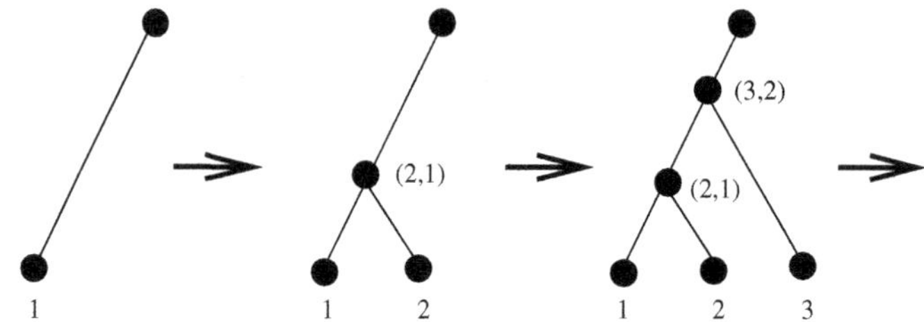

Fig. 3. Modification of the suffix tree construction.

Now we have a set of nodes $M_i = \{v|v$ is an internal node of $ST(T_i')$ and $L(v)$ is a supermaximal repeat of $T_i'\}$. We compute the set of corresponding nodes $V_i = \{v'|v'$ is an internal node of $GST(T_1'..T_\ell')$ and it is the corresponding node of $v \in M_i\}$. To do so, we use the information obtained during the construction of $ST(T_i')$. Figure 4 illustrates the idea. We read the information (j, j') at v computed in Step 2. Then we compute the LCA v' of two leaves in $GST(T_1'..T_\ell')$ representing $T_i'[j..|T_i'|]$ and $T_i'[j'..|T_i'|]$, respectively. It is easy to show that v' is the corresponding node of v. After $O(\sum_{i=1}^{\ell} |T_i'|)$-time preprocessing, finding a corresponding node takes constant time [6, 11, 2]. The total time complexity is $O(\sum_{i=1}^{\ell} |T_i'|)$.

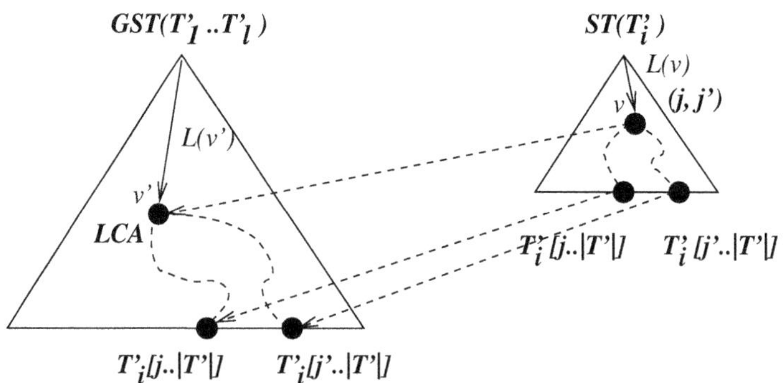

Fig. 4. Finding the corresponding node of v.

Step 4: Now we explain the hard part of the algorithm, modifying $GST(T_1'..T_\ell')$ into the generalized suffix tree of the supermaximal repeats in linear time. At this point we have sets V_i's, where $L(v)$ for each $v \in V_i$ $(1 \le i \le \ell)$ is a supermaximal repeat of T_i'.

The outline of Step 4 is as follows.

1. For each supermaximal repeat S, insert the suffixes of $S\$$ into $GST(T_1'..T_\ell')$.
2. Identify the nodes of the current tree which should be included in the generalized suffix tree of the supermaximal repeats.
3. Remove the unnecessary nodes and edges of the tree.

We first insert the suffixes of the supermaximal repeats into $GST(T'_1..T'_\ell)$. For each $i = 1, 2, \ldots, \ell$, we traverse $GST(T'_1..T'_\ell)$ from each element of V_i to the root node following the suffix links. Whenever we meet a node previously unvisited during the traversal, we create a new leaf node with ID i. These new leaves are stored in a set $N_i = \{v | v$ is a leaf node of the tree and $L(v)$ is a suffix of a supermaximal repeat of T'_i followed by $\$\}$. We also link the current node and the new leaf with an edge labeled by \$. The trick is that we stop the traversal when we meet a previously visited node and move to the next element of V_i. Figure 5 illustrates the idea. Suppose T'_1 has two supermaximal repeats, $GGTC$ and CTC. First we handle $GGTC$. The visiting order is $1 \rightarrow 2 \rightarrow 3 \rightarrow 4 \rightarrow 5$. After visiting node 5, which is the root node, we are done with $GGTC$ and we handle CTC. After visiting node 6, we visit node 3 again, following the suffix link. Then we are done with CTC. This procedure runs in $O(|T'_i|)$ time and $|N_i| = O(|T'_i|)$.

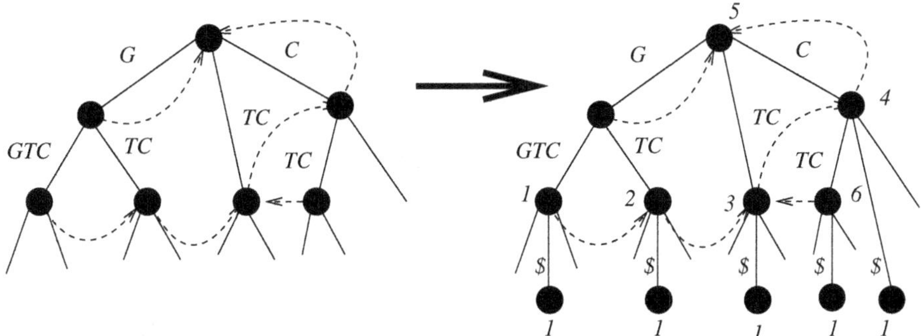

Fig. 5. Inserting the suffixes of $GGTC$ and CTC into $GST(T'_1..T'_\ell)$.

Now we identify the nodes of the tree which should be included in the the generalized suffix tree of the supermaximal repeats. To do so, for each $i = 1, 2, \ldots, \ell$, we traverse the tree from each element of N_i to the root node upward and mark the nodes on the path. We stop the traversal if we meet a marked node and go on to process the next element of N_i. The generalized suffix tree of the supermaximal repeats consists of the marked node and edges linking them in the tree.

Finally, we remove the unnecessary nodes and edges which are not in the generalized suffix tree of the supermaximal repeats. We traverse the tree from original leaves (not the new leaves created in Step 4) to the root node upward and delete the nodes and edges on the path if they are not marked. We move to the next original leaf of the tree if we meet a marked node. After deleting all the unnecessary nodes and edges, we get the generalized suffix tree of the supermaximal repeats. This procedure runs in $O(\sum_{i=1}^{\ell} |T'_i|)$ time.

Step 5: The remaining problem is to find the longest common substring among k supermaximal repeats with distinct IDs with the generalized suffix tree of the supermaximal repeats. Unlike the longest common substring problem, two or more supermaximal repeats can have the same ID here.

Still we can use Hui's algorithm for the longest common substring problem in this case, because it solves a rather general problem [7]. The problem is that each leaf of the tree has a color (an ID in our problem) and that we want to find the deepest node (in the length of $L(v)$) whose subtree has leaves with at least k colors. We do not mention the details of Hui's algorithm here. Rather we show an example in Figure 6. Suppose T_1' has two supermaximal repeats $GGTC$ and CTC, T_2' has two supermaximal repeats CTC and TCA, and T_3' has two supermaximal repeats TCG and ATC. For each internal node of the generalized suffix tree of the supermaximal repeats, we compute the number of different IDs in its subtrees. The internal nodes with rectangles (nodes γ and δ) have leaves with three different IDs in their subtrees. The internal nodes with circles (nodes α, β, and ϵ) have leaves with two different IDs in their subtrees. For the $(3,3)$ longest common repeat problem, we compare the lengths of $L(\gamma) = TC$ and $L(\delta) = C$. The answer is TC. For the $(2,3)$ longest common repeat problem, the answer is $L(\epsilon) = CTC$. It runs in $O(\sum_{i=1}^{\ell} |T_i'|)$ time, reporting the answer of (k,ℓ) longest common repeat problem for all $1 \le k \le \ell$.

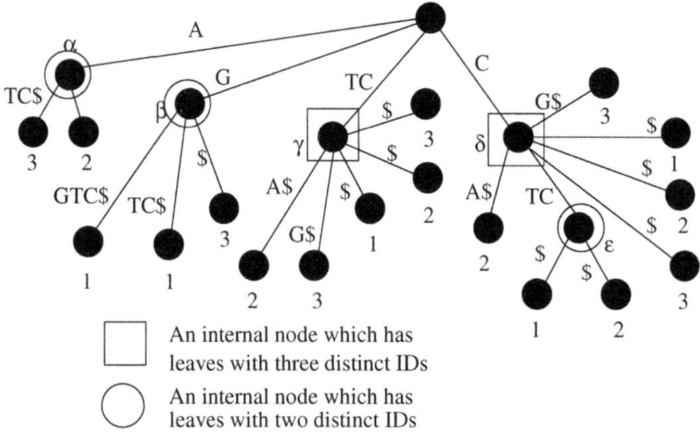

Fig. 6. An example of the longest common repeat problem.

Theorem 1. *The (k,ℓ) longest common repeat problem can be solved in $O(\sum_{i=1}^{\ell} |T_i|)$ time and space for all $1 \le k \le \ell$.*

Proof. We showed that all the steps run in $O(\sum_{i=1}^{\ell} |T_i'|)$ time and space. And $|T_i'| = O(|T_i|)$.

4 Conclusion

We have defined the longest common repeat problem and presented a linear time algorithm for the problem, allowing reversed and reverse-complemented repeats.

A remaining work is to devise a space-efficient algorithm for the longest common repeat problem. Another possibility is the longest common approximate repeat problem.

References

1. A. Apostolico, F. Gong, and S. Lonardi. Verbumculus and the discovery of unusual words. *Journal of Computer Science and Technology*, 19(1):22–41, 2003.
2. M. A. Bender and M. Farach-Colton. The LCA problem revisited. In *Proceedings of the Fourth Latin American Symposium*, pages 88–94, 2000.
3. L. Falquet, M. Pagini, P. Bucher, N. Hulo, C. J. Sigrist, K. Hofmann, and A. Bairoch. The PROSITE database, its status in 2002. *Nucleic Acids Research*, 30:235–238, 2002.
4. M. Farach-Colton, P. Ferragina, and S. Muthukrishnan. On the sorting-complexity of suffix tree construction. *Journal of the ACM*, 47(6):987–1011, 2000.
5. D. Gusfield. *Algorithms on strings, trees and sequences: computer science and computational biology*. Cambridge University Press, Cambridge, 1997.
6. D. Harel and R. E. Tarjan. Fast algorithms for finding nearest common ancestor. *SIAM Journal on Computing*, 13(2):338–355, 1984.
7. L. C. K. Hui. Color set size problem with applications to string matching. In *Proceedings of the Third Annual Symposium on Combinatorial Pattern Matching*, pages 230–243. Springer-Verlag, Berlin, 1992.
8. R. M. Karp, R. E. Miller, and A. L. Rosenberg. Rapid identification of repeated patterns in strings, trees and arrays. In *Proceedings of the Fourth Annual ACM Symposium on Theory of Computing*, pages 125–136, 1972.
9. G. M. Landau and J. P. Schmidt. An algorithm for approximate tandem repeats. In *Proceedings of the Fourth Combinatorial Pattern Matching*, pages 120–133, 1993.
10. E. M. McCreight. A space-economical suffix tree construction algorithm. *Journal of the ACM*, 23(2):262–272, April 1976.
11. B. Schieber and U. Vishkin. On finding lowest common ancestors: Simplification and parallelization. *SIAM Journal on Computing*, 17:1253–1262, 1988.
12. J. P. Schmidt. All highest scoring paths in weighted grid graphs and its application to finding all approximate repeats in strings. *SIAM Journal on Computing*, 27(4):972–992, 1998.
13. E. Ukkonen. On-line construction of suffix trees. *Algorithmica*, 14:249–260, 1995.

Automaton-Based Sublinear Keyword Pattern Matching

Loek Cleophas, Bruce W. Watson, and Gerard Zwaan

Software Construction Group / FASTAR Research Group
Department of Mathematics and Computer Science
Technische Universiteit Eindhoven
P.O. Box 513 NL-5600 MB Eindhoven, The Netherlands
loek@loekcleophas.com, bruce@bruce-watson.com, g.zwaan@tue.nl
http://www.fastar.org

Abstract. We show how automaton-based sublinear[1] keyword pattern matching (skpm) algorithms appearing in the literature can be seen as different instantiations of a general automaton-based skpm algorithm skeleton. Such algorithms use finite automata (FA) for efficient computation of string membership in a certain language. The algorithms were formally derived as part of a new skpm algorithm taxonomy, based on an earlier suffix-based skpm algorithm taxonomy [1]. Such a taxonomy is based on deriving the algorithms from a common starting point by successively adding algorithm and problem details and has a number of advantages. It provides correctness arguments, clarifies the working of the algorithms and their interrelationships, helps in implementing the algorithms, and may lead to new algorithms being discovered by finding gaps in the taxonomy. We show how to arrive at the general algorithm skeleton and derive some instantiations, leading to well-known factor- and factor oracle-based algorithms. In doing so, we show the shift functions used for them can be (strengthenings of) shift functions used for suffix-based algorithms. This also results in a number of previously undescribed factor-based skpm algorithm variants, whose performance remains to be investigated.

1 Introduction

The (exact) keyword pattern matching (kpm) problem can be described as "the problem of finding all occurrences of keywords from a given set as substrings in a given string" [1]. Watson and Zwaan (in [1], [2, Chapter 4]) derived well-known solutions to the problem from a common starting point, factoring out their commonalities and presenting them in a common setting to better comprehend and compare them. Other overviews of kpm are given in [3, 4] and many others.

Although the original taxonomy contained many skpm algorithms, a new category of skpm algorithms – based on factors instead of suffixes of keywords

[1] By sublinear, we mean that the number of symbol comparisons may be sublinear in input string length.

A. Apostolico and M. Melucci (Eds.): SPIRE 2004, LNCS 3246, pp. 18–29, 2004.

– has emerged in the last decade. This category includes algorithms such as (Set) Backward DAWG Matching [5] and (Set) Backward Oracle Matching [6, 7], which were added to the existing taxonomy by Cleophas [8].

In this paper, we show how suffix, factor and factor oracle automaton-based skpm algorithms can be seen as instantiations of a general algorithm skeleton. We show how this skeleton is derived by successively adding algorithm details to a naïve, high-level algorithm. Since the suffix-based algorithms have been extensively described in the past [1, 2, 8], we focus our attention on the factor- and factor oracle-based algorithms.

Figure 1 shows the new skpm taxonomy. Nodes represent algorithms, while edges are labeled with the detail they represent. Most of the details are introduced in the course of the text; for those that are not, please refer to [9].

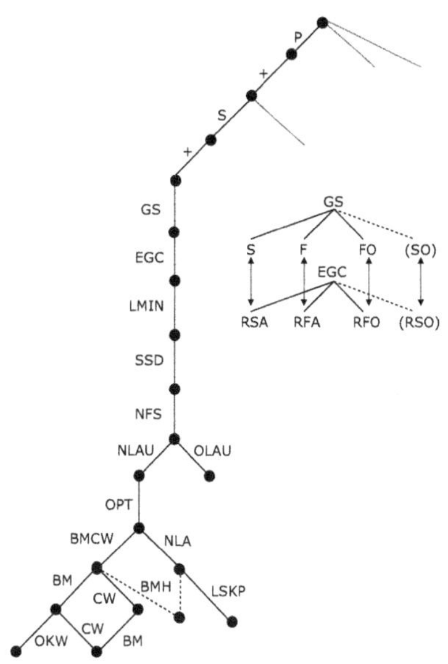

Fig. 1. A new automaton-based skpm algorithm taxonomy.

1.1 Related Work

The complete original taxonomy is presented in [2, Chapter 4] and [1]. The additions and changes are described in Cleophas's MSc thesis [8, Chapter 3]. The new skpm taxonomy part is completely described in [9].

The SPARE TIME (String PAttern REcognition) toolkit implements most algorithms in the taxonomy. It is discussed in detail in [8, Chapter 5] and will be available from `http://www.fastar.org`.

1.2 Taxonomy Construction

In our case, a taxonomy is a classification according to essential details of algorithms or data structures from a certain field, taking the form of a *(directed acylic) taxonomy graph*. The construction of a taxonomy has a number of goals:

- Providing algorithm correctness arguments, often absent in literature
- Clarifying the algorithms' working and interrelationships
- Helping in correctly and easily implementing the algorithms [10, 2]
- Leading to new algorithms, by finding and filling gaps in the taxonomy

The process of taxonomy construction is preceded by surveying the existing literature of algorithms in the problem field. Based on such a survey, one may try to bring order to the field by placing the algorithms found in a taxonomy.

The various algorithms in a taxonomy are derived from a common starting point by adding details indicating the variations between different algorithms. The common starting point is a naïve algorithm whose correctness is easily shown. Associated with this algorithm are requirements in the form of a pre- and postcondition, invariant and a specification of (theoretical) running time and/or memory usage, specifying the problem under consideration. The details distinguishing the algorithms each belong to one of the following categories:

- *Problem details* involve minor pre- and postcondition changes, restricting in- or output
- *Algorithm details* are used to specify variance in algorithmic structure
- *Representation details* are used to indicate variance in data structures, internally to an algorithm or also influencing in- and output representation.
- *Performance details* i.e. running time and memory consumption variance.

As the representation and performance details mainly influence implementation but do not influence the other goals stated above, problem and algorithm details are most important. These details form the taxonomy graph edges.

Taxonomy construction is often done bottom-up, starting with single-node taxonomies for each algorithm in the problem domain literature. As one sees commonalities among them, one may find generalizations which allow combining multiple taxonomies into one larger one with the new generalization as the root. Once a complete taxonomy has been constructed, it is presented top-down. Associated with the addition of a detail, correctness arguments showing how the more detailed algorithm is derived from its predecessor are given. To indicate a particular algorithm and form a taxonomy graph, we use the sequence of details in order of introduction. Sometimes an algorithm can be derived in multiple ways. This causes the taxonomy to take the form of a directed acyclic graph instead of a directed tree.

This type of taxonomy development was also used for garbage collection [11], FA construction and minimization [2, 12], graph representations [13] and others.

1.3 Notation and Definitions Used

Since a large part of this paper consists of derivations of existing algorithms, we will often use notations corresponding to their use in existing literature on those algorithms. We use A and B for arbitrary sets, $\mathcal{P}(A)$ for the powerset of a set A, V for the (non-empty and finite) alphabet and V^* for words over the alphabet, $P = \{p_0, p_1, \ldots p_{|P|-1}\} \subseteq V^*$ for a finite, non-empty pattern set with $lmin_P = (\mathbf{MIN}\, p : p \in P : |p|)$, as well as R for predicates, M for finite automata and Q for state sets. States are represented by q and q_0. Symbols $a, b, \ldots, e$ represent alphabet symbols from V, while $p, s, \ldots z$ represent words over alphabet V. Symbols $i, j, \ldots, n$ represent integer values. We use $\perp$ ('bottom') to denote an undefined value. Sometimes functions, relations or predicates are used that have names longer than just a single character.

A (deterministic) FA is a 5-tuple $M = \langle Q, V, \delta, q_0, F\rangle$ where Q is a finite set of states, $\delta \in Q \times V \rightarrow Q$ is the transition relation, $q_0 \in Q$ is a start state and

$F \subseteq Q$ is a set of final states. We extend δ to $\delta^* \in Q \times V^* \to Q$ defined by $\delta^*(q, \varepsilon) = q$ and $\delta^*(q, wa) = \delta(\delta^*(q, w), a)$.

We use p^R for the reversal of a string p, and use string reversal on a set of strings as well. A string u is a *factor* (resp. *prefix*, *suffix*) of a string v if $v = sut$ (resp. $v = ut$, $v = su$). We use functions **fact**, **pref** and **suff** for the set of factors, prefixes and suffixes of a (set of) string(s) respectively. We write $u \leq_p v$ to denote that u is a prefix of v. The infix operators $\upharpoonleft$, $\downharpoonleft$, $\upharpoonright$, $\downharpoonright$ (pronounced 'left take', 'left drop', 'right take' and 'right drop' respectively) for $0 \leq k$ are defined as: $w \upharpoonleft k$ is the $k\,\mathbf{min}\,|w|$ leftmost symbols of w, $w \downharpoonleft k$ is the $(|w| - k)\,\mathbf{max}\,0$ rightmost symbols of w, $w \upharpoonright k$ is the $k\,\mathbf{min}\,|w|$ rightmost symbols of w and $w \downharpoonright k$ is the $(|w| - k)\,\mathbf{max}\,0$ leftmost symbols of w. For example, $(hers)\upharpoonleft 3 = her$, $(hers)\downharpoonleft 1 = ers$, $(hers)\upharpoonright 5 = hers$ and $(hers)\downharpoonright 10 = \varepsilon$.

Our notation for quantifications is introduced in Appendix A. We use predicate calculus in derivations [14] and present algorithms in an extended version of (part of) the guarded command language [15]. In that language, $x, y := X, Y$ is used for multiple-variable assignment, while **if** $b \to S \; [\!] \; \neg b \to T$ **fi** represents executing S if b evaluates to true, and T if $\neg b$ evaluates to true. The extensions of the basic language are **as** $b \to S$ **sa** as a shortcut for **if** $b \to S \; [\!] \; \neg b \to$ skip **fi**, and **for** $x : R \to S$ **rof** for executing statement list S once for each value of x initially satisfying R (assuming there is a finite number of such values for x), in arbitrarily chosen order [16].

2 An Automaton-Based Algorithm Skeleton for Sublinear Keyword Pattern Matching

In this section, we work towards an automaton-based algorithm skeleton for skpm, by adding details to a naïve solution.

The kpm problem, given input string $S \in V^*$, and pattern set P, is to establish (see Appendix A for our notation for quantifications)

$$R: \; O = \left(\bigcup l, v, r : lvr = S \wedge v \in P : \{(l, v, r)\}\right)$$

i.e. to let O be the set of triples forming a splitting of S in three such that the middle part is a keyword in P. A trivial (but unrealistic) solution is

Algorithm 1()

$$O := \left(\bigcup l, v, r : lvr = S \wedge v \in P : \{(l, v, r)\}\right) \{ \; R \; \}$$

The sequence of details describing this algorithm is the empty sequence. We may proceed by considering a substring of S as "suffix of a prefix of S" or as "prefix of a suffix of S". We choose the first possibility as this is the way that the algorithms we consider treat substrings of input string S (the second leads to algorithms processing S from right to left instead). Applying "examine prefixes of a given string in any order" (algorithm detail (P)) to S, we obtain:

Algorithm 2(P)

$O := \varnothing;$
for $(u, r) : ur = S \rightarrow$
  $O := O \cup \left(\bigcup l, v : lv = u \wedge v \in P : \{(l, v, r)\}\right)$
rof$\{ R \}$

This algorithm is used in [8, 2] to derive (non-sublinear) prefix-based algorithms such as Aho-Corasick, Knuth-Morris-Pratt and Shift-And/-Or.

The update of O in the repetition of Algorithm 2 can be computed with another repetition, considering suffixes of u. Applying "examine suffixes of a given string in any order" (algorithm detail (S)) to string u we obtain:

Algorithm 3(P, S)

$O := \varnothing;$
for $(u, r) : ur = S \rightarrow$
  for $(l, v) : lv = u \rightarrow$
    as $v \in P \rightarrow O := O \cup \{(l, v, r)\}$ **sa**
  rof
rof$\{ R \}$

Algorithm (P, S) consists of two nested non-deterministic repetitions. Each can be determinized by considering prefixes (or suffixes as the case is) in increasing (called detail (+)) or decreasing (detail (−)) order of length. Since the algorithms we consider achieve sublinear behaviour by examining string S from left to right, and patterns in P from right to left, we focus our attention on:

Algorithm 4(P_+, S_+)

$u, r := \varepsilon, S;$
if $\varepsilon \in P \rightarrow O := \{(\varepsilon, \varepsilon, S)\}$ $[\!]$ $\varepsilon \notin P \rightarrow O := \varnothing$ **fi**;
$\{$ invariant: $ur = S \wedge O = \left(\bigcup x, y, z : xyz = S \wedge xy \leq_p u \wedge y \in P : \{(x, y, z)\}\right) \}$
do $r \neq \varepsilon \rightarrow$
  $u, r := u(r{\upharpoonright}1), r{\downharpoonright}1;\ l, v := u, \varepsilon;$
  as $\varepsilon \in P \rightarrow O := O \cup \{(u, \varepsilon, r)\}$ **sa**;
  $\{$ invariant: $u = lv \}$
  do $l \neq \varepsilon \rightarrow$
    $l, v := l{\downharpoonleft}1, (l{\upharpoonleft}1)v;$
    as $v \in P \rightarrow O := O \cup \{(l, v, r)\}$ **sa**
  od
od$\{ R \}$

To arrive at a more efficient algorithm, we strengthen the inner loop guard $l \neq \varepsilon$. In [1, 2], this was done by adding **cand** $(l{\upharpoonleft}1)v \in \textbf{suff}(P)$ [2]. A more general

[2] We use **cand** (**cor**) for *conditional con-* resp. *disjunction*, i.e. the second operand is evaluated if and only if necessary to determine the value of the con- or disjunction.

strengthening is possible however. Suppose we have a function $\mathbf{f} \in \mathcal{P}(V^*) \to \mathcal{P}(V^*)$ satisfying $P \subseteq \mathbf{f}(P) \wedge \mathbf{suff}(\mathbf{f}(P)) \subseteq \mathbf{f}(P)$ (i.e. $\mathbf{f}$ is such that P is included in $\mathbf{f}(P)$ and $\mathbf{f}(P)$ is suffix-closed) then we have (for all $w, x \in V^*$) $w \notin \mathbf{f}(P) \Rightarrow w \notin P$ and $w \notin \mathbf{f}(P) \Rightarrow xw \notin P$ (application of right conjunct followed by left one). We may therefore strengthen the guard to $l \neq \varepsilon$ **cand** $(l\upharpoonright 1)v \in \mathbf{f}(P)$ (algorithm detail (GS), for guard strengthening). This leads to:

Algorithm 5(P+, S+, GS)

$u, r := \varepsilon, S;$
if $\varepsilon \in P \to O := \{(\varepsilon, \varepsilon, S)\} \,[\!]\, \varepsilon \notin P \to O := \varnothing$ **fi**;
$\{$ invariant: $ur = S \wedge O = \left(\bigcup x, y, z : xyz = S \wedge xy \leq_p u \wedge y \in P : \{(x, y, z)\}\right) \}$
do $r \neq \varepsilon \to$
  $u, r := u(r\upharpoonright 1), r\downharpoonright 1;\; l, v := u, \varepsilon;$
  as $\varepsilon \in P \to O := O \cup \{(u, \varepsilon, r)\}$ **sa**;
  $\{$ invariant: $u = lv \wedge v \in \mathbf{f}(P) \}$
  do $l \neq \varepsilon$ **cand** $(l\upharpoonright 1)v \in \mathbf{f}(P) \to$
    $l, v := l\downharpoonright 1, (l\upharpoonright 1)v;$
    as $v \in P \to O := O \cup \{(l, v, r)\}$ **sa**
  od$\{ l = \varepsilon$ **cor** $(l\upharpoonright 1)v \notin \mathbf{f}(P) \}$
od$\{ R \}$

Observe that $v \in \mathbf{f}(P)$ is now an invariant of the inner repetition, initially established by $v := \varepsilon$ (since $P \neq \varnothing$ and thus $\varepsilon \in \mathbf{f}(P)$).

Several choices for $\mathbf{f}(P)$ are possible, of which we mention:

- $\mathbf{suff}(P)$, leading to the original taxonomy [1, 2]. In [9], those algorithms are derived using an automaton-based algorithm skeleton.
- $\mathbf{fact}(P)$, discussed in Section 3.
- $\mathbf{factoracle}(P^R)^R$, a superset of $\mathbf{fact}(P^R)^R$ ($= \mathbf{fact}(P)$), see Section 4.
- A function returning a superset of **suff**. This could be implemented using a *suffix oracle* [6, 7]. We will not explore this option here.

Direct evaluation of $(l\upharpoonright 1)v \in \mathbf{f}(P)$ is expensive and this is where automata come in: to efficiently compute this guard conjunct, the transition function $\delta_{R,\mathbf{f},P}$ of a finite automaton recognizing $\mathbf{f}(P)^R$ is used, with the property:

Property 1 (Transition function of automaton recognizing $\mathbf{f}(P)^R$*).* The transition function $\delta_{R,\mathbf{f},P}$ of a deterministic FA $M = \langle Q, V, \delta_{R,\mathbf{f},P}, q_0, F\rangle$ recognizing $\mathbf{f}(P)^R$ has the property that $\delta^*_{R,\mathbf{f},P}(q_0, w^R) \neq \perp \equiv w^R \in \mathbf{f}(P)^R$. □

Property 1 requires $\mathbf{pref}(\mathbf{f}(P)^R) \subseteq \mathbf{f}(P)^R$, i.e. $\mathbf{suff}(\mathbf{f}(P)) \subseteq \mathbf{f}(P)$. Also note that $w^R \in \mathbf{f}(P)^R \equiv w \in \mathbf{f}(P)$. Since we will always refer to the same set P, we will use $\delta_{R,\mathbf{f}}$ for $\delta_{R,\mathbf{f},P}$. Transition function $\delta_{R,\mathbf{f}}$ can be computed beforehand.

By making $q = \delta^*_{R,\mathbf{f}}(q_0, ((l\upharpoonright 1)v)^R)$ an invariant of the algorithm's inner repetition, guard conjunct $(l\upharpoonright 1)v \in \mathbf{f}(P)$ can be changed to $q \neq \perp$. We call this algorithm detail (EGC), for efficient guard computation. This algorithm detail leads to the following algorithm skeleton:

Algorithm 6(P$_+$, S$_+$, GS, EGC)

$u, r := \varepsilon, S$;
if $\varepsilon \in P \rightarrow O := \{(\varepsilon, \varepsilon, S)\} \;[\!]\; \varepsilon \notin P \rightarrow O := \varnothing$ **fi**;
{ invariant: $ur = S \wedge O = \big(\bigcup x, y, z : xyz = S \wedge xy \leq_p u \wedge y \in P : \{(x, y, z)\}\big)$ }
do $r \neq \varepsilon \rightarrow$
    $u, r := u(r{\upharpoonright}1), r{\downharpoonright}1$; $l, v := u, \varepsilon$; $q := \delta_{R,\mathbf{f}}(q_0, l{\upharpoonright}1)$;
    as $\varepsilon \in P \rightarrow O := O \cup \{(u, \varepsilon, r)\}$ **sa**;
    { invariant: $u = lv \wedge v \in \mathbf{f}(P) \wedge q = \delta^*_{R,\mathbf{f}}(q_0, ((l{\upharpoonright}1)v)^R)$ }
    do $l \neq \varepsilon$ **cand** $q \neq \perp \rightarrow$
        $l, v := l{\downharpoonright}1, (l{\upharpoonright}1)v$;
        $q := \delta_{R,\mathbf{f}}(q, l{\upharpoonright}1)$;
        as $v \in P \rightarrow O := O \cup \{(l, v, r)\}$ **sa**
    od{ $l = \varepsilon$ **cor** $(l{\upharpoonright}1)v \notin \mathbf{f}(P)$ }
od{ R }

The particular automaton choices for this detail will be discussed together with the corresponding choices for detail (GS) in Sections 3 and 4. Note that guard $v \in P$ can be efficiently computed, i.e. computed in $\Theta(1)$, by providing a map from automaton states to booleans.

In practice, the algorithms often use automata recognizing $\mathbf{f}(P')^R$ where $P' = \{v : v \in \mathbf{pref}(P) \wedge |v| = lmin_P\}$ instead of $\mathbf{f}(P)^R$. Informally, an automaton is built on the prefixes of length $lmin_P$, to obtain smaller automata (see [9] for more information). To save memory usage, the automata are sometimes constructed on-the-fly as well.

Starting from the above algorithm, we derive an automaton-based skpm algorithm skeleton. The basic idea is to make shifts of more than one symbol. Given k satisfying $1 \leq k \leq \big(\mathbf{MIN}\, n : 1 \leq n \wedge \mathbf{suff}(u(r{\upharpoonright}n)) \cap P \neq \varnothing : n\big)$, we can replace $u, r := u(r{\upharpoonright}1), r{\downharpoonright}1$ by $u, r := u(r{\upharpoonright}k), r{\downharpoonright}k$. The upperbound on k is the distance to the next match, the maximal safe shift distance (mssd). Any smaller k is safe as well, and we thus define a safe shift distance as a shift distance k satisfying $1 \leq k \leq \big(\mathbf{MIN}\, n : 1 \leq n \wedge \mathbf{suff}(u(r{\upharpoonright}n)) \cap P \neq \varnothing : n\big)$. The use of assignment $u, r := u(r{\upharpoonright}k), r{\downharpoonright}k$ for a safe shift distance k forms algorithm detail (SSD).

Since shift functions may depend on l, v and r, we will write $k(l, v, r)$. We aim to approximate the mssd from below, since computing the distance itself essentially amounts to solving our original problem. To do this, we weaken the predicate $\mathbf{suff}(u(r{\upharpoonright}n)) \cap P \neq \varnothing$. This results in safe shift distances that are easier to compute. In the derivation of such weakening steps, the $u = lv \wedge v \in \mathbf{f}(P)$ part of the invariant of the inner repetition in Algorithm 6 is used. By adding $l, v := \varepsilon, \varepsilon$ to the initial assignments, we turn this into an outer repetition invariant. This also turns $l = \varepsilon$ **cor** $(l{\upharpoonright}1)v \notin \mathbf{f}(P)$ – the negation of the inner repetition guard – into an outer repetition invariant. Hence, we arrive at the following algorithm skeleton:

Algorithm 7(P$_+$, S$_+$, GS, EGC, SSD)

$u, r := \varepsilon, S;$
if $\varepsilon \in P \rightarrow O := \{(\varepsilon, \varepsilon, S)\} \;[\!]\; \varepsilon \notin P \rightarrow O := \varnothing$ **fi**;
$l, v := \varepsilon, \varepsilon;$
$\{$ invariant: $ur = S \wedge O = \left(\bigcup x, y, z : xyz = S \wedge xy \leq_p u \wedge y \in P : \{(x, y, z)\}\right)$
$\quad\quad \wedge\, u = lv \wedge v \in \mathbf{f}(P) \wedge \left(l = \varepsilon \ \mathbf{cor}\ (l{\upharpoonright}1)v \notin \mathbf{f}(P)\right)$ $\}$
do $r \neq \varepsilon \rightarrow$
 $u, r := u(r{\upharpoonright}k(l,v,r)), r{\downharpoonright}k(l,v,r);\ l, v := u, \varepsilon;\ q := \delta_{R,\mathbf{f}}(q_0, l{\upharpoonright}1);$
 as $\varepsilon \in P \rightarrow O := O \cup \{(u, \varepsilon, r)\}$ **sa**;
 $\{$ invariant: $q = \delta^*_{R,\mathbf{f}}(q_0, ((l{\upharpoonright}1)v)^R)$ $\}$
 do $l \neq \varepsilon$ **cand** $q \neq \bot \rightarrow$
  $l, v := l{\lfloor}1, (l{\upharpoonright}1)v;$
  $q := \delta_{R,\mathbf{f}}(q, l{\upharpoonright}1);$
  as $v \in P \rightarrow O := O \cup \{(l, v, r)\}$ **sa**
 od
od$\{$ R $\}$

Using this algorithm skeleton, various sublinear algorithms may be obtained by choosing appropriate $\mathbf{f}(P)$ and function k. For lack of space, we do not consider the choice of **suff**(P) for $\mathbf{f}(P)$ in this paper (see [9] instead).

In [17], an alternative algorithm skeleton for (suffix-based) skpm is presented, in which the update to O in the inner loop has been moved out of that loop. This requires the use of a precomputed output function, but has the potential to substantially reduce the algorithms' running time. This alternative skeleton is not considered in this paper.

3 Factor-Based Sublinear Pattern Matching

We now derive a family of algorithms by using the set of factors of P, **fact**(P). We use detail choice (GS=F), i.e. we choose **fact**(P) for $\mathbf{f}(P)$. The inner repetition guard then becomes $l \neq \varepsilon$ **cand** $(l{\upharpoonright}1)v \in \mathbf{fact}(P)$.

As direct evaluation of $(l{\upharpoonright}1)v \in \mathbf{fact}(P)$ is expensive, the transition function of an automaton recognizing the set $\mathbf{fact}(P)^R$ is used (detail choice (EGC=RFA)). Using function $\delta_{R,\mathbf{fact}}$ of Section 2 and making $q = \delta^*_{R,\mathbf{fact}}(q_0, ((l{\upharpoonright}1)v)^R)$ an invariant of the inner repetition, the guard becomes $l \neq \varepsilon$ **cand** $q \neq \bot$.

Note that various automata exist whose transition functions can be used for $\delta_{R,\mathbf{fact}}$, including the trie built on $\mathbf{fact}(P)^R$ and the *suffix automaton* or the *dawg* (for directed acyclic word graph) on $\mathbf{fact}(P)^R$ [3].

The use of detail choices (GS=F) and (EGC=RFA) in Algorithm 7 has two effects. Firstly, more character comparisons will in general be performed: in cases where $(l{\upharpoonright}1)v \notin \mathbf{suff}(P)$ yet $(l{\upharpoonright}1)v \in \mathbf{fact}(P)$, factor-based algorithms will extend v to the left more than strictly necessary. On the other hand, when the guard of the inner loop becomes false, $(l{\upharpoonright}1)v \notin \mathbf{fact}(P)$ holds, which gives potentially more information to use in the shift function than $(l{\upharpoonright}1)v \notin \mathbf{suff}(P)$.

Since $(l{\restriction}1)v \notin \mathbf{fact}(P) \Rightarrow (l{\restriction}1)v \notin \mathbf{suff}(P)$, we may use *any* safe shift function derived for suffix-based sublinear algorithms, discussed in [1, 2, 8]). This results in a large number of new algorithms, since most such shift functions have not been used with a factor-based algorithm before. In using such a shift function, we replace the $\mathbf{suff}(P)$ part of their domain by $\mathbf{fact}(P)$, meaning that precomputation changes.

3.1 The No-Factor Shift

We can get potentially larger shifts than by simply using suffix-based shift functions, since $(l{\restriction}1)v \notin \mathbf{fact}(P)$ is stronger than $(l{\restriction}1)v \notin \mathbf{suff}(P)$. In [9] we show that we may use any shift function satisfying

$$\begin{aligned}&\big(\mathbf{MIN}\, n : 1 \le n \wedge Weakening(\mathbf{suff}(u(r{\upharpoonright}n)) \cap P \neq \varnothing) : n\big)\\ &\mathbf{max}(1\,\mathbf{max}(lmin_P - |v|))\end{aligned} \tag{1}$$

The left operand of the outer **max** corresponds to any suffix-based safe shift function, while the right operand corresponds to the shift in case $(l{\restriction}1)v$ is not a factor of a keyword. We introduce shift function $k_{ssd,nfs}(l,v,r)$ where $k_{ssd,nfs} \in V^* \times \mathbf{fact}(P) \times V^* \to \mathbb{N}$ is defined by $k_{ssd,nfs}(l,v,r) = k_{ssd}(l,v,r)$ **max** (1 **max** $(lmin_P - |v|)$) for any suffix-based safe shift function k_{ssd} (algorithm detail (NFS)). We call it the no-factor shift, since it uses $(l{\restriction}1)v \notin \mathbf{fact}(P)$. In particular, we may use safe shift distance 1 with the no-factor shift to get shift distance 1 **max** (1 **max** $(lmin_P - |v|)$) $=$ 1 **max** $(lmin_P - |v|)$.

This equals the shift distance used in the basic ideas for backward DAWG matching [18, page 27] and – combined with algorithm detail (LMIN) mentioned in Section 2 – set backward DAWG matching [18, page 68]. The actual algorithms described in the literature use an improvement based on a property of DAWGs. We discuss this in Subsection 3.2.

The shift function 1 **max** $(lmin_P - |v|)$ just requires precomputation of $lmin_P$, yet gives quite large shift distances. This is the reason why factor-based skpm algorithms have gotten a lot of attention since their first descriptions in literature. The algorithms in literature do not combine it with any of the more involved precomputed shift functions as those described in [9, 1, 2]. If precomputation time is not an important issue however, combining such a shift function and the no-factor shift may be advantageous, potentially yielding larger shifts. As far as we know, such a combination has not been described or used before. Since about ten shift functions are given in [9], the combination of a single one with the no-factor shift already gives us about ten new factor-based skpm algorithms. It remains to be investigated whether these algorithms indeed improve over the running time of the algorithms from literature.

3.2 Cheap Computation of a Particular Shift Function

We now consider a different weakening of $\mathbf{suff}(u(r{\upharpoonright}n)) \cap P \neq \varnothing$ in the safe shift function predicate. In [9] we show that this leads to shift 1 $\mathbf{max}(lmin_P - last_{v,P})$ where $last_{v,P} = \big(\mathbf{MAX}\, m : 0 \le m \le |v| \wedge v{\restriction}m \in \mathbf{pref}(P) : m\big)$.

It seems to be rather difficult to compute $last_{v,P}$. When using a DAWG to implement transition function $\delta_{R,\mathbf{fact}}$ of algorithm detail (EGC=RFA) however, we may use a property of this automaton to compute $last_{v,P}$ 'on the fly': the final states of the DAWG correspond to suffixes of some $p^R \in P^R$, i.e. to prefixes of some $p \in P$. Thus, $last_{v,P}$ equals the length of v at the moment the most recent final state was visited.

We introduce shift function $k_{lskp} \in \mathbf{fact}(P) \to \mathbb{N}$ defined by $k_{lskp} = 1$ **max** $(lmin_P - last_{v,P})$. This function does not depend on l and can therefore be seen as a variant of the shift function represented by algorithm detail (NLA) in [9, 1]. Calculating the shift distance using k_{lskp} (and variable $last_{v,P}$) is algorithm detail (LSKP) (longest suffix which is keyword prefix). Due to lack of space, the complete algorithm is not presented here; please refer to [9, 8] for this.

The algorithm is a variant of Set Backward DAWG Matching [5], [18, page 68], which adds algorithm detail (LMIN). Adding algorithm detail (OKW) results in (single-keyword) Backward DAWG Matching.

Algorithm detail (NFS) is included in neither detail sequence, since the no-factor shift can never be larger than the k_{lskp} shift.

4 Factor Oracle-Based Sublinear Pattern Matching

We now derive a family of algorithms by using $\mathbf{factoracle}(P^R)^R$ for $\mathbf{f}(P)$. We may do so since $\mathbf{factoracle}(P^R)^R \supseteq \mathbf{fact}(P^R)^R$ and **factoracle** is suffix-closed [19, 6, 7]. We strengthen the inner repetition guard, which now becomes $l \neq \varepsilon$ **cand** $(l{\upharpoonright}1)v \in \mathbf{factoracle}(P^R)^R$.

Since direct evaluation of $(l{\upharpoonright}1)v \in \mathbf{factoracle}(P^R)^R$ is impossible[3], the transition function of the factor oracle [19, 6, 7] recognizing the set $\mathbf{factoracle}(P^R)$ is used. Using function $\delta_{\mathbf{factoracle}(P^R)}$[4] and making $q = \delta^*_{\mathbf{factoracle}(P^R)}(q_0, ((l{\upharpoonright}1)v)^R)$ an invariant of the inner repetition, the guard becomes $l \neq \varepsilon$ **cand** $q \neq \perp$.

The use of detail choices (GS=FO) and (EGC=RFO) in Algorithm 7 has two important effects. Firstly, the factor oracle recognizing $\mathbf{factoracle}(P^R)$ is easier to construct and may have less states and transitions than an automaton recognizing $\mathbf{fact}(P^R)$ [19, 6, 7]. On the other hand, even more character comparisons may be performed than when using an automaton recognizing $\mathbf{fact}(P^R)$ (let alone when using an automaton recognizing $\mathbf{suff}(P^R)$): When $(l{\upharpoonright}1)v \notin \mathbf{fact}(P)$ yet $(l{\upharpoonright}1)v \in \mathbf{factoracle}(P^R)^R$, the algorithm will go on extending v to the left more than strictly necessary.

However, $(l{\upharpoonright}1)v \notin \mathbf{factoracle}(P^R)^R \Rightarrow (l{\upharpoonright}1)v \notin \mathbf{fact}(P^R)^R$ and hence $(l{\upharpoonright}1)v \notin \mathbf{fact}(P)$ and therefore any shift function may be used satisfying Equation 1. In particular, both the safe shift functions for the suffix-based algorithms as well as the no-factor shift introduced in Section 3 may be used.

---

[3] The language of a factor oracle so far has not been described separately from the automaton construction.

[4] Since $\mathbf{factoracle}(P)^R \neq \mathbf{factoracle}(P^R)$ could hold, we cannot use $\delta_{R,\mathbf{factoracle}}$ to describe the transition function. We introduce $\delta_{\mathbf{factoracle}(P^R)}$, the transition function of the automaton recognizing $\mathbf{factoracle}(P^R)$.

The Set Backward Oracle Matching algorithm [7], [18, pages 69-72] equals our algorithm (P$_+$, S$_+$, GS=FO, EGC=RFO, LMIN, SSD, NFS, ONE), while adding detail (OKW) gives the single keyword Backward Oracle Matching algorithm [6], [18, pages 34-36], [19].

5 Final Remarks

We showed how suffix, factor and factor oracle automaton-based sublinear keyword pattern matching algorithms appearing in the literature can be seen as instantiations of a general automaton-based skpm algorithm skeleton. The algorithms were formally derived as part of a new taxonomy, presenting correctness arguments and clarity on their working and interrelationships.

We discussed the algorithm skeleton and some instantiations leading to well-known algorithms such as (Set) Backward DAWG Matching and (Set) Backward Oracle Matching. In addition, we showed the shift functions used for suffix-based algorithms to be in principle reusable for factor- and factor oracle-based algorithms. This results in a number of previously undescribed factor automaton-based skpm algorithm variants. Their practical performance remains to be investigated and compared to the more basic factor-based skpm algorithms known from the literature and described in this paper as well.

The algorithms described here could also be described using a generalization of the alternative Commentz-Walter algorithm skeleton presented in [17], in which the output variable update is moved out of a loop to increase performance. In addition to changes to the algorithms in the taxonomy to accomodate this idea, benchmarking would also need to be performed to study the effects.

We have not considered precomputation of the various shift functions used in the algorithms discussed in this paper. Precomputation of these functions for suffix-based algorithms was described in [1], but extending this precomputation to factor- and factor oracle-based algorithms remains to be done.

References

1. Watson, B.W., Zwaan, G.: A taxonomy of sublinear multiple keyword pattern matching algorithms. Science of Computer Programming **27** (1996) 85–118
2. Watson, B.W.: Taxonomies and Toolkits of Regular Language Algorithms. PhD thesis, Faculty of Computing Science, Technische Universiteit Eindhoven (1995)
3. Crochemore, M., Rytter, W.: Jewels of Stringology - Text Algorithms. World Scientific Publishing (2003)
4. Apostolico, A., Galil, Z.: Pattern Matching Algorithms. Oxford University Press (1997)
5. Crochemore, M., Czumaj, A., Gasieniec, L., Jarominek, S., Lecroq, T., Plandowski, W., Rytter, W.: Speeding up two string matching algorithms. Algorithmica **12** (1994) 247–267
6. Allauzen, C., Crochemore, M., Raffinot, M.: Efficient Experimental String Matching by Weak Factor Recognition. In: Proceedings of the 12th conference on Combinatorial Pattern Matching. Volume 2089 of LNCS. (2001) 51–72

7. Allauzen, C., Raffinot, M.: Oracle des facteurs d'un ensemble de mots. Technical Report 99-11, Institut Gaspard-Monge, Université de Marne-la-Vallée (1999)
8. Cleophas, L.G.: Towards SPARE Time: A New Taxonomy and Toolkit of Keyword Pattern Matching Algorithms. Master's thesis, Department of Mathematics and Computer Science, Technische Universiteit Eindhoven (2003)
9. Cleophas, L., Watson, B.W., Zwaan, G.: A new taxonomy of sublinear keyword pattern matching algorithms. Technical Report 04/07, Department of Mathematics and Computer Science, Technische Universiteit Eindhoven (2004)
10. Watson, B.W., Cleophas, L.: SPARE Parts: A C++ toolkit for String PAttern REcognition. Software – Practice & Experience **34** (2004) 697–710
11. Jonkers, H.: Abstraction, specification and implementation techniques, with an application to garbage collection. Technical Report 166, Mathematisch Centrum, Amsterdam (1983)
12. Watson, B.W.: Constructing minimal acyclic deterministic finite automata. PhD thesis, Department of Computer Science, University of Pretoria (2004)
13. Barla-Szabo, G.: A taxonomy of graph representations. Master's thesis, Department of Computer Science, University of Pretoria (2002)
14. Dijkstra, E.W., Scholten, C.S.: Predicate Calculus and Program Semantics. Springer, New York, NY (1990)
15. Dijkstra, E.W.: A Discipline of Programming. Prentice Hall, Englewood Cliffs, NJ (1976)
16. van den Eijnde, J.: Program derivation in acyclic graphs and related problems. Technical Report 92/04, Faculty of Computing Science, Technische Universiteit Eindhoven (1992)
17. Watson, B.W.: A new family of Commentz-Walter-style multiple-keyword pattern matching algorithms. In: Proceedings of the Prague Stringology Club Workshop 2000, Department of Computer Science and Engineering, Czech Technical University, Prague (2000) 71–76
18. Navarro, G., Raffinot, M.: Flexible pattern matching in strings: practical on-line search algorithms for texts and biological sequences. Cambridge University Press (2002)
19. Cleophas, L., Zwaan, G., Watson, B.W.: Constructing Factor Oracles. In: Proceedings of the Prague Stringology Conference 2003, Department of Computer Science and Engineering, Czech Technical University, Prague (2003)

A Quantifications

A basic understanding of the meaning of *quantifications* is assumed. We use the notation $(\oplus a : R(a) : E(a))$ where $\oplus$ is the associative and commutative *quantification operator* (with unit $e_\oplus$), a is the *quantified variable* introduced, R is the *range predicate* on a, and E is the *quantified expression*. By definition, we have $(\oplus a : false : E(a)) = e_\oplus$.

The following table lists some of the most commonly quantified operators, their quantified symbols, and their units:

Operator	$\vee$	$\wedge$	$\cup$	**min**	**max**	$+$
Symbol	$\exists$	$\forall$	$\bigcup$	**MIN**	**MAX**	Σ
Unit	$false$	$true$	$\varnothing$	$+\infty$	$-\infty$	0

Techniques for Efficient Query Expansion

Bodo Billerbeck and Justin Zobel

School of Computer Science and Information Technology
RMIT University, Melbourne, Australia
{bodob,jz}@cs.rmit.edu.au

Abstract. Query expansion is a well-known method for improving average effectiveness in information retrieval. However, the most effective query expansion methods rely on costly retrieval and processing of feedback documents. We explore alternative methods for reducing query-evaluation costs, and propose a new method based on keeping a brief summary of each document in memory. This method allows query expansion to proceed three times faster than previously, while approximating the effectiveness of standard expansion.

1 Introduction

Standard ranking techniques in information retrieval return documents that contain the same terms as the query. While the insistence on exact vocabulary matching is often effective, identification of some relevant documents involves finding alternative query terms. Previous work has shown that through query expansion (QE) effectiveness is often significantly improved (Rocchio, 1971, Robertson and Walker, 1999, Carpineto et al., 2001).

Local analysis has been found to be one of the most effective methods for expanding queries (Xu and Croft, 2000). For those methods the original query is used to determine top-ranked documents from which expansion terms are subsequently extracted. A major drawback of such methods is the need to retrieve those documents during query evaluation, greatly increasing costs. In other work (Billerbeck et al., 2003), we explored the use of surrogates built from past queries as a cheap source of expansion terms, but such surrogates require large query logs to be usable.

In this paper, we identify the factors that contribute to the cost of query expansion, and explore in principle the alternatives for reducing these costs. Many of these approaches compromise effectiveness so severely that they are not of practical benefit. However, one approach is consistently effective: use of brief summaries – a pool of the most important terms – of each document. These *surrogates* are much smaller than the source documents, and can be rapidly processed during expansion. In experiments with several test sets, we show that our approach reduces the time needed to expand and evaluate a query by a factor of three, while approximately maintaining effectiveness compared to standard QE.

A. Apostolico and M. Melucci (Eds.): SPIRE 2004, LNCS 3246, pp. 30–42, 2004.

2 Background

Relevance feedback is used to refine a query using knowledge of whether documents retrieved by this query are relevant. Weighted terms from judged documents are added to the original query, where they act as positive and negative examples of the terms that should occur in relevant and non-relevant documents. The modified query is then reissued, in the hope of ranking the remaining relevant documents more highly (Rocchio, 1971, Ruthven and Lalmas, 2003). Interactive QE can significantly increase effectiveness (Magennis and van Rijsbergen, 1997), although on average – for non expert users – automatic expansion is more likely to lead to better performance (Ruthven, 2003).

In automatic QE, also called pseudo relevance feedback, the query is augmented with expansion terms from highly-ranked documents (Robertson and Walker, 1999). An alternative (Qiu and Frei, 1993, Gauch and Wang, 1997) is to examine the document collection ahead of time and construct similarity thesauri to be accessed at query time. The use of thesauri in general has been shown to be less successful than automatic QE (Mandala et al., 1999), though the two approaches can be successfully combined (Xu and Croft, 2000).

An effective method for QE, used throughout this paper, is based on the Okapi BM25 measure (Robertson and Walker, 1999, Robertson et al., 1992). Slightly modified, this measure is as follows:

$$bm25(q,d) = \sum_{t \in q} \log \left(\frac{N - f_t + 0.5}{f_t + 0.5} \right) \times \frac{(k_1 + 1) f_{d,t}}{K + f_{d,t}}$$

where terms t appear in query q; the collection contains N documents d; f_t documents contain a particular term and a particular document contains a particular term $f_{d,t}$ times; K is $k_1((1-b)+b \times L_d/AL)$; constants k_1 and b respectively are set to 1.2 and 0.75; and L_d and AL are measurements in a suitable unit for the document length and average document length respectively. The modifications to the original formulation (see Sparck-Jones et al. (2000) for a detailed explanation) is the omission of a component that deals with repeated query terms. In the queries we use, term repetitions are rare.

In this paper we use the expansion method proposed by Robertson and Walker (1999) where E terms with the lowest *term selection value* are chosen from the top R ranked documents:

$$TSV_t = \left(\frac{f_t}{N} \right)^{r_t} \binom{R}{r_t}$$

where a term t is contained in r_t of the top ranked R documents. The expansion terms get added to the original query, but instead of using their Okapi value, their weight (Robertson and Walker, 1999) is chosen by the formula[1]:

[1] The factor of $\frac{1}{3}$ was recommended by unpublished correspondence with the authors. It de-emphasises expansion terms and prevents query drift, that is, "alteration of the focus of a search topic caused by improper expansion" (Mitra et al., 1998). We confirmed in unpublished experiments that the value of the factor is suitable.

$$\frac{1}{3} \times \log\left(\frac{(r_t + 0.5)/(R - r_t + 0.5)}{(f_t - r_t + 0.5)/(N - f_t - R + r_t + 0.5)}\right)$$

We have shown previously that best choices of R and E depend on the collection used and should in principle be carefully optimised (Billerbeck and Zobel, 2004); to reduce the complexity of the experiments, in this paper we use the standard values of $R = 10$ and $E = 25$.

Although there has been a great deal of research on efficient evaluation of ranked queries (Witten et al., 1999, pages 207–210), there is no prior work on efficient QE for text retrieval, the focus of this paper.

3 Query Expansion Practicalities

In most expansion methods making use of local analysis, there are five key stages. First, the original query is used to rank an initial set of documents. This set is then retrieved from disk and all terms are extracted from those documents. Terms are evaluated and ranked in order of their potential contribution to the query. The top ranked terms are appended to the query, and finally the reformulated query is reissued and a final set of documents is ranked.

Each phase of the ranking process has scope for efficiency gains, but some of the gains involve heuristics that can compromise effectiveness. In this section we explore these options; this exploration provides a focus for the experiments reported later in this paper. Some of the concepts introduced here – in particular, associations and surrogates – are described in more detail in the next section.

Initial Ranking. During the first stage, documents are ranked according to the original query. For each query term the inverted list is retrieved, if it hasn't been cached, and processed. For each document referenced in the list, a score is calculated and added to a list of scores that is kept for (say) 20,000 documents (Moffat and Zobel, 1996). Once all query terms have been processed, the top R documents are used for the next stage.

The cost of accessing an inverted list depends on the disk access time. For a long list, the costs are directly proportional to list size. If the list is organised by document identifier, the whole list must be fetched for each query term.

A way of reducing the cost of retrieving and processing the inverted lists is to cut down the volume of list information that has to be retrieved. This has been achieved by, for example, Anh and Moffat (2002), where documents are not stored in the order they are encountered during indexing, but in order of the *impact* a term has in a particular document. For instance, a term has more impact in a document in which it occurs twice, than another of the same length in which it occurs once. Using this ordering means that either the processing of lists can be stopped once a threshold is reached, or that the lists arc capped to begin with, leading to lower storage requirements, reduced seek times, and allowing more lists to be cached in memory. We have not used impacts in our experiments, but the gains that they provide are likely to be in addition to the gains that we achieve with our methods.

Another way to reduce list length, discussed in more detail later, is to index only a fraction of the document collection for the initial ranking. Initial ranking is traditionally on the document collection, but there is no particular reason why other collections should not be used. Another option, also explored later, of this kind is to use document surrogates. A drawback of these approaches is that the full index still needs to be available for the final ranking and thus is loaded at the same time as auxiliary indexes. This means that some of the advantage of using shorter lists is negated by having less space available to cache them.

Fetching Documents. Having identified the highly ranked documents, these need to be fetched. In the vast majority of cases these documents are not cached from a previous expansion or retrieval process (assuming a typical memory size), and therefore have to be fetched from disk, at a delay of a few milliseconds each.

Traditionally, full-text documents are fetched. This is the most expensive stage of expansion and therefore the area where the greatest gains are available. We have shown previously that surrogates – which are a fraction of the size of the documents – can be more effective than full-text documents (Billerbeck et al., 2003). Using surrogates such as query associations is more efficient, provided that those surrogates can be pre-computed, as discussed later.

Another approach is limiting the number of documents available for extraction of terms, which should result in higher efficiency, due to reduced cache misses when retrieving the remaining documents and otherwise smaller seek times as it can be expected that the limited number of documents are clustered on disk. Documents could be chosen by, for example, discarding those that are the least often accessed over a large number of queries (Garcia et al., 2004).

A more radical measure is to use in-memory document surrogates that provide a sufficiently large pool of expansion terms, as described in the following section. If such a collection can be made sufficiently small, the total cost of expansion can be greatly reduced. Typically full text document collections don't fit into main memory, but well-constructed surrogates may be only a small fraction of the size of the original collection. Our surrogates are designed to be as small as possible while maintaining effectiveness.

Extracting Candidate Terms. Next, *candidate terms* (that is, potential expansion terms) are extracted from the fetched documents. These documents need to be parsed, and terms need to be stopped. (We do not use stemming, since in unpublished experiments we have found that stemming does not make a significant difference to effectiveness.)

This phase largely depends on the previous phase; if full text documents have been fetched, these need to be parsed and terms need to be stopped. In the case of query associations, the surrogates are pre-parsed and pre-stopped and extraction is therefore much more efficient.

The in-memory surrogates we propose can be based on pointers rather than the full terms in memory. The pointers reference terms in the dictionary used for finding and identifying statistics and inverted lists. They have a constant size

(4 bytes) and are typically smaller than a vocabulary term. This approach also eliminates the lookups needed in the next stage.

Selecting Expansion Terms. The information (such as the inverse document frequency) necessary for calculation of a term's TSV is held in the vocabulary, which may be held on disk or (as in our implementation) in memory; even when held on disk, the frequency of access to the vocabulary means that typically much of it is cached. As a result, this phase is the fastest and can only be sped up by providing fewer candidate terms for selection.

Query associations typically consist of 20–50 terms, as opposed to the average of 200 or more for web documents. Use of surrogates could make this stage several times more efficient than the standard approach. Surrogates are a strict subset of full text documents, and usually are a tiny fraction thereof, ensuring that selection is efficient.

Final Ranking. Finally the document collection is ranked against the reformulated query. Similar considerations as in the first phase are applicable here. We have shown previously (Billerbeck et al., 2003) that final ranking against surrogates is, unsurprisingly, ineffective. The only option for efficiency gains at this stage is to use an approach such as impact-ordering, as discussed earlier.

4 Methods of Increasing Efficiency for QE

In the previous section we identified costs and plausible approaches for reducing them. In this section, we consider the most promising methods in more detail, setting a framework for experiments. In particular, we propose the novel strategy of using bag-of-word summaries as a source of expansion terms.

Query Associations. Query associations (Scholer and Williams, 2002) capture the topic of a document by associating past user queries with the documents that have been highly ranked by that query. We have previously shown (Billerbeck et al., 2003) that associations are effective when useful query logs are available. A disadvantage of using associations is that an extra index needs to be loaded and referenced during query evaluation. However, this penalty is small, as associations are likely to be a small fraction of collection size. The advantages are that associations are usually pre-stemmed and stopped, stored in a parsed form, and cheap to retrieve.

Rather than indexing the associations, it would be possible in principle to rank using the standard index, then fetch and expand from the associations, but in our earlier work (Billerbeck et al., 2003) we found that it was necessary to rank against the associations themselves.

Reducing Collection Size for Sourcing Expansion Terms. The intuition underlying expansion is that, in a large collection, there should be multiple documents on the same topic as the query, and that these should have other pertinent terms.

However, there is no logical reason why the whole collection should have to be accessed to identify such documents. Plausibly, documents sampled at random from the collection should represent the overall collection in respect of the terminology used. In our experiments, we sampled the collection by choosing every nth document, for n of 2 and 4. Other options would be to use centroid clusters or other forms of representative chosen on the basis of semantics. Documents could also be stored in a pre-parsed format (such as a forward index), which we have not tested.

In-Memory Document Summaries. The major bottleneck of local analysis is the reliance on the highly ranked documents for useful expansion terms. These documents typically need to be retrieved from disk. We propose that summaries of all documents be kept in memory, or in a small auxiliary database that is likely to remain cached. A wide range of document summarisation techniques have been investigated (Goldstein et al., 1999), and in particular Lam-Adesina and Jones (2001) have used summarisation for QE. In this work, representative sentences are selected, giving an abbreviated human-readable document.

However, summaries to be used for QE are not for human consumption. We propose instead that the summaries consist of the terms with the highest $tf.idf$ values, that is, the terms that the expansion process should rank highest as candidates if given the whole document. To choose terms, we use the function:

$$tf.idf = \log\left(\frac{N}{f_t}\right) \times \log\left(1 + f_{d,t}\right)$$

where N is the number of documents in the collection, f_t of which contain term t, and $f_{d,t}$ is the number of occurrences of t in document d.

Given these values, we can then build summaries in two ways. One is to have a fixed number S of highly-ranked terms per document. The other is to choose a global threshold C, in which case each summary consists of all the document terms whose $tf.idf$ value exceeds C. Instead of representing summaries as sequences of terms, it is straightforward to instead use lists of pointers to the vocabulary representation of the term, reducing storage costs and providing rapid access to any statistics needed for the TSV. During querying, all terms in the surrogates that have been ranked against the original query are then used for selection. This not only avoids long disk I/Os, but also the original documents – typically stored only in their raw form – do not need to be parsed. S or C can be chosen depending on collection size or available memory.

Although it is likely that query-biased summaries (Tombros and Sanderson, 1998) – as provided in most contemporary web search engines – would be more effective (Lam-Adesina and Jones, 2001), such a method cannot be applied in the context of efficient QE, as query-biased summaries cannot be precomputed.

Other Approaches. Since the original query terms effectively get processed twice during the ranking process, it seems logical to only process the original query terms during the initial ranking, and then, later, process the expansion terms without clearing the accumulator table that was used for the initial ranking.

However, as explored previously (Moffat and Zobel, 1996), limiting the number of accumulators aids efficiency and effectiveness. To support this strategy, query terms must be sorted by their inverse document frequency before the query is processed. Because most expansion terms have a high inverse document frequency – that is, they appear in few documents and are relatively rare – it is important that they be processed before most of the original query terms, which typically have lower values. (The effect is similar – albeit weaker – to that of impact ordered indexes as discussed previously.) This means that the original query must be processed again with the expansion terms for final ranking. Intuition suggests that this argument is incorrect, and the original query terms should be allowed to choose the documents; however, in preliminary experiments we found that it was essential to process the original terms a second time. Processing only expansion terms in the second phase reduced costs, but led to poor effectiveness.

Other strategies could also lead to reduced costs. Only some documents, perhaps chosen by frequency of access (Garcia et al., 2004) or sampling, might be included in the set of surrogates. A second tier of surrogates could be stored on disk, for retrieval in cases where the highly-ranked documents are not amongst those selected by sampling. Any strategy could be further improved by compressing the in-memory surrogates, for example with d-gapping (Witten et al., 1999, page 115) and a variable-byte compression scheme (Scholer et al., 2002).

Note that our summaries have no contextual or structural information, and therefore cannot be used – without major modifications – in conjunction with methods using such information, such as the local context analysis method of Xu and Croft (2000) or the summarisation method of Goldstein et al. (1999).

5 Experiments

Evaluating these approaches to QE requires that we test whether the heuristics degrade effectiveness, and whether they lead to reduced query evaluation time. To ensure that the time measurements were realistic, we used Lucy[2] as the underlying search engine.

The test data is drawn from the TREC conferences (Harman, 1995). We used two collections. The first was of newswire data, from TREC 7 and 8. The second was the WT10g collection, consisting of 10 gigabytes of web data crawled in 1997 (Bailey et al., 2003) for TREC 9 and 10. Each of these collections has two sets of 50 topics and accompanying relevance judgements. As queries, we used the title field from each TREC topic. We use the Wilcoxon signed rank test to evaluate the significance of the effectiveness results (Zobel, 1998).

For timings, we used 10,000 stopped queries taken from two query logs collected for the Excite search engine (Spink et al., 2002); these are web queries and thus are suitable for the WT10g runs. Since we were not able to obtain appropriate query logs for the newswire data, we used the same 10,000 queries

[2] Lucy/Zettair is an open source search engine being developed at RMIT by the Search Engine Group. The primary aim in developing Lucy is to test techniques for efficient information retrieval. Lucy is available from http://www.seg.rmit.edu.au/.

Table 1. Performance of expansion techniques of TREC queries on the TREC newswire and WT10g collections, for TREC 8 and TREC 10 queries. Effectiveness results shown are average precision (AvP), precision at 10 (P@10), and R-Precision (R-P). Also shown is the average query time over 10,000 queries and the amount of overhead memory required for each method; "index" marks the need to refer to an auxiliary index during expansion. A † marks results that are significantly different to the baseline of no expansion at the 0.10 level, and ‡ at the level of 0.05. S is the number of summary terms used, and C specifies the cutoff threshold for the selection value.

TREC	Expansion Method	Time (ms)	AvP	P@10	R-P	Mem (MB)
8	None	23	0.221	0.442	0.260	n/a
8	Standard	211	0.247‡	0.466	0.288‡	n/a
8	Assoc.	179	0.219	0.400	0.263	index
8	Half1	201	0.241‡	0.436	0.283‡	index
8	Half2	185	0.235†	0.430	0.275‡	index
8	Quarter1	167	0.221	0.382‡	0.255	index
8	Quarter2	183	0.237	0.430	0.278	index
8	Quarter3	175	0.220	0.434	0.268	index
8	Quarter4	174	0.218	0.390‡	0.273	index
8	$S = 1$	46	0.231‡	0.446	0.267‡	6
8	$S = 10$	54	0.238‡	0.438	0.271‡	24
8	$S = 25$	59	0.244‡	0.456	0.277‡	54
8	$S = 40$	61	0.245‡	0.452	0.275‡	83
8	$S = 50$	64	0.243‡	0.454	0.281‡	102
8	$S = 100$	72	0.240‡	0.450	0.282‡	183
8	$C = 1.0$	58	0.243‡	0.448	0.280‡	56
10	None	62	0.163	0.290	0.190	n/a
10	Standard	615	0.180	0.288	0.202	n/a
10	Assoc.	835	0.180	0.272†	0.209	index
10	$S = 1$	139	0.138	0.218	0.150	19
10	$S = 10$	177	0.153†	0.227	0.169	76
10	$S = 25$	202	0.156	0.224	0.170	166
10	$S = 28$	204	0.185	0.308	0.217†	183
10	$S = 50$	221	0.156	0.224	0.170	296
10	$S = 100$	245	0.156	0.224	0.170	296
10	$C = 1.0$	217	0.185‡	0.312†	0.213†	190

for this collection. The machine used for our timings is a dual Intel Pentium III 866 MHz with 768 MB of main memory running Fedora Core 1.

Results

We used the TREC 8 and TREC 10 query sets to explore the methods. Results for this exploration are shown in Table 1. We applied the best methods found in Table 1 to the TREC 7 and TREC 9 query sets, as shown in Table 2. The tables detail the collection, the method of expansion, average precision, precision at 10, and r-precision values, as well as auxiliary memory required. A second index

Table 2. As in Table 1, but showing results only for the methods that worked best on TREC 8 and TREC 10.

TREC	Expansion Method	Time (ms)	AvP	P@10	R-P	Mem (MB)
7	None	23	0.191	0.456	0.248	n/a
7	Standard	211	0.232‡	0.452	0.286‡	n/a
7	$S = 40$	61	0.220‡	0.426†	0.279‡	83
7	$C = 1.0$	58	0.215‡	0.426†	0.272‡	56
9	None	62	0.193	0.267	0.223	n/a
9	Standard	615	0.177	0.260	0.200	n/a
9	$S = 28$	204	0.161	0.269	0.176	183
9	$C = 1.0$	217	0.162	0.256	0.169‡	190

is needed for the runs where associations or fractional collections are used for initial ranking and candidate term extraction.

For TREC 8 and to a lesser extent TREC 10, standard QE improves over the baseline, but in both cases query evaluation takes around nine times as long. Several of the methods proposed do not succeed in our aims. Associations take as long as standard QE, and effectiveness is reduced. For TREC 8 the surrogates are arguably inappropriate, as the web queries may not be pertinent to the newswire data; however, this issue highlights the fact that without a query log associations cannot be used.

Using halves ($n = 2$) or quarters ($n = 4$) of the collection also reduces effectiveness, and has little impact on expansion time; this is due to the need to load and access a second index. Larger n led to smaller improvements in QE; in experiments with $n = 8$, not reported here, QE gave no improvements. Reducing R to roughly a quarter of its original size in order to cater for a smaller number of relevant documents – as intuition might suggest – only further degrades results. This is consistent with previous work which shows that retrievel effectiveness especially in the top ranked documents is greater for larger collections than sub-collections (Hawking and Robertson, 2003) which means that there is a higher likelihood of sourcing expansion terms from relevant documents when using local analysis QE. It was also found that QE works best when expansion terms are sourced from collections that are a superset of documents of the one targeted (Kwok and Chan, 1998).

However, our simple *tf.idf* summaries work well. Even one-word ($S = 1$) summaries yield significantly improved average precision on TREC 8, for a memory overhead of a few megabytes. The best cases were $S = 40$ on TREC 8 and $S = 28$ on TREC 10, where processing costs were only a third those of standard QE. These gains are similar to those achieved by (Lam-Adesina and Jones, 2001) with summaries of 6–9 sentences each, but our summaries are considerably more compact, showing the advantage of a form of summary intended only for QE. While the memory overheads are non-trivial – over 180 megabytes for TREC 10 – they are well within the capacity of a small desktop machine.

Results on TREC 7 for the summaries are equally satisfactory, with good effectiveness and low overheads. Results on TREC 9 are, however, disappoint-

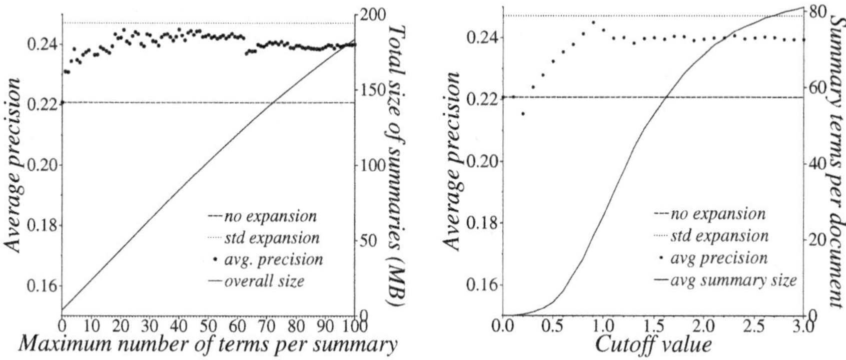

Fig. 1. Varying average precision and associated memory cost with the number and cutoff value of summary terms respectively. Using the TREC 8 collection and queries.

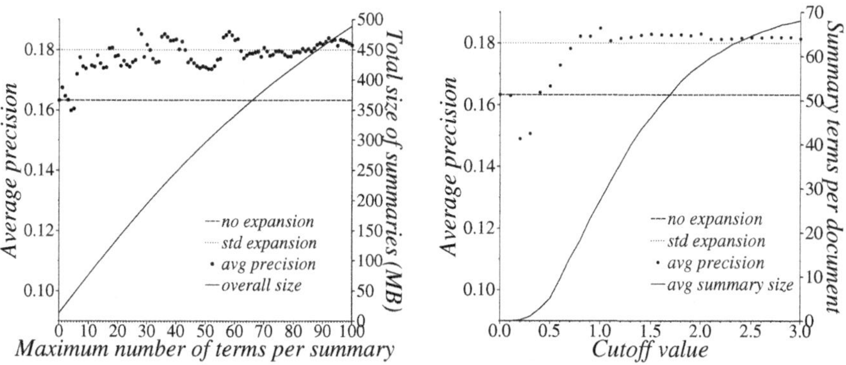

Fig. 2. As in previous figure, but using the TREC 10 collection and queries.

ing. We had already discovered that expansion on TREC 9 does not improve effectiveness (Billerbeck and Zobel, 2004); our results here are, in that light, unsurprising. The principal observation is that QE based on summaries is still of similar effectiveness to that based on full documents.

We show only one value for the cutoff threshold, $C = 1.0$. This leads to the same effectiveness for similar memory overhead. Summaries and choice of S and C are further examined in Figures 1 and 2 for newswire and web data respectively. These show that a wide range of S values (left figure) and C values (right figure) lead to improved effectiveness, in some cases exceeding that of standard QE.

6 Conclusions

We have identified the main costs of query expansion and, for each stage of the query evaluation process, considered options for reducing costs. Guided by preliminary experiments, we explored two options in detail: expansion via reduced-size collections and expansion via document surrogates. Two forms of surrogates were considered: query associations, consisting of queries for which each document was highly ranked, and *tf.idf* summaries.

The most successful method was the *tf.idf* summaries. These are much smaller than the original collections, yet are able to provide effectiveness close to that of standard QE. The size reduction and simple representation means that they can be rapidly processed. Of the two methods for building summaries, slightly better performance was obtained with those consisting of terms whose selection value exceeded a global threshold. The key to the success of this method is that it eliminates several costs: there is no need to fetch documents after the initial phase of list processing, and selection and extraction of candidate terms is trivial.

Many of the methods we explored were unsuccessful. Associations can yield good effectiveness if a log is available, but are expensive to process. Reduced-size collections yielded no benefits; it is possible that choosing documents on a more principled basis would lead to different effectiveness outcomes, but the costs are unlikely to be reduced. Streamlining list processing by carrying accumulator information from one stage to the next led to a collapse in effectiveness. Our *tf.idf* summaries, in contrast, maintain the effectiveness of QE while reducing time by a factor of three.

Acknowledgements

This research is supported by the Australian Research Council and by the State Government of Victoria. Thanks to Nick Lester and William Webber from the SEG group for their help with Lucy. Thanks also to Falk Scholer for letting us use his pre-built associated queries.

References

V. N. Anh and A. Moffat. Impact transformation: effective and efficient web retrieval. In *Proc. ACM-SIGIR Int. Conf. on Research and Development in Information Retrieval*, pages 3–10. ACM Press, New York, 2002.

P. Bailey, N. Craswell, and D. Hawking. Engineering a multi-purpose test collection for web retrieval experiments. *Information Processing & Management*, 39(6):853–871, 2003.

B. Billerbeck, F. Scholer, H. E. Williams, and J. Zobel. Query expansion using associated queries. In *Proc. Int. Conf. on Information and Knowledge Management*, pages 2–9. ACM Press, New York, 2003.

B. Billerbeck and J. Zobel. Questioning query expansion: An examination of behaviour and parameters. In K.-D. Schewe and H. E. Williams, editors, *Proc. Australasian Database Conf.*, volume 27, pages 69–76. CRPIT, 2004.

C. Carpineto, R. de Mori, G. Romano, and B. Bigi. An information-theoretic approach to automatic query expansion. *ACM Transactions on Information Systems*, 19(1): 1–27, 2001.

S. Garcia, H. E. Williams, and A. Cannane. Access-ordered indexes. In V. Estivill-Castro, editor, *Proceedings of the 27th Australasian Computer Science Conference*, volume 26, pages 7–14, Dunedin, New Zealand, January 2004.

S. Gauch and J. Wang. A corpus analysis approach for automatic query expansion. In *Proc. Int. Conf. on Information and Knowledge Management*, pages 278–284. ACM Press, New York, 1997.

J. Goldstein, M. Kantrowitz, V. Mittal, and J. Carbonell. Summarizing text documents: sentence selection and evaluation metrics. In *Proc. ACM-SIGIR Int. Conf. on Research and Development in Information Retrieval*, pages 121–128. ACM Press, New York, 1999.

D. Harman. Overview of the second Text REtrieval Conference (TREC-2). *Information Processing & Management*, 31(3):271–289, 1995.

D. Hawking and S. E. Robertson. On collection size and retrieval effectiveness. *Kluwer International Journal of Information Retrieval*, 6(1):99–150, 2003.

K. L. Kwok and M. Chan. Improving two-stage ad-hoc retrieval for short queries. In *Proc. ACM-SIGIR Int. Conf. on Research and Development in Information Retrieval*, pages 250–256. ACM Press, 1998.

A. M. Lam-Adesina and G. J. F. Jones. Applying summarization techniques for term selection in relevance feedback. In *Proc. ACM-SIGIR Int. Conf. on Research and Development in Information Retrieval*, pages 1–9, New Orleans, Louisiana, United States, 2001. ACM Press, New York.

M. Magennis and C. J. van Rijsbergen. The potential and actual effectiveness of interactive query expansion. In *Proc. ACM-SIGIR Int. Conf. on Research and Development in Information Retrieval*, pages 324–332. ACM Press, New York, 1997.

R. Mandala, T. Tokunaga, and H. Tanaka. Combining multiple evidence from different types of thesaurus for query expansion. In *Proc. ACM-SIGIR Int. Conf. on Research and Development in Information Retrieval*, pages 191–197, Berkeley, California, United States, 1999. ACM Press, New York.

M. Mitra, A. Singhal, and C. Buckley. Improving automatic query expansion. In W. B. Croft, A. Moffat, C. J. van Rijsbergen, R. Wilkinson, and J. Zobel, editors, *Proc. ACM-SIGIR Int. Conf. on Research and Development in Information Retrieval*, pages 206–214, Melbourne, Australia, August 1998. ACM Press, New York.

A. Moffat and J. Zobel. Self-indexing inverted files for fast text retrieval. *ACM Transactions on Information Systems*, 14(4):349–379, October 1996.

Y. Qiu and H.-P. Frei. Concept based query expansion. In *Proc. ACM-SIGIR Int. Conf. on Research and Development in Information Retrieval*, pages 160–169. ACM Press, New York, 1993.

S. E. Robertson and S. Walker. Okapi/Keenbow at TREC-8. In *Proc. Text Retrieval Conf. (TREC)*, pages 151–161, Gaithersburg, Maryland, 1999. NIST Special Publication 500-264.

S. E. Robertson, S. Walker, M. Hancock-Beaulieu, A. Gull, and M. Lau. Okapi at TREC. In *Proc. Text Retrieval Conf. (TREC)*, pages 21–30, 1992.

J. J. Rocchio. Relevance feedback in information retrieval. In E. Ide and G. Salton, editors, *The Smart Retrieval System — Experiments in Automatic Document Processing*, pages 313–323. Prentice-Hall, Englewood Cliffs, New Jersey, 1971.

I. Ruthven. Re-examining the potential effectiveness of interactive query expansion. In *Proc. ACM-SIGIR Int. Conf. on Research and Development in Information Retrieval*, pages 213–220. ACM Press, New York, 2003.

I. Ruthven and M. Lalmas. A survey on the use of relevance feedback for information access systems. *Knowledge Engineering Review*, 18(2):95–145, 2003.

F. Scholer and H. E. Williams. Query association for effective retrieval. In C. Nicholas, D. Grossman, K. Kalpakis, S. Qureshi, H. van Dissel, and L. Seligman, editors, *Proc. Int. Conf. on Information and Knowledge Management*, pages 324–331, McLean, Virginia, 2002.

F. Scholer, H. E. Williams, J. Yiannis, and J. Zobel. Compression of inverted indexes for fast query evaluation. In *Proc. ACM-SIGIR Int. Conf. on Research and Development in Information Retrieval*, pages 222–229. ACM Press, New York, 2002.

K. Sparck-Jones, S. Walker, and S. E. Robertson. A probabilistic model of information retrieval: development and comparative experiments. Parts 1&2. *Information Processing & Management*, 36(6):779–840, 2000.

A. Spink, D. Wolfram, Major B. J. Jansen, and T. Saracevic. From e-sex to e-commerce: Web search changes. *IEEE Computer*, 35(3):107–109, March 2002.

A. Tombros and M. Sanderson. Advantages of query biased summaries in information retrieval. In *Proc. ACM-SIGIR Int. Conf. on Research and Development in Information Retrieval*, pages 2–10. ACM Press, New York, 1998.

I. H. Witten, A. Moffat, and T. C. Bell. *Managing Gigabytes: Compressing and Indexing Documents and Images*. Morgan Kaufman, San Francisco, California, United States, 2nd edition, 1999.

J. Xu and W. B. Croft. Improving the effectiveness of information retrieval with local context analysis. *ACM Transactions on Information Systems*, 18(1):79–112, 2000.

J. Zobel. How reliable are the results of large-scale information retrieval experiments? In W. B. Croft, A. Moffat, C. J. van Rijsbergen, R. Wilkinson, and J. Zobel, editors, *Proc. ACM-SIGIR Int. Conf. on Research and Development in Information Retrieval*, pages 307–314, Melbourne, Australia, August 1998. ACM Press, New York.

Inferring Query Performance Using Pre-retrieval Predictors

Ben He and Iadh Ounis

Department of Computing Science
University of Glasgow
{ben,ounis}@dcs.gla.ac.uk

Abstract. The prediction of query performance is an interesting and important issue in Information Retrieval (IR). Current predictors involve the use of relevance scores, which are time-consuming to compute. Therefore, current predictors are not very suitable for practical applications. In this paper, we study a set of predictors of query performance, which can be generated prior to the retrieval process. The linear and non-parametric correlations of the predictors with query performance are thoroughly assessed on the TREC disk4 and disk5 (minus CR) collections. According to the results, some of the proposed predictors have significant correlation with query performance, showing that these predictors can be useful to infer query performance in practical applications.

1 Introduction

Robustness is an important measure reflecting the retrieval performance of an IR system. It particularly refers to how an IR system deals with poorly-performing queries. As stressed by Cronen-Townsend et. al. [4], poorly-performing queries considerably hurt the effectiveness of an IR system. Indeed, this issue has become important in IR research. For example, in 2003, TREC proposed a new track, namely the Robust Track, which aims to investigate the retrieval performance of poorly-performing queries. Moreover, the use of reliable query performance predictors is a step towards determining for each query the most optimal corresponding retrieval strategy. For example, in [2], the use of query performance predictors allowed to devise a selective decision methodology avoiding the failure of query expansion.

In order to predict the performance of a query, the first step is to differentiate the highly-performing queries from the poorly-performing queries. This problem has recently been the focus of an increasing research attention.

In [4], Cronen-Townsend et. al. suggested that query performance is correlated with the *clarity* of a query. Following this idea, they used a clarity score as the predictor of query performance. In their work, the clarity score is defined as the Kullback-Leibler divergence of the query model from the collection model. In [2], Amati et. al. proposed the notion of *query-difficulty* to predict query performance. Their basic idea is that the query expansion weight, which is the divergence of the query terms' distribution in the top-retrieved documents

A. Apostolico and M. Melucci (Eds.): SPIRE 2004, LNCS 3246, pp. 43–54, 2004.

from their distribution in the whole collection, provides evidence of the query performance.

Both methods mentioned above select a feature of a query as the predictor, and estimate the correlation of the predictor with the query performance. However, it is difficult to incorporate these methods into practical applications because they are post-retrieval approaches, involving the time-consuming computation of relevance scores.

In this paper, we study a set of predictors that can be computed before the retrieval process takes place. The retrieval process refers to the process where the IR system looks through the inverted files for the query terms and assigns a relevance score to each retrieved document. The experimental results show that some of the proposed predictors have significant correlation with query performance. Therefore, these predictors can be applied in practical applications.

The remainder of this paper is organised as follows. Section 2 proposes a set of predictors of query performance. Sections 3 and 4 study the linear and non-parametric correlations of the predictors with average precision. Section 5 presents a smoothing method for improving the most effective proposed predictor and the obtained results. Finally, Section 6 concludes this work and suggests further research directions.

2 Predictors of Query Performance

In this section, we propose a list of predictors of query performance. Similar to previous works mentioned in Section 1, we consider the intrinsic statistical features of queries as the predictors and use them in inferring the query performance. Moreover, these features should be computed prior to the retrieval process. The proposed list of predictors is inspired by previous works related to probabilistic IR models, including the language modelling approach [11] and Amati & van Rijsbergen's Divergence From Randomness (DFR) models [3]:

- **Query length.** According to Zhai & Lafferty's work [15], in the language modelling approach, the query length has a strong effect on the smoothing methods. In our previous work, we also found that the query length heavily affects the length normalisation methods of the probabilistic models [7]. For example, the optimal setting for the so-called normalisation 2 in Amati & van Rijsbergen's probabilistic framework is query-dependent [3]. The empirically obtained setting of its parameter c is $c = 7$ for short queries and $c = 1$ for long queries, suggesting that the optimal setting depends on the query length. Therefore, the query length could be an important characteristic of the queries. In this paper, we define the query length as:

  Definition 1 (ql): *The query length is the number of non-stop words in the query.*
- **The distribution of informative amount in query terms.** In general, each term can be associated with an inverse document frequency ($idf(t)$)

describing the informative amount that a term t carries. As stressed by Pirkola and Jarvelin, the difference between the *resolution power* of the query terms, which is given as the $idf(t)$ values, could affect the effectiveness of the retrieval performance [9]. Therefore, the distribution of the $idf(t)$ factors in the composing query terms might be an intrinsic feature that affects the retrieval performance. In this paper, we investigate the following two possible definitions for the distribution of informative amount in query terms:

Definition 2 ($\gamma 1$): *Given a query Q, the distribution of informative amount in its composing terms, called $\gamma 1$, is represented as:*

$$\gamma 1 = \sigma_{idf} \tag{1}$$

where σ_{idf} is the standard deviation of the idf of the terms in Q.

For *idf*, we use the INQUERY's *idf* formula [1]:

$$idf(t) = \frac{\log_2(N + 0.5)/N_t}{\log_2(N + 1)} \tag{2}$$

where N_t is the number of documents in which the query term t appears and N is the number of documents in the whole collection.
Another possible definition representing the distribution of informative amount in the query terms is:

Definition 3 ($\gamma 2$): *Given a query Q, the distribution of informative amount in its composing terms, called $\gamma 2$, is represented as:*

$$\gamma 2 = \frac{idf_{max}}{idf_{min}} \tag{3}$$

where idf_{max} and idf_{min} are the maximum and minimum idf among the terms in Q respectively.

The *idf* of Definition 3 is also given by the INQUERY's *idf* formula.

- **Query clarity.** Query clarity refers to the speciality/ambiguity of a query. According to the work by Cronen-Townsend et. al. [4], the clarity (or on the contrary, the ambiguity) of a query is an intrinsic feature of a query, which has an important impact on the system performance. Cronen-Townsend et. al. proposed the clarity score of a query to measure the coherence of the language usage in documents, whose models are likely to generate the query [4]. In their definition, the clarity of a query is the sum of the Kullback-Leibler divergence of the query model from the collection model. However, this definition involves the computation of relevance scores for the query model, which is time-consuming. In this paper, we simplify the clarity score by proposing the following definition:

Definition 4 (SCS): *The simplified query clarity score is given by:*

$$SCS = \sum_{Q} P_{ml}(w|Q) \cdot log_2 \frac{P_{ml}(w|Q)}{P_{coll}(w)} \tag{4}$$

In the above definition, $P_{ml}(w|Q)$ is given by $\frac{qtf}{ql}$. It is the maximum likelihood of the query model of the term w in query Q. qtf is the number of occurrences of a query term in the query and ql is the query length. $P_{coll}(w)$ is the collection model, which is given by $\frac{tf_{coll}}{token_{coll}}$, where tf_{coll} is the number of occurrences of a query term in the whole collection and $token_{coll}$ is the number of tokens in the whole collection.
Although the above definition seems simple and naive, it would be very easy to compute. In Sections 3 and 4, we will show that this simplified definition has significant linear and non-parametric correlations with query performance. Moreover, in Section 5, the proposed simplified clarity score is improved by smoothing the query model.
- **Query scope.** Similar to the clarity score, an alternative indication of the generality/speciality of a query is the size of the document set containing at least one of the query terms. As stressed in [10], the size of this document set is an important property of the query. Following [10], in this work, we define the query scope as follows:

  Definition 5 (ω): *The query scope is:*

$$\omega = -\log(n_Q/N) \tag{5}$$

  where n_Q is the number of documents containing at least one of the query terms, and N is the number of documents in the whole collection.

In the following sections, we will study the correlations of the predictors with query performance. In order to fully investigate the predictors, we check both linear and non-parametric dependance of the predictors with query performance. The latter is a commonly used measure for the query performance predictors, since the distribution of the involved variables are usually unknown. On the contrary, the linear dependance assumes a linear distribution of the involved variables. Although this strong assumption is not always true, the linear fitting of the variables can be straightforwardly applied in practical applications.

3 The Linear Dependence Between the Predictors and Average Precision

In this section, we measure the linear correlation r of each predictor with the actual query performance, and the p-value associated to this correlation [5]. We use average precision (AP) as the focus measure representing the query performance in all our experiments. Again, note that the linear correlation assumes a linear distribution of the involved variables, which is not always true.

The correlation r varies within [-1, 1]. It indicates the linear dependence between the two pairs of variables. A value of $r = 0$ indicates that the two variables are independent. $r > 0$ and $r < 0$ indicates that the correlation between the two variables is positive and negative, respectively. The p-value is the probability of randomly getting a correlation as large as the observed value, when the true correlation is zero. If p-value is small, usually less than 0.05, then the correlation is significant. A significant correlation of a predictor with AP indicates that this predictor could be useful to infer the query performance in practical applications.

3.1 Test Data and Settings

The document collection used to test the efficiency of the proposed predictors is the TREC disk4&5 test collections (minus the Congressional Record on disk4). The test queries are the TREC topics 351-450, which are used in the TREC7&8 ad-hoc tasks. For all the documents and queries, the stop-words are removed using a standard list and the Porter's stemming algorithm is applied.

Each query consists of three fields, i.e. Title, Description and Narrative. In our experiments, we define three types of queries with respect to the different combinations of these three fields:

- **Short query**: Only the titles are used.
- **Normal query**: Only the descriptions are used.
- **Long query**: All the three fields are used.

The statistics of the length of the three types of queries are provided in Table 1. We run experiments for the three types of queries to check the impact of the query type on the effectiveness of the predictors, including the query length.

In the experiments of this section, given the AP value of each query, we compute r and the corresponding p-value of the linear dependance between the two variables, i.e. AP and each of the predictors. The AP values of the test queries are given by the PL2 and BM25 term weighting models, respectively. We use two statistically different models in order to check if the effectiveness of the predictors is independent of the used term-weighting models.

PL2 is one of the Divergence From Randomness (DFR) term weighting models developed within Amati & van Rijsbergen's probabilistic framework for IR [3]. Using the PL2 model, the relevance score of a document d for query term t is given by:

$$w(t,d) = tf \cdot \log_2 \frac{tf}{\lambda} + (\lambda + \frac{1}{12 \cdot tf} - tf) \cdot \log_2 e + 0.5 \cdot \log_2(2 \cdot tf) \cdot \frac{1}{tf+1} \quad (6)$$

where λ is the mean and variance of a Poisson distribution.

The within document term frequency tf is then normalised using the *normalisation 2*:

$$tfn = tf \cdot \log_2(1 + c \cdot \frac{avg\_l}{l}), (c > 0) \quad (7)$$

where l is the document length and avg_l is the average document length in the whole collection.

Table 1. The statistics of the length of the three types of queries. avg_ql is the average query length. $Var(ql)$ is the variance of the length of the queries

	Short Query	Normal Query	Long Query
avg_ql	2.42	7.55	21.13
$Var(ql)$	0.42	10.19	55.77

Table 2. The settings of the free parameters for different types of queries

Parameter	Short Query	Normal Query	Long Query
c of PL2	5.90	1.61	1.73
b of BM25	0.09	0.25	0.64

Replacing the raw term frequency tf by the normalised term frequency tfn in Equation (6), we obtain the final weight. c is a free parameter. It is automatically estimated by measuring the normalisation effect [7]. The first row of Table 2 provides the applied c value for the three types of queries.

As one of the most well-established IR systems, Okapi uses BM25 to measure the term weight, where the *idf* factor $w^{(1)}$ is normalised as follows [12]:

$$w(t,d) = w^{(1)} \frac{(k_1+1)tf}{K+tf} \frac{(k_3+1)qtf}{k_3+qtf} \tag{8}$$

where w is the final weight. K is given by $k_1((1-b)+b\frac{l}{avg\_l})$, where l and avg_l are the document length and the average document length in the collection, respectively. For the parameters k_1 and k_3, we use the standard setting of [14], i.e. $k_1 = 1.2$ and $k_3 = 1000$. qtf is the number of occurrences of a given term in the query and tf is the within document frequency of the given term. b is the free parameter of BM25's term frequency normalisation component. Similar to the parameter c of the normalisation 2, it is estimated by the method provided in [7]. However, due to the "out of range" problem mentioned in [7], we applied a new formula for the normalisation effect (see Appendix). The second row of Table 2 provides the applied b values in all reported experiments.

3.2 Discussion of Results

In Table 3, we summarise the results of the linear correlations of the predictors with AP. From the results, we could derive the following observations:

- Query length (see Definition 1) does not have a significant linear correlation with AP. This might be due to the fact that the length of queries of the same type are very similar (see $Var(ql)$ in Table 1). To check the assumption, we computed the correlation of AP with the length of a mixture of three types of queries. Thus, we had $100 \times 3 = 300$ observations of both AP and query length. Measuring the correlation, we obtained $r = 0.0585$ and a p-value of 0.3124, which again indicates a very low correlation. Therefore, query length seems to be very weakly correlated with AP.

Table 3. The correlations r of the predictors with AP, and the related p-values. The results are given separately with respect to the three types of queries. Significant correlations are shown in bold. The test queries are the topics used in TREC7&8

	PL2, Short Query					BM25, Short Query				
	ql	$\gamma 1$	$\gamma 2$	ω	SCS	ql	$\gamma 1$	$\gamma 2$	ω	SCS
r	-0.1839	**0.2398**	0.0569	**0.3772**	**0.4484**	-0.1773	0.1860	0.0332	**0.3746**	**0.4208**
p-value	0.0670	**0.0163**	0.5738	**0.0001**	**3.037e-6**	0.0776	0.0639	0.7430	**0.0001**	**1.351e-5**
	PL2, Normal Query					BM25, Normal Query				
	ql	$\gamma 1$	$\gamma 2$	ω	SCS	ql	$\gamma 1$	$\gamma 2$	ω	SCS
r	0.0830	**0.3017**	0.1259	0.1895	**0.2602**	0.0876	**0.2946**	0.1436	0.1629	**0.2293**
p-value	0.4116	**0.0023**	0.2120	0.0590	**0.0089**	0.3862	**0.0029**	0.1542	0.1054	**0.0217**
	PL2, Long Query					BM25, Long Query				
	ql	$\gamma 1$	$\gamma 2$	ω	SCS	ql	$\gamma 1$	$\gamma 2$	ω	SCS
r	0.0543	**0.3227**	**0.3029**	0.0910	**0.2401**	0.0790	**0.2822**	**0.2753**	0.0843	**0.2066**
p-value	0.5915	**0.0011**	**0.0022**	0.3679	**0.0161**	0.4349	**0.0044**	**0.0056**	0.4044	**0.0392**

- $\gamma 1$ (see Definition 2) has significant linear correlation with AP in all cases except for the short queries when BM25 is used. It is also interesting to see that the correlations for normal and long queries are stronger than that for short queries.
- The linear correlation of $\gamma 2$ (see Definition 3) with AP is only significant for long queries. Also, the correlation is positive, which indicates that a larger gap of informative amount between the query terms would result into a higher AP. Moreover, the results show that on the used test collection, $\gamma 1$ is more effective than $\gamma 2$ in inferring query performance.
- For ω, the query scope (see Definition 4), its linear correlation with AP is only significant for short queries. Perhaps this is because when queries are getting longer, the query scope tends to be stable. Figure 1 supports this assumption. We can see that the ω of normal and long queries are clearly more stable than those of short queries.
- The simplified clarity score (SCS, see Definition 5) has significant linear correlation with AP in all circumstances. For the short queries, the use of PL2 results in the highest linear correlation among all the predictors (the linear fitting is given in Figure 2). However, when the query length increases, the correlation gets weaker.
- Moreover, it seems that the predictors are generally less effective when BM25 is used as the term-weighting model. For the same predictor, the AP given by BM25 is usually less correlated with it than the AP given by PL2.

In summary, query type has a strong impact on the effectiveness of the predictors. Indeed, the correlation of a predictor with AP varies for diverse query types. For short queries, SCS and ω have strong linear correlations with AP. For normal queries, $\gamma 1$ has moderately significant linear correlation with AP. For long queries, $\gamma 1$ and $\gamma 2$ have significant linear correlations with AP.

In general, among the five proposed predictors, SCS is the most effective one for short queries, and $\gamma 1$ is the most effective one for normal and long queries.

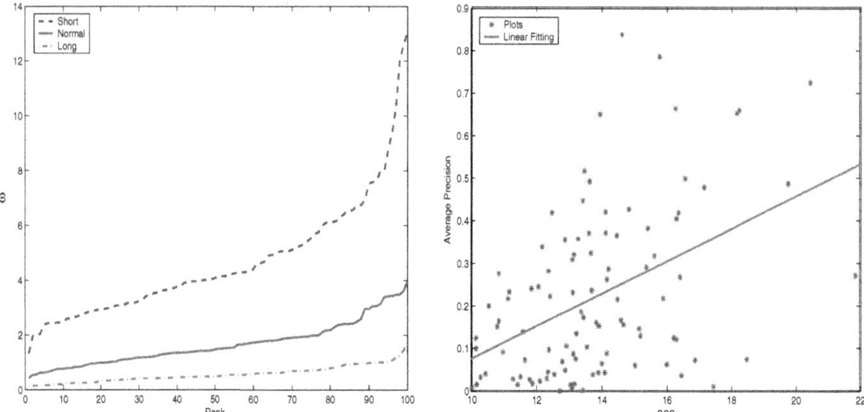

Fig. 1. The ranked ω values in ascending order for the three types of queries

Fig. 2. The linear correlation of SCS with AP using PL2 for short queries

For all the three types of queries, $\gamma 1$ is more effective than $\gamma 2$ in inferring query performance. Moreover, since ω was proposed for Web IR [10] and SCS is more effective than ω, SCS could also be a good option for Web IR. Note that, although some previous works found that query length affects the retrieval performance [7, 15], it seems that query length is not significantly correlated with AP, at least on the used collection.

Finally, we found that, in most cases, the predictors are slightly less correlated with the AP obtained using BM25 than that obtained using PL2. The difference of correlations is usually marginal, except for short queries, where $\gamma 1$ is significantly correlated with the AP obtained using PL2, but not BM25. Overall, the use of different term-weighting models does not considerably affect the correlations of the proposed predictors with AP.

4 Non-parametric Correlation of the Predictors with Average Precision

In this section, instead of the linear correlation, we check the non-parametric correlations of the predictors with AP. An appropriate measure for the non-parametric test is the Spearman's rank correlation [6]. In this paper, we denote the Spearman's correlation between variables X and Y as $rs(X, Y)$.

The test data and experimental setting for checking the Spearman's correlation are the same as the previous section. As shown in Table 4, the results are very similar to the linear correlations provided in Table 3. SCS is again the most effective predictor, which has significant Spearman's correlations with AP for the three types of queries. Also, $\gamma 1$ seems to be the most effective predictor for normal and long queries. Moreover, the predictors are generally slightly less correlated with the AP obtained using BM25 than that obtained using PL2. Again,

Table 4. The Spearman's correlation rs of the predictors with AP for three types queries using PL2 and BM25 respectively. Significant correlations are shown in bold. The test queries are the topics used in TREC7&8

	PL2, Short Query					BM25, Short Query				
	ql	$\gamma1$	$\gamma2$	ω	SCS	ql	$\gamma1$	$\gamma2$	ω	SCS
rs	-0.0476	**0.2141**	0.0279	**0.3627**	**0.4236**	-0.0354	0.1449	-0.0217	**0.3393**	**0.3752**
p-value	0.6359	**0.0331**	0.7794	**0.0003**	**2.504e-5**	0.7243	0.1497	0.8280	**0.0007**	**0.0002**
	PL2, Normal Query					BM25, Normal Query				
	ql	$\gamma1$	$\gamma2$	ω	SCS	ql	$\gamma1$	$\gamma2$	ω	SCS
rs	-0.0646	**0.3627**	0.1240	0.1790	**0.2721**	-0.0640	**0.3439**	0.1129	0.1647	**0.2583**
p-value	0.5203	**0.0003**	0.2183	0.0748	**0.0068**	0.5242	**0.0006**	0.2615	0.1013	**0.0102**
	PL2, Long Query					BM25, Long Query				
	ql	$\gamma1$	$\gamma2$	ω	SCS	ql	$\gamma1$	$\gamma2$	ω	SCS
rs	0.0132	**0.3272**	**0.2236**	0.1324	**0.2668**	-2.1e-05	**0.2972**	0.1875	0.1544	**0.2556**
p-value	0.8958	**0.0011**	**0.0266**	0.1861	**0.0079**	0.9998	**0.0030**	0.0628	0.1238	**0.0110**

the difference of correlations is usually marginal, except the correlation of $\gamma1$ with short queries, where $rs(\gamma1, AP)$ for PL2 is significant, while $rs(\gamma1, AP)$ for BM25 is not. Finally, $\gamma1$ is still more effective than $\gamma2$ as a query performance predictor.

We also compare $rs(SCS, AP)$ with the $rs(CS, AP)$ for the TREC7&8 and TREC4 ad-hoc tasks reported in [4]. CS stands for Cronen-Townsend et. al.'s clarity score. To do the comparison, besides $rs(SCS, AP)$ for TREC7&8 provided in Table 4, we also run experiments checking the $rs(SCS, AP)$ values for the queries used in TREC4. The test queries for TREC4 are the TREC topics 201-250, which are normal queries as they only consist of the descriptions. There was no experiment for long queries reported in [4]. The parameter c of the normalisation 2 (see Equation (7)) is also automatically set to 1.64 in our experiments for TREC4.

Regarding the generation of AP, Cronen-Townsend et. al. apply Song & Croft's multinomial language model for CS [13], and we apply PL2 for SCS. Since $rs(SCS, AP)$ is stable for statistically diverse term-weighting models, i.e. PL2 and BM25 (see Table 4), we believe that the use of the two different term-weighting models won't considerably affect the comparison.

Table 5 compares $rs(SCS, AP)$ with the $rs(CS, AP)$ reported in [4]. We can see that for normal queries, $rs(CS, AP)$ is clearly higher than $rs(SCS, AP)$. However, for short queries, although $rs(CS, AP)$ is larger than $rs(SCS, AP)$, the latter is still a significant high correlation.

In summary, SCS is effective in inferring the performance of short queries. Since the actual queries on the World Wide Web are usually very short, SCS can be useful for Web IR, or for other environments where queries are usually short. Moreover, SCS is very practical as the cost of its computation is indeed insignificant. However, comparing with CS, SCS seems to be moderately weak in inferring the performance of longer queries, including normal queries, although the obtained $rs(SCS, AP)$ values are still significant according to the corresponding p-values.

Table 5. The Spearman's correlations of clarity score (CS) and SCS with AP. For SCS and CS, AP is obtained using PL2 and Song & Croft's multinomial language model, respectively. For TREC7&8, the queries are of short type. For TREC4, the queries are of normal type as they only consist of descriptions. The data in the first row are taken from [4]

	TREC7&8 Short Query		TREC4 Normal Query	
	rs	p-value	rs	p-value
CS	0.536	4.8e-8	0.490	3.0e-4
SCS	0.424	2.5e-5	0.252	0.0779

The moderately weak correlations of SCS with AP for longer queries might be due to the fact that the maximum likelihood of the query model ($P_{ml}(w|Q)$) is not reliable when the query length increases. As mentioned before, the effectiveness of those predictors, which are positively correlated with the query length, decreases as the query gets longer. Therefore, we might be able to increase the correlation by smoothing the query model, which is directly related to the query length. We will discuss this issue in the next section.

5 Smoothing the Query Model of SCS

In this section, we present a method for smoothing the query model of SCS. For the estimation of the query model $P(w|Q)$, instead of introducing the document model by a total probability formula [4], we model the qtf density of query length ql directly, so that the computation of SCS does not involve the use of relevance scores. Note that qtf is the frequency of the term in the query Q.

Let us start with assuming an increasing qtf density of query length ql, then we would have the following density function:

$$\rho = C \cdot ql^{\beta} \tag{9}$$

where ρ is the density and C is a constant of the density function. The exponential β should be larger than 0. An appropriate value is $\beta = 0.5$.

Let the average query length be the interval of the integral of ρ, we then have the following smoothing function:

$$qtfn = \int_{ql}^{ql+avg\_ql} \rho d(ql) = \nu \cdot ((ql + avg\_ql)^{1.5} - ql^{1.5}) \tag{10}$$

where $qtfn$ is the smoothed qtf. Replacing qtf with $qtfn$ in Definition 4, we will obtain the smoothed query model. avg_ql is the average query length. ν is a free parameter. It is empirically set in our experiments (see the third column of Table 6).

Table 6 summarises the obtained $rs(SCS, AP)$ values using the smoothing function. For short queries, no significant effect is noticed. However, for normal and long queries, the rs values are considerably larger than the values obtained

Table 6. The Spearman's correlation of SCS with AP for different types of queries using the smoothing function. AP is obtained using PL2

Task	Query Type	ν	rs	p-value
TREC7&8	Short	e-5	0.4268	2.471e-5
TREC7&8	Normal	2.5e-4	0.3017	0.0027
TREC7&8	Long	2.5e-4	0.3002	0.0028
TREC4	Normal	5e-5	0.2847	0.0463

without the use of the smoothing function (see Table 4). It is also encouraging to see that for TREC4, compared to the rs value in Table 5, the obtained rs value using the smoothing function is significant. Therefore, the effectiveness of SCS has improved for normal and long queries by smoothing the query model.

6 Conclusions and Future Work

We have studied a set of pre-retrieval predictors for query performance. The predictors can be generated before the retrieval process takes place, which is more practical than current approaches to query performance prediction. We have measured the linear and non-parametric correlations of the predictors with AP. According to the results, the query type has an important impact on the effectiveness of the predictors. Among the five proposed predictors, a simplified definition of clarity score (SCS) has the strongest correlation with AP for short queries. $\gamma 1$ is the most correlated with AP for normal and long queries. Also, we have shown that SCS can be improved by smoothing the query model. Taking the complexity of generating a predictor into consideration, SCS and $\gamma 1$ can be useful for practical applications. Moreover, according to the results, the use of two statistically diverse term-weighting models does not have an impact on the overall effectiveness of the proposed predictors.

In the future, we will investigate improving the predictors using various methods. For example, we plan to develop a better smoothing function for the query model of SCS. We will also incorporate the proposed predictors into our query clustering mechanism, which has been applied to select the optimal term-weighting model, given a particular query [8]. The use of better predictors would hopefully allow the query clustering mechanism to be improved. As a consequence, the query-dependence problem of the term frequency normalisation parameter tuning, stressed in [7], could be overcome.

Acknowledgments

This work is funded by the Leverhulme Trust, grant number F/00179/S. The project funds the development of the Smooth project, which investigates the term frequency normalisation (URL: http://ir.dcs.gla.ac.uk/smooth). The experimental part of this paper has been conducted using the Terrier framework (EPSRC, grant GR/R90543/01, URL: http://ir.dcs.gla.ac.uk/terrier). We would also like to thank Gianni Amati for his helpful comments on the paper.

References

1. J. Allan, L. Ballesteros, J. Callan, W. Croft. Recent experiments with INQUERY. In *Proceedings of TREC-4*, pp. 49-63, Gaithersburg, MD, 1995.
2. G. Amati, C. Carpineto, G. Romano. Query difficulty, robustness, and selective application of query expansion. In *Proceedings of ECIR'04*, pp. 127-137, Sunderland UK, 2004.
3. G. Amati and C. J. van Rijsbergen. Probabilistic models of information retrieval based on measuring the divergence from randomness. In *TOIS*, 20(4), pp. 357-389, 2002.
4. S. Cronen-Townsend, Y. Zhou, W. B. Croft. Predicting query performance. In *Proceedings of SIGIR'02*, pp. 299-306, Tampere, Finland, 2002.
5. M. DeGroot. *Probability and Statistics.* Addison Wesley, 2nd edition, 1989.
6. J. D. Gibbons and S. Chakraborti. *Nonparametric statistical inference.* New York, M. Dekker, 1992.
7. B. He and I. Ounis. A study of parameter tuning for term frequency normalization. In *Proceedings of CIKM'03*, pp. 10-16, New Orleans, LA, 2003.
8. B. He and I. Ounis. A query-based pre-retrieval model selection approach to information retrieval. In *Proceedings of RIAO'04*, pp. 706-719, Avignon, France, 2004.
9. A. Pirkola and K. Jarvelin. Employing the resolution power of search keys. *JASIST*, 52(7):575-583, 2001.
10. V. Plachouras, I. Ounis, G. Amati, C. J. van Rijsbergen. University of Glasgow at the Web Track: Dynamic application of hyperlink analysis using the query scope. In *Proceedings of TREC2003*, pp. 248-254, Gaithersburg, MD, 2003.
11. J. M. Ponte and W. B. Croft. A language modeling approach to information retrieval. In *Proceedings of SIGIR'98*, pp. 275-281, Melbourne, Australia, 1998.
12. S. Robertson, S. Walker, M. M. Beaulieu, M. Gatford, A. Payne. Okapi at TREC-4. In *Proceedings of TREC-4*, pp. 73-96, Gaithersburg, MD, 1995.
13. F. Song and W.Croft. A general language model for information retrieval. In *Proceedings of SIGIR'99*, pp. 279-280, Berkeley, CA, 1999.
14. K. Sparck-Jones, S. Walker, S. Robertson. A probabilistic model of information retrieval: Development and comparative experiments. *IPM*, 36(2000):779-840, 2000.
15. C. Zhai and J. Lafferty. A study of smoothing methods for language models applied to ad hoc information retrieval. In *Proceedings of SIGIR'01*, pp. 334-342, New Orleans, LA, 2001.

Appendix

The new formula for the normalisation effect NE_D is the following:

$$NE_D = Var\left(\frac{NE_{d_i}}{NE_{d,max}}\right), d_i \in D \tag{11}$$

where D is the set of documents containing at least one of the query terms. d_i is a document in D. $NE_{d,max}$ is the maximum NE_{d_i} in D. Var denotes the variance. NE_{d_i} is given by:

$$\frac{1}{(1-b) + b \cdot \frac{l}{avg\_l}} \tag{12}$$

where l is the length of the document d_i. b is a free parameter of BM25. avg_l is the average document length in the whole collection.

A Scalable System for Identifying Co-derivative Documents

Yaniv Bernstein and Justin Zobel

School of Computer Science and Information Technology
RMIT University, Melbourne, Australia
{ybernste,jz}@cs.rmit.edu.au

Abstract. Documents are co-derivative if they share content: for two documents to be co-derived, some portion of one must be derived from the other or some portion of both must be derived from a third document. The current technique for concurrently detecting all co-derivatives in a collection is document fingerprinting, which matches documents based on the hash values of selected document subsequences, or chunks. Fingerprinting is currently hampered by an inability to accurately isolate information that is useful in identifying co-derivatives. In this paper we present SPEX, a novel hash-based algorithm for extracting duplicated chunks from a document collection. We discuss how information about shared chunks can be used for efficiently and reliably identifying co-derivative clusters, and describe DECO, a prototype system that makes use of SPEX. Our experiments with several document collections demonstrate the effectiveness of the approach.

1 Introduction

Many document collections contain sets of documents that are *co-derived*. Examples of co-derived documents include plagiarised documents, document revisions, and digests or abstracts. Knowledge of co-derivative document relationships in a collection can be used for returning more informative results from search engines, detecting plagiarism, and managing document versioning in an enterprise.

Depending on the application, we may wish to identify all pairs of co-derived documents in a given collection (the $n \times n$ or *discovery* problem) or only those documents that are co-derived with a specified query document (the $1 \times n$ or *search* problem). We focus in this research on the more difficult discovery problem. While it is possible to naïvely solve the discovery problem by repeated application of an algorithm designed for solving the search problem, this quickly becomes far too time-consuming for practical use.

All current feasible techniques for solving the discovery problem are based on document fingerprinting, in which a compact representation of a selected subset of contiguous text *chunks* occurring in each document – its *fingerprint* – is stored. Pairs of documents are identified as possibly co-derived if enough of the chunks in their respective fingerprints match. Fingerprinting schemes differentiate themselves largely on the way in which chunks to be stored are selected.

A. Apostolico and M. Melucci (Eds.): SPIRE 2004, LNCS 3246, pp. 55–67, 2004.

In this paper we introduce SPEX, a novel and efficient algorithm for identifying those chunks that occur more than once within a collection. We present the DECO package, which uses the shared phrase indexes generated by SPEX as the basis for accurate and efficient identification of co-derivative documents in a collection. We believe that DECO effectively addresses some of the deficiencies of existing approaches to this problem. Using several collections, we experimentally demonstrate that DECO is able to reliably and accurately identify co-derivative documents within a collection while using fewer resources than previous techniques of similar capability. We also have data to suggest that DECO should scale well to very large collections.

2 Co-derivatives and the Discovery Problem

We consider two documents to be co-derived if some portion of one document is derived from the other, or some portion that is present in both documents is derived from a third document. Broder (1997) defines two measures of co-derivation – *resemblance* and *containment* – in terms of the number of *shingles* (we shall use the term *chunks*) a pair of documents have in common. A chunk is defined by Broder as 'a contiguous subsequence'; that is, each chunk represents a contiguous set of words or characters within the document. An example chunk of length six taken from this document would be 'each chunk represents a contiguous set'. The intuition is that, if a pair of documents share a number of such chunks, then they are unlikely to have been created independently. Such an intuition is what drives fingerprinting-based approaches, described later.

We can conceptualise the co-derivation relationships within a collection as a graph, with each node representing a single document and the presence or absence of an edge between two nodes representing the presence or absence of a co-derivation relationship between the documents represented by those nodes. We call this the *relationship graph* of the collection. The task of the discovery problem is to discover the structure of this graph. Note that, as the number of edges in a graph is quadratic in the number of nodes, the task of discovering the structure of the relationship graph is a formidable one: for example, a collection of 100,000 documents contains nearly 5 billion unique document pairings.

3 Strategies for Co-derivative Discovery

There are several approaches to solving the search problem, in particular fingerprinting systems and ranking-based systems. Ranking-based systems such as relative frequency matching (Shivakumar & García-Molina 1995) and the identity measure (Hoad & Zobel 2003) make use of document statistics such as the relative frequency of words between documents to give a score for how likely a pair of documents is to be co-derived. In comparisons between such methods and fingerprinting, the ranking-based methods tended to perform better, though it is worth noting that the comparisons were carried out by the proponents of these systems. However, the only computationally feasible algorithms for the discovery problem to date have used the process of document fingerprinting.

3.1 Fingerprinting

The key observation underlying document fingerprinting (Manber 1994, Brin et al. 1995, Heintze 1996, Broder et al. 1997, Hoad & Zobel 2003) mirrors that behind the definitions of Broder (1997): if documents are broken down into small contiguous chunks, then co-derivative documents are likely to have a large number of these chunks in common, whereas independently derived documents with overwhelming probability will not. Fingerprinting algorithms store a selection of chunks from each document in a compact form and flag documents as potentially co-derived if they have some common chunks in their fingerprints.

While fingerprinting algorithms vary in many details, their basic process is as follows: documents in a collection are parsed into units (typically either characters or individual words); representative chunks of contiguous units are selected through the use of a heuristic; the selected chunks are then hashed for efficient retrieval and/or compact storage; the hash-keys, and possibly also the chunks themselves, are then stored, often in an inverted index structure (Witten et al. 1999). The index of hash-keys contains all the fingerprints for a document collection and can be used for the detection of co-derivatives.

The principal way in which document fingerprinting algorithms differentiate themselves is in the choice of selection heuristic, that is, the method of determining which chunks should be selected for storage in each document's fingerprint. The range of such heuristics is diverse, as reviewed by Hoad & Zobel (2003). The simplest strategies are full selection, in which every chunk is selected, and random selection, where a given proportion or number of chunks is selected at random from each document to act as a fingerprint. Other strategies pick every nth chunk, or only pick chunks that are rare across the collection (Heintze 1996). Taking a different approach is the *anchor* strategy (Manber 1994), in which chunks are only selected if they begin with certain pre-specified combinations of letters. Simpler but arguably as effective is the *modulo* heuristic, in which a chunk is only selected if its hash-key *modulo* a parameter k is equal to zero. The *winnowing* algorithm of Schleimer et al. (2003) passes a window over the collection and selects the chunk with the lowest hash-key in each window. Both the *anchor* and *modulo* heuristics ensure a level of synchronisation between fingerprints in different documents, in that if a particular chunk is selected in one document, it will be selected in all documents.

In their comparative experiments, Hoad & Zobel (2003) found that few of the fingerprinting strategies tested could reliably identify co-derivative documents in a collection. Of those that could, Manber's *anchor* heuristic was the most effective, but its performance was inferior to their ranking-based identity measure system. Similarly, Shivakumar & García-Molina (1995) found that the COPS fingerprinting system (Brin et al. 1995) was far more likely than their SCAM ranking-based system to fail to identify co-derivative documents.

Several techniques use fingerprinting for the discovery problem:

Manber (1994) counts the number of identical postings lists in the chunk index, arguing this can be used to identify clusters of co-derived documents in the collection. However, as Manber points out, there are many cases in which the results produced by his method can be extremely difficult to interpret.

Broder et al. (1997) describe an approach in which each postings list is broken down to a set of document-pair tokens, one for each possible pairing in the list. The number of tokens for each pair of documents is counted and used as the basis for a set of discovery results. While this approach can yield far more informative results, taking the Cartesian product of each postings list means that the number of tokens generated is quadratic in the length of the postings list; this can easily cause resource blowouts and introduces serious scalability problems for the algorithm.

Shivakumar & García-Molina (1999) addressed the scalability problems of the previous algorithm by introducing a hash-based *probabilistic counting* technique. For each document pair, instead of storing a token, a counter in a hashtable is incremented. A second pass generates a list of candidate pairs by discarding any pair that hashes to a counter that recorded insufficient hits. Assuming the hashtable is of sufficient size, this pruning significantly reduces the number of tokens that must be generated for the exact counting phase.

A fundamental weakness of fingerprinting strategies is that they cannot identify and discard chunks that do not contribute towards the identification of any co-derivative pairs. Unique chunks form the vast majority in most collections, yet do not contribute toward solving the discovery problem. We analysed the *LATimes* newswire collection (see section 6) and found that out of a total of 67,808,917 chunks of length eight, only 2,816,822 were in fact instances of duplicate chunks: less than 4.5% of the overall collection. The number of distinct duplicated chunks is 907,981, or less than 1.5% of the collection total.

The inability to discard unused data makes full fingerprinting too expensive for most practical purposes. Thus, it becomes necessary to use chunk-selection heuristics to keep storage requirements at a reasonable level. However, this introduces *lossiness* to the algorithm: current selection heuristics are unable to discriminate between chunks that suggest co-derivation between documents in the collection and those that do not. There is a significant possibility that two documents sharing a large portion of text are passed over entirely.

For example, Manber (1994), uses character-level granularity and the *modulo* selection heuristic with $k = 256$ Thus, any chunk has an unbiased one-in-256 chance of being stored. Consider a pair of documents that share an identical 1 KB (1024 byte) portion of text. On average, four of the chunks shared by these documents will be selected. Using the Poisson distribution with $\lambda = 4$, we can estimate the likelihood that C chunks are selected as $P(C = 0) = e^{-4} \cdot 4^0/0! =$ 1.8% and $P(C = 1) = e^{-4} \cdot 4^1/1! = 7.3\%$. This means that a pair of documents containing a full kilobyte of identical text have nearly a 2% chance of not having a single hash-key in common in their fingerprints, and a greater than 7% chance of only one hash key in common. The same results obtain for an identical 100-word sequence with a word-level chunking technique and $k = 25$, as used by Broder et al. (1997). Such lossiness is unacceptable in many applications.

Schleimer et al. (2003) make the observation that the *modulo* heuristic provides no guarantee of storing a shared chunk no matter how long the match. Whatever the match length, there is a nonzero probability that it will be overlooked. Their winnowing selection heuristic is able to guarantee that any contiguous run of shared text greater than a user-specifiable size w will register at least one identical hash-key in the fingerprints of the documents in question. However, a document that contains fragmented duplication below the level of w can still escape detection by this scheme: it is still fundamentally a lossy algorithm.

3.2 Algorithms for Lossless Fingerprinting

We make the observation that as only chunks that occur in more than one document contribute towards identifying co-derivation, a selection strategy that selected all such chunks would provide functional equivalence to full fingerprinting, but at a fraction of the storage cost for most collections. The challenge is to find a way of efficiently and scalably discriminating between duplicate and unique chunks.

Hierarchical dictionary-based compression techniques like SEQUITUR (Nevill-Manning & Witten 1997) and RE-PAIR (Larsson & Moffat 2000) are primarily designed to eliminate redundancy by replacing strings that occur more than once in the data with a reference to an entry in a ruleset. Thus, passages of text that occur multiple times in the collection are identified as part of the compression process. This has been used as the basis for phrase-based collection browsing tools such as PHIND (Nevill-Manning et al. 1997) and RE-STORE (Moffat & Wan 2001). However, the use of these techniques in most situations is ruled out by their high memory requirements: the PHIND technique needs about twice the memory of the total size of the collection being browsed (Nevill-Manning et al. 1997). To keep memory use at reasonable levels, the input data is generally segmented and compressed block-by-block; however, this negates the ability of the algorithm to identify globally duplicated passages. Thus, such algorithms are not useful for collections of significant size.

Suffix trees are another potential technique for duplicate-chunk identification, and are used in this way in computational biology (Gusfield 1997). However, the suffix tree is an in-memory data structure that consumes a quantity of memory equal to several times the size of the entire collection. Thus, this technique is also only suitable for small collections.

4 The SPEX Algorithm

Our novel hash-based SPEX algorithm for duplicate-chunk extraction has much more modest and flexible memory requirements than the above and is thus the first selection algorithm that is able to provide *lossless* chunk selection within large collections. The fundamental observation behind the operation of SPEX is that if any subchunk of a given chunk can be shown to be unique, then the chunk in its entirety must be unique. For example, if the chunk 'quick brown' occurs only once in the collection, there is no possibility that the chunk 'quick brown fox' is repeated. SPEX uses an iterated hashing approach to discard unique chunks and leave only those that are very likely to be duplicates.

The basic mechanics of the algorithm are shown in Algorithm 1. At the core of SPEX is a pair of hashcounters – hashtable accumulator arrays – designed to

Algorithm 1 The SPEX algorithm.

```
// C: Collection of chunks
// l: Target chunk length
// c_n: chunk of length n
// c_n{p...q}: The chunk composed of words p through q of chunk c_n
// #(c): The hash value of chunk c
// h_n: Hashcounter for chunks of length n

for all c_1 ∈ C do
  h_1[#(c_1)] ← h_1[#(c_1)] + 1
end for
for n ∈ [2, l] do
  for all c_n ∈ C do
    if h_{n-1}[#(c_n{1...n-1})] > 1 and h_{n-1}[#(c_n{2...n})] > 1 then
      h_n[#(c_n)] ← h_n[#(c_n)] + 1
    end if
  end for
end for
```

count string occurrences. Each time a string is inserted into a hashcounter, it is hashed and a counter at that location is incremented. Collisions are not resolved. For the purposes of the SPEX algorithm, we care about only three counter values: 0, 1 and '2 or more'. As such, each field in the hashcounter need be only two bits wide. If the same string is inserted into a hashcounter more than once, the hashcounter will indicate this. The hashcounter can also return false positives, indicating a string occurs multiple times when it in fact does not. A small number of such false positives can be tolerated by SPEX; the number can be kept small because the two-bit wide fields allow for extremely large hashcounters to reside in a relatively modest amount of memory

When a document collection is presented to SPEX, the first step is to sequentially scan the collection and insert each word encountered into a hashcounter. This hashcounter thus indicates (with the possibility of false positives) whether a word occurs multiple times in the collection. Following this, we pass a sliding window of size two words over the collection. Each two-word chunk is broken down into two single word subchunks and compared against the hashcounter. If the hashcounter indicates that both subchunks occur multiple times then the chunk is inserted into the second hashcounter. Otherwise, the chunk is rejected. After this process is complete, the second hashcounter indicates whether a particular chunk of size two is a possible duplicate chunk. For chunks of size three, we pass a sliding window of length three over the collection and decompose the candidate chunks into two subchunks of length two. We similarly accept a chunk only if it is indicated by the hashcounter that both subchunks occur multiple times within the collection. Figure 1 illustrates this process.

The algorithm can be extended to any desired chunk size l by iteration, at each phase incrementing the chunk size by one. We only ever require two hashcounters because the hashcounter for chunks of size $n-2$ is no longer re-

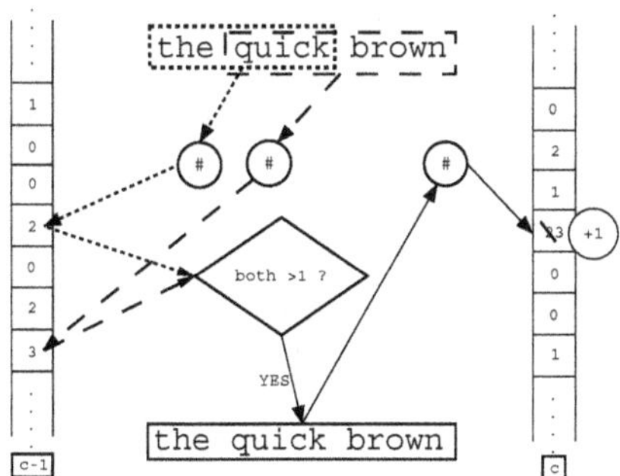

Fig. 1. The process for inserting a new chunk into the hashcounter in SPEX. The chunk "the quick brown" is divided into two sub-chunks "the quick" and "quick brown" They are each hashed into the old hash table. If the count for both sub-chunks is greater than one, the full chunk is hashed and the counter at that location in the new hashcounter is incremented.

quired when searching for chunks of size n and may be reused. We are not overly concerned about false positives, because subsequent iterations tend to have a dampening rather than an amplifying effect on their presence. SPEX is thus able to provide an accurate representation of duplicate chunks of length u in a time proportional to $O(uv)$, where v is the length of the document collection.

5 The DECO Package

Our DECO system for co-derivative detection presents a number of innovations. The most significant of these is the use of SPEX for creating shared-chunk indexes. Another addition is the inclusion of more sophisticated scoring functions for determining whether documents are co-derived. DECO operates in two phases: index building and relationship graph generation. In the index building phase, SPEX is used as described earlier. At the final iteration of the algorithm, the chunks that are identified as occurring more than once are stored in an inverted index structure (Witten et al. 1999). This index contains an entry for each duplicate chunk and a list of each document where it occurs. We call this index the *shared-chunk index.*

In the relationship graph generation phase, DECO uses the shared-chunk index and an approximate counting technique similar to that proposed by Shivakumar & García-Molina (1999) in order to identify co-derived document pairs. Several parameters must be specified to guide this process: the most important of these are the *scoring function* and the *inclusion threshold.* Given documents u and v, the scoring function may at present be one of the following:

$$S_1(u,v) = \sum_{c \in u \wedge c \in v} 1 \qquad S_2(u,v) = \sum_{c \in u \wedge c \in v} 1/\min \bar{u}, \bar{v}$$
$$S_3(u,v) = \sum_{c \in u \wedge c \in v} 1/\operatorname{mean} \bar{u}, \bar{v} \qquad S_4(u,v) = \sum_{c \in u \wedge c \in v} \frac{1/f_c}{\operatorname{mean} \bar{u}, \bar{v}}$$

where $\bar{u}$ is the length (in words) of a document u, and f_c is the number of collection documents a given chunk c appears in. Function S_1 above simply counts the number of chunks common to the two documents; this elementary scoring method is how fingerprinting algorithms have worked up to now. Functions S_2 and S_3 attempt to normalise the score relative to the size of the documents, so that larger documents don't dominate smaller ones in the results. They are very similar to the resemblance measure of Broder (1997) but are modified for more efficient computation. Function S_4 gives greater weight to phrases that are rare across the collection. These scoring functions are all simple heuristics; further refinement of these functions and the possible use of statistical models is desirable and a topic of future research.

The inclusion threshold is the minimum value of $S(u, v)$ for which an edge between u and v will be included in the relationship graph. We wish to set the threshold to be such that pairs of co-derived documents score above the threshold while pairs that are not co-derived score below the threshold.

6 Experimental Methodology

We use three document collections in our experiments. The *webdata+xml* and *linuxdocs* collections were accumulated by Hoad & Zobel (2003). The *webdata+xml* collection consists of 3,307 web documents totalling approximately 35 megabytes, into which have been seeded nine documents (the *XML documents*), each of which is a substantial edit by a different author of a single original report discussing XML technology. Each of these nine documents shares a co-derivation relationship with each of the other eight documents, though in some cases they only have a relatively small quantity of text in common. The *linuxdocs* collection consists of 78,577 documents (720 MB) drawn from the documentation included with a number of distributions of RedHat Linux. While the *webdata+xml* collection serves as an artificial but easily-analysed testbed for co-derivative identification algorithms, the *linuxdocs* collection, rich in duplicate and near-duplicate documents, is a larger and more challenging real-world collection.

The *LATimes* collection is a 476 megabyte collection of newswire articles from the Los Angeles Times, one of the newswire collections created for the TREC conference (Harman 1995). This collection is used as an example of a typical document collection and is used to investigate the index growth we may expect from such a typical collection.

We define a collection's *reference graph* as the relationship graph that would be generated by a human judge for the collection[1]. The *coverage* of a given computer-generated relationship graph is the proportion of edges in the reference graph that are also contained in that graph, and the *density* of a relationship graph is the proportion of edges in that graph that also appear in the reference graph. While these two concepts are in many ways analogous to the traditional recall and precision metrics used in query-based information retrieval (Baeza-Yates & Ribeiro-Neto 1999), we choose the new terminology to emphasise that the task is quite different to querying: we are not trying to meet an explicit

[1] Although the concept of an 'ideal' underlying relationship graph is a useful artifice, the usual caveats of subjectivity and relativity must be borne in mind.

information need, but are rather attempting to accurately identify existing information relationships within the collection.

To estimate the density of a relationship graph, we take a random selection of edges from the graph and judge whether the documents they connect are in fact co-derived. To estimate the coverage of a relationship graph, we select a number of representative documents and manually determine a list of documents with which they are co-derived. The coverage estimate is then the proportion of the manually determined pairings that are identified in the relationship graph. A third metric, average precision, is simply the average proportion of co-derivative edges to total edges for the documents selected to estimate coverage. While it is an inferior measure to average density, it plays a role in experimentation because it is far less time-consuming to calculate.

7 Testing and Discussion

Index Growth Rate. In order to investigate the growth trend of the shared-chunk index as the source collection grows, we extracted subcollections of various sizes from the *LATimes* collection and the *linuxdocs* collection, and observed the number of duplicate chunks extracted as the size of the collection grew.

This growth trend is important for the scalability of SPEX and by extension the DECO package: if the growth trend were quadratic, for example, this would set a practical upper bound on the size of the collection which could be submitted to the algorithm, whereas if the trend were linear or $n \log(n)$ then far larger collections would become practical. We found that, for this collection at least, the growth rate follows a reasonably precise linear trend. For the *LATimes* collection, 40 MB of data yielded 54,243 duplicate chunks; 80 MB yielded 126,542; 160 MB 268,128; and 320 MB 570,580 duplicate chunks. While further testing is warranted, a linear growth trend suggests that the algorithm has potential to scale extremely well.

Webdata+XML Experiments. Because the *webdata+xml* collection contains the nine seed documents for which we have exact knowledge of co-derivation relationships, it makes a convenient collection for proving the effectiveness of the DECO package and determining good parameter settings. Using DECO to create a shared-chunk index with a chunk size of eight took under one minute on an Intel Pentium 4 PC with 512 MB of RAM. For this collection, we tested DECO using the four scoring functions described in section 5. For each scoring function, we tested a range of five inclusion thresholds, named – in order of increasing value – T_1 to T_5; the values vary between the scoring functions and were chosen based on preliminary experiments. Each of the 20 generated relationship graphs were then tested for the presence of the 36 edges connecting the XML documents to each other.

As can be seen in Table 1, the estimated coverage values strongly favour the lower inclusion thresholds. Indeed, for all scoring functions using the inclusion threshold T_1, 100% of the pairings between the XML documents were

Table 1. Coverage estimates, as percentages, for the *webdata+xml* collection calculated on the percentage of XML document pairings identified. The average precision was 100% in all cases.

	T_1	T_2	T_3	T_4	T_5
S_1	100.0	97.2	36.1	8.3	0.0
S_2	100.0	100.0	83.3	58.3	25.0
S_3	100.0	91.7	72.2	52.8	16.7
S_4	100.0	97.2	91.7	58.3	22.2

Table 2. Coverage and average precision estimates, as a pair X/Y of percentages, for DECO applied to the *linuxdocs* collection, using a full shared-chunk index and for indexes that store chunks only if their hash-key equals zero *modulo* 16 and 256.

	T_1	T_2	T_3	T_4	T_5
Full chunk indexing					
S_1	100/ 70	89/ 71	56/ 93	36/ 95	34/100
S_2	100/ 57	100/ 75	100/ 92	89/ 94	57/100
S_3	98/ 75	96/ 84	94/100	84/100	47/100
S_4	99/ 83	96/ 91	94/100	78/100	30/100
Fingerprinting modulo *16*					
S_1	90/ 72	88/ 76	56/ 94	36/ 96	34/100
S_2	90/ 75	90/ 75	80/ 94	78/100	57/100
S_3	88/ 82	86/ 91	74/100	74/100	47/100
S_4	88/ 85	86/ 93	86/ 93	69/100	60/100
Fingerprinting modulo *256*					
S_1	54/ 95	54/ 95	54/ 95	54/ 95	34/ 97
S_2	54/ 97	54/ 97	54/ 97	54/ 97	44/ 97
S_3	54/ 97	54/100	54/100	51/100	42/100
S_4	54/ 97	54/100	54/100	44/100	31/100

included in the relationship graph. In all cases the average precision was also 100%. These values – 100% coverage and 100% density – suggest a perfect result, but are certainly overestimates. The nature of the test collection – nine co-derived documents seeded into an entirely unrelated background collection – made it extremely unlikely that spurious edges would be identified. This not only introduced an artificially high density estimate but also strongly biased the experiments in favour of the lower inclusion thresholds, because they allowed all the correct edges to be included with very little risk that incorrect edges would likewise be admitted.

Experiments on the Linux Documentation Collection. For the *linuxdocs* collection, we used DECO to create a shared-chunk index with a chunk size of eight, taking approximately 30 minutes on an Intel Pentium 4 PC with 512 MB of RAM. For generation of relationship graphs we used the same range of scoring functions and inclusion thresholds as in the previous section. We wished also to investigate the level of deterioration witnessed in a fingerprinting strategy as the selectivity of the fingerprint increased; to this end, we experimented with relationship graphs generated from indexes generated using the *modulo* heuristic with $k = 16$ and $k = 256$. The inclusion threshold for these experiments were adjusted downward commensurately.

To estimate the coverage of the relationship graphs, we selected ten documents from the collection representing a variety of different sizes and types, and manually collated a list of co-derivatives for each of these documents. This was done by searching for other documentation within the collection that referred to the same program or concept; thus, the lists may not be entirely comprehensive. Estimated coverage and average precision results for this set of experiments are given in Table 2. Several trends are observable in the results. The first of these is that in general, scoring functions S_2, S_3, and S_4 were more effective than the simple chunk-counting S_1 scoring function Another trend is that performance is noticeably superior with the full shared-chunk index than with the selective shared-chunk indexes. Note in particular that, for the *modulo* 256 index, no configuration was able to find more than 54% of the relevant edges. This is almost certainly because the other 46% of document pairs do not have any chunks in common that evaluate to 0 *modulo* 256 when hashed. This illustrates the dangers of using lossy selection schemes when a high degree of reliability is desired.

We had insufficient human resources to complete an estimate of density for all of the relationship graphs generated. Instead, we selected a range of configurations that seemed to work well and estimated the density for these configurations. This was done by picking 30 random edges from the relationship graph and manually assessing whether the two documents in question were co-derived. The results were pleasingly high: $S_2/T_3/1$, $S_3/T_2/256$, and $S_4/T_3/16$ all scored a density of 93.3% (28 out of 30) while $S_4/T_3/1$ and $S_2/T_1/16$ both returned an estimated density of 100%. Other combinations were not tested.

8 Conclusions

There are many reasons why one may wish to discover co-derivation relationships amongst the documents in a collection. Previous feasible solutions to this task have been based on fingerprinting algorithms that used heuristic chunk selection techniques. We have argued that, with these techniques, one can have either reliability or acceptable resource usage, but not both at once.

We have introduced the SPEX algorithm for efficiently identifying shared chunks in a collection. Unique chunks represent a large proportion of all chunks in the collection – over 98% in one of the collections tested – but play no part in discovery of co-derivatives. Identifying and discarding these chunks means that document fingerprints only contain data that is relevant to the co-derivative discovery process. In the case of the *LATimes* collection, this allows us to create an index that is functionally equivalent to full fingerprinting but is one fiftieth of the size of a full chunk index. Such savings allow us to implement a system that is effective and reliable yet requires only modest resources.

Tests of our DECO system, which used the SPEX algorithm, on two test collections demonstrated that the package is capable of reliably discovering co-derivation relationships within a collection, and that introducing heuristic chunk-selection strategies degraded reliability.

There is significant scope for further work and experimentation with DECO. One area of particular importance is the scalability of the algorithm. We have demonstrated that the system performs capably when presented with a highly redundant 700 MB collection and are confident that it can handle much larger collections, but this needs to be experimentally demonstrated. Another important further development is the design of an adjunct to the SPEX algorithm that would make it possible to add new documents to a collection without rebuilding the entire shared-chunk index. The difficulty of extending the index is the one major defect of SPEX compared to many other fingerprinting selection heuristics. However, the sensitivity, reliability and efficiency of SPEX make it already a valuable tool for analysis of document collections.

Acknowledgements

This research was supported by the Australian Research Council.

References

Baeza-Yates, R. & Ribeiro-Neto, B. (1999), *Modern Information Retrieval*, Addison-Wesley Longman.

Brin, S., Davis, J. & García-Molina, H. (1995), Copy detection mechanisms for digital documents, *in* 'Proceedings of the ACM SIGMOD Annual Conference', pp. 398–409.

Broder, A. Z. (1997), On the Resemblance and Containment of Documents, *in* 'Compression and Complexity of Sequences (SEQUENCES'97)', pp. 21–29.

Broder, A. Z., Glassman, S. C., Manasse, M. S. & Zweig, G. (1997), 'Syntactic clustering of the Web', *Computer Networks and ISDN Systems* **29**(8-13), 1157–1166.

Gusfield, D. (1997), *Algorithms on strings, trees, and sequences: computer science and computational biology*, Cambridge University Press.

Harman, D. (1995), 'Overview of the second text retrieval conference (TREC-2)', *Information Processing and Management* **31**(3), 271–289.

Heintze, N. (1996), Scalable Document Fingerprinting, *in* '1996 USENIX Workshop on Electronic Commerce'.

Hoad, T. C. & Zobel, J. (2003), 'Methods for Identifying Versioned and Plagiarised Documents', *Journal of the American Society for Information Science and Technology* **54**(3), 203–215.

Larsson, N. J. & Moffat, A. (2000), 'Offline Dictionary-Based Compression', **88**(11), 1722–1732.

Manber, U. (1994), Finding Similar Files in a Large File System, *in* 'Proceedings of the USENIX Winter 1994 Technical Conference', San Fransisco, CA, USA, pp. 1–10.

Moffat, A. & Wan, R. (2001), Re-Store: A System for Compressing, Browsing, and Searching Large Documents, *in* 'Proceedings of the International Symposium on String Processing and Information Retrieval', IEEE Computer Society, pp. 162–174.

Nevill-Manning, C. G. & Witten, I. H. (1997), 'Compression and Explanation Using Hierarchical Grammars', *The Computer Journal* **40**(2/3), 103–116.

Nevill-Manning, C. G., Witten, I. H. & Paynter, G. W. (1997), Browsing in digital libraries: a phrase-based approach, *in* 'Proceedings of the second ACM international conference on Digital libraries', ACM Press, pp. 230–236.

Schleimer, S., Wilkerson, D. S. & Aiken, A. (2003), Winnowing: local algorithms for document fingerprinting, *in* 'Proceedings of the 2003 ACM SIGMOD international conference on on Management of data', ACM Press, pp. 76–85.

Shivakumar, N. & García-Molina, H. (1995), SCAM: A Copy Detection Mechanism for Digital Documents, *in* 'Proceedings of the Second Annual Conference on the Theory and Practice of Digital Libraries'.

Shivakumar, N. & García-Molina, H. (1999), Finding Near-Replicas of Documents on the Web, *in* 'WEBDB: International Workshop on the World Wide Web and Databases, WebDB', Springer-Verlag.

Witten, I. H., Moffat, A. & Bell, T. C. (1999), *Managing Gigabytes: Compressing and Indexing Documents and Images*, Morgan Kauffman.

Searching for a Set of Correlated Patterns

Extended Abstract

Shmuel T. Klein and Riva Shalom

Department of Computer Science, Bar Ilan University, Ramat-Gan 52900, Israel
{tomi,gonenr1}@cs.biu.ac.il

We concentrate in this paper on multiple pattern matching, in which a *set* of patterns $S = \{P_1, \ldots, P_k\}$, rather than a single one, is to be located in a given text T. This problem has been treated in several works, including Aho and Corasick, Commentz-Walter, Uratani and Takeda and Crochemore et al. None of these algorithms assumes any relationships between the individual patterns. Nevertheless, there are many situations where the given strings are not necessarily independent.

Consider, for example, a large full text information retrieval system, to which queries consisting of terms to be located are submitted. If a user wishes to retrieve information about `computers`, he might not want to restrict his query to this term alone, but include also grammatical variants and other related terms, such as `under-computerized`, `recomputation`, `precompute`, `computability`, etc. Using wild-cards, one could formulate this as `*comput*`, so that all the patterns to be searched for share some common substring. A similar situation arises in certain biological applications, where several genetic sequences have to be located in DNA strings, and these sequences may have considerable overlaps.

The basic idea is the following: if we can find a substantial overlap s, shared by all the patterns in the set, it is for s that we start searching in the text, using any single pattern matching algorithm, for example BM. If no occurrence of s is found, none of the patterns appears and we are done. If s does occur $t > 0$ times, it is only at its t locations that we have to check for the appearance of the set of prefixes of s in the set of patterns and of the corresponding set of suffixes. This can be done locally at the t positions where s has been found, e.g., with the AC algorithm, but with no need to use its *fail* function.

More formally, let the set S consist of patterns P_i, where $P_i = l_i \, s \, r_i$, and l_i and r_i are the (possibly empty) prefixes and suffixes of P_i which are left after removing the substring s. For our example, $\{l_i\}$ = {`under-`, `re`, `pre`, Λ}, where Λ denotes the empty string, and $\{r_i\}$ = {`erized`, `ation`, `e`, `ability`}. Denote also the length of P_i by m_i and the total length $\sum_{i=1}^{k} m_i$ by M. The algorithm starts by identifying s, the longest common substring shared by $P_1, \ldots, P_k$. The search algorithm is then given by:

```
OVERLAP_MATCHING(s, S)
search for s in text T using KMP or BM
for each i such that s is found starting at position i
        check at position i + |s| − 1 for an occurrence of an element of {r_j}
                    using an AC automaton
        for each matching r_j found
                check if l_j matches T at position i − |l_j|
                if yes, declare match at i − |l_j|
```

A. Apostolico and M. Melucci (Eds.): SPIRE 2004, LNCS 3246, pp. 68–69, 2004.

The dominant part of the time complexity will generally be for the search of s, which can be done in time $O(|T|)$. Applying the AC automaton is not really a search, since it is done at well-known positions. Its time complexity is therefore bounded $O(t \cdot \max\{m_i\})$, where t is the number of occurrences of the overlap s. Only in case the occurrences of s are so frequent that the potential positions of the patterns cover a large part of the string T may $O(t \cdot \max\{m_i\})$ be larger than $O(|T|)$, but this will rarely occur for a natural language input string.

Consider now as example the dictionary $S = \{P_1 =$ `dxyz`, $P_2 =$ `wdxyza`, $P_3 =$ `bcdxyzw`, $P_4 =$ `bcdzw`$\}$, showing a major deficiency of the suggested algorithm. The longest substring shared by *all* the patterns is just a single character, `d` or `z`. One can of course circumvent the case, which is even worse from our point of view, when the longest common substring is empty, by invoking then the standard AC routine. But if there is a non-empty string s, but it is too short, it might occur so often that the benefit of our procedure could be lost.

In the above example, the string `dxyz` is shared by only three of the four elements of the dictionary S, but its length is much longer than the string shared by all the elements. This suggests that it might be worthwhile not to insist on having the overlap cover the entire dictionary, but maybe to settle for one shared not by all, but at least by a high percentage of the patterns, which may allow us to choose a longer overlap. An alternative approach could be to look for two or more substrings $s_1, s_2, \ldots$, each longer than s and each being shared by the patterns of some proper subset of S, but which together cover the entire dictionary. For our example we could, e.g., use the pair of substrings $\{$`dxyz`, `bcd`$\}$. In Information Retrieval applications, such an approach could be profitable in case the query consists of the grammatical variants of two or more terms, or in case of irregularities, as in the set $\{$`go`, `goes`, `undergoing`, `went`$\}$.

To get a general feeling of how the algorithms behave in some real-life applications, we ran a set of tests on several text and DNA files. As a measure for the efficiency, we defined a *rate* as the number of symbol comparisons divided by the length of the text. The Aho Corasick algorithm served as benchmark, yielding always a rate of 1. The graphs in Figure 1 give the rate, for each of the algorithms we considered, as a function of the overlap size.

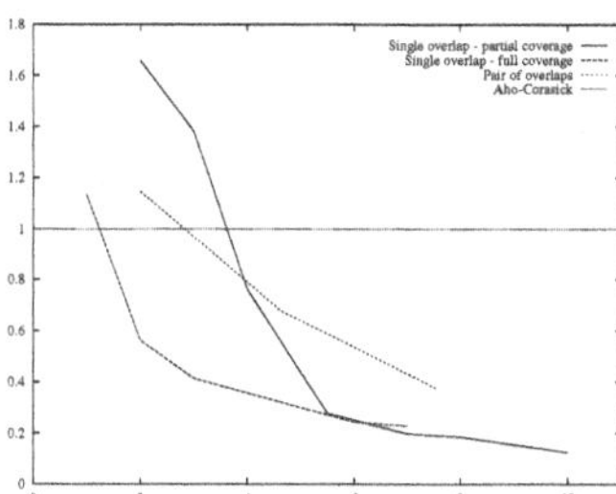

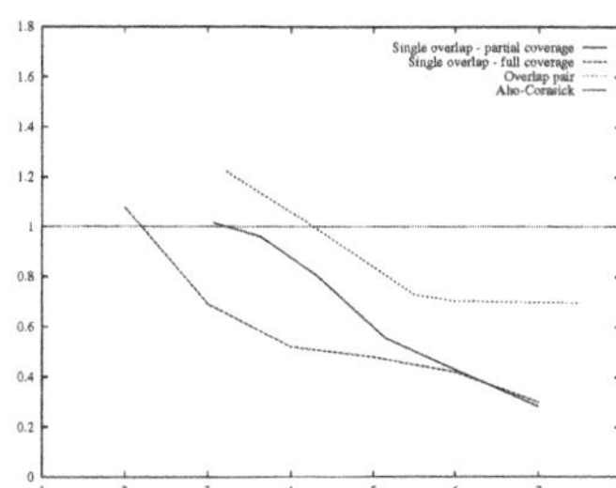

Fig. 1. Comparative performance for text and DNA files

As can be seen, the rate is strictly decreasing with the overlap size, and rates as low as 0.4 on the average can be reached already for relatively short overlaps of size 4–5.

Linear Nondeterministic Dawg String Matching Algorithm (Abstract)

Longtao He and Binxing Fang

Research Center of Computer Network and Information Security Technology
Harbin Institute of Technology, Harbin 150001, P.R. China

The exact *string matching* problem is to find all the occurrences of a given pattern $x = x_1 x_2 \cdots x_m$ in a large text $y = y_1 y_2 \cdots y_n$, where both x and y are sequences of symbols drawn from a finite character set Σ of size σ.

Various good solutions have been presented during years. Among them, BNDM [1] is a very efficient and flexible algorithm. It simulates the BDM algorithm using bit-parallelism. BNDM first builds a mask table B for each symbol c. The mask in $B[c]$ has the i-th bit set if and only if $x_i = c$. The search state is kept in a computer word $L = L_m \cdots L_1$, where the bit L_i at iteration l is set if and only if $x_i \cdots x_{i+l-1} = y_{j-l+1} \cdots y_j$, where j is the end position of the current window. Each time we position the window in the text we initialize $L = 1^m$ and scan the window backward. For each new text character we update L with the formula:

$$L \leftarrow (L \ \& \ B[y_{j-l}]) >> 1 \tag{1}$$

Each time we find a prefix of the pattern ($L_1 = 1$) we remember the position in the window. If we run out of 1's in L, there cannot be a match and we suspend the scanning and then shift the window to the right. If we can perform m iterations then we report a match.

BNDM uses only one computer word to keep the search state. The overflow bits in the shift right of the search state are lost. This is why BNDM has a quadratic worst case time complexity. We present a new purely bit-parallel variant of BNDM, which we call the Linear Nondeterministic Dawg Matching algorithm (LNDM). LNDM makes use of two computer words L and R. L is the traditional state. The additional computer word R keeps the overflow bits in the shift right of the search state L during the backward scan. The formulas to update the search state are changed to:

$$L \leftarrow L \ \& \ B[y_{j-l}] \tag{2}$$

$$(LR) \leftarrow (LR) >> 1 \tag{3}$$

where (LR) means concatenation of L and R. Instead of checking if $L_1 = 1$, LNDM just right-shifts (LR). The scan goes until L is equal to 0^m. Then, if $R \neq 0^m$, we resume a forward scan after the end of current window with a nondeterministic automaton initialized by the saved bits $R << (m-l)$.

In the additional forward scan stage, LNDM runs as a reverse Backward Nondeterministic Dawg, to be precise, a Forward Nondeterministic Dawg. For each new text symbol we update R with the formula:

$$R \leftarrow (R << 1) \ \& \ B[y_{j+r}] \tag{4}$$

A. Apostolico and M. Melucci (Eds.): SPIRE 2004, LNCS 3246, pp. 70–71, 2004.

```
LNDM (x = x1 x2 ··· xm, y = y1 y2 ··· yn)
Preprocessing
    For c ∈ Σ do B[c] ← 0^m
    For i ∈ 1···m do
        B[x_i] ← B[x_i] | 0^(m-i) 1 0^(i-1)
Search
    For k ∈ 1···⌊n/m⌋ do
        l ← 0, r ← 0
        L ← 1^m, R ← 0^m
        While L ≠ 0^m do
            L ← L & B[y_(km-l)]
            l ← l + 1
            (LR) ← (LR) >> 1
        End of while
        R ← R >> (m − l)
        While R ≠ 0^m do
            r ← r + 1
            If R&10^(m-1) ≠ 0^m then
                output km + r − m
            End of if
            R ← (R << 1) & B[y_(km+r)]
        End of while
    End of for
```

Fig. 1. The Pseudo-code of LNDM.

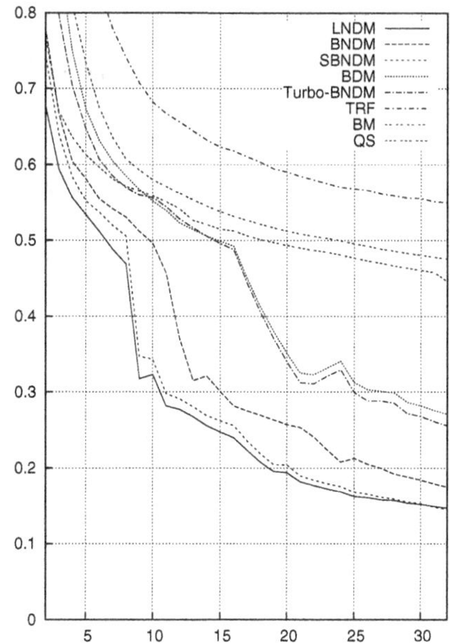

Fig. 2. Running time for alphabet size 256.

Since LNDM scans in the reverse direction against BNDM in this stage, the formula differs from that of BNDM in the shift direction. Each time we meet the situation $R_m = 1$ we report a match. If we run out of 1's in R, there cannot be a match and the algorithm shifts to next window.

The algorithm is summarized in Fig.1. With this approach, LNDM can safely shift by m fixedly after each attempt. This important improvement enables LNDM to have optimal time complexities respectively in the worst, best and average cases: $O(n)$, $O(n/m)$ and $(O(n(\log_\sigma m)/m))$ for the pattern not longer than computer word.

We compared the following algorithms with LNDM: BM, QS, BDM, Turbo-BDM, BNDM, Turbo-BNDM, and SBNDM. Fig.2 shows the experimental results over alphabet size 256. The results over large alphabets is similar. The x axis is the length of the patterns, and the y axis shows the average running time in second per pattern per MB text of each algorithm. The results show that LNDM is very fast in practice for large alphabet. Among the worst case linear time algorithms, LNDM is the most efficient one.

References

1. Navarro, G., Raffinot, M.: Fast and flexible string matching by combining bit-parallelism and suffix automata. ACM Journal of Experimental Algorithmics (JEA) **5** (2000)

Permuted and Scaled String Matching

Extended Abstract

Ayelet Butman[1], Revital Eres[2], and Gad M. Landau[2,*]

[1] Holon Academic Institute of Technology, Israel
butmosh@zahav.net.il

[2] Dept. of Computer Science, University of Haifa, Mount Carmel, Haifa 31905 Israel
{revitale,landau}@cs.haifa.ac.il

The goal of *scaled permuted string matching* is to find all occurrences of a pattern in a text, in all possible scales and permutations. Given a text of length n and a pattern of length m we present an $O(n)$ algorithm.

Definition 1 Scaled permuted string matching
Input: *A pattern* $P = p_1 \cdots p_m$ *and a text* $T = t_1 \cdots t_n$ *both over alphabet* Σ.
Output: *All positions in* T *where an occurrence of a permuted copy of the pattern* P, *scaled to* k, *starts* ($k = 1, \ldots, \lfloor \frac{n}{m} \rfloor$). *The pattern is first permuted and then scaled.*

Example: The string *bbbbaabbaaccaacc* is a scaled (to 2) permutation of *baabbacc*.

1 Permuted String Matching over Run-Length Encoded Text

The permuted string matching problem over uncompressed text is simply solved. A sliding window of size $|P|$ can be moved over T to count, for each location of T the order of statistics of the characters. Obviously, this can be done in $O(n)$ time. Let T' be the run-length compressed version of T where $T' = \sigma_1^{r_1} \cdots \sigma_{|T^{\blacksquare}|}^{r_{|T^{\blacksquare}|}}$. Similarly, P' is the permuted run-length compressed pattern. The pattern can be permuted, and therefore, in each location of the text we check if the order of statistics of the characters is equal to that of the pattern. As a result, a better compression can be achieved. Symbols with the same character are compressed. For example, let $P = aabbbaccaab$, its run-length compressed version is $a^2b^3a^1c^2a^2b^1$ and its permuted run-length compressed version is $P' = a^5b^4c^2$. The technique we use is similar to the sliding window technique: a window is shifted on T' from left to right in order to locate all the matches. The window is a substring of T' that represents a candidate for a match. Unlike the simple algorithm, this time the window size is not fixed.

We will define a *valid* window as a substring of T' that fulfills the following two properties: *sufficient* – The number of times each character appears in the window is at least the number of times it appears in the pattern. *minimal*

* Partially supported by NSF grant CCR-0104307, by the Israel Science Foundation grant 282/01, and by IBM Faculty Award.
A full version of the paper appears in http://cs.haifa.ac.il/LANDAU/public.html

A. Apostolico and M. Melucci (Eds.): SPIRE 2004, LNCS 3246, pp. 72–73, 2004.

– Removing the rightmost or the leftmost symbol of the window violates the *sufficient* property.

The algorithm scans the text, locates all *valid* windows and finds the ones in which a permuted copy of the pattern occurs. During the scan of the text, given a *valid* window, it is trivial to check if it contains a match. Hence, we will describe only how to locate all *valid* windows. The *valid* windows are found by scanning the text from left to right, using two pointers, *left* and *right*. To discover each *valid* window, the *right* pointer moves first to find a *sufficient* window and then the *left* pointer moves to find the *valid* window within the *sufficient* window. The *right* pointer moves as long as deleting the leftmost symbol of the window violates the *sufficient* property of the window. When this symbol can finally be removed, the *right* pointer stops and the *left* pointer starts moving. The *left* pointer moves as long as deleting the leftmost symbol of the window does not violate the *sufficient* property of the window. At this point, a new *valid* window has been found.

Example: Let $P' = a^2b^3c^2d^2$ and $T' = c^3a^2c^2a^3d^2b^3c^1$ then $c^3a^2c^2a^3d^2b^3$ is the first *sufficient* window, and $c^2a^3d^2b^3$ is the first *valid* window (but not a match).

Time Complexity: We assume that $|\Sigma|$ is $O(|P'|)$, hence, the time complexity of the algorithm is $O(|P'| + |T'|)$.

2 A Linear Time Algorithm for the Scaled Permuted String Matching Problem

The algorithm is composed of two stages: 1. Preprocessing the text T'. Computing compact copies of the text for each possible scale $1 \leq s \leq \frac{n}{m}$. 2. Applying the permuted string matching over the run-length encoded text algorithm (section 1) on the copies of the text.

We observe that if a permutation of P scaled to s occurs in ${\sigma_i}^{j_i} \cdots {\sigma_k}^{j_k}$ then $j_{i+1}, \ldots, j_{k-1}$ are multiple of s, and $j_i, j_k \geq s$. Hence, we compute for each scale s a compact text T'_s in the following two steps: (In order to simplify the computation of Stage 2, a symbol ${t_j}^{r_j}$ of T' is replaced in T'_s by ${t_j}^{\lfloor \frac{r_j}{s} \rfloor}$.)

Step 1. Locating the regions – T' is scanned from left to right. Consider a symbol ${t_i}^{r_i}$. A new symbol ${t_i}^{\frac{r_i}{s}}$ is added to T'_s if r_i is a multiple of s. It may continue a region or start a new one, in the second case we add a separator ($) between the regions.

Step 2. Expansion of the regions – The last refinement is done by scanning each T'_s text from left to right and expanding all the regions we generated in step 1.

Example: Let $T' = a^6b^2c^4a^3d^5b^9d^2c^8b^4a^7$, the new text after applying step 2 is: $T'_1 = \$\ a^6b^2c^4a^3d^5b^9d^2c^8b^4a^7\$$, $T'_2 = \$a^3b^1c^2a^1\$b^4d^1c^4b^2a^3\$$, $T'_3 = \$a^2\$c^1a^1d^1\ \$d^1b^3\$$, $T'_4 = \$c^1\$c^2b^1a^1\$$, $T'_5 = \$d^1b^1\$$ $T'_6 = \$a^1\$$, $T'_7 = \$a^1\$$, $T'_8 = \$c^1\$$, $T'_9 = \$b^1\$$

Stage 2 runs the permuted string matching over a run-length encoded text algorithm (section 1) on all the new compact texts.

Time Complexity: The running time of both Stage 1 and Stage 2 is bounded by the total length ($O(n)$) of the new texts, therefore, the total time complexity is $O(n)$.

Bit-Parallel Branch and Bound Algorithm for Transposition Invariant LCS

Kjell Lemström[1], Gonzalo Navarro[2], and Yoan Pinzon[3,4]

[1] Department of Computer Science, University of Helsinki, Finland
[2] Department of Computer Science, University of Chile
[3] Department of Computer Science, King's College, London, UK
[4] Department of computer Science
Autonomous University of Bucaramanga, Colombia

Main Results. We consider the problem of longest common subsequence (LCS) of two given strings in the case where the first may be shifted by some constant (i.e. transposed) to match the second. For this longest common transposition invariant subsequence (LCTS) problem, that has applications for instance in music comparison, we develop a branch and bound algorithm with best case time $O((m^2 + \log\log\sigma)\log\sigma)$ and worst case time $O((m^2 + \log\sigma)\sigma)$, where m and σ are the length of the strings and the number of possible transpositions, respectively. This compares favorably against the $O(\sigma m^2)$ naive algorithm in most cases and, for large m, against the $O(m^2 \log\log m)$ time algorithm of [2].

Technical Details. Let $A = a_1, \ldots, a_n$ and $B = b_1, \ldots, b_m$ be two strings, over a finite numeric alphabet $\Sigma = \{0 \ldots \sigma\}$. A subsequence of string A is obtained by deleting zero, one or several characters of A. The length of the *longest common subsequence* of A and B, denoted $LCS(A, B)$, is the length of the longest string that is a subsequence both of A and B.

The conventional dynamic programming approach computes $LCS(A, B)$ in time $O(mn)$, using a well-known recurrence that can be easily adapted to compute $LCS(A + c, B)$, where $A + c = (a_1 + c), \ldots, (a_n + c)$, for some transposition c, where $-\sigma \leq c \leq \sigma$:

$$LCS^c_{i,0} = 0; \;\; LCS^c_{0,j} = 0;$$
$$LCS^c_{i,j} = \textbf{if } a_i + c = b_j \textbf{ then } 1 + LCS^c_{i-1,j-1} \textbf{ else } \max(LCS^c_{i-1,j}, LCS^c_{i,j-1}).$$

Our goal is to compute the length of the *longest common transposition invariant subsequence*,

$$LCTS(A, B) = \max_{c \in -\sigma \ldots \sigma} LCS^c(A, B).$$

Let X denote a subset of transpositions and $LCS^X(A, B)$ be such that a_{i+1} and b_{j+1} match whenever $b_{j+1} - a_{i+1} \in X$. Now, it is easy to see that $LCS^X(A, B) \geq \max_{c \in X} LCS^c(A, B)$, so $LCS^X(A, B)$ may not contain the actual maximum $LCS^c(A, B)$ for $c \in X$ but gives an upper bound. Our aim is to find the maximum $LCS^c(A, B)$ value by successive approximations.

A. Apostolico and M. Melucci (Eds.): SPIRE 2004, LNCS 3246, pp. 74–75, 2004.

We form a binary tree whose nodes have the form $[I, J]$ and represent the range of transpositions $X = \{I \dots J\}$. The root is $[-\sigma, \sigma]$. The leaves have the form $[c, c]$. Every internal node $[I, J]$ has two children $[I, \lfloor (I+J)/2 \rfloor]$ and $[\lfloor (I+J)/2 \rfloor + 1, J]$.

The hierarchy is used to upper bound the $LCS^c(A, B)$ values. For every node $[I, J]$ of the tree, if we compute $LCS^{\{I \dots J\}}(A, B)$, the result is an upper bound to $LCS^c(A, B)$ for any $I \leq c \leq J$. Moreover, $LCS^X(A, B)$ is easily computed in $O(mn)$ time if $X = \{I \dots J\}$ is a continuous range of values:

$$LCS^X_{i,0} = 0;\;\; LCS^X_{0,j} = 0;$$

$$LCS^X_{i,j} = \textbf{if } b_j - a_i \in X \textbf{ then } 1 + LCS^X_{i-1,j-1} \textbf{ else } \max(LCS^c_{i-1,j}, LCS^c_{i,j-1}).$$

We already know that the LCS value of the root is $\min(m, n)$, since every pair of characters match. The idea is now to compute its two children, and continue with the most promising one (higher LCS^X upper bound). For this most promising one, we compute its two children, and so on. At any moment, we have a set of subtrees to consider, each one with its own upper bound on the leaves it contains. At every step of the algorithm, we take the most promising subtree, compute its two children, and add them to the set of subtrees under consideration. If the most promising subtree turns out to be a leaf node $[c, c]$, then the upper bound value is indeed the exact LCS^c value. At this point we can stop the process, because all the upper bounds of the remaining subtrees are smaller or equal than the actual LCS^c value we have obtained. So we are sure of having obtained the highest value.

For the analysis, we have a best case of $\log_2(2\sigma + 1) = O(\log \sigma)$ iterations and a worst case of $2(2\sigma + 1) - 1 = 4\sigma + 1 = O(\sigma)$ until we obtain the first leaf element. Our priority queue, which performs operations in logarithmic time, contains $O(\log \sigma)$ elements in the best case and $O(\sigma)$ in the worst case. Hence every iteration of the algorithm takes $O(m^2 + \log\log \sigma)$ at best and $O(m^2 + \log \sigma)$ at worst. This gives an overall best case complexity of $O((m^2 + \log\log\sigma)\log\sigma)$ and $O((m^2 + \log\sigma)\sigma)$ for the worst case. The worst case is not worse than the naive algorithm for $m = \Omega(\sqrt{\log \sigma})$, which is the case in practice.

By using bit-parallel techniques that perform several LCS^X computations at the same time [1], the algorithm can be extended to use a t-ary tree.

This technique can be applied also to any distance d satisfying $\min_{c \in X} d^c(A, B) \leq d^X(A, B)$, where $d^X(A, B)$ is computed by considering that a_{i+1} and b_{j+1} match whenever $b_{j+1} - a_{i+1} \in X$. This includes δ-LCS, general weighted edit distance, polyphony, etc., so it enjoys of more generality than most of the previous approaches. It cannot, however, be easily converted into a search algorithm.

References

1. K. Lemström and G. Navarro. Flexible and efficient bit-parallel techniques for transposition invariant approximate matching in music retrieval. In *Proc. SPIRE'03*, LNCS 2857, pp. 224–237, 2003.
2. V. Mäkinen, G. Navarro, and E. Ukkonen. Algorithms for transposition invariant string matching. In *Proc. STACS'03*, LNCS 2607, pp. 191–202, 2003.

A New Feature Normalization Scheme Based on Eigenspace for Noisy Speech Recognition

Yoonjae Lee and Hanseok Ko

Dept. of Electronics and Computer Engineering, Korea University, Seoul, Korea
yjlee@ispl.korea.ac.kr, hsko@korea.ac.kr

Abstract. We propose a new feature normalization scheme based on eigenspace, for achieving robust speech recognition. In particular, we employ the Mean and Variance Normalization (MVN) in eigenspace using unique and independent eigenspaces to cepstra, delta and delta-delta cepstra respectively. We also normalize training data in eigenspace and get the model from the normalized training data. In addition, a feature space rotation procedure is introduced to reduce the mismatch of training and test data distribution in noisy condition. As a result, we obtain a substantial recognition improvement over the basic eigenspace normalization.

1 Proposed Scheme

We separated the feature vector into three classes as cepstra, delta and delta-delta cepstra because each class has its own definition and characteristics. Then we implemented a separated-eigenspace normalization (SEN) scheme.

When cepstral features are distorted by noisy conditions, their distribution can be moved as well as rotated by some amount from their original distribution.[2] When we rotate only the dominant eigenvector that has the largest variance or eigenvalue, the first eigenvectors of training and test features become the same and the mismatch between the training and test data distribution can be reduced. Only the first eigenvector rotation procedure is presented here simply as follows. First, we need to obtain the eigenvalue and eigenvector of full training corpus. $\tilde{v}$ denotes the first dominant eigenvector of the training distribution and v denotes the first dominant eigenvector of one test utterance. Then the rotation angle α, between the two eigenvectors, is computed from their dot product, $\alpha = \arccos(\tilde{v} \cdot v)$ and $R = \begin{pmatrix} \cos(\alpha) & \sin(\alpha) \\ -\sin(\alpha) & \cos(\alpha) \end{pmatrix}$ where R denotes a rotation matrix. Since the two eigenvectors are not orthogonal, the Gram-Schmidt is applied to $\tilde{v}$ in order to obtain the orthonormal basis vector $\hat{v}$ lying in the same plane of rotation, $\hat{v} = \dfrac{v - (\tilde{v} \cdot v) \cdot \tilde{v}}{\| v - (\tilde{v} \cdot v) \cdot \tilde{v} \|}$. Then we project the test features onto the plane spanned by $\tilde{v}$ and $\hat{v}$. The projection

A. Apostolico and M. Melucci (Eds.): SPIRE 2004, LNCS 3246, pp. 76–78, 2004.

matrix consists of $\tilde{v}$ and $\hat{v}$, thus $J = (\tilde{v}, \hat{v})$. Finally, a correction matrix $I - JJ^T$ with the identity matrix I has to be applied in order to restore the dimensions lost in the projection procedure. Then the full rotation matrix Q is derived as: $Q = JRJ^T + I - JJ^T$. Finally, the rotated feature is obtained by: $\hat{X}_t^c = QX_t^c$.

2 Experiments and Results

Recognition Task: The feature normalization method has been tested with the Aurora2.0 database that contains English connected digits recorded in clean environments. Three sets of sentences under several conditions (e.g. SetA: subway, car noise, SetB: restaurant, street and train station noise, SetC: subway and street noise) were prepared by contaminating them with SNRs ranging from -5dB to 20dB and clean condition. A total of 1001 sentences are included in each noise condition.

Experiments Procedure and Results: We followed the Aurora2.0 evaluation procedure for performance verification along with identical conditions suggested in the Aurora2.0 procedure. Note that we use a c0 coefficient instead of log-energy to induce improved performance, because eigenspace is defined consistently when some of elements have large variance. First we examine the baseline performance (clean condition training). We then apply MVN [3] and the eigenspace MVN to only the test data and to both training and test data together. Next, we experimented on separated-eigenspace normalization (SEN). The feature space rotation with SEN was examined also. The experiment notations of Tables are as follows: 1) MVN : mean and variance normalization in cepstral domain, 2) EIG : mean and variance in eigenspace.[1] (eigenspace normalization), 3) SEN : separated-eigenspace normalization, 4) SEN_Ro_20 : separated-eigenspace normalization +feature space rotation. The first eigenvector of the test is obtained from training noisy set's 20dB data of each.

From Table 1, we can see that SEN with feature rotation and training data normalization is more effective than basic eigenspace normalization.

We initially expected the best performance when each dominant eigenvector obtained from each SNR was applied to the corresponding SNR test set. However, it turns out that such method does not guarantee the improvement. At low SNR, the performance becomes slightly degraded. We achieved the best performance when applying an eigenvector of 20dB set to all SNR data of same test set.

Table 1. Average word accuracy for the proposed scheme of all data set in Aurora2.0(%) (_T denotes the normalization of training data)

	Baseline	MVN	EIG	EIG_T	SEN	SEN_T	SEN_Ro_20_T
SetA	59.58	77.90	79.81	80.43	80.27	80.51	81.08
SetB	57.18	79.49	81.21	82.87	81.77	82.49	-
SetC	66.81	77.90	78.96	79.23	79.32	79.10	-

At lower SNR, the data distribution in cepstral domain becomes more compressed. Consequently, their discriminative shapes (e.g. large variance) is diminished as the SNR becomes lower. That's the reason why 20dB statistics yielded the best performance. From a 20dB noisy training database, we estimated the characteristics of corresponding noise and compensated for the feature reliably. Through the proposed methods, we obtained average word accuracy up to 81.08% on the setA of Aurora2.0.

Acknowledgement

Research supported by No. 10011362 MCIE of Korea.

References

1. K. Yao, E. Visser, O. Kwon, and T. Lee, :A Speech Processing Front-End with Eigenspace Normalization for Robust Speech Recognition in Noisy Automobile Environments, Eurospeech2003 (2003) 9-12
2. S. Molau, D. Keysers and H. Ney, : Matching training and test data distributions for robust speech recognition, Speech Communication, Vol.41, No4 (2003) 579-601
3. P.Jain and H.Hermansky, : Improved Mean and Variance Normalization for Robust Speech Recognition, Proc.of ICASSP (2001)

Fast Detection of Common Sequence Structure Patterns in RNAs

Rolf Backofen and Sven Siebert

Friedrich-Schiller Universität
Ernst-Abbe Platz 2, 07743 Jena, Germany
{backofen,siebert}@inf.uni-jena.de

Abstract. We developed a dynamic programming approach of computing common sequence/structure patterns between two RNAs given by their sequence and secondary structures. Common patterns between two RNAs are meant to share the same local sequential and structural properties. Nucleotides which are part of an RNA are linked together due to their phosphodiester or hydrogen bonds. These bonds describe the way how nucleotides are involved in patterns and thus delivers a bond-preserving matching definition. Based on this definition, we are able to compute all patterns between two RNAs in time $O(nm)$ and space $O(nm)$, where n and m are the lengths of the RNAs, respectively. Our method is useful for describing and detecting local motifs and for detecting local regions of large RNAs although they do not share global similarities. An implementation is available in C++ and can be obtained by contacting one of the authors.

1 Introduction

RNAs are polymers consisting of the four nucleotides A,C,G and U which are linked together by their phosphodiester bonds. This chain of nucleotides is called the primary structure. Bases which are part of the nucleotides form hydrogen bonds within the same molecule leading to structure formation. One major challenge is to find (nearly) common patterns in RNAs since they suggest functional similarities of these molecules. For this purpose, one has to investigate not only sequential features, but also structural features. The structure in combination with the sequence of a molecule dictates its function. Finding common RNA motifs is currently a hot topic in bioinformatics since RNA has been identified as one of the most important research topics in life sciences. RNA was selected as *the* scientific breakthrough of the year 2002 by the reader of the science journal.

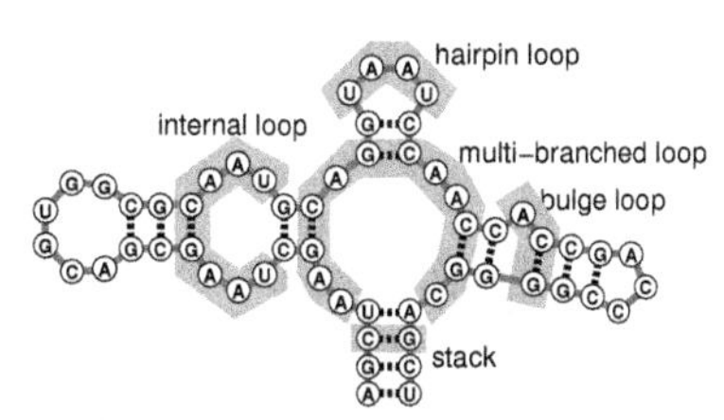

Fig. 1. Structure elements of an RNA secondary structure.

A. Apostolico and M. Melucci (Eds.): SPIRE 2004, LNCS 3246, pp. 79–92, 2004.

Most approaches on finding RNA sequence/structure motifs are based on (locally) aligning two RNAs of lengths n. They use dynamic programming methods with a high complexity between $O(n^4)$ and $O(n^6)$ ([1], [9]). Hence, these approaches are suited for RNAs with just moderate sizes. For that reason, we want to use a general approach that is inspired by the DIALIGN [10] method for multiple sequence alignments. The basic idea is to find exact patterns in large RNAs first, and then to locally align only subsequences containing many exact patterns by using a more complex approach like [1].

So far, the problem of finding local, exact common sequence/structure patterns was unsolved. This is the problem which is considered in this paper. We can list all patterns between two RNAs in time $O(nm)$ and space $O(nm)$, where n and m are the lengths of the RNAs, respectively. The key idea is a dynamic programming method that describes secondary structures not only as base pairing interactions but at a higher level of structure elements known as hairpin loops, right bulges, left bulges, internal loops or multi-branched loops (see Figure 1). The computation of RNA patterns is performed on loop regions from inside to outside. Base-pairs which enclose loops occur in a nested fashion, i.e nested base-pairs fulfill for any two base-pairs (i_1, i_2) and (j_1, j_2) either $i_1 < i_2 < j_1 < j_2$ or $i_1 < j_1 < j_2 < i_2$. Hence, we are able to obtain an elegant solution to the pattern search problem.

Fig. 2. Alternative matching.

A naive attempt is to consider all combinations of positions i in the first RNA and positions j in the second RNA and to extend these starting patterns by looking at neighbouring nucleotides sharing the same sequential and structural properties. If these properties are fulfilled then the nucleotides are taken into the pattern. At a first glance, this idea may work, but the crucial point are the loops. Consider e.g. the case shown in Figure 2. Suppose the algorithm starts at position 1 in the first RNA and position 1 in the second RNA and is working towards the multiple loop in the first RNA. The lower stem has been successfully matched. But now there is no clear decision to match the upper part of the stem-loop of the second RNA either to the left side or to the right side of the multiple loop. This decision depends on how a common pattern is defined, of course, and how to reach a maximally extended pattern. Therefore, the only solution is to make some pre-computations of sequential and structural components of RNAs. Finally, we end up in a dynamic programming approach which compares inner parts of RNAs first, stores the results in different matrices and build up the solutions successively. Note, that it is also a mistake to compute common sequential parts first and then to recompose these parts by their structural properties. This problem is obviously a computational intractable problem because of considering all combinations of subsets of sequence parts.

Related Work: Wang et al.[13] published an algorithm for finding a largest approximately common substructure between two trees. This is an inexact pattern matching algorithm suitable for RNA secondary structures. A survey of computing similarity between RNAs with and without secondary structures until 1995 is given by Bafna et al.[2]. Gramm et al. [5] formulated the arc-preserving problem: given two nested RNAs S_1 and S_2 with lengths n and m $(n \geq m)$, respectively, does S_2 occurs in S_1 such that S_2 can be obtained by deleting bases from S_1 with the property that the arcs are preserved ? This problem can not be seen as biological motivated because the structure of S_2 would be found splitted in S_1. It has been shown by Jiang et al. [8] that finding the longest common arc-preserving subsequence for arc-annotated sequences (LAPCS), where at least one of them has crossing arc structure is MAXSNP-hard. Exact pattern matching on RNAs has been done by Gendron et al. [4]. They propose a backtracking algorithm, similar to an algorithm from Ullman [11] solving the subgraph isomorphism problem from graph theory. It aims at finding recurrent patterns in one RNA.

The paper is organized as follows: In section 2, we introduce the reader into definitions and notations of RNAs. In section 3, we define matchings between two RNAs such that they can be described by matching and matched paths. In Section 4, a bond preserving matching is proposed which is used for the dynamic programming matrices (section 5). The matrices are computed by recursion equations in section 6. The pseudo code is given in section 7.

2 Definitions and Notations

An *RNA* is a tuple (S, P), where S is a string of length n over the alphabet $\Sigma = \{A, C, G, U\}$. We denote $S(i)$ as the base at position i. P is a set of base-pairs (i, i'), $1 \leq i < i' \leq n$, such that $S(i)$ and $S(i')$ are complementary bases. Here, we refer to Watson-Crick base-pairs A—U and C—G, as well as the non-standard base-pair G—U. In the following, we write $i \overset{P}{\text{—}} i'$ instead of $(i, i') \in P$ meaning that the two bases S(i) and S(i') are linked together by a bond. For the rest of the paper, we restrict our set of base-pairs to secondary structures holding the following property: for any two base-pairs (i, i') and (j, j') either $i < i' < j < j'$ *(independent)* or $i < j < j' < i'$ *(nested)*. The nestedness condition allows us to partially order the bases of an RNA.

Definition 1 (Stacking Order). *Let (S, P) be an RNA. The* stacking order *of a base S(i) (abbr. as $stord_P(i)$) is the number of bonds $k \overset{P}{\text{—}} l$ with $k < i < l$, plus one.*

Hence, we are able to partition a secondary structure into structure elements with the same stacking order. We call them loops. See e.g. Figure 1 for various loop names. For our algorithmic approach, we have to look at neighbouring bases belonging to the same loop. This is achieved by a function right (left) of an RNA (S, P):

$$\text{right}_P(i) = \begin{cases} j & \text{if } (i, j) \in P \\ i + 1 & \text{otherwise} \end{cases}$$

and analogously for $\text{left}_P(i)$. The function $\text{right}_P^k(i)$ (resp. $\text{left}_P^k(i)$) is a short term of applying the right function (resp. left) to i k-times. We define $\text{rbd}_P(i)$

(resp. $\text{lbd}_P(i)$) to be true if there is a bond $i \overset{P}{\text{——}} i'$ (resp. $i' \overset{P}{\text{——}} i$), false otherwise. Thus, we can describe loops mathematically as follows.

Definition 2 (Loop). *Let (S, P) be an RNA. The* loop *which is enclosed by a bond $i \overset{P}{\text{——}} i'$ is the set of positions*

$$loop(i \overset{P}{\text{——}} i') = \{r \mid i < r < i' \wedge \exists k : r = right_P^k(i)\}.$$

3 Matchings

Suppose we are given two RNAs (S_1, P_1) and (S_2, P_2). The sets $V_1 = \{i \mid 1 \leq i \leq |S_1|\}$ and $V_2 = \{j \mid 1 \leq j \leq |S_2|\}$ contains the positions of both RNAs.

Definition 3 (Matching). *A* matching *M between two RNAs (S_1, P_1) and (S_2, P_2) is a set of pairs $M = \{(i, j) \mid i \in V_1 \wedge j \in V_2\}$ which describes a partial bijection from V_1 to V_2 and satisfies the following conditions:*

1. ***structure condition:** for each $(i, j) \in M$, it follows $rbd_{P_1}(i) \Leftrightarrow rbd_{P_2}(j) \wedge lbd_{P_1}(i) \Leftrightarrow lbd_{P_2}(j)$*
2. ***base condition:** for each $(i, j) \in M$ it follows $S_1(i) = S_2(j)$*

The matching definition is applied to single bases. Since bases are sometimes part of base-pairs, we may see them as units given as an additional bond condition:

3. **bond condition:** for each $\{(i, j), (i', j')\} \subseteq M$ with $i \overset{P_1}{\text{——}} i'$ and $j \overset{P_2}{\text{——}} j'$ it follows $S_1(i) = S_2(j) \wedge S_1(i') = S_2(j')$

The range of the first RNA is given as the set $\text{ran}_1(M) = \{i \mid \exists j : (i, j) \in M\}$. It describes the pattern found in the first RNA which is matched to the same pattern in the second RNA. Given an element $i \in \text{ran}_1(M)$, we denote $M(i)$ as the uniquely determined element j with $(i, j) \in M$. Similarly, given an element $j \in \text{ran}_2(M)$, we denote $M^{-1}(j)$ as the uniquely determined element i with $(i, j) \in M$.

The first two points of the definition can be easily written as a matching predicate between two bases at positions i and j:

$$\text{match}(i, j) = [S(i) = S(j)] \wedge [\text{lbd}_{P_1}(i) \leftrightarrow \text{lbd}_{P_2}(j)] \wedge [\text{rbd}_{P_1}(i) \leftrightarrow \text{rbd}_{P_2}(j)]$$

The bond condition provides a structure conserving requirement based on base-pairs. It can be extended by a bond checking such that the predicate of $\text{match}(i \overset{P_1}{\text{——}} i', j \overset{P_2}{\text{——}} j')$ is given as

$$[i \overset{P_1}{\text{——}} i'] \wedge [j \overset{P_2}{\text{——}} j'] \wedge [S_1(i) = S_2(j)] \wedge [S_1(i') = S_2(j')]$$

The matching conditions are applied to single bases or base-pairs so far. Now, we want to merge bases and base-pairs such that special relations among them are fulfilled. They provide a definition for matchings. We make use of a *transition type* function on two positions i and i' which is $+1$, -1 or 0 depending on whether $i = i' + 1$, $i = i' - 1$ or $i \overset{P}{\text{—}} i'$. A path in an RNA is a sequence of positions $i_1 \ldots i_k$, such that the bases $S(i_l)$ and $S(i_{l+1})$ for $l = 1, \ldots, k-1$ are connected due to the bond conditions or due to the backbone of this RNA.

Definition 4 (Matching/Matched Path). *Let (S_1, P_1) and (S_2, P_2) be two RNAs and M a matching between them. An M-*matching path *is a list of pairs $(i_1, j_1) \ldots (i_k, j_k) \in M$ such that*

1. *$i_1 \ldots i_k$ is a path in (S_1, P_1)*
2. *$j_1 \ldots j_k$ is a path in (S_2, P_2)*
3. *for each $1 \leq l < k$ the transition types of (i_l, i_{l+1}) and (j_l, j_{l+1}) are equal.*

A matching is connected *if there is a M-matching path between any two pairs in M. A path in only one of the RNAs consisting of only matched bases is called M-*matched path.

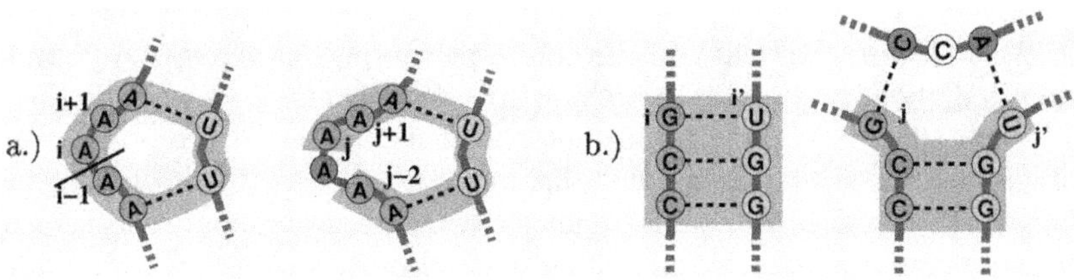

Fig. 3. Unpreserved bonds (backbone and secondary). a.) the backbone bonds $i-1, i$ is not preserved. b.) the bond $i \overset{P_1}{\text{—}} i'$ is not preserved. The matching is indicated by blue and green nodes. In both cases, the the corresponding bases in the second structure are connected with nodes (in red) that are not part of the matching.

Note the difference between *matching* paths and *matched* paths. A matched path is a path occurring in one structure, but there must not be necessarily a corresponding path in the other structure. Furthermore, the restriction of *matching* paths to some structure clearly produces a *matched* path. But the contrary is not true. There are matched paths, where the image of the path (under the matching) is not a path in the other structure. To clarify this, consider the simplest matched paths, which are edges (backbone connections or bonds) between matched bases. By definition, they are matched paths, but there might not be a matching path associated with. This happens for bases which mark the "ends" of the matching. The two cases for backbone edges and bond edges are shown in Figure 3.

From the definitions of matchings, it is not clear whether they respect the backbone order, i.e. $i < i'$ implies $M(i) < M(i')$. One can show that this holds for connected matchings. Since we will restrict ourself to matchings that preserve bonds later, and the proofs are simpler for these kind of matchings, we omit the proof for the general case here. We treat only the simple case for preserving the stacking order for general connected matchings.

Proposition 1. *Let* $(i_1, j_1) \dots (i_k, j_k) \in M$ *be a matching path. Then the path preserves the relative stacking order, i.e. for all* $1 \leq r \leq k$ *we have* $stord_{P_1}(i_1) - stord_{P_2}(j_1) = stord_{P_1}(i_r) - stord_{P_2}(j_r)$.

4 Bond Preserving Matching

As Figure 3b indicates, a matched bond $i \overset{P_1}{\text{—}} i'$ which does not correspond to a matching path only occurs if we have a stem in the first structure that is matched to a multiple loop in the second structure (or vice versa). This is biologically unwanted, since it is very unlikely that this pattern could have been generated by evolution. For that reason, we are interested in matchings that preserve bonds.

Definition 5 (Bond-Preserving Matching). *A connected matching* M *is said to be bond-preserving if every matched bond in* P_1 *or* P_2 *is also a matching path, i.e. if* $\{(i, j), (i', j')\} \subseteq M$ *and* $i \overset{P_1}{\text{—}} i'$*, then* $j \overset{P_2}{\text{—}} j'$*, and vice versa.*

In the following, we will consider bond-preserving matchings. We say that a connected, bond-preserving matching M is *maximally extended*, if there is no M' such that $M \subsetneq M'$. We are interested in finding all (non-overlapping) maximally extended matchings. For this purpose, we need to show some properties. We start with a proposition that allows us to decompose the problem of finding a maximally extended matching into subproblems of finding maximally extended loop matchings. The next proposition shows that the backbone order is respected. And the third proposition shows that if we do not exceed a loop, then maximally extended matchings (in this loop) are uniquely determined by one element.

Proposition 2. *Let* $i, i' \in loop(r \overset{P_1}{\text{—}} s)$*, and let* M *be a bond-preserving matching with* $\{(i, j), (i', j')\} \subseteq M$*. Then any shortest matching path between* (i, j) *and* (i', j') *uses only elements of* $loop(r \overset{P_1}{\text{—}} s) \cup \{r, s\}$.

Proof (Sketch). By contradiction. If there would be a path not satisfying this, then this path has to use a bond twice, either the same element or both elements of the bond. In the first case, we have an immediate contradiction to the minimality. In the second case, the bond is a matched bond. Since M is bond-preserving, one gets a shorter matching path by using this bond.

Proposition 3 (Backbone Order). *Let* M *be a connected matching, and* $(i, j), (i', j') \in M$*. Then* $i < i'$ *if and only if* $j < j'$.

The proof is given in the appendix.

Proposition 4. *Let* $i \overset{P_1}{\text{—}} i'$ *and* $j \overset{P_2}{\text{—}} j'$ *be two bonds, and let* $r \in loop(i \overset{P_1}{\text{—}} i')$ *and* $s = loop(j \overset{P_2}{\text{—}} j')$*. Let* M, M' *with* $i, i' \notin ran_1(M) \cup ran_1(M')$ *and* $(r, s) \in M \cap M'$*. Then* $ran_1(M) \cup loop(i \overset{P_1}{\text{—}} i') = ran_1(M') \cup loop(i \overset{P_1}{\text{—}} i')$ *and* $ran_2(M) \cup loop(j \overset{P_2}{\text{—}} j') = ran_2(M') \cup loop(j \overset{P_2}{\text{—}} j')$.

Proof (Sketch). Follows from Proposition 2 and the fact that if one does not use the closing bond of a loop, then there is only one unique connecting path between two elements of the loop. Hence, there cannot be any conflicting paths that are matched to different elements, and the two matchings must agree on the loop elements.

5 Dynamic Programming Matrices

We want to find all non-overlapping, maximally extended, bond-preserving matchings. For overlapping matchings, we choose the one with maximal size. If there are overlapping matchings of the same size, then only one is selected.

We use a dynamic programming approach by filling a matrix $M(r,s)$, with the following interpretation. We define an order $\prec$ on elements as follows:

$$i \prec j \equiv \begin{cases} i < j & \text{if } \mathrm{stord}_{P_1}(i) = \mathrm{stord}_{P_1}(j) \\ \mathrm{stord}_{P_1}(i) < \mathrm{stord}_{P_1}(j) & \text{otherwise} \end{cases}$$

For pairs (r,s) and (k,l) we define $(r,s) \prec (k,l)$ if and only if $r \prec k$. Then

$$M(r,s) = \max\left\{ |M| \;\middle|\; \begin{array}{l} \text{M is a maximally extended matching} \\ \text{with } (r,s) \in M \text{ and there is no} \\ (r',s') \in M \text{ with } (r',s') \prec (r,s) \end{array} \right\}$$

contains the size of an maximal matching. For simplicity, we assume the maximum value over an empty set to be 0. Note that the size is stored only for the left-most, bottom-most pair (r,s) in M. For calculating $M(r,s)$, we will additionally need auxiliary matrices M^{r_end}, M^{bb} and M^{rb}, which are defined as follows.

Definition 6 (Auxiliary Matrices). *Let $R_1 = (S_1, P_1)$ and $R_2 = (S_2, P_2)$ be two RNAs. Let r (resp. s) be an element of loop($i \overset{P_1}{\text{——}} i'$) (resp. loop($j \overset{P_2}{\text{——}} j'$)). Then $M_{\prec}^{loop}(r,s)$ is the size of the maximal matching within the loops that contain (r,s), and is extended to the right or above (r,s), i.e.*

$$M_{\prec}^{loop}(r,s) = \max\left\{ |M| \;\middle|\; \begin{array}{l} M \subseteq [i..i'] \times [j..j'] \textit{ is a connected} \\ \textit{matching with } (r,s) \in M \textit{ and} \\ \forall (r',s') \in M \backslash \{(i,i'),(j,j')\} : (r,s) \preceq (r',s') \end{array} \right\}$$

In addition, we define for every i,j such that $i \overset{P_1}{\text{——}} i'$ and $j \overset{P_2}{\text{——}} j'$ the matrix element $M^{bb}(i \overset{P_1}{\text{——}} i', j \overset{P_2}{\text{——}} j')$ to be the maximal matching that matches the bonds $i \overset{P_1}{\text{——}} i'$ and $j \overset{P_2}{\text{——}} j'$, i.e.

$$M^{bb}(i \overset{P_1}{\text{——}} i', j \overset{P_2}{\text{——}} j') = \max\left\{ |M| \;\middle|\; \begin{array}{l} M \subseteq [i..i'] \times [j..j'] \textit{ is a} \\ \textit{connected matching with} \\ (i,j) \in M \text{ and } (i',j') \in M \end{array} \right\}$$

In addition, we define $M^{rb}(i \xrightarrow{P_1} i', j \xrightarrow{P_2} j')$ *to be the maximal matching containing the right partners* i' *and* j' *of the bonds only, i.e.*

$$M^{rb}(i \xrightarrow{P_1} i', j \xrightarrow{P_2} j') = \max \left\{ |M| \;\middle|\; \begin{array}{l} M \in [i+1..i'] \times [j+1..j'] \\ \textit{is a connected matching} \\ \textit{with } (i',j') \in M \end{array} \right\}$$

The first procedure calculates $M^{loop}_{\prec}(r,s)$ for a matching of two loops associated with the bonds $i \xrightarrow{P_1} i'$ and $j \xrightarrow{P_2} j'$, given that $M^{loop}_{\prec}$, M^{bb} and M^{rb} is already calculated for all bonds that are contained in the two loops. For calculating $M^{bb}(i \xrightarrow{P_1} i', j \xrightarrow{P_2} j')$, we use additional auxiliary variables. The variable $RDist$ stores the loop distance to the right-end of the loop. Thus, for given $RDist$, we consider elements r and s which have distance $RDist$ to i' and j', respectively. Looking from the right end (i',j') of the loop this implies that

$$r = \mathrm{left}_{R_1}^{RDist}(i') \quad \text{and} \quad s = \mathrm{left}_{R_2}^{RDist}(j').$$

First, we need to know whether there is a matching connecting (r,s) with the right ends of the loop (i',j'):

$$Reach^{r\_end}(RDist) = \begin{cases} \text{true} & \text{if } \exists \text{ connected matching} \\ & \quad M \subseteq [i..i'] \times [j..j'] \text{ with} \\ & \quad (r,s) \in M \text{ and } (i',j') \in M \\ \text{false} & \text{otherwise} \end{cases} \tag{1}$$

Since we don't need the matrix entries any further, we only store the current value in the variable *Reach*. In addition, we store the size of the matching that used in the definition of $Reach^{r\_end}(RDist)$. If $Reach^{r\_end}(RDist)$ is false, then we use the size of the last entry $Reach^{r\_end}(RDist')$ with $RDist' < RDist$ and $Reach^{r\_end}(RDist') = true$. Technically, this is achieved by an array $M^{r\_end}(RDist)$ with

$$M^{r\_end}(RDist) = \max \left\{ |M| \;\middle|\; \begin{array}{l} M \subseteq [i..i'] \times [j..j'] \text{ is a connected} \\ \text{matching with } (i',j') \in M \text{ and} \\ \forall (r',s') \in M \backslash \{(i,i'),(j,j')\} : \\ \hfill (r,s) \preceq (r',s') \end{array} \right\} \tag{2}$$

6 Recursion Equations

The auxiliary matrices and arrays can be easily calculated via the following recursion equations. For $M^{loop}_{\prec}(r,s)$ we have

$$M^{loop}_{\prec}(r,s) = \tag{3}$$
$$\begin{cases} M^{bb}(r,s) + M^{loop}_{\prec}(r'+1, s'+1) & \text{if match}(r \xrightarrow{P_1} r', s \xrightarrow{P_2} s') \\ M^{rb}(r,s) + M^{loop}_{\prec}(r+1, s+1) & \text{else if } \mathrm{rbd}_{P_1}(r) \wedge \mathrm{rbd}_{P_2}(s) \wedge \mathrm{match}(r,s) \\ 1 + M^{loop}_{\prec}(r+1, s+1) & \text{else if match}(r,s) \\ 0 & \text{otherwise} \end{cases}$$

Note that if r and s are the left ends of the bonds $r \overset{P_1}{\text{---}} r' \wedge s \overset{P_2}{\text{---}} s'$, but the bonds are not matchable, then this case is covered by the third case. Here, $r+1$ and $s+1$ are *not* in the same loop as r, s. Therefore, we consider the case where the maximal matching extends to the next loop via the left ends of two bonds. This case is depicted in Figure 4. r and s do match, whereas the bonding partners r' and s' do not match. The currently considered loop is encircled. Since $r+1$ and $s+1$ in the contiguous loop do match, we know that we can calculate $M_{\prec}^{loop}(r, s)$ recursively by calculating $M_{\prec}^{loop}(r+1, s+1)$.

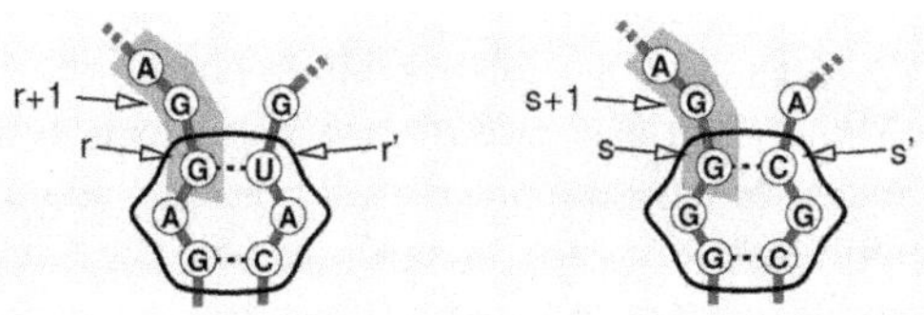

Fig. 4. Extension to next loop.

The next step is to define the auxiliary arrays $Reach^{r\_end}(RDist)$ and $M^{r\_end}(RDist)$ for a given loop. $RDist$ is the distance to the right end of the closing bond. Consider the case where we want to match two loops associated with the bonds $i \overset{P_1}{\text{---}} i'$ and $j \overset{P_2}{\text{---}} j'$. Let len be the minimum of the two loop lengths, and $0 \leq RDist < len$. Then

$$Reach^{r\_end}(0) = \begin{cases} true & \text{if match}(i', j') \\ false & \text{otherwise} \end{cases} \quad \text{and}$$

$$M^{r\_end}(0) = \begin{cases} 1 & \text{if match}(i', j') \\ 0 & \text{otherwise} \end{cases}$$

For $1 \leq RDist \leq len_{min}$, let $r = \text{left}_{R_1}^{RDist}(i')$ and $s = \text{left}_{R_2}^{RDist}(j')$ be the two positions with distance $RDist$ to the right end of the considered loops. Then we obtain

$$Reach^{r\_end}(RDist) = Reach^{r\_end}(RDist - 1) \wedge \text{match}(r, s)$$

$$M^{r\_end}(RDist) = \begin{cases} M_{\prec}^{loop}(r, s) & \text{if } Reach^{r\_end}(RDist) \\ M^{r\_end}(RDist - 1) & \text{otherwise.} \end{cases}$$

The matrix $M^{rb}(i \overset{P_1}{\text{---}} i', j \overset{P_2}{\text{---}} j')$ can be easily defined by

$$M^{rb}(i \overset{P_1}{\text{---}} i', j \overset{P_2}{\text{---}} j') = \max_{0 \leq Rdist < len_{min}} \left\{ M^{r\_end}(RDist) \right\}$$

For the M^{bb} matrix, there are two different cases as shown in Figure 5. In the first case a.), the extensions from the initial matching (i, i') to the right, and the

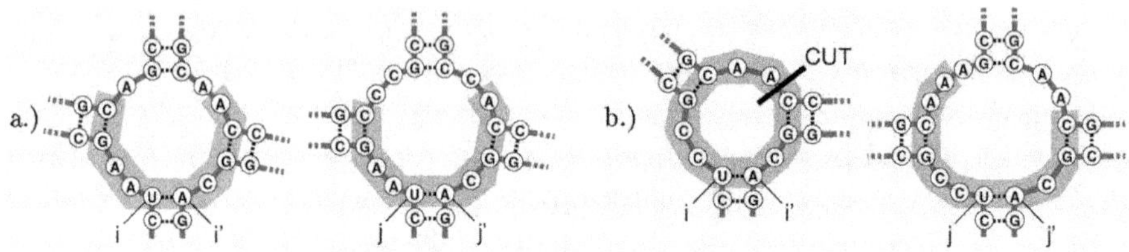

Fig. 5. The two possible cases for $M^{rb}(i \overset{P_1}{\rule{2em}{2pt}} i', j \overset{P_2}{\rule{2em}{2pt}} j')$.

extension from (j, j') to the left do not overlap, whereas they do overlap in the second case b). For the second case, we do not know exactly how to match the overlapping part. Hence, we have to consider all possible *cuts* in the smaller loop, marking the corresponding ends of the extensions from the left ends and from the right ends of the loop. The extensions from the right ends are already calculated in the M^{r_end} matrix. Only for the definition of the recursion equation, we define $M^{l\_end}(LDist)$ and $Reach^{l\_end}(LDist)$ analogously to equations (2) and (1), respectively. For the implementation, we need to store only the current values M^{l_end} and $Reach^{l\_end}$.

Now let $len_{i,i'}$ (resp $len_{j,j'}$) be $|\text{loop}(i \overset{P_1}{\rule{2em}{2pt}} i')|$ (resp. $|\text{loop}(i \overset{P_1}{\rule{2em}{2pt}} i')|$), and let $len_{min} = \min\{len_{i,i'}, len_{j,j'}\}$. Then we have

$$M^{bb}(i \overset{P_1}{\rule{2em}{2pt}} i', j \overset{P_2}{\rule{2em}{2pt}} j') = \max_{\substack{0 \leq LDist < Len_{Min} \\ \text{with } right_{P_1}^{LDist}(i) \text{ is not} \\ \text{a left end of a bond}}} \left\{ M^{l\_end}(LDist) + M^{r\_end}(RDist) \right\} \quad (4)$$

where $RDist = \begin{cases} len_{i,i'} - LDist & \text{if } len_{min} = len_{i,i'} \\ len_{i,i'} + (len_{i,i'} - len_{j,j'}) - LDist & \text{else} \end{cases}.$

The condition $right_{P_1}^{LDist}(i)$ *is not a left end of a bond* guarantees that we do not cut in the middle of a bond, which is excluded since we are considering bond-preserving matchings only. The term $(len_{i,i'} - len_{j,j'})$ in the second part of the definition of $RDist$ is to compensate for the longer length of the first loop[1].

Finally, we consider the $M(r, s)$ entries. Let r and s again be two bases of the loops defined $i \overset{P_1}{\rule{2em}{2pt}} i'$ and $j \overset{P_2}{\rule{2em}{2pt}} j'$ with distance $RDist$ to the right loop ends i' and j', respectively. The values of $M(r, s)$ and $Mloop(r, s)$ are equal for all entries $M(r, s) \neq 0$. $M(r, s)$ is zero if there is some $(r', s') \prec (r, s)$ that is matchable. This leads to the following equation:

[1] In the case that $i \overset{P_1}{\rule{2em}{2pt}} i'$ is the smaller loop, then overlapping of the left and right match extensions is already excluded by definition, and we do not need to compensate for it.

```
1: procedure START-LOOP-WALKING(i, i', j, j')
       ▷ Right loop ends of both RNAs
2:     reach = INIT-LOOP-MATRICES(i', j', i', j')
3:     (loop_size, loop_dist) := LOOP-WALKING(i', j', i, j, i', j', reach, true)
       ▷ Only right loop end of first RNA
4:     k := i'
5:     while k > i + 1 do
6:         k := left_R1(k)
7:         INIT-LOOP-MATRICES(k, j', i', j')
8:         LOOP-WALKING(k, j', i, j, i', j', false, false)
9:     end while
       ▷ Only right loop end of second RNA
10:    l := j'
11:    while l > j + 1 do
12:        l := left_R2(l)
13:        INIT-LOOP-MATRICES(i', l, i', j')
14:        LOOP-WALKING(i', l, i, j, i', j', false, false)
15:    end while
16:    return (loop_size, loop_dist)
17: end procedure
```

Fig. 6. Starting points of loop walking

$$M(r,s) = \begin{cases} 0 & \text{if } \neg\text{match}(r,s) \vee \text{match}(\text{left}_{R_1}(r), \text{left}_{R_2}(s)) \\ & \quad \vee Reach^{r\_end}(RDist) \\ M_{\prec}^{loop}(r,s) & \text{otherwise} \end{cases}$$

7 Pseudo-code

The main procedure consists of two for-loops, each calling a base-pair from the first and second RNA, and performs the pattern search from inner to outer loops. It calls the procedure START-LOOP-WALKING which initiates the calculation of all matrices except $M^{bb}(i \xrightarrow{P_1} i', j \xrightarrow{P_2} j')$ for two bonds $i \xrightarrow{P_1} i'$ and $j \xrightarrow{P_2} j'$, assuming that all matrix entries for loops above are already calculated. In addition, it calculates the loop length of the smaller loop and the distance of the two loop lengths (which is done in sub-procedure CALC-REMAIN-LOOP-LEN).

The real calculation of these matrices is done in the sub-procedure LOOP-WALKING, which traverses the loop from right to left (via the application of left.(·) function). The function LOOP-WALKING has two modes concerning whether we started the loop-traversal with both right ends i, i' or not. In the first mode (initiated in line of START-LOOP-WALKING), we calculate also the array M^{r_end}, and move the $M(r,s)$ down to (i', j') for all (r,s) where $Reach^{r\_end}$ is true. This part is done by the subprocedure LOOP-REACH. In the second mode, when LOOP-WALKING is called with only one right end (lines 8 and 14 of

START-LOOP-WALKING), then we know the right ends cannot be in any matching considered there. Hence, we may not calculate the M^{r_end} array.

The subprocedure MLOOP-RECURSION is just an implementation of recursion Equation (3) for $M_{\prec}^{loop}$. The sub-procedure INIT-LOOP-MATRICES just initializes the matrices for the starting points. In most case, the initial values are 0 (since we cannot have a match if we do not start with the right-ends due to the structure condition). The only exception is if we start with both right ends, and these rights ends do match. In this case, we initialize the corresponding matrix entries with 1. The sub-procedure INIT-LOOP-MATRICES is listed in the appendix.

```
procedure LOOP-WALKING(r, s, i, j, i', j', reach, right_ends)
    RDist = 0
    while r > i ∧ s > j do
        r' := r;   s' := s
        r := left_R1(r');   s := left_R2(s');   RDist = RDist + 1
        if BASE-MATCH(r, s) ∨ BOND-MATCH(r^r, r, s^r, s) then
            MLOOP-RECURSION(r^r, r, s^r, s')
            M(r, s) := M_≺^loop(r, s);   M(r', s') := 0
            if right_ends then
                LOOP-REACH(r, s, i, j, i', j', reach, RDist)
            end if
        else
            M_≺^loop(r, s) := 0;   M(r, s) := 0;   reach := false
            if right_ends then
                M^r_end(RDist) := M^r_end(RDist − 1)
            end if
        end if
    end while
    if right_ends then
        return CALC-REMAIN-LOOP-LEN(r, s, i, j, RDist)
    end if
end procedure
```

Fig. 7. The procedure loop walking is going from one base to the next

The next step is to calculate $M^{bb}(i \overset{P_1}{\longleftrightarrow} i', j \overset{P_2}{\longleftrightarrow} j')$, which is done by the procedure LOOP-MATCHING. LOOP-MATCHING is called *after* START-LOOP-WALKING is finished. In principle, this is just an implementation of the recursion equation (4). Since we do not want want to maintain another array $M^{l\_end}(LDist)$, we store only value for the current $LDist$ in the variable M^{l_end}. The procedure maintains three neighbouring cells (r^l, s^l), (r, s) and (r^r, s^r). (r^l, s^l) correspond to $LDist - 1$, and (r, s) to $LDist$. The cut will be between (r, s) and (r^r, s^r). The sub-procedure MLEND-RECURSION is in principle only an implementation of the recursion equation for M^{l_end} under the condition that that $Reach^{l\_end}$ is true. As it can be seen from the definition of M^{r_end} in Equation (2), the recursion equation under this condition is in principle analogous to the recursion equation for $M_{\prec}^{loop}$ given in Equation (3).

```
procedure LOOP-MATCHING(i, i', j, j', i_i'_lens, lens_dist)
    LDist := 0
    if BOND-MATCH(i, i', j, j') then
        M^l_end := 0;   Reach^l_end := true
        r^r := i;   r := i;   r^l := i
        s^r := j;   s := j;   s^l := j
        while r^r < i' ∧ s^r < j' ∧ Reach^l_end := true do
            r^l := r;   r := r^r;   r^r := right_R1(r^r);
            s^l := s;   s := s^r;   s^r := right_R2(s^r);
            if BASE-MATCH(r, s) ∨ BOND-MATCH(r^r, r, s^r, s) then
                M^l_end = MLEND-RECURSION(r^l, r, r^r, s^l, s, s^r, M^l_end)
            else
                Reach^l_end := false
            end if
            if Reach^l_end ∧ ¬BOND-MATCH(r^l, r, s^l, s) then
                FILL-MBB(i, i', j, j', M^l_end, LDist, i_i'_len, lens_dist)
            end if
            LDist := LDist + 1
        end while
    else
        M^bb(i, j) := 0
    end if
end procedure
```

Fig. 8. Calculation of M^{bb}

The maximally extended matchings are finally calculated from the $M(r, s)$ matrix by an usual traceback. The space complexity of the algorithm is $O(nm)$. The time complexity is $O(nm)$ for the following reason. Every pair (r, s) with $1 \leq r \leq |S_1|$ and $1 \leq s \leq |S_2|$ is considered at most twice in START-LOOP-WALKING and LOOP-WALKING, with an $O(1)$ complexity for calculating the corresponding matrix entries. Similarly, every pair (r, s) is considered at most twice in LOOP-WALKING. Since there are $O(nm)$ many pairs (r, s), we get a total complexity of $O(nm)$.

8 Conclusion

We have presented a fast dynamic programming approach in time $O(nm)$ and space $O(nm)$ for detecting common sequence/structure patterns between two RNAs given by their primary and secondary structures. These patterns are derived from exact matchings and can be used for local alignments ([1]). The most promising advantage is clearly to investigate large RNAs of several thousand bases in reasonable time. Here, one can think of detecting local sequence/structure regions of several RNAs sharing the same biological function.

References

1. Rolf Backofen and Sebastian Will. Local sequence-structure motifs in RNA. *Journal of Bioinformatics and Computational Biology (JBCB)*, 2004. accepted for publication.
2. V. Bafna, S. Muthukrishnan, and R. Ravi. Computing similarity between rna strings. In *Proc. 6th Symp. Combinatorical Pattern Matching*, pages -16, 1995.
3. David Eppstein. Subgraph isomorphism in planar graphs and related problems. *J. Graph Algorithms & Applications*, 3(3):1–27, 1999.
4. P. Gendron, D. Gautheret, and F. Major. Structural ribonucleic acid motifs identification and classification. In *High Performance Computing Systems and Applications*. Kluwer Academic Press, 1998.
5. Gramm, Guo, and Niedermeier. Pattern matching for arc-annotated sequences. *FSTTCS: Foundations of Software Technology and Theoretical Computer Science*, 22, 2002.
6. I. L. Hofacker, B. Priwitzer, and P. F. Stadler. Prediction of locally stable RNA secondary structures for genome-wide surveys. *Bioinformatics*, 20(2):186–190, 2004.
7. Matthias Höchsmann, Thomas Töller, Robert Giegerich, and Stefan Kurtz. Local similarity in rna secondary structures. In *Proceedings of Computational Systems Bioinformatics (CSB 2003)*, 2003.
8. Tao Jiang, Guo-Hui Lin, Bin Ma, and Kaizhong Zhang. The longest common subsequence problem for arc-annotated sequences. In *Proceedings of the 11th Annual Symposium on Combinatorial Pattern Matching (CPM2000)*, 2000.
9. Tao Jiang, Guohui Lin, Bin Ma, and Kaizhong Zhang. A general edit distance between RNA structures. *Journal of Computational Biology*, 9(2):371–88, 2002.
10. B. Morgenstern, K. Frech, A. Dress, and T. Werner. DIALIGN: finding local similarities by multiple sequence alignment. *Bioinformatics*, 14(3):290–4, 1998.
11. J. R. Ullmann. An algorithm for subgraph isomorphism. *Journal of the ACM*, 23(1):31–42, January 1976.
12. Juris Viksna and David Gilbert. Pattern matching and pattern discovery algorithms for protein topologies. In O. Gascuel and B. M. E. Moret, editors, *Proceedings of the First International Workshop on Algorithms in Bioinformatics (WABI 2001)*, number 2149, pages 98–111, 2001.
13. Jason Tsong-Li Wang, Bruce A. Shapiro, Dennis Shasha, Kaizhong Zhang, and Kathleen M. Currey. An algorithm for finding the largest approximately common substructures of two trees. *IEEE Transactions on Pattern Analysis and Machine Intelligence*, 20(8):889–895, 1998.

An Efficient Algorithm for the Longest Tandem Scattered Subsequence Problem

Adrian Kosowski

Department of Algorithms and System Modeling
Gdańsk University of Technology, Poland
kosowski@sphere.eti.pg.gda.pl

Abstract. The paper deals with the problem of finding a tandem scattered subsequence of maximum length (LTS) for a given character sequence. A sequence is referred to as tandem if it can be split into two identical sequences. An efficient algorithm for the LTS problem is presented and is shown to have $O(n^2)$ computational complexity and linear memory complexity with respect to the length n of the analysed sequence. A conjecture is put forward and discussed, stating that the complexity of the given algorithm may not be easily improved. Finally, the potential application of the solution to the LTS problem in approximate tandem substring matching in DNA sequences is discussed.

1 Introduction

A *perfect single repeat tandem sequence* (referred to throughout this article simply as a *tandem sequence*) is one which can be expressed as the concatenation of two identical sequences. Tandem sequences are well studied in literature. The problem of finding the longest tandem substring (the longest subsequence composed of consecutive elements) of a given sequence was solved by Main and Lorentz [7], who showed an $O(n \log n)$ algorithm, later improved to $O(n)$ complexity by Kolpakov and Kucherov [3]. A lot of attention has also been given to finding longest approximate tandem substrings of sequences, where the approximation criterium of the match is given either in terms of the Hamming distance or the so called edit distance between the substring and the sequence.

This paper deals with a related problem, concerning determining the longest tandem subsequence (which need not be a substring) of a given sequence (the so called LTS problem). A formal definition of LTS is in Subsection 2.1 and an efficient algorithm which solves LTS in $O(n^2)$ using $O(n)$ space is outlined in subsections 2.1 and 2.2. This result is a major improvement on the hitherto extensively used naive algorithm, which reduces the solution LTS to n iterations of an algorithm solving the longest common subsequence problem (LCS), yielding $O(n^3)$ computational complexity.

Finally, in Section 3 we consider the application of LTS as a relatively fast (but not always accurate) criterium for finding approximate tandem substrings of sequences and judging how well they match the original sequence.

A. Apostolico and M. Melucci (Eds.): SPIRE 2004, LNCS 3246, pp. 93–100, 2004.

2 An Efficient Algorithmic Approach to the *LTS* Problem

2.1 Notation and Problem Definition

Throughout the paper, the set of nonnegative integers is denoted by $\mathbb{N}$. Sets of consecutive elements of $\mathbb{N}$ are referred to as *discrete intervals* and denoted by the symbol $\langle i, j\rangle$, which is equivalent to $\{i, i+1, \ldots, j\}$.

Definition 1. *A* character sequence *s of length n over nonempty alphabet Ω is a function $s : \langle 1, n\rangle \longrightarrow \Omega$. The* length *$|s|$ of sequence s is the number of elements of the sequence, $|s| = n$. The symbol s_i, where $1 \leq i \leq n$, is used to denote $s(i)$, the i-th element of sequence s.*

Sequence s is expressed in compact form as $s = [s_1 s_2 \ldots s_n]$.

Definition 2. *Sequence s of length $|s| = n$ is called a* tandem sequence *if n is an even number and $\forall_{1\leq i\leq n/2}\ s_i = s_{i+n/2}$.*

Definition 3. *Sequence t, $|t| = k$, is called a* subsequence *of sequence s, $|s| = n$, if it is possible to indicate an increasing function $h : \langle 1, k\rangle \to \langle 1, n\rangle$, such that $\forall_{1\leq i\leq k}\ t_i = s_{h(i)}$. This relation between sequences t and s is written in the form $t \subseteq s$.*

Definition 4. *The* Longest Tandem Subsequence *problem (LTS for short) for a given sequence s is the problem of finding a tandem sequence t such that $t \subseteq s$ and the length of sequence t is the maximum possible.*

The suggested approach to the *LTS* problem reduces *LTS* for sequence s to the problem of determining the longest common subsequence of two sequences not longer than s.

Definition 5. *The* longest common subsequence *$LCS(p, q)$ of sequences p and q is a sequence t, such that $t \subseteq p$ and $t \subseteq q$, of the maximum possible length.*

The *LTS* problem for sequence $s = [s_1 s_2 \ldots s_n]$ can be solved by means of an algorithm consisting of the following two stages.

Algorithm 1. Longest Tandem Subsequence

1. Determine an index l, $1 \leq l < n$ for which $|LCS([s_1 \ldots s_l],\ [s_{l+1} \ldots s_n])|$ takes the maximum possible value.
2. Compute sequence $t = LCS([s_1 \ldots s_l],\ [s_{l+1} \ldots s_n])$ and return as output.

The computational time and memory complexity of Algorithm 1 is dependent on the implementation of Stages 1 and 2. Both these steps will be analysed individually and shown to be solvable in $O(n^2)$ time using $\Theta(n)$ memory.

Stage 2 of Algorithm 1 can be implemented using Hirschberg's approach [1], who presented an algorithm which, given two character sequences p and q ($|p| = m$, $|q| = k$), computes the sequence $LCS(p, q)$ in $\Theta(mk)$ time and requires

$\Theta(m+k)$ memory. The strings whose longest common subsequence is determined in Stage 2 of Algorithm 1 have a total length of n, which closes the analysis of the complexity of this stage of the algorithm.

An efficient approach to Stage 1 of the algorithm is the subject of consideration in the following subsection. Since the problem of finding the index l for sequence s is of some significance and may even in certain applications be considered separately from the *LTS* problem (i.e. related to DNA sequencing, Section 3), it is useful to call it by its own name, referring to it as the *LTSsplit* problem.

2.2 A $\Theta(n^2)$ Time Algorithm for the *LTSsplit* Problem

Definition 6. *LTSsplit is the problem in which, given a sequence s ($|s| = n$), we have to determine an index l, $1 \leq l \leq n$, such that the length of the string $LCS([s_1 \dots s_l],\ [s_{l+1} \dots s_n])$ is the maximum possible.*

The suggested algorithmic solution to the *LTSsplit* problem is based on dynamic programming. In order to describe the lengths of the analyzed subsequences, it is convenient to define the family of functions f_k, for $1 \leq k \leq n$. For a given k, function $f_k : \mathbb{Z} \times \mathbb{Z} \longrightarrow \mathbb{N}$ is given as follows:

$$f_k(i,j) := \begin{cases} |LCS([s_1 \dots s_i], [s_j \dots s_k])|, & \text{for } 1 \leq i < j \leq k \\ 0, & \text{in all other cases when } i,j \geq 0 \\ -1, & \text{when } i,j < 0 \end{cases} \quad (1)$$

Index l may be expressed in terms of the function f_k by the following set of conditions:

$$\begin{cases} f_n(l, l+1) = \max_{r:\ 1 \leq r < n} (f_n(r, r+1)) \\ 1 \leq l < n \end{cases} \quad (2)$$

The values of function $f_k(i,j)$, for $1 \leq i < j \leq k \leq n$, can be expressed using a simple recursive formula:

$$f_k(i,j) = \begin{cases} \max\ \{f_k(i-1,j),\ f_{k-1}(i,j)\} & \text{when } s_i \neq s_k \\ f_{k-1}(i-1,j) + 1 & \text{when } s_i = s_k \end{cases} \quad (3)$$

In order to express values of function f_k using values of function f_{k-1} it is helpful to introduce the index $\gamma_k(i)$, defined as the largest value of r such that $r \leq i$ and $s_r = s_k$, or 0 if no such value exists. From formula (3) we have

$$f_k(i,j) = \max\ \{f_{k-1}(\gamma_k(i) - 1, j) + 1,\ f_{k-1}(i,j)\} \quad (4)$$

Let us now consider the family of functions $d_k : \mathbb{N}^+ \times \mathbb{N} \rightarrow \{0,1\}$, defined for $1 \leq k \leq n$ as follows: $d_k(i,j) = f_k(i,j) - f_k(i-1,j)$. For the range of arguments $1 \leq i < j \leq k$ the value of function f_k may be expressed as

$$f_k(i,j) = \sum_{r=1}^{i} d_k(r,j) \quad (5)$$

A convenient characterization of function d is given by the following property.

Property 1. Let $1 \le i < j \le k$. The following statements hold

1. Suppose that $d_{k-1}(i,j) = 1$.
   Then $d_k(i,j) = 0$ iff $\forall_{\gamma_k(i-1) \le r < i}\ d_{k-1}(r,j) = 0$.
2. Suppose that $d_{k-1}(i,j) = 0$.
   Then $d_k(i,j) = 1$ iff $s_i = s_k$ and $\exists_{\gamma_k(i-1) \le r < i}\ d_{k-1}(r,j) = 1$.

Proof. Both claims of the property are proven below.

(Claim 1.) Let us assume that $d_{k-1}(i,j) = 1$ and let $d = \sum_{r=\gamma_k(i-1)}^{i-1} d_{k-1}(r,j)$ and $w = f_{k-1}(\gamma_k(i-1)-1,j)$. By using formulae (5) and (4) we obtain $f_{k-1}(i-1,j) = w+d$ and $f_k(i-1,j) = \max\{w+1, w+d\} = w + \max\{1,d\}$ respectively. Moreover, since $f_{k-1}(\gamma_k(i)-1,j)+1 \le f_{k-1}(i-1,j)+1 = f_{k-1}(i,j) = w+d+1$, by formula (4) $f_k(i,j) = w+d+1$. Therefore $f_k(i,j) = f_k(i-1,j)$ iff $d = 0$.

(Claim 2.) First, assume that $d_{k-1}(i,j) = 0$ and $s_i = s_k$. Let w and d be defined as in the proof of claim 1. Acting identically as last time, we get $f_{k-1}(i-1,j) = w+d$ and $f_k(i-1,j) = w+\max\{1,d\}$. By formula (3) $f_k(i,j) = f_{k-1}(i-1,j)+1 = w+d+1$. Therefore $f_k(i,j) = f_k(i-1,j)+1$ iff $d > 0$.
Let us now assume that $d_{k-1}(i,j) = 0$ and $s_i \ne s_k$. Suppose that $f_k(i,j) = f_k(i-1,j)+1$. From formula (3) we have $f_k(i,j) = f_{k-1}(i,j) = f_{k-1}(i-1,j) \le f_k(i-1,j)$, a contradiction.

At this point it is essential to notice that function d_k has another interesting property, which is useful in the construction of an efficient algorithm for *LTSsplit*.

Property 2. Given i and k, $1 \le i < k \le n$, the value of $d_k(i,j)$ is equal to 1 iff $j \in \langle i+1, a_k(i) \rangle$, for some function $a_k : \mathbb{N} \to \mathbb{N}$.

For an illustration of the function a_k, see Fig. 1.

Proof. For given i, the observation that the set $S = \{j : i < j \le k \wedge d_k(i,j) = 1\}$ is a discrete interval whose left end equals $i+1$ is a consequence of the property

$F_k=\{f_k(i,j)\}$

i \ j	1	2	3	4	5	6
1 B	0	1	1	1	0	0
2 A	0	0	2	2	1	1
3 B	0	0	0	2	1	1
4 B	0	0	0	0	1	1
5 C	0	0	0	0	0	1
6 A	0	0	0	0	0	0

$D_k=\{d_k(i,j)\}$

i \ j	1	2	3	4	5	6
1 B	0	1	1	1	0	0
2 A	0	0	1	1	1	1
3 B	0	0	0	0	0	0
4 B	0	0	0	0	0	0
5 C	0	0	0	0	0	0
6 A	0	0	0	0	0	0

$A_k=\{a_k(i)\}$

i	
1 B	4
2 A	6
3 B	0
4 B	0
5 C	0
6 A	0

Fig. 1. Values of functions f_k, d_k and a_k for sequence s beginning with BABBCA and $k = 6$

of monotonicity. More formally speaking, the proof proceeds by induction with respect to k.

If $k = 1$ then S is empty.

Let $k > 1$ and suppose that the inductive assumption holds for $k-1$. It suffices to show that if $d_k(i,j) = 1$, then for an arbitrarily chosen t, $i < t < j$, we have $d_k(i,t) = 1$. We will consider two separate cases.

First, let $d_k(i,j) = 1$ and $d_{k-1}(i,j) = 1$. By claim 1 of Property 1, for some r, $\gamma_k(i-1) \le r < i$, we obtain $d_{k-1}(r,j) = 1$. By the inductive assumption we conclude that $d_{k-1}(r,t) = 1$ and $d_{k-1}(i,t) = 1$. The equality $d_k(i,t) = 1$ is a conclusion from claim 1 of Property 1.

Now, suppose $d_k(i,j) = 1$ and $d_{k-1}(i,j) = 0$. By claim 2 of Property 1 we have $s_i = s_k$ and for some r, $\gamma_k(i-1) \le r < i$, we have $d_{k-1}(r,j) = 1$. As in the previous case, $d_{k-1}(r,t) = 1$. The equality $d_k(i,t) = 1$ is a conclusion from either claim 1 or claim 2 of Property 1, depending on whether $d_{k-1}(i,t) = 1$ or $d_{k-1}(i,t) = 0$, respectively.

By definition of function d_k, $d_k(i,j) = 0$ when $j \le i$, which completes the proof.

As a direct conclusion from Property 2, the values of function a_k uniquely determine all values of function d_k. It is possible to consider a unique representation of matrix $D_k = \{d_k(i,j)\}$ of dimension $n \times n$ $(1 \le i,j \le n)$ in the form of the column of numbers $A_k = \{a_k(i)\}$ of dimension n $(1 \le i \le n)$.

Theorem 1. *There exists an algorithm solving the LTSsplit problem for a given sequence s of length n in $O(n^2)$ time and using $\Theta(n)$ memory.*

Proof. The algorithm for solving the *LTSsplit* problem consists of the following steps:

1. For all k, $1 \le k \le n$, compute the column A_k by modifying column A_{k-1}, making use of Property 2.
2. Determine an *LTSsplit* index l from the values of column A_n using the following equation (directly inferred from the definitions of A_n, d_n, f_n):

$$f_n(i, i+1) = |\{p : 1 \le p \le i \ \wedge \ a_n(p) \ge i+1\} \tag{6}$$

using condition (2) to guarantee the suitable choice of l.

The linear memory complexity of Steps 1 and 2 of the algorithm is evident. It is also obvious that Step 2 of the algorithm can be performed in $O(n^2)$ time (in fact, Step 2 can even be implemented with $O(n)$ running time, yet this is irrelevant to the proof). It now suffices to present a $O(n^2)$ approach to the problem of finding the column A_n in Step 1 of the algorithm.

To clarify this step, we will consider a geometrical presentation of column A_k as a set $P_k = \{p_1, \ldots, p_k\}$ of k closed horizontal segments of the plane, where the segment p_i has vertical coordinate i, left horizontal coordinate 0 and right horizontal coordinate $a_k(i)$. For some k, consider a pair of values i, j, where $1 \le i < j \le k$. By definition of column A_k and set P_k, the value of $d_k(i,j)$ is 1 iff the point (i, j) belongs to some segment of P_k. We define the *visible section of segment* p_i *at height* r, $0 < r < i$, as a segment $q \subseteq p_i$ whose projection π_x to the horizontal axis fulfills the condition: $\pi_x(q) = \pi_x(p_i) \setminus \bigcup_{t=r}^{i-1} \pi_x(p_t)$. For the sake of completeness of the definition, the visible section of any segment at height 0 is assumed to be empty. The following corollary is a direct conclusion resulting from the analysis of Property 2.

Corollary 1. *Given set* P_{k-1}*, the set* P_k *may be constructed from* P_{k-1} *by performing the following transformations:*

1. *for all* i, $1 \leq i \leq k$, *such that* $s_i = s_k$, *remove segment* p_i *from the set and insert a segment with vertical coordinate* i *and horizontal coordinates* 0 *and* k.
2. *for all* i, *truncate the right part of segment* p_i *by removing the visible section of* p_i *at height* $\gamma_k(i-1)$ *of* P_{k-1} *from* p_i.

An example of the transformation of set P_{k-1} into set P_k is presented in Fig. 2. Since the operations described in Corollary 1 only modify the right endpoints of segments from P_k, the described procedure may be considered in terms of introducing appropriate modifications to the column A_k. The transformation from A_{k-1} to A_k can be performed in $O(k)$ time in two sweeps, once to detect the indices i for which $s_i = s_k$ and update the values as in Step 1 of the transformation, the other – to perform Step 2 of the transformation. Thus the column A_n can be obtained in $O(n^2)$ operations and the proof is complete.

In order to formalise the adopted approach, a complete implementation of both steps of the algorithm for *LTSsplit* is given below. To simplify the code, the two sweeps corresponding to Steps 1 and 2 of the transformation from A_{k-1} to A_k are performed in slightly modified order, which does not influence the correctness of the algorithm.

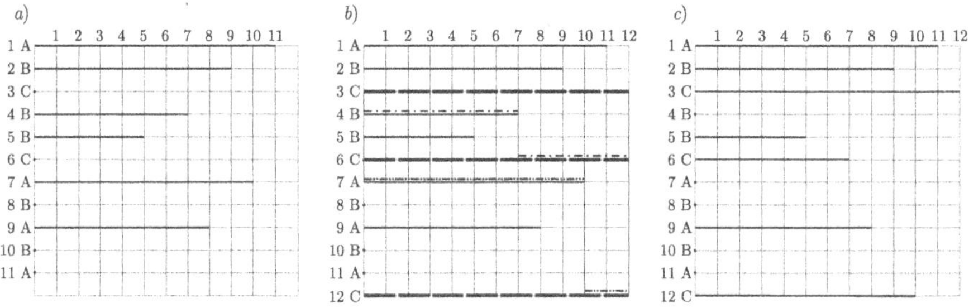

Fig. 2. An illustration of the transformation of set P_{k-1} into set P_k for a sequence beginning with ABCBBCABABAC ($k = 12$)
a) the set P_{k-1} *b)* the set after Step 1 of conversion (newly added segments are marked with a bold dashed line; segment fragments to be truncated are denoted by a dash-dot line) *c)* the set P_k

```
algorithm LTSsplit (s : array 1..n of character) : integer;
var a, c, k, l, t : integer;
A := [0, ..., 0] : array 1..n of integer;
begin
  {(⋆) Compute column A_k for k = 1, 2, ..., n}
  for k in (1, 2, ..., n) do
    for a in (k − 1, k − 2, ..., 1) do
      if s[a] = s[k] then begin
        t := A[a];
        c := a + 1;
        {Perform Step 2 of Corollary 1 using a downward sweep technique}
        while (t < k) and (c < k) do begin
          {Trim the segment corresponding to p_c to length t,
           removing the section of it which is visible at height a}
          (A[c], t) := (min{A[c], t}, max{A[c], t});
          c := c + 1;
        end;
        A[a] := k;
      end;
  {(⋆⋆) Calculate index l using the column A_n}
  c := 0;
  l := 1;
  for k in (1, 2, ..., n − 1) do begin
    t := 0;
    for a in (1, 2, ..., k) do
      if A[a] > k then t := t + 1;
    if t > c then begin
      c := t;
      l := k;
    end;
  end;
  return l;
end.
```

2.3 Remarks on the Efficiency of the Algorithm for *LTS*

The approach to the *LTS* problem described in Algorithm 1 decomposes it into the *LTSsplit* and *LCS* subproblems, both of which can be solved using $O(n^2)$ algorithms with a low coefficient of proportionality (similar for both algorithms on most system architectures).

The existence of faster algorithms for the problem appears unlikely, since no algorithm with $o(n^2)$ complexity is known for *LCS* in the case of general sequences. This may formally be stated as the following conjecture.

Conjecture 1. It is believed that the computational complexity of an algorithm solving the *LTS* problem is never lesser than the complexity of an optimal algorithm solving *LCS* for general sequences.

3 Final Remarks

One of the major issues of DNA string matching deals is the problem of finding the longest approximate tandem substring of a given DNA sequence. Formally speaking, a *longest approximate single tandem string repeat* in sequence s is defined as a substring $p \subseteq s$ (a subsequence composed of consecutive elements of s) of maximum possible length, which can be split into two similar substrings p_1, p_2 [4,5]. The criterium of similarity may have varying degrees of complexity. Typically described criteria include the Hamming distance, the Levenshtein edit distance (elaborated on in [6]), as well as more complex criteria (expressing the distance in terms of weights of operations required to convert one sequence to the other, [2,8]).

In some applications, the criterium used to describe the similarity of p_1 and p_2 is the length of $LCS(p_1, p_2)$. Given the sequence p, the $LTSsplit$ algorithm can be applied to find the best point for splitting p so as to maximise $LCS(p_1, p_2)$. In consequence the output of the algorithm solving LTS directly leads to the answer to the two most relevant problems, namely whether p can be split into two similar fragments and, if so, what those fragments are.

Acknowledgement

The author would like to express his gratitude to Michał Małafiejski, Ph.D., from the Gdańsk University of Technology, for phrasing the LTS problem in its simplest form and for his kind and helpful contribution to the improvement of this paper.

References

1. Hirschberg D.S., A linear space algorithm for computing maximal common subsequences, Information Processing Letters (1975) **18**.
2. Kannan S.K., Myers E.W., An Algorithm for Locating Nonoverlapping Regions of Maximum Alignment Score. SIAM Journal of Computing, pp. 648–662 (1996) **25**.
3. Kolpakov R.M., Kucherov G., Finding Maximal Repetitions in a Word in Linear Time. Symposium on Foundations of Computer Science FOCS'99, New-York, pp. 596–604 (1999).
4. Kolpakov R.M., Kucherov G., Finding approximate repetitions under Hamming distance. Theoretical Computer Science, pp. 135–156 (2003) **303**.
5. Landau G.M., Schmidt J.P., An algorithm for approximate tandem repeats, Proceedings of the 4th Annual Symposium on Combinatorial Pattern Matching pp. 120–133, Springer-Verlag (1993) **684**.
6. Levenshtein V.I., Binary codes capable of correcting deletions, insertions, and reversals. Soviet Phys. Dokl, pp. 707–710 (1966) **10**.
7. Main M.G., Lorentz R.J., An $O(n \log n)$ algorithm for finding all repetitions in a string. Journal of Algorithms, pp. 422–432 (1984) **5**.
8. Schmidt J.P., All highest scoring paths in weighted grid graphs and their application to finding all approximate repeats in strings. SIAM Journal of Computing, pp. 972–992 (1998) **27**.

Automatic Document Categorization Based on k-NN and Object-Based Thesauri*

Sun Lee Bang[1], Hyung Jeong Yang[2], and Jae Dong Yang[1]

[1] Department of Computer Science, Chonbuk National University
Jeonju, 561-756, South Korea
{slbang,jdyang}@chonbuk.ac.kr

[2] Department of Computer Science, Carnegie Mellon University
Pisttsburgh, 15213, USA
hjyang@cs.cmu.deu

Abstract. The k-NN classifier(k-NN) is one of the most popular document categorization methods because of its simplicity and relatively good performance. However, it significantly degrades precision when ambiguity arises - there exist more than one candidate category for a document to be assigned. To remedy the drawback, we propose a new method, which incorporates the relationships of object-based thesauri into the document categorization using k-NN. Employing the thesaurus entails structuring categories into taxonomies, since their structure needs to be conformed to that of the thesaurus for capturing relationships between themselves. By referencing relationships in the thesaurus which correspond to the structured categories, k-NN can be drastically improved, removing the ambiguity. In this paper, we first perform the document categorization by using k-NN and then employ the relationships to reduce the ambiguity. Experimental results show that the proposed approach improves the precision of k-NN up to 13.86% without compromising its recall.

1 Introduction

Recently with the advent of digital libraries containing a huge amount of documents, the importance of document categorization is ever increasing as a solution for effective retrieval. Document categorization is the task of assigning a document to an appropriate category in a predefined set of categories. Traditionally, the document categorization has been performed manually. However, as the number of documents explosively increases, the task becomes no longer amenable to the manual categorization, requiring a vast amount of time and cost. This has led to numerous researches for automatic document classification including bayesian classifiers, decision trees, k-nearest neighbor (k-NN) classifiers, rule learning algorithms, neural networks, fuzzy logic based algorithms and support vector machines [1][4][5][7][8][9][10][11]. For the classification, they usually create feature vectors from terms frequently occurring in documents and

* This work was supported by Korea Science and Engineering Foundation(KOSEF) Grant No. R05-2003-000-11986-0.

A. Apostolico and M. Melucci (Eds.): SPIRE 2004, LNCS 3246, pp. 101–112, 2004.

then repeatedly refine the vectors through document learning [12]. However, since they only train the classifiers with the vectors, they usually incur ambiguity when determining categories, which significantly degrades their precision [6]. For example, suppose there is a document which reviews overall features of display equipment. Apparently, most terms occurring in this document would be related to the categories *LCD*, *CRT* and *PDP*. Simply considering document vectors alone without considering relationship between categories, they fail to capture the fact that LCD, CRT and PDP are commonly the examples of the display equipment, suffering from the ambiguity between the categories.

To tackle the problem, we propose a new method to improve the precision of k-NN by incorporating the relationships of object-based thesauri into document categorization using k-NN. The reason we choose k-NN is that it shows relatively good performance in general in spite of its simplicity [2][12][13]. Employing the thesaurus entails structuring categories into taxonomies, since their structure needs to be conformed to that of the thesaurus for capturing relationships between themselves. By referencing relationships in the thesaurus which correspond to the structured categories, k-NN can be improved, removing the ambiguity. In this paper, we first perform the document classification by using k-NN and then, if a document is to be classified into more than one category, we employ the relationships of the thesaurus to reduce the ambiguity. Experimental results show that this method enhances the precision of k-NN up to 13.86% without compromising its recall.

This paper proceeds as follows. In Section 2, we review research related to our classification method. Section 3 describes a way of hierarchical classification employing the object-based thesaurus. Section 4 shows experimental results, and conclusion and future researches follow in Section 5.

2 Preliminaries

2.1 Document Classification Based on k-NN

As in most research work, we use the vector space model for representing a document. Let D be a set of documents and T be a set of distinct terms that appear in the set of documents D. d is represented by a vector of term weights [12].

To get the weight of a term $t_i \in T$, we use *tfidf* weighting scheme that is generally used. Also, term weights are normalized by cosine normalization [12]. Let w_{ki} be a normalized weight with respect to $d_k \in D$ and t_i. Based on this weighting scheme, the following vector for d_k can be constructed:

$$term(d_k) = \{t_1/w_{k1}, t_2/w_{k2}, \cdots, t_{|T|}/w_{k|T|}\}$$

where $|T|$ is the cardinality of T.

To classify a document d, k-NN selects its similar neighbors among the training documents and uses the categories assigned by the neighbors to judge the category of d [2][5][13]. To explain how k-NN determines the category of d, we provide a definition.

Definition 1. Let $Near(d)$ be the set of k nearest neighbor documents with respect to d and $d^{Near} \in Near(d)$. Assignment of d^{Near} to $c_i \in C = \{c_1, c_2, \cdots, c_m\}$ is denoted by

$$c_i(d^{Near}) = \begin{cases} 1, & \text{if } d^{Near} \text{ belongs to } c_i \\ 0, & \text{otherwise} \end{cases}$$

Since each d^{Near} is a document similar to d, we can estimate the weight w_{c_i} with which d may belong to c_i by calculating $w_{c_i} = \sum_{j=1}^{k} c_i(d_j^{Near})$. The weight may be viewed as the degree of proper category to which d belongs.

Example 1. Let k=11 and $c_i \in \{c_1, c_2, \cdots, c_8\}$. From k-NN, suppose we obtain $c_i(d_j^{Near}), j = 1, 2, \cdots, 11$ and w_{c_i} as shown in Fig. 1.

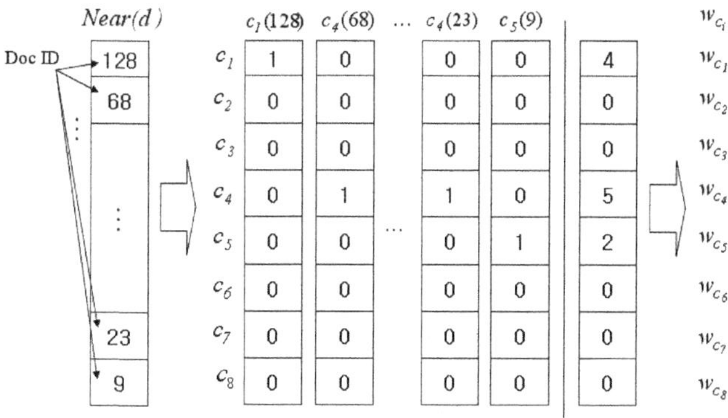

Fig. 1. Document classification by k-NN

Since w_{c_4} is the largest value, k-NN simply selects c_4 as the target category for d. But, what if d's actual category turns out to be c_1 after appropriately exploiting relationships between c_1 and c_5? In the following section we briefly explore the object-based thesauri that offer such relationships used in our method.

2.2 Object-Based Thesauri [3]

The semantic interpretation of the object-based thesaurus may be identified from the two perspectives: object perspective and relationship perspective.

In the object perspective, in contrast to conventional thesauri treating nodes as terms, our thesaurus views the nodes as objects taking the terms as their names. An object may be an object class or an instance of some object classes. It is taken as an instance, if it can be an example of object classes - for example, in Fig. 2, "TFT-LCD" is an instance, since it is an example of "LCD." It may take other more specialized objects as its sub-classes or instances, depending on whether they can be its examples or not. Since the direct or indirect sub-classes of an object class c can, in turn, have their own instances, c may form a class hierarchy together with the sub-classes and their instances.

In the relationship perspective, the object-based thesaurus refines traditional relationships, BT(Broader Term)/NT(Narrower Term) and RT(Related Term) into generalization/specialization, composite, and association according to their semantics. Fig. 2 is an example thesaurus to be used in this paper. To distinguish object classes for instances, we call the classes as concepts. Additionally, when the objects form a class hierarchy rooted at c, we call it concept hierarchy and call c top level concept respectively. Refer to [3] for the detailed description of this thesaurus including various strategies to effectively construct it.

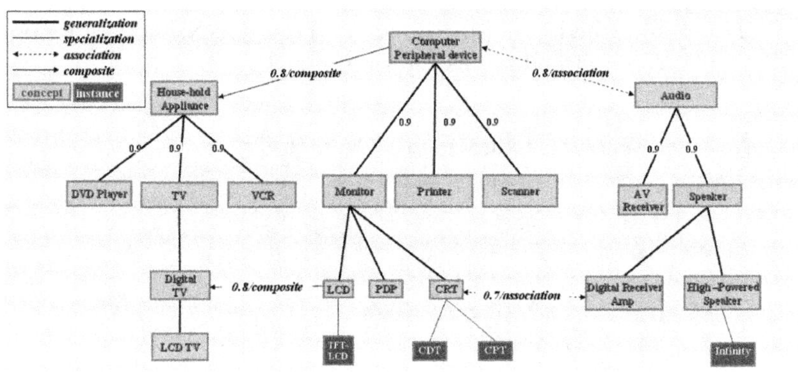

Fig. 2. Example of the object-based thesaurus

3 Document Classification with k-NN and Thesauri

In this section we demonstrate that generalization, composite, association and instance relationships in the object-based thesauri may serve to enhance the precision of k-NN.

3.1 Structuring the Set of Categories

A subset C of concepts or instances in a thesaurus Th is defined as follows.

Definition 2. Let $C = \{c_{i_1 i_2 \cdots i_l} | i_l \in I^+, l = 1, 2, \cdots, n\}$ where n is the maximum concept level of Th. Then for a category $c_{i_1 i_2 \cdots i_l}$, c_{i_1} is the i_1th top-level concept and $c_{i_1 i_2 \cdots i_l}$ is the i_lth sub concept of $c_{i_1 i_2 \cdots i_{l-1}}$ in the level $l-1$, $2 \leq l \leq n$.

If we need to emphasize that c_{i_1} is a top-level concept, we denote it by $c_{i_1}^{top}$. Since Th also has instances for each $c_{i_1 i_2 \cdots i_l}$, we denote the instance set by $I(c_{i_1 i_2 \cdots i_l})$. Fig.3 depicts an example of $C = \{c_1, c_2, c_{11}, \cdots, c_{212}\}$, which is structured like Th.

Since we use concepts in C as categories, from now on we call concepts and categories interchangeably. But we don't adopt any instance in $I(c)$ for $c \in C$ as a category, since not only the instances are too specific to be categories but

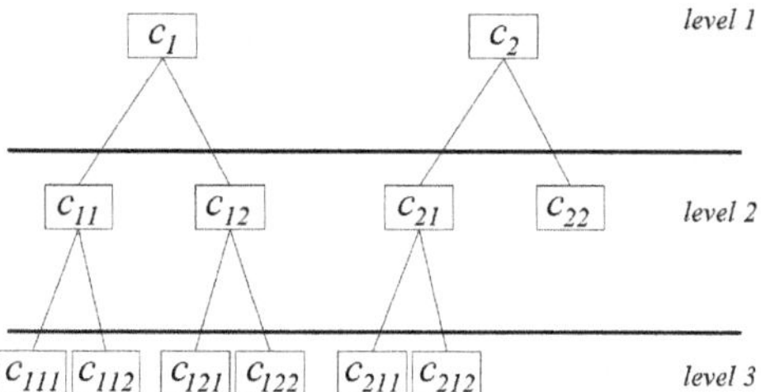

Fig. 3. Category structure conforming to *Th*

also their number tends to be large in general. We hence use $\{I(c) \mid c \in C\}$ as a local dictionary of c characterising c.

For $d \in D$, a category $c \in C$ has the implication property from generalization that if $c_{i_1 i_2 i_3}(d)$=1, then $c_{i_1 i_2}(d)$=1. This means that if d is included in the category $c_{i_1 i_2 i_3}$, then d should also be included in its super category $c_{i_1 i_2}$. We formally define this property in the following definition.

Definition 3. For $c_{i_1 i_2 \cdots i_l} \in C$, if $c_{i_1 i_2 \cdots i_l}(d) = 1$, then $c_{i_1 i_2 \cdots i_{l-1}}(d) = 1, 2 \leq l \leq n$.

The following proposition generalizes this property.

Proposition 1. For $c_{i_1 i_2 \cdots i_l} \in C$, if $c_{i_1 i_2 \cdots i_l}(d) = 1$, then $c_{i_1 i_2 \cdots i_s}(d) = 1$, where $s = 1, 2, \cdots, l-1, 2 \leq l \leq n$.

Proof. If $c_{i_1 i_2}(d)$=1, then $c_{i_1}(d)$=1 for $s = 1$ by Definition 3. Suppose the following holds as the inductive hypothesis:

$$\text{If } c_{i_1 i_2 \cdots i_{l-1}}(d)\text{=1, then } c_{i_1 i_2 \cdots i_{s'}}(d)\text{=1, } s' = 1, 2, \cdots, l-2,\ 3 \leq l \leq n. \quad (1)$$

Since if $c_{i_1 i_2 \cdots i_l}(d)$=1, then $c_{i_1 i_2 \cdots i_{l-1}}(d)$=1 by Definition 3, we can conclude this proposition holds by using (1).

According to Proposition 1, once a document is assigned to a lower level category, our algorithm would automatically assign it to its direct or indirect super categories along the corresponding hierarchy. However, this automatic assignment could incur a problem that weights of the higher level categories are always larger. This problem is formally specified in Proposition 2.

Proposition 2. Let $w_{c_{i_1 i_2 \cdots i_l}}$ be a weight of $c_{i_1 i_2 \cdots i_l} \in C$, $1 \leq l \leq n$. Then the following holds; if $w_{c_{i_1 i_2 \cdots i_l}} > 0$, then $w_{c_{i_1 i_2 \cdots i_s}} \geq w_{c_{i_1 i_2 \cdots i_l}}$, $s = 1, 2, \cdots, l-1$.

Proof. Let's apply Proposition 1 to $w_{i_1 i_2 \ldots i_l} = \sum_{j=1}^{k} c_{i_1 i_2 \cdots i_l}(d_j^{Near})$. Then since if $c_{i_1 i_2 \cdots i_l}(d_j^{Near}) = 1$, then $c_{i_1 i_2 \cdots i_s}(d_j^{Near}) = 1$, we can conclude $w_{i_1 i_2 \cdots i_s} \geq w_{i_1 i_2 \cdots i_l}$ for $s = 1, 2, \cdots, l-1$, $2 \leq l \leq n$.

Generally, since assigning documents to the lower level categories is more useful classification, in the subsequent section we develop a notion called reduced candidate category set not to neglect the categories when assigning.

3.2 Reducing Ambiguity with Thesaurus

We begin this section by defining a set of candidate categories for $d \in D$.

Definition 4. A set of candidate categories with a predefined threshold value α is denoted by

$$C_\alpha(d) = \{c_{i_1 i_2 \cdots i_l} | c_{i_1 i_2 \cdots i_l} \in C,\ w_{c_{i_1 i_2 \cdots i_l}} \geq \alpha,\ 1 \leq l \leq n\}.$$

Additionally, we denote the cardinality of $C_\alpha(d)$ by $|C_\alpha(d)|$. $C_\alpha(d)$ is denoted by simply $C(d)$ when α is unimportant.

For notational convenience, we call $Sup(c)$ as the super category set of $c \in C$.

Definition 5. The super category set of $c_{i_1 i_2 \cdots i_l} \in C$ is defined by

$$Sup(c_{i_1 i_2 \cdots i_l}) = \{c_{i_1 i_2 \cdots i_s} | c_{i_1 i_2 \cdots i_s} \in C, 1 \leq s \leq l-1\},$$
$$Sup(c_{i_1}^{top}) = \{c_{i_1}^{top}\} \text{ when } l = 1.$$

We now define a reduced candidate category set $C_R(d)$ as the minimal set of candidate categories for d.

Definition 6. A reduced candidate category set is defined by

$$C_R(d) = C(d) - \cup_{l=1}^{n} Sup(c_{i_1 i_2 \cdots i_l}) \text{ where } c_{i_1 i_2 \cdots i_l} \in C(d).$$

$C_R(d)$ is the minimal set curtailing every candidate category in $C(d)$ deducible from each category of the most lowest level. The minimal property of $C_R(d)$ can remove some ambiguity to which $C(d)$ may lead otherwise - for example, the ambiguity incurred from $C(d) = \{c_{11}, c_{111}\}$ may be removed by curtailing the higher category c_{11} from $C(d)$: $C_R(d) = \{c_{111}\}$. Hence, we refer to ambiguity only when $|C_R(d)| \geq 2$ from now on.

We first deal with definite category assignment and then develop a way of resolving the ambiguity appearing in each case by exploiting relationships available in the object-based thesaurus. Definition 7 shows a way for any $c \in C_R(d)$ to systematically use the related category set $\{c' | c' \notin C_R(d)\}$. Each $c' \notin C_R(d)$ may act a crucial role in resolving the ambiguity, though it is not selected as a candidate category of d.

Definition 7. Let $C^{\square}(d) = C_{\alpha^{\square}}(d) - C_\alpha(d)$ for another threshold value α' satisfying $\alpha > \alpha' > 0$ and call it second candidate category set for d. Then a reduced second candidate category set is defined by

$$C_R^{\square}(d) = C^{\square}(d) - \cup_{l=1}^{n} Sup(c_{i_1 i_2 \cdots i_l}) \text{ where } c_{i_1 i_2 \cdots i_l} \in C^{\square}(d).$$

To develop our algorithm, consider a document d, which deals with a topic about *Digital TV*, *LCD* and *PDP*. The following structured category set depicted in Fig. 4 involves them as categories.

Example 2. Suppose we get $w_{c_{111}} = 4, w_{c_{112}} = 4, w_{c_{211}} = 1$, with $k = 9, \alpha = 4$ and $\alpha^{\square} = 1$. Then $C_4(d) = \{c_1, c_{11}, c_{111}, c_{112}\}$, $C_R(d) = \{c_{111}, c_{112}\}$ and $C_R^{\square}(d) = \{c_{211}\}$.

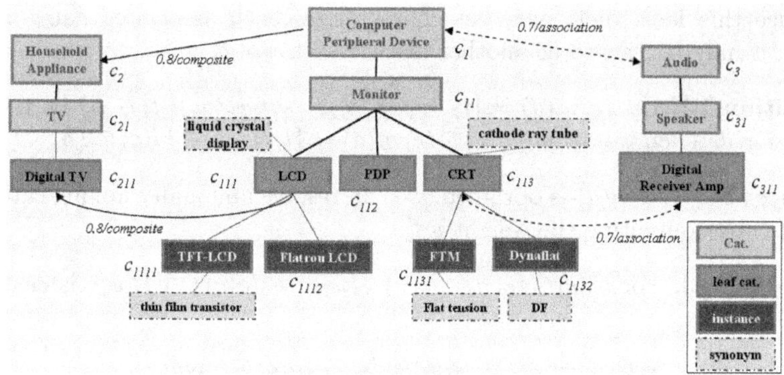

Fig. 4. Example of the structured category set

Our algorithm tries to select one between $LCD(c_{111})$ and $PDP(c_{112})$, depending on which one has composite or association relationships with *Digital TV*. Though *Digital TV* does not belong to $C_R(d)$, it may act as a crucial clue to determine a correct category, due to the fact that $DigitalTV(d) \in C_R^{\square}(d)$. We now provide the following definition for elaborating this selection process.

Definition 8. $r(c_i) = comp(c_i) \cup assoc(c_i)$ where $comp(c_i)$ and $assoc(c_i)$ return the set of categories related to c_i with composite and association relationship respectively. They are specified in the thesaurus *Th*.

Definition 9. Let $w_{c_ic_j}/comp$ and $w_{c_ic_j}/assoc$ denote weights estimating the weight of composite and association relationship between $c_j \in r(c_i)$ and c_i respectively.

The following definition is used to adjust weight of each $c_i \in C_R(d)$ by $r(c_i)$.

Definition 10. Let $c_i \in C_R(d)$ and $c_j \in C_R^{\square}(d)$ for $d \in D$. Then weight of c_i considering $r(c_i)$ is calculated by

$$w^r_{c_i} = w_{c_i} + \Sigma_{c_j \in comp(c_i)} w_{c_ic_j}/comp \times w_{c_j} + \Sigma_{c_j \in assoc(c_i)} w_{c_ic_j}/assoc \times w_{c_j}.$$

Example 3. In *Example 2*, w^r_{LCD} and w^r_{PDP} for $LCD, PDP \in C_R(d)$ exploiting $DigitalTV \in comp(LCD)$ may be calculated as follows.

$$w^r_{LCD} = 4 + w_{LCD,DigitalTV}/comp \times w_{DigitalTV} = 4 + 0.8 \times 1 = 4.8.$$
$$w^r_{PDP} = 4 + w_{PDP,DigitalTV}/comp \times w_{DigitalTV} = 4 + 0 \times 1 = 4.$$

Based on $w^r_{LCD} > w^r_{PDP}$, we may decide *d* belongs to *LCD* rather than *PDP*. Unfortunately, if this process fails to select a unique category, we need to use a local dictionary of $C_R(d)$. In the following definition we introduce a data set called local dictionary set gathered to further differentiate the categories.

Definition 11. A local dictionary set for $c \in C_R(d)$ is defined by $ld(c) = \{c\} \cup assoc(c) \cup comp(c) \cup sym(c) \cup I(c) \cup sym(I(c))$ where $sym(c)$ is the set of c's synonyms.

Since this local dictionary set characterizes each associated category $c \in C_R(d)$, it may be viewed as another feature vector of c.

Definition 12. Let $term(d) = \{t_1/w_1, t_2/w_2, \cdots, t_{|T|}/w_{|T|} | t_i \in T\}$ be the term vector for d. Then we define $ld(c) \sqcap term(d) = \{t_i/w_i | t_i \in ld(c) \cap T\}$.

Once $ld(c) \sqcap term(d)$ is obtained, we can resolve ambiguity among categories in $C_R(d)$ by computing the weight w_c^{ld}.

Definition 13. For $ld(c) \sqcap term(d) = \{t_i/w_i | t_i \in ld(c) \cap T\}$, w_c^{ld} is calculated by

$$w_c^{ld} = w_c^r + \Sigma w_i \ for \ \forall t_i/w_i \in ld(c) \sqcap term(d).$$

Example 4. In Fig. 4, suppose we get $w_{c_{111}} = 4, w_{c_{112}} = 1, w_{c_{113}} = 4$, with $k = 9$. Then $C_R(d) = \{LCD, CRT\}$ with α=4. Since $w_{c_{111}}^r = w_{c_{113}}^r = 4$, our algorithm would fail to get the unique category. So, local dictionaries are exploited for distinguishing *LCD* from *CRT*. Hence,

$ld(LCD) = \{LCD\} \cup assoc(LCD) \cup comp(LCD) \cup sym(LCD) \cup I(LCD)$
$\cup sym(I(LCD))$
$= \{$"LCD," "Digital TV," "TFT-LCD," "Flatron LCD,"
"liquid crystal display," "thin film transistor"$\}$.

Similarly, we can get

$ld(CRT) = \{$"CRT," "Digital Receiver Amp," "FTM," "Dynaflat,"
"cathode ray tube," "Flat tension," "DF"$\}$.

If we let

$term(d) = \{$"crt"/0.36,"digital tv"/0.23, "display"/0.33,"flat tension"/0.19, $\cdots$,
"flatron lcd"/0.21, "lcd" /0.64, "monitor"/0.35, "pdp"/0.19, $\cdots$,
"tft-lcd"/0.53, $\cdots\}$,

then

$ld(LCD) \sqcap term(d) = \{$"digital tv"/0.23, "flatron lcd"/0.21,"lcd"/0.64,
"tft-lcd"/0.53$\}$.
$ld(CRT) \sqcap term(d) = \{$"crt"/0.36,"flat tension"/0.19$\}$.

We now get $w_{LCD}^{ld} = 4 + 1.61 = 5.61$ and $w_{CRT}^{ld} = 4 + 0.55 = 4.55$.

To ensure that the difference between w_{LCD}^{ld} and w_{CRT}^{ld} is not negligibly small, we may need the third threshold value β denoting meaningful weight difference. For example, *LCD* could be our choice only if $\beta = 0.5$.

If the process still fails to select a unique category, the final alternative is to assign d to the super category of the categories which generalizes them. We provide the following proposition without proof to show a way of identifying the direct super category, which does not exist in $C_R(d)$.

Proposition 3. Let $|C_R(d)| \geq 2$ and s be its cadinality. Then for $\forall c_{i_1 i_2 \cdots i_{l-1} i_s} \in C_R(d)$, a category which directly generalizes each of them is $c_{i_1 i_2 \cdots i_{l-1}}$. It is denoted by

$$Sup_{direct}(\{c_{i_1 i_2 \cdots i_{l-1} i_s} | c_{i_1 i_2 \cdots i_{l-1} i_s} \in C_R(d)\}) = c_{i_1 i_2 \cdots i_{l-1}}.$$

In *Example 4*, if $w^{ld}_{LCD} = w^{ld}_{CRT}$, then the alternative category would be monitor (c_{11}), which generalizes $LCD(c_{111})$ and $CRT(c_{113})$; $Sup_{direct}(\{c_{111}, c_{113}\}) = c_{11}$.

We are now in a position to propose the final version of our algorithm.

Algorithm 1 Resolve $(C_R(d), C_R^{\square}(d), d, Th)$
Begin

1. Let $c, c' \in C_R(d), |C_R(d)| \geq 2$ and a predefined threshold value $\beta > 0$. Compute w^r_c and $w^r_{c^\square}$ respectively for all $c'' \in (r(c) \cup r(c')) \wedge c'' \in C_R^{\square}(d)$ by referring to Th.
2. If $w^r_c > w^r_{c^\square}$ for every $c' \in C_R(d) \wedge c \neq c'$, then Return($c$) else $C_R(d) \longleftarrow \{c, c' | w^r_c = w^r_{c^\square}\}$.
3. For each $c \in C_R(d)$, calculate $w^{ld}_c = w^r_c + \sum w_i$ for $\forall t_i/w_i \in ld(c) \sqcap term(d)$.
4. If $w^{ld}_c - w^{ld}_{c^\square} \geq \beta$ for every $c' \in C_R(d)$, then Return(c).
5. If $|C_R(d)| \geq 2$ and $c \longleftarrow Sup_{direct}(C_R(d)) \neq \emptyset$, then Return ($c$) else assign d to each $c \in C_R(d)$ simultaneously.

End

4 Experimental Results

In this experiment, we collected 427 documents from electronic-product review directories in Yahoo Korean Web site[1]. We held out 30% of the documents for the testing and used the remaining 70% for training, respectively. We used the six top level categories such as household appliance, computer, computer peripheral device, computer component, audio equipment and video equipment and in turn 24 sub categories were made of them. The object-based thesaurus we used contains about 340 terms that were extracted from the data set. Categorization results with k-NN differ according to parameters such as the number of neighbors and the threshold values of candidate category sets. Different numbers of neighbors and threshold values are examined in this experiment. We first perform modified k-NN on the hierarchically structured categories; if a document is assigned to a unique category, it is automatically assigned to its super categories by proposition 1. Next, the relationships of the thesaurus are employed with the modified k-NN according to Algorithm 1. Table 1 shows the experimental results of k-NN, modified k-NN and modified k-NN with the thesaurus(or briefly k-NN + Thesaurus). The threshold value of the candidate category sets α and the number of neighbors k are 7 and 17, respectively.

Even in classifying with k-NN, since categories on higher levels tend to have high weight, in most cases, documents are assigned to them if each document should have only one target category. Therefore, the precision of k-NN becomes abnormally high by 90.7%, while its recall is 47.9% which is considerably low. The modified k-NN which is allowed to take more than one category can boost up

[1] http://kr.yahoo.com/Computers_and_Internet/Product_Reviews

Table 1. Result of classification with k=17 and $\alpha = 7$

	Method	Precision	Recall	F-measure
classification with hierarchical structure	k-NN	90.73%	47.94%	62.73%
	modified k-NN	84.03%	88.14%	86.04%
	k-NN+Thesaurus	89.58%	93.04%	91.27%
classification with the lowest level categories	k-NN	72.85%	80.29%	76.39%
	modified k-NN	71.26%	90.51%	79.74%
	k-NN+Thesaurus	86.71%	90.51%	88.57%

Table 2. Result of classification with k-NN on the lowest level categories

k-NN	Precision	Recall	F-Measure
k=14	76.82%	84.67%	80.56%
k=15	75.51%	81.02%	78.17%
k=16	74.15%	79.56%	76.76%
k=17	72.85%	80.29%	76.39%
k=18	75.17%	81.75%	78.32%

Table 3. Result of classification with "k-NN + Thesaurus" on the lowest level categories

k-NN + Thesaurus	Precision	Recall	F-Measure
k=14, α=6	87.77%	89.05%	88.41%
k=15, α=6	86.52%	89.05%	87.77%
k=16, α=7	84.89%	86.13%	85.51%
k=17, α=7	86.71%	90.51%	88.57%
k=18, α=7	87.05%	88.32%	87.68%

the recall up to 88.14%. The precision of "k-NN+Thesaurus" is improved about 5.5% when compared with the modified k-NN - its enhancement in precision is not prominent in the hierarchical structure. The reason is that the modified k-NN can assign a document automatically to the super categories of a category c as well as c, i.e., even though the categorization on lower levels is not correct, on higher levels it remains correct. However, if we experiment the categorization on the lowest level categories, "k-NN + Thesaurus" can improve the precision of k-NN about 13.86%. It shows that with the modified k-NN, documents are fortunately assigned to proper categories on higher levels, but the same is not usually true on lower levels.

For the comparison, Table 2 shows the result of k-NN with different number of neighbors considering the lowest level categories alone.

Table 3 shows the result of "k-NN+Thesaurus" considering the lowest level categories with different number of neighbors and different threshold values.

As shown in Table 2 and Table 3, our method drastically improves the precision due to the removal of the ambiguity, which remained unsolved in k-NN. Fig. 5 clearly shows the enhancement of the recall and precision listed in Table 3.

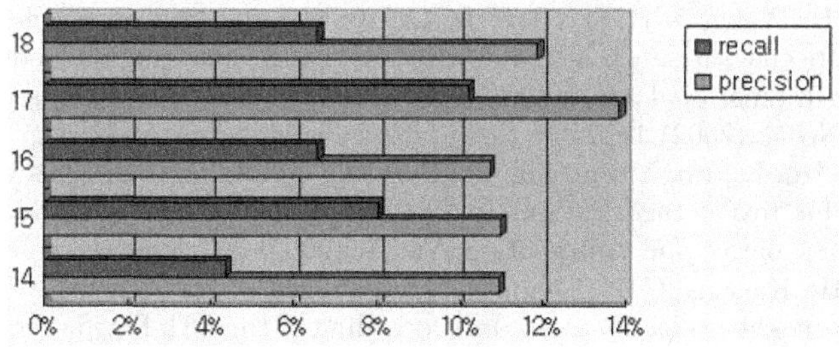

Fig. 5. Enhancement of recall and precision

Remark the drastic enhancement of the precision in comparison with that of the recall. It is due to the effect of resolving ambiguity. To be specific, the enhancement is apparent especially when k=17, i.e., when maximal ambiguity arises. The reason is that since the average number of training documents for each category ranges from 10 to 15, most of them are likely to participate in k neighbors of a document *d*, whenever it needs to be assigned to some categories.

F-measure of our method wholly relies on the number of thesaurus terms used in an experiment. Therefore, if refining the object-based thesaurus with more terms, we may expect more improved performance. Readers may refer to [3], which deals with semi-automatic construction technique available to easily create such sophisticated thesauri.

5 Conclusions and Future Research

In this paper, we proposed an automatic text classification method to enhance the classification performance of k-NN with the object-based thesaurus. By reducing ambiguity frequently appearing in k-NN, our method drastically improved the precision of k-NN, preserving its recall. Since the ambiguity problem is inherent in other automatic document classifiers, we expect that out method can also be adopted to enhance their performance if appropriately coupled with them.

As future research, applying our method to semantic web application would be more meaningful. For example, labeled hyperlinks encoded in the semantic web documents could provide more fruitful clue to removing the ambiguity.

References

1. Antonie, M. L. and Zaiane, O. R.: Text document categorization by term association. In Proceeding of the second IEEE Intenational Conference on Data Mining(ICDM). (2002) 19–26
2. Bao, Y. and Ishii, N.: Combining multiple k-nearest neighbor classifier for text classification by reducts. Discovery Science. (2002) 340–347

3. Choi, J. H., Yang, J. D. and Lee, D. G.: An object-based approach to managing domain specific thesauri: semiautomatic thesauri construction and query-based browsing. Intenational Journal of Software Engineering & Knowledge Engineering, Vol. 10, No. 4. (2002) 1–27
4. Diao, L., Hu, K., Lu, Y. and Shi, C.: Boosting simple decision trees with bayesian learning for text categorization. In Proceeding of the fourth World Congress on Intelligent Control and Automation. Vol. 1. (2002) 321–325
5. Han, E. H., Karypis, G. and Kumar, V.: Text categorization using weight adjusted k-nearest neighbor classification. In Proceeding of the fifth Pacific-Asia Conference on Advances in Knowledge Discovery and Data Mining(PAKDD). (2001) 53-65
6. Hiroshi, U., Takao, M. and Shioya, I.: Improving text categorization by resolving semantic ambiguity. In Proceeding of the IEEE Pacific Rim Conference on Communications, Computers and Signal processing (PACRIM). (2003) 796–799
7. Hu, J. and Huang, H.: An algorithm for text categorization with SVM. In Processing the tenth IEEE Region Conference on Computers, Communications, Control and Power Engineering, Vol. 1. (2002) 47–50
8. Joachims, T.: Text categorization with support vector machines: learning with many relevant features. In Proceeding of the tenth European Conference on Machine Learning(ECML). (1998) 137–142
9. Lam, W. and Han, Y.: Automatic textual document categorization based on generalized instance sets and a metamodel. In Proceeding of the IEEE Transactions on Pattern Analysis and Machine Intelligence, Vol. 25, No. 5. (2003) 628-633
10. Sasaki, M. and Kita, K.: Rule-based text categorization using hierarchical categories. In Proceeding of the IEEE International Conference on System, Man and Cybernetics, Vol. 3. (1998) 2827–2830
11. Schapire, R. E. and Singer, Y.: Text categorization with the concept of fuzzy set of informative keywords. In Proceeding of the IEEE International Fuzzy Systems Conference(FUZZ-IEEE), Vol. 2. (1999) 609–614
12. Sebastiani, F.: Machine learning in automated text categorization. ACM Computing Surveys, Vol. 34, No. 1. (2000) 1–47
13. Soucy, P. and Mineau, G. W.: A simple KNN algorithm for text categorization. In Proceeding of the first IEEE International Conference on Data Mining(ICDM). Vol. 28. (2001) 647–648

Indexing Text Documents Based on Topic Identification

Manonton Butarbutar and Susan McRoy

Department of Electrical Engineering and Computer Science
University of Wisconsin – Milwaukee, USA
{anton,mcroy}@cs.uwm.edu

Abstract. This work provides algorithms and heuristics to index text documents by determining important topics in the documents. To index text documents, the work provides algorithms to generate topic candidates, determine their importance, detect similar and synonym topics, and to eliminate incoherent topics. The indexing algorithm uses topic frequency to determine the importance and the existence of the topics. Repeated phrases are topic candidates. For example, since the phrase 'index text documents' occurs three times in this abstract, the phrase is one of the topics of this abstract. It is shown that this method is more effective than either a simple word count model or approaches based on term weighting.

1 Introduction

One of the key problems in indexing texts by topics is to determine which set of words constitutes a topic. This work provides algorithms to identify topics by determining which sets of words appear together within a certain proximity and how often those words appear together in the texts.

To count the frequencies of topics in texts accurately, a system must be able to detect topic repetition, similarity, synonymy, parallelism, and implicit references. However, these factors are not all equally important. We have found that topic repetition and topic similarity are the most useful and are sufficient to produce good indices.

The work described in this paper provides algorithms to detect similar topics in texts. For example, if a text contains the phrase 'a native American history book' and 'this book is about the history of native Americans', our system, *iIndex*, detects both phrases as similar, counts the frequency of topic 'native American history book' as two, and makes the phrase a candidate topic. The iIndex system also detects topics that are synonyms and sums their frequencies to represent the synonyms together as one meaning. This is important because the same topic can be expressed in several different ways. For example, the phrases 'topic identification', 'topic determination', 'topic discovery', 'finding topic', 'locating topic', and 'topic spotting' can all serve as synonyms.

Among similar phrases, the iIndex system extracts shorter and best phrases from texts as topic candidates. For example, the phrase 'blood pressure' is selected over 'pressure of the blood'. In addition, unlike previous approaches, such as [WEK01], iIndex extracts *any* important phrases from texts, not just simple noun phrases. For example, expressions such as 'high blood pressure has no symptoms' and 'blood

A. Apostolico and M. Melucci (Eds.): SPIRE 2004, LNCS 3246, pp. 113–124, 2004.

pressure should be monitored more frequently' are extracted from texts; these expressions would be missed by a noun phrase indexer.

The major contributions of this work are techniques and algorithms to determine and to order the most important topics in text documents and to index text documents efficiently based on important topics in the texts without employing linguistic parsing. It efficiently solves the problem of finding important topics in texts, a problem that requires exponential computation time, by carefully selecting subsets of the problem that are practical to compute, yet useful as they cover 97% of the problem domain. The approach also provides a method that defines topic synonyms with inference complexity *O(log n)* or better.

2 Background

Over the past 30 years, a number of approaches to information retrieval have been developed, including word-based ranking, link-based ranking, phrase-based indexing, concept-based indexing, rule-based indexing, and logical inference-based indexing [Ha92, Sa89].

The closest work to iIndex is that of Johnson [JCD+99] and Aronson [ABC+00]; iIndex, however, applies a much richer set of techniques and heuristics than these two approaches. For example, iIndex allows one to configure the maximum number of words in a phrase, whereas in prior work the phrase size has been fixed (3 in Johnson and 6 in Aronson). The iIndex system also uses *limited stemming* as opposed to standard stemming. (We describe both methods and explain the weaknesses of standard stemming, in Section 3.3.) iIndex also considers complete documents as its input, while Aronson uses only the titles and abstracts. Finally, iIndex uses a set of configurable matching techniques, while Johnson uses just one.

Fagan [Fa87] is one of the first to examine the effectiveness of using phrases for document retrieval. He reports improvements in precision from –1.8% to 20.1%. As in other prior work, his phrase construction is limited to 2-word phrases and uses standard stemming. Similarly, Kelledy and Smeaton [KS97] report that the use of phrases improves the precision of information retrieval. They use up to 3-word phases and employ standard stemming. They also require that phrases appear in at least 25 different documents, whereas iIndex uses any phrases that are repeated in any document. Consequently, their approach would miss newly coined phrases that are repeated in only one document, such as 'limited stemming' in this document. Also, unlike iIndex, they do not consider phrase variants such as 'department of defense' and 'defense department' as equivalent. Mitra et al. [MBSC97] describes a repetition of the experiments by Fagan with a larger set of about 250,000 documents, limiting the approach to 2-word phrases that appear in at least 25 documents, employing standard stemming, and ignoring word order. They conclude that the use of phrases does not have a significant effect on the precision of the high rank retrieval results, but is useful for the low rank results.

The work by Wacholder [WEK01] indexes only noun phrases, whereas iIndex considers all types of phrases. Moreover, Wacholder ranks the topics by the frequency of the head noun alone, whereas iIndex ranks the topics by the frequency of the whole phrase.

Woods [Wo97] provides another approach to topic identification, but, unlike iIndex, does not use frequency in determining topic rankings.

3 Indexing by Topic

A *topic* is a set of words, normally a phase, that has meaning. Topics are *determined* by detecting sets of words that appear together within certain proximity and counting how often those words appear together. The more frequent a set of words in the document, the better the chance that set of words represents an important concept or topic in the document. Generally, the more (significant) words in a topic the more specific the topic. Similar topics are grouped (and later stored) by a process that we call *topic canonization.* This process involves converting the words in a phrase to their base forms and then ordering the words alphabetically. The resulting phrase is called the *canonical phrase*. We discuss our methods for determining topic length, topic proximity, and topic frequency below.

A *sentence* or a *phrase* is a string of characters between topic separators. *Topic separators* are special characters such as period, semicolon, question mark, and exclamation mark that separate one topic from another. A *word* is a string of characters consisting of only a-z, A-Z, and 0-9. The approach ignores tokens that are numbers, hyphens, possessive apostrophes and blank characters.

The *topic length* is the number of *significant words* that constitute a topic (sentence or phrase.) Significant words are those that have not been predefined as stop words. A *stop word* is high-frequency word that has no significant meaning in a phrase [Sa89]. iIndex uses 184 stop words. They are manually selected as follows: all single characters from a to z, all pronouns, terms frequently used as variable names such as *t1*, *t2*, *s1*, *s2*, and words that were selected manually, after evaluating the results of indexing several documents using iIndex.

The maximum and minimum values for topic length are configurable parameters of iIndex (discussed in Section 4). iIndex also provides default settings. The default maximum length is 10 and the minimum length is 2. These values were selected because it has been reported that the average length of large queries to a major search engine (Alta Vista) is 2.3 words [SHMM98].

Topic proximity is the maximum distance of words apart that constitute a topic. For example, the phrase ‘a topic must be completely within a sentence’ is about ‘sentence topic’ and the two words are 6 positions apart. Thus, for this example, the topic proximity is 6.

The *topic frequency,* or reference count, is the number of times that a topic, similar topic, or synonymous topic is repeated in the document. In our approach, the importance of a topic is measured by its frequency. A topic is *relevant* to a unit of a document if the topic is referenced more than once in the unit. A *unit* of a document can be the whole document, a section, or a paragraph.

3.1 Indexing Algorithm

The goal of this algorithm is, given a set of documents *D*, to find a set of *w*-word topics that are repeated *r* times in the documents. The words that constitute a topic should not be separated by more than *p* positions.

For example, given document *D* = “abcdbc”, where each letter represents a word, the list of phrases of any 2 words at most 1 position apart is {ab, bc, cd, db, bc}. Each phrase has frequency 1, except phrase ‘bc’ which has frequency 2. The phrases with the highest frequency are the most important topics. In this case, the only topic is 'bc', as a topic must have a frequency of at least 2.

Let u be a unit of a document d in D. By default, u is the whole document. Let X be the *index* of D, which is the set of topics that are repeated at least r times in u. Each index entry x in X represents a relation between topic t, unit u, and the frequency of t in u and is denoted as $x(t, u, f)$. The index is represented by $X(T, U, F)$ where T is the set of all topics in D, U is the set of all units in D, and F is a set of integers. By definition, $\{x(t, u, f1)\}$ union $\{x(t, u, f2)\} = \{x(t, u, f1+f2)\}$ i.e. we sum the frequencies of t in u. The frequency of topic t in unit u is denoted by $x(f)$ for a given index entry $x(t, u, f)$.

Algorithm 1 Indexing Algorithm

1. For each u in d, do the following.
   a. Let Xu be the index of u. Initialize Xu to empty.
   b. Let s be a sentence in u.
   c. Remove stop words and numbers from s. Ignore s if it is one word or less.
   d. For each sentence s in u do the following.
      i. Generate topic candidates T from s (Section 3.2).
      ii. For each topic t in T, do the following.
         1. Perform limited stemming on t (Algorithm 2).
         2. Perform topic canonization on t.
      iii. Eliminate topics in T that are overlapping in position.
      iv. Merge and sum the frequencies of topics T that are the same, similar or synonyms, to produce index entry $x(t, u, f)$ and add it into Xu. Notice that $x(t, u, f1+f2)$ replaces both $x(t, u, f1)$ and $x(t, u, f2)$ in Xu.
   e. Remove index entries x from Xu that do not satisfy any of the following conditions:
      i. Topic t consists of significant words less than w.
      ii. Topic t contains duplicate words.
      iii. Topic t is a subset of other topics and t is not a stand-alone topic.
   f. For each topic t in Xu, remove extraneous words from t (Algorithm 5). Remove t if it is reduced to one word or less.
2. For each document d in D do the following.
   g. Let Xd be the index of d. Set Xd is the union of Xu from each u in d. In doing so, replace u with d in index entry $x(t, u, f)$.
   h. Remove x from Xd if $x(f) < r$.
3. The index X is the union of Xd and Xu from each u in d and from each d in D.

3.2 Topic Generation

Given a sentence of length s, this algorithm generates all possible phrases (topics) of length 2 to w words with words up to p positions apart. The algorithm systematically generates all possible phrases as described in the following example.

3.2.1 An Example

Let's generate all 3-word phrases of at most 3 positions apart from a text document "abcde…z". In this case, each letter represents a word. For a 3-word phrase, there are only 2 possible slots inside the phrase as shown in pattern *XzXzX*, where *X* represents one word and *z* represents a slot. For each slot *z*, we may skip 0, 1, or 2 words, i.e. at most 3 positions apart. The list of patterns is shown in **Table 1**. The dash signs in the patterns represent words that are skipped.

Table 1. List of patterns for generating topic candidates

#	Slots	Patterns	Phrases	#Phrases
1	0 0	XXX	abc, bcd, cde, …	24 = 26-3+1-(0+0)
2	0 1	XX-X	abd, bce, cdf, …	23 = 26-3+1-(0+1)
3	0 2	XX--X	abe, bcf, cdg, …	22 = 26-3+1-(0+2)
4	1 0	X-XX	acd, bde, cef, …	23 = 26-3+1-(1+0)
5	1 1	X-X-X	ace, bdf, ceg, …	22 = 26-3+1-(1+1)
6	1 2	X-X--X	…	21 = 26-3+1-(1+2)
7	2 0	X--XX	…	22 = 26-3+1-(2+0)
8	2 1	X--X-X	…	21 = 26-3+1-(2+1)
9	2 2	X--X--X	…	20 = 26-3+1-(2+2)

The number of patterns is 3^2 = 9. The number of phrases, 24 + 23 +… + 20 = 198, is less than 9 * 24 = 216, because there are 9 patterns each of which cannot generate more than 24 phrases (each phrase contains at least 3 words).

3.2.2 Computational Complexity

The number of patterns consist of *w* words at most *p* positions apart is p^{w-1}. An upper bound of the number of phrases of *w* words at most *p* positions apart generated from one sentence of length *s* is $(s-w+1)p^{w-1}$. Thus, the number of phrases $f(s,w,p)$ is less than $(s-w+1)p^{w-1}$. The number of phrases consisting of 2 to *w* words is $g(s,w,p)=\sum_{i=2}^{w} f(s,i,p)$.

3.2.3 Computational Performance

Worst Case

Table 2 shows the performance of iIndex on the worst-case scenario of generating all possible phrases from *one* sentence of unique words w1, w2, …, w124. The value of *s* = 124 is the longest sentence found among all text documents evaluated in this work. The value of *w* = 10 is the default value set for iIndex.

The numbers in the table were computed by iIndex. The computer specified in Section 4 ran out of memory when the iIndex tried to compute g(124, 10, 3). Therefore, the computation time for g(124, 10, 3) is an estimate as indicated by the asterisk.

Average Case

Although the worst case scenarios are almost impossible to compute, the average cases can be computed efficiently, as shown in Table 3. The table shows the performance of generating all possible phrases from one sentence consisting of 15 unique words. The value of s = 15 and w = 3 are based on the average sentence length and average topic length of all text documents evaluated in this work.

Table 2. The performance of a worst-case scenario

g(s, w, p)	Patterns	Phrases	Minutes
g(124, 10, 1)	9	1071	0
g(124, 10, 2)	1,022	114,437	14
g(124, 10, 3)	29,523	3,158,934	*386
g(124, 10, 4)	349,524	35,767,926	*4,371
g(124, 10, 5)	2,441,405	238,647,305	*29,161

Table 3. The performance of an average-case scenario

g(s, w, p)	Patterns	Phrases	Milliseconds
g(15, 3, 1)	2	27	30
g(15, 3, 2)	6	75	40
g(15, 3, 3)	12	138	40
...	...	...	...
g(15, 3, 12)	111	555	90

Best Case

The best-case scenario is when almost all problem instances are covered in a reasonable amount of time. In this work, 97% of sentences had 43 words or less and 97% of the topics generated from all the documents had length 6. Based on those values, the performance of the algorithm is computed as shown in Table 4. The empirical results show that we can compute g(43, 6, 3) in 7 seconds. That means it is practical to compute the index of text documents that contain sentences up to 43 words long, topics up to 6 words long, and topic proximities up to 3 positions apart.

Table 4. The performance of the best-case scenario

g(s, w, p)	Patterns	Phrases	Seconds
g(43, 6, 1)	5	200	0
g(43, 6, 2)	62	2,279	0
g(43, 6, 3)	363	12,327	7
g(43, 6, 4)	1,364	42,722	53
g(43, 6, 5)	3,905	112,250	156

With this approach, we efficiently solve the problem of finding important topics in texts, a problem that requires exponential computation time, by carefully selecting subsets of the problem that are practical to compute, yet cover 97% of the problem.

3.3 Similar Topic Detection

Topic *t1* is *similar* to topic *t2* if they have the same significant base words. *Significant* words are those that are not stop words. *Base* words are those that have been converted to their root forms by a process called limited stemming, described below. Examples of similar topics are 'repeated term', 'repeated terms', 'term repetition', and 'repetition of terms'.

Limited stemming is the process of converting word forms to their base forms (stems, roots) according to a set of conversion rules, *F,* as part of the simple grammar

G described in Section 3.4. Only those words in *F* are converted to their base forms, in addition to the automatic conversion of regular forms as described in the following algorithm.

Set *F* includes a list of irregular forms and their corresponding base forms as defined in the WordNet [Mi96] list of exceptions (adj.exc, adv.exc, noun.exc, verb.exc). Examples of irregular forms are 'goes', 'went', and 'gone' with base form 'go'. The stemming is represented by one rule: go → goes | went | gone.

Word forms that have the same sense in all phrases, but are not included in the WordNet list of exceptions are manually added to *F*. Examples of such word forms are 'repetition' with base form 'repeat' and the word 'significance' with base 'significant'.

Algorithm 2 Limited Stemming Algorithm

This algorithm returns the base form of a given word *w* or null.

1. If word *w* is defined in *F* then return its base form.
2. Else
    a. If either suffix 's', 'ed', or 'ing' exists at the end of word *w* then truncate the suffix from *w* to produce *w'*.
    b. If length of *w'* is at least 2 then return *w'*.
    c. Return null.

The limited stemming algorithm above has been developed to avoid some of the errors that arise when a *standard stemming* algorithm (such as described in [Sa89]) predicts that two words have the same meaning when they do not [Ha92, Fa87]. For example, the word 'importance' should not be stemmed to 'import' because the two words are semantically unrelated.

As mentioned above, stop words and word order are ignored when determining topics. When these ideas are combined with limited stemming, the following phrases are detected as similar: 'repeated terms', 'repeated term', 'term repetition', 'repetition of terms'. This heuristic will not always work. For example, it will never be able to distinguish between 'absence of evidence' and 'evidence of absence'. However, we have found very few cases of this sort.

Algorithm 3 Similar Topic Detection

The following algorithm determines if topic *t1* is similar to topic *t2*.

1. Remove stop words from *t1* and *t2*.
2. Perform limited stemming on *t1* and *t2*.
3. Order words in *t1* alphabetically.
4. Order words in *t2* alphabetically.
5. Return true if *t1* is identical to *t2*.

3.4 Synonymous Topic Detection

Phrases that have the same meaning are called *phrase synonyms* or *topic synonyms*. In addition to topic canonization, phrase synonyms can be defined explicitly by adding production rules, *S*, to the simple grammar *G* defined below. For example, the following production rule specifies that phrases ‘topic identification’, ‘determine topics’, ‘discover topics’, and ‘topic spotting’ are synonyms: topic identification → determine topics | discover topics | topic spotting .

The rules in *S* are manually constructed to improve the quality of the index. However, the iIndex produces good indices without defining any rules in *S*.

Phrase synonyms share one meaning called the *synonym meaning*, which is represented by the string at the head of the production rule. In the above example, the synonym meaning is string ‘topic identification’. Each phrase (node) in the production rule represents a set of similar phrases.

Topic *t1* is *synonymous* to topic *t2* if and only if the synonym meaning of *t1* is literally the same as the synonym meaning of *t2*.

A *simple grammar*, *G*, is used to represent both stems for words and synonyms for topics. It is called a simple grammar because it can be implemented with a simple look up table with logarithmic complexity *O(log n)* where *n* is the number of entries in the table (the same as the number of terms in the production rules.) The grammar could be implemented with constant complexity *O(1)* using hashing.

There are 4519 rules defined in the current implementation of iIndex. The rules define 11452 mappings of one string to another.

Algorithm 4 Synonymous Topic Detection

1. Remove stop words from *t1* and *t2*.
2. Convert topic *t1* and *t2* to their canonical phrases.
3. Let *g1* be the set of synonym rules with *t1*. Let *g2* be the set of synonym rules with *t2*. (Both *g1* and *g2* are subsets of the simple grammar *G*.)
4. If intersection of *g1* and *g2* is not empty, then *t1* and *t2* are synonyms, otherwise they are not.

3.5 Topic Elimination

The iIndex generates some *incoherent* phrases, such as ‘algorithm for determining’ and ‘automatic indexing involves’, during the indexing process. Those phrases need to be removed from the index.

Topics that contain duplicate words are also removed because we have found that they are mostly incoherent. An example phrase with duplicate words is ‘string the string’. The iIndex generates the phrase from [Ka96] because the phrase is repeated twice (ignoring stop words) as follows.

“... denotes the empty *string, the string* containing no elements ...”

“... machine has accepted the *string or that the string* belongs ...”

3.5.1 Remove Extra Words from Topics

This section describes heuristics to remove some incoherent phrases or to transform them into coherent phrases.

Define *B* as the set of words and phrases to be eliminated from the beginning of topics and *E* as the set from the end of the topics. *S* is the set of stop words. Sets *B* and *E* are constructed manually. Examples are *B* = {according to, based on, following, mentioned in} and *E* = {using, the following, involves, for combining, for determining, to make}.

Algorithm 5 Removal of Extraneous Words from Topics

1. Remove consecutive words or phrases from the beginning of topic t if they are in B or S.
2. Remove consecutive words or phrases from the end of t if they are in E or S.
3. If t is reduced to one word or less then do not use t, otherwise use t.

4 Implementation

The iIndex system has been written in C++. Experiments were performed on a laptop with the following hardware and software: Pentium 4, 2 GHz, Microsoft Windows 2000 Professional, 768 MB memory, and 37 GB hard drive.

The inputs to iIndex are plain text documents in ASCII format. The limited stemming is defined in a file forms.txt, topic synonyms in rules.txt, stop words in stopWords.txt, and topic separators in topicSeparator.txt. Parameters with default values such as $s = 50$, $w = 10$, $p = 1$, $r = 2$ are configurable in param.txt, where s is the maximum length of sentences, w is the maximum length of topics, p is the proximity of topics, and r is the minimum phrase frequency needed to be considered a topic.

5 Results and Evaluation

The iIndex correctly and efficiently finds the most important topics in various types and lengths of text documents, from individual sentences and paragraphs to short papers, extended papers, training manuals, and PhD dissertations. Titles and abstracts were not marked in any special way and thus are not known to iIndex. The topics extracted from texts are ordered by their importance (topic frequencies).

The iIndex finds 477 topics in [Wi98], a training manual, as shown in Table 5. (N = sequence number, TF = topic frequency, WF = word frequency average). It correctly extracts the topic 'blood pressure measurement' as the third most important topic, the topic mentioned in the title of the text. It is indeed true that the text is about blood pressure, high blood pressure, and blood pressure measurement as suggested by the first 3 most important topics.

Table 5. List of important topics in blood pressure measurement manual

N	TF	WF	Topics
1	250	306	blood pressure
2	56	227	high blood pressure
3	46	217	blood pressure measurement
4	19	38	american heart association
5	19	157	blood vessels

The iIndex finds 42 topics in [Ka96], a short paper. It correctly extracts the topic 'finite state technology' as the second most important topic, which is exactly the title of the paper. It is indeed true that the paper is about finite state, finite state technology, and regular language as suggested by the first 3 most important topics.

The iIndex finds 2172 topics in [Wo97], an extended paper. It correctly extracts the topic 'conceptual indexing' as the most important topic, which is exactly the title of the paper. It is indeed true that the text is about conceptual indexing, conceptual taxonomy, and retrieval system as suggested by the first 3 most important topics.

The iIndex finds 2413 topics in [Li97], a PhD thesis. It correctly extracts the phrase 'topic identification' as the second most important topic, the topic mentioned in the title. It is indeed true that the text is about topic signatures, topic identification, precision and recall as suggested by the first 3 most important topics.

5.1 Speed of Indexing

Overall, the iIndex is very effective and very efficient in finding the most important topics in text documents. It takes 34 seconds to index a 100-page (46145-word) text [Wo97]. It takes only 3 seconds to find 482 important topics among 23166 possible phrases in the [Wi98] training manual and less than 1 second to find 43 important topics among 5017 possible phrases in [Ka96].

5.2 Comparisons to the Word Count Model

The word count model ranks the topics based on the word frequency average listed in column WF of Table 6. The word count model ranks the topic 'blood pressure cuff' extremely high (2nd), a topic that is mentioned just 2 times in [Wi98]. It ranks this topic higher than the topic 'blood pressure measurement', a topic that is mentioned 46 times. It is unlikely that topic 'blood pressure cuff' is more important than topic 'blood pressure measurement' in the document. On the other hand, the iIndex correctly infers that topic 'blood pressure measurement' is much more important (3rd) than topic 'blood pressure cuff' (262nd) in the document as shown in Table 5. The iIndex thus determines the importance of topics in this document more accurately than the word count model does.

Table 6. List of important topics in blood pressure measurement manual by word count average order

N	TF	WF	Topics
1	250	306	blood pressure
2	2	242	blood pressure cuff
3	8	229	blood pressure to clients
4	56	227	high blood pressure
5	17	221	elevated blood pressure

5.3 Comparisons to the TFIDF / Term Weighting Model

The best term weighting model is *tfidf* according to Salton and Buckley [SB88] who evaluated 287 different combinations of term-weighting models. However, *tfidf* fails to find the most important topic 'voting power' from a Wall Street Journal text, according to [Li97, page 73] while the iIndex correctly finds it as shown in Table 7.

The iIndex finds more specific and meaningful topics such as voting power, million shares, and eastern labor costs, while *tfidf* finds less specific topics such as Lorenzo, holder, voting, proposal, etc. The iIndex is thus better at identifying important and specific topics than *tfidf.*

Table 7. List of important topics in Wall Street Journal text identified by tfidf and iIndex

Rank	*tfidf*		**iIndex**	
	Term	Weight	Phrase	Frequency
1	Lorenzo	19.90	voting power	2
2	holder	9.66	million shares	2
3	voting	9.05	eastern labor costs	2
4	proposal	8.03		
5	50.7%	7.61		
...				
16	power	5.01		
...				

6 Conclusions

This paper presents iIndex, an effective and efficient approach to indexing text documents based on topic identification. A topic is any meaningful set of words that is repeated at least twice in the texts. The determination of topics is based on the repetition of the words that appear together within texts. To measure topic frequencies in texts more accurately, iIndex detects topics that are similar or synonymous. It is also highly configurable.

iIndex allows users to configure the length of phrases, the maximum gap between words in a phrase, the maximum sentence length, the sets of words to be considered as synonyms, the stems of irregular words, the set of stop words, the set of topic separators, and the minimum phrase frequency for topics. iIndex also provides useful defaults for these values; for example by choosing a sentence maximum of 50 words, a phrase length of 10, and a word proximity of 1, it can produce a good index of a 100-page (about 46145-word) text in 34 seconds.

References

[ABC+00] A. R. Aronson, O. Bodenreider, H. F. Chang, S. M. Humphrey, J. G. Mork, S. J. Nelson, et al. The NLM indexing initiative. *Proc AMIA Symp 2000*(20 Suppl):17-21.

[Fa87] J. L. Fagan. Automatic Phrase Indexing for Document Retrieval: An Examination of Syntactic and Non-Syntactic Methods. *Proceedings of the Tenth ACM SIGIR Conference on Research and Development in Information Retrieval*, pages 91-108, June 1987.

[Ha92] D. Harman. Ranking Algorithms. In William B. Frakes and Richardo Baeza-Yates, editors, *Information Retrieval Data Structures & Algorithms*, pages 363-392, Prentice Hall, New Jersey, 1992.

[JCD+99] D. B. Johnson, W. W. Chu, J. D. Dionisio, R. K. Taira, H. Kangarlo. Creating and Indexing Teaching Files from Text Patient Reports. *Proc AMIA Symp 1999*:814-8.

[Ka96] R. M. Kaplan. Finite State Technology. In Ronald A. Cole, Editor in Chief, *Survey of the State of the Art in Human Language Technology*, Chapter 11.6, Center for Spoken Language Understanding, Oregon Graduate Institute, USA, 1996.

[KS97] F. Kelledy, A. F. Smeaton. Automatic Phrase Recognition and Extraction from Text. *Proceedings of the 19th Annual BCS-IRSG Colloqium on IR Research*, Aberden, Scottland, April 1997.

[Li97] C. Y. Lin. Robust Automated Topic Identification. *PhD Thesis*, University of Southern California, 1997.

[MBSC97] M. Mitra, C. Buckley, A. Singhal, C. Cardie. An Analysis of Statistical and Syntactic Phrases. Proceedings of RIAO97, Computer-Assisted Information Searching on the Internet, pages 200-214, Montreal, Canada, June 1997.

[Mi96] G. A. Miller. WordNet: A Lexical Database for English. *Communications of the ACM*, 38(11):39-41, 1996.

[SB88] G. Salton, C. Buckley. Term-weighting approaches in automatic text retrieval. *Information Processing and Management*, pages 513-523, 1988.

[Sa89] G. Salton. Automatic Text Processing. Addison-Wesley, 1989.

[SHMM98] C. Silverstein, M. Henzinger, H. Marais, M. Moricz. Analysis of a very large AltaVista query log. Tech. rep. 1998-014, Digital Systems Research Center, 1998.

[WEK01] N. Wacholder, D. K. Evans, J. L Klavans. Automatic Identification and Organization of Index Terms for Interactive Browsing. *Joint Conference on Digital Libraries 2001*:126-34.

[Wi98] Blood Pressure Affiliate Faculty of the American Heart Association of Wisconsin. Blood Pressure Measurement Education Program Manual. American Heart Association of Wisconsin, Milwaukee,1998

[Wo97] A. W. Woods. Conceptual Indexing: A Better Way to Organize Knowledge. Technical Report SMLI TR 97-61, Sun Microsystems Laboratories, Mountain View, CA, 1997.

Cross-Comparison for Two-Dimensional Text Categorization

Extended Abstract

Giorgio Maria Di Nunzio

Department of Information Engineering, University of Padua
dinunzio@dei.unipd.it
http://www.dei.unipd.it/~dinunzio/

The organization of large text collections is the main goal of automated text categorization. In particular, the final aim is to classify documents into a certain number of pre-defined categories in an efficient way and with as much accuracy as possible. On-line and run-time services, such as personalization services and information filtering services, have increased the importance of effective and efficient document categorization techniques. In the last years, a wide range of supervised learning algorithms have been applied to this problem [1]. Recently, a new approach that exploits a two-dimensional summarization of the data for text classification was presented [2]. This method does not go through a selection of words phase; instead, it uses the whole dictionary to present data in intuitive way on two-dimensional graphs. Although successful in terms of classification effectiveness and efficiency (as recently showed in [3]), this method presents some unsolved key issues: the design of the training algorithm seems to be ad hoc for the *Reuters-21578*[1] collection; the evaluation has only been done only on the 10 most frequent classes of the Reuters-21578 dataset; the evaluation lacks measure of significance in most parts; the method adopted lacks a mathematical justification. We focus on the first three aspects, leaving the fourth as the future work.

The definitions and the experimental setup of [3] were adopted in this work. The baseline was the support vector machines (SVM) learning method using the SVM^{Light} implementation[2]. The *Focused Angular Region* (FAR) algorithm [3] was compared with SVM. For the experimental evaluation, we added two more datasets to the above mentioned Reuters-21578 (see the details in [3]): first, the *20Newsgroups*[3] which contains about 20,000 articles evenly divided among 20 UseNet discussion group. We randomly divided the collection in two subset: the 70% was used to train the classifier and the remainder to test the performance. Second, the new *RCV1*[4] Reuters corpus. We focused here on the 21 non-empty sub-categories of the main category named GCAT. We trained on the first month (Aug 20 1996, Sept 19 1996) with 23,114 documents, and tested on the last month (Jul 20 1997, Aug 19 1997) with 19,676 documents. Standard

[1] http://www.daviddlewis.com/resources/testcollections/reuters21578/
[2] http://svmlight.joachims.org/
[3] http://www.ai.mit.edu/~jrennie/20Newsgroups/
[4] http://about.reuters.com/researchandstandards/corpus/

A. Apostolico and M. Melucci (Eds.): SPIRE 2004, LNCS 3246, pp. 125–126, 2004.

Table 1. Upper half: F_1 macro- and micro-averaged comparison between SVM and FAR algorithm together with training times. Lower half: *sign test* (ST) and *signed rank test* (SRT) results. ">" means $0.01 < \text{P-value} \leq 0.05$. "∼" means P-value > 0.05. The last row reports the P-value

	Reuters-21578	*20Newsgroups*	*RCV1*
	SVM - FAR	SVM - FAR	SVM - FAR
F_1-macro	.866 - .801	.685 - .623	.754 - .701
F_1-micro	.923 - .868	.687 - .606	.577 - .552
Training time (seconds)	16.09 - 4.29	813.01 - 14.88	439.76 - 24.57
	ST - SRT	ST - SRT	ST - SRT
$m_0 = .02$	∼ - ∼	> - >	∼ - ∼
$m_0 = .03$	∼ - ∼	∼ - ∼	∼ - ∼
$m_0 = .04$ (P-value)	(.377) - (.492)	(.252) - (.277)	(.668) - (.892)

IR evaluation measures have been computed. Recall ρ_i and Precision π_i were calculated for each category c_i, together with micro- and macro-averaged estimates of the collections. The F_1 measure was calculated for each category as well as the overall F_1 macro- and micro-averaged measures (see definitions in [1]). A controlled study using two statistical significance tests was made to compare the two classification methods: the *sign test* (ST) and the *signed rank test* (SRT) (see [4]). The paired F_1 measures for individual categories and the magnitude of the differences between paired observations as well as their signs were used. For the ST, the null hypotheses was $H_0 : m \leq m_0$, where m is the simple average of the differences between paired F_1, while for SRT the null hypothesis was H_0 : *the distribution of the differences is symmetric with respect to* m_0.

The final results are reported in Tab. 1. FAR algorithm demonstrates to be effective and efficient on different collections. The training time is one order of magnitude less than SVM (there are also some cross-validation aspects in favor of FAR given in [3]), and the difference in performance with respect to the baseline appears to be constant. Significance tests clearly show that FAR algorithm performs no worse than four point percentage on average with respect to SVM. It is worth noting that the P-value of the last row of Tab. 1 indicates a strong evidence for not rejecting H_0 when $m_0 = .04$.

References

1. Sebastiani, F.: Machine learning in automated text categorization. ACM Computing Surveys **34** (2002) 1–47
2. Di Nunzio, G.M.: A bidimensional view of documents for text categorisation. In: Proceedings of the 26th European Conference on Information Retrieval (ECIR–04), Sunderland, UK (2004) 112–126
3. Di Nunzio, G.M., Micarelli, A.: Pushing "underfitting" to the limit: Learning in bidimensional text categorization. In: Proceedings of the 16th European Conference on Artificial Intelligence (ECAI–04), Valencia, Spain (2004) Forthcoming.
4. Ross, S.: Introduction to Probability and Statistics for Engineers and Scientists. Academic Press (2000)

DDOC: Overlapping Clustering of Words for Document Classification

Guillaume Cleuziou, Lionel Martin, Viviane Clavier, and Christel Vrain

LIFO, Laboratoire d'Informatique Fondamentale d'Orléans
Rue Léonard de Vinci B.P. 6759, 45067 Orléans cedex2, France
{cleuziou,martin,clavier,cv}@lifo.univ-orleans.fr

Abstract. In this paper we study the interest of integration of an overlapping clustering approach rather than traditional hard-clustering ones, in the context of dimensionality reduction of the description space for document classification.
The Distributional Divisive Overlapping Clustering (DDOC) method is briefly presented and compared to Agglomerative Distributional Clustering (ADC) [2] and Information-Theoretical Divisive Clustering (ITDC) [3] on the two corpus *Reuters-21578* and *20Newsgroup*.

1 Introduction

Document classification is usually based on word distributions into a collection of documents. However, the size of the vocabulary leads to a very large description space which can be reduced from different ways: word selection, re-parameterisation or word clustering. The last method aims at indexing the documents with clusters of words which present similar distributions under the class labels $p(c|w)$. The two main algorithms are: the Agglomerative Distributional Clustering (ADC) [2] and the Information-Theoretical Divisive Clustering (ITDC) [3].

Rather than build disjoint clusters, we propose here to produce overlapping clusters of words. We claim that "soft-clusters" match better with the natural non-exclusive membership of words to semantic concepts.

2 The DDOC Method

The Distributional Divisive Overlapping Clustering (DDOC) method is inspired from the clustering algorithm PoBOC [1]. This algorithm has three main advantages: first it produces overlapping clusters, then the number of clusters is not given as a parameter and finaly, it only requires a similarity matrix over the dataset. Nevertheless PoBOC is not suitable for very large databases (VLDB) then a traditional sampling is applied. An overview of the DDOC method is proposed in figure 1.

First experiments aim at observing the power of overlapping word clusters indexing combined with a bayesian classifier. Figure 2 presents the results obtained on the Reuters corpus. Experiments on the Newsgroup dataset lead to almost identical results.

A. Apostolico and M. Melucci (Eds.): SPIRE 2004, LNCS 3246, pp. 127–128, 2004.

Input: The vocabulary V, a similarity matrix S, two parameters M and t,
Output: A set of overlapping word clusters $\mathcal{W} = \{W_1, \ldots, W_k\}$,

1. Select the M words with higher mutual information with the class variable,
2. Apply PoBOC over this set of M words, resulting in k overlapping clusters,
3. Assign the other words to these k clusters with a multi-assignment heuristic (cf. PoBOC),
4. Iterate a reallocation stage from each word to one or several clusters until no change is observed or t iterations are achieved.

Fig. 1. The DDOC algorithm.

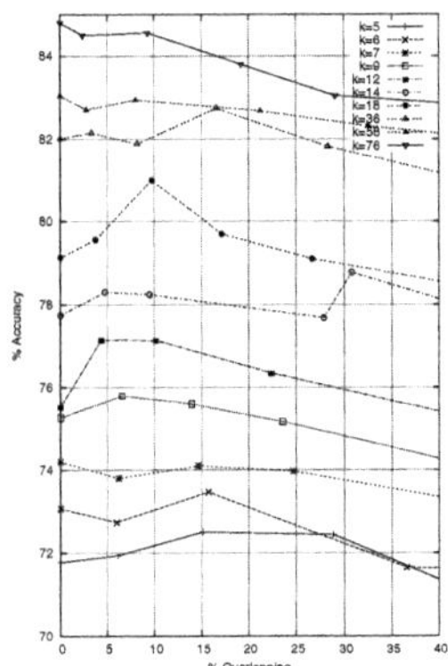

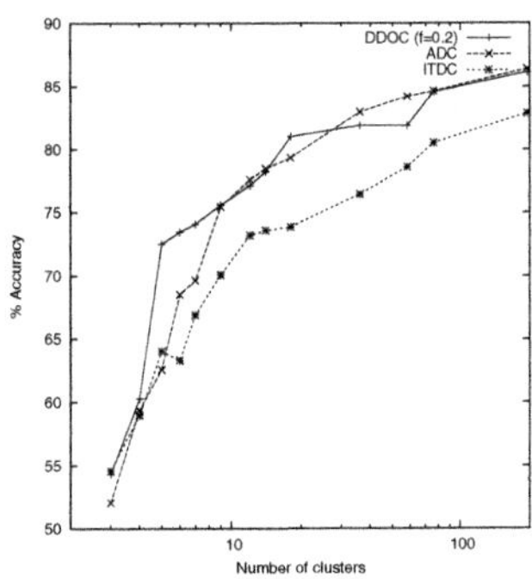

Fig. 2. (left) Classification Accuracy w.r.t importance of overlaps with DDOC. (right) Classification Accuracy: comparison between ADC, ITDC and DDOC.

3 Conclusion

Empirical evaluations of the DDOC method tend to conclude that the overlaps between word clusters can help at indexing better the documents, inducing a slightly better classifier than ADC or ITDC algorithms. Further works will concern a more formal study in the context of information theory and the use of Support Vector Machine (SVM) classifiers in our framework.

References

1. Cleuziou, G., Martin, L., Clavier, L. and Vrain, C., *PoBOC: an Overlapping Clustering Algorithm, Application to Rule-Based Classification and Textual Data.* In Proceedings of the 16th European Conference on Artificial Intelligence ECAI, Valencia, Spain, Aug. 22-27, 2004, (to appear).
2. Baker, L.D. and McCallum, A.K., *Distributional clustering of words for text classification.* In Proceedings of the 21st ACM International Conference on Research and Development in Information Retrieval, Melbourne, AU, 1998, p. 96-103.
3. Dhillon, I.S., Mallela, S. and Kumar, R., *A divisive information theoretic feature clustering algorithm for text classification.* Journal of Machine Learning Ressources, 2003, vol. 3, p. 1265-1287.

Evaluation of Web Page Representations by Content Through Clustering*

Arantza Casillas[1], Víctor Fresno[2],
M. Teresa González de Lena[2], and Raquel Martínez[2]

[1] Dpt. Electricidad y Electrónica. UPV-EHU
arantza@we.lc.ehu.es
[2] Dpt. Informática, Estadística y Telemática, URJC
{v.fresno,m.t.gonzalez,r.martinez}@escet.urjc.es

Abstract. In order to obtain accurate information from Internet web pages, a suitable representation of this type of document is required. In this paper, we present the results of evaluating 7 types of web page representations by means of a clustering process.

1 Web Document Representation

This work is focused on web page representation by text content. We evaluate 5 representations based solely on the plain text of the web page, and 2 more which in addition to plain text use HTML tags for emphasis and the "title" tag. We represent web documents using the vector space model. First, we create 5 representations of web documents which use only the text plain of the HTML documents. These functions are: Binary (B), Term Frequency (TF), Binary Inverse Document Frequency (B-IDF), TF-IDF, and weighted IDF (WIDF). In addition we use 2 more which combine several criteria: word frequency in the text, the words appearance in the title, positions throughout the text, and whether or not the word appears in emphasized tags. These representations are the Analitic Combination of Criteria (ACC) and the Fuzzy Combination of Criteria (FCC). The first one [Fresno & Ribeiro 04] uses a linear combination of criteria, whereas the second one [Ribeiro et al. 03] combines them by using a fuzzy system.

2 Experiments and Conclusions

We use 3 subsets of the BankSearch Dataset [Sinka & Corne] as the web page collections to evaluate the representations: (1) ABC&GH is made up of 5 categories belonging to 2 more general themes; (2) G&H groups 2 categories that belong to a more general theme; and (3) A&D comprises 2 separated categories. Thus, the difficulty of clustering the collections is not the same. We use 2 feature reduction methods: (1) considering only the terms that occur more than a minimum times ("Mn", 5 times); (2) removing all features that appear in more than x documents ("Mx", 1000 times). For ACC and FCC we use the proper

* Work supported by the Madrid Research Agency, project 07T/0030/2003 1.

A. Apostolico and M. Melucci (Eds.): SPIRE 2004, LNCS 3246, pp. 129–130, 2004.

Table 1. Clustering results with the different collections and representations

Represent.	ABC&GH				G&H				A&D			
	N. Feat.	F-me.	Entr.	T. s.	N. Feat.	F-me.	Entr.	T. s.	N. Feat.	F-me.	Entr.	T. s.
ACC (10)	5,188	0.805	0.175	26	3,802	0.891	0.149	7	2,337	0.988	0.026	4
ACC (7)	4,013	0.803	0.176	18	2,951	0.869	0.168	5	1,800	0.988	0.026	3
ACC (5)	3,202	0.763	0.184	16	2,336	0.888	0.152	4	1,409	**0.989**	**0.025**	3
ACC (4)	2,768	0.818	0.170	13	1,999	**0.898**	**0.143**	4	1,228	**0.989**	**0.025**	2
FCC (10)	5,620	0.959	0.071	34	3,933	0.879	0.153	8	2,580	0.974	0.048	4
FCC (7)	4,114	0.952	0.080	19	2,813	0.851	0.167	5	1,886	0.972	0.051	3
FCC (5)	3,076	0.951	0.082	15	2,047	0.831	0.176	4	1,422	0.978	0.044	2
FCC (4)	2,544	0.955	0.077	11	1,654	0.823	0.194	3	1,188	0.972	0.051	2
B(Mn-Mx)	12,652	0.960	0.073	85	11,175	0.667	0.272	24	4,684	0.985	0.089	9
B(Mn)	13,250	0.963	0.066	61	11,499	0.774	0.228	31	4,855	0.975	0.045	8
B-IDF(Mn-Mx)	12,652	0.976	0.047	80	11,175	0.740	0.247	22	4,684	0.982	0.039	9
B-IDF(Mn)	13,250	**0.979**	**0.043**	65	11,499	0.814	0.202	30	4,855	0.974	0.048	9
TF(Mn-Mx)	12,652	0.938	0.096	89	11,175	0.775	0.230	23	4,684	0.975	0.046	8
TF(Mn)	13,250	0.937	0.095	62	11,499	0.856	0.178	30	4,855	0.953	0.073	8
TF-IDF(Mn-Mx)	12,652	0.466	0.255	91	11,175	0.858	0.176	21	4,684	0.982	0.034	9
TF-IDF(Mn)	13,250	0.966	0.062	62	11,499	0.880	0.159	28	4,855	0.975	0.037	11
WIDF(Mn-Mx)	12,652	0.907	0.127	88	11,175	0.771	0.230	22	4,684	0.905	0.136	9
WIDF(Mn)	13,250	0.924	0.111	69	11,499	0.776	0.228	29	4,855	0.916	0.114	9

weighting function of each one as the reduction function, by selecting the n most relevant features on each web page (i. e. ACC(4) means that only the 4 most relevant features of each page are selected). Notice that only B, TF, ACC and FCC are independent of the collection information. A good representation is one which leads to a good clustering solution. Since we work with a known, small number of classes (2 in these collections) we use a partition clustering algorithm of the CLUTO library [Karypis]. We carry out an external evaluation by means of F-measure and entropy measures.

The results can be seen in Table 1. It shows the number of features, the values of the external evaluation and the time taken in the clustering process. The experiments show that no single representation is the best in all cases. ACC is involved in the best results of 2 collections and the results of FCC are similar or, in some cases, better than with the others. These results suggest that using light information from the HTML mark-up combined with textual information leads to good results in clustering web pages. The ACC representation optimizes the web page's representation using less terms, and does not need collection information.

References

[Fresno & Ribeiro 04] Fresno, V., Ribeiro, A.: "An Analytical Approach to Concept Extraction in HTML Environments". *JIIS.* Kluwer A. Pub., (2004) 215-235.

[Karypis] Karypis G. "CLUTO: A Clustering Toolkit". Technical Report: 02-017. University of Minnesota, Department of Computer Science, Minneapolis, MN 55455.

[Ribeiro et al. 03] Ribeiro, A., Fresno, V., García-Alegre, M., and Guinea, D.: "A Fuzzy System for the Web page Representation". *Intelligent Exploration of the Web*, Springer-Verlag, (2003) 19-38.

[Sinka & Corne] Sinka, M. P., Corne, D. W. BankSearch Dataset. `http://www.pedal.rdg.ac.uk/banksearchdataset/`

Evaluating Relevance Feedback and Display Strategies for Searching on Small Displays

Vishwa Vinay[1], Ingemar J. Cox[1], Natasa Milic-Frayling[2], and Ken Wood[2]

[1] Department of Computer Science, University College London, UK
v.vinay@cs.ucl.ac.uk, ingemar@ieee.org
[2] Microsoft Research Ltd, 7 J J Thomson Avenue, Cambridge, UK
{natasamf,krw}@microsoft.com

Extended Abstract

Searching information resources using mobile devices is affected by displays on which only a small fraction of the set of ranked documents can be displayed. In this study we explore the effectiveness of relevance feedback methods in assisting the user to access a predefined target document through searching on a small display device. We propose an innovative approach to study this problem. For small display size and, thus, limited decision choices for relevance feedback, we generate and study the complete space of user interactions and system responses. This is done by building a tree - the documents displayed at any level depend on the choice of relevant document made at the earlier level. Construction of the tree of all possible user interactions permits an evaluation of relevance feedback algorithms with reduced reliance on user studies. From the point of view of real applications, the first few iterations are most important – we therefore limit ourselves to a maximum depth of six in the tree.

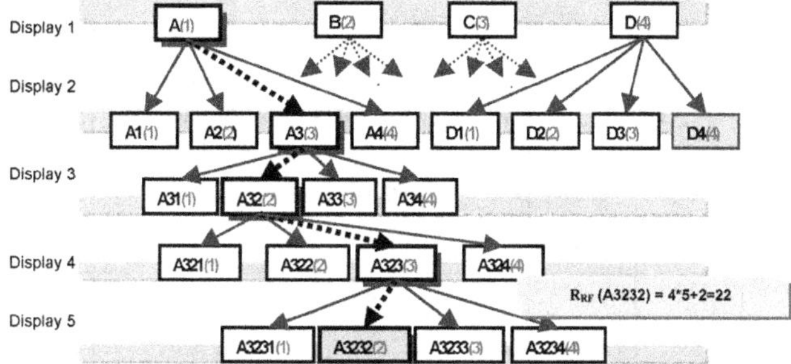

Fig. 1. Decision tree for iterative relevance feedback, showing nodes in which the target document is reached, the rank of a document within each display, and the calculation of RF-rank for the target. This branch is expanded only till depth 5 because the target has been found

We use the Rocchio relevance feedback scheme in conjunction with the *tf-idf* scheme where documents and queries are represented as vectors of term weights normalized for length, and similarity is measured by the cosine distance between these vectors. We only consider relevant documents, with the Rocchio feedback weights all being 1. The search task is to *find* a randomly chosen *target* in the database using an initial *query* of four randomly chosen words from the target. The

A. Apostolico and M. Melucci (Eds.): SPIRE 2004, LNCS 3246, pp. 131–133, 2004.

evaluation metric is the total number of documents *seen* before the target is found. The baseline is the rank of the document after the initial query (R_{Scroll}), i.e. before any relevance feedback is applied. The *minimum feedback rank* (min R_{RF}) for a given target document corresponds to the best case scenario where the user always provides the system with the optimal choice of document for relevance feedback, thus providing an upper bound on the effectiveness of relevance feedback. The *number of target document occurrences* in a tree provides a measure of the likelihood of a non-ideal user locating the target document. At each search iteration, we display K=4 documents to the user. The most obvious strategy is to display the K documents with the highest rank which is likely to result in a set of documents all very similar to one another. An alternative approach is to display a selection of documents such that a user's response maximizes the *immediate information gain* to the system and helps to minimize the number of search iterations. This is approximated by sampling K documents from the underlying distribution of similarity. In the experiments we use the Reuters-21578 collection of textual documents. Using the 19,043 documents that have non-empty "Title" and "Body" fields, we remove the stop words and create a vector representation of documents with *tf-idf* weights. Table 1 contains the statistics of *successful searches*, ie; trees which contain the target. The RF rank of an *ideal user* is the minimum path length from the root of the tree to a node with the target, whereas the mean length of all paths leading to the target represents the average performance of successful users. For the Top-K scheme, 52 of the 100 trees contained the target, whereas the corresponding number was 97 for the sampled scheme. However, 4.49% of paths in successful searches led to the target for Sampled displays as opposed to 46.67% for the Top-K.

Table 1. Performance of Rocchio RF Algorithm based on the Initial Query

Scroll Rank Range	Number of Targets	Number of Targets Found		Avg. No. of Documents seen without RF		Avg. No. of Documents seen by the 'ideal user' using RF		No. of Docs. seen with RF averaged over all successful users	
		Top-K	Sampled	Top-K	Sampled	Top-K	Sampled	Top-K	Sampled
1 – 20	45	45(100%)	45(100%)	4.37778	4.37778	4.31111	5.33333	16.5418	19.1322
21 – 40	14	6(42.8%)	14(100%)	25.5	29.7857	20.6667	13.0714	21.6236	21.919
41 – 60	5	0(0%)	5(100%)	-	54.2	-	16.6	-	21.9912
61 – 80	4	0(0%)	4(100%)	-	66.5	-	16.5	-	21.8056
81 – 100	6	0(0%)	6(100%)	-	92.8333	-	15.3333	-	21.4944
>100	26	1(3.84%)	23(89%)	367	341.304	20	18.5652	20.7828	22.1351

The results indicate that if the user's query is sufficiently accurate, then the initial rank of the target document is likely to be high and scrolling or relevance feedback with a greedy display performs almost equally well. However, if the user's initial query is poor, then scrolling is futile and relevance feedback with a display strategy that maximizes information gain is preferable. Amongst the two display strategies, the success of the greedy update relies on a good initial query, whereas the sampled update provides performance almost independent of the initial query but is very sensitive to feedback. Future work includes the examination of other display strategies, including hybrid strategies that attempt to optimally combine the exploratory properties of maximizing information gain with the exploitative properties of greedy displays, and also to verify our results with a user trial.

References

1. Cox, I. J., Miller, M.L., Minka, T.P., Papathomas, T.V., and Yianilos, P.N. The Bayesian Image Retrieval System, PicHunter: Theory, Implementation and Psychophysical Experiments. IEEE Transactions on Image Processing, 9(1):20-37, 2000.
2. Harman, D. Relevance feedback revisited. Proceedings of 15th annual international ACM SIGIR conference on research and development in information retrieval, Copenhagen, 1.10, 1992.
3. Rocchio, J. Relevance feedback information retrieval. In Gerard Salton (ed.): The Smart Retrieval System – Experiments in Automatic Document Processing, pp. 313–323. Prentice-Hall, Englewood Cliffs, N.J., 1971.
4. Robertson, S.E., Sparck Jones, K. Relevance weighting of search terms. Journal of the American Society for Information Science 27, 1976, pp. 129-146.
5. Sparck Jones, K., Walker, S., and Robertson, S.E. A probabilistic model of information retrieval: development and comparative experiments. Information Processing and Management 36 (2000) 779-808, 809-840.

Information Extraction by Embedding HMM to the Set of Induced Linguistic Features

Hyun Chul Lee[1] and Jian Chang Mao[2]

[1] Department of Computer Science
University of Toronto
Toronto, Ontario, M5S 3G4, Canada
leehyun@cs.toronto.edu
[2] Verity, Inc.
892 Ross Drive, Sunnyvalle, California 94089, USA
jmao@verity.com

Abstract. We propose and evaluate an approach for automatic information extraction(IE) by representing the extracted grammatical patterns as states of a Hidden Markov Model(HMM). Our experiments suggest that with the incorporation of simple extraction rules, the reliability and the performance of HMM based IE system are greatly enhanced.

1 Introduction

Recently, several research efforts have been devoted to the automatization of IE from text. While most of works fall into the category of extraction pattern learning methods [1], HMMs have shown to be a powerful alternative. Nevertheless, none of the previous HMM-based IE methods does fully explore the wide array of linguistic information as the extraction pattern learning methods aim to do. We propose a novel HMM-based IE method in which a document is represented as a sequence of extracted grammatical patterns instead of a simple sequence of tokens. We call our model as eHMM for the reference purpose.

2 Our Approach

First, we induce the linguistic features from the candidate instances by constructing rules out of them. We employ a covering algorithm which is motivated by *Crystal* [2]. Based on a similarity measure which is similar in spirit to the euclidean L_1 norm and a simple induction rule, our algorithm greedily finds and generalizes rules while eliminating those instances that are already covered from the search space. The set of linguistic features are produced as the union of these induced rules. Next, our HMM is trained using this set of linguistic features. The topology of our model is based on that proposed by [3] which distinguishes background, prefix, target and suffix states. Since a single and unambiguous path is possible under this particular topology, the transition probabilities are easily

A. Apostolico and M. Melucci (Eds.): SPIRE 2004, LNCS 3246, pp. 134–135, 2004.

computed by the standard maximum likelihood with ratios of counts. The emission probabilities, on the other hand, are estimated by weighting each element of the set of linguistic features according to its similarity to the token being estimated. Extraction is performed by 2 steps: (1) each word of the document is mapped to the set of linguistic features, and then (2) the most likely state sequence is discovered using the standard *Viterbi algorithm*. More details are found at http://www.cs.toronto.edu/~leehyun/extraction.pdf.

3 Experimental Results

Our approach was tested on the CMU seminar announcement corpus which has been investigated by various researchers. This corpus consists of 485 documents whose task consists of uniquely identifying speaker name, starting time, ending time and location of each seminar.

Table 1.

System	stime	etime	location	speaker
	F-me.	F-me.	F-me.	F-me.
eHMM	95.9	95.4	88.6	70.3
$(LP)^2$	99.0	95.4	75.0	77.5
HMM	99.1	59.5	83.9	71.1
Rapier	95.9	96.7	73.4	52.9
SNoW-IE	99.6	96.3	75.2	73.8

Similar to other experiments [3, 4] concerning this dataset, we report the results on Table 1 which are based on 50/50 split of the corpus being averaged over five runs. Our system performs comparably to the best system in each category, while clearly outperforming all other systems in finding location whose extraction is particularly boosted by our approach. Moreover, the eHMM does not show the same drawback as that of the traditional HMM method [3] in which sparsely trained states tend to emit those tokens that have never seen during training.

4 Conclusion

We have proposed an approach to learning models for IE by combining the previous HMM-based IE method with the extraction pattern learning method. A natural extension of our work is to find a more complete way of merging HMM and extraction pattern learning into one single model.

References

1. Muslea, I.: Extraction patterns for information extraction tasks: a survey. In: AAAI-99 Workshop on Machine Learning for IE, Menlo Park, California, AAAI (1999) 1–6
2. Soderland, S., Fisher, D., Aseltine, J., Lehnert, W.: Crystal: inducing a conceptual dictionary. In: the 14th IJCAI, Montreal, Canada, MK (1995) 1314–1319
3. Freitag, D., McCallum, A.: Information extraction using hmms and shrinkage. In: AAAI-99 Workshop on ML for IE, Menlo Park, California, AAAI (1999) 31–36
4. Ciravegna, F.: Adaptive information extraction from text by rule induction and generalization. In: the 17th IJCAI, Washington, D.C., Morgan Kaufmann (2001)

Finding Cross-Lingual Spelling Variants

Krister Lindén

Helsinki University, Department of General Linguistics
P.O.Box 9 (Siltavuorenpenger 20 A)
FIN-00014 University of Helsinki, Finland
Krister.Linden@helsinki.fi

Finding term translations as cross-lingual spelling variants on the fly is an important problem for cross-lingual information retrieval (CLIR). CLIR is typically approached by automatically translating a query into the target language. For an overview of cross-lingual information retrieval, see [1]. When automatically translating the query, specialized terminology is often missing from the translation dictionary. The analysis of query properties in [2] has shown that proper names and technical terms often are prime keys in queries, and if not properly translated or transliterated, query performance may deteriorate significantly. As proper names often need no translation, a trivial solution is to include the untranslated keys as such into the target language query. However, technical terms in European languages often have common Greek or Latin roots, which allows for a more advanced solution using approximate string matching to find the word or words most similar to the source keys in the index of the target language text database [3].

In European languages the loan words are often borrowed with minor but language specific modifications of the spelling. A comparison of methods applied to cross-lingual spelling variants in CLIR for a number of European languages is provided in [4]. They compare exact match, simple edit distance, longest common subsequence, digrams, trigrams and tetragrams as well as skipgrams, i.e. digrams with gaps. Skipgrams perform best in their comparison with a relative improvement of 7.5 % on the average on the simple edit distance baseline. They also show that among the baselines, the simple edit distance baseline is in general the hardest baseline to beat. They use no explicit n-gram transformation information. In [5], explicit n-gram transformations are based on digrams and trigrams. Trigrams are better than digrams, but no comparison is made to the edit distance baseline. In both of the previous studies on European languages most of the distance measures for finding the closest matching transformations is based on a bag of n-grams ignoring the order of the n-grams.

Between languages with different writing systems foreign words are often borrowed based on phonetic rather than orthographic transliterations. In [6], a generative model is introduced which transliterates words from Japanese to English using weighted finite-state transducers. The transducer model only uses context-free transliterations which do not account for the fact that a sound may be spelled differently in different contexts. This is likely to produce heavily overgenerating systems.

Assume that we have a word in a foreign language. We call this the source word S. We want to know the possible meanings of the word in a language known to us without having a translation dictionary. We take the word and compare it to all the words in a word list L of the target language in order to determine which target word T is most similar to the unknown word. In the beginning we only compare how many letters or sounds are similar. As we learn the regularities involved, we observe that the likelihood

A. Apostolico and M. Melucci (Eds.): SPIRE 2004, LNCS 3246, pp. 136–137, 2004.

for insertion, deletion and replacement for each letter or sound is different in different contexts. To find the most likely target word for any given source word, we need to maximize the probability $P(T|S)$, i.e. $\arg\max_{T \in L} P(T|S)$.

The first contribution of this work is to show that a distance measure which explicitly accounts for the order of the letter or sound n-grams, significantly outperforms models based on unordered bags of n-grams. The second contribution is to efficiently implement an instance of the the general edit distance with weighted finite-state transducers using context sensitive transliterations. The costs for the edit distance are learned from a training sample of term pairs. The third contribution of this work is to demonstrate that the model needs little or no adaptation for covering new language pairs and that the model is robust, i.e. adding a new language does not adversely affect the performance of the model for the already trained languages.

Against an index of a large English newspaper database we achieve 80-91 % precision at the point of 100 % recall for a set of medical terms in Danish, Dutch, French, German, Italian, Portuguese and Spanish. On the average this is a relative improvement of 26 % on the simple edit distance baseline. Using the medical terms as training data we achieve 64-78 % precision at the point of 100 % recall for a set of terms from varied domains in French, German, Italian, Spanish, Swedish and Finnish. On the average this is a relative improvement of 23 % on the simple edit distance baseline. For Swedish there is no training data and for Finnish, i.e. a language from a different language family, we need only a small amount of training data for adapting the model. In addition, the model is reasonably fast.

Acknowledgements

The research was done in cooperation with the Information Science Department of the Tampere University. I am grateful to Heikki Keskustalo, Kalervo Järvelin, Ari Pirkola as well as Mathias Creutz of the Helsinki University of Technology and Lauri Carlson of the Helsinki University for helpful discussions.

References

1. Oard, D., Diekma, A.: Cross language information retrieval. In: Annual Review of Information Science and Technology. Volume 33. (1998) 223–256
2. Pirkola, A., Järvelin, K.: Employing the resolution power of search keys. Journal of the American Society of Information Science **52** (2001) 575–583
3. Pirkola, A., Hedlund, T., Keskustalo, H., Järvelin, K.: Dictionary-based cross-language information retrieval: Problems, methods, and research findings. Information Retrieval **4** (2001) 209–230
4. Keskustalo, H., Pirkola, A., Visala, K., Leppänen, E., Järvelin, K.: Non-adjacent digrams improve matching of cross-lingual spelling variants. In: SPIRE 2003 - 10th International Symposium on String Processing and Information Retrieval, Manaus, Brazil (2003)
5. Pirkola, A., Toivonen, J., Keskustalo, H., Visala, K., Järvelin, K.: Fuzzy translation of cross-lingual spelling variants. In: Proceedings of the 26th annual international ACM SIGIR conference on Research and development in informaion retrieval, ACM Press (2003) 345–352
6. Knight, K., Graehl, J.: Machine transliteration. Computational Linguistics **24** (1998) 599–612

An Efficient Index Data Structure with the Capabilities of Suffix Trees and Suffix Arrays for Alphabets of Non-negligible Size*

Dong Kyue Kim[1], Jeong Eun Jeon[1], and Heejin Park[2]

[1] School of Electrical and Computer Engineering, Pusan National University
Busan 609-735, South Korea
[2] College of Information and Communications, Hanyang University
Seoul 133-791, South Korea
hjpark@hanyang.ac.kr

Abstract. The suffix tree and the suffix array are fundamental full-text index data structures and many algorithms have been developed on them to solve problems occurring in string processing and information retrieval. Some problems are solved more efficiently using the suffix tree and others are solved more efficiently using the suffix array. We consider the index data structure with the capabilities of both the suffix tree and the suffix array without requiring much space. For the alphabets whose size is negligible, Abouelhoda et al. developed the enhance suffix array for this purpose. It consists of the suffix array and the child table. The child table stores the parent-child relationship between the nodes in the suffix tree so that every algorithm developed on the suffix tree can be run with a small and systematic modification. Since the child table consumes moderate space and is constructed very fast, the enhanced suffix array is almost as time/space-efficient as the suffix array. However, when the size of the alphabet is not negligible, the enhance suffix array loses the capabilities of the suffix tree. The pattern search in the enhanced suffix array takes $O(m|\Sigma|)$ time where m is the length of the pattern and Σ is the alphabet, while the pattern search in the suffix tree takes $O(m \log |\Sigma|)$ time.

In this paper, we improve the enhanced suffix array to have the capabilities of the suffix tree and the suffix array even when the size of the alphabet is not negligible. We do this by presenting a new child table, which improves the enhanced suffix array to support the pattern search in $O(m \log |\Sigma|)$ time. Our index data structure is almost as time/space-efficient as the enhanced suffix array. It consumes the same space as the enhanced suffix array and its construction time is slightly slower ($< 4\%$) than that of the enhanced suffix array. In a different point of view, it can be considered the first practical one facilitating the capabilities of suffix trees when the size of the alphabet is not negligible because the suffix tree supporting $O(m \log |\Sigma|)$-time pattern search is not easy to implement and thus it is rarely used in practice.

* This research was supported by the Program for the Training of Graduate Students in Regional Innovation which was conducted by the Ministry of Commerce, Industry and Energy of the Korean Government.

A. Apostolico and M. Melucci (Eds.): SPIRE 2004, LNCS 3246, pp. 138–149, 2004.

1 Introduction

The full-text index data structure for a text incorporates the indices for all the suffixes of the text. It is used in numerous applications [7], which are exact string matching, computing matching statistics, finding maximal repeats, finding longest common substrings, and so on. Two fundamental full-text index data structures are the suffix tree and the suffix array.

The suffix tree of text T due to McCreight [15] is a compacted trie of all suffixes of T. It was designed as a simplified version of Weiner's position tree [17]. If the size of the alphabet is negligible, the suffix tree for text T of length n, consumes $O(n)$ space and can be constructed in $O(n)$ time [4, 5, 15, 16]. In addition, a pattern P of length m can be found in $O(m)$ time in the suffix tree. If the size of the alphabet is not negligible, the size of the suffix tree and the search time in the suffix tree is affected by the data structure for node branching. There are three different types of such data structures which are the array, the linked list, and the balanced search tree. If the data structure is an array, the size of the suffix tree is $O(n|\Sigma|)$ where Σ is the set of alphabets and searching the pattern P takes $O(m)$ time. If it is a linked list, the size and of the suffix tree is $O(n)$ and searching the pattern P takes $O(m|\Sigma|)$ time. If the data structure is a balanced search tree, the size of the suffix tree is $O(n)$ and searching the pattern P takes $O(m \log |\Sigma|)$ time. Thus, when the size of the alphabet is not negligible, only the balanced search tree is an appropriate data structure for node branching. However, using the balanced search tree as the data structure for node branching makes the suffix tree hard to implement and it also contributes a quite large hidden constant to the space complexity of the suffix tree. Thus, the suffix tree supporting $O(m \log |\Sigma|)$-time pattern search is rarely used in practice.

The suffix array due to Manber and Myers [14] and independently due to Gonnet et al. [6] is basically a sorted list of all the suffixes of the string. The suffix array is developed as a space-efficient alternative to the suffix tree. It consumes only $O(n)$ space even though the size of the alphabet is not negligible. Since it is developed as a space-efficient full-text index data structure, it was not so time-efficient as the suffix tree when it was introduced. It took $O(n \log n)$ time for constructing the suffix array[1] and $O(m + \log n)$ time for pattern search even with the lcp (longest common prefix) information. However, researchers have tried to make the suffix array as time-efficient as the suffix tree. Recently, almost at the same time, three different algorithms have been developed to directly construct the suffix array in $O(n)$ time by Kim et al [12], Ko and Aluru [13], and Kärkkäinen and Sanders [10]. In addition, practically fast algorithms for suffix array construction have been developed by Larsson and Sadakane [8], and Kim, Jo, and Park [11].

Although the suffix array is becoming more time-efficient, the suffix tree still has merits because some problems can be solved in a simple and efficient

[1] The suffix array could be constructed in $O(n)$ time if we first constructed the suffix tree and then the suffix array from the suffix tree. However, constructing the suffix array in this way is not space-efficient.

manner using the suffix tree. Thus, there has been an effort to develop a full-text index data structure that has the capabilities of the suffix tree and the suffix array without requiring much space. When the size of the alphabet is negligible, Abouelhoda et al. [1, 2] developed the enhanced suffix array for this purpose. It consists of the suffix array and the child table. The child table stores the parent-child relationship between the nodes in the suffix tree whose data structure for node branching is *the linked list*. On the enhanced suffix array, every algorithm developed on the suffix tree can be run with a small and systematic modification. Since the child table is an array of n elements and it is constructed very fast, the enhanced suffix array is still space-efficient. However, when the size of the alphabet is not negligible, the enhance suffix array loses the power of the suffix tree. The pattern search in the enhanced suffix array takes $O(m|\Sigma|)$ time, while the pattern search in the suffix tree takes $O(m \log |\Sigma|)$ time. This is because the child table stores the information about the suffix tree whose data structure for node branching is the linked list.

In this paper, we present an efficient index data structure having the capabilities of the suffix tree and the suffix array even when the size of the alphabet is not negligible. We do this by presenting a new child table storing the parent-child relationship between the nodes in the suffix tree whose data structure for node branching is *the complete binary tree*. With this new child table, one can search the pattern P in $O(m \log |\Sigma|)$ time. Our index data structure is almost as time/space-efficient as the enhanced suffix array. It consumes the same space as the enhanced suffix array and its construction time is slightly slower ($< 3\%$) than that of the enhanced suffix array. In addition, since the construction time of the enhanced suffix array is also slightly slower than that of the suffix array, our index data structure can be constructed almost as fast as the suffix arrays. In a different point of view, it can be considered the first practical one facilitating the capabilities of suffix trees when the size of the alphabet is not negligible because the suffix tree supporting $O(m \log |\Sigma|)$-time pattern search is not easy to implement and thus it is rarely used in practice.

We describe the main difficulties to make our index data structure almost as time/space-efficient as the enhanced suffix array, and the techniques to overcome the difficulties.

- Our child table is an incorporation of *four* conceptual arrays `up`, `down`, `lchild`, and `rchild`, while the previous child table is that of *three* conceptual arrays `up`, `down`, and `nextlIndex`: We developed a new incorporation technique that can store the four conceptual arrays into an array of n elements which is the same space as the previous child table consumes.
- The structural information of the complete binary tree is not easily obtained directly from the lcp table: We developed an *lcp extension* technique that extends the lcp to reflect the structure of the complete binary tree. This lcp extension technique requires the right-to-left scan of the bit representations of n integers to find the rightmost 1 in the bit representations. It seems to take $O(n \log n)$ time at first glance, however, it can be shown that it takes $O(n)$ time by resorting to amortized analysis.

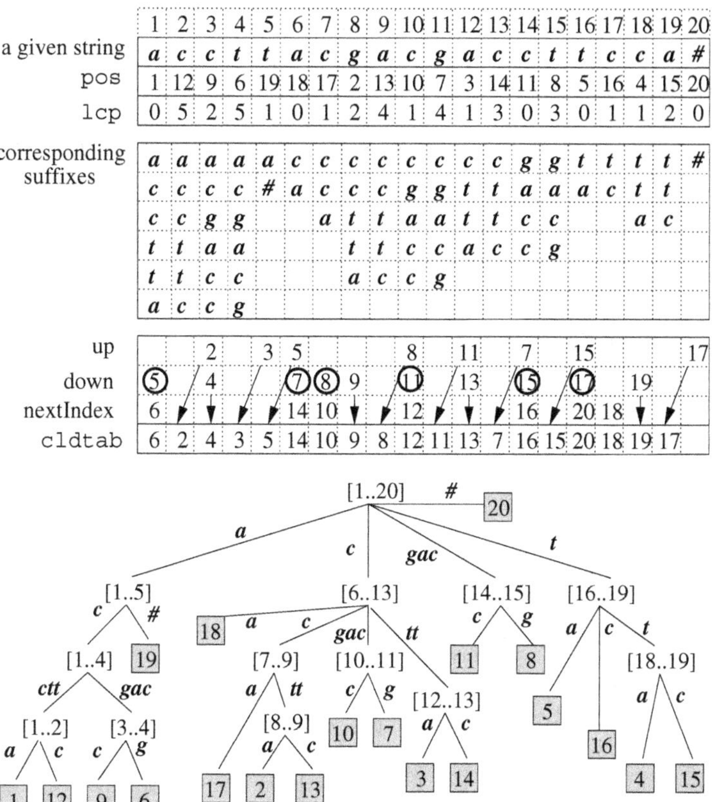

1 2 3 4 5 6 7 8 9 10 11 12 13 14 15 16 17 18 19 20
a given string a c c t t a c g a c g a c c t t c c a #
pos 1 12 9 6 19 18 17 2 13 10 7 3 14 11 8 5 16 4 15 20
lcp 0 5 2 5 1 0 1 2 4 1 4 1 3 0 3 0 1 1 2 0
corresponding suffixes
up 2 3 5 8 11 7 15 17
down 5 4 7 8 9 11 13 15 17 19
nextIndex 6 14 10 12 16 20 18
cldtab 6 2 4 3 5 14 10 9 8 12 11 13 7 16 15 20 18 19 17
[1..20]
[1..5]
[1..4]
[1..2]
[3..4]
[6..13]
[7..9]
[8..9]
[10..11]
[12..13]
[14..15]
[16..19]
[18..19]

Fig. 1. The enhanced suffix array and the suffix tree of *accttacgacgaccttcca#*. The suffix tree uses the linked list for node branching.

- During the pattern search, we have to distinguish the elements of child table from `up` or `down` and the elements from `lchild` or `rchild`. However, the child table does not indicate this. To solve this problem, we use the `lcp` array. If `lcp`$[i]$ = `lcp`[`cldtab`$[i]$], `cldtab`$[i]$ is from `lchild` or `rchild`. Otherwise, `cldtab`$[i]$ is from `up` or `down`.

We introduce some notations and definitions in Section 2. In Section 3, we introduce the enhanced suffix array. In Section 4, we describe our index data structure and an algorithm to generate it. In Section 5, we measure the performance of our index data structure by experiments and compare it with that of the enhanced suffix array. We conclude in Section 6.

2 Preliminaries

Consider a string S of length n over an alphabet Σ. Let $S[i]$ for $1 \leq i \leq n$ denote the ith symbol of string S. We assume that $S[n]$ is a special symbol # which is lexicographically larger than any other symbol in Σ. The *suffix array* of S consists of the pos and lcp arrays. The array pos$[1..n]$ is basically a sorted list of all the suffixes of S. However, suffixes themselves are too heavy to be stored and thus only the starting positions of the suffixes are stored in the pos array. Figure 1 shows an example of the pos array of *accttacgacgaccttcca#*. We will consider, in this paper, the starting position of a suffix as the suffix itself.

The array lcp$[1..n]$ is an array that stores the lengths of the longest common prefix of two adjacent suffixes in the pos array. We store in lcp$[i]$, $2 \leq i \leq n$, the length of the longest common prefix of pos$[i-1]$ and pos$[i]$. We store 0 in lcp$[1]$. For example, in Fig. 1, lcp$[3] = 2$ because the length of the longest common prefix of pos$[2]$ and pos$[3]$ is 2.

The lcp-interval of the suffix array of S, corresponding to the node in the suffix tree of S, is defined as follows [1, 2].

Definition 1. *Interval $[i..j]$, $0 \leq i \leq j \leq n$, is an lcp-interval of lcp-value l (l-interval), if*

1. lcp$[i] < l$,
2. lcp$[k] \geq l$ *for all* $i+1 \leq k \leq j$,
3. lcp$[k] = l$ *for some* $i+1 \leq k \leq j$ *if* $i \neq j$ *and* $l = n-i+1$ *if* $i = j$, *and*
4. lcp$[j+1] < l$.

For example, in Fig. 1, interval $[1..4]$ is a 2-interval because lcp$[1] < 2$, lcp$[k] \geq 2$ for all $2 \leq k \leq 4$, lcp$[3] = 2$, and lcp$[5] < 2$. *The prefix* of an lcp-interval $[i..j]$ is the longest common prefix of the suffixes in pos$[i..j]$. Fig. 1 shows the one-to-one correspondence between the lcp-intervals in the suffix array and the nodes in the suffix tree. The parent-child relationship between the lcp-intervals are the same as that between the corresponding nodes in suffix trees. That is, an lcp-interval $[i..j]$ is a *child interval* of another lcp-interval $[k..l]$ if the corresponding node of $[i..j]$ is a child of the corresponding node of $[k..l]$. An lcp-interval $[i..j]$ is the *parent interval* of an lcp-interval $[k..l]$ if $[k..l]$ is a child interval of $[i..j]$. For example, in Fig. 1, $[1..4]$ is a child interval of $[1..5]$ and $[1..5]$ is the parent interval of $[1..4]$.

3 The Enhanced Suffix Array

The enhanced suffix array due to Abouelhoda et al. [1, 2] consists of the suffix array and the child table. The child table cldtab is an incorporation of three conceptual arrays up, down, and nextlIndex. They store the information about the structure of the suffix tree whose data structure for node branching is the linked list. This suffix tree is slightly differ from the traditional suffix tree in that the linked list does not include the first child interval. A tree edge connects an lcp-interval to its second child interval and a link in the list connects an ith, $i \geq 2$, child interval to its next sibling, i.e., the $(i+1)$st child interval. The information about the tree edges is stored by the arrays up and down and the information about the links in the linked list is stored by the array nextlIndex.

The meanings of formal definitions[2] of arrays up, down, and nextlIndex are as follows.

- The element up$[i]$ stores the first index of the second child interval of the longest lcp-interval ending at index $i-1$.
- The element down$[i]$ stores the first index of the second child interval of the longest lcp-interval starting at index i.
- The element nextlIndex$[i]$ stores the first index of the next sibling interval of the longest lcp-interval starting at index i if and only if the interval is neither the first child nor the last child of its parent.

In Fig. 1, up[14] stores 7 which is the first index of [7..9] that is the second child interval of [6..13] which is the longest lcp-interval ending at index 13. Element down[7] stores 8 which is the first index of [8..9] that is the second child interval of [7..9] which is the longest lcp-interval starting at index 7. Element nextlIndex[7] stores 10 which is the first index of [10..11] that is the next sibling interval of [7..9] which is the longest lcp-interval starting at index 7.

We first show how to find the first child interval of an lcp-interval and then other child intervals. To find the first child interval of a given lcp-interval $[i..j]$, we compute the first index α of the second child interval of $[i..j]$. (If α is computed, one can find the first child interval $[i..\alpha-1]$ easily.) The value α is stored in up$[j+1]$ or down$[i]$. It is stored in up$[j+1]$ if $[i..j]$ is not the last child interval of its parent and in down$[i]$, otherwise. If $[i..j]$ is not the last child interval of its parent, $[i..j]$ is the longest interval ending at index j and thus up$[j+1]$ stores α. Otherwise, $[i..j]$ is shorter than its parent interval $[k..j]$, $k<i$, and thus $[i.j]$ is not the longest interval ending at j. In this case, however, $[i..j]$ is the longest interval starting at i and thus down$[i]$ stores α.

We show how to find the kth, $k \geq 2$, child interval of $[i..j]$. We first define $\texttt{nextlIndex}^r[\alpha]$ as $\texttt{nextlIndex}[\texttt{nextlIndex}^{r-1}[\alpha]]$ recursively. Then, the first index of the kth child interval is represented by $\texttt{nextlIndex}^{k-2}[\alpha]$ where α is the first index of the second child interval. The last index of the kth child interval is $\texttt{nextlIndex}^{k-1}[\alpha]-1$ if it is not the last child and it is j, otherwise.

Abouelhoda et al. [1,2] showed that only n elements among the $3n$ elements of arrays up, down, and nextlIndex, are necessary and we get the following lemma.

Lemma 1. *Only n elements among the $3n$ elements of arrays* up, down, *and* nextlIndex *are necessary and they can be stored in the child table of n elements [1, 2].*

The procedures UP-DOWN and NEXT in Fig. 2 compute the arrays up and down, and nextlIndex respectively. Each procedure runs in $O(n)$ time. The analysis of running time of these procedures, in addition to the proof of their correctness, are given in [1].

---

[2] $\texttt{up}[i] = \min\{q \in [0..i-1] | \texttt{lcp}[q] > \texttt{lcp}[i] \text{ and } \forall k \in [q+1..i-1] : \texttt{lcp}[k] \geq \texttt{lcp}[q]\}$.
$\texttt{down}[i] = \max\{q \in [i+1..n] | \texttt{lcp}[q] > \texttt{lcp}[i] \text{ and } \forall k \in [i+1..q-1] : \texttt{lcp}[k] > \texttt{lcp}[q]\}$.
$\texttt{nextlIndex}[i] = \min\{q \in [i+1..n] | \texttt{lcp}[q] = \texttt{lcp}[i] \text{ and } \forall k \in [i+1..q-1] : \texttt{lcp}[k] > \texttt{lcp}[i]\}$.

```
Procedure UP-DOWN
    lastIndex := −1;
    push(0);
    for i := 1 to n do
        while lcp[i] < lcp[top] do
            lastIndex := pop;
            if lcp[i] ≤ lcp[top] and lcp[top] ≠ lcp[lastIndex] then
                down[top] := lastIndex
        if lastIndex ≠ −1 then
            up[i] := lastIndex;
            lastIndex := −1;
        push(i)
end

Procedure NEXT
    push(0);
    for i := 1 to n do
        while lcp[i] < lcp[top] do
            pop;
            if lcp[i] = lcp[top] then
                lastIndex := pop;
                nextlIndex := i
            push(i)
end
```

Fig. 2. Procedures UP-DOWN and NEXT.

4 The New Child Table

Our index data structure consists of the suffix array and a new child table. The new child table `cldtab`, stores the information about the suffix tree whose data structure for node branching is the complete binary tree. Figure 3 shows a suffix tree for *accttacgacgaccttcca#* whose data structure for node branching is the complete binary tree. In this suffix tree, the child intervals except the first child interval of an lcp-interval $[i..j]$ form a complete binary tree. Let the *root child* of $[i..j]$ denote the root lcp-interval of the complete binary tree. In Fig. 3, each solid line is the edge connecting an lcp-interval to its root child interval and dashed lines are the edges connecting the sibling intervals such that they form complete binary trees. Our child table is an incorporation of four conceptual arrays `up`, `down`, `lchild`, and `rchild`. The arrays `up` and `down` stores the information about the solid edges and the arrays `lchild` and `rchild` stores the information about the dashed edges.

We describe the definitions of the arrays `up`, `down`, `lchild`, and `rchild`. The element `up`$[i]$ stores the first index of the root child of the longest interval ending at index $i-1$ and the element `down`$[i]$ stores the first index of the root child of the longest interval starting at i. The element `lchild`$[i]$ (resp. `rchild`$[i]$) stores the first index of the left (resp. right) child of the longest interval starting at i in the complete binary tree, which is a sibling in the suffix tree.

We show that only n elements of the $4n$ elements of those arrays `up`, `down`, `lchild`, and `rchild` are necessary and they can be stored in the child table of

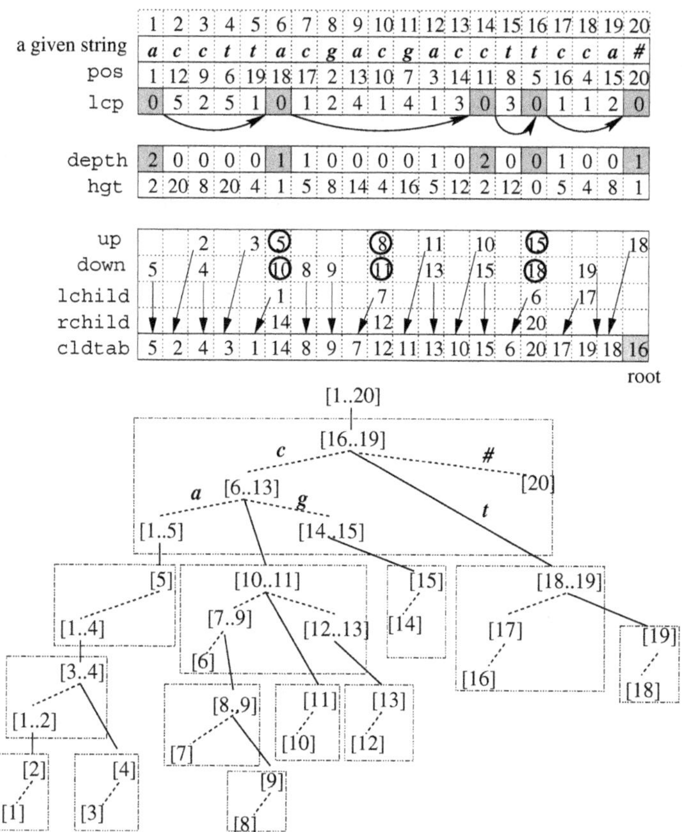

Fig. 3. Our index data structure and the suffix tree of *accttacgacgaccttcca#*. The suffix tree uses the complete binary tree for node branching.

n elements. We have only to show that the number of solid and dashed edges are n. We first count the number of outgoing edges from all the children of an lcp-interval in the following lemma.

Lemma 2. *The number of outgoing edges from the children of a non-singleton lcp-interval x are $2q_x - q'_x - 2$ where q_x is the number of children of x and q'_x is the number of singleton children of x.*

Proof. The number of outgoing edges from the children of x are equal to $C + R$, where C is the number of dashed edges in the complete binary tree for the children of x and R is the number of solid edges to the root children of the children of x. Since C is $q_x - 2$ (because there are $q_x - 1$ children of x in the complete binary tree and a complete binary tree with $q_x - 1$ nodes has $q_x - 2$ edges) and R is $q_x - q'_x$ (because singleton children have no root children), $C + R$ becomes $2q_x - q'_x - 2$.

From Lemma 2, we can derive the following theorem.

Theorem 1. *Only n elements among $4n$ elements of arrays* `up`, `down`, `lchild`, *and* `rchild` *are necessary and they can be stored in the child table of n elements.*

Proof. The main part of this proof is to show that the total number of outgoing edges from every non-singleton interval is n. The details are omitted.

We show how to compute the child table. The main idea is that arrays `lchild` and `rchild` are not different from the arrays `up` and `down` if we do not differentiate the edges of the suffix trees and those of the complete binary trees. Not to differentiate those edges, we use the lcp extension technique. We use a temporary array `depth` to store the extended part of the lcp. For easy explanation, we use a conceptual array `hgt` where `hgt`$[i]$ is a concatenation of `lcp`$[i]$ and `depth`$[i]$. The computation of the arrays consists of the following three steps.

1. *Compute the number of children for every lcp-interval*: We can do this in $O(n)$ time by running the procedure NEXT in Fig. 2.
2. *For each child interval except the first child interval of lcp-interval $[i..j]$, compute the depth of it in the complete binary tree*: Let $[c_k..c_{k+1}-1]$, $k \geq 2$, denote the kth child interval. We compute the depth of the interval $[c_k..c_{k+1}-1]$ and store it in `depth`$[c_k]$. We only describe how to compute the depth when all leaves are at the same level. (Computation of the depth is slightly different when all leaves are not at the same level.) We compute the depth D of the complete binary tree, and the level L_k of the kth child in the complete binary tree. Once D and L_k is computed, the depth the kth child is easily computed because it is $D - L_k$. Since computing D is straightforward, we only describe how to compute L_k. The L_k corresponds to the number of tailing 0's in the bit representation of k. For example, every odd numbered child has no tailing 0's and thus the level of it is 0. We consider the running time of computing the depths of all q children in the complete binary tree. To determine the depths of all q nodes, we have to scan the bit representation from the right until we reach the rightmost 1 for all integers $1, 2, ..., q$. One can show this takes $O(q)$ time overall by resorting to the amortized analysis which is very similar to the one used to count the bit-flip operations of a binary counter [3]. Overall, this step takes $O(n)$ time.
3. *Compute the arrays* `up'` *and* `down'` *with the* `hgt` *and store them in the child table*: We do this in $O(n)$ time by running the procedure UP-DOWN in Fig. 2, and storing `up'`$[i]$ in `cldtab`$[i-1]$ and `down'`$[i]$ in `cldtab`$[i]$. The elements of arrays `up'` and `down'` correspond to the elements of arrays `up`, `down`, `lchild`, and `rchild` computed from the `lcp`. If the longest interval starting at index i is an internal node, `up'`$[i]$ = `lchild`$[i]$ and `down'`$[i]$ = `rchild`$[i]$. If it is a leaf, `down'`$[i]$ = `down`$[i]$ or `up'`$[j+1]$ = `up`$[j+1]$.

Theorem 2. *The new child table* `cldtab` *can be constructed in $O(n)$ time.*

We consider the pattern search in our index data structure. The pattern search starts at the root child $[i..j]$ of $[1..n]$. If a prefix of the pattern matches

	Pattern search in ESA				Pattern search in ours			
length	$\|\Sigma\| = 2$	$\|\Sigma\| = 20$	$\|\Sigma\| = 64$	$\|\Sigma\| = 128$	$\|\Sigma\| = 2$	$\|\Sigma\| = 20$	$\|\Sigma\| = 64$	$\|\Sigma\| = 128$
1M	5.05	8.95	16.89	28.80	6.60	6.31	6.59	6.41
10M	6.15	14.11	24.52	38.61	8.10	8.98	8.77	7.98
30M	6.48	17.13	26.47	46.78	8.77	10.63	9.50	10.59
50M	6.77	18.02	35.81	54.34	8.74	11.56	13.19	12.22

Fig. 4. The experimental results for the pattern search in the enhanced suffix array and ours. We measured the running time for performing the pattern search for 10^6 number of patterns of lengths between 300 and 400.

the prefix of $[i..j]$, we move to the the root child of $[i..j]$ using `up`$[j+1]$ or `down`$[i]$. Otherwise (if a mismatch occurs), we move to one of the sibling using `lchild`$[i]$ or `rchild`$[i]$. In this way, we proceeds the pattern search until we find the pattern or we are certain that the pattern does not exist. However, the child table does not indicate whether an element of the child table is from `up` or `down`, or from `lchild` or `rchild`. To solve this problem, we use the `lcp` array. If `lcp`$[i]$ = `lcp`[`cldtab`$[i]$], `cldtab`$[i]$ is from `lchild` or `rchild`. Otherwise, `cldtab`$[i]$ is from `up` or `down`. Thus, with exploiting both arrays `cldtab` and `lcp`, we can search a pattern in $O(m \log |\Sigma|)$ time.

Theorem 3. *The new child table* `cldtab` *and* `lcp` *array support the* $O(m \log |\Sigma|)$ *-time pattern search in the worst case.*

5 Experimental Results

We measure the search time in our index data structure and that in the enhanced suffix array. In addition, we also measure the construction time of the suffix array, the enhanced suffix array, and our index data structure. We generated different kinds of random strings which are differ in lengths (1M, 10M, 30M, and 50M) and in the sizes of alphabets (2, 4, 20, 64, and 128) from which they are drawn. We measured the running time in second on the 2.8Ghz Pentium IV with 2GB main memory.

Figure 4 compares the pattern search time in the enhanced suffix array with that in our index data structure. It shows that the pattern search in our index data structure is faster when the size of alphabet is larger than 20 regardless of the length of the random string. Moreover, the ratio of the pattern search time of the enhanced suffix array to that of ours becomes larger as the size of alphabet becomes large. These experimental results are consistent with the time complexity analysis of the pattern search.

Figure 5 compares the construction time of the suffix array, the enhanced suffix array, and our index data structure. The construction time of our index data structure is at most 4% slower than that of the enhanced suffix array. In addition, the construction time for the child table is almost negligible compared with the construction time for the `pos` and `lcp` arrays. Thus, we can conclude

length	pos (LS)	pos (KS)	pos (KJP)	lcp	cldtab	new cldtab	ESA	ours	%
				$\lvert\Sigma\rvert = 2$					
1 M	4.15	2.05	1.72	0.33	0.03	0.11	2.08	2.16	104
10 M	60.20	25.50	18.48	3.43	0.34	0.93	22.25	22.84	103
30 M	206.19	79.14	59.82	11.84	1.02	2.79	72.68	74.45	102
50 M	364.30	137.91	103.72	20.83	1.62	4.74	126.16	129.29	102
				$\lvert\Sigma\rvert = 4$					
1 M	3.81	2.55	1.67	0.33	0.04	0.11	2.04	2.11	103
10 M	53.79	30.39	19.63	3.44	0.36	0.98	23.43	24.05	103
30 M	180.42	97.74	62.66	11.58	1.03	2.84	75.27	77.08	102
50 M	347.10	162.59	108.42	21.39	1.65	4.77	131.46	134.58	102
				$\lvert\Sigma\rvert = 64$					
1 M	0.75	1.81	2.15	0.38	0.05	0.11	2.58	2.64	102
10 M	50.98	40.10	26.41	3.65	0.53	1.18	30.59	31.24	102
30 M	185.32	122.75	81.71	11.75	1.30	3.25	94.76	96.71	102
50 M	335.77	211.79	141.28	21.53	1.96	5.45	164.77	168.26	102
				$\lvert\Sigma\rvert = 128$					
1 M	0.63	1.96	2.24	0.37	0.04	0.11	2.65	2.72	103
10 M	20.35	43.16	29.35	3.84	0.55	1.23	33.74	34.42	102
30 M	169.58	129.87	86.23	11.93	1.42	3.49	99.58	101.65	102
50 M	319.53	226.43	152.25	21.76	2.22	5.59	176.23	179.60	102

Fig. 5. We computed the percentage of the construction time of our index data structure over that of the enhanced suffix array. The construction time for the enhanced suffix array (ESA) is the construction time for the arrays `pos`, `lcp`, and `cldtab`. The construction time for our data structure is the construction time for the arrays `pos`, `lcp`, and new `cldtab`. To construct the `pos` array, we considered Larsson and Sadakane's [8] (LS) algorithm, Kärkkäinen and Sanders' [10] (KS) algorithm, and Kim, Jo, and Park's [11] (KJP) algorithm. Among the algorithms, KJP algorithm is the fastest in most cases, we used KJP algorithm to construct the `pos` array. To construct the `lcp` array, we used Kasai et al. [9]'s algorithm.

that our data structure can be constructed almost as fast as the suffix array and the enhanced suffix array.

6 Conclusion

We presented an index data structure with the capabilities of the suffix tree and the suffix array even when the size of the alphabet is not negligible by improving the enhanced suffix array. Our index data structure support the pattern search in $O(m \log |\Sigma|)$ time and it is almost as time/space-efficient as the enhanced suffix array. In a different point of view, it can be considered the first practical one facilitating the capabilities of suffix trees when the size of the alphabet is not negligible because the suffix tree supporting $O(m \log |\Sigma|)$-time pattern search is not easy to implement and thus it is rarely used in practice.

References

1. M.I. Abouelhoda, S. Kurtz, and E. Ohlebusch, Replacing suffix trees with enhanced suffix arrays, *J. of Discrete Algorithms* (2004), 53–86.
2. M. Abouelhoda, E. Ohlebusch, and S. Kurtz, Optimal exact string matching based on suffix arrays, *Symp. on String Processing and Information Retrieval* (2002), 31–43.
3. T. H. Cormen, C. E. Leiserson, R. L. Rivest, C. Stein, Introduction to Algorithms (Second Edition), *MIT Press* (2001)
4. M. Farach, Optimal suffix tree construction with large alphabets, *IEEE Symp. Found. Computer Science* (1997), 137–143.
5. M. Farach-Colton, P. Ferragina and S. Muthukrishnan, On the sorting-complexity of suffix tree construction, *J. Assoc. Comput. Mach.* 47 (2000), 987-1011.
6. G. Gonnet, R. Baeza-Yates, and T. Snider, New indices for text: Pat trees and pat arrays. In W. B. Frakes and R. A. Baeza-Yates, editors, Information Retrieval: Data Structures & Algorithms, *Prentice Hall* (1992), 66–82.
7. D. Gusfield, Algorithms on Strings, Trees, and Sequences, *Cambridge Univ. Press* 1997.
8. N. J. Larsson and K. Sadakane, Faster Suffix Sorting, Technical Report, number LU-CS-TR:99-214, Department of Computer Science, Lund University, Sweden, (1999).
9. T. Kasai, G. Lee, H. Arimura, S. Arikawa, and K. Park, Linear-time longest-common-prefix computation in suffix arrays and its applications, *Symp. Combinatorial Pattern Matching* (2001), 181–192.
10. J. Kärkkäinen and P. Sanders, Simpler linear work suffix array construction, *Int. Colloq. Automata Languages and Programming* (2003), 943–955.
11. D. K. Kim, J. Jo, and H. Park, A fast algorithm for constructing suffix arrays for fixed-size alphabets, *Workshop on Efficient and Experimental Algorithms* (2004), 301–314.
12. D. K. Kim, J. S. Sim, H. Park and K. Park, Linear-time construction of suffix arrays, *Symp. Combinatorial Pattern Matching* (2003), 186–199.
13. P. Ko and S. Aluru, Space-efficient linear time construction of suffix arrays, *Symp. Combinatorial Pattern Matching* (2003), 200–210.
14. U. Manber and G. Myers, Suffix arrays: A new method for on-line string searches, *SIAM J. Comput.* 22 (1993), 935–938.
15. E.M. McCreight, A space-economical suffix tree construction algorithm, *J. Assoc. Comput. Mach.* 23 (1976), 262–272.
16. E. Ukkonen, On-line construction of suffix trees, *Algorithmica* 14 (1995), 249–260.
17. P. Weiner, Linear pattern matching algorithms, *Proc. 14th IEEE Symp. Switching and Automata Theory* (1973), 1–11.

An Alphabet-Friendly FM-Index*

Paolo Ferragina[1], Giovanni Manzini[2], Veli Mäkinen[3], and Gonzalo Navarro[4]

[1] Dipartimento di Informatica, University of Pisa, Italy
[2] Dipartimento di Informatica, University of Piemonte Orientale, Italy
[3] Department of Computer Science, University of Helsinki, Finland
[4] Department of Computer Science, University of Chile, Chile

Abstract. We show that, by combining an existing compression boosting technique with the wavelet tree data structure, we are able to design a variant of the FM-index which scales well with the size of the input alphabet Σ. The size of the new index built on a string $T[1,n]$ is bounded by $nH_k(T)+O\big((n\log\log n)/\log_{|\Sigma|} n\big)$ bits, where $H_k(T)$ is the k-th order empirical entropy of T.
The above bound holds simultaneously for all $k \leq \alpha \log_{|\Sigma|} n$ and $0 < \alpha < 1$. Moreover, the index design does not depend on the parameter k, which plays a role only in analysis of the space occupancy.
Using our index, the counting of the occurrences of an arbitrary pattern $P[1,p]$ as a substring of T takes $O(p\log|\Sigma|)$ time. Locating each pattern occurrence takes $O(\log|\Sigma|\ (\log^2 n/\log\log n))$ time. Reporting a text substring of length ℓ takes $O((\ell + \log^2 n/\log\log n)\log|\Sigma|)$ time.

1 Introduction

A *full-text index* is a data structure built over a text string $T[1,n]$ that supports the efficient search for an arbitrary pattern as a *substring* of the indexed text. A *self-index* is a full-text index that encapsulates the indexed text T, without hence requiring its explicit storage.

The FM-index [3] has been the first self-index in the literature to achieve a space occupancy close to the k-th order entropy of T—hereafter denoted by $H_k(T)$ (see Section 2.1). Precisely, the FM-index occupies at most $5nH_k(T) + o(n)$ bits of storage, and allows the search for the *occ* occurrences of a pattern $P[1,p]$ within T in $O(p + occ\log^{1+\epsilon} n)$ time, where $\epsilon > 0$ is an arbitrary constant fixed in advance. It can display any text substring of length ℓ in $O(\ell + \log^{1+\epsilon} n)$ time. The design of the FM-index is based upon the relationship between the Burrows-Wheeler compression algorithm [1] and the suffix array data structure [16, 9]. It is therefore a sort of *compressed suffix array* that takes advantage of the compressibility of the indexed text in order to achieve space occupancy close to the Information Theoretic minimum. Indeed, the design of the FM-index does not depend on the parameter k and its space bound holds *simultaneously*

* Partially supported by the Italian MIUR projects `ALINWEB` and `ECD` and `Grid.it` and ``Piattaforma distribuita ad alte prestazioni'', and by the Chilean Fondecyt Grant 1-020831.

A. Apostolico and M. Melucci (Eds.): SPIRE 2004, LNCS 3246, pp. 150–160, 2004.

over all $k \geq 0$. These remarkable theoretical properties have been validated by experimental results [4, 5] and applications [14, 21].

The above bounds on the FM-index space occupancy and query time have been obtained assuming that the size of the input alphabet is a constant. Hidden in the big-O notation there is an exponential dependency on the alphabet size in the space bound, and a linear dependency on the alphabet size in the time bounds. More specifically, the search time is $O(p + occ\ |\Sigma|\ \log^{1+\epsilon} n)$ and the time to display a text substring is $O((\ell + \log^{1+\epsilon} n)\ |\Sigma|)$. Although in practical implementations of the FM-index [4, 5] these dependencies are removed with only a small penalty in the query time, it is worthwhile to investigate whether it is possible to build a more "alphabet-friendly" FM-index.

In this paper we use the compression boosting technique [2, 7] and the wavelet tree data structure [11] to design a version of the FM-index which scales well with the size of the alphabet. Compression boosting partitions the Burrows-Wheeler transformed text into contiguous areas in order to maximize the overall compression achievable with zero-order compressors used over each area. The wavelet tree offers a zero-order compression and also permits answering some simple queries over the compressed area.

The resulting data structure indexes a string $T[1, n]$ drawn from an alphabet Σ using $nH_k(T) + O\big((n \log\log n)/\log_{|\Sigma|} n\big)$ bits of storage. The above bound holds simultaneously for all $k \leq \alpha \log_{|\Sigma|} n$ and $0 < \alpha < 1$. The structure of our index is extremely simple and does not depend on the parameter k, which plays a role only in the analysis of the space occupancy. With our index, the counting of the occurrences of an arbitrary pattern $P[1, p]$ as a substring of T takes $O(p \log |\Sigma|)$ time. Locating each pattern occurrence takes $O(\log |\Sigma|\ (\log^2 n/\log\log n))$ time. Displaying a text substring of length ℓ takes $O((\ell + \log^2 n/\log\log n) \log |\Sigma|)$ time. Compared to the original FM-index, we note that the new version scales better with the alphabet size in all aspects. Albeit the time to count pattern occurrences has increased, that of locating occurrences and displaying text substrings has decreased.

Recently, various compressed full-text indexes have been proposed in the literature achieving several time/space trade-offs [13, 20, 18, 11, 12, 10]. Among them, the one with the smallest space occupancy is the data structure described in [11] (Theorems 4.2 and 5.2) that achieves $O(p \log |\Sigma| + \text{polylog}(n))$ time to count the pattern occurrences, $O(\log |\Sigma|\ (\ell + \log^2 n/\log\log n))$ time to locate and display a substring of length ℓ, and uses $nH_k(T) + O\big((n \log\log n)/\log_{|\Sigma|} n\big)$ bits of storage. The space bound holds for *a fixed k* which must be chosen in advance, i.e., when the index is built. The parameter k must satisfy the constraint $k \leq \alpha \log_{|\Sigma|} n$ with $0 < \alpha < 1$, which is the same limitation that we have for our space bound. An alternative way to reduce the alphabet dependence of the FM-index has been proposed in [10], where the resulting space bound is the higher $O((H_0 + 1)n)$ although based on a simpler solution to implement.

To summarize, our data structure is extremely simple, has the smallest known space occupancy, and counts the occurrences faster than the data structure in [11], which is the only other compressed index known to date with a $nH_k(T) + o(n)$ space occupancy.

2 Background and Notation

Hereafter we assume that $T[1,n]$ is the text we wish to index, compress and query. T is drawn from an alphabet Σ of size $|\Sigma|$. By $T[i]$ we denote the i-th character of T, $T[i,n]$ denotes the ith text suffix, and $T[1,i]$ denotes the ith text prefix. We write $|w|$ to denote the length of string w.

2.1 The k-th Order Empirical Entropy

Following a well established practice in Information Theory, we lower bound the space needed to store a string T by using the notion of *empirical entropy.* The empirical entropy is similar to the entropy defined in the probabilistic setting with the difference that it is defined in terms of the character frequencies observed in T rather than in terms of character probabilities. The key property of empirical entropy is that it is defined *pointwise* for *any* string T and can be used to measure the performance of compression algorithms as a function of the *string structure*, thus *without* any assumption on the input source. In a sense, compression bounds produced in terms of empirical entropy are *worst-case measures*.

Formally, the *zero-th order* empirical entropy of T is defined as $H_0(T) = -\sum_i (n_i/n)\log(n_i/n)$, where n_i is the number of occurrences of the i-th alphabet character in T, $n = \sum_i n_i = |T|$, and all logarithms are taken to the base 2 (with $0 \log 0 = 0$). To introduce the concept of k-*th order* empirical entropy we need to define what is a *context.* A length-k context w in T is one of its substrings of length k. Given w, we denote by $\vec{w}_T$ the string formed by concatenating all the symbols following the occurrences of w in T, taken from left to right. For example, if $T = \texttt{mississippi}$ then $\vec{\texttt{s}}_T = \texttt{sisi}$ and $\vec{\texttt{si}}_T = \texttt{sp}$. The k-th order empirical entropy of T is defined as:

$$H_k(T) = \frac{1}{n} \sum_{w \in \Sigma^k} |\,\vec{w}_T\,|\, H_0(\vec{w}_T). \tag{1}$$

The k-th order empirical entropy $H_k(T)$ is a lower bound to the output size of any compressor which encodes each character of T using a uniquely decipherable code that depends only on the character itself and on the k characters preceding it. For any $k \geq 0$ we have $H_k(T) \leq \log|\Sigma|$. Note that for strings with many regularities we may have $H_k(T) = o(1)$. This is unlike the entropy defined in the probabilistic setting which is always a constant. As an example, for $T = (ab)^{n/2}$ we have $H_0(T) = 1$ and $H_k(T) = O((\log n)/n)$ for any $k \geq 1$.

2.2 The Burrows-Wheeler Transform

In [1] Burrows and Wheeler introduced a new compression algorithm based on a reversible transformation now called the *Burrows-Wheeler Transform* (BWT

```
                              F             T^bwt
----------------              -----------------
mississippi#                  # mississipp i
ississippi#m                  i #mississip p
ssissippi#mi                  i ppi#missis s
sissippi#mis                  i ssippi#mis s
issippi#miss                  i ssissippi# m
ssippi#missi       ==>        m ississippi #
sippi#missis                  p i#mississi p
ippi#mississ                  p pi#mississ i
ppi#mississi                  s ippi#missi s
pi#mississip                  s issippi#mi s
i#mississipp                  s sippi#miss i
#mississippi                  s sissippi#m i
----------------              -----------------
```

Fig. 1. Example of Burrows-Wheeler transform for the string $T=$ `mississippi`. The matrix on the right has the rows sorted in lexicographic order. The output of the BWT is the last column; in this example the string `ipssm#pissii`.

from now on). The BWT consists of three basic steps (see Figure 1): (1) append at the end of T a special character # smaller than any other text character; (2) form a *conceptual* matrix $\mathcal{M}_T$ whose rows are the cyclic shifts of the string $T\#$ sorted in lexicographic order; (3) construct the transformed text T^{bwt} by taking the last column of matrix $\mathcal{M}_T$. Notice that every column of $\mathcal{M}_T$, hence also the transformed text T^{bwt}, is a permutation of $T\#$. In particular the first column of $\mathcal{M}_T$, call it F, is obtained by lexicographically sorting the characters of $T\#$ (or, equally, the characters of T^{bwt}).

We remark that the BWT by itself is not a compression algorithm since T^{bwt} is just a permutation of $T\#$. However, if T has some regularities the BWT will "group together" several occurrences of the same character. As a result, the transformed string T^{bwt} contains long runs of identical characters and turns out to be highly compressible (see e.g. [1, 17] for details).

Because of the special character #, when we sort the rows of $\mathcal{M}_T$ we are essentially sorting the suffixes of T. Therefore there is a strong relation between the matrix $\mathcal{M}_T$ and the suffix array built on T. The matrix $\mathcal{M}_T$ has also other remarkable properties; to illustrate them we introduce the following notation:

- Let $C[\cdot]$ denote the array of length $|\Sigma|$ such that $C[c]$ contains the total number of text characters which are alphabetically smaller than c.
- Let $\mathsf{Occ}(c,q)$ denote the number of occurrences of character c in the prefix $T^{bwt}[1,q]$.
- Let $LF(i)=C[T^{bwt}[i]]+\mathsf{Occ}(T^{bwt}[i],i)$.

$LF(\cdot)$ stands for *Last-to-First* column mapping since the character $T^{bwt}[i]$, in the last column of $\mathcal{M}_T$, is located in the first column F at position $LF(i)$. For example in Figure 1 we have $LF(10)=C[\mathtt{s}]+\mathsf{Occ}(\mathtt{s},10)=12$; and in fact $T^{bwt}[10]$ and $F[LF(10)]=F[12]$ both correspond to the first `s` in the string `mississippi`.

The $LF(\cdot)$ mapping allows us to scan the text T backward. Namely, if $T[k] = T^{bwt}[i]$ then $T[k-1] = T^{bwt}[LF(i)]$. For example in Fig. 1 we have that $T[3] = \mathtt{s}$ is the 10th character of T^{bwt} and we correctly have $T[2] = T^{bwt}[LF(10)] = T^{bwt}[12] = \mathtt{i}$ (see [3] for details).

2.3 The FM-Index

The FM-index is a *self-index* that allows to efficiently search for the occurrences of an arbitrary pattern $P[1,p]$ as a *substring* of the text $T[1,n]$. Pattern P is provided on-line whereas the text T is given to be preprocessed in advance. The number of pattern occurrences in T is hereafter indicated with *occ*. The term *self-index* highlights the fact that T is not stored explicitly but it can be derived from the FM-index.

The FM-index consists of a compressed representation of T^{bwt} together with some auxiliary information which makes it possible to compute in $O(1)$ time the value $\mathsf{Occ}(c,q)$ for any character c and for any q, $0 \le q \le n$. The two key procedures to operate on the FM-index are: the *counting* of the number of pattern occurrences (shortly get_rows), and the *location* of their positions in the text T (shortly get_position). Note that the counting process returns the value *occ*, whereas the location process returns *occ* distinct integers in the range $[1,n]$.

Algorithm get_rows($P[1,p]$)

```
i ← p, c ← P[p], First ← C[c] + 1, Last ← C[c + 1];
while ((First ≤ Last)  and (i ≥ 2)) do
    c ← P[i − 1];
    First ← C[c] + Occ(c, First − 1) + 1;
    Last ← C[c] + Occ(c, Last);
    i ← i − 1;
if (Last < First) then return "no rows prefixed by P[1, p]" else return
  (First, Last).
```

Fig. 2. Algorithm get_rows for finding the set of rows prefixed by $P[1,p]$, and thus for counting the pattern's occurrences $occ = \mathsf{Last} - \mathsf{First} + 1$. Recall that $C[c]$ is the number of text characters which are alphabetically smaller than c, and that $\mathsf{Occ}(c,q)$ denotes the number of occurrences of character c in $T^{bwt}[1,q]$.

Figure 2 sketches the pseudocode of the counting operation that works in p phases, numbered from p to 1. The i-th phase preserves the following invariant: *The parameter* First *points to the first row of the BWT matrix* $\mathcal{M}_T$ *prefixed by* $P[i,p]$, *and the parameter* Last *points to the last row of* $\mathcal{M}_T$ *prefixed by* $P[i,p]$. After the final phase, P prefixes the rows between First and Last and thus, according to the properties of matrix $\mathcal{M}_T$ (see Section 2.2), we have $occ = \mathsf{Last} - \mathsf{First} + 1$. It is easy to see that the running time of get_rows is dominated by the cost of the $2p$ computations of the values Occ( ).

Algorithm get_position(i)

1. $i' \leftarrow i$, $t \leftarrow 0$;
2. **while** row i' is not marked **do**
3. $\quad i' \leftarrow LF[i']$;
4. $\quad t \leftarrow t + 1$;
5. **return** $\mathsf{Pos}(i') + t$;

Fig. 3. Algorithm get_position for the computation of $\mathsf{Pos}(i)$.

Given the range ($\mathsf{First}, \mathsf{Last}$), we now consider the problem of retrieving the positions in T of these pattern occurrences. We notice that every row in $\mathcal{M}_T$ is prefixed by some suffix of T. For example, in Fig. 1 the fourth row of $\mathcal{M}_T$ is prefixed by the text suffix $T[5, 11] =$ `issippi`. Then, for $i = \mathsf{First}, \mathsf{First}+1, \ldots, \mathsf{Last}$ we use procedure get_position(i) to find the position in T of the suffix that prefixes the i-th row $\mathcal{M}_T[i]$. Such a position is denoted hereafter by $\mathsf{Pos}(i)$, and the pseudocode of get_position is given in Figure 3. The intuition underlying its functioning is simple. We scan backward the text T using the $LF(\cdot)$ mapping (see Section 2.2) until a *marked* position is met. If we mark one text position every $\Theta(\log^2 n/\log\log n)$, the `while` loop is executed $O(\log^2 n/\log\log n)$ times. Since the computation of $LF(i)$ can be done via at most $|\Sigma|$ computations of Occ(), we have that get_position takes $O(|\Sigma|\ (\log^2 n/\log\log n))$ time. Finally, we observe that marking one position every $\Theta(\log^2 n/\log\log n)$ takes $\Theta(n \log\log n/\log n)$ bits overall. Combining the observations on get_position with the ones for get_rows, we get [3]:

Theorem 1. *For any string $T[1, n]$ drawn from a constant-sized alphabet Σ, the FM-index counts the occurrences of any pattern $P[1, p]$ within T taking $O(p)$ time. The location of each pattern occurrence takes $O(|\Sigma|\ \log^2 n/\log\log n)$ time. The size of the FM-index is bounded by $5nH_k(T) + o(n)$ bits, for any $k \geq 0$.*

In order to retrieve the content of $T[l, r]$, we must first find the row in $\mathcal{M}_T$ that corresponds to r, and then issue $\ell = r - l + 1$ backward steps in T, using the $LF(\cdot)$ mapping. Starting at the lowest marked text position that follows r, we perform $O(\log^2 n/\log\log n)$ steps until reaching r. Then we perform ℓ additional LF-steps to collect the text characters. The resulting complexity is $O((\ell + \log^2 n/\log\log n)\ |\Sigma|)$.

We point out the existence [6] of a variant of the FM-index that achieves $O(p + occ)$ query time and uses $O(nH_k(T)\log^\epsilon n) + o(n)$ bits of storage. This data structure exploits the interplay between the Burrows-Wheeler compression algorithm and the `LZ78` algorithm [22]. Notice that this is first full-text index achieving $o(n \log n)$ bits of storage, possibly $o(n)$ on highly compressible texts, and *output sensitivity* in the query execution.

As we mentioned in the Introduction, the main drawback of the FM-index is that, hidden in the $o(n)$ term of the space bound, there are constants which depend exponentially on the alphabet size $|\Sigma|$. In Section 3 we describe a simple alternative representation of T^{bwt} which takes $nH_k(T) + O(\log|\Sigma| \frac{n \log\log n}{\log n})$ bits and allows the computation of $\mathsf{Occ}(c, q)$ and $T^{bwt}[i]$ in $O(\log|\Sigma|)$ time.

2.4 Compression Boosting

The concept of *compression boosting* has been recently introduced in [2, 7, 8] opening the door to a new approach to data compression. The key idea is that one can take an algorithm whose performance can be bounded in terms of the 0-th order entropy and obtain, via the booster, a new compressor whose performance can be bounded in terms of the k-th order entropy, *simultaneously for all* k. Putting it another way, one can take a compression algorithm that uses no context information at all and, via the boosting process, obtain an algorithm that automatically uses the "best possible" contexts.

To simplify the exposition, we now state a boosting theorem in a form which is slightly different from the version described in [2, 7]. However, the proof of Theorem 2 can be obtained by a straightforward modification of the proof of Theorem 4.1 in [7].

Theorem 2. *Let $\mathcal{A}$ be an algorithm which compresses any string s in less than $|s|H_0(s) + f(|s|)$ bits, where $f(\cdot)$ is a non decreasing concave function. Given $T[1, n]$ there is a $O(n)$ time procedure that computes a partition $s_1, s_2, \ldots, s_z$ of T^{bwt} such that, for any $k \geq 0$, we have*

$$\sum_{i=1}^{z} |\mathcal{A}(s_i)| \leq \sum_{i=1}^{z} (|s_i|H_0(s_i) + f(|s_i|)) \leq nH_k(T) + |\Sigma|^k f(n/|\Sigma|^k).$$

Proof. (Sketch). According to Theorem 4.1 in [7], the booster computes the partition that minimizes the function $\sum_{i=1}^{z} |s|H_0(s_i) + f(|s_i|)$. To determine the right side of the above inequality, we consider the partition $\hat{s}_1, \hat{s}_2, \ldots, \hat{s}_m$ induced by the contexts of length k in T. For such partition we have $m \leq |\Sigma|^k$ and $\sum_{i=1}^{m} |\hat{s}_i|H_0(\hat{s}_i) = nH_k(T)$. The hypothesis on f implies that $\sum_{i=1}^{m} f(|\hat{s}_i|) \leq |\Sigma|^k f(n/|\Sigma|^k)$ and the theorem follows. ∎

To understand the relevance of this result suppose that we want to compress $T[1, n]$ and that we wish to exploit the zero-th order compressor $\mathcal{A}$. Using the booster we can first compute the partition $s_1, s_2, \ldots, s_z$ of T^{bwt}, and then compress each s_i using $\mathcal{A}$. By the above theorem, the overall space occupancy would be bounded by $\sum_i |\mathcal{A}(s_i)| \leq nH_k(T) + |\Sigma|^k f(n/|\Sigma|^k)$. Note that the process is reversible, because the decompression of each s_i retrieves T^{bwt}, and from T^{bwt} we can retrieve T using the inverse BWT. Summing up, the booster allows us to compress T up to its k-th order entropy using only the zero-th order compressor $\mathcal{A}$. Note that the parameter k is neither known to $\mathcal{A}$ nor to the booster, it comes into play only in the space complexity analysis. Additionally, the space bound in Theorem 2 holds *simultaneously* for all $k \geq 0$. The only information that is required by the booster is the function $f(n)$ such that $|s|H_0(s) + f(|s|)$ is an upper bound on the size of the output produced by $\mathcal{A}$ on input s.

2.5 The Wavelet Tree

Given a binary sequence $S[1,m]$ and $b \in \{0,1\}$, consider the following operations: $\mathsf{Rank}_b(S,i)$ computes the number of b's in $S[1,i]$, and $\mathsf{Select}_b(S,i)$ computes the position of the i-th b in $S[1,i]$. In [19] it has been proven the following:

Theorem 3. *Let $S[1,m]$ be a binary sequence containing t occurrences of the digit 1. There exists a data structure (called* FID*) that supports $\mathsf{Rank}_b(S,i)$ and $\mathsf{Select}_b(S,i)$ in constant time, and uses $\lceil \log \binom{m}{t} \rceil + O((m \log\log m)/\log m) = mH_0(S) + O((m \log\log m)/\log m)$ bits of space.*

If, instead of a binary sequence, we have a sequence $W[1,w]$ over an arbitrary alphabet Σ, a compressed and indexable representation of W is provided by the wavelet tree [11] which is a clever generalization of the FID data structure.

Theorem 4. *Let $W[1,w]$ denote a string over an arbitrary alphabet Σ. The wavelet tree built on W uses $wH_0(W) + O(\log|\Sigma|\,(w \log\log w)/\log w)$ bits of storage and supports in $O(\log|\Sigma|)$ time the following operations:*
- *given q, $1 \le q \le w$, the retrieval of the character $W[q]$;*
- *given $c \in \Sigma$ and q, $1 \le q \le w$, the computation of the number of occurrences $\mathsf{Occ}_W(c,q)$ of c in $W[1,q]$.*

To make the paper more self-contained we recall the basic ideas underlying the wavelet tree. Consider a balanced binary tree $\mathcal{T}$ whose leaves contain the characters of the alphabet Σ. $\mathcal{T}$ has depth $O(\log|\Sigma|)$. Each node u of $\mathcal{T}$ is associated with a string W_u that represents the subsequence of W containing *only* the characters that descend from u. The root is thus associated with the entire W. To save space and be alphabet-friendly, the wavelet tree does not store W_u but a binary image of it, denoted by B_u, that is computed as follows: $B_u[i] = 0$ if the character $W_u[i]$ descends from the left child of u, otherwise $B_u[i] = 1$. Assume now that every binary sequence B_u is implemented with the data structure of Theorem 3; then it is an exercise to derive the given space bounds and to implement $\mathsf{Occ}_W(c,q)$ and retrieve $W[q]$ in $O(\log|\Sigma|)$ time.

3 Alphabet-Friendly FM-Index

We now have all the tools we need in order to build a version of the FM-index that scales well with the alphabet size. The crucial observation is the following. To build the FM-index we need to solve two problems: a) to compress T^{bwt} up to $H_k(T)$, and b) to compute $\mathsf{Occ}(c,q)$ in time independent of n. We use the boosting technique to transform problem a) into the problem of compressing the strings $s_1, s_2, \ldots, s_z$ up to their zero-th order entropy, and we use the wavelet tree to create a compressed (up to H_0) and indexable representation of each s_i thus solving simultaneously problems a) and b). The details of the construction are given in Figure 4.

To compute $T^{bwt}[q]$, we first determine the substring s_y containing the q-th character of T^{bwt} by computing $y = \mathsf{Rank}_1(\mathcal{B},q)$. Then we exploit the wavelet

1. Use Theorem 2 to determine the optimal partition $s_1, s_2, \ldots, s_z$ of T^{bwt} with respect to $f(t) = (Kt \log |\Sigma| \log\log t)/\log t + (1 + |\Sigma|)\log n$, where K is such that $(Kt \log |\Sigma| \log\log t)/\log t$ is larger than the $O((t \log |\Sigma| \log\log t)/\log t)$ term in Theorem 4.
2. Build a binary string $\mathcal{B}$ that keeps track of the starting positions in T^{bwt} of the s_i's. The entries of $\mathcal{B}$ are all zeroes except for the bits at positions $\sum_{j=1}^{i} |s_j|$ for $i = 1, \ldots, z$ which are set to 1. Construct the data structure of Theorem 3 over the binary string $\mathcal{B}$.
3. For each string s_i, $i = 1, \ldots, z$ build:
   (a) the array $\mathcal{C}_i[1, |\Sigma|]$ such that $\mathcal{C}_i[c]$ stores the occurrences of character c within $s_1 s_2 \cdots s_{i-1}$;
   (b) the wavelet tree $\mathcal{T}_i$.

Fig. 4. Construction of an alphabet-friendly FM-index.

tree $\mathcal{T}_y$ to determine $T^{bwt}[q]$. By Theorem 3 the former step takes $O(1)$ time, and by Theorem 4 the latter step takes $O(\log |\Sigma|)$ time.

To compute $\mathsf{Occ}(c, q)$, we initially determine the substring s_y where the row q occurs, $y = \mathsf{Rank}_1(\mathcal{B}, q)$. Then we exploit the wavelet tree $\mathcal{T}_y$ and the array $\mathcal{C}_y[c]$ to compute $\mathsf{Occ}(c, q) = \mathsf{Occ}_{s_y}(c, q') + \mathcal{C}_y[c]$, where $q' = q - \sum_{j=1}^{y-1} |s_j|$. Again, by Theorems 3 and 4 this computation takes overall $O(\log |\Sigma|)$ time.

Combining these bounds with the results stated in Section 2.3, we obtain that the alphabet-friendly FM-index takes $O(p \log |\Sigma|)$ time to count the occurrences of a pattern $P[1, p]$ and $O(\log |\Sigma| (\log^2 n / \log\log n))$ time to retrieve the position of each occurrence.

Concerning the space occupancy we observe that by Theorem 3, the storage of $\mathcal{B}$ takes $\lceil \log \binom{n}{z} \rceil + O((n \log\log n)/\log n)$ bits. Each array $\mathcal{C}_i$ takes $O(|\Sigma| \log n)$ bits, and each wavelet tree $\mathcal{T}_i$ occupies $|s_i| H_0(s_i) + O\Big(|s_i| \frac{\log |\Sigma| \log\log |s_i|}{\log |s_i|}\Big)$ bits (Theorem 4). Since $\log \binom{n}{z} \le z \log n$, the total occupancy is bounded by

$$\sum_{i=1}^{z} \Big(|s_i| H_0(s_i) + K |s_i| \frac{\log |\Sigma| \log\log |s_i|}{\log |s_i|} + (1 + |\Sigma|) \log n \Big) + O((n \log\log n)/\log n) \, .$$

Function $f(t)$ defined at Step 1 of Figure 4 was built to match exactly the overhead space bound we get for each partition, so the partitioning was optimally built for that overhead. Hence we can apply Theorem 2 to get that the above summation is bounded by

$$nH_k(T) + O\Big(n \frac{\log |\Sigma| \log\log n}{\log(n/|\Sigma|^k)} \Big) + O\big(|\Sigma|^{k+1} \log n\big) \, . \tag{2}$$

We are interested in bounding the space occupancy in terms of H_k only for $k \le \alpha \log_{|\Sigma|} n$ for some $\alpha < 1$. In this case we have $|\Sigma|^k \le n^\alpha$ and (2) becomes

$$nH_k(T) + O(\log |\Sigma| (n \log\log n)/\log n) \, . \tag{3}$$

We achieve the following result[1]:

Theorem 5. *The data structure described in Figure 4 indexes a string* $T[1,n]$ *over an arbitrary alphabet* $|\Sigma|$*, using a storage bounded by*

$$nH_k(T) + O(\log|\Sigma|(n\log\log n)/\log n)$$

bits for any $k \leq \alpha \log_{|\Sigma|} n$ *and* $0 < \alpha < 1$*. We can count the number of occurrences of a pattern* $P[1,p]$ *in* T *in* $O(p\log|\Sigma|)$ *time, locate each occurrence in* $O(\log|\Sigma|(\log^2 n/\log\log n))$ *time, and display a text substring of length* ℓ *in* $O((\ell + \log^2 n/\log\log n)\log|\Sigma|)$ *time.*

It is natural to ask whether a more sophisticated data structure can achieve a $nH_k(T) + o(n)$ space bound without any restriction on the alphabet size or context length. The answer to this question is negative. To see this, consider the extreme case in which $|\Sigma| = n$, that is, the input string consists of a permutation of n distinct characters. In this case we have $H_k(T) = 0$ for $k \geq 1$. Since the representation of such string requires $\Theta(n\log n)$ bits, a self index of size $nH_k(T) + o(n)$ bits cannot exist.

Finally, we note that the wavelet tree alone, over the full BWT transformed text T^{bwt}, would be enough to obtain the time bounds we achieved. However, the resulting structure size would depend on $H_0(T)$ rather than $H_k(T)$. The partitioning of the text into areas is crucial to obtain the latter space bounds. A previous technique combining wavelet trees with text partitioning [15] takes each run of equal letters in T^{bwt} as an area. It requires $2n(H_k \log|\Sigma| + 1 + o(1))$ bits of space and counts pattern occurrences in the optimal $O(p)$ time. It would be interesting to retain the optimal space complexity obtained in this work and the optimal search time $O(p)$.

References

1. M. Burrows and D. Wheeler. A block sorting lossless data compression algorithm. Technical Report 124, Digital Equipment Corporation, 1994.
2. P. Ferragina, R. Giancarlo, G. Manzini, and M. Sciortino. Boosting textual compression in optimal linear time. Technical Report 240, Dipartimento di Matematica e Applicazioni, University of Palermo, Italy, 2004.
3. P. Ferragina and G. Manzini. Opportunistic data structures with applications. In *IEEE Symposium on Foundations of Computer Science (FOCS '00)*, pages 390–398, 2000.
4. P. Ferragina and G. Manzini. An experimental study of a compressed index. *Information Sciences: special issue on "Dictionary Based Compression"*, 135:13–28, 2001.
5. P. Ferragina and G. Manzini. An experimental study of an opportunistic index. In *ACM-SIAM Symposium on Discrete Algorithms (SODA '01)*, pages 269–278, 2001.

[1] If we mark one text position every $\log^{1+\epsilon} n$, the location of each occurrence would take $O(\log|\Sigma|\log^{1+\epsilon} n)$ time and additional $O(n/\log^{\epsilon} n)$ bits of storage.

6. P. Ferragina and G. Manzini. On compressing and indexing data. Technical Report TR-02-01, Dipartimento di Informatica, University of Pisa, Italy, 2002.
7. P. Ferragina and G. Manzini. Compression boosting in optimal linear time using the Burrows-Wheeler transform. In *ACM-SIAM Symposium on Discrete Algorithms (SODA '04)*, 2004.
8. R. Giancarlo and M. Sciortino. Optimal partitions of strings: A new class of Burrows-Wheeler compression algorithms. In *Combinatorial Pattern Matching Conference (CPM '03)*, pages 129–143, 2003.
9. G. H. Gonnet, R. A. Baeza-Yates, and T. Snider. New indices for text: PAT trees and PAT arrays. In B. Frakes and R. A. Baeza-Yates and, editors, *Information Retrieval: Data Structures and Algorithms*, chapter 5, pages 66–82. Prentice-Hall, 1992.
10. Sz. Grabowski, V. Mäkinen, and G. Navarro. First Huffman, then Burrows-Wheeler: an alphabet-independent FM-index. In *Symposium on String Processing and Information Retrieval (SPIRE 2004)*, 2004. Appears in this same volume.
11. R. Grossi, A. Gupta, and J. Vitter. High-order entropy-compressed text indexes. In *ACM-SIAM Symposium on Discrete Algorithms (SODA '03)*, pages 841–850, 2003.
12. R. Grossi, A. Gupta, and J. Vitter. When indexing equals compression: Experiments on compressing suffix arrays and applications. In *ACM-SIAM Symp. on Discrete Algorithms (SODA '04)*, 2004.
13. R. Grossi and J. Vitter. Compressed suffix arrays and suffix trees with applications to text indexing and string matching. In *ACM Symposium on Theory of Computing (STOC '00)*, pages 397–406, 2000.
14. J. Healy, E.E. Thomas, J.T. Schwartz, and M. Wigler. Annotating large genomes with exact word matches. *Genome Research*, 13:2306–2315, 2003.
15. V. Mäkinen and G. Navarro. New search algorithms and time/space tradeoffs for succinct suffix arrays. Technical Report C-2004-20, University of Helsinki, Finland, 2004.
16. U. Manber and G. Myers. Suffix arrays: a new method for on-line string searches. *SIAM Journal on Computing*, 22(5):935–948, 1993.
17. G. Manzini. An analysis of the Burrows-Wheeler transform. *Journal of the ACM*, 48(3):407–430, 2001.
18. G. Navarro. Indexing text using the Ziv-Lempel trie. *Journal of Discrete Algorithms*, 2(1):87–114, 2004.
19. R. Raman, V. Raman, and S.Srinivasa Rao. Succinct indexable dictionaries with applications to encoding k-ary trees and multisets. In *ACM-SIAM Symposium on Discrete Algorithms (SODA '02)*, pages 233–242, 2002.
20. K. Sadakane. Succinct representations of LCP information and improvements in the compressed suffix arrays. In *ACM-SIAM Symposium on Discrete Algorithms (SODA '02)*, pages 225–232, 2002.
21. K. Sadakane and T. Shibuya. Indexing huge genome sequences for solving various problems. *Genome Informatics*, 12:175–183, 2001.
22. J. Ziv and A. Lempel. Compression of individual sequences via variable length coding. *IEEE Transaction on Information Theory*, 24:530–536, 1978.

Concurrency Control and I/O-Optimality in Bulk Insertion

Kerttu Pollari-Malmi and Eljas Soisalon-Soininen

Department of Computer Science and Engineering
Helsinki University of Technology, P.O.Box 5400, FIN-02015 HUT, Finland
{kerttu,ess}@cs.hut.fi

Abstract. In a bulk update of a search tree a set of individual updates (insertions or deletions) is brought into the tree as a single transaction. In this paper, we present a bulk-insertion algorithm for the class of (a, b)-trees (including B^+-trees). The keys of the bulk to be inserted are divided into subsets, each of which contains keys with the same insertion place. From each of these sets, together with the keys already in the insertion place, an (a, b)-tree is constructed and substituted for the insertion place. The algorithm performs the rebalancing task in a novel manner minimizing the number of disk seeks required. The algorithm is designed to work in a concurrent environment where concurrent single-key actions can be present.

1 Introduction

Bulk insertion is an important index operation, for example in document databases and data warehousing. Document databases usually apply indices containing words and their occurrence information. When a new document is inserted into the database, a bulk insertion containing words in this document will be performed. Experiments of a commercial system designed for a newspaper house in Finland [15] have shown that a bulk insertion can be up to two orders of magnitude faster than the same insertions individually performed.

Additions to large data warehouses may number in the hundreds of thousands or even in the millions per day, and thus indices that require a disk operation per insertion are not acceptable. As a solution, a new B-tree like structure for indexing huge warehouses with frequent insertions is presented in [8]. This structure is similar to the buffer tree structure of [1, 2]; the essential feature is that one advancing step in the tree structure always means a search phase step for a set of several insertions.

In this paper, we consider the case in which the bulk, i.e., the set of keys to be inserted, fits into the main memory. This assumption is reasonable in most applications. Only some extreme cases of frequent insertions into warehouses do not fulfil this requirement. We present a new bulk-insertion algorithm, in which the possibility of concurrent single-key operations are taken into account. The bulk insertion is performed by local operations that involve only a constant number of nodes at a time. This makes it possible to design efficient concurrency

A. Apostolico and M. Melucci (Eds.): SPIRE 2004, LNCS 3246, pp. 161–170, 2004.

control algorithms, because only a constant number of nodes need be latched at a time. Allowing concurrent searches is vital in document databases [15] and in www-search-engine applications.

The search trees to be considered are a class of multi-way trees, called (a, b)-trees [6, 12]. The class of (a, b)-trees is a generalization of B$^+$-trees: in an (a, b)-tree, $b \geq 2a - 1$, a and b denote the minimum and the maximum number of elements in a node. The trees considered are external, i.e., keys are stored in the leaves and internal nodes contain routing information.

For our model of I/O-complexity we assume that each node of the tree is stored in one disk page. We assume that the current path from the root to a leaf (or the path not yet reached a leaf but advancing towards a leaf) is always found in the main memory, but otherwise accessing a node requires one I/O-operation. Moreover, in our model we count writing (or reading) of several consecutive disk pages as one I/O-operation. This is justified whenever the number of consecutive pages is "reasonable" because the seek time has become a larger and larger factor in data transfer to/from disk [17]. In our paper this property of the model comes into use when a portion of the bulk goes into the same leaf, and this (usually a relatively small) part of the bulk will be written on disk.

2 General Bulk Insertion

In a *level-linked* (a, b)*-tree* [6, 12], $a \geq 2, b \geq 2a - 1$, all paths from the root to a leaf have the same length. The leaves contain at least a and at most b keys, and, similarly, the internal nodes have at least a and at most b children. The root of the tree is an exception and has at least 2 and at most b children. In leaves each key is coupled with a data record (or with a pointer to data). An internal node v with n children is of the form

$$(p_0)(r_1, p_1)(r_2, p_2) \dots (r_n, p_n)(r_{n+1}, p_{n+1}),$$

where for $i = 1, \dots, n$, p_i is the pointer to the ith child of v. This ith child is the root of the subtree that contains the keys in the interval $(r_i, r_{i+1}]$. Values r_i, $1 \leq i \leq n + 1$, in an internal node are called *routers*. We say that node v *covers* the interval $(r_1, r_{n+1}]$.

Router r_1 is smaller than any key in the subtree rooted at v, called the *lowvalue* of node v, denoted *lowvalue*(v), and router r_{n+1} is the largest possible key value in this subtree, called the *highvalue* and denoted *highvalue*(v). Pointer p_0 points to the node that precedes, and p_{n+1} points to the node that follows node v at the same level. If node v is the parent of a leaf l and pointer $p_i, i = 1, \dots, n$, in v points to l, then the *lowvalue* of leaf l is r_i and the *highvalue* is r_{i+1}.

The basic idea of our I/O-optimal bulk-insertion algorithm is that the keys of the bulk sorted in the main memory will efficiently be divided into subsets, each of which contains keys that have the same insertion place (which is a node in the leaf level). From each of these sets, called *simple bulks*, together with the keys already in the insertion place, an (a, b)-tree, called an *insertion tree*, is constructed and substituted for the insertion place. After this process, called *bulk insertion without rebalancing*, has been completed, the structure contains all keys of the bulk and can already be used as a search tree with logarithmic search time. In order to retain the (a, b)-tree properties the structure needs, of course, rebalancing.

Moreover, we aim at a solution where concurrency is allowed and concurrency control is *efficient* in the sense that each process will latch only a constant number of nodes at a time and that a latch on a node is held only for a constant time. The concurrency control needed before rebalancing is simple latch coupling in the same way as for single-key updates (insertions or deletions). The efficient latch coupling in the search phase of an update (bulk or single) applies *might-write* latches, which exclude other updates but allow readers to apply their shared latches. *Shared* or *read* latches applied by readers exclude only the exclusive latches required on nodes to be written.

Given an (a, b)-tree T and a bulk with m keys, denoted $k_1, \ldots, k_m$, in ascending order, the bulk insertion into T without rebalancing works as follows.

Algorithm BI (Bulk Insertion)

Step 1. Set $i = 1$, and set $p =$ the root of T.

Step 2. Starting at node p search for the insertion place l_i of key k_i. Push each node in the path from node p to l_i onto stack S. In the search process apply latch coupling in the might-write mode. When leaf l_i is found, the latch on it will be upgraded into an exclusive latch. The latch on the parent of l_i will be released.

Step 3. Let k_{i+j} be the largest key in the input bulk that is less than or equal to the highvalue of l_i. From the keys $k_i, \ldots, k_{i+j}$ together with the keys already in l_i, an (a, b)-tree B_i is constructed and substituted for l_i in T. This will be done by storing the contents of the root of B_i into node l_i, so that no changes is needed in the parent of l_i. Release the latch on the node that is now the root of B_i.

Step 4. Set $i = i + j + 1$. If $i > m$, then continue to Step 5. Otherwise pop nodes from stack S until the popped node p covers the key k_i. If such a node is not found in the stack (this may occur if the root has been split after the bulk insertion started), set p as the new root. The nodes which are popped from the stack are latched in the shared mode, but latch-coupling is not used. Return to Step 2.

Step 5. Now all insertion positions have been replaced by the corresponding insertion trees. Rebalance the constructed tree by performing Algorithm SBR (given below) for each B_i in turn.

If concurrent single-key updates are allowed, it may happen that in Step 4 the algorithm must return even to the root although in the original tree only a few steps upward would have been enough in order to find the node from which to continue.

The algorithm composed of the first 4 steps of the above algorithm is called Algorithm BIWR (Bulk Insertion Without Rebalancing). In the following discussion of the complexity of Algorithm BIWR we assume that the concurrency is limited to concurrent searches.

If searching must be done in the standard way, that is, only pointers from parents to children are followed, it is clear that Algorithm BIWR is optimal as to nodes visited in T and thus in the number of nodes accessed. This is because each node in the paths from the root to the insertion positions must be accessed at least once, and this is exactly what the above algorithm does. If parent links together with level links are applied, a better performance can be obtained in some special cases, but from results in [3] it is straightforward to derive that no asymptotic improvement can be obtained.

The insertion tree B_i is constructed in the main memory, but I/O-operations are needed in writing it on disk as a part of the whole tree. For doing this only one disk seek is needed and in our model thus only one operation. We have:

Theorem 1. *Let T be an (a, b)-tree, and assume that a bulk of m keys is inserted into T by Algorithm BIWR (Bulk Insertion Without Rebalancing, the first four steps of Algorithm BI). Then the resulting tree (which has logarithmic depth but does not fulfil the (a, b)-balance conditions) contains exactly the keys that were originally in T or were members of the bulk. The I/O-complexity of Algorithm BIWR is*

$$\Theta(k + L) = \Theta(L),$$

where k denotes the number of insertion trees B_i constructed in Step 3 of the algorithm and L denotes the number of different nodes that appear in the paths from the root of the original tree T to the insertion places l_i.

3 Rebalancing

Our next task is to perform rebalancing. Our solution for rebalancing is designed such that concurrent searches and single-key updates are possible.

We assume first that we are given a situation in which the whole bulk to be inserted has the same insertion place l_1, and Algorithm BIWR has produced a new tree T, in which l_1 has been replaced by an insertion tree B_1 (Step 3 in Algorithm BIWR). Before we can start the rebalancing task we must have obtained a shared lock on the key interval $[k, k']$, where k and k', respectively, are the smallest and the largest key in B_1. This lock is requested in Step 3 in Algorithm BIWR before the replacement of l_1 by B_1 can take place. This guarantees that no updates that would affect B_1 could occur during rebalancing, provided that performing updates requires obtaining an exclusive lock on the key to be inserted or deleted, see e.g. [9]. (The locks are not the same as the latches; latches are for physical entities of a database, and locks for logical entities. Latches are short duration semaphores, and locks are usually held until the commit of the transaction involved.)

Now if B_1 contains one leaf only, we are done, and the lock on $[k, k']$ can be released. Otherwise, we perform the *simple bulk rebalancing* in the following way.

Algorithm SBR (Simple Bulk Rebalancing)

Step 1. Latch exclusively the parent of the root of B_1 and denote the latched node by p. Set $h = 1$.

Step 2. Split node p such that the left part contains all pointers to children that store keys smaller than the smallest key in B_1, and the right part all pointers to children that store keys larger than the largest key in B_1. Denote the nodes thus obtained by p_l and p_r. Observe that both p_l and p_r exist; in the extreme case node p_l contains only the lowvalue and the level link to the left and p_r only the highvalue and the level link to the right. In all cases p is set to p_l; that is, p_l is the node that remains latched, and $p = p_l$ does not point to the root of B_1 (or its ancestor) any more. Moreover, notice that neither p_l nor p_r can contain more than b elements, even though, when returning from Step 3, p could contain $b + 1$ elements. See Fig. 1 for illustration.

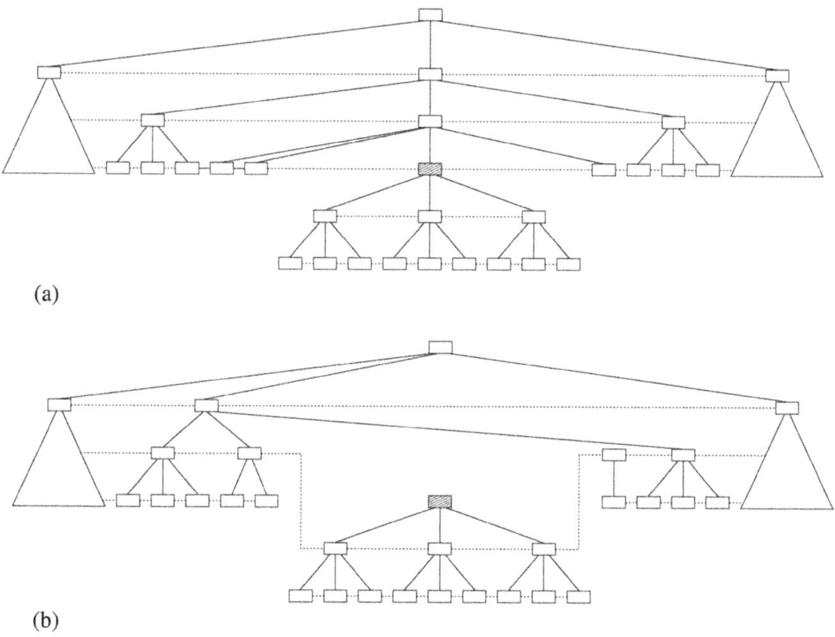

Fig. 1. Splitting the parent of the root of the insertion tree, $a = 2$ and $b = 4$. (a) Original tree. The root of the insertion tree is shaded. (b) Split tree with updated level links at height 1.

Exclusively latch p_r, and the leftmost and rightmost nodes, denoted q_l and q_r, respectively, at the height h in B_1. Then compress (by applying fusing or sharing) node p_l together with node q_l, node p_r together with q_r, and also adjust the level links appropriately. (The nodes in T and nodes in B_1 at height h are all linked together by level links and no violations against the (a, b)-tree property occur in these nodes.) Release all latches held.

Step 3. Set h = h + 1. At height h in T latch exclusively the node, denoted p, that has lowvalue smaller than the smallest key in B_1 and highvalue larger than the largest key in B_1. If in Step 2 node p_r, one level below, was not fused with q_r but remained (perhaps shortened because of sharing), add this node as a new child to p. For the moment, allow p grow one too large, if necessary. If h is smaller than the height of B_1, then return to Step 2.

Step 4. Now the insertion tree B_1 has been properly level-linked with the rest of the tree, with the exception of the root and the leaf level. As in Step 2, split node p appropriately into p_l and p_r such that the root of B_1 can be put between them. The nodes at the leaf level which thus far has been level-linked to the root of B_1 must now be level-linked with the leftmost and, respectively, the rightmost leaf node in B_1. For the operation, all changed nodes must be exclusively latched. At the end, all latches held are released.

Step 5. The whole insertion tree B_1 has now been correctly level-linked, but it might be that the root of B_1 and its right brother have no parent, that is, they can be reached only by level links and not by child links from their parents. (See Fig. 2.) Thus rebalancing is still needed above the root of B_1, and the need of splits may propagate up to the root of the whole tree. In a concurrent environment this remaining rebalancing can be done exactly as for single inserts in $\mathrm{B}^{\mathrm{link}}$-trees [16]. Figure 3 shows the final rebalanced tree.

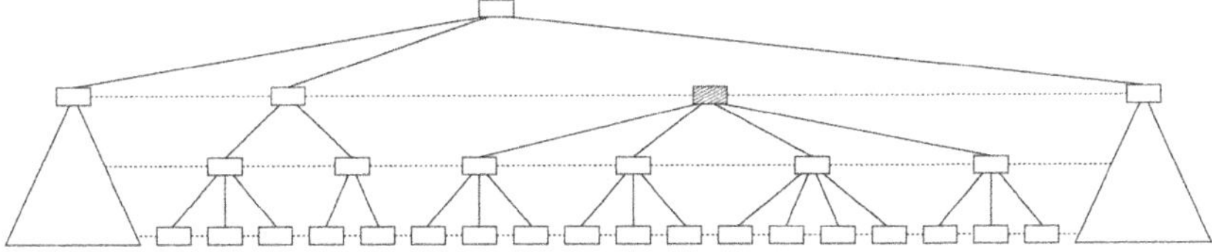

Fig. 2. Tree of Fig. 1 after the insertion tree has been correctly level-linked.

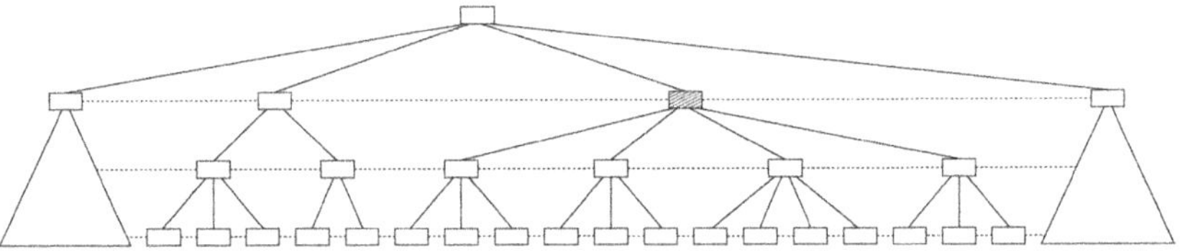

Fig. 3. Tree of Fig. 2 when bulk rebalancing has been finished.

It is important to note that, for rebalancing, we cannot simply cut the tree T starting from the insertion place up to the height of B_1, and then lift B_1 to its right position. Such an algorithm would need too much simultaneous latching in order to set the level links correctly. The level links are essential because they guarantee the correctness of concurrent searching at all times. The simpler solution to "merge" B_1 with T by cutting T at l_1, joining the left part with B_1, and joining the result with the right part [13] is not applicable in a concurrent environment, either.

First, for the correctness and complexity (Theorem 2–6), we consider Algorithm SBR in an environment, where only concurrent searches are allowed.

Notice that then node p as specified in Step 2 is directly obtained from the stack of nodes constructed in the search phase of Algorithm BI.

The following theorem is immediate. Notice that in Step 3 of Algorithm SBR compressing of nodes as described is always possible because the insertion tree B_1 is in balance. Compressing two nodes means, in the same way as in standard B-tree rebalancing, that two nodes are either made as one node (fusing) or their contents are redistributed (sharing) such that both nodes meet the (a, b)-tree conditions.

Theorem 2. *Let T be a tree yielded by Algorithm BIWR such that from the inserted bulk of size m only one insertion tree was constructed. Algorithm SBR (Simple Bulk Rebalancing) rebalances T, that is, yields an (a, b)-tree that contains exactly the keys originally in T. The worst case I/O-complexity of Algorithm SBR (when only concurrent searches are present) is $\Theta(\log m)$ (Steps 1–3), plus $\Theta(\log n)$ (Step 4), where n denotes the size of T.*

Notice that the worst case complexity $\Theta(\log n)$ of Step 5 comes from the fact that nodes above the root of B_1 may be full; this worst case may occur also for single insertions. Thus, and because it may be necessary to split h nodes, where h denotes the height of B_1, the above algorithm is asymptotically optimal.

Step 5 in Algorithm SBR can be considered as an elimination of an $b+1$- or $b+2$-node (node that contains $b+1$ or $b+2$ elements) from the tree. This is because the parent of the root of B_1 can have got one or two new children. But, as shown in [5], elimination of a $b+1$-node takes amortized constant time, provided that $b \geq 2a$. (By *amortized time* we mean the time of an operation averaged over a worst-case sequence of operations starting with an empty structure. See [12, 18].) The same holds, of course, for the elimination of a $b+2$-node. Thus Theorem 2 implies:

Theorem 3. *Let T be a tree yielded by Algorithm BIWR such that from the inserted bulk of size m only one insertion tree was constructed. Algorithm SBR (Simple Bulk Rebalancing) rebalances T, that is, yields an (a, b)-tree that contains exactly the keys originally in T. The amortized I/O-complexity of Algorithm SBR (when only concurrent searches are present) is $\Theta(\log m)$.*

The result of Theorem 3 requires that each B_i in Algorithm BI is constructed so that at most two nodes at each level of B_i contain exactly a or b keys or have exactly a or b children. This is possible since $a \geq 2$ and $b \geq 2a$, see [7].

Assume that a bulk insertion of m keys without rebalancing has been applied to an (a, b)-tree yielding a tree denoted by T. Assume that the bulk was divided into k insertion trees, denoted $B_1, B_2, \ldots, B_k$. Rebalancing T, that is, the final step of Algorithm BI, can now be performed by applying Algorithm SBR for $B_1, B_2, \ldots$, and B_k, in turn. The cost of rebalancing includes (i) the total cost of Steps 1–3 of Algorithm SBR for $B_1, \ldots, B_k$ and (ii) the total cost of rebalancing (Step 4) above node p_i that has become the parent of B_i, $i = 1, \ldots, k$. Part (i) has I/O-complexity $O(\Sigma_{i=1}^{k} \log m_i)$, where m_i denotes the size of B_i, and part (ii) has the obvious lower bound $\Omega(L)$, where L denotes the number of different nodes appearing in the paths from the root to the insertion places in the original tree. It is easy to see that $O(L + \Sigma_{i=1}^{k} \log m_i)$ bounds from above part (ii). Of those nodes that are full before the rebalancing starts only L can be split because of rebalancing. Rebalancing of one B_i cannot produce more than $O(\log m_i)$ new full nodes that may need be split by rebalancing a subsequent B_j. Thus the total number by splits and also the number of I/Os needed for the whole rebalancing task is $O(L + \Sigma_{i=1}^{k} \log m_i)$.

We have:

Theorem 4. *Assume that a bulk insertion without rebalancing has been applied to an (a, b)-tree, and assume that the bulk was divided into k insertion trees with sizes $m_1, m_2, \ldots, m_k$. Then the worst case I/O-complexity of rebalancing (the final step of Algorithm BI), provided that only concurrent searches are present, is*

$$\Theta(\Sigma_{i=1}^{k} \log m_i + L),$$

where L is number of different nodes in the paths from the root to the insertion places (roots of the insertion trees) before the rebalancing starts.

For the amortized complexity we have:

Theorem 5. *Assume that a bulk insertion without rebalancing has been applied to an (a, b)-tree, $b \geq 2a$, and assume that the bulk was divided into k insertion trees with sizes $m_1, m_2, \ldots, m_k$. Then the amortized I/O-complexity of rebalancing, provided that only concurrent searches are present, is*

$$\Theta(\Sigma_{i=1}^{k} \log m_i).$$

Theorems 1 and 4 imply:

Theorem 6. *The worst case I/O-complexity of a bulk insertion into an (a, b)-tree is*

$$\Theta(\Sigma_{i=1}^{k} \log m_i + L),$$

where m_i is the size of the ith simple bulk and L is the number of different nodes in the paths from the root to the insertion places.

Our concurrent algorithm is meant to be used together with key searches that do not change the structure and with single-key operations. The pure searches are the most important operations that must be allowed together with bulk insertion. This is certainly important for www search engines, and it was vital for the commercial text database system reported in [15]. For the correctness, the issues to be taken care of are that no search paths (for pure searches or the search phases of insertions or deletions) cannot get lost, and that the possible splits or compress operations performed by concurrent single-key actions do not cause any incorrectness.

Because a shared lock on the key interval of the insertion tree must have been obtained before rebalancing, no changes in the interval trees caused by concurrent processes can occur during the bulk insertion. Thus the only possibility for incorrectness (due to bulk insertion) is that a search path gets lost when a node above the insertion tree is split and the search would go through this node and end in a leaf of the insertion tree B_i, or in a leaf right to B_i, cf. Fig. 1 (b). But when this kind of a split occurs, the exclusive latches as defined in Step 3 of the algorithm prevents the search path losses. After Step 3 has been completed, all leaves of B_i, and all leaves to the right of B_i that have lost their parent path to the root (in Fig. 1 (b) one leaf to the right of the insertion tree) are again reachable because of the level links set. The possible splits or compress operations of concurrent single-key actions imply the possibility that the nodes of the search path to the insertion place pushed on stack are not always parents of the split nodes. Thus the parent must be searched, see Step 3, by a left-to-right traverse starting from the node that is popped from the stack. (Cf. [16].)

The pure searches and the search phases of single-key actions and the search phase of the bulk insertion apply latch coupling in the appropriate mode, and all changes in nodes are made under an exclusive latch, which prevents all other possible path losses.

We have:

Theorem 7. *The concurrent algorithm BI and standard concurrent searches and concurrent single-key actions all applied to the same level-linked (a, b)-tree run correctly with each other.*

4 Conclusion

We have presented an I/O-optimal bulk insertion algorithm for (a, b)-trees, a general class of search trees that include B-trees. Some ideas of the new algorithm stem from earlier papers on bulk updates [11,15]. The new aspect in the present paper is that we couple efficient concurrency control with an I/O-optimal algorithm, and the I/O-complexity is carefully analyzed in both worst case and amortized sense.

The same amortized time bound has been proved for relaxed (a, b)-trees in [10], but with linear worst case time. In addition, although [10] gives operations to locally decrease imbalance in certain nodes, it does not give any deterministic algorithm to rebalance the whole tree after group insertion. Algorithms based on relaxed balancing also have the problem that they introduce new almost empty nodes at intermediate stages.

The idea of performing bulk insertion by inserting small trees [14] is independently presented for R-trees in [4]. In [4] concurrency control is not discussed, whereas our main contribution is to introduce efficient concurrency control into I/O-optimal bulk insertion.

Our method of bulk rebalancing can also be applied for buffer trees [1,2]. Buffer trees are a good choice for efficient bulk insertion in the case in which the bulk is large and does not fit into the main memory.

References

1. L.Arge. The buffer tree: a technique for designing batched external data structures. *Algorithmica* **37** (2003), 1–24.

2. L.Arge, K.H.Hinrichs, J.Vahrenhold, and J.S.Vitter. Efficient bulk operations on dynamic R-trees. *Algorithmica* **33** (2002), 104–128.
3. M.R.Brown and R.E.Tarjan. Design and analysis of a data structure for representing sorted lists. *SIAM Journal of Computing* **9** (1980), 594–614.
4. L.Chen, R.Choubey, and E.A.Rundensteiner. Merging R-trees: Efficient strategies for local bulk insertion. *GeoInformatica* **6** (2002), 7–34.
5. K.Hoffmann, K.Mehlhorn, P.Rosenstiehl, and R.E.Tarjan: Sorting Jordan sequences in linear time using level-linked search trees. *Information and Control* **68** (1986), 170–184.
6. S.Huddleston and K.Mehlhorn. A new data structure for representing sorted lists. *Acta Informatica* **17** (1982), 157–184.
7. L.Jacobsen, K.S.Larsen, and M.N.Nielsen. On the existence and construction of non-extreme (a,b)-trees. *Information Processing Letters* **84** (2002), 69–73.
8. C.Jermaine, A.Datta, and E.Omiecinski. A novel index supporting high volume data warehouse insertion. In: *Proceedings of the 25th International Conference on Very Large Databases.* Morgan Kaufmann Publishers, 1999, pp. 235–246.
9. M.Kornacker, C.Mohan, and J.M.Hellerstein. Concurrency and recovery in generalized search trees. In: *Proceedings of the 1997 SIGMOD Conference, SIGMOD Record* **26**. ACM Press 1997, pp. 62–72.
10. K.S.Larsen. Relaxed multi-way trees with group updates. *Journal of Computer and System Sciences* **66** (2003), 657–670.
11. L.Malmi and E.Soisalon-Soininen. Group updates for relaxed height-balanced trees. In: *Proceedings of the 18th ACM SIGMOD-SIGACT-SIGART Symposium on Principles of Database Systems.* ACM Press, 1999, pp. 358–367.
12. K.Mehlhorn. *Data Structures and Algorithms, Vol. 1: Sorting and Searching,* Springer-Verlag, 1984.
13. A.Moffat, O.Petersson, and N.C.Wormald. A tree-based mergesort. *Acta Informatica* **35** (1998), 775–793.
14. K.Pollari-Malmi. Batch updates and concurrency control in B-trees. Ph.D.Thesis, Helsinki University of Technology, Department of Computer Science and Engineering, Report A38/02, 2002.
15. K.Pollari-Malmi, E.Soisalon-Soininen, and T.Ylönen. Concurrency control in B-trees with batch updates. *IEEE Transactions on Knowledge and Data Engineering* **8** (1996), 975–984.
16. Y.Sagiv. Concurrent operations on B*-trees with overtaking. *Journal of Computer and System Sciences* **33** (1986), 275–296.
17. Y.Tao and D.Papadias. Adaptive index structures. In: *Proceedings of the 28th Conference on Very Large Data Bases.* Morgan Kaufmann Publishers, 2002, pp. 418–429.
18. R.E.Tarjan. Amortized computational complexity. *SIAM Journal on Algebraic and Discrete Methods* **6** (1985), 306–318.

Processing Conjunctive and Phrase Queries with the Set-Based Model*

Bruno Pôssas, Nivio Ziviani, Berthier Ribeiro-Neto, and Wagner Meira Jr.

Departamento de Ciência da Computação
Universidade Federal de Minas Gerais
30161-970 Belo Horizonte-MG, Brazil
{bavep,nivio,berthier,meira}@dcc.ufmg.br

Abstract. The objective of this paper is to present an extension to the set-based model (SBM), which is an effective technique for computing term weights based on co-occurrence patterns, for processing conjunctive and phrase queries. The intuition that semantically related term occurrences often occur closer to each other is taken into consideration. The novelty is that all known approaches that account for co-occurrence patterns was initially designed for processing disjunctive (OR) queries, and our extension provides a simple, effective and efficient way to process conjunctive (AND) and phrase queries. This technique is time efficient and yet yields nice improvements in retrieval effectiveness. Experimental results show that our extension improves the average precision of the answer set for all collection evaluated, keeping computational cost small. For the TReC-8 collection, our extension led to a gain, relative to the standard vector space model, of 23.32% and 18.98% in average precision curves for conjunctive and phrase queries, respectively.

1 Introduction

Users of the World Wide Web are not only confronted by an immense overabundance of information, but also by a plethora of tools for searching for the web pages that suit their information needs. Web search engines differ widely in interface, features, coverage of the web, ranking methods, delivery of advertising, and more. Different search engines and portals have different (default) semantics of handling a multi-word query. Although, all major search engines, such as Altavista, Google, Yahoo, Teoma, uses the AND semantics, i.e. conjunctive queries, (it is mandatory for all the query words to appear in a document for it to be considered).

In this paper we propose a extension to the set-based model [1, 2] to process conjunctive and phrase queries. The set-based model uses a term-weighting scheme based on association rules theory [3]. Association rules are interesting because they provide all the elements of the $tf \times idf$ scheme in an algorithmically efficient and parameterized approach. Also, they naturally provide for quantification of representative term co-occurrence patterns, something that is not present in the $tf \times idf$ scheme.

* This work was supported in part by the GERINDO project-grant MCT/CNPq/CT-INFO 552.087/02-5 and by CNPq grant 520.916/94-8 (Nivio Ziviani).

A. Apostolico and M. Melucci (Eds.): SPIRE 2004, LNCS 3246, pp. 171–182, 2004.

We evaluated and validated our extension of the set-based model (SBM) for processing conjunctive and phrase queries through experimentation using two reference collections. Our evaluation is based on a comparison to the standard vector space model (VSM) adapted to handle the these type of queries. Our experimental results show that the SBM yields higher retrieval performance, which is superior for all query types and collections considered. For the TReC-8 collection [4], containing 2 gigabytes of size and approximately 530,000 documents, the SBM yields, respectively, an average precision that are 23.32% and 18.98% higher than the VSM for conjunctive and phrase queries. The set-based model is also competitive in terms of computing performance. For the WBR99 collection, containing 16 gigabytes of size and approximately 6,000,000 web pages, using a log with 100,000 queries, the increase in the average response time is, respectively, 6.21% and 14.67% for conjunctive and phrase queries.

The paper is organized as follows. The next section describes the representation of co-occurrence patterns based on a variant of association rules. A review of the set-based model is presented in the Section 3. Section 4 presents our extension of the set-based model for processing conjunctive and phrase queries. In section 5 we describe the reference collections and the experimental results comparing the VSM and the SBM for processing disjunctive and phrase queries. Related works are discussed in Section 6. Finally, we present some conclusions and future work in Section 7.

2 Preliminaries

In this section we introduce the concept of termsets as a basis for computing term weights. In the set-based model a document is described by a set of termsets, where termset is simply an ordered set of terms extracted from the document itself.

Let $T = \{\mathrm{k}_1, \mathrm{k}_2, ..., \mathrm{k}_t\}$ be the vocabulary of a collection of documents D, that is, the set of t unique terms that may appear in a document from D. There is a total ordering among the vocabulary terms, which is based on the lexicographical order of terms, so that $\mathrm{k}_i < \mathrm{k}_{i+1}$, for $1 \leq i \leq t-1$.

Definition 1. *An n-termset s is an ordered set of n unique terms, such that $s \subseteq T$. Notice that the order among terms in s follows the aforementioned total ordering.*

Let $S = \{\mathrm{s}_1, \mathrm{s}_2, ..., \mathrm{s}_{2^t}\}$ be the vocabulary-set of a collection of documents D, that is, the set of 2^t unique termsets that may appear in a document from D. Each document j from D is characterized by a vector in the space of the termsets. With each termset s_i, $1 \leq i \leq 2^t$, we associate an inverted list ls_i composed of identifiers of the documents containing that termset. We also define the frequency ds_i of a termset s_i as the number of occurrences of s_i in D, that is, the number of documents where $s_i \subseteq d_j$ and $d_j \in D$, $1 \leq j \leq N$. The frequency ds_i of a termset s_i is the length of its associated inverted list ($| \, ls_i \, |$).

Definition 2. *A termset s_i is a frequent termset if its frequency ds_i is greater than or equal to a given threshold, which is known as support in the scope of association rules [3], and referred as minimal frequency in this work. As presented in the original Apriori algorithm [5], an n-termset is frequent if and only if all of its $n-1$-termsets are also frequent.*

The proximity information is used as a pruning strategy to find only the termsets occurrences bounded by an specified proximity threshold (referred as minimal proximity), conforming with the assumption that semantically related term occurrences often occur closer to each other.

Definition 3. *A* <u>*closed termset*</u> cs_i *is a frequent termset that is the largest termset among the termsets that are subsets of* cs_i *and occur in the same set of documents. That is, given a set* $\mathcal{D} \subseteq D$ *of documents and the set* $\mathcal{S}_{\mathcal{D}} \subseteq S$ *of termsets that occur in all documents from* $\mathcal{D}$ *and only in these, a closed termset* cs_i *satisfies the property that* $\nexists s_j \in \mathcal{S}_{\mathcal{D}} | cs_j \subset s_j$.

For sake of processing disjunctive queries (OR), closed termsets are interesting because they represent a reduction on the computational complexity and on the amount of data that has to be analyzed, without loosing information, since all frequent termsets in a closure are represented by the respective closed termset [1, 2].

Definition 4. *A* <u>*maximal termset*</u> ms_i *is a frequent termset that is not a subset of any other frequent termset. That is, given the set* $\mathcal{S}_{\mathcal{D}} \subseteq S$ *of frequent termsets that occur in all documents from* $\mathcal{D}$*, a maximal termset* ms_i *satisfies the property that* $\nexists s_j \in \mathcal{S}_{\mathcal{D}} | ms_i \subset s_j$.

Let FT be the set of all frequent termsets, and CFT be the set of all closed termsets and MFT be the set of all maximal termsets. It is straightforward to see that the following relationship holds: $MFT \subseteq CFT \subseteq CT$. The set MFT is orders of magnitude smaller than the set CFT, which itself is orders of magnitude smaller than the set FT. It is proven that the set of maximal termsets associated with a document collection are the minimum amount of information necessary to derive all frequent termsets associated with that collection [6].

Generating maximal termsets is a problem very similar to mining association rules and the algorithms employed for the latter is our starting point [3]. Our approach is based on an efficient algorithm for association rule mining, called GENMAX [7], which has been adapted to handle terms and documents instead of items and transactions, respectively. GENMAX uses backtracking search to enumerate all MFT.

3 Review of the Set-Based Model (SBM)

In the set-based model, a document is described by a set of termsets, extracted from the document itself. With each termset we associate a pair of weights representing (a) its importance in each document and (b) its importance in the whole document collection. In a similar way, a query is described by a set of termsets with a weight representing the importance of each termset in the query. The algebraic representation of the set of termsets for both documents and queries correspond to vectors in a 2^t-dimensional Euclidean space, where t is equal to the number of unique index terms in the document collection.

3.1 Termset Weights

Term weights can be calculated in many different ways [8, 9]. The best known term weighting schemes use weights that are function of (i) $tf_{i,j}$, the number of times that an index term i occurs in a document j and (ii) df_i, the number of documents that an index term i occurs in the whole document collection. Such term-weighting strategy is called $tf \times idf$ schemes. The expression for idf_i represents the importance of term i in the collection, it assigns a high weight to terms which are encountered in a small number of documents in the collection, supposing that rare terms have high discriminating value.

In the set-based model, the association rules scheme naturally provides for quantification of representative patterns of term co-occurrences, something that is not present in the $tf \times idf$ approach. To determine the weights associated with the termsets, we also use the number of occurrences of a termset in a document, in a query, and in the whole collection. Formally, the weight of a termset i in a document j is defined as:

$$w_{i,j} = (1 + \log sf_{i,j}) \times ids_i = (1 + \log sf_{i,j}) \times \log\left(1 + \frac{N}{ds_i}\right) \tag{1}$$

where N is the number of documents in the collection, $sf_{i,j}$ is the number of occurrences of the termset i in document d_j, and ids_i is the inverted frequency of occurrence of the termset s_i in the collection. $sf_{i,j}$ generalizes $tf_{i,j}$ in the sense that it counts the number of times that the termset s_i appears in document d_j. The component ids_i also carries the same semantics of idf_i, but accounting for the cardinality of the termsets as follows. High-order termsets usually have low frequency, resulting in large inverted frequencies. Thus, this strategy assigns large weights to termsets that appear in small number of documents, that is, rare termsets result in greater weights.

3.2 Similarity Calculation

Since documents and queries are represented as vectors, we assign a similarity measure to every document containing any of the query termsets, defined as the normalized scalar product between the set of document vectors $\boldsymbol{d_j}$, $1 \leq j \leq N$, and the query vector $\boldsymbol{q}$. This approach its equivalent to the cosine of the angle between these two vectors. The similarity between a document d_j and a query q is defined as:

$$sim(q, d_j) = \frac{\boldsymbol{d_j} \bullet \boldsymbol{q}}{|\boldsymbol{d_j}| \times |\boldsymbol{q}|} = \frac{\sum_{s \in S_q} w_{s,j} \times w_{s,q}}{|\boldsymbol{d_j}| \times |\boldsymbol{q}|}, \tag{2}$$

where $w_{s,j}$ is the weight associated with the termset s in document d_j, $w_{s,q}$ is the weight associated with the termset s in query q, S_q is the set of all termsets such that all $s \subseteq q$. We observe that the normalization (i.e., the factors in the denominator) was not expanded, as usual. The normalization is done using only the 1-termsets that compose the query and document vectors. This is important to reduce computational costs because computing the norm of a document using termsets might be prohibitively costly.

3.3 Searching Algorithm

The steps performed by the set-based model to the calculation of the similarity metrics are equivalent to the standard vector space model. Figure 1 presents the searching algorithm. First we create the data structures (line 4) that are used for calculating the document similarities A among all termsets S_q of a document d_j. Then, for each query term, we retrieve its inverted list, and determine the first frequent termsets, i.e., the frequent termsets of size equal to 1, applying the minimal frequency threshold mf (lines 5 to 10). The next step is the enumeration of all termsets based on the 1-termsets, filtered by the minimal frequency and proximity threshold (line 11). After enumerating all termsets, we evaluated its inverted lists, calculating the partial similarity of a termset $s_i \in S_q$ to a document d_j (lines 12 to 17). After evaluating termsets, we normalize the document similarities A by dividing each document similarity $A_j \in A$ by the norm of the document d_j (line 18). The final step is to select the k largest similarities and return the corresponding documents (line 19).

```
SBM(Q, mf, mp, k)
     Q : a set of query terms
     mf : minimum frequency threshold
     mp : minimum proximity threshold
     k : number of documents to be returned
1.   Let A be a set of accumulators
2.   Let C_q be a set of 1-termsets
3.   Let S_q be a set of termsets
4.   A = ∅,  S = ∅
5.   for each query term t ∈ Q do begin
6.       if df_t ≥ mf then begin
7.           Obtain the 1-termset s_t from term t
8.           C_q = C_q ∪ {s_t}
9.       end
10.  end
11.  S_q = Termsets_Gen(C_q, mf, mp)
12.  for each termset s_i ∈ S_q do begin
13.      for each [d_j, sf_{i,j}] in ls_i do begin
14.          if A_j ∉ A then A = A ∪ {A_j}
15.          A_j = A_j + w_{s_i,j} × w_{s_i,q}, from Eq. (1).
16.      end
17.  end
18.  for each accumulator A_j ∈ A do A_j = A_j ÷ |d_j|
19.  determine the k largest A_j ∈ A and return the corresponding documents
20.  end
```

Fig. 1. The set-based model searching algorithm

3.4 Computational Complexity

The complexity of the standard vector space model and the set-based model is linear with respect to the number of documents in the collection. Formally, the upper bound on the number of operations performed for satisfying a query in the vector space model is $O(|q| \times N)$, where $|q|$ is the number of terms in the query and N is the number of documents in the collection. The worst case scenario for the vector space model is a query comprising the whole vocabulary t ($|q| = t$), which results in a merge of all inverted lists in the collection. The computational complexity for set-based model is $O(cN)$, where c is the number of termsets, a value that is $O(2^{|q|})$, where $|q|$ is the number of terms in the query. These are worst case measures and the average measures for the constants involved are much smaller [1, 2].

4 Modeling Conjunctive and Phrase Queries in SBM

In this section we show how to model conjunctive and phrase queries using the framework provided by the original set-based model (see Section 3). Our approach does not modify its algebraic representation, and the changes to the original model are minimal.

4.1 Conjunctive Queries

The main modification of set-based model for the conjunctive and phrase query processing is related to the enumeration of termsets. In the original version of the set-based model, the enumeration algorithm determines all closed termsets for a given user query, and the minimal frequency and proximity thresholds. Each mined closed termset represents a valid co-occurrence pattern in the space of documents defined by the terms of the query. For disjunctive queries, each one of these patterns contributes for the similarity between a document and a query. The conjunctive query processing requires that only the co-occurrence pattern defined for the query can be found, i.e., the occurrence of all query terms in a given document must be valid. If so, this document can be added to the response set.

A maximal termset corresponds to a frequent termset that is not a subset of any other frequent termset (see definition 4). Based on this definition, we can extend the original set-based model enumerating the set of maximal termsets for a given user query instead of the set of closed termsets. To verify if the enumerated set is valid, we check the following conditions. First, the mined set of maximal termsets must be composed by an unique element. Second, this element must have all query terms. If all these conditions are true, we can evaluate the inverted list of maximal termset found, calculating its partial similarity to each document d_j (lines 12 to 17 of the algorithm of Figure 1). The final steps are the normalization of document similarities and the selection of the k largest similarities, returning the corresponding documents.

The proximity information is used as a pruning strategy to find only the maximal termset occurrences bounded by the minimal proximity threshold, conforming with the assumption that semantically related term occurrences often occur closer to each other. This pruning strategy is incorporated in the maximal termsets enumeration algorithm.

4.2 Phrase Queries

Search engines are used to find data in response to ad hoc queries. However, a significant fraction of the queries include phrases, where the user has indicated that some of the query terms must be adjacent, typically by enclosing them in quotation marks. Phrases have the advantage of being unambiguous concept markers and are therefore viewed as a valuable addition to ranked queries.

A standard way to evaluate phrase queries is to use an inverted index, in which for each index term there is a list of postings, and each posting includes a document identifier, an in-document frequency, and a list of ordinal word positions at which term occurs in the document. Given such a word-level inverted index and a phrase query, it is straightforward to combine the postings lists for the query to identify matching documents and to rank them using the standard vector space model.

The original set-based model can be easily adapted to handle phrase queries. To achieve this, we enumerate the set of maximal termsets instead of the set of closed termsets, using the same restrictions applied for conjunctive queries. To verify if the query terms are adjacent, we just check if its ordinal word positions are adjacents. The proximity threshold is then set to one and is used to evaluated this referential constraint.

We may expect that this extension to the set-based model is suitable for selecting just maximal termsets representing strong correlations, increasing the retrieval effectiveness of both type of the queries. Our experimental results(see Section 5.3) confirm such observations.

5 Experimental Evaluation

In this section we describe experimental results for the evaluation of the set-based model (SBM) for conjunctive and phrase queries in terms of both effectiveness and computational efficiency. Our evaluation is based on a comparison to the standard vector space model (VSM). We first present the experimental setup and the reference collections employed, and then discuss the retrieval performance and the computational efficiency.

5.1 Experimental Setup

In this evaluation we use two reference collections that comprise not only the documents, but also a set of example queries and the relevant responses for each query, as selected by experts. We quantify the retrieval effectiveness of the various approaches through standard measures of average recall and precision. The computational efficiency is evaluated through the query response time, that is, the processing time to select and rank the documents for each query.

The experiments were performed on a Linux-based PC with a AMD-athlon 2600+ 2.0 GHz processor and 512 MBytes RAM. Next we present the reference collections used, followed by the results obtained.

5.2 The Reference Collections

In our evaluation we use two reference collections WBR99 and TReC-8 [4]. Table 1 presents the main features of these collections.

The WBR99 reference collection is composed of a database of Web pages, a set of example Web queries, and a set of relevant documents associated with each example query. The database is composed of 5,939,061 pages of the Brazilian Web, under the

Table 1. Characteristics of the reference collections

Characteristics	Collection	
	TReC-8	WBR99
Number of Documents	528,155	5,939,061
Number of Distinct Terms	737,833	2,669,965
Number of Topics	450	100,000
Number of Used Topics	50 (401-450)	50
Average Terms per Query	4.38	1.94
Average Relevants per Query	94.56	35.40
Size (GB)	2	16

domain ".br". We decided to use this collection because it represents a highly connected subset of the Web, that is large enough to provide good prediction of the results if the whole Web was used, and, at the same time, is small enough to be handled by our available computational resources.

A total of 50 example queries were selected from a log of 100 000 queries submitted to the *TodoBR* search engine[1]. The queries selected were the 50 most frequent ones with more than two terms. Some frequent queries related to sex were not considered. The mean number of keywords per query is 3.78. The sets of relevant documents for each query were build using pooling method used for the Web-based TREC collection [10]. We compose a query pool formed by the top 15 documents generated by each evaluated model for both query types. Each query pool contained an average of 19.91 documents for conjunctive queries and 18.77 for phrase queries. All documents present in each query pool were submitted to a manual evaluation by a group of 9 users, all of them familiar with Web searching. The average number of relevant documents per query is 12.38 and 6.96 for conjunctive and phrase queries, respectively.

The TReC-8 collection [4] has been growing steadily over the years. At TREC-8, which is used in our experiments, the collection size was roughly 2 gigabytes. The documents presents in the TReC-8 collection are tagged with SGML to allow easy parsing, and come from the following sources: The Financial Times, Federal Register, Congressional Record, Foreign Broadcast Information Service and LA Times.

The TReC collection includes a set of example *information requests* (queries) which can be used for testing a new ranking algorithm. Each request is a description of an information need in natural language. The TReC-8 has a total of 450 queries, usually referred as a topic. Our experiments are performed with the 401-450 range of topics. This range of topics has 4.38 index terms per query.

5.3 Retrieval Performance

We start our evaluation by verifying the precision-recall curves for each model when applied to the reference collection. Each curve quantifies the precision as a function of the percentage of documents retrieved (recall). The results presented for SBM for both query types were obtained by setting the minimal frequency threshold to a one

[1] http://www.todobr.com.br

document. The minimal proximity threshold was not used for the conjunctive queries evaluation, and set to one for the phrase queries.

As we can see in Table 2, SBM yields better precision than VSM, regardless of the recall level. Further, the gains increase with the size of queries, because large queries allow computing a more representative termset, and are consistently greater for the both query types. Furthermore, accounting for correlations among terms never degrades the quality of the response sets. We confirm such observations by verifying the overall average precision achieved for each model. The gains provided by SBM over the VSM in terms of overall precision was 7.82% and 23.32% for conjunctive queries and 9.73% and 18.98% for phrase queries for WBR99 and TReC-8 collections, respectively.

Table 2. Recall-precision curves for VSM and SBM

(a) Conjunctive queries results

Recall (%)	**Precision(%)**			
	WBR99		TReC-8	
	VSM	*SBM*	*VSM*	*SBM*
0	44.14	48.81	63.17	74.41
10	43.03	48.81	44.06	53.63
20	42.23	46.13	33.87	38.56
30	38.40	41.93	26.36	31.81
40	37.41	39.66	20.11	25.69
50	37.41	39.32	15.35	21.24
60	36.71	37.74	10.22	16.66
70	33.97	36.53	7.63	10.88
80	29.62	32.55	6.48	7.24
90	27.27	28.25	3.90	5.13
100	25.00	26.29	3.67	4.32
Average	35.92	38.73	21.35	26.33
Improvement	-	7.82	-	23.32

(b) Phrase queries results

Recall (%)	**Precision(%)**			
	WBR99		TReC-8	
	VSM	*SBM*	*VSM*	*SBM*
0	48.71	51.38	42.41	45.15
10	41.48	43.58	20.21	28.61
20	27.83	31.91	16.07	21.71
30	21.13	23.35	12.47	15.70
40	17.59	18.67	11.19	13.92
50	10.54	11.71	9.25	10.47
60	4.18	5.22	7.64	8.85
70	2.94	3.49	6.62	6.97
80	2.09	2.96	3.92	4.00
90	1.03	1.57	3.30	3.44
100	0.23	1.23	3.24	3.37
Average	16.16	17.73	12.39	14.75
Improvement	-	9.73	-	18.98

In summary, set-based model (SBM) is the first information retrieval model that exploits term correlations and term proximity effectively and provides significant gains in terms of precision, regardless of the query type. In the next section we discuss the computational costs associated with SBM.

5.4 Computational Efficiency

In this section we compare our model to the standard vector space model regarding the query response time, in order to evaluate its feasibility in terms of computational costs. This is important because one major limitation of existing models that account for term correlations is their computational cost. Several of these models cannot be applied to large or even mid-size collections since their costs increase exponentially with the vocabulary size.

We compared the response time for the models and collections considered, which are summarized in Table 3. We also calculated the increase of the response time of SBM when compared to VSM for both query types. All 100,000 queries submitted to the *TodoBR* search engine, excluding the unique term queries, was evaluated for the WBR99 collection. We observe that SBM results in a response time increase of 6.21% and 24.13% for conjunctive queries and 14.67% and 23.68% for phrase queries when compared to VSM for WBR99 and TReC-8, respectively.

Table 3. Average response time for VSM and SBM

Query Type	Avg. Response Time (s)			
	WBR99		TReC-8	
	VSM	*SBM*	*VSM*	*SBM*
conjunctive	0.632	0.671	0.029	0.036
phrase	1.491	1.709	0.038	0.047

We identify one main reason for the relatively small increase in execution time for SBM. Determining maximal termsets and calculating their similarity do not increase significantly the cost associated with queries. This fact happens due to the small number of query related termsets in the reference collections, especially for WBR99. As a consequence, the inverted lists associated tend to be small and are usually manipulated in main memory in our implementation of SBM. Second, we employ pruning techniques that discard irrelevant termsets early in the computation, as described in [1].

6 Related Work

The vector space model was proposed by Salton [11, 12], and different weighting schemes were presented [8, 9]. In the vector space model, index terms are assumed to be mutually independent. The independence assumption leads to a linear weighting function which, although not necessarily realistic, is ease to compute.

Different approaches to account for co-occurrence among index terms during the information retrieval process have been proposed [13, 14, 15]. The work in [16] presents an interesting approach to compute index term correlations based on automatic indexing schemes, defining a new information retrieval model called generalized vector space model. Wong et al. [17] extended the generalized vector space model to handle queries specified as boolean expressions.

The set-based model was the first information retrieval model that exploits term correlations and term proximity effectively and provides significant gains in terms of precision, regardless of the size of the collection and of the size of the vocabulary [1, 2]. Experimental results showed significant and consistent improvements in average precision curves in comparison to the vector space model and to the generalized vector space model, keeping computational cost small.

Our work differs from that presented in the following way. First, all known approaches that account for co-occurrence patterns was initially designed for processing disjunctive (OR) queries. Our extension to the set-based model provides a simple, effective and efficient way to process conjunctive (AND) and phrase queries. Experimental results show significant and consistent improvements in average precision curves in comparison to the standard vector space model adapted to process these types of queries, keeping processing times close to the times to process the vector space model.

The work in [18] introduces a theoretical framework for the association rules mining based on a boolean model of information retrieval known as Boolean Retrieval Model. Our work differs from that presented in the following way. In our work we use association rules to define a new information retrieval model that provides not only the main term weights and assumptions of the $tf \times idf$ scheme, but also provides for quantification of term co-occurrence and can be successfully used in processing of disjunctive, conjunctive and phrase queries.

Ahonen-Myka [19] employs a versatile technique, based on maximal frequent sequences, for finding complex text phrases from full text for further processing and knowledge discovery. Our work also use the concept of maximal termsets/sequences to account for term co-occurrence patterns in documents, but the termsets are, successfully, used as a basis for an information retrieval model.

7 Conclusions and Future Work

We presented an extension for the set-based model to consider correlations among index terms in conjunctive and phrase queries. We show that it is possible to significantly improve retrieval effectiveness, while keeping extra computational costs small. The computation of correlations among index terms using maximal termsets enumerated by an algorithm to generate association rules leads to a direct extension of the set-based model. Our approach does not modify its algebraic representation, and the changes to the original model are minimal.

We evaluated and validated our proposed extension for the set-based model for conjunctive and phrase queries in terms of both effectiveness and computational efficiency using two test collections. We show through curves of recall versus precision that our extension presents results that are superior for all query types considered and the additional computational costs are acceptable. In addition to assessing document relevance, we also showed that the proximity information has application in identifying phrases with a greater degree of precision.

Web search engines are rapidly emerging into the most important application of the World Wide Web, and query segmentation is one of the most promising techniques to improve search precision. This technique reduce the query into a form that is more likely to express the topic(s) that are asked for, and in a suitable manner for a word-based or phrase-based inverse lookup, and thus improve precision of the search. We will use the set-based model for automatic query segmentation.

References

1. Pôssas, B., Ziviani, N., Meira, W., Ribeiro-Neto, B.: Set-based model: A new approach for information retrieval. In: The 25th ACM-SIGIR Conference on Research and Development in Information Retrieval, Tampere, Finland (2002) 230–237

2. Pôssas, B., Ziviani, N., Meira, W.: Enhancing the set-based model using proximity information. In: The 9th International Symposium on String Processing and Information Retrieval, Lisbon, Portugal (2002)
3. Agrawal, R., Imielinski, T., Swami, A.: Mining association rules between sets of items in large databases. In: Proceedings of the ACM SIGMOD International Conference Management of Data, Washington, D.C. (1993) 207-216
4. Voorhees, E., Harman, D.: Overview of the eighth text retrieval conference (trec 8). In: The Eighth Text Retrieval Conference, National Institute of Standards and Technology (1999) 1–23
5. Agrawal, R., Srikant, R.: Fast algorithms for mining association rules. In: The 20th International Conference on Very Large Data Bases, Santiago, Chile (1994) 487-499
6. Zaki, M.J.: Generating non-redundant association rules. In: 6th ACM SIGKDD International Conference on Knowledge Discovery and Data Mining, Boston, MA, USA (2000) 34-43
7. Gouda, K., Zaki, M.J.: Efficiently mining maximal frequent itemsets. In: Proceedings of the 2001 IEEE International Conference on Data Mining. (2001) 163-170
8. Yu, C.T., Salton, G.: Precision weighting – an effective automatic indexing method. In: Journal of the ACM. Volume 23(1). (1976) 76–88
9. Salton, G., Buckley, C.: Term-weighting approaches in automatic retrieval. In: Information Processing and Management. Volume 24(5). (1988) 513–523
10. Hawking, D., Craswell, N.: Overview of TREC-2001 web track. In: The Tenth Text REtrieval Conference (TREC-2001), Gaithersburg, Maryland, USA (2001) 61–67
11. Salton, G., Lesk, M.E.: Computer evaluation of indexing and text processing. In: Journal of the ACM. Volume 15(1). (1968) 8–36
12. Salton, G.: The SMART retrieval system – Experiments in automatic document processing. Prentice Hall Inc., Englewood Cliffs, NJ (1971)
13. Raghavan, V.V., Yu, C.T.: Experiments on the determination of the relationships between terms. In: ACM Transactions on Databases Systems. Volume 4. (1979) 240–260
14. Harper, D.J., Rijsbergen, C.J.V.: An evaluation of feedback in document retrieval using co-occurrence data. In: Journal of Documentation. Volume 34. (1978) 189–216
15. Salton, G., Buckley, C., Yu, C.T.: An evaluation of term dependencies models in information retrieval. In: The 5th ACM-SIGIR Conference on Research and Development in Information Retrieval. (1982) 151-173
16. Wong, S.K.M., Ziarko, W., Raghavan, V.V., Wong, P.C.N.: On modeling of information retrieval concepts in vector spaces. In: The ACM Transactions on Databases Systems. Volume 12(2). (1987) 299–321
17. Wong, S.K.M., Ziarko, W., Raghavan, V.V., Wong, P.C.N.: On extending the vector space model for boolean query processing. In: Proceedings of the 9th Annual International ACM SIGIR Conference on Research and Development in Information Retrieval, Pisa, Italy, September 8-10, 1986, ACM (1986) 175–185
18. Bollmann-Sdorra, P., Hafez, A., Raghavan, V.V.: A theoretical framework for association mining based on the boolean retrieval model. In: Data Warehousing and Knowledge Discovery: Third International Conference, Munich, Germany (2001) 21–30
19. Ahonen-Myka, H., Heinonen, O., Klemettinen, M., Verkamo, A.: Finding co-occurring text phrases by combining sequence and frequent set discovery. In Feldman, R., ed.: Proceedings of 16th International Joint Conference on Artificial Intelligence IJCAI-99 Workshop on Text Mining: Foundations, Techniques and Applications, Stockholm, Sweden (1999) 1–9

Metric Indexing for the Vector Model in Text Retrieval

Tomáš Skopal[1], Pavel Moravec[2], Jaroslav Pokorný[1], and Václav Snášel[2]

[1] Charles University in Prague, Department of Software Engineering, Malostranské nám. 25, 118 00 Prague, Czech Republic, EU
tomas@skopal.net, jaroslav.pokorny@mff.cuni.cz

[2] VŠB – Technical University of Ostrava, Department of Computer Science, 17. listopadu 15, 708 33 Ostrava, Czech Republic, EU
{pavel.moravec,vaclav.snasel}@vsb.cz

Abstract. In the area of Text Retrieval, processing a query in the vector model has been verified to be qualitatively more effective than searching in the boolean model. However, in case of the classic vector model the current methods of processing many-term queries are inefficient, in case of LSI model there does not exist an efficient method for processing even the few-term queries. In this paper we propose a method of vector query processing based on metric indexing, which is efficient especially for the LSI model. In addition, we propose a concept of approximate semi-metric search, which can further improve the efficiency of retrieval process. Results of experiments made on moderate text collection are included.

1 Introduction

The Text Retrieval (TR) models [4, 3] provide a formal framework for retrieval methods aimed to search huge collections of text documents. The classic vector model as well as its algebraic extension LSI have been proved to be more effective (according to precision/recall measures) than the other existing models[1]. However, current methods of vector query processing are not much efficient for many-term queries, while in the LSI model they are inefficient at all. In this paper we propose a method of vector query processing based on metric indexing, which is highly efficient especially for searching in the LSI model.

1.1 Classic Vector Model

In the classic vector model, each document D_j in a collection C ($0 \leq j \leq m$, $m = |C|$) is characterized by a single vector d_j, where each coordinate of d_j is associated with a term t_i from the set of all unique terms in C ($0 \leq i \leq n$, where n is the number of terms). The value of a vector coordinate is a real number $w_{ij} \geq 0$ representing the *weight* of the i-th term in the j-th document. Hence,

[1] For a comparison over various TR models we refer to [20, 11].

A. Apostolico and M. Melucci (Eds.): SPIRE 2004, LNCS 3246, pp. 183–195, 2004.

a collection of documents can be represented by an $n \times m$ *term-by-document* matrix A. There are many ways how to compute the term weights w_{ij} stored in A. A popular weight construction is computed as $tf * idf$ (see e.g. [4]).

Queries. The most important problem about the vector model is the querying mechanism that searches matrix A with respect to a query, and returns only the relevant document vectors (appropriate documents respectively). The query is represented by a vector q the same way as a document is represented. The goal is to return the most similar (relevant) documents to the query. For this purpose, a similarity function must be defined, assessing a similarity value to each pair of query and document vectors (q, d_j). In the context of TR, the *cosine measure* $\text{SIM}_{cos}(q, d_j) = \frac{\sum_{k=1}^{n} q_k \cdot w_{kj}}{\sqrt{\sum_{k=1}^{n} {q_k}^2 \cdot \sum_{k=1}^{n} {w_{kj}}^2}}$ is widely used. During a query processing, the columns of A (the document vectors) are compared against the query vector using the cosine measure, while the sufficiently similar documents are returned as a result. According to the query extent, we distinguish *range queries* and *k-nearest neighbors (k-NN) queries.* A range query returns documents similar to the query more than a given similarity threshold. A k-NN query returns the k most similar documents.

Generally, there are two ways how to specify a query. First, a *few-term query* is specified by the user using a few terms, while an appropriate vector for such a query is very sparse. Second, a *many-term query* is specified using a text document, thus the appropriate query vector is usually more dense. In this paper we focus just on the many-term queries, since they better satisfy the similarity search paradigm which the vector model should follow.

1.2 LSI Vector Model (Simplified)

Simply said, the LSI (latent semantic indexing) model [11, 4] is an algebraical extension of the classic vector model. First, the term-by-document matrix A is decomposed by singular value decomposition (SVD) as $A = U \Sigma V^T$. The matrix U contains *concept vectors*, where each concept vector is a linear combination of the original terms. The concepts are *meta-terms* (groups of terms) appearing in the original documents. While the term-by-document matrix A stores document vectors, the *concept-by-document* matrix ΣV^T stores *pseudo-document* vectors. Each coordinate of a pseudo-document vector represents a weight of an appropriate concept in a document.

Latent Semantics. The concept vectors are ordered with respect to their significance (appropriate singular values in Σ). Consequently, only a small number of concepts is really significant – these concepts represent (statistically) the main themes present in the collection – let us denote this number as k. The remaining concepts are unimportant (noisy concepts) and can be omitted, thus the dimensionality is reduced from n to k. Finally, we obtain an approximation (rank-k SVD) $A \approx U_k \Sigma_k V_k^T$, where for sufficiently high k the approximation error will be negligible. Moreover, for a low k the effectiveness can be subjectively even higher (according to the precision/recall values) than for a higher k [3]. When searching in a real-world collection, the optimal k is usually ranged from several tens to several hundreds. Unlike the term-by-document matrix A, the concept-by-document matrix $\Sigma_k V_k^T$ as well as the concept base matrix U are dense.

Queries. Searching for documents in the LSI model is performed the same way as in the classic vector model, the difference is that matrix $\Sigma_k V_k^T$ is searched instead of A. Moreover, the query vector q must be projected into the concept base, i.e. $U_k^T q$ is the *pseudo-query vector* used by LSI. Since the concept vectors of U are dense, a pseudo-query vector is dense as well.

1.3 Vector Query Processing

In this paper we focus on efficiency of vector query processing. More specifically, we can say that a query is processed efficiently in case that only a small proportion of the matrix storage volume is needed to load and process. In this section we outline several existing approaches to the vector query processing.

Document Vector Scanning. The simplest method how to process a query is the sequential scanning of all the document vectors (i.e. the columns of A, $\Sigma_k V_k^T$ respectively). Each document vector is compared against the query vector using the similarity function, while sufficiently similar documents are returned to the user. It is obvious that for any query the whole matrix must be processed. However, sequential processing of the whole matrix is sometimes more efficient (from the disk management point of view) than a random access to a smaller part of the matrix used by some other methods.

Term Vector Filtering. For sparse query vectors (few-term queries respectively), there exists a more efficient scanning method. Instead of the document vectors, the term vectors (i.e. the rows of the matrix) are processed. The cosine measure is computed simultaneously for all the document vectors, "orthogonally" involved in the term vectors. Due to the simultaneous cosine measure evaluation a set of m accumulators (storing the evolving similarities between each document and the query) must be maintained in memory. The advantage of term filtering is that only those term vectors must be scanned, for which the appropriate term weights in the query vector are nonzero. The term vector filtering can be easily provided using an inverted file – as a part of the boolean model implementation [15].

The simple method of term filtering has been improved by an approximate approach [19] reducing the time as well as space costs. Generally, the improvement is based on early termination of query processing, exploiting a restructured inverted file where the term entries are sorted according to the decreasing occurrences of a term in document. Thus, the most relevant documents in each term entry are processed first. As soon as the first document is found in which the number of term occurrences is less than a given addition threshold, the processing of term entry can stop, because all the remaining documents have the same or less importance as the first rejected document. Since some of the documents are never reached during a query processing, the number of used accumulators can be smaller than m, which saves also the space costs. Another improvement of the inverted file exploiting *quantized weights* was proposed recently [2], even more reducing the search costs.

Despite the above mentioned improvements, the term vector filtering is generally not so much efficient for many-term queries, because the number of filtered term vectors is decreased. Moreover, the term vector filtering is completely useless for the LSI model, since each pseudo-query vector is dense, and none of the term vectors can be skipped.

Signature Methods. Signature files are a popular filtering method in the boolean model [13], however, there were only few attempts made to use them in the vector model. In that case, the usage of signature files is not so straightforward due to the term weights. Weight-partitioned signature files (WPSF) [14] try to solve the problem by recording the term weights in so-called TF-groups. A sequential file organization was chosen for the WPSF which caused excessive search of the signature file. An improvement was proposed recently [16] using the S-trees [12] to speedup the signature file search. Another signature-like approach is the VA-file [6]. In general, usage of the signature methods is still complicated for the vector model, and the results achieved so far are rather poor.

2 Metric Indexing

Since in the vector model the documents are represented as points within an n-dimensional vector space, in our approach we create an index for the term-by-document matrix (for the concept-by-document matrix in case of LSI) based on metric access methods (MAMs) [8]. A property common to all MAMs is that they exploit only a metric function for the indexing. The metric function stands for a similarity function, thus metric access methods provide a natural way for similarity search. Among many of MAMs, we have chosen the M-tree.

2.1 M-Tree

The M-tree [9, 18, 21] is a dynamic data structure designed to index objects of metric datasets. Let us have a metric space $\mathcal{M} = (\mathbb{U}, d)$ where $\mathbb{U}$ is an object universe (usually a vector space), and d is a function measuring distance between two objects in $\mathbb{U}$. The function d must be a metric, i.e. it must satisfy the axioms of reflexivity, positivity, symmetry and triangular inequality. Let $\mathbb{S} \subseteq \mathbb{U}$ be a dataset to be indexed. In case of the vector model in TR, an object $O_i \in \mathbb{S}$ is represented by a (pseudo-)document vector of a document D_i. The particular metric d, replacing the cosine measure, will be introduced in Section 2.2.

Like the other indexing trees based on B^+-tree, the M-tree structure is a balanced hierarchy of nodes. In M-tree the objects are distributed in a hierarchy of *metric regions* (each node represents a single metric region) which can be, in turn, interpreted as a hierarchy of object clusters. The nodes have a fixed capacity and a minimum utilization threshold. The leaf nodes contain *ground entries* $grnd(O_i)$ of the indexed objects themselves, while in the inner nodes the *routing entries* $rout(O_j)$ are stored, representing the metric regions and routing to their covering subtrees. Each routing entry determines a metric region in space $\mathcal{M}$ where the object O_j is a center of that region and r_{O_j} is a radius bounding the region. For the hierarchy of metric regions (routing entries $rout(O_j)$ respectively) in the M-tree, the following requirement must be satisfied:

All the objects of ground entries stored in the leaves of the covering subtree of $rout(O_j)$ *must be spatially located inside the region defined by* $rout(O_j)$.

The most important consequence of the above requirement is that many regions on the same M-tree level may overlap. An example in Figure 1 shows several objects partitioned among metric regions and the appropriate M-tree. We can see that the regions defined by $rout_1(O_1)$, $rout_1(O_2)$, $rout_1(O_4)$ overlap. Moreover, object O_5 is located inside the regions of $rout_1(O_1)$ and $rout_1(O_4)$ but it is stored just in the subtree of $rout_1(O_4)$. Similarly, the object O_3 is located even in three regions but it is stored just in the subtree of $rout_1(O_2)$.

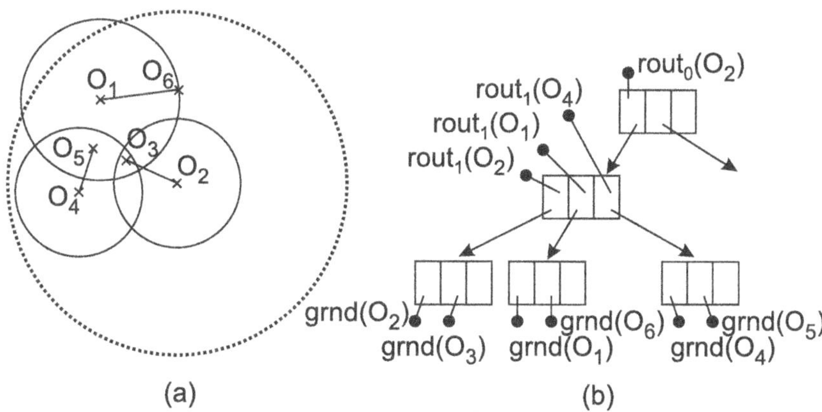

Fig. 1. Hierarchy of metric regions (a) and the appropriate M-tree (b)

Similarity Queries in the M-Tree. The structure of M-tree natively supports similarity queries. The similarity function is represented by the metric function d where the close objects are interpreted as similar.

A range query `RangeQuery(`Q`,`r_Q`)` is specified as a *query region* given by a query object Q and a query radius r_Q. The purpose of a range query is to retrieve all such objects O_i satisfying $d(Q, O_i) \leq r_Q$. A k-nearest neighbours query (k-NN query) `kNNQuery(`Q`,`k`)` is specified by a query object Q and a number k. A k-NN query retrieves the first k nearest objects to Q.

During the range query processing (k-NN query processing respectively), the M-tree hierarchy is being traversed down. Only if a routing entry $rout(O_j)$ (its metric region respectively) overlaps the query region, the covering subtree of $rout(O_j)$ is relevant to the query and thus further processed.

2.2 Application of M-Tree in the Vector Model

In the vector model the objects O_i are represented by (pseudo-)document vectors d_i, i.e. by columns of term-by-document or concept-by-document matrix, respectively. We cannot use the cosine measure $\text{SIM}_{cos}(d_i, d_j)$ as a metric function directly, since it does not satisfy the metric axioms. As an appropriate metric, we define the *deviation metric* $d_{dev}(d_i, d_j)$ as a vector deviation

$$d_{dev}(d_i, d_j) = arccos(\text{SIM}_{cos}(d_i, d_j))$$

The similarity queries supported by M-tree (utilizing d_{dev}) are exactly those required for the vector model (utilizing SIM_{cos}). Specifically, the range query will return all the documents that are similar to a query more than some given threshold (transformed to the query radius) while the k-NN query will return the first k most similar (closest respectively) documents to the query.

In the M-tree hierarchy similar documents are clustered among metric regions. Since the triangular inequality for d_{dev} is satisfied, many irrelevant document clusters can be safely pruned during a query processing, thus the search efficiency is improved.

3 Semi-metric Search

In this section we propose the concept of semi-metric search – an approximate extension of metric search applied to M-tree. The semi-metric search provides even more efficient retrieval, considerably resistant to the curse of dimensionality.

3.1 Curse of Dimensionality

The metric indexing itself (as is experimentally verified in Section 4) is beneficial for searching in the LSI model. However, searching in a collection of high-dimensional document vectors of the classic vector model is negatively affected by a phenomenon called *curse of dimensionality* [7, 8]. In the M-tree hierarchy (even the most optimal hierarchy) the curse of dimensionality causes that clusters of high-dimensional vectors are not distinct, which is reflected by huge overlaps among metric regions.

Intrinsic Dimensionality. In the context of metric indexing, the curse of dimensionality can be generalized for general metric spaces. The major condition determining the success of metric access methods is the *intrinsic dimensionality* of the indexed dataset. The intrinsic dimensionality of a metric dataset (one of the interpretations [8]) is defined as

$$\rho = \frac{\mu^2}{2\sigma^2}$$

where μ and σ^2 are the mean and the variance of the dataset's *distance distribution histogram*. In other words, if all pairs of the indexed objects are almost equally distant, then the intrinsic dimensionality is maximal (i.e. the mean is high and/or the variance is low), which means the dataset is poorly intrinsically structured. So far, for datasets of high intrinsic dimensionality there still does not exist an efficient MAM for exact metric search. In case of M-tree, a high intrinsic dimensionality causes that almost all the metric regions overlap each other, and searching in such an M-tree deteriorates to sequential search.

In case of vector datasets, the intrinsic dimensionality negatively depends on the correlations among coordinates of the dataset vectors. The intrinsic dimensionality can reach up to the value of the classic (embedding) dimensionality. For example, for uniformly distributed (i.e. not correlated) n-dimensional vectors the intrinsic dimensionality tends to be maximal, i.e. $\rho \approx n$.

In the following section we propose a concept of semi-metric modifications that decrease the intrinsic dimensionality and, as a consequence, provide a way to efficient approximate similarity search.

3.2 Modification of the Metric

An increase of the variance of distance distribution histogram is a straightforward way how to decrease the intrinsic dimensionality. This can be achieved by a suitable modification of the original metric, preserving the similarity ordering among objects in the query result.

Definition 1. Let us call the *increasing modification* d^f_{dev} of a metric d_{dev} a function

$$d^f_{dev}(O_i, O_j) = f(d_{dev}(O_i, O_j))$$

where $f : \langle 0, \pi \rangle \rightarrow R^+_0$ is an increasing function and $f(0) = 0$. For simplicity, let $f(\pi) = 1$.

Definition 2. Let $s : \mathbb{U} \times \mathbb{U} \rightarrow R^+_0$ be a similarity function (or a distance function) and $SimOrder_s : \mathbb{U} \rightarrow \mathcal{P}(\mathbb{S} \times \mathbb{S})$ be a function defined as

$$\langle O_i, O_j \rangle \in SimOrder_s(Q) \Leftrightarrow s(O_i, Q) < s(O_j, Q)$$

$\forall O_i, O_j \in \mathbb{S}, \forall Q \in \mathbb{U}$. In other words, the function $SimOrder_s$ orders the objects of dataset $\mathbb{S}$ according to the distances to the query object Q.

Proposition. For the metric d_{dev} and every increasing modification d^f_{dev} the following equality holds:

$$SimOrder_{d_{dev}}(Q) = SimOrder_{d^f_{dev}}(Q), \forall Q \in \mathbb{U}$$

Proof:
"$\subset$": The function f is increasing. If for each $O_i, O_j, O_k, O_l \in \mathbb{U}$, $d_{dev}(O_i, O_j) > d_{dev}(O_k, O_l)$ holds, then $f(d_{dev}(O_i, O_j)) > f(d_{dev}(O_k, O_l))$ must also hold.
"$\supset$": The second part of proof is similar. □

As a consequence of the proposition, if we process a query sequentially over the entire dataset $\mathbb{S}$, then it does not matter if we use either d_{dev} or d^f_{dev}, since both of the ways will return the same query result.

If the function f is additionally *subadditive*, i.e. $f(a) + f(b) \geq f(a+b)$, then f is *metric-preserving* [10], i.e. $f(d(O_i, O_j))$ is still metric. More specifically, concave functions are metric-preserving (see Figure 2a), while convex (even partially convex) functions are not – let us call them *metric-violating* functions (see Figure 2b). A metric modified by a metric-violating function f is a *semi-metric*, i.e. a function satisfying all the metric axioms except the triangular inequality.

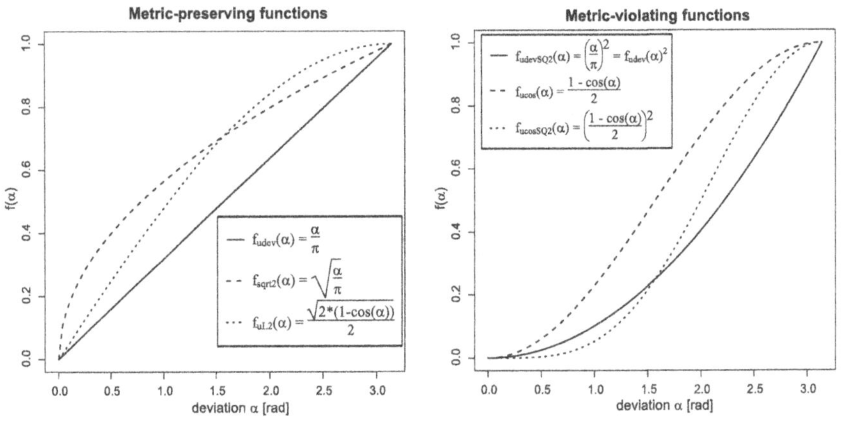

Fig. 2. (a) Metric-preserving functions (b) Metric-violating functions

Clustering Properties. Let us analyze the clustering properties of modifications d^f_{dev} (see also Figure 2). For concave f, two objects close to each other according to d_{dev} are more distant according to d^f_{dev}. Conversely, for convex f, the close objects according to d_{dev} are even closer according to d^f_{dev}. As a consequence, the concave modifications d^f_{dev} have a negative influence on clustering, since the object clusters become indistinct. On the other side, the convex modifications d^f_{dev} even more tighten the object clusters, making the cluster structure of the dataset more evident. Simply, the convex modifications increase the distance histogram variance, thereby decreasing the intrinsic dimensionality.

3.3 Semi-metric Indexing and Search

The increasing modifications d^f_{dev} can be utilized in the M-tree instead of the deviation metric d_{dev}. In case of a semi-metric modification d^f_{dev}, the query processing is more efficient because of smaller overlaps among metric regions in the M-tree. Usage of metric modifications is not beneficial, since their clustering properties are worsen, and the overlaps among metric regions are larger.

Semi-metric Search. A semi-metric modification d^f_{dev} can be used for all operations on the M-tree, i.e. for M-tree building as well as for M-tree searching. With respect to M-tree construction principles (we refer to [21]) and the proposition in Section 3.2, the M-tree hierarchies built either by d or d^f_{dev} are the same. For that reason, an M-tree built using a metric d can be queried using any modification d^f_{dev}. Such *semi-metric queries* must be extended by the function f, which stands for an additional parameter. For a range query the query radius r_Q must be modified to $f(r_Q)$. During a semi-metric query processing, the function f is applied to each value computed using d as well as it is applied to the metric region radii stored in the routing entries.

Error of the Semi-metric Search. Since the semi-metric d^f_{dev} does not satisfy the triangular inequality property, a semi-metric query will return more or less approximate results. Obviously, the error is dependent on the convexity of a modifying function f. As an output error, we define a *normed overlap error*

$$E_{NO} = 1 - \frac{|result_{Mtree} \cap result_{scan}|}{max(|result_{Mtree}|, |result_{scan}|)}$$

where $result_{Mtree}$ is a query result returned by the M-tree (using a semi-metric query), and $result_{scan}$ is a result of the same query returned by sequential search over the entire dataset. The error E_{NO} can be interpreted as a *relative precision* of the M-tree query result with respect to the result of full sequential scan.

Semi-metric Search in Text Retrieval. In the context of TR, the searching is naturally approximate, since precision/recall values do never reach up to 100%. From this point of view, the approximate character of semi-metric search is not a serious limitation – acceptable results can be achieved by choosing such a modifying function f, for which the error E_{NO} will not exceed some small value, e.g. 0.1. On the other side, semi-metric search significantly improves the search efficiency, as it is experimentally verified in the following section.

4 Experimental Results

For the experiments we have chosen the Los Angeles Times collection (a part of TREC 5) consisting of 131,780 newspaper articles. The entire collection contained 240,703 unique terms. As "rich" many-term queries, we have used articles consisting of at least 1000 unique terms. The experiments were focused on disk access costs (DAC) spent during k-NN queries processing. Each k-NN query was repeated for 100 different query documents and the results were averaged. The access to disk was aligned to 512B blocks, considering both access to the M-tree index as well as to the respective matrix. The overall query DAC are presented in megabytes. The entries of M-tree nodes have contained just the document vector identifiers (i.e. pointers to the matrix columns), thus the M-tree storage volume was minimized. In Table 1 the M-tree configuration used for experiments is presented (for a more detailed description see [21]).

The labels of form Devxxx in the figures below stand for modifying functions f used by semi-metric search. Several functions of form DevSQ$p(\alpha) = \left(\frac{\alpha}{\pi}\right)^p$ were chosen. The queries labeled as Dev represent the original metric queries presented in Section 2.2.

Table 1. The M-tree configuration

Page size: 512 B; Capacity (leaves: 42, nodes: 21)
Construction: MinMax + SingleWay + SlimDown
Tree height: 4; Avg. util. (leaves: 56%, nodes: 52%)

4.1 Classic Vector Model

First, we performed tests for the classic vector model. The storage of the term-by-document matrix (in CCS format [4]) took 220 MB. The storage of M-tree index was about 4MB (i.e. 1.8% of the matrix storage volume (MSV)).

In Figure 3a the comparison of document vector scanning, term vector filtering as well as metric and semi-metric search is presented. It is obvious that using document vector scanning the whole matrix (i.e. 220 MB DAC) was loaded and processed. Since the query vectors contained many zero weights, the term vector filtering worked more efficiently (76 MB DAC, i.e. 34% of MSV).

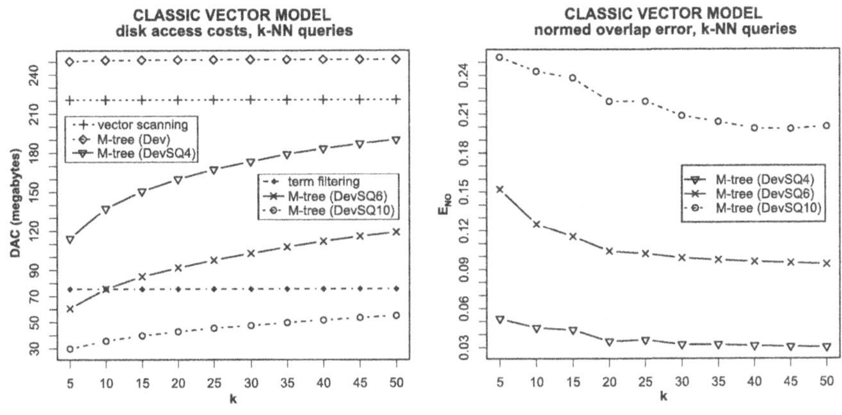

Fig. 3. Classic vector model: (a) Disk access costs (b) E_{NO} error

The metric search Dev did not performed well – the curse of dimensionality ($n = 240{,}703$) forced almost 100% of the matrix to be processed. The extra 30 MB DAC overhead (beyond the 220 MB of MSV) was caused by the non-sequential access to the matrix columns. On the other side, the semi-metric search performed better. The DevSQ10 queries for $k = 5$ consumed only 30 MB

DAC (i.e. 13.6% of MSV). Figure 3b shows the normed overlap error E_{NO} of the semi-metric search. For DevSQ4 queries the error was negligible. The error for DevSQ6 remained below 0.1 for $k > 35$. The DevSQ10 queries were affected by a relatively high error from 0.25 to 0.2 (with increasing k).

4.2 LSI Model

The second set of tests was made for the LSI model. The target (reduced) dimensionality was chosen to be 200. The storage of the concept-by-document matrix took 105 MB, while the size of M-tree index was about 3 MB (i.e. 2.9 % of MSV).

Because the size of term-by-document matrix was very large, the direct calculation of SVD was impossible. Therefore, we have used a two-step method [17], which in first step calculates a *random projection* [1, 5] of document vectors into a smaller dimensionality of *pseudo-concepts*. This is done by multiplication of a zero-mean unit-variance random matrix and the term-by-document matrix. Second, a rank-$2k$ SVD is calculated on the resulting *pseudoconcept-by-document* matrix, giving us a very good approximation of the classic rank-k SVD.

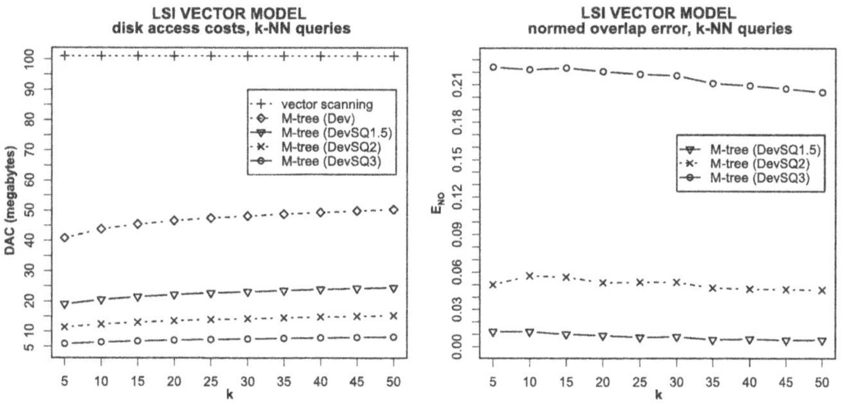

Fig. 4. LSI model: (a) Disk access costs (b) E_{NO} error

The Figure 4a shows that metric search Dev itself was more than twice as efficient as the document vector scanning. Even better results were achieved by the semi-metric search. The DevSQ3 queries for $k = 5$ consumed only 5.8 MB DAC (i.e. 5.5% of MSV). Figure 4b shows the error E_{NO}. For DevSQ1.5 queries the error was negligible, for DevSQ2 it remained below 0.06. The DevSQ3 queries were affected by a relatively high error.

5 Conclusion

In this paper we have proposed a metric indexing method for an efficient search of documents in the vector model. The experiments have shown that metric indexing itself is suitable for an efficient search in the LSI model. Furthermore, the approximate semi-metric search allows us to provide quite efficient similarity search in the classic vector model, and a remarkably efficient search in the LSI model. The output error of semi-metric search can be effectively tuned by choosing such modifying functions, that preserve an expected accuracy sufficiently.

In the future we would like to compare the semi-metric search with some other methods, in particular with the VA-file (in case of LSI model). We also plan to develop an analytical error model for the semi-metric search in M-tree, allowing to predict and control the output error E_{NO}.

This research has been partially supported by GAČR grant No. 201/00/1031.

References

1. D. Achlioptas. Database-friendly random projections. In *Symposium on Principles of Database Systems*, 2001.
2. V. N. Anh, O. de Kretser, and A. Moffat. Vector-space ranking with effective early termination. In *Proceedings of the 24th annual international ACM SIGIR*, pages 35–42. ACM Press, 2001.
3. R. Baeza-Yates and B. Ribeiro-Neto. *Modern Information Retrieval.* Addison Wesley, New York, 1999.
4. M. Berry and M. Browne. *Understanding Search Engines, Mathematical Modeling and Text Retrieval.* Siam, 1999.
5. E. Bingham and H. Mannila. Random projection in dimensionality reduction: applications to image and text data. In *Knowledge Discovery and Data Mining*, pages 245–250, 2001.
6. S. Blott and R. Weber. An Approximation-Based Data Structure for Similarity Search. Technical report, ESPRIT, 1999.
7. C. Böhm, S. Berchtold, and D. Keim. Searching in High-Dimensional Spaces – Index Structures for Improving the Performance of Multimedia Databases. *ACM Computing Surveys*, 33(3):322–373, 2001.
8. E. Chávez and G. Navarro. A probabilistic spell for the curse of dimensionality. In *Proc. 3rd Workshop on Algorithm Engineering and Experiments (ALENEX'01), LNCS 2153.* Springer-Verlag, 2001.
9. P. Ciaccia, M. Patella, and P. Zezula. M-tree: An Efficient Access Method for Similarity Search in Metric Spaces. In *Proceedings of the 23rd Athens Intern. Conf. on VLDB*, pages 426–435. Morgan Kaufmann, 1997.
10. P. Corazza. Introduction to metric-preserving functions. *Amer. Math Monthly*, 104(4):309–23, 1999.
11. S. C. Deerwester, S. T. Dumais, T. K. Landauer, G. W. Furnas, and R. A. Harshman. Indexing by latent semantic analysis. *Journal of the American Society of Information Science*, 41(6):391–407, 1990.
12. U. Deppisch. S-tree: A Dynamic Balanced Signature Index for Office Retrieval. In *Proceedings of ACM SIGIR*, 1986.
13. C. Faloutsos. Signature-based text retrieval methods, a survey. *IEEE Computer society Technical Committee on Data Engineering*, 13(1):25–32, 1990.
14. D. L. Lee and L. Ren. Document Ranking on Weight-Partitioned Signature Files. In *ACM TOIS 14*, pages 109–137, 1996.
15. A. Moffat and J. Zobel. Fast ranking in limited space. In *Proceedings of ICDE 94*, pages 428–437. IEEE Computer Society, 1994.

16. P. Moravec, J. Pokorný, and V. Snášel. Vector Query with Signature Filtering. In *Proc. of the 6th Bussiness Information Systems Conference, USA*, 2003.
17. C. H. Papadimitriou, H. Tamaki, P. Raghavan, and S. Vempala. Latent semantic indexing: A probabilistic analysis. In *Proocedings of the ACM Conference on Principles of Database Systems (PODS), Seattle*, pages 159–168, 1998.
18. M. Patella. *Similarity Search in Multimedia Databases.* Dipartmento di Elettronica Informatica e Sistemistica, Bologna, 1999.
19. M. Persin. Document filtering for fast ranking. In *Proceedings of the 17th annual international ACM SIGIR*, pages 339–348. Springer-Verlag New York, Inc., 1994.
20. G. Salton and M. McGill. *Introduction to Modern Information Retrieval.* McGraw Hill Publications, 1st edition, 1983.
21. T. Skopal, J. Pokorný, M. Krátký, and V. Snášel. Revisiting M-tree Building Principles. In *ADBIS 2003, LNCS 2798, Springer, Dresden, Germany*, 2003.

Negations and Document Length in Logical Retrieval

David E. Losada[1] and Alvaro Barreiro[2]

[1] Intelligent Systems Group, Department of Electronics and Computer Science
University of Santiago de Compostela, Spain
dlosada@dec.usc.es

[2] AIlab, Department of Computer Science,
University of A Coruña, Spain
barreiro@udc.es

Abstract. Terms which are not explicitly mentioned in the text of a document receive often a minor role in current retrieval systems. In this work we connect the management of such terms with the ability of the retrieval model to handle partial representations. A simple logical indexing process capable of expressing negated terms and omitting some other terms in the representation of a document was designed. Partial representations of documents can be built taking into account document length and global term distribution. A propositional model of information retrieval is used to exemplify the advantages from such expressive modeling. A number of experiments applying these partial representations are reported. The benefits of the expressive framework became apparent in the evaluation.

1 Introduction

For many retrieval systems the set of terms that determines the rank of a certain document given a query is solely composed of the terms in common between document and query. Nevertheless, it is well known that documents are often vague, imprecise and lots of relevant terms are not mentioned. Since topicality is a key component of retrieval engines, models of Information Retrieval (IR) should avoid to take strong decisions about the relationship between terms and document's semantics.

Current practice in IR tends to limit unfairly the impact of terms which are not explicitly mentioned by a given document. Although the vector-space model maintains a dimension for every term of the vocabulary, popular weighting schemes assign a null weight for those terms not explicitly mentioned. Similarly, probabilistic approaches, whose basic foundations allow to consider all the terms of the alphabet to do retrieval, tend to reduce the computation to the set of terms explicitly mentioned by a given document [14]. A notable exception is located in the context of the Language Modeling (LM) approaches [9, 2]: a term t which is not present in a document d is not considered as impossible in connection with the document's semantics but t receives a probability value greater than zero. This value grows with the global distribution of the term in the document collection, i.e. if t is frequently used by documents in the collection then it is possibly related to the document d. This is a valuable approach because it opens a new way to handle terms not explicitly mentioned in a given document but, on the other hand, the opposite problem arises: no one term can be considered totally unrelated to

A. Apostolico and M. Melucci (Eds.): SPIRE 2004, LNCS 3246, pp. 196–207, 2004.

a given document. This is because all the probability values coming from every query term are multiplied together and, hence, if zero probabilities are allowed then we would assign a null probability to any document that regards one or more of the query terms as unrelated.

In this work we propose an alternative way for handling both situations. A term t which is not explicitly mentioned by a document d may be considered as: a) totally unrelated to d and, hence, if a query uses t then the document d is penalized (this penalization should not be as extreme as assigning a retrieval status value of 0 for d) or b) possibly related to d and, hence, a non-zero contribution is computed for modeling the possible connection between t and d.

A formalism allowing partiality can distinguish between: a) lack of information about the actual connection between a given topic and a particular document, b) certainty that a given topic is completely out of the scope of a given document and c) certainty that a given topic is totally connected to the contents of a given document. In particular, logic-based models [15, 1] supply expressive representations in which these situations can be adequately separated. In this work we use a logical model of IR based on Propositional Logic and Belief Revision (PLBR) [6, 8] to exemplify the advantages of the logical modeling. We design a novel logical indexing method which builds expressive document representations. The logical indexing is driven by global term distribution and document length. In this way, intuitions applied in the context of document length normalization [13, 11] and LM smoothing techniques [9] can be incorporated into the logical formalism. This indexing approach was empirically evaluated revealing the advantages of the approach taken.

The rest of this paper is organized as follows. In section 2 the foundations of the logical model are presented. This section is intentionally brief because further details can be found in the literature. Section 3 addresses the construction of partial representations for documents in connection with global term distribution and document length. Experiments are reported in section 4 and section 5 offers an analysis a posteriori of the behaviour of the indexing method. Some conclusions and possible avenues of further research are presented in section 6.

2 The Model

Given a document and a query represented as propositional formulas d and q, respectively, it is well known that the notion of logical consequence (i.e. $d \models q$) is rather strict for retrieval because it yields a binary relevance decision [15]. The PLBR model defines a measure of closeness between d and q which can straightforwardly be used to build a formal rank of documents induced by the query [6, 8].

Dalal's Belief Revision measure of distance between logical interpretations [3] stands on the basis of the PLBR approach. A query q can be seen as the set of logical interpretations satisfying q, i.e. the set of *models* of q. The distance from each model of the document to the query is computed as the minimum distance from the model of the document to the query models. The final distance from the document to the query is the average distance from document models to the query.

Given a model of the document and a model of the query, the original PLBR distance basically counts the number of *disagreements*, i.e. the number of propositional letters with different interpretation[1]. This approach was later extend to define a new measure of distance between logical interpretations that takes into account inverse document frequency (idf) information [4]. Within this measure, every letter mapped into the same truth value by both interpretations produces an increment to the final distance that depends on its idf value. Note that this extension maintains the propositional formalism for representing documents and queries but introduces idf information for distance computation. As it will be explained later, in this paper we will use idf information for producing negated terms in the logical document representations. Observe that both uses of idf information are different because the former is done at matching time whereas the latter is done at indexing time.

The PLBR distance can be computed in polynomial time provided that d and q are in disjunctive normal form (DNF) [7]. A prototype logical system was implemented to evaluate the PLBR model against large collections. The experiments conducted revealed important benefits when handling expressions involving both logical conjunctions and disjunctions [5].

Nevertheless, the logical indexing applied so far was rather simplistic. No major attention was paid to the design of evolved techniques to produce more expressive document logical representations. In particular, the use of logical negations was left aside, which is precisely the aim of this work.

3 Partial Representations for Documents

The PLBR model has provision for establishing a distinction between a term for which we do not know whether or not it is significant with respect to a given document's semantics and a term for which we have positive evidence that it is not related at all with document's contents. The latter case naturally leads to a negated expression of the term within document's representation whereas the most sensible decision regarding the former case is to omit the term in the document's representation.

We first present some heuristics that can be applied to identify appropriate terms to be negated and then we give a further step to connect the new logical indexing with document's length.

3.1 Negative Term Selection

Let us consider a logical representation of a document in which only the terms that appear in the text of the document are present as positive literals[2] (let us call this conservative setting as *negate-nothing approach*). Of course, many of the terms not mentioned by the document (*unseen* terms) will undoubtedly be disconnected with document's contents and, hence, to omit those terms within the document's representation does not seem to be the best choice. On the contrary, a negated representation of those terms appears as a good alternative. To negate every unseen term is also unfair (*negate-all approach*) because there will be many topics that, although not explicitly mentioned, are strongly connected with document's semantics.

[1] Note that every indexing term is modelled as a propositional letter in the alphabet.

[2] A literal is a propositional letter or its negation.

We propose a logical indexing strategy that negates *some* unseen terms selected on the basis of their distribution in the whole collection. Note that this global information is also used in the context of LM smoothing strategies for quantifying the relatedness between unseen terms and document's contents. More specifically, a null probability is not assigned for a term which was not seen in the text of a document. The fact that we have not seen it does not make it impossible. It is often assumed that a non-occurring term is possible, but no more likely than what would be expected by chance in the collection.

If a given term is infrequent in the document base then it is very unlikely that documents that do not mention it are actually related to this topic (and, thus, very unlikely that any user that wants to retrieve those documents finds the term useful when expressing her/his information need). On the other hand, frequent terms are more generic and have more chance to present connections with the topics of documents even in the case when they are not explicitly mentioned. This suggests that unseen infrequent terms are good candidates to formulate negations in the logical indexing process.

The obvious intention when negating a term in a document's representation is to move the document away from queries mentioning the term. Consider a query term which is missing in the text of a given document. If the query term is globally infrequent and, thus, it had been negated within the document's representation then the document will be penalized. On the contrary, if the term is globally frequent and it was omitted in the document's representation, then the penalization is much lower. This is intuitive because frequent terms have much more chance of being connected with the contents of documents that do not explicitly mentioned them.

3.2 Document Length

We now pay attention to the issue of the number of terms that should be negated in the representation of every document. In this respect, a first question arises: is it fair to negate the same number of terms for all documents? In the following we try to give a motivated answer.

Let T_d be the subset of terms of the alphabet (T) that are present in the text of a document d. Consider that we decide to introduce k negated terms in the logical representation of d. That is, every term in T_d will form a positive literal and k terms in $T \backslash T_d$ (the k terms in $T \backslash T_d$ most infrequent in the collection) produce k negated literals. If we introduce the same number of negations for all documents in the collection we would be implicitly assuming that all documents had the same chance of mentioning explicitly all their relevant topics. This assumption is not appropriate.

A long document may simply cover more material than a short one. We can even think on a long document as a sequence of unrelated short documents concatenated together. This view is called the *scope hypothesis* and contrasts with the *verbosity hypothesis*, in which a long document is supposed to cover a similar scope than a short document but simply uses more words [11]. It is accepted that the verbosity hypothesis prevails over the scope hypothesis. Indeed, the control of verbosity stands behind the success of high performance document length normalization techniques [13, 11].

This also connects with recent advances on smoothing strategies for Language Modeling. For instance, a bayesian predictive smoothing approach takes into account the difference of data uncertainty in short and long documents [16]. As documents are larger, the uncertainty in the estimations becomes narrower. A similar idea will drive our logical indexing process because long documents are supposed to indicate more exhaustively their contents and, hence, more assumptions on the non-related terms will be taken.

A fixed number of negations for every document is also not advisable from a practical perspective. Think that the sets $T \setminus T_d$ are very large (because $T_d << T$) and, hence, there will surely be many commom terms in the sets $T \setminus T_d$ across all documents. As a consequence, there will likely be little difference between the negated terms introduced by two different documents and, therefore, the effect on retrieval performance will be unnoticeable.

In this work we propose and evaluate a simple strategy in which the number of negations grows linearly with the size of the document. In our logical indexing process, the size of a document will be measured as the number of different terms mentioned by the document.

Another important issue affects the maximum and minimum number of negations that the logical indexing will apply. Let us assume that, for a given document d, we decide to include 1000 negated literals in its logical representation. Since the number of negations is relatively low (w.r.t. current term spaces), the involved terms will be very infrequent, most of them mentioned by a single document in the whole collection and, therefore, it is also very unlikely that any query finds them useful to express an information need. As a consequence, a low number of negations will definitely not produce any effect on retrieval performance because the negated terms are rare and will be hardly used by any query. This advances that significant changes on the retrieval behaviour of the logical model will be found when the number of negations is high. Inspired by this, we designed our logical indexing technique starting from a total closed-world assumption (i.e. we negate every unseen term) and we reduce the number of negations as document's size decreases. That is, instead of starting from a representation with 0 negated terms which is repeteadly populated by negations involving infrequent terms, we start from a logical formula with $T \setminus T_d$ negated terms and we repeteadly omit globally frequent terms[3].

We define now the number of terms that will be omitted in the logical representation of a given document as a function of the size of the document:

$$OT_d = \frac{max\_dl - dl_d}{max\_dl - min\_dl} \cdot MAX\_OT \tag{1}$$

where dl_d is the size of the document d, max_dl (min_dl) is the size of the largest (shortest) document and MAX_OT is a constant that determines the maximum number of terms for which the logical indexing will not make any strong decision and, hence, no literal, either positive or negative, will be expressed[4].

[3] In the future we also plan to articulate an indexing process which skips globally infrequent terms and, hence, these procedures will be revisited.

[4] Of course, MAX_OT should be lower or equal than the smallest value of $|T \setminus T_d|$ computed across all documents. Otherwise, the indexing process could suggest a value of OT_d, such that $OT_d > |T \setminus T_d|$. This indexing could only be implemented by considering some explicit terms in T_d as non-informative words that should be omitted the representation of the document. Obviously, this is not the intention pursued here.

To sum up, every document will be represented as a logical formula in which:

- Terms appearing explicitly in the text of the document, $t \in T_d$, will be positive literals in the representation of the document.
- Terms not mentioned explicitly, $t \in T \setminus T_d$ are ranked in decreasing order of appearances within the whole collection and:
  - Top OT_d terms will be omitted in the representation of d.
  - The remaining terms will be negative literals in the logical formula representing d.

$$T = \{a, b, c, d, e, f, g, h, i, j, l, m, n, o, p, q, r, s, t, u\}$$

Document	T_d (explicit terms)
d_1	a, r
d_2	a, c, d, e, u, t
...	...

$$max\_dl = 10$$
$$min\_dl = 2$$
$$MAX\_OT = 10$$

$$OT_{d_1} = \frac{10-2}{10-2} \cdot 10 = 10$$
$$OT_{d_2} = \frac{10-6}{10-2} \cdot 10 = 5$$

Document	omitted terms	negated terms
d_1	$u, t, s, q, p, o, n, m, l, j$	i, h, g, f, e, d, c, b
d_2	s, r, q, p, o	$n, m, l, j, i, h, g, f, b$
...	...	...

Document	Logical representation
d_1	$a \wedge r \wedge \neg i \wedge \neg h \wedge \neg g \wedge \neg f \wedge \neg e \wedge \neg d \wedge \neg c \wedge \neg b$
d_2	$a \wedge c \wedge d \wedge e \wedge u \wedge t \wedge \neg n \wedge \neg m \wedge \neg l \wedge \neg j \wedge \neg i \wedge \neg h \wedge \neg g \wedge \neg f \wedge \neg b$
...	...

Fig. 1. Logical indexing process

Figure 1 illustrates an example of this logical indexing process. The vocabulary of 20 terms is supposed to be ordered in increasing order of appearance within the whole collection. The largest document is supposed to have 10 terms whereas the shortest one (d_1) mentions just two terms. The constant MAX_OT is assumed to be equal to 10. Observe that, a *closed-world assumption indexing* would assign 18 and 14 negations to d_1 and d_2, respectively, whereas the length-dependent indexing assigns 8 negations to the short document d_1 and 9 negations to the long document. Note that the final logical representation of a long document is more complete because there will be few omitted terms and, on the contrary, representations of short documents are more partial.

The tuning constant MAX_OT is an instrument to make explicit control on partiality. If $MAX\_OT = 0$ then the system does not allow partiality in the logical repre-

Table 1. Training phase - Tuning partiality

Topics #151-#200								
	cwa indexing	MAX_OT	MAX_OT	MAX_OT	MAX_OT	MAX_OT	MAX_OT	MAX_OT
α		1000	2000	3000	4000	5000	10000	50000
0.4	0.0719	0.1320	0.1544	0.1475	0.1420	0.1422	0.1136	0.0736
	1533	2013	2090	1849	1912	1845	1639	1539
0.5	0.1055	0.1470	**0.1687**	0.1562	0.1537	0.1613	0.1526	0.1075
	1760	2010	**2048**	1786	1837	1950	1810	1764
0.6	**0.1520**	0.1561	0.1513	0.1289	0.1041	0.1290	0.1426	0.1452
	1751	1864	1738	1447	1298	1578	1522	1748

sentations and, therefore, all the vocabulary terms have to be mentioned either positive or negative. As MAX_OT grows logical representations become more partial. Obviously, very low values of MAX_OT will not permit to establish significant differences between the indexing of short and long documents.

4 Experiments

This logical indexing was evaluated against the WSJ subset of the TREC collection in discs 1&2. This collection constains 173252 articles published in the Wall Street Journal between 1987 and 1992.

We took 50 TREC topics for training the MAX_OT parameter (TREC topics #151 - #200) and a separate set of topics is later used for validating previous findings (TREC topics #101 - #150). For each query, top 1000 documents were used for evaluation.

Documents and topics were preprocessed with a stoplist of 571 common words and remaining terms were stemmed using Porter's algorithm [10]. Logical queries are constructed by simply connecting their stems through logical conjunctions. Queries are long because the subparts Title, Description and Narrative were all considered. Stemmed document terms are directly incorporated as positive literals and some negated terms are included in the conjunctive representation of a document depending on document's length and term's global frequency. In order to check whether or not this new logical indexing improves the top performance obtained by the PLBR model so far, we first ran a number of experiments following a closed-world assumption (i.e. all terms which are not mentioned by the document are incorporated as negated literals). Recall that the PLBR model handles idf information when measuring distances between logical interpretations. This effect is controlled by a parameter α. We tried out values for α from 0.9 to 0.1 in steps of 0.1. Since the major benefits were found when $0.4 \leq \alpha \leq 0.6$, we only present performance results for $\alpha = 0.4, 0.5, 0.6$. On the second column of table 1 (cwa indexing) we show performance ratios (non-interpolated average precision & total number of relevant retrieved documents) for the cwa indexing approach on the training set. The best results were found for a value of α equal to 0.6 (in bold).

Columns 3rd to 9th of table 1 depict performance results for the more evolved logical indexing with varied number of omitted terms. Not surprinsingly, for high values of omitted terms ($\geq$ 50000) performance tends to the performance obtained with the basic

Table 2. Test phase - Effect of partiality

Topics #101-#150		
Recall	cwa indexing trained $\alpha = 0.6$	dl indexing not trained $MAX\_OT = 2000, \alpha = 0.5$
0.00	0.4576	0.5379
0.10	0.2842	0.3317
0.20	0.2154	0.2639
0.30	0.1788	0.2075
0.40	0.1445	0.1600
0.50	0.1195	0.1240
0.60	0.0923	0.0993
0.70	0.0717	0.0684
0.80	0.0397	0.0373
0.90	0.0188	0.0131
1.00	0.0098	0.0035
Avg.prec. (non-interpolated)	0.1319	0.1482
% change		+12.4%
Total relevant retrieved	1828	2301
% change		+25.9%

indexing (first column). This is because the ratio $negated\_terms/omitted\_terms$ is so low that almost every query term is either matched by a document or it was omitted. There are very few negations and, hence, the distinction between those classes of terms is unnoticeable. On the other hand, for relatively low values of MAX_OT (between 1000 and 5000) performance tends to improve with respect to cwa indexing. The best training run is obtained when $MAX\_OT = 2000, \alpha = 0.5$ (0.1687 vs 0.152, 11% improvement in non-interpolated average precision and 2048 vs 1751, 17% more relevant documents retrieved).

In order to confront previous findings, we ran additional experiments with the test set of topics. We fixed a value of 2000 omitted terms and $\alpha = 0.5$ for the new indexing approach. Although this is the test phase, we trained again the parameter α for the basic indexing policy (cwa) and we show here the best results ($\alpha = 0.6$). This is to assure that the new document length indexing without training can improve the best results attainable with the basic cwa indexing. The results are depicted in table 2. Major benefits are found when partial representations are handled. It seems clear that the consideration of document length to omit up to 2000 terms improves significantly the retrieval performance of the logical model.

This experimentation suggests to omit a relatively low number of omitted terms with respect to the total vocabulary size. This means that the shortest document will be able to have 2000 omitted terms within its logical representation. These 2000 terms will be those more globally used that are not present in that small document. It is well known [12] that the large majority of the words occurring in a corpus have very low document frequency. This means that most terms are used just once in the whole collection and, hence, it is also unlikely that any query makes use of them. That is, only a small fragment of the vocabulary (the most frequent ones) makes a significant impact on retrieval performance. Indeed, in the WSJ collection that we indexed, 76839 terms out of 163656 (which is the vocabulary size after preprocessing) are only mentioned in a single document. This explains why the major differents in performance are found for small values of MAX_OT.

5 Analysis

In this section we provide an additional analysis of the logical indexing keeping track of its behaviour against document length. We will follow the methodology designed by Singhal, Buckley and Mitra [13] to analyze the likelihood of relevance/retrieval for documents of all lengths and plot these likelihoods against the document length to compare the relevance pattern and the retrieval pattern.

First, the document collection is ordered by document's length and documents are divided into equal-sizes chunks, which are called bins. For our case, the 173252 WSJ documents were divided into 173 bins containing one thousand documents each and an additional bin contained the 252 largest documents. For the test topics (#101-#150) we then took the 4556 (query, relevant document) pairs and counted how many pairs had their document from the ith bin. These values allow to plot a relevance pattern against document length. Specifically, the conditional probability $P(D \in ith\ bin | D\ is\ relevant)$ can be computed as the ratio of the number of pairs that have the document from the ith bin and the total number of pairs.

A given retrieval strategy will present a good behaviour against document's length provided that its probability of retrieval for the documents of a given length is very close to the probability of finding a relevant document of that length. Therefore, once we have a relevance pattern, we can compute the retrieval pattern and compare them graphically. We will compute the retrieval pattern for both the cwa PLBR run and the PLBR run with document length-dependent indexing. Comparing them with the relevance pattern we will be able to validate the adequacy of our document's length-dependent indexing and, possibly, identify further avenues of research.

The retrieval pattern's computation is also very simple. For each query the top one thousand documents retrieved are selected (for our case, 50.000 (query, retrieved documents) pairs) and, for each bin, we can directly obtain $P(D \in ith\ bin | D\ is\ retrieved)$.

Figure 2 shows the probability of relevance and the probability of retrieval of the cwa PLBR run plotted against the bin number (2(a)). The probability of relevance and the probability of retrieval applying the document length-dependent logical indexing are plotted in fig. 2(b). Recall that bin #1 contains the smallest documents and bin #174 containst the largest documents. Following that figure, there is no clear evidence about the distinction between both approaches. In figure 3 we plot cwa indexing and dl indexing against document length. Although the curves are very similar, some trends can be identified. For bins #1 to #100 the dl indexing approach retrieves documents with higher probability than the cwa approach. On the other hand, very long documents (last 20 bins) are retrieved with higher probability if the cwa strategy is applied. This demonstrates that the dl indexing procedure does its job because it tends to favour short doc-

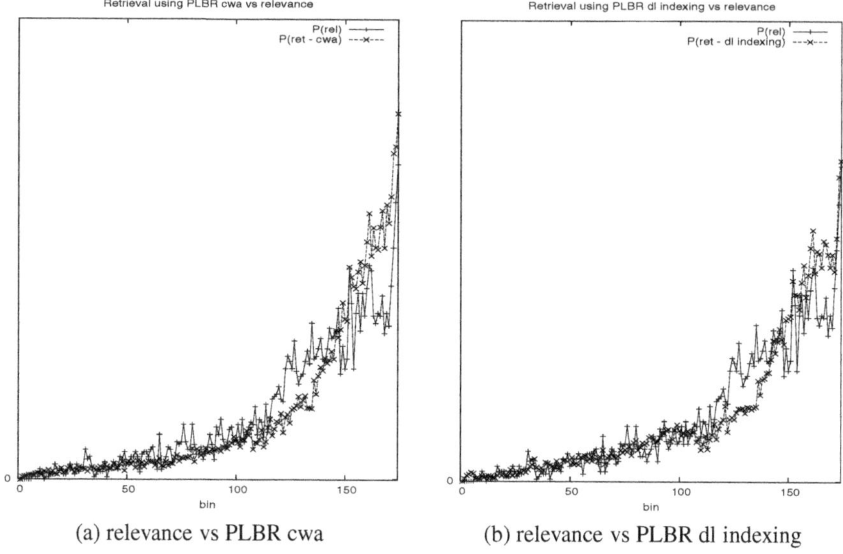

(a) relevance vs PLBR cwa

(b) relevance vs PLBR dl indexing

Fig. 2. Probability of relevance vs probability of retrieval

uments w.r.t. long ones. Nevertheless, this analysis also suggests new ways to improve the document length logical indexing. The most obvious is that very long documents do still present a probability of being retrieved which is much greater than the probability of relevance (see fig. 2(b), last 20 bins). This suggests that the formula that computes the number of omitted terms (equation 1, section 3.2) should be adapted accordingly. As a consequence, subsequent research effort will be directed to the fine tuning of the document length-dependent indexing.

6 Conclusions and Future Work

In this work we have proposed a novel logical indexing technique which yields a natural way to handle terms not explicitly mentioned by documents. The new indexing approach is assisted by popular IR notions such as document length normalization and global term distribution. The combination of those classical notions and the expressiveness of the logical apparatus leads to a precise modeling of the document's contents. The evaluation conducted confirms empirically the advantages of the approach taken.

Future work will be focused in a number of lines. First, as argued in the previous section, document length contribution should be optimized. Second, more evolved techniques to negate terms will also be investigated. In this respect, the application of term similarity information is especially encouraging for avoiding negated terms whose semantics is close to some of the terms which appear explicitly in the text of a document.

Our present document length strategy captures verbosity by means of document length. Although it is sensible to think that there is a correlation between document

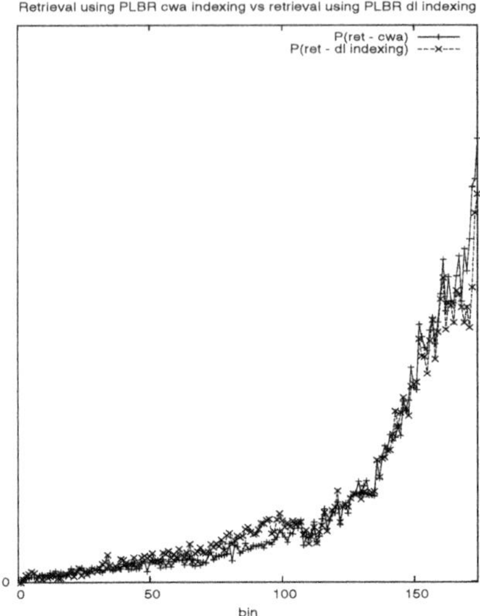

Fig. 3. cwa indexing vs dl indexing

length and verbosity, it is also very interesting to study new methods to identify verbose/scope documents and tune the model accordingly.

Acknowledgements

This work was supported by projects TIC2002-00947 (from "Ministerio de Ciencia y Tecnología") and PGIDT03PXIC10501PN (from "Xunta de Galicia"). The first author is supported in part by "Ministerio de Ciencia y Tecnología" and in part by FEDER funds through the "Ramón y Cajal" program.

References

1. F. Crestani, M. Lalmas, and C. J. van Rijsbergen (editors). *Information Retrieval, Uncertainty and Logics: advanced models for the representation and retrieval of information.* Kluwer Academic, Norwell, MA., 1998.
2. W. B. Croft and J. Lafferty. *Language Modeling for Information Retrieval.* Kluwer Academic, 2003.
3. M. Dalal. Investigations into a theory of knowledge base revision:preliminary report. In *Proceedings of the 7th National Conference on Artificial Intelligence (AAAI'88)*, pages 475–479, Saint Paul, USA, 1988.
4. D. Losada and A. Barreiro. Embedding term similarity and inverse document frequency into a logical model of information retrieval. *Journal of the American Society for Information Science and Technology, JASIST*, 54(4):285–301, February 2003.
5. D. Losada and A. Barreiro. Propositional logic representations for documents and queries: a large-scale evaluation. In F. Sebastiani, editor, *Proc. 25th European Conference on Information Retrieval Research, ECIR'2003*, pages 219–234, Pisa, Italy, April 2003. Springer Verlag, LNCS 2663.

6. D. E. Losada and A. Barreiro. Using a belief revision operator for document ranking in extended boolean models. In *Proc. SIGIR-99, the 22nd ACM Conference on Research and Development in Information Retrieval*, pages 66–73, Berkeley, USA, August 1999.
7. D. E. Losada and A. Barreiro. Efficient algorithms for ranking documents represented as dnf formulas. In *Proc. SIGIR-2000 Workshop on Mathematical and Formal Methods in Information Retrieval*, pages 16–24, Athens, Greece, July 2000.
8. D. E. Losada and A. Barreiro. A logical model for information retrieval based on propositional logic and belief revision. *The Computer Journal*, 44(5):410–424, 2001.
9. J. Ponte and W. B. Croft. A language modeling approach to information retrieval. In *Proc. 21st ACM Conference on Research and Development in Information Retrieval, SIGIR'98*, pages 275–281, Melbourne, Australia, 1998.
10. M.F. Porter. An algorithm for suffix stripping. *Program*, 14(3):130–137, 1980.
11. S. Robertson and S. Walker. Some simple effective approximations to the 2-poisson model for probabilistic weighted retrieval. In *Proc. SIGIR-94, the 17th ACM Conference on Research and Development in Information Retrieval*, pages 232–241, Dublin, Ireland, July 1994.
12. G. Salton, A. Wong, and C. Yang. A vector space model for automatic indexing. *Communications of the ACM*, 18:613–620, 1975.
13. A Singhal, C. Buckley, and M Mitra. Pivoted document length normalization. In *Proc. SIGIR-96, the 19th ACM Conference on Research and Development in Information Retrieval*, pages 21–29, Zurich, Switzerland, July 1996.
14. C. J. van Rijsbergen. A theoretical basis for the use of co-occurrence data in information retrieval. *Journal of Documentation*, 33(2):106–119, 1977.
15. C.J. van Rijsbergen. A non-classical logic for information retrieval. *The Computer Journal*, 29:481–485, 1986.
16. H. Zaragoza, D. Hiemstra, and M. Tipping. Bayesian extension to the language model for ad hoc information retrieval. In *Proc. 26th ACM Conference on Research and Development in Information Retrieval, SIGIR'03*, pages 4–9, Toronto, Canada, 2003.

An Improvement and an Extension on the Hybrid Index for Approximate String Matching

Heikki Hyyrö[1,2,⋆]

[1] PRESTO, Japan Science and Technology Agency
[2] Department of Computer Sciences, University of Tampere, Finland
Heikki.Hyyro@cs.uta.fi

Abstract. In [2] Navarro and Baeza-Yates found their so-called hybrid index to be the best alternative for indexed approximate search in English text. The original hybrid index is based on Levenshtein edit distance. We propose two modifications to the hybrid index. The first is a way to accelerate the search. The second modification is to make the index permit also the error of transposing two adjacent characters ("Damerau distance"). A full discussion is presented in Section 11 of [1].

Let $ed(A, B)$ denote the edit distance between strings A and B, $|A|$ denote the length of A, A_i denote the ith character of A, and $A_{i..j}$ denote the substring of A that begins from its ith and ends at it jth character. Given a length-m pattern string P, a length-n text string T, and an error limit k, the task of approximate string matching is to find such text positions j where $ed(P, T_{h..j}) \leq k$ and $h \leq j$. Levenshtein edit distance $ed_L(A, B)$ is the minimum number of single-character insertions, deletions and substitutions needed in transforming A into B or vice versa. Damerau edit distance $ed_D(A, B)$ is otherwise similar but permits also the operation of transposing two permanently adjacent characters.

Using an index structure during the search can accelerate approximate string matching. One such index is the hybrid index of Navarro & Baeza-Yates [2] for Levenshtein edit distance, which they found to be the best choice for searching English text. It uses *intermediate partitioning*, where the pattern is partitioned into j pieces $P^1, .., P^j$, and then each piece P^i is searched for with $d^i = \lfloor k/j \rfloor$ errors. If $j > 1$ and a hit $T_{j-h..j}$ is found so that $ed_L(P^i, T_{j-h..j}) \leq d^i$, the text area $T_{j-m-k..j+m+k}$ will be included in a check for a complete match of P with k errors. The hits for each piece P^i are found by a depth-first search (DFS) over a suffix tree[1] built for the text. This involves filling a dynamic programming table D, where $D[r, l] = ed(P^i_{1..r}, T_{j+1..j+l})$, during the DFS. When the DFS arrives at a node that corresponds to the text substring $T_{j+1..j+l}$, the distances $ed_L(P^i_{1..r}, T_{j+1..j+l})$ are computed for $r = 1 \ldots m^i$, where $m^i = |P^i|$.

Our main proposal for accelerating the DFS is as follows. When the DFS reaches a depth-l node that corresponds to the text substring $T_{j+1..j+l}$ and

⋆ Supported by Tampere Graduate School in Information Science and Engineering.

[1] A trie of all suffixes of the text in which each suffix has its own leaf node and the position of each suffix is recorded into the corresponding leaf.

A. Apostolico and M. Melucci (Eds.): SPIRE 2004, LNCS 3246, pp. 208–209, 2004.

a)

		t	h	e	r	e			
	0	1	2	3	4	5	6	7	8
t	1	0	1	2	3	4			
h	2	1	0	1	2	3			
e	3	2	1	0	1	**2**			
s	4	3	2	1	1	**2**	2		
i	5	4	3	2	2	**2**	2	2	
s	6	5	4	3	3	3	2	2	2

b)

$m^i = m$	$d^i = k$	OURS/NBY (WSJ)	OURS/NBY (yeast)
5	1	0,23	0,66
5	2	0,33	0,74
10	1	0,19	0,20
10	2	0,33	0,31
10	3	0,41	0,39
15	1	0,19	0,19
15	2	0,34	0,27
15	3	0,43	0,36
15	4	0,50	0,49

Fig. 1. Figure a): Matrix D for computing $ed_L(P^i_{1..r}, T_{j+1..})$, where $P^i_{1..m^i}$ = "thesis", $T_{j+1..}$ = "there..", and $d^i = 2$. Now $D[r,5] \geq d^i = 2$ for $r = 1 \ldots m^i$, and the only way to reach a cell value $D[m^i, x] \leq 2$, where $x > 5$, is to have only matches at the remaining parts of the top-left-to-bottom-right diagonals with the value $D[h,5] = 2$. The cells in these diagonal extensions have the value $d^i = 2$ underlined, and the pattern suffixes corresponding to the cell values $D[3,5]$, $D[4,5]$ and $D[5,5]$ (shown in bold) are $P^i_{4..6}$ = "sis", $P^i_{5..6}$ = "is" and P^i_6 = "s", respectively. Figure b): The ratio between the running time of our improved DFS (OURS) and the runtime of the original DFS of Navarro and Baeza-Yates (NBY). We tested with two $\approx$ 10 MB texts: Wall Street Journal articles (WSJ) and the DNA of baker's yeast (yeast). The computer was a 600 Mhz Pentium 3 with 256 MB RAM, Linux OS and GCC 3.2.1 compiler.

where $D[r,l] \geq d^i$ for $r = 1..m^i$, the only strings that have $T_{j+1..j+l}$ as a prefix and match P^i with d^i errors are of form $T_{j+1..j+l} \circ P^i_{h+1..m^i}$, where $\circ$ denotes concatenation and h fulfills the condition $D[h,l] = d^i$. In this situation we check directly for the presence of any of these concatenated substrings, and then let the DFS backtrack. Fig. 1a illustrates, and Fig. 1b shows experimental results from a comparison against the original DFS of [2] when $P^i = P$ and $d^i = k$.

In addition we propose the following lemma for partitioning P under Damerau distance. It uses *classes of characters*, which refers to permitting a pattern position to match with any character enumerated inside square brackets. For example P = "thes[ei]s" matches with the strings "theses" and "thesis".

Lemma 1. *Let P^i, $i = 1..j$, be j non-overlapping substrings of the pattern P that are ordered so that P^{i+1} occurs on the right side of P^i in P. Also let B be some string for which $ed_D(P, B) \leq k$, let each P^i be associated with the corresponding number of errors d^i, and let strings $\bar{P}^i$, $i = 1..j$, be defined as follows:*

$\bar{P}^i = P^i$, if $i = j$ or P^i and P^{i+1} do not occur consecutively in P.
$\bar{P}^i = P^i_{1..m^i-1} \circ [P^i_{m^i} P^{i+1}_1]$, otherwise.

If $\sum_{i=1}^{j} d^i \geq k - j + 1$, then one of the strings $\bar{P}^i$ matches inside B with at most d^i errors.

References

1. H. Hyyrö. *Practical Methods for Approximate String Matching.* PhD thesis, Department of Computer Sciences, University of Tampere, Finland, December 2003.
2. G. Navarro and R. Baeza-Yates. A hybrid indexing method for approximate string matching. *Journal of Discrete Algorithms (JDA)*, 1(1):205–239, 2000.

First Huffman, Then Burrows-Wheeler: A Simple Alphabet-Independent FM-Index

Szymon Grabowski[1], Veli Mäkinen[2], and Gonzalo Navarro[3]

[1] Computer Engineering Dept., Tech. Univ. of Łódź, Poland
[2] Dept. of Computer Science, Univ. of Helsinki, Finland
[3] Dept. of Computer Science, Univ. of Chile, Chile

Main Results. The basic string matching problem is to determine the occurrences of a short pattern $P = p_1p_2 \ldots p_m$ in a large text $T = t_1t_2 \ldots t_n$, over an alphabet of size σ. Indexes are structures built on the text to speed up searches, but they used to take up much space. In recent years, *succinct* text indexes have appeared. A prominent example is the FM-index [2], which takes little space (close to that of the *compressed* text) and *replaces* the text, as it can search the text (in optimal $O(m)$ time) and reproduce any text substring without accessing it. The main problem of the FM-index is that its space usage depends exponentially on σ, that is, $5H_kn + \sigma^\sigma o(n)$ for any k, H_k being the k-th order entropy of T.

In this paper we present a simple variant of the FM-index, which removes its alphabet dependence. We achieve this by, essentially (but not exactly), Huffman-compressing the text and FM-indexing the binary sequence. Our index needs $2n(H_0 + 1)(1 + o(1))$ bits, independent of σ, and it searches in $O(m(H_0 + 1))$ average time, which can be made $O(m \log \sigma)$ in the worst case. Moreover, our index is considerably simpler to implement than most other succinct indexes.

Technical Details. The Burrows-Wheeler transform (BWT) [1] T^{bwt} of T is a permutation of T such that $T^{bwt}[i]$ is the character preceding the i-th lexicographically smallest suffix of T. The FM-index finds the number of occurrences of P in T by running the following algorithm [2]:

Algorithm FM_Search(P,T^{bwt})
 $i = m$; $sp = 1$; $ep = n$;
 while (($sp \leq ep$) **and** ($i \geq 1$) **do**
  $c = P[i-1]$;
  $sp = C[c] + Occ(T^{bwt}, c, sp-1)+1$;
  $ep = C[c] + Occ(T^{bwt}, c, ep)$;
  $i = i - 1$;
 if ($ep < sp$) **then return** "not found" **else return** "found ($ep - sp + 1$) occs".

The index is actually formed by array $C[\cdot]$, such that $C[c]$ is the number of characters smaller than c in T, and function $Occ(T^{bwt}, \cdot, \cdot)$, such that $Occ(T^{bwt}, c, i)$ is the number of occurrences of c in $T^{bwt}[1 \ldots i]$. The exponential alphabet dependence of the FM-index is incurred in the implementation of Occ in constant time.

A. Apostolico and M. Melucci (Eds.): SPIRE 2004, LNCS 3246, pp. 210–211, 2004.

Our idea is first to Huffman-compress T so as to obtain T', a binary string of length $n' < n(H_0 + 1)$. Then, if we encode P to P' with the same codebook used for T, it turns out that any occurrence of P in T is also an occurrence of P' in T' (but not vice versa, as P' may match in the middle of a code in T').

We apply the BWT to T' to obtain array $B = (T')^{bwt}$, of n' bits. Another array Bh signals which bits of B correspond to beginning of codewords in T'. If we apply algorithm FM_Search(P',B), the result is the number of occurrences of P' in T'. Moreover, the algorithm yields the range $[sp, ep]$ of occurrences in B. The real occurrences of P in T correspond to the bits set in $Bh[sp \ldots ep]$.

Function $rank(Bh, i)$, which tells how many bits are set in $Bh[1 \ldots i]$, can be implemented in constant time by storing $o(n')$ bits in addition to Bh [4]. So our number of occurrences is $rank(Bh, ep) - rank(Bh, sp - 1)$.

The advantage over the original FM-index is that this time the text T' is binary and thus $Occ(B, 1, i) = rank(B, i)$ and $Occ(B, 0, i) = i - rank(B, i)$. Hence we can implement Occ in constant time using $o(n')$ additional bits, independently of the alphabet size.

Overall we need $2n(H_0+1)(1+o(1))$ bits, and can search for P in $O(m(H_0+1))$ time if P distributes as T. By adding $1+\varepsilon$ bits, for any $\varepsilon > 0$, we can find the text position of each occurrence in worst case time $O((1/\varepsilon)(H_0 + 1) \log n)$, and display any text substring of length L in $O((1/\varepsilon)(H_0 + 1)(L + \log n))$ average time. By adding other $2n$ bits, we can ensure that all $O(H_0 + 1)$ values become $O(\log \sigma)$ in the worst case times. For further details and experimental results refer to [3].

References

1. M. Burrows and D. J. Wheeler. A block-sorting lossless data compression algorithm. *DEC SRC Research Report 124*, 1994.
2. P. Ferragina and G. Manzini. Opportunistic data structures with applications. In *Proc. FOCS'00*, pp. 390–398, 2000.
3. Sz. Grabowski, V. Mäkinen and G. Navarro. *First Huffman, then Burrows-Wheeler: A Simple Alphabet-Independent FM-Index.* Technical Report TR/DCC-2004-4, Dept. of Computer Science, University of Chile. `ftp://ftp.dcc.uchile.cl/pub/users/gnavarro/huffbwt.ps.gz`
4. I. Munro. Tables. In *Proc. FSTTCS'96*, pp. 37–42, 1996.

Metric Indexes for Approximate String Matching in a Dictionary

Kimmo Fredriksson

Depart. of CS, University of Joensuu, PO Box 111, FIN–80101 Joensuu, Finland
kfredrik@cs.joensuu.fi

We consider the problem of finding all approximate occurrences of a given string q, with at most k differences, in a finite database or *dictionary* of strings. The strings can be e.g. natural language words, such as the vocabulary of some document or set of documents. This has many important application in both off-line (indexed) and on-line string matching. More precisely, we have a universe $\mathbb{U}$ of *strings*, and a non-negative distance function $d : \mathbb{U} \times \mathbb{U} \rightarrow \mathbb{N}$. The distance function is metric, if it satisfies (i) $d(x, y) = 0 \Leftrightarrow x = y$; (ii) $d(x, y) = d(y, x)$; (iii) $d(x, y) \leq d(x, z) + d(z, y)$. The last item is called the "triangular inequality", and is the most important property in our case. Many useful distance functions are known to be metric, in particular edit (Levenshtein) distance is metric, which we will use for d.

Our dictionary S is a finite subset of that universe, i.e. $S \subseteq \mathbb{U}$. S is preprocessed in order to efficiently answer range queries. Given a query string q, we retrieve all strings in S that are close enough to q, i.e. we retrieve the set $\{u \in S \mid d(q, u) \leq k\}$ for some k.

To solve the problem, we build a metric index over the dictionary, and use the triangular inequality to efficiently prune the search. This is not a new idea, huge number of different indexes have been proposed over the years, see [2] for a recent survey. An example of such an index is the Burkhard-Keller tree [1]. They build a hierarchy as follows. Some arbitrary string (called *pivot*) $p \in S$ is chosen for the root of the tree. The child number e is recursively built using the set $S_e = \{u \in S \setminus \{p\} \mid d(p, u) = e\}$. This is repeated until there are only one, or in general b (for a *bucket*), strings left, which are stored into the leaves of the tree. The tree has $O(n)$ nodes, where $n = |S|$, and the construction requires $O(n \log n)$ distance computations on average. The search with the query string q and range k first evaluates the distance $d(q, p)$, where p is the string in the root of the tree. If $d(q, p) \leq k$, then p is put into the output list. The search then recursively enters into each child e such that $d(q, p) - k \leq e \leq d(q, p) + k$. Whenever the search reaches a leaf, the stored bucket of strings are directly compared against q. The search requires $O(n^\alpha)$ distance computations on average, where $0 < \alpha < 1$.

Another example is Approximating Eliminating Search Algorithm (AESA) [4], which is an extreme case of pivot based algorithms. This time there is not any hierarchy, but the data structure is simply a precomputed matrix of all the $n(n-1)/2$ distances between the n strings in S. The space complexity is therefore $O(n^2)$ and the matrix is computed with $O(n^2)$ edit distance computations. This makes the structure highly impractical for large n. The benefit comes from search time, empirical results have shown that it needs only a constant number of

A. Apostolico and M. Melucci (Eds.): SPIRE 2004, LNCS 3246, pp. 212–213, 2004.

distance evaluations on average. However, each distance evaluation takes $O(n)$ "extra CPU time".

The problem with AESA is its high preprocessing and space complexities. For small dictionaries this is not a problem, so we propose using AESA to implement additional search algorithm for the buckets of b strings stored into the leaves of the tree based indexes such as BKT. This means that the space complexity becomes $O(nb)$, and the construction time $O(n(b + \log(n/b)))$. In effect this makes the index memory adaptive. We can adjust b to make a good use of the available memory to reduce the number of distance computations. We call the resulting algorithm ABKT. Another way to trade space for time is to collapse children $d(q,p) - k \leq e \leq d(q,p) + k$ into a single branch, and at the search time enter only into child $(d(q,p), k)$. This can be done only for levels up to ℓ of the tree to keep the memory requirements low. We call this algorithm E(BP)BKT.

The recent bit-parallel on-line string matching algorithm in [3] can be easily modified to compute several edit distances in parallel for short strings, i.e. we can compute the edit distance between q and r other strings, each of length m, in time $O(|q|)$, where $r = \lfloor w/m \rfloor$ and w is the number of bits in computer word (typically 32 or 64, or even 128 with the SIMD extensions of recent processors). Simplest application of this technique in BKT is to store a bucket of r strings into each node, instead of only one (the pivot), and use one of them as the pivot string for building the hierarchy and guiding the search. In the preprocessing phase the effect is that the tree has only $O(n/r)$ nodes (assuming $b = 1$). At the search time, we evaluate the distance between the query string and the pivot as before, but at the same time, without any additional cost, we evaluate $r - 1$ other distances. For these $r - 1$ other distances we just check if they are close enough to the query (this can be done in parallel in $O(1)$ time), but do not use them for any other purpose. We call this algorithm BPBKT.

We have implemented the algorithms in C/C++ and run experiments in 2GHz Pentium 4. We used a dictionary of 98580 English words for the experiments. We selected 10,000 query words from the dictionary. For ABKT we used $b = 1000$, for BPBKT $r = 8$ (and $w = 128$) and for EBPBKT $\ell = 1$. The average number of distance evaluations / total query time in seconds for $k = 1$ were 2387 / 20.58 (BKT), 495 / 14.74 (ABKT), 729 / 8.93 (BPBKT) and 583 / 7.09 (EBPBKT). The ratio between the performance of the algorithms remained approximately the same for $k = 1..4$.

References

1. W. A. Burkhard and R. M. Keller. Some approaches to best-match file searching. *Commun. ACM*, 16(4):230–236, 1973.
2. E. Chávez, G. Navarro, R. Baeza-Yates, and J.L. Marroquin. Searching in metric spaces. *ACM Computing Surveys*, 33(3):273–321, September 2001.
3. H. Hyyrö, K. Fredriksson, and G. Navarro. Increased bit-parallelism for approximate string matching. In *WEA '04*, LNCS 3059, pages 285–298, 2004.
4. E. Vidal. An algorithm for finding nearest neighbors in (approximately) constant average time. *Pattern Recognition Letters*, 4:145–157, 1986.

Simple Implementation of String B-Trees*

Joong Chae Na and Kunsoo Park

School of Computer Science and Engineering
Seoul National University
{jcna,kpark}@theory.snu.ac.kr

1 Introduction

The String B-tree [2] due to Ferragina and Grossi is a well-known external-memory index data structure which handles arbitrarily long strings and performs search efficiently. It is essentially a combination of B^+-trees and Patricia tries. From a high-level point of view, the String B-tree of a string T of length N is a B^+-tree, where the keys are *pointers* to the suffixes of string T, and they are sorted in lexicographically increasing order of the suffixes. A Patricia trie is used for each node of the String B-tree. By plugging in Patricia tries at nodes, the branch/search/update operations can be carried out efficiently. Due to Patricia tries, however, the String B-tree is rather heavy and complex.

In this paper we propose a new implementation of the String B-tree, which is simpler and easier to implement than the original String B-tree, and that supports as efficient search as the original String B-tree. Instead of a Patricia trie, each node contains an array, lcp_i, of integers and an array, lnc_i, of characters. Once the number of keys in a node is given, arrays lcp_i and lnc_i occupy a fixed space, while the space required for a Patricia trie can vary within a constant factor. Because arrays are simple and occupy a fixed space, they are easy to handle and suitable for external-memory data structure.

We present an efficient branching algorithm at a node that uses only the two arrays lcp_i and lnc_i. Ferguson [1] gave a branching algorithm for binary strings. We extend this algorithm so as to do the branch operation efficiently for strings over a general alphabet. The search algorithm based on our branching algorithm requires $O(\log_B N + \frac{M+occ}{B})$ disk accesses as in the original String B-tree, where M is the length of a pattern, occ is the number of occurrences, and B is the disk page size. The branching algorithm can be also used as a basic algorithm of the insertion, deletion, and construction algorithms of the original String B-tree.

2 Branching Algorithm

Let T be a string of length N over an alphabet Σ, which is stored in external memory. We denote the ith character of string T by $T[i]$. We define the ith *suffix* as the substring $T[i]T[i+1]\cdots T[N]$ and call the index i a *suffix pointer*. Given two strings α and β, $\alpha \prec \beta$ if α is lexicographically smaller than β, and $\alpha \preceq \beta$

* Work supported by IMT 2000 Project AB02.

A. Apostolico and M. Melucci (Eds.): SPIRE 2004, LNCS 3246, pp. 214–215, 2004.

if α is lexicographically smaller than or equal to β. We denote by $lcp(\alpha, \beta)$ the length of the *longest common prefix* (lcp) of α and β.

We explain additional data stored in nodes. Let $s_0, s_1, \ldots, s_n$ be suffixes represented by suffix pointers stored in a node v, where $s_0 \prec s_1 \prec \cdots \prec s_n$. For efficient branching, we store additional data lcp_i and lnc_i in node v, which are defined as follows for $1 \leq i \leq n$:

- $lcp_i = lcp(s_{i-1}, s_i)$, and
- $lnc_i = s_i[lcp_i + 1]$.

Given a pattern P of length M, the branching algorithm finds an index j such that $s_{j-1} \prec P \preceq s_j$ at node v. Let L be the value of $\max(lcp(P, s_0), lcp(P, s_n))$. At node v, the algorithm requires that:

C1. $s_0 \prec P \prec s_n$, and
C2. L is given as a input parameter and $L < M$.

When the branching algorithm is used as a basic operation of the search in the String B-tree, the above conditions are satisfied. We omit the details. For simplicity, we define $P[i]$ as an empty character for $i > M$, which is lexicographically smaller than any other character in Σ.

The algorithm consists of the following three stages.

Stage A: Find the suffix s_x using lcp_i and lnc_i such that s_x is one of suffixes that share the longest lcp with P among suffixes stored in node v.
Starting with $i = 1$, we scan arrays lcp_i and lnc_i from left to right and maintain x as the desired index inductively. We initialize x to 0. At step i, we compare $P[l+1]$ with lnc_i (i.e., $s_i[l+1]$), where $l = lcp_i$. If $lnc_i \preceq P[l+1]$, then we set x to i and increase i by one. Otherwise, we increase i until $lcp_i < l$. We repeat this process until i reaches n. Then, s_x is the desired suffix.

Stage B: Find the value of $lcp(P, s_x)$.
We load disk pages where s_x is stored and compare P with s_x character-by-character from the $(L+1)$st character. As a result, we get the value of $lcp(P, s_x)$. Let L' be the value of $lcp(P, s_x)$. In this stage, we access $O(\frac{L^{\square}-L}{B})$ disk pages.

Stage C: Find the index j such that $s_{j-1} \prec P \preceq s_j$.
If $P \preceq s_x$, then we decrease i until $lcp_i \leq L'$, starting with $i = x$. If $P \succ s_x$, then, we increase i until $lcp_i \leq L'$, starting with $i = x + 1$. Then, the value of i is the desired index j.

References

1. D. E. Ferguson. Bit-Tree: A data structure for fast file processing. *Communications of the ACM*, 35(6):114–120, 1992.
2. P. Ferragina and R. Grossi. The String B-tree: A new data structure for string search in external memory and its applications. *Journal of the ACM*, 46(2):236–280, 1999.

Alphabet Permutation for Differentially Encoding Text (Extended Abstract)

Gad M. Landau[1], Ofer Levi[1], and Steven Skiena[2]

[1] Dept. of Computer Science, University of Haifa, Mount Carmel, Haifa 31905 Israel,
{landau,oferl}@cs.haifa.ac.il

[2] Dept. of Computer Science, SUNY Stony Brook, NY 11794-4400
skiena@cs.sunysb.edu

One degree of freedom not usually exploited in developing high-performance text-processing algorithms is the encoding of the underlying atomic character set. Here we consider a text compression method where the specific character set collating-sequence employed in encoding the text has a big impact on performance. We demonstrate that permuting the standard character collating-sequences yields a small win on Asian-language texts over *gzip*. We also show improved compression with our method for English texts, although not by enough to beat standard methods. However, we also design a class of artificial languages on which our method clearly beats *gzip*, often by an order of magnitude.

1 Differential Encoding

Differential coding is a common preprocessing step for compressing numerical data associated with sampled signals and other time series streams. The temporal coherence of such signals implies that the value at time t_i likely differs little from that at t_{i+1}. Thus representing the signal as an initial value followed a stream of difference (i.e. $t_{i+1} - t_i$ for $0 \leq i < n$) should consist primarily of small differences. Such streams should be more compressible using standard techniques like run-length encoding, Huffman coding, and gzip than the original data stream.

The most relevant previous work is [1], where alphabet permutation was employed to improve the performance of compression algorithms based on the Burrows-Wheeler transform.

2 Experiments on English Texts

The key to successful differential encoding lies in identifying the best collating sequence. We seek the circular n-permutation π which minimizes

$$\min_{\pi \in \Pi} \sum_{i=1}^{n} \sum_{j=1}^{n} d(i,j) p(\sigma_i, \sigma_j)$$

where $p(i,j)$ is the probability that symbol j immediately follows symbol i, i.e. $p(i,j) = P(j|i)$, and $d(i,j)$ is the shortest "distance" from i to j around the circular permutation. Thus $d(i,j) = \min(|j-i|, n - |j-i|)$.

A. Apostolico and M. Melucci (Eds.): SPIRE 2004, LNCS 3246, pp. 216–217, 2004.

To estimate the conditional character-probabilities for the optimized collating sequence for English text, we used letter-pair (bigram) frequencies derived from a large corpus of text including the famous Brown corpus. The *Discropt* system was run for 10 hours optimizing the permutation over these frequencies, resulting in the following collating sequence:

`. V G W C D I N H E T ' ' S A R O L F M P U Y B J Q Z X K`

We compared differential compression using both the standard and optimized collating sequence, with both standard Huffman codes and gzip employed for encoding. The permuted collating sequence typically reduces the size of the Huffman-encoded differential sequences by 3-4%, and gzip-encoded differential sequences by about 1% – however, both encoding algorithms work substantially better on the original text instead of the differential text.

3 Experiments on Asian-Language Texts

We reasoned that differential encoding might perform better on Asian-language texts, because the larger size of the alphabet makes such texts more closely resemble quantized signals. We experimented on Chinese, Japanese, and Korean UNICODE texts with both 8-bit and 16-bit recoded alphabets. The 8-bit alphabet permutation produced worse results than the original alphabet encoding for both gzip and Huffman codes, but permuting the full 16-bit alphabet encoding did permit the differential gzip encoding to beat the conventional gzip encodings by 1-2% on almost all files.

4 Experiments on Martian-Language Texts

To demonstrate that gzip can be significantly beaten via differential encoding, we define a class of artificial languages which we will call *Martian*. Martian words evolve in *families*. Each family is defined by a length-$(l-1)$ sequence of differences from 0 to $\alpha - 1$, where $\alpha = |\Sigma|$ for alphabet Σ. There are α distinct length-l words in each family, formed by prepending each $\sigma \in \Sigma$ to the difference sequence. For example, for $\Sigma = \{a, \ldots, z\}$ the family $(+2, +3, -6)$ defines the words *acfz*, *bdga*, *cehb*, and so forth.

We achieve our greatest improvement in differentially encoding relatively short Martian texts drawn from large families of long words. We demonstrated that differential encoded gzip results in 5.8 times better compression than plaintext gzip on files from 2500 to 50,000 words for 20 families of 20-character words. Even more extreme performance is obtainable by further lengthening the words.

References

1. B. Chapin and S. Tate. Higher compression from the burrows-wheeler transform by modified sorting. In *IEEE Data Compression Conference*, 1998.

A Space-Saving Linear-Time Algorithm for Grammar-Based Compression

Hiroshi Sakamoto[1], Takuya Kida[2], and Shinichi Shimozono[1]

[1] Kyushu Institute of Technology, Kawazu 680-4, Iizuka 820-8502, Japan
{hiroshi,sin}@ai.kyutech.ac.jp
[2] Hokkaido University, Kita 14, Nishi 9, Kita-ku, Sapporo, 060-0814 Japan
kida@ist.hokudai.ac.jp

Abstract. A space-efficient linear-time approximation algorithm for the grammar-based compression problem, which requests for a given string to find a smallest context-free grammar deriving the string, is presented. The algorithm consumes only $O(g_* \log g_*)$ space and achieves the worst-case approximation ratio $O(\log g_* \log n)$, with the size n of an input and the optimum grammar size g_*. Experimental results for typical benchmarks demonstrate that our algorithm is practical and efficient.

1 Introduction

The grammar-based compression problem is to find a smallest context-free grammar that generates only the given string. Such a CFG requires that every nonterminal is derived from only one production rule, say, deterministic. The problem deeply relates to factoring problems for strings, and the complexity of similar minimization problems have been rigorously studied. For example, Storer [20] introduced a factorization for a given string and showed the problem is NP-hard. De Agostino and Storer [2] defined several online variants and proved that those are also NP-hard.

As non-approximability results, Lehman and Shelat [12] showed that the problem is APX-hard, i.e. it is hard to approximate this problem within a constant factor (see [1] for definitions). They also mentioned its interesting connection to the semi-numerical problem [9], which is an algebraic problem of minimizing the number of different multiplications to compute the given integers and has no known polynomial-time approximation algorithm achieving a ratio $o(\log n / \log \log n)$. Since the problem is a special case of the grammar-based compression, an approximation better than this ratio seems to be computationally hard.

On the other hand, various practical algorithms for the grammar-based compression have been devised so far. LZ78 [24] including LZW [21], and BISECTION [8] are considered as algorithms that computes straight-line programs, CFGs formed from Chomsky normal form formulas. Also algorithms for restricted CFGs have been presented in [6, 10, 14, 15, 22]. Lehman and Shelat [12] proved the upper bounds of the approximation ratio of these practical algo-

A. Apostolico and M. Melucci (Eds.): SPIRE 2004, LNCS 3246, pp. 218–229, 2004.

rithms, as well as the lower bounds with the worst-case instances. For example, BISECTION algorithm achieves an approximation ratio no more than $O((n/\log n)^{1/2})$. All those ratios, including the lower-bounds, are larger than $O(\log n)$.

Recently polynomial-time approximation algorithms for the grammar-based compression problem have been widely studied and the worst-case approximation ratio has been improved. The first $\log n$-approximation algorithm was developed by Charikar et al. [3]. Their algorithm guarantees the ratio $O(\log(n/g_*))$, where g_* is the size of a minimum deterministic CFG for an input. Independently, Rytter presented in [16] another $O(\log(n/g_*))$-approximation algorithm that employs a suffix tree and the LZ-factorization technique for strings. Sakamoto also proposed in [17] a simple linear-time algorithm based on Re-pair [10] and achieving ratio $O(\log n)$; Now this ratio has been improved to $O(\log(n/g_*))$.

The ratio $O(\log(n/g_*))$ achieved by these new algorithms is theoretically sufficiently small. However, all these algorithms require $O(n)$ space, and it prevents us to apply the algorithms to huge texts, which is crucial to obtain a good compression ratio in practice. For example, the algorithm Re-pair [10] spends $5n + n^{1/2}$ space on unit-cost RAM with the input size n.

This state motivates us to develop a linear-time, sub-linear space $O(\log n)$-approximation algorithm for grammar-based compression. We present a simple algorithm that repeats substituting one new nonterminal symbol to all the same and non-overlapping two contiguous symbols occurring in the string. This is carried out by utilizing idea of the lowest common ancestor of balanced binary trees, and no real special data structure, such as suffix tree or occurrence frequency table, is requested. In consequence, the space complexity of our algorithm is nearly equal to the total number of created nonterminal symbols, each of which corresponds to a production rule in Chomsky normal form.

The size of the final dictionary of the rules is proved by LZ-factorization and its compactness [16]. Our algorithm runs in linear-time with $O(g_* \log g_*)$ space, and guarantees the worst-case approximation ratio $O(\log g_* \log n)$ on unit-cost RAM model. The memory space is devoted to the dictionary that maps a contiguous pair of symbols to a nonterminal. Practically, in randomized model, space complexity can be reduced to $O(g_* \log g_*)$ by using a hash table for the dictionary. In the framework of dictionary-based compression, the lower-bound of memory space is usually estimated by the size of a possible smallest dictionary, and thus our algorithm is nearly optimal in space complexity. Compared to other practical dictionary-based compression algorithms, such as LZ78, which achieves the ratio $\Omega(n^{2/3}/\log n)$, the lower-bound of memory space of our algorithm is considered to be sufficiently small. We confirm practical efficiency of our algorithm by computational experiments on several benchmark texts.

The remaining part of this paper is organized as follows. In Section 2, we prepare the definitions related to the grammar-based compression. In Section 3, we introduce the notion of lowest common ancestors in a complete binary tree defined by alphabet symbols. Using this notion, our algorithm decides a fixed priority of all pairs appearing in a current string and replaces them according to the priority. The algorithm is presented in Section 4 and we analyze the approximation ratio and estimate the space efficiency. In Section 5, we show the experimental results by applying our algorithm to typical benchmarks. In Section 6, we summarize this study.

2 Notions and Definitions

We assume a finite alphabet for the symbols forming input strings throughout this paper. Let Σ be a finite alphabet. The set of all strings over Σ is denoted by Σ^*, and Σ^i denotes the set of all strings of length i. The length of a string $w \in \Sigma^*$ is denoted by $|w|$, and also for a set S, the notion $|S|$ refers to the size (cardinality) of S. The ith symbol of w is denoted by $w[i]$. For an interval $[i, j]$ with $1 \leq i \leq j \leq |w|$, the substring of w from $w[i]$ to $w[j]$ is denoted by $w[i, j]$.

A *repetition* is a string x^k for some $x \in \Sigma$ and some positive integer k. A repetition $w[i, j]$ in w of a symbol $x \in \Sigma$ is *maximal* if $w[i-1] \neq x$ and $w[j+1] \neq x$. It is simply referred by x^+ if there is no ambiguity in its interval in w. Intervals $[i, j]$ and $[i', j']$ with $i < i'$ are *overlapping* if $i' \leq j < j'$, and are *independent* if $j < i'$. A *pair* $u \in \Sigma^*$ is a string of length two, and an interval $[i, i+1]$ is a *segment of* u *in* w if $w[i, i+1] = u$. Two segments $[i-1, i]$ and $[i+1, i+2]$ are said to be the *left segment* and the *right segment of* $[i, j]$, respectively.

A *context-free grammar* (*CFG*) is a quadruple $G = (\Sigma, N, P, s)$ of disjoint finite alphabets Σ and N, a finite set $P \subseteq N \times (N \cup \Sigma)^*$ of *production rules*, and the *start symbol* $s \in N$. Symbols in N are called *nonterminals*. A production rule $a \to b_1 \cdot \cdots \cdot b_k$ in P *derives* $\beta \in (\Sigma \cup N)^*$ *from* $\alpha \in (\Sigma \cup N)^*$ by replacing an occurrence of $a \in N$ in α with $b_1 \cdot \cdots \cdot b_k$. In this paper, we assume that any CFG is *deterministic*, that is, for each nontermial $a \in N$, exactly one production rule from a is in P. Thus, the language $L(G)$ defined by G is a singleton set. We say a CFG G *derives* $w \in \Sigma^*$ if $L(G) = \{w\}$. The *size of* G is the total length of strings in the right hand sides of all production rules, and is denoted by $|G|$.

The aim of grammar-based compression is formalized as a combinatorial optimization problem, as follows:

Problem 1 GRAMMAR-BASED COMPRESSION
INSTANCE: *A string* $w \in \Sigma^*$.
SOLUTION: *A deterministic CFG* G *that derives* w.
MEASURE: *The size of* G.

From now on, we assume that every deterministic CFG is in Chomsky normal form, i.e. the size of strings in the right-hand side of production rules is two, and we use $|N|$ for the size of a CFG. Note that for any CFG G there is an equivalent CFG G' in Chomsky normal form whose size is no more than $2 \cdot |G|$.

It is known that there is an important relation between a deterministic CFG and the factorization. The *LZ-factorization* $LZ(w)$ *of* w is the decomposition of w into $f_1 \cdot \cdots \cdot f_k$, where $f_1 = w[1]$, and for each $1 < \ell \leq k$, f_ℓ is the longest prefix of the suffix $w[|f_1 \cdots f_{\ell-1}| + 1, |w|]$ that appears in $f_1 \cdots f_{\ell-1}$. Each f_ℓ is called a *factor*. The size $|LZ(w)|$ of $LZ(w)$ is the number of its factors. The following result is used in the analysis of the approximation ratio of our algorithm.

Theorem 1 ([16]). For any string w and its deterministic CFG G, the inequality $|LZ(w)| \leq |G|$ holds.

3 Compression by the Alphabetical Order

In this section we describe the central idea of our grammar-based compression utilizing information only available from individual symbols. The aim is to minimize the number of different nonterminals generated by our algorithm.

A *replacement* $[i, i+1] \rightarrow a$ *for* w is an operation that replaces a pair $w[i, i+1]$ with a nonterminal $a \in N$. A set R of replacements is, by assuming some order on R, regarded as an operation that performs a series of replacements to w. In the following we introduce a definition of a set of replacements whose effect on a string is independent of the order.

Definition 1. A set R of replacements for w is *appropriate* if it satisfies the following: (1) At most one of two overlapping segments $[i, i+1]$ and $[i+1, i+2]$ is replaced by replacements in R, (2) At least one of three overlapping segments $[i, i+1]$, $[i+1, i+2]$ and $[i+2, i+3]$ is replaced by replacements in R, and (3) For any pair of replacements $[i, i+1] \rightarrow a$ and $[j, j+1] \rightarrow b$ in R, $a = b$ if and only if $w[i, i+1] = w[j, j+1]$.

Clearly, for any string w, an appropriate replacement R for w generates the string w' uniquely. In such a case, we say that R *generates* w' *from* w, and write $w' = R(w)$. Now we consider the following problem:

Problem 2 MINIMUM APPROPRIATE REPLACEMENT
INSTANCE: A string w.
SOLUTION: An appropriate replacement R for w.
MEASURE: The number of kinds of nonterminals newly introduced by R.

Here we explain the strategies for making pairs in our algorithm. Let d be a positive integer, and let k be $\lceil \log_2 d \rceil$. An *alphabet tree* T_d *for* $\Sigma = \{a_1, \ldots, a_d\}$ is the rooted, ordered complete binary tree whose leaves are labeled with $1, \ldots, 2^k$ from left to right. The *height* of an internal node refers to the number of edges of a path from the node to a descendant leaf. Let $lca(i, j)_d$ denote the height of the lowest common ancestor of the leaves i and j. For the simplicity, we omit the index d and use $lca(i, j)$ if there is no ambiguity.

Definition 2. Let Σ be a finite alphabet with a fixed order. A string $\alpha \in \Sigma^*$ is *increasing* if the symbols in α are in increasing order, and is *decreasing* if the symbols are decreasing with the order of Σ. A string is *monotonic* if it is either increasing or decreasing.

By using the above notion, we factorize a string $w \in \Sigma^*$ into the sequence $w_1, \ldots, w_n$ of monotonic strings uniquely, as follows: w_1 is the longest and monotonic prefix of w, and if $w_1, \ldots, w_i$ are decided, then w_{i+1} is the longest and monotonic prefix of the string $w' = w[|w_1 \cdots w_i| + 1, |w|]$. The sequence $w_1, \ldots, w_n$ is called the *Σ-factoring of w*.

Definition 3. Let $w_1, \ldots, w_n$ be the Σ-factoring of w. A pair $a \cdot b$ is a *boundary pair between w_j and w_{j+1}* if a is the rightmost symbol of w_j and b is the leftmost symbol of w_{j+1}.

The first idea for MINIMUM APPROPRIATE REPLACEMENT is to replace all the boundary pairs. Let w be a string over an alphabet Σ' and α a substring in w appearing at least twice. If α is longer than $2|\Sigma'|$, then it contains at least two boundary pairs. Let b_L and b_R be the leftmost and the rightmost boundary pairs in α, respectively, and let $[i, i+1]$ and $[j, j+1]$ be the corresponding segments of b_L and b_R. Then we can write $\alpha = X \cdot \alpha[i, i+1] \cdot Y \cdot \alpha[j, j+1] \cdot Z$ with strings X, Y and Z. Let R be an appropriate replacement that replaces all the boundary pairs (and other remained pairs, for example by left-to-right scheme) in Y. In any occurrence of α, the substring $\alpha[i, i+1] \cdot Y \cdot \alpha[j, j+1]$ is uniquely replaced by R. Thus, for any two occurrences of α, the differences of their replacement by R occur only in X and Z. Notice that $|X|$ and $|Y|$ are bounded by the current alphabet size $k = |\Sigma'|$. Next, we reduce the length of such X and Y to $O(\log k)$ by another technique.

Definition 4. Let w be a string in Σ^*, and let $w[i-1, i+2] = a_{j_1} a_{j_2} a_{j_3} a_{j_4}$ be a monotonic substring of w with $a_{j_1}, a_{j_2}, a_{j_3}, a_{j_4} \in \Sigma$. If $lca(j_1, j_2) < lca(j_2, j_3)$ and $lca(j_2, j_3) > lca(j_3, j_4)$, then the pair $w[i, i+1]$ is called a *locally maximum pair*.

Our second idea is to replace all locally maximum pairs. Since any locally maximum pair shares no symbol with neither other locally maximum pairs nor boundary pairs, all boundary pairs and locally maximum pairs in w can be included in an appropriate replacement R. Assume a substring having no locally maximum pair. The length of such a string is $O(\log k)$, where k is the height of the tree T_d, because there are at most $\log k$ different values of $lca(i, j)$. Thus, any two occurrences of α are replaced by R with the same string except their prefices and suffices of length at most $O(\log k)$. If a string consists of only short Σ-factors, then there may be no locally maximum pairs in the string. Therefore, not only locally maximum pairs but also the boundary pairs are necessary. In the next section we describe the algorithm utilizing the ideas given above.

4 Algorithm and Analysis

In this section we introduce an approximation algorithm for the grammar-based compression problem and analyze its approximation ratio to the optimum as well as its space efficiency.

4.1 Algorithm LCA

The algorithm LCA(w) is presented in Fig. 1. We describe the outline of LCA(w) below.

1. **Algorithm** LCA(w)
2. $m = 0$;
3. Initialize the mth dictionary $D_m = \emptyset$;
4. Replace all maximal repetitions $w[i, i+j]$ by $A_{(a,j)}$ and add '$A_{(a,j)} \to B_{(a,j)} C_{(a,j)}$'
5. to D_m, where $B_{(a,j)}$, $C_{(a,j)}$ and their productions are recursively defined below;
6. For each $i = 1, \ldots, |w| - 2$ do:
7.   If the pair $w[i, i+1]$ is boundary or locally maximum, then
8.   replace $w[i, i+1]$ by a consistent A_k;
9. $D_m \leftarrow \{`A_k \to w[i, i+1]'\}$;
10.   else
11.   replace $w[i]$ and $w[i+1, i+2]$ by *consistent* nonterminals A_k and A_{k+1};
12. $D_m \leftarrow \{`A_k \to w[i]', `A_{k+1} \to w[i+1, i+2]'\}$;
13. Increment m;
14. Goto 3. until all pairs in w are mutually different;
15. Output $D \cup \{S \to w\}$ for $D = D_0 \cup \cdots \cup D_m$;

$$B_{(a,j)} C_{(a,j)} = \begin{cases} A^2_{(a,j/2)}, & \text{if } j \geq 4 \text{ is even} \\ A_{(a,j-1)} \cdot a, & \text{if } j \geq 3 \text{ is odd} \\ a^2, & \text{otherwise} \end{cases}$$

Fig. 1. The approximation algorithm for grammar-based compression. A segment $w[i, i+1]$ must be replaced by a nonterminal *consistent* with a current dictionary D_m, i.e. $w[i, i+1]$ is replaced by A if a production $A \to BC$ ($BC = w[i, i+1]$) is already registered to D_m and a new nonterminal is created to replace $w[i, i+1]$ otherwise.

Phase 1 (Line 4 – 5): The algorithm finds out all maximum repetitions and replace them with nonterminal symbols. As a result, a maximal repetition a^+ will be divided into two strings. This process continues until the length of any repetition becomes two or less.

Phase 2 (Line 6 – 12): Since all repetitions have been already removed, every Σ-factor has length at least two, and boundary and locally maximum pairs do not overlap each other. Obviously, the algorithm will find such an appropriate set R of replacements. Then according to R, the algorithm replaces w, and add all productions in R to the current dictionary D_m. Note that any symbol in w will be replaced by an operation in either line 8 or 11: this trick plays an important role to reduce space complexity.

Phase 3 (Line 14 – 15): The algorithm repeats the above steps until all pairs in the current string become being mutually different, and then outputs the final dictionary.

Since the algorithm replaces either $w[i, i+1]$ or $w[i+1, i+2]$, or both, the outer loop in LCA(w) repeats at most $O(\log |w|)$ times. Moreover, for each iteration of the outer loop, the length of a string becomes at least $2/3$ times the previous one. We can verify whether a segment is locally maximum by its *lca* in $O(1)$ time[1]. Thus, LCA(w) runs in linear time with $|w|$.

Theorem 2. The running time of LCA(w) is bounded by $O(|w|)$.

4.2 Performance Analysis

Lemma 1. Let w be a string in Σ^*, and let $[l,r]$ and $[l',r']$ be intervals of w of the same substring $\alpha = w[l,r] = w[l',r']$. Let R be the appropriate replacement for w specified by the dictionary D produced by LCA(w). Then, for each index $\lceil \log|\Sigma|\rceil + 1 \le i \le |\alpha| - \lceil \log|\Sigma|\rceil$, a replacement "$[l+i-1, l+i] \to a$" with some $a \in N$ is in R if and only if "$[l'+i-1, l'+i] \to a$" is in R.

Proof. All locally maximum and boundary pairs are independent of each other. Thus, R contains all locally maximum and boundary pairs in w. Every segment between those pairs is replaced by a nonterminal as to maintain consistency with the up-to-date dictionary, by the left-to-right scheme. A prefix and a suffix of α having no locally maximum pair are no longer than $\lceil \log|\Sigma|\rceil$. Thus, any pair of the ith segments in $w[l,r]$ and $w[l',r']$, except the first $\lceil \log|\Sigma|\rceil$ segments and the last $\lceil \log|\Sigma|\rceil$ ones, is going to be replaced by the same nonterminal, or is not going to be replaced. □

Theorem 3. The worst-case approximation ratio of the size of a grammar produced by the algorithm LCA to the size of a minimum grammar is $O(\log g_* \log n)$, where g_* is the size of a minimum grammar.

Proof. We first estimate the number of different nonterminals produced by an appropriate replacement R for an input string $w \in \Sigma^*$. Let g_* be the size of a minimum grammar for w, and let $w_1 \cdots w_m$ be the LZ-factorization of w. We denote by $\#(w)_R$ the number of different nonterminals produced by R. From the definition of LZ-factorization, any factor w_i occurs in $w_1 \cdots w_{i-1}$, or $|w_i| = 1$. With lemma 1, any factor w_i and its left-most occurrence are compressed into almost the same strings $\alpha\beta\gamma$ and $\alpha'\beta\gamma'$, such that $|\alpha\gamma|$ and $|\alpha'\gamma'|$ are $O(\log|\Sigma|)$. Thus, we can estimate $\#(w)_R = \#(w_1 \cdots w_{m-1})_R + O(\log|\Sigma|) = O(m \log|\Sigma|) = O(g_* \log|\Sigma|)$. Therefore, we can apply the above estimation for the occurrences of β whenever $|\beta| \ge 2$. Since Σ is initially a constant alphabet, $\#(w)_R$ converges to $O(g_* \log g_*)$. Hence, $O(g_* \log g_*)$ is the maximum number of different nonterminals produced by a set of appropriate replacement by LCA(w). The main loop of LCA(w) is executed at most $O(\log n)$ times. Therefore, the total number of different nonterminals produced by LCA(w) is $O(g_* \log g_* \log n)$. This derives the approximation ratio.

The memory space required by LCA(w) can be bounded by the size of data structure to answer the membership query: input is a pair A_iA_j; output is an integer k if $A_k \to A_iA_j$ is already created and no otherwise. By Theorem 3,

[1] We can get the *lca* of any two leaves i and j of complete binary trees by an **xor** operation between binary numbers in $O(1)$ time under our RAM model [5].

the size of a current dictionary D_m is bounded by $O(g_* \log g_*)$ for each $m \geq 0$. Moreover, each symbol A_i in a current string is replaced by a rule of the form $A_j \to A_i$ or $A_j \to YZ$, where $A_i \in \{Y, Z\}$. Thus, $O((g_* \log g_*)^2)$-space algorithm is obtained by a naive implementation. Finally we show that the memory space can be improved to $O(g_* \log g_*)$.

4.3 Improving the Space Efficiency

An idea for improving space complexity of the algorithm is to recycle nonterminals created in the preceding iteration. Let $D(\alpha)$ be the string obtained by applying a dictionary D to a string α. Let D_1 and D_2 be dictionaries such that any symbol in w is replaced by D_1 and any symbol in $D_1(w)$ is replaced by D_2. Then, the decoding of the string $D_2(D_1(w))$ is uniquely determined, even if D_2 reuses nonterminals in D_1 like "$A \to AB$." Thus, we consider that the final dictionary D is composed of $D_1, \ldots, D_m$, where D_i is the dictionary constructed in the ith iteration. Since any symbol $w[i]$ is replaced with a nonterminal in line 8 or 11 in the algorithm, the decoding is unique and $D_m(\cdots D_1(w')\cdots) = w$ for the final string w'. Such a dictionary is computed by the following function and data structures.

Let D_i be the set of productions, N_i the set of alphabet symbols created in the ith iteration, and k_i the cardinality $|N_i|$. We define the function $f_i(x, y) = (x-1)k_i + y$ for $1 \leq x, y \leq k_i$. This is a one-to-one mapping from $\{1, \ldots, k_i\} \times \{1, \ldots, k_i\}$ to $\{1, \ldots, k_i^2\}$, and is used to decide an index of a new nonterminal associated to a pair $A_x A_y$, where A_x denotes the xth created nonterminal in N_i.

The next dictionary D_{i+1} is constructed from D_i, N_i, and f_i as follows. In the algorithm LCA, there are two cases of replacements: one is for replacements of pairs, and the other is for replacements of individual symbols in line 11. We first explain the case of replacements of pairs. Let a pair $A_x A_y$ in a current string be decided to be replaced. The algorithm LCA computes the integer $z = f(x, y)$, and looks up a hash table H for z. If $H(z)$ is absent and $N_i = \{A_1, \ldots, A_k\}$, then set $N_i = N_i \cup \{A_{k+1}\}$, $D_i = D_i \cup \{A_{k+1} \to A_x A_y\}$, $H(z) = k+1$, and replace the pair $A_x A_y$ with A_{k+1}. If $H(z) = k+1$ is present, then only replace the pair $A_x A_y$ by A_{k+1}. We next explain the case of replacements of individual symbols. Since all maximal repetitions like A^+ are removed in line 4-5, there is no pair like AA in a current string. Thus, for a replacement of a single symbol A_x, we can use the nonterminal A_{k+1} such that $z = f_i(x, x)$ and $H(z) = k+1$. The dictionary D_i constructed in the ith iteration can be divided to D_{i_1} and D_{i_2} such that D_{i_1} is the dictionary for repetitions and $D_{i_2} = D_i \setminus D_{i_2}$. Thus, we can create all productions without collisions, and decode a current string w_{i+1} to the previous string w_i by the manner $D_i(w_{i+1}) \equiv D_{i_1}(D_{i_2}(w_{i+1})) = w_i$.

Theorem 4. The space required by LCA(w) is $O(g_* \log g_*)$.

Proof. Let n be the size $|w|$ and m the number of iterations of outer loops executed in LCA(w). By theorem 3, the number $|N_i|$ of new nonterminals created in the ith iteration is $O(g_* \log g_*)$ for each $i \leq m$. To decide the index of a

Table 1. Result for the canterbury corpus.

File	Category	Size (byte)	Repeat times	Size of w	Size of D	Compressed size(bytes)	gzip (bytes)
alice29.txt	English text	152089	6	5053	45243	176956	54435
asyoulik.txt	Shakespeare	125179	7	2523	42562	156220	48951
cp.html	HTML source	24603	7	470	9010	28980	7999
fields.c	C source	11150	9	71	4418	12616	3143
grammar.lsp	LISP source	3721	6	122	1730	4408	1246
kennedy.xls	Excel Spreadsheet	1029744	5	41600	139118	980832	206779
lcet10.txt	Technical writing	426754	7	8167	113760	477268	144885
plrabn12.txt	Poetry	481861	7	9779	138353	593988	195208
ptt5	CCITT test set	513216	6	2759	40784	154836	56443
sum	SPARC Executable	38240	11	77	14349	46260	12924
xargs.1	GNU manual page	4227	5	262	2122	5804	1756

new nonterminal from a pair A_xA_y, LCA computes $z = f_i(x,y)$, $H(z)$, and $k = |N_i|$ for the current N_i. Since $|z| \leq O(\log n)$ and the number of different z is $O(g_* \log g_*)$, the space for H is $O(g_* \log g_*)$ and $k = O(g_* \log g_*)$. Thus, the construction of D_i requires only $O(g_* \log g_*)$ space. We can release whole the memory space for D_i in the next loop. Hence, the total size of the space for constructing D is also $O(g_* \log g_*)$.

5 Experiments

To estimate the performance of LCA(w), we implemented the algorithm and tested it. We used a PC with Intel Xeon 3.06GHz dual-CPU and 3.5GB memory running Cygwin on Windows XP, and used Gcc version 3.3.1 for the implementation. We used the canterbury corpus and the artificial corpus, which are from the Canterbury Corpus (http://corpus.canterbury.ac.nz/).

Tables 1 and 2. show the results for each corpus. In the tables, 'Repeat times' means how many times the algorithm processed the lines from 3 to 11 in Fig. 1. Note that it corresponds to the height of the syntax tree of the grammar generated by the algorithm. 'Size of w' and 'Size of D' indicate respectively the length of the sequence w and the total number of rules in the dictionary D, which are obtained at the last. 'Compressed size' indicates the whole output file size, where w and D are encoded in a simple way: each element in them is represented by an integer with the smallest length of bits so that it can be distinguished from the others.

As we see from Table 1, LCA(w) gives rather worse compression ratios than gzip. One of the reasons is because of our poor way of encoding. Another main reason is that D becomes very large when a target text is long and has few repetitions. If we thin out useless rules in D like Sequitur algorithm[15] and apply more efficient encodings, it can be improved. On the other hand, from Table 2, we see that there are cases that LCA(w) is better than gzip, because that the texts have many repetitions.

Table 2. Result for the artificial corpus.

File	Category	Size (byte)	Repeat times	Size of w	Size of D	Compressed size(bytes)	gzip (bytes)
a.txt	The letter 'a'	1	1	1	1	16	27
aaa.txt	The letter 'a', repeated 100,000 times	100000	1	1	22	64	141
alphabet.txt	Enough repetitions of the alphabet to fill 100,000 characters	100000	6	3	77	136	315
random.txt	100,000 characters, randomly selected from $[a-z\|A-Z\|0-9\|!\|\ ]$ (alphabet size 64)	100000	3	17696	42500	191672	75689

Table 3. Maximum memory consumption for the dictionary.

text size (bytes)	Sequitur (bytes)	LCA(w) (bytes)
10	132	2056
100	1344	2056
1000	14352	6740
10000	98796	46800
100000	726828	428480
1000000	6903468	2880300

Table 4. Compression time.

text size (bytes)	Sequitur (s)	LCA(w) (s)
10	0.030	0.093
100	0.030	0.077
1000	0.046	0.061
10000	0.061	0.077
100000	0.390	0.186
1000000	4.311	0.874

Our algorithm runs in $O(n)$ time and the size of dictionary is bounded by $O(g_* \log g_*)$ in average. To estimate time and space efficiency, we compared LCA(w) with Sequitur (Tables 3 and 4). We used random texts with $|\Sigma| = 26$ as target texts. Since the memory consumptions of both algorithms increase and decrease during running, we measured the maximum memory consumptions. The results show that LCA(w) is superior to Sequitur when the text is sufficiently long.

6 Conclusion

We presented a linear-time algorithm for the grammar-based compression. This algorithm guarantees the approximation ratio $O(\log g_* \log n)$ and the memory space $O(g_* \log g_*)$. This space bound is considered to be sufficiently small since $\Omega(g_*)$ space is a lower bound for *non-adaptive* dictionary-based compression. In particular, the upper bound of memory space is best in the previously known linear-time *polylog*-approximation algorithms. We also show the scalability of our algorithm for large text data.

References

1. G. Ausiello, P. Crescenzi, G. Gambosi, V. Kann, A. Marchetti-Spaccamela, and M. Protasi. *Complexity and Approximation: Combinatorial Optimization Problems and Their Approximability Properties.* Springer, 1999.
2. S. De Agostino and J. A. Storer. On-Line versus Off-Line Computation in Dynamic Text Compression. *Inform. Process. Lett.*, 59:169–174, 1996.
3. M. Charikar, E. Lehman, D. Liu, R. Panigrahy, M. Prabhakaran, A. Rasala, A. Sahai, and A. Shelat. Approximating the Smallest Grammar: Kolmogorov Complexity in Natural Models. In *Proc. 29th Ann. Sympo. on Theory of Computing*, 792-801, 2002.
4. M. Farach. Optimal Suffix Tree Construction with Large Alphabets. In *Proc. 38th Ann. Sympo. on Foundations of Computer Science*, 137-143, 1997.
5. D. Gusfield. *Algorithms on Strings, Trees, and Sequences.* Computer Science and Computational Biology. Cambridge University Press, 1997.
6. T. Kida, Y. Shibata, M. Takeda, A. Shinohara, and S. Arikawa. Collage System: a Unifying Framework for Compressed Pattern Matching. *Theoret. Comput. Sci.* (to appear).
7. J. C. Kieffer and E.-H. Yang. Grammar-Based Codes: a New Class of Universal Lossless Source Codes. *IEEE Trans. on Inform. Theory*, 46(3):737–754, 2000.
8. J. C. Kieffer, E.-H. Yang, G. Nelson, and P. Cosman. Universal Lossless Compression via Multilevel Pattern Matching. *IEEE Trans. Inform. Theory*, IT-46(4), 1227–1245, 2000.
9. D. Knuth. Seminumerical Algorithms. Addison-Wesley, 441-462, 1981.
10. N. J. Larsson and A. Moffat. Offline Dictionary-Based Compression. *Proceedings of the IEEE*, 88(11):1722-1732, 2000.
11. E. Lehman. Approximation Algorithms for Grammar-Based Compression. PhD thesis, MIT, 2002.
12. E. Lehman and A. Shelat. Approximation Algorithms for Grammar-Based Compression. In *Proc. 20th Ann. ACM-SIAM Sympo. on Discrete Algorithms*, 205-212, 2002.
13. M. Lothaire. *Combinatorics on Words*, volume 17 of *Encyclopedia of Mathematics and Its Applications*. Addison-Wesley, 1983.
14. C. Nevill-Manning and I. Witten. Compression and Explanation Using Hierarchical Grammars. *Computer Journal*, 40(2/3):103–116, 1997.
15. C. Nevill-Manning and I. Witten. Identifying hierarchical structure in sequences: a linear-time algorithm. *J. Artificial Intelligence Research*, 7:67–82, 1997.
16. W. Rytter. Application of Lempel-Ziv Factorization to the Approximation of Grammar-Based Compression. In *Proc. 13th Ann. Sympo. Combinatorial Pattern Matching*, 20-31, 2002.
17. H. Sakamoto. A Fully Linear-Time Approximation Algorithm for Grammar-Based Compression. *Journal of Discrete Algorithms*, to appear.

18. D. Salomon. *Data compression: the complete reference*. Springer, second edition, 1998.
19. J. Storer and T. Szymanski. Data compression via textual substitution. *J. Assoc. Comput. Mach.*, 29(4):928–951, 1982.
20. J. A. Storer and T. G. Szymanski. The Macro Model for Data Compression. In *Proc. 10th Ann. Sympo. on Theory of Computing*, pages 30-39, San Diego, California, 1978. ACM Press.
21. T. A. Welch. A Technique for High Performance Data Compression. *IEEE Comput.*, 17:8-19, 1984.
22. E.-H. Yang and J. C. Kieffer. Efficient Universal Lossless Data Compression Algorithms Based on a Greedy Sequential Grammar Transform–Part One: without Context Models. *IEEE Trans. on Inform. Theory*, 46(3):755-777, 2000.
23. J. Ziv and A. Lempel. A Universal Algorithm for Sequential Data Compression. *IEEE Trans. on Inform. Theory*, IT-23(3):337-349, 1977.
24. J. Ziv and A. Lempel. Compression of Individual Sequences via Variable-Rate Coding. *IEEE Trans. on Inform. Theory*, 24(5):530-536, 1978.

Simple, Fast, and Efficient Natural Language Adaptive Compression*

Nieves R. Brisaboa[1], Antonio Fariña[1], Gonzalo Navarro[2], and José R. Paramá[1]

[1] Database Lab., Univ. da Coruña, Facultade de Informática
Campus de Elviña s/n, 15071 A Coruña, Spain
{brisaboa,fari,parama}@udc.es

[2] Center for Web Research, Dept. of Computer Science, Univ. de Chile
Blanco Encalada 2120, Santiago, Chile
gnavarro@dcc.uchile.cl

Abstract. One of the most successful natural language compression methods is word-based Huffman. However, such a two-pass semi-static compressor is not well suited to many interesting real-time transmission scenarios. A one-pass adaptive variant of Huffman exists, but it is character-oriented and rather complex. In this paper we implement word-based adaptive Huffman compression, showing that it obtains very competitive compression ratios. Then, we show how End-Tagged Dense Code, an alternative to word-based Huffman, can be turned into a faster and much simpler adaptive compression method which obtains almost the same compression ratios.

1 Introduction

Transmission of compressed data is usually composed of four processes: *compression*, *transmission*, *reception*, and *decompression*. The first two are carried out by a *sender* process and the last two by a *receiver*. This abstracts from communication over a network, but also from writing a compressed file to disk so as to load and decompress it later. In some scenarios, especially the latter, compression and transmission usually complete before reception and decompression start.

There are several interesting *real-time* transmission scenarios, however, where those processes should take place concurrently. That is, the sender should be able to start the transmission of compressed data without preprocessing the whole text, and simultaneously the receiver should start reception and decompress the text as it arrives. Real-time transmission is usually of interest when communicating over a network. This kind of compression can be applied, for example, to interactive services such as remote login or talk/chat protocols, where small

* This word is partially supported by CYTED VII.19 RIBIDI Project. It is also funded in part (for the Spanish group) by MCyT (PGE and FEDER) grant(TIC2003-06593) and (for the third author) by Millennium Nucleus Center for Web Research, Grant (P01-029-F), Mideplan, Chile.

A. Apostolico and M. Melucci (Eds.): SPIRE 2004, LNCS 3246, pp. 230–241, 2004.

messages are exchanged during the whole communication time. It might also be relevant to transmission of Web pages, so that the exchange of (relatively small) pages between a server and a client along the time enables adaptive compression by installing a browser plug-in to handle decompression. This might be also interesting for wireless communication with hand-held devices with little bandwidth and processing power.

Real-time transmission is handled with so-called *dynamic* or *adaptive* compression techniques. These perform a single pass over the text (so they are also called *one-pass*) and begin compression and transmission as they read the data. Currently, the most widely used adaptive compression techniques belong to the Ziv-Lempel family [1]. When applied to natural language text, however, the compression ratios achieved by Ziv-Lempel are not that good (around 40%).

Statistical *two-pass* techniques, on the other hand, use a *semi-static* model. A first pass over the text to compress gathers global statistical information, which is used to compress the text in a second pass. The computed model is transmitted prior to the compressed data, so that the receiver can use it for decompression. Classic Huffman code [11] is a well-known two-pass method. Its compression ratio is rather poor for natural language texts (around 60%). In recent years, however, new Huffman-based compression techniques for natural language have appeared, based on the idea of taking the words, not the characters, as the source symbols to be compressed [13]. Since in natural language texts the frequency distribution of words is much more biased than that of characters, the gain in compression is enormous, achieving compression ratios around 25%-30%. Additionally, since in Information Retrieval (IR) words are the atoms searched for, these compression schemes are well suited to IR tasks. Word-based Huffman variants focused on fast retrieval are presented in [7], where a byte- rather than bit-oriented coding alphabet speeds up decompression and search.

Two-pass codes, unfortunately, are not suitable for real-time transmission. Hence, developing an adaptive compression technique with good compression ratios for natural language texts is a relevant problem. In [8, 9] a dynamic Huffman compression method was presented. This method was later improved in [12, 14]. In this case, the model is not previously computed nor transmitted, but rather computed and updated on the fly both by sender and receiver.

However, those methods are character- rather than word-oriented, and thus their compression ratios on natural language are poor. Extending those algorithms to build a dynamic word-based Huffman method and evaluating its compression efficiency and processing cost is the first contribution of this paper. We show that the compression ratios achieved are in most cases just 0.06% over those of the semi-static version. The algorithm is also rather efficient: It compresses 4 megabytes per second in our machine. On the other hand, it is rather complex to implement.

Recently, a new word-based byte-oriented method called End-Tagged Dense Code (ETDC) was presented in [3]. ETDC is not based on Huffman at all. It is simpler and faster to build than Huffman codes, and its compression ratio is only 2%-4% over the corresponding word-based byte-oriented Huffman code.

For IR purposes, ETDC is especially interesting because it permits direct text searching, much as the Tagged Huffman variants developed in [7]. However, ETDC compresses better than those fast-searchable Huffman variants.

The second contribution of this paper is to show another advantage of ETDC compared to Huffman codes. We show that an adaptive version of ETDC is much simpler to program and 22%-26% faster than word-oriented dynamic Huffman codes. Moreover, its compression ratios are only 0.06% over those of semi-static ETDC, and 2%-4% over semi-static Huffman code. From a theoretical viewpoint, dynamic Huffman complexity is proportional to the number of target symbols output, while dynamic ETDC complexity is proportional to the number of source symbol processed. The latter is never larger than the former, and the difference increases as more compression is obtained.

As a sanity check, we also present empirical results comparing our dynamic word-based codes against two well-known compression techniques such as *gzip* (fast compression and decompression, but poor compression) and *bzip2* (good compression ratio, but slower). These results show that our two techniques provide a well balanced trade-off between compression ratio and speed.

2 Word-Based Semi-static Codes

Since in this paper we focus on word-based natural language text compression, we speak indistinctly of *source symbols* and *words*, and sometimes call *vocabulary* the set of source symbols.

2.1 Word-Based Huffman Codes

The idea of Huffman coding [11] is to compress the text by assigning shorter codes to more frequent symbols. Huffman algorithm obtains an optimal (shortest total length) *prefix code* for a given text. A code is a *prefix code* if no codeword is a prefix of any other codeword. A prefix code can be decoded without reference to future codewords, since the end of a codeword is immediately recognizable.

The word-based Huffman byte oriented codes proposed in [7] obtain compression ratios on natural language close to 30% by coding with bytes instead of bits (in comparison to the bit oriented approach that achieves ratios close to 25%). In exchange, decompression and searching are much faster with byte-oriented Huffman code because no bit manipulations are necessary. This word-based byte-oriented Huffman code will be called *Plain Huffman* code in this paper.

Another code proposed in [7] is *Tagged Huffman* code. This is like Plain Huffman, except that the first bit of each byte is reserved to flag whether the byte is the first of its codeword. Hence, only 7 bits of each byte are used for the Huffman code. Note that the use of a Huffman code over the remaining 7 bits is mandatory, as the flag is not useful by itself to make the code a prefix code. The tag bit permits direct searching on the compressed text by simply compressing the pattern and then running any classical string matching algorithm. On Plain

Huffman this does not work, as the pattern could occur in the text not aligned to any codeword [7].

While searching Plain Huffman compressed text requires inspecting all its bytes from the beginning, Boyer-Moore type searching (that is, skipping bytes) [2] is possible over Tagged Huffman code. On the other hand, Tagged Huffman code pays a price in terms of compression performance of approximately 11%, as it stores full bytes but uses only 7 bits for coding.

2.2 End-Tagged Dense Codes

End-Tagged Dense code (ETDC) [3] is obtained by a seemingly dull change to Tagged Huffman code. Instead of using a flag bit to signal the *beginning* of a codeword, the *end* of a codeword is signaled. That is, the highest bit of any codeword byte is 0 except for the last byte, where it is 1. By this change there is no need at all to use Huffman coding in order to maintain a prefix code.

In general, ETDC can be defined over symbols of b bits, although in this paper we focus on the byte-oriented version where $b = 8$. ETDC is formally defined as follows.

Definition 1 Given source symbols $\{s_1, \ldots, s_n\}$*, End-Tagged Dense Code assigns number* $i-1$ *to the* i*-th most frequent symbol. This number is represented in base* 2^{b-1}*, as a sequence of digits, from most to least significant. Each such digit is represented using* b *bits. The exception is the least significant digit* d_0*, where we represent* $2^{b-1} + d_0$ *instead of just* d_0.

That is, the first word is encoded as $\underline{1}0000000$, the second as $\underline{1}0000001$, until the 128th as $\underline{1}1111111$. The 129th word is coded as $\underline{0}0000000{:}\underline{1}0000000$, 130th as $\underline{0}0000000{:}\underline{1}0000001$ and so on until the $(128^2 + 128)^{th}$ word $\underline{0}1111111{:}\underline{1}1111111$, just as if we had a 14-bit number.

As it can be seen, the computation of codes is extremely simple: It is only necessary to sort the source symbols by decreasing frequency and then sequentially assign the codewords. The coding phase is faster than using Huffman because obtaining the codes is simpler. Empirical results comparing ETDC against Plain and Tagged Huffman can be found in [3].

Note that the code depends on the rank of the words, not on their actual frequency. As a result, it is not even necessary to transmit the code of each word, but just the sorted vocabulary, as the model to the receiver. Hence, End-Tagged Dense Codes are simpler, faster, and compress better than Tagged Huffman codes. Since the last bytes of codewords are distinguished, they also permit direct search of the compressed text for the compressed pattern, using any search algorithm.

On-the-Fly Coding and Decoding. We finally observe that, for compression and decompression, we do not really have to start by sequentially assigning the codes to the sorted words. An on-the-fly encoding is also possible.

Given a word ranked i in the sorted vocabulary, the encoder can run a simple *encode* function to compute the codeword $C_i = encode(i)$. It is a matter of

```
Sender ( )
  Vocabulary ← {C_new-Symbol};
  Initialize CodeBook;
  for i ∈ 1...n do
    read s_i from the text;
    if s_i ∉ Vocabulary then
      send C_new-Symbol;
      send s_i in plain form;
      Vocabulary ← Vocabulary ∪ {s_i};
      f(s_i) ← 1;
    else
      send CodeBook(s_i);
      f(s_i) ← f(s_i) + 1;
    Update CodeBook;
```

```
Receiver ( )
  Vocabulary ← {C_new-Symbol};
  Initialize CodeBook;
  for i ∈ 1...n do
    receive C_i;
    if C_i = C_new-Symbol then
      receive s_i in plain form;
      Vocabulary ← Vocabulary ∪ {s_i};
      f(s_i) ← 1;
    else
      s_i ← CodeBook^-1(C_i);
      f(s_i) ← f(s_i) + 1;
    output s_i;
    Update CodeBook;
```

Fig. 1. Sender and receiver processes in statistical dynamic text compression.

expressing $i - 1$ in base 2^{b-1} (which requires just bit shifts and masking) and outputting the sequence of digits. Function *encode* takes just $O(l)$ time, where $l = O(\log(i)/b)$ is the length in digits of codeword C_i.

At decompression time, given codeword C_i of l digits and the sorted vocabulary, it is also possible to compute, in $O(l)$ time, function $i = decode(C_i)$, essentially by interpreting C_i as a base 2^{b-1} number and finally adding 1. Then, we retrieve the i-th word in the sorted vocabulary.

3 Statistical Dynamic Codes

Statistical dynamic compression techniques are one-pass. Statistics are collected as the text is read, and consequently, the model is updated as compression progresses. They do not transmit the model, as the receiver can figure out the model by itself from the received codes.

In particular, *zero-order* compressors model the text using only the information on source symbol frequencies, that is, $f(s_i)$ is the number of times source symbol s_i appears in the text (read up to now). In the discussion that follows we focus on zero-order compressors.

In order to maintain the model up to date, dynamic techniques need a data structure to keep the vocabulary of all symbols s_i and their frequencies $f(s_i)$ up to now. This data structure is used by the encoding/decoding scheme, and is continuously updated during compression/decompression. After each change in the vocabulary or frequencies, the codewords assigned to *all* source symbols may have to be recomputed due to the frequency changes. This recomputation must be done both by the sender and the receiver.

Figure 1 depicts the sender and receiver processes, highlighting the symmetry of the scheme. *CodeBook* stands for the model, used to assign codes to source symbols or vice versa.

3.1 Dynamic Huffman Codes

In [8, 9] an adaptive character-oriented Huffman coding algorithm was presented. It was later improved in [12], being named *FGK* algorithm. *FGK* is the basis of the UNIX *compact* command.

FGK maintains a Huffman tree for the source text already read. The tree is adapted each time a symbol is read to keep it optimal. It is maintained both by the sender, to determine the code corresponding to a given source symbol, and by the receiver, to do the opposite. Thus, the Huffman tree acts as the *CodeBook* of Figure 1. Consequently, it is initialized with a unique special node called *zeroNode* (corresponding to *new-Symbol*), and it is updated every time a new source symbol is inserted in the vocabulary or a frequency increases. The codeword for a source symbol corresponds to the path from the tree root to the leaf corresponding to that symbol. Any leaf insertion or frequency change may require reorganizing the tree to restore its optimality.

The main challenge of Dynamic Huffman is how to reorganize the Huffman tree efficiently upon leaf insertions and frequency increments. This is a complex and potentially time-consuming process that must be carried out both by the sender and the receiver.

The main achievement of *FGK* is to ensure that the tree can be updated by doing only a constant amount of work per node in the path from the affected leaf to the tree root. Calling $l(s_i)$ the path length from the leaf of source symbol s_i to the root, and $f(s_i)$ its frequency, then the overall complexity of algorithm *FGK* is $\sum f(s_i)l(s_i)$, which is exactly the length of the compressed text, measured in number of target symbols.

3.2 Word-Based Dynamic Huffman Codes

We implemented a word-based version of algorithm *FGK*. This is by itself a contribution because no existing adaptive technique obtains similar compression ratio on natural language. As the number of text words is much larger than the number of characters, several challenges arised to manage such a large vocabulary. The original *FGK* algorithm pays little attention to these issues because of its underlying assumption that the source alphabet is not very large.

However, the most important difference between our word-based version and the original *FGK* is that we chose the code to be byte rather than bit-oriented. Although this necessarily implies some loss in compression ratio, it gives a decisive advantage in efficiency. Recall that the algorithm complexity corresponds to the number of target symbols in the compressed text. A bit-oriented approach requires time proportional to the number of bits in the compressed text, while ours requires time proportional to the number of bytes. Hence byte-coding is almost 8 times faster.

Being byte-oriented implies that each internal node can have up to 256 children in the resulting Huffman tree, instead of 2 as in a binary tree. This required extending *FGK* algorithm in several aspects.

4 Dynamic End-Tagged Dense Code

In this section we show how ETDC can be made adaptive. Considering again the general scheme of Figure 1, the main issue is how to maintain the *CodeBook* up to date upon insertions of new source symbols and frequency increments. In the case of ETDC, the *CodeBook* is essentially the array of source symbols sorted by frequencies. If we are able to maintain such array upon insertions and frequency changes, then we are able to code any source symbol or decode any target symbol by using the on-the-fly *encode* and *decode* procedures explained at the end of Section 2.2.

Bytes = 36

Plain text: t h e # r o s e # r o s e # i s # b e a u t i f u l # b e a u t i f u l

Input order	0	1	2	3	4	5	6
Word parsed		the	rose	rose	is	beautiful	beautiful
In vocabulary?		no	no	yes	no	no	yes
Data sent		$C_1$the	C_2rose	C_2	$C_3$is	C_4beautiful	C_4
Vocabulary state 1	--	the 1	the 1	rose 2	rose 2	rose 2	rose 2
Vocabulary state 2	--	--	rose 1	the 1	the 1	the 1	beautiful 2
Vocabulary state 3	--	--	--	--	is 1	is 1	is 1
Vocabulary state 4	--	--	--	--	--	beautiful 1	the 1

Bytes = 28

Compressed text: C_1 t h e # C_2 r o s e # C_2 C_3 i s # C_4 b e a u t i f u l # C_4

Fig. 2. Transmission of message "the rose rose is beautiful beautiful".

Figure 2 shows how the compressor operates. At first (step 0), no words have been read so *new-Symbol* is the only word in the vocabulary (it is implicitly placed at position 1). In step 1, a new symbol "the" is read. Since it is not in the vocabulary, C_1 (the codeword of *new-Symbol*) is sent, followed by "the" in plain form (bytes 't', 'h', 'e' and some terminator '#'). Next, "the" is added to the vocabulary (array) with frequency 1, at position 1. Implicitly, *new-Symbol* has been displaced to array position 2. Step 2 shows the transmission of "rose", which is not yet in the vocabulary. In step 3, "rose" is read again. As it was in the vocabulary at array position 2, only codeword C_2 is sent. Now, "rose" becomes more frequent than "the", so it moves upward in the array. Note that a hypothetical new occurrence of "rose" would be transmitted as C_1, while it was sent as C_2 in step 1. In steps 4 and 5, two more new words, "is" and "beautiful", are transmitted and added to the vocabulary. Finally, in step 6, "beautiful" is read again, and it becomes more frequent than "is" and "the". Therefore, it moves upward in the vocabulary by means of an exchange with "the".

The main challenge is how to efficiently maintain the sorted array. In the sequel we show how we obtain a complexity equal to the number of source symbols transmitted. This is always lower than *FGK* complexity, because at least one target symbol must be transmitted for each source symbol, and usually several more if some compression is going to be achieved. Essentially, we must be able to identify *groups* of words with the same frequency in the array, and be able of fast promoting of a word to the next group when its frequency increases.

The data structures used by the sender and their functionality are shown in Figure 3. The hash table of words keeps in *word* the source word characters, in *posInVoc* the position of the word in the vocabulary array, and in *freq* its frequency. In the vocabulary array (*posInHT*) the words are not explicitly represented, but a pointer to *word* is stored. Finally, arrays *top* and *last* tell, for each possible frequency, the vocabulary array positions of the first and last word with that frequency. It always holds $top[f-1] = last[f]+1$ (so actually only one array is maintained). If no words of frequency f exist, then $last[f] = top[f]-1$.

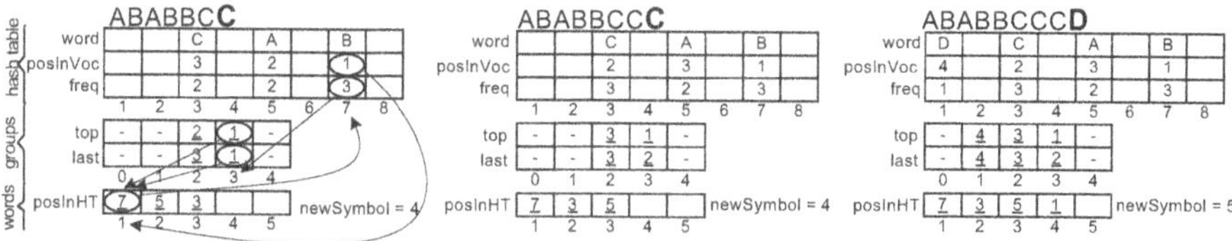

Fig. 3. Transmission of words: ABABBCC, ABABBCCC and ABABBCCCD.

When the sender reads word s_i, it uses the hash function to obtain its position p in the hash table, so that $word[p] = s_i$. After reading $f = freq[p]$, it increments $freq[p]$. The index of s_i in the vocabulary array is also obtained as $i = posInVoc[p]$ (so it will send code C_i). Now, word s_i must be promoted to its next group. For this sake, it finds the head of its group $j = top[f]$ and the corresponding word position $h = posInHT[j]$, so as to swap words i and j in the vocabulary array. The swapping requires exchanging $posInHT[j]$ with $posInHT[i]$, setting $posInVoc[p] = j$ and setting $posInVoc[h] = i$. Once the swapping is done, we promote j to the next group by setting $last[f+1] = j$ and $top[f] = j+1$.

If s_i turns out to be a new word, we set $word[p] = s_i$, $freq[p] = 1$, and $posInVoc[p] = n$, where n is the number of source symbols known prior to reading s_i (and considering *new-Symbol*). Then exactly the above procedure is followed with $f = 0$ and $i = n$. Also, n is incremented.

The receiver works very similarly, except that it starts from i and then it obtains $p = posInHT[i]$. Figure 4 shows the pseudocode.

Implementing dynamic ETDC is simpler than building dynamic word-based Huffman. In fact, our implementation of the Huffman tree update takes about 120 C source code lines, while the update procedure takes only about 20 lines in dynamic ETDC.

5 Empirical Results

We tested the different compressors over several texts. As representative of short texts, we used the whole Calgary corpus. We also used some large text collections from TREC-2 (AP Newswire 1988 and Ziff Data 1989-1990) and from TREC-4 (Congressional Record 1993, Financial Times 1991 to 1994). Finally, two larger collections, ALL_FT and ALL, were used. ALL_FT aggregates all texts from

```
Sender (s_i)
p ← hash(s_i);
if word[p] = nil then // new word
   word[p] ← s_i;
   freq[p] ← 0;
   posInVoc[p] ← n;
   posInHT[n] ← p;
   n ← n + 1;
f ← freq[p];
freq[p] ← freq[p] + 1;
i ← posInVoc[p];
j ← top[f];
h ← posInHT[j];
posInHT[i] ↔ posInHT[j];
posInVoc[p] ← j;
posInVoc[h] ← i;
last[f + 1] ← j;
top[f] ← j + 1;
```

```
Receiver (i)
p ← posInHT[i];
ifword[p] = nil then // new word
   word[p] ← s_i;
   freq[p] ← 0;
   posInVoc[p] ← n;
   posInHT[n] ← p;
   n ← n + 1;
f ← freq[p];
freq[p] ← freq[p] + 1;
i ← posInVoc[p];
j ← top[f];
h ← posInHT[j];
posInHT[i] ↔ posInHT[j];
posInVoc[p] ← j;
posInVoc[h] ← i;
last[f + 1] ← j;
top[f] ← j + 1;
```

Fig. 4. Sender and receiver processes to update *CodeBook* in ETDC.

Table 1. Compression ratios of dynamic versus semi-static techniques.

CORPUS	TEXT SIZE	Plain Huffman			End-Tagged Dense Code			$diff_{ETDC}$
		2-pass	dynamic	Increase	2-pass	dynamic	Increase	$-$
	bytes	ratio %	ratio %	$diff_{PH}$	ratio %	ratio %	$diff_{ETDC}$	$diff_{PH}$
CALGARY	2,131,045	46.238	46.546	0.308	47.397	47.730	0.332	0.024
FT91	14,749,355	34.628	34.739	0.111	35.521	35.638	0.116	0.005
CR	51,085,545	31.057	31.102	0.046	31.941	31.985	0.045	-0.001
FT92	175,449,235	32.000	32.024	0.024	32.815	32.838	0.023	-0.001
ZIFF	185,220,215	32.876	32.895	0.019	33.770	33.787	0.017	-0.002
FT93	197,586,294	31.983	32.005	0.022	32.866	32.887	0.021	-0.001
FT94	203,783,923	31.937	31.959	0.022	32.825	32.845	0.020	-0.002
AP	250,714,271	32.272	32.294	0.021	33.087	33.106	0.018	-0.003
ALL_FT	591,568,807	31.696	31.710	0.014	32.527	32.537	0.011	-0.003
ALL	1,080,719,883	32.830	32.849	0.019	33.656	33.664	0.008	-0.011

Financial Times collection. ALL collection is composed by Calgary corpus and all texts from TREC-2 and TREC-4.

A dual Intel®Pentium®-III 800 Mhz system, with 768 MB SDRAM-100Mhz was used in our tests. It ran Debian GNU/Linux (kernel version 2.2.19). The compiler used was gcc version 3.3.3 20040429 and `-O9` compiler optimizations were used. Time results measure CPU user-time. The spaceless word model [6] was used to model the separators.

Table 1 compares the compression ratios of two-pass versus one-pass techniques. Columns labeled **diff** measure the increase, in percentual points, in the compression ratio of the dynamic codes compared against their semi-static version. The last column shows those differences between Plain Huffman and ETDC.

To understand the increase of size of dynamic versus semi-static codes, two issues have to be considered: (*i*) each new word s_i parsed during dynamic compression is represented in the compressed text (or sent to the receiver) as a pair $\langle C_{new\text{-}Symbol}, s_i \rangle$, while in two-pass compression only the word s_i needs to be stored/transmitted in the vocabulary; (*ii*) on the other hand, some low-frequency words can be encoded with shorter codewords by dynamic techniques, since by the time they appear the vocabulary may still be small.

Compression ratios are around 30-35% for the larger texts. For the smaller ones, compression is poor because the size of the vocabulary is proportionally

Table 2. Comparison between dynamic ETDC and dynamic PH.

CORPUS	TEXT SIZE bytes	n	Dyn PH time (sec)	Dyn PH ratio%	Dyn ETDC time (sec)	Dyn ETDC ratio %	Increase size %	Decrease time %
CALGARY	2,131,045	30,995	0.520	46.546	0.384	47.730	2.543	22.892
FT91	14,749,355	75,681	3.428	34.739	2.488	35.638	2.588	22.685
CR	51,085,545	117,713	11.450	31.102	8.418	31.985	2.839	22.629
FT92	175,449,235	284,892	41.330	32.024	31.440	32.838	2.542	26.404
ZIFF	185,220,215	237,622	44.628	32.895	33.394	33.787	2.710	22.559
FT93	197,586,294	291,427	47.118	32.005	36.306	32.887	2.755	20.840
FT94	203,783,923	295,018	48.260	31.959	36.718	32.845	2.774	22.006
AP	250,714,271	269,141	60.702	32.294	47.048	33.106	2.514	22.796
ALL_FT	591,568,807	577,352	143.050	31.710	111.068	32.537	2.609	23.796
ALL	1,080,719,883	886,190	268.983	32.849	213.068	33.664	2.481	25.927

Table 3. Comparison of compression ratio against gzip and bzip2.

CORPUS	TEXT SIZE bytes	Dyn PH	Dyn ETDC	gzip -f	gzip -b	bzip2 -f	bzip2 -b
		compression ratio %					
CALGARY	2,131,045	46.546	47.730	43.530	36.840	32.827	28.924
FT91	14,749,355	34.739	35.638	42.566	36.330	32.305	27.060
CR	51,085,545	31.102	31.985	39.506	33.176	29.507	24.142
FT92	175,449,235	32.024	32.838	42.585	36.377	32.369	27.088
ZIFF	185,220,215	32.895	33.787	39.656	32.975	29.642	25.106
FT93	197,586,294	32.005	32.887	40.230	34.122	30.624	25.322
FT94	203,783,923	31.959	32.845	40.236	34.122	30.535	25.267
AP	250,714,271	32.294	33.106	43.651	37.225	33.260	27.219
ALL_FT	591,568,807	31.710	32.537	40.988	34.845	31.152	25.865
ALL	1,080,719,883	32.849	33.664	41.312	35.001	31.304	25.981

too large with respect to the compressed text size (as expected from Heaps' law [10]). This means that proportionally too many words are transmitted in plain form.

The increase of size of the compressed texts in ETDC compared to PH is always under 1 percentage point, in the larger texts. On the other hand, the dynamic versions lose very little in compression (maximum 0.02 percentage points, 0.06%) compared to their semi-static versions. This shows that the price paid by dynamism in terms of compression ratio is negligible. Note also that in most cases, and in the larger texts, dynamic ETDC loses even less compression than dynamic Plain Huffman.

Table 2 compares the time performance of our dynamic compressors. The latter two columns measure the increase in compression ratio (in percentage) of ETDC versus Plain Huffman, and the reduction in processing time, in percentage.

As it can be seen, dynamic ETDC loses less than 1 percentage point (3%) of compression ratio compared to dynamic Plain Huffman, in the larger texts. In exchange, it is 22%-26% faster and considerably simpler to implement. Dynamic Plain Huffman compresses 4 megabytes per second, while dynamic ETDC reaches 5.

Tables 3 and 4 compare both dynamic Plain Huffman and dynamic ETDC against *gzip* (Ziv-Lempel family) and *bzip2* (Burrows-Wheeler [5] type technique). Experiments were run setting *gzip* and *bzip2* parameters to "best" (-b) and "fast" (-f) compression.

As expected "bzip2 -b" achieves the best compression ratio. It is about 6 and 7 percentage points better than dynamic PH and dynamic ETDC respectively. However, it is much slower than the other techniques tested in both compression and decompression processes. Using the "fast" *bzip2* option seems to be undesirable, since compression ratio gets worse (it becomes closer to dynamic PH) and compression and decompression speeds remain poor.

On the other hand, "gzip -f" is shown to achieve good compression speed, at the expense of compression ratio (about 40%). It is shown that dynamic ETDC is also a fast technique. It is able to beat "gzip -f" in compression speed (except in the ALL corpus). Regarding to compression ratio, dynamic ETDC achieves also best results than "gzip -b" (except in CALGARY and ZIFF corpora). However, *gzip* is clearly the fastest method in decompression.

Hence, dynamic ETDC is either much faster or compresses much better than *gzip*, and it is by far faster than *bzip2*.

Table 4. Comparison of compression and decompression time against gzip and bzip2.

CORPUS	compression time (sec)					decompression time (sec)				
	Dyn PH	Dyn ETDC	gzip -f	bzip2 -f	bzip2 -b	Dyn PH	Dyn ETDC	gzip -f	bzip2 -f	bzip2 -b
CALGARY	0,498	0,384	0,360	2,180	2,660	0,330	0,240	0,090	0,775	0,830
FT91	3,218	2,488	2,720	14,380	18,200	2,350	1,545	0,900	4,655	5,890
CR	10,880	8,418	8,875	48,210	65,170	7,745	5,265	3,010	15,910	19,890
FT92	42,720	31,440	34,465	166,310	221,460	30,690	19,415	8,735	57,815	71,050
ZIFF	43,122	33,394	33,550	174,670	233,250	30,440	11,690	9,070	58,790	72,340
FT93	45,864	36,306	36,805	181,720	237,750	32,780	21,935	10,040	62,565	77,860
FT94	47,078	36,718	37,500	185,107	255,220	33,550	22,213	10,845	62,795	80,370
AP	60,940	47,048	50,330	231,785	310,620	43,660	27,233	15,990	81,875	103,010
ALL_FT	145,750	91,068	117,255	558,530	718,250	104,395	66,238	36,295	189,905	235,370
ALL	288,778	213,905	188,310	996,530	1342,430	218,745	126,938	62,485	328,240	432,390

6 Conclusions

In this paper we have considered the problem of providing adaptive compression for natural language text, with the combined aim of competitive compression ratios and good time performance.

We built an adaptive version of word-based Huffman codes. For this sake, we adapted an existing algorithm so as to handle very large sets of source symbols and byte-oriented output. The latter decision sacrifices some compression ratio in exchange for an 8-fold improvement in time performance. The resulting algorithm obtains compression ratio very similar to its static version (0.06% off) and compresses about 4 megabytes per second on a standard PC.

We also implemented a dynamic version of the End-Tagged Dense Code (ETDC). The resulting adaptive version is much simpler than the Huffman-based one, and 22%-26% faster, compressing typically 5 megabytes per second. The compressed text is only 0.06% larger than with semi-static ETDC and 3% larger than with Huffman.

As a result, we have obtained adaptive natural language text compressors that obtain 30%-35% compression ratio, and compress more than 4 megabytes per second. Empirical results show their good performance when they are compared against other compressors such as *gzip* and *bzip2*.

Future work involves building an adaptive version of (s,c)-Code [4], an extension to ETDC where the number of byte values that signal the end of a codeword can be adapted to optimize compression, instead of being fixed at 128 as in ETDC. An interesting problem in this case is how to efficiently maintain the optimal (s,c), which now vary as compression progresses.

References

1. T. C. Bell, J. G. Cleary, and I. H. Witten. *Text Compression.* Prentice Hall, 1990.
2. R.S. Boyer and J.S. Moore. A fast string searching algorithm. *Communications of the ACM*, 20(10):762–772, October 1977.
3. N. Brisaboa, E. Iglesias, G. Navarro, and J. Paramá. An efficient compression code for text databases. In *25th European Conference on IR Research (ECIR 2003)*, LNCS 2633, pages 468–481, 2003.
4. N.R. Brisaboa, A. Fariña, G. Navarro, and M.F. Esteller. (s,c)-dense coding: An optimized compression code for natural language text databases. In *Proc. 10th International Symposium on String Processing and Information Retrieval (SPIRE 2003)*, LNCS 2857, pages 122–136, 2003.
5. M. Burrows and D. J. Wheeler. A block-sorting lossless data compression algorithm. Technical Report 124, 1994.
6. E. de Moura, G. Navarro, N. Ziviani, and R. Baeza-Yates. Fast searching on compressed text allowing errors. In *Proc. 21st Annual International ACM SIGIR Conference on Research and Development in Information Retrieval (SIGIR-98)*, pages 298–306, 1998.
7. E. de Moura, G. Navarro, N. Ziviani, and R. Baeza-Yates. Fast and flexible word searching on compressed text. *ACM Transactions on Information Systems (TOIS)*, 18(2):113–139, 2000.
8. N Faller. An adaptive system for data compression. In *In Record of the 7th Asilomar Conference on Circuits, Systems, and Computers*, pages 593–597, 1973.
9. R.G Gallager. Variations on a theme by Huffman. *IEEE Trans. on Inf. Theory*, 24(6):668–674, 1978.
10. H. S. Heaps. *Information Retrieval: Computational and Theoretical Aspects.* Academic Press, New York, 1978.
11. D. A. Huffman. A method for the construction of minimum-redundancy codes. *Proc. Inst. Radio Eng.*, 40(9):1098–1101, 1952.
12. D.E. Knuth. Dynamic Huffman coding. *Journal of Algorithms*, 2(6):163–180, 1985.
13. A. Moffat. Word-based text compression. *Software - Practice and Experience*, 19(2):185–198, 1989.
14. J.S. Vitter. Design and analysis of dynamic Huffman codes. *Journal of the ACM (JACM)*, 34(4):825–845, 1987.
15. J.S. Vitter. Algorithm 673: dynamic Huffman coding. *ACM Transactions on Mathematical Software (TOMS)*, 15(2):158–167, 1989.

Searching XML Documents Using Relevance Propagation

Karen Sauvagnat, Mohand Boughanem, and Claude Chrisment

IRIT- SIG, 118 route de Narbonne
31 062 Toulouse Cedex 4, France
{sauvagna,bougha,chrisment}@irit.fr

Abstract. The issue of information retrieval in XML documents was first investigated by the database community. Recently, the Information Retrieval (IR) community started to investigate the XML search issue. For this purpose, traditional information retrieval models were adapted to process XML documents and rank results by relevance. In this paper, we describe an IR approach to deal with queries composed of content and structure conditions. The XFIRM model we propose is designed to be as flexible as possible to process such queries. It is based on a complete query language, derived from Xpath and on a relevance values propagation method. The value of this proposed method is evaluated thanks to the INEX evaluation initiative. Results show a relative high precision of our system.

1 Introduction

Users looking for precise information do not want to be submerged by noisy subjects, as it can be in long documents. One of the main advantages of the XML format is its capacity to combine structured and un-structured (i.e. text) data. As a consequence, XML documents allow information to be processed at another granularity level than the whole document. The main challenge in XML retrieval is to retrieve the most exhaustive[1] and specific[2] information unit [12]. Approaches dealing with this challenge can be divided into two main sub-groups [5]. On the one hand, the data-oriented approaches use XML documents to exchange structured data. The database community was the first to propose solutions for the XML retrieval issue, using the data-oriented approaches. In the Xquery language proposed by the W3C [25], SQL functionalities on tables (collection of tuples) are extended to support similar operations on forests (collection of trees), as XML documents can be seen as trees. Unfortunately, most of the proposed approaches typically expect binary answers to very specific queries. However, an extension of XQuery with full-text search features is expected [26]. On the other hand, the document-oriented approaches consider that tags are used to describe the logical structure of documents. The IR community has adapted traditional IR approaches to address the user information needs in XML collection.

[1] An element is exhaustive to a query if it contains all the required information.

[2] An element is specific to a query if all its content concerns the query.

A. Apostolico and M. Melucci (Eds.): SPIRE 2004, LNCS 3246, pp. 242–254, 2004.

The goal of this paper is to show that the approach we proposed, which belongs to the document-centric view, can also give good results for specific queries (regarding structure) containing content conditions. The following section gives a brief view of related work. Then, in section 3, we present the XFIRM *(XML Flexible Information Retrieval Model)* model and the associated query language. Section 4 presents the INEX initiative for XML retrieval evaluation and evaluates our approach via experiments carried out on the INEX collection.

2 Related Work: Information Retrieval Approaches for XML Retrieval

One of the first IR approaches proposed for dealing with XML documents was the "fetch and browse" approach [3, 4], saying that *a system should always retrieve the most specific part of a document answering a query*. This definition assumes that the system first searches whole documents answering the query in an exhaustive way (the *fetch* phase) and then extracts the most specific information units (the *browse* phase). Most of the Information Retrieval Systems (IRS) dealing with XML documents allow information units to be directly searched, without first processing the whole documents. Let us describe some of them.

The *extended boolean model* uses a new non-commutative operator called "contains", that allows queries to be specified completely in terms of content and structure [11].

Regarding the *vector space model*, the similarity measure is extended in order to evaluate relations between structure and content . In this case, each index term should be encapsulated by one or more elements. The model can be generalized with the aggregation of relevance scores in the documents hierarchy [7]. In [22], the query model is based on tree matching: it allows the expression of queries without perfectly knowing the data structure.

The *probabilistic model* is applied to XML documents in [12, 24, 5]. The XIRQL query language [5] extends the Xpath operators with operators for relevance-oriented search and vague searches on non-textual content. Documents are then sorted by decreasing probability that their content is the one specified by the user.

Language models are also adapted for XML retrieval [1, 15]. Finally, *bayesian networks* are used in [17].

In [9], Fuhr and al. proposed an augmentation method for dealing with XML documents. In this approach, standard term weighting formulas are used to index so called "index nodes" of the document. Index nodes are not necessarily leaf nodes, because this structure is considered to be too fine-grained. However, index nodes are disjoint. In order to allow nesting of nodes, in case of high-level index nodes comprising other index nodes, only the text that is not contained within the other index nodes is indexed. For computing the indexing weights of inner nodes, the weights from the most specific index-nodes are propagated towards the inner nodes. During propagation, however, the weights are down-weighted by multiplying them with a so-called augmentation factor. In case a term at an inner node receives propagated weights from several leaves, the overall term weight is computed by assuming a probabilistic disjunction of the leaf term weights. This way, more specific elements are preferred during retrieval.

The approach we describe in this paper is also based on an augmentation method. However, in our approach, all leaf nodes are indexed, because we think that even the smallest leaf node can also contain relevant information. Moreover, the way relevance values are propagated in the document tree is function of the distance that separates nodes in the tree. The following section describes our model.

3 The XFIRM Model

3.1 Data Representation

A structured document sd_i is a tree, composed of simple nodes n_j, leaf nodes ln_j and attributes a_j. Formally, this can be written as follows : $sd_i = (tree_i) = (\{n_j\}, \{ln_j\}, \{a_j\})$. This representation is a simplification of Xpath and Xquery data model [27], where a node can be a *document*, an *element*, *text*, a *namespace*, an *instruction* or a *comment*. In order to easy browse the document tree and to quickly find ancestors-descendants relationships, the XFIRM model uses the following representation of nodes and attributes, based on the Xpath Accelerator approach [10]:

Node: n_j =*(pre, post, parent, attribute)*

Leaf node: ln_j = *(pre, post, parent,* $\{t_1,t_2,...t_n\}$*)*

Attribute: a_j=*(pre, val)*

A node is defined thanks to its pre-order and post-order value (*pre* and *post*), the pre-order value of its parent node (*parent*), and depending on its type (simple node of leaf node), by a field indicating the presence or absence of attributes (*attribute*) or by the terms it contains ($\{t_1,t_2,...,t_n\}$). An attribute is defined by the pre-order value of the node containing it (*pre*) and by its value (*val*). Pre-order and post-order values are assigned to nodes thanks respectively to a prefixed and post-fixed traversal of the document tree, as illustrated in the following figure.

<article> <fm> <title> Search engines : how to find a needle in a haystack</title> <author > J. Dupont </author> <year> 1998 </year> </fm> <bdy> <sec > <st> Introduction </st>	<p> Internet growth…</p> </sec> <sec > <st> Search engines </st> <p> Yahoo! is …</p> <p> Google is a full-text search engine </p> </sec> </bdy> </article>

Fig. 1. Example of XML document

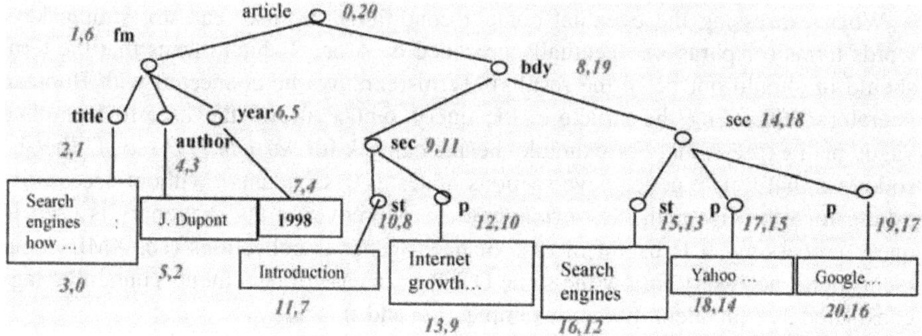

Fig. 2. Tree representation of the XML document in Figure 1. Each node is assigned a pre-order and post-order value

If we transpose nodes in a two-dimensions space based on the pre and post order coordinates, we can exploit the following properties, given a node *n*:

- all ancestors of *n* are to the upper left of *n*'s position in the plane
- all its descendants are to the lower right,
- all preceding nodes in document order are to the lower left, and
- the upper right partition of the plane comprises all following nodes (regarding document order)

In contrast to other path index structures for XML, Xpath Accelerator efficiently supports path expressions that do not start at the document root. As explained in [19], all data are stored in a relational database. The *Path Index* (PI) allows the reconstruction of the document structure (thanks to the Xpath Accelerator model). The *Term Index* (TI) is a traditional inverted file. The *Element Index* (IE) describes the content of each leaf node, the *Attribute Index* (AI) gives the values of attributes, and the *Dictionary* (DICT) allows the grouping of tags having the same signification.

3.2 The XFIRM Query Language

XFIRM is based on a complete query language, allowing the expression of queries with simple keywords terms and/or with structural conditions [20]. In its more complex form, the language allows the expression of hierarchical conditions on document structure and the element to be returned to the user can be specified (thanks to the *te: (target element)* operator). For example, the following XFIRM queries:
(i) // te: p [weather forecasting systems]
(ii) // article[security] // te: sec ["facial recognition"]
(iii) // te: article [Petri net] //sec [formal definition] AND sec[algorithm efficiency]
(iv) // te: article [] // sec [search engines]
respectively mean that (i) the user wants a paragraph about *weather forecasting systems*, (ii) a section about *facial recognition* in an article about *security* , (iii) an article about *Petri net* containing a section giving a *formal definition* and another section talking about *algorithm efficiency,* and *(iv)* an article containing a section about *search engines.*

When expressing the eventual content conditions, the user can use simple keywords terms (or phrases), eventually preceded by + or - (which means that the term should or should not be in the results). Terms can also be connected with Boolean operators. Regarding the structure, the query syntax allows the user to formulate vague path expressions. For example, he/she can ask for "*article [] // sec []*" (he/she so knows that article nodes have sections nodes as descendants), without necessarily asking for a precise path, i.e. *article/bdy/sec*. Moreover, a tag dictionary is used in query processing. It is useful in case of heterogeneous collections (i.e. XML documents don't necessary follow the same DTD) or in case of documents containing tags considered as equivalent, like for example, *title* and *sub-title*.

3.3 Query Processing

The approach we propose for dealing with queries containing content and structure conditions is based on relevance weights propagation. The query evaluation is carried out as follows:

1. queries are decomposed in elementary sub-queries
2. relevance values are assigned to leaf nodes
3. relevance values are propagated through ther document tree
4. original queries are evaluated thanks to elementary sub-queries

Query Decomposition

Each XFIRM query can be decomposed in sub-queries SQ_i as follows:

$$Q = // SQ_1 // SQ_2 //...// te : SQ_j //...// SQ_n \quad (1)$$

Where *te:* indicates which element is the target element. Each sub-query SQ_i can then be re-decomposed in elementary sub-queries $ESQ_{i,j}$, eventually linked with boolean operators and of the form:

$$ESQ_{i,j} = tg\ [q] \quad (2)$$

Where tg is a tag name and $q = \{t_1, ...t_n\}$ is a set of keywords, i.e. a content condition.

Evaluating Leaf Nodes Relevance Values

The first step in query processing is to evaluate the relevance value of leaf nodes *ln* according to the content conditions (if they exist). Let $q=\{t_1,...,t_n\}$ be a content condition. Relevance values are evaluated thanks to a similarity function called $RSV_m(q,nf)$, where m is an IR model. XFIRM authorizes the implementation of many IR models. As the purpose of this article is to evaluate the interest of relevance values propagation, we choose to take the vector space model as reference. So:

$$RSV(q,\ln) = \sum_{i=1}^{n} w_i^q * w_i^{\ln} \text{, with } w_i^q = tf_i^q * ief_i \quad \text{And } w_i^{\ln} = tf_i^{\ln} * ief_i \quad (3)$$

Where: tf_i is the term frequency in the query q or in the leaf node *ln*, ief_i is the inverse element frequency of term i, i.e. $log\ (N/n+1)+1$, n is the number of leaf nodes containing i and N is the total number of leaf nodes.

Elementary Sub-queries $ESQ_{i,j}$ Processing

The result set $R_{i,j}$ of $ESQ_{i,j}$ is a set of pairs *(node, relevance)* defined as follows:

$$R_{i,j} = \{ (n, r_n) / n \in \{construct(tg)\} \text{ and } r_n = F_k (RSV_m(q, nf_k), dist(n,nf_k)) \} \quad (4)$$

Where: r_n is the relevance weight of node n ; the *construct(tg)* function allows the creation of the set of all nodes having *tg* as tag name ; the F_k $(RSV_m(q, nf_k), dist(n,nf_k))$ function allows the propagation and aggregation of relevance values of leaf nodes nf_k , descendants of node *n,* in order to form the relevance value of node *n.* This propagation is function of distance $dist(n,nf_k)$ which separates node *n* from leaf node nf_k in the document tree (i.e. the number of arcs that are necessary to join *n* and nf_k).

Subqueries SQ_i Processing

Once each $ESQ_{i,j}$ has been processed, subqueries SQ_i are evaluated thanks to the commutative operators $\oplus_{AND}$ et $\oplus_{OR}$ defined below:

Definition 1 : Let $N = \{ (n, r_n) \}$ and $M = (m, r_m) \}$ be two sets of pairs (node, relevance)

$N \oplus_{AND} M = \{ (l, r_l) /$ *l is the nearest common ancestor of m and n or l=m (respectively n) if m (resp .n) is ancestor of n (resp. m) ,* $\forall m$*, n being in the same document and* $r_l = aggreg_{AND}(r_n , r_{m'} , dist(l,n), dist(l,m))\}$ (5)

$N \oplus_{OR} M = \{ (l, r_l) / \; l=n \in N \text{ or } l=m \in M \text{ and } r_l = r_n \text{ or } r_m \}$ (6)

Where $aggreg_{AND}(r_n , r_m , dist(l,n),dist(l,m))= r_l$ defines the way relevance values r_n and r_m of nodes *n* and *m* are aggregated in order to form a new relevance r_l.

Let R_i be the result set of SQ_i. Then:

If $SQ_i = ESQ_{i,j}$, then $R_i = R_{i,j}$ (7)

If $SQ_i = ESQ_{i,j}$ AND $ESQ_{i,k}$, then $R_i = R_{i,j} \oplus_{AND} R_{i,k}$ (8)

If $SQ_i = ESQ_{i,j}$ OR $ESQ_{i,k}$, then $R_i = R_{i,j} \oplus_{OR} R_{i,k}$ (9)

Whole Queries Processing

The result set of sub-queries SQ_i are then used to process whole queries. In each query, a target element is specified, as defined above.

$Q =// SQ_1 // SQ_2 //...//te : SQ_j //...//SQ_n$

Thus, the aim in whole query processing will be to propagate the relevance values of sub-queries SQ_i to nodes belonging to the result set of the sub-query SQ_j which defines the target element. This is obtained thanks to the non-commutative operators ∇ and Δ defined below:

Definition 2 : Let $R_i = \{(n, r_n)\}$ and $R_{i+1} = \{\{m, r_m)\}$ be two sets of pairs (node, relevance)

$$R_i \nabla R_{i+1} = \{(n, r_n) / n\in R_i \text{ is ancestor of } m\in R_{i+1} \text{ and } r_n=prop\_agg(r_n, r_m, dist(m,n))\} \quad (10)$$

$$R_i \Delta R_{i+1} = \{(n, r_n) / n \in \text{ is descendant of } m \in R_{i+1} \text{ and } r_n = prop\_agg(r_n, r_m, dist(m,n))\} \quad (11)$$

Where $prop\_agg(r_n , r_m, dist(m,n))\text{->} r_n$ allows the aggregation of relevance weights r_m of node m and r_n of node n according to the distance that separates the 2 nodes, in order to obtain the new relevance weight r_n of node n .

The result set R of a query Q is then defined as follows:

$$R = R_j \nabla (R_{j+1} \nabla (R_{j+2}\nabla \ldots)) \quad (12)$$

$$R = R_j \Delta (R_{j-1} \Delta (R_{j-2}\Delta \ldots))$$

In fact, this is equivalent to propagate relevance values of results set $R_{j+1}, \ldots, R_n$ and $R_1,\ldots,R_n$ respectively upwards and downwards in the document tree.

4 Experiments and Results

4.1 The SCAS Task in the INEX Initiative

Evaluating the effectiveness of XML retrieval systems requires a test collection (XML documents, task/queries, and relevance judgments) where the relevance assessments are provided according to a relevance criterion that takes into account the imposed structural aspects [6]. The Initiative for the Evaluation of XML Retrieval tends to reach this aim. INEX collection, 21 IEEE Computer Society journals from 1995-2002 consists of 12 135 documents with extensive XML-markup.

Participants to INEX SCAS task (Strict Content and Structure Task) have to perform CAS (Content and Structure) queries, which contain explicit references to the XML structure, and restrict the context of interest and/or the context of certain search concepts. One can found an example of INEX 2003 CAS query below.

```
<inex_topic topic_id="64" query_type="CAS">
<title> //article[about(./,'hollerith')] // sec[about(./, 'DEHOMAG')] </title>
<description> In articles discussing Herman Hollerith find sections that mention DEHOMAG </description>
<narrative> Relevant sections deal with DEHOMAG in documents that discuss work or life of Herman Hollerith </narrative>
<keywords> Hollerith, DEHOMAG, Deutsche Hollerith Maschinen Gesellschaft </keywords>
</inex_topic>
```

Fig. 5. Example of CAS query

The INEX metric for evaluation is based on the traditional recall and precision measures. To obtain recall/precision figures, the two dimensions of relevance (exhaustivity and specificity) need to be quantised onto a single relevance value. Quantisation functions for two user standpoints were used: (i) a "strict" quantisation to evaluate whether a given retrieval approach is capable of retrieving highly exhaustive and highly specific document components, (ii) a "generalised" quantisation has been used in order to credit document components according to their degree of relevance.

Some Approaches

In INEX 2003, most of the approaches used IR models to answer the INEX tasks, which shows the increased interest of the IR community to XML retrieval.

Some approaches used a fetch and browse strategy [21, 16], which didn't give as good results as expected. The Queensland University of Technology used a filtering method to find the most specific information units [8]. The vector space model was adapted in [14], using 6 different index for terms (article, section, paragraph, abstract,...). Finally language models were used in [2, 13] and [23]. Last cited obtained the best of all performances, using one language model per element.

In the following, we present the results of the experiments we conducted in the INEX collection in order to evaluate several possible implementations of our model.

4.2 Various Propagation Functions

5 propagation functions have been evaluated.

- $F_k(RSV_m(q, nf_k), dist(n,nf_k))$ ***(4)*** is set to:

$$F_k(RSV(q, nf_k), dist(n, nf_k)) = \sum_{k=1..n} \alpha^{dist(n, nf_k)} * RSV(n, nf_k) \quad (13)$$

- $aggreg_{AND}(r_n, r_m, dist(l,n), dist(l,m))$ ***(5)*** is either set to :

$$aggreg_{AND}(r_n, r_m, dist(l,n), dist(l,m)) = \frac{r_n}{dist(l,n)} + \frac{r_m}{dist(m,l)} \quad (14)$$

$$aggreg_{AND}(r_n, r_m, dist(l,n), dist(l,m)) = \alpha^{dist(l,n)} * r_n + \alpha^{dist(l,m)} * r_m \quad (15)$$

- And finally, $prop\_agg(dist(m,n), r_n, r_m)$ ***(10)*** is either set to:

$$prop\_agg(dist(m,n), r_n, r_m) = \frac{r_n + r_m}{dist(m,n)} \quad (16)$$

$$prop\_agg(dist(m,n), r_n, r_m) = \alpha^{dist(m,n)} * r_m + r_n \quad (17)$$

Where $\alpha \in]0..1]$ is a parameter used to adjust the importance of the distance between nodes in the different functions and *dist(x,y)* is the distance which separates node *x* from node *y* in the document tree.

4.3 Implementation Issues

The transformation of INEX CAS queries to XFIRM queries was fairly easy. Table1 gives some correspondences:

Table 1. Transformation of INEX topics into XFIRM queries

INEX topic	XFIRM query
//article [about(.,'clustering + distributed') and about(.//sec,'java')]	// te: article [clustering + distributed] // sec [java]
//article[about(./sec,'"e- commerce"') // abs[about(., 'trust authentication')]	//article [] AND sec["e- commerce"] // te: abs [trust authentication]
//article[(.//yr='2000' OR .//yr='1999') AND about(., "intelligent transportation system"') // sec [about(.,'automation +vehicle)]	//article ["intelligent transportation system"] // te: sec [automation + vehicle]

During $ESQ_{i,j}$ processing, the most relevant leaf nodes are found, and for each of these leaf nodes, XFIRM looks for ancestors. In order to have a correct response time of the system, the propagation is stopped when 1500 "correct" ancestors are found (i.e. ancestors having a correct tag name).

When a INEX topic contains a condition on the article publication date (as its the case in the last query of Table 1), this condition is not translated in the XFIRM language, because propagation with a very common term (like a year) is too long. To solve this issue, queries are processed by XFIRM without this condition, and results are then filtered on the article publication date.

Finally, the Dictionary index is used to find equivalent tags. For example, according to INEX guidelines, *sec* (section) nodes are equivalent to *ss1*, *ss2* and *ss3*.

4.4 Runs

We evaluated 5 runs, combining the different functions:

Run name	Prop. functions	α	Topic Fields
xfirm.TK.alpha=0.7	(13) (15) (17)	0.7.	Title+Keywords
xfirm.TK.alpha=0.9	(13) (15) (17)	0.9.	Title+Keywords
xfirm.TK.alpha=1	(13) (15) (17)	$\alpha = 1$	Title+Keywords
xfirm.TK.mix	(13) (14) (16)	$\alpha = 0.9$ for (13).	Title+Keywords
xfirm.T.mix:	(13) (14) (16)	$\alpha = 0.9$ for (13)	Title

In addition, these runs were compared to the best run we performed last year in the Inex SCAS task with our fetch and browse method: **Mercure2.pos_cas_ti** [21].

4.5 Analysis of the Results

Table 2 shows the average precision (for strict and generalized quantization) obtained by each run over 30 queries. The associated recall-precision curves for strict quantization are plotted in Figure 6.

The first point to be noticed is the relatively high precision for all runs. Table 3 shows our runs if they were integrated in the official INEX results for strict quantization. Best results were obtained by the University of Amsterdam, using language

Table 2. Average precision for our 6 runs

	Average precision (strict quantization)	Average precision (generalized quantization)
Xfirm.TK.alpha=0.7	0,2346	0,2253
Xfirm.TK.alpha=0.9	0,2766	0,2279
Xfirm.TK.alpha=1	0,2783	0,2257
Xfirm.TK.mix	**0,2898**	**0,2300**
Xfirm.T.mix	0,2675	0,2276
Mercure2.pos_cas_ti	0,1620	0,1637

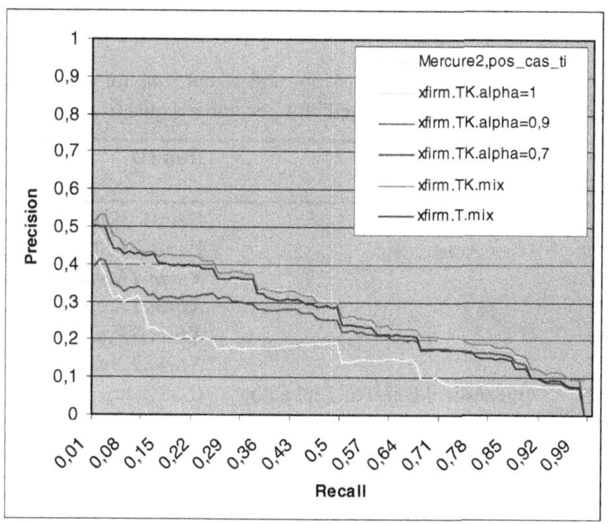

Fig. 6. Average/precision curves for strict quantization

models [23]. Most of our runs would have been ranked between the second and third position, before the Queensland University of Technology [16], who processed queries with a fetch and browse approach.

The propagation method we used increases in a very significant way the results we obtained with our "fetch and browse" method (run *Mercure2.pos_cas_ti*). This is not really surprising, because the XFIRM model is able to process all the content conditions, whereas the run performed with Mercure system only verify that conditions on the target element are respected. Moreover, the processing time for each query is of course lower (because thanks to the index structure, the XFIRM model has not to browse each exhaustive document to find the specific elements). The use of distance between nodes seems to be a useful parameter for the propagation functions. It can be noticed that the *Xfirm.TK.mix* run where distance is considered, obtains best average precision than the *Xfirm.TK.alpha=1* run, where the distance had no importance. However, the three runs evaluated with different values of α *(Xfirm.TK.aplha= 0.7, Xfirm.TK.aplha=0.9 , Xfirm.TK.alpha=1*) show that the distance should be considered carefully. Indeed, when relevance values are too down-weighted by the distance, the performances decrease.

Finally, the use of title and keywords fields of INEX topics increases the average precision of the *xfirm.TK.mix* run comparing to the *.xfirm.T.mix* run, even if it decreases the precision for some particular queries.

So, the relevance propagation method seems to give good results, using all leaf nodes as start point to the propagation. Our methods have to be explored on other topics/collections to confirm these performances. Moreover, the IR model (i.e. the vector space model) used for relevance value calculation needs more investigations, the formula used for these experiments being not normalized. Further experiments will be necessary, for example with the *bm25* formula [18].

Table 3. Ranking of official INEX submissions and of our runs for strict quantization. Please note that most of them are too in the "top ten" for generalized quantization

rank	Avg precision	Organisation	Run ID
1	0.3182	U. of Amsterdam	UamsI03-SCAS-MixedScore
2	0.2987	U. of Amsterdam	UamsI03-SCAS-ElementScore
	0.2898		***Xfirm.TK.mix***
	0.2783		***Xfirm.TK.alpha=1***
	0.2766		***Xfirm.TK.alpha=0.9***
	0.2675		***Xfirm.T.mix***
3	0.2601	Queensland Univ. of Technology	CASQuery_1
4	0.2476	University of Twente and CWI	LMM-ComponentRetrieval-SCAS
5	0.2458	IBM, Haifa Research lab	SCAS-TK-With-Clustering
6	0.2448	Universität Duisburg-Essen	Scas03-way1-alias
7	0.2437	RMIT University	RMIT_SCAS_1
8	0.2419	RMIT University	RMIT_SCAS_2
9	0.2405	IBM, Haifa Research lab	SCAS-TK-With-No- Clustering
10	0.2352	RMIT University	RMIT_SCAS_3
	0.2346		***Xfirm.TK.alpha=0.7***
…	…	…	…
24	*0.1641*	*IRIT*	*Mercure2.pos_cas_ti*

5 Conclusion

We have presented here an approach for XML content and structure-oriented search that addresses the search issue from an IR viewpoint. We have described the XFIRM model and a relevance values propagation method that allows the ranking of information units according to their degree of relevance. This propagation method is based on relevance values calculation for each leaf node (thanks to the vector space model) and then on propagation functions using the distance between nodes to aggregate the relevance values. The XFIRM model decomposes each query in elementary subqueries to process them and then recomposes the original query to respect the eventual hierarchical conditions.

This method achieves good results on the INEX topics. Further experiments should be achieved to evaluate the impact of the IR model used for leaf nodes relevance values calculation and to confirm results on other topics/collections.

References

1. Abolhassani, M., Fuhr, N. : Applying the Divergence From Randomness Approach for Content-Only Search in XML Documents. In: ECIR 04. 2004.
2. Abolhassani M., Fuhr, N., Malik, S. : HyREX at INEX 03. . In Proceedings of INEX 2003 Workshop, 2003.
3. Afrati, Foto N., Koutras, Constantinos D.: A Hypertext Model Supporting Query Mechanisms. Proceedings of the European Conference on Hypertext, 1990.
4. Chiaramella, Y. , Mulhem, P. , Fourel, F. A model for multimedia search information retrieval. Technical report, Basic Research Action FERMI 8134, University of Glasgow, 1996.
5. Fuhr, N., Grossjohann, K. "XIRQL: A query Language for Information Retrieval in XML Documents". In Proc. of the 24th annual ACM SIGIR conference, 2001.
6. Fuhr, N., Malik, S., Lalmas, M : Overview of the Initiative for the Evaluation of XML Retrieval (INEX) 2003. In Proceedings of INEX 2003 Workshop, 2003.
7. M. Fuller, E. Mackie, R. Sacks-Davis, R. Wilkinson *: Structural answers for a large structured document collection.* In Proc. ACM SIGIR, 1993.
8. Geva, S., Murray L-S. : Xpath inverted file for information retrieval. . In Proceedings of INEX 2003 Workshop, 2003.
9. Gövert Norbert, Abolhassani, M., Fuhr, N., Grossjohann, K. : Content-oriented XML retrieval with HyREX. In Proceedings of the first INEX Workshop, 2002.
10. Grust, T, "Accelerating XPath Location Steps". In M. J. Franklin, B. Moon, and A. Ailamaki, editors, *Proceedings of the 2002 ACM SIGMOD International Conference on Management of Data*, USA, 2002.
11. Hayashi, Y. , Tomita , J., Kikoi, G , "Searching text-rich XML documents with relevance ranking". *In Proc ACM SIGIR 2000 Workshop on XML and IR* . Athens 2000.
12. Lalmas, M., "Dempster-Shafer theory of evidence applied to structured documents: modeling uncertainty". In Proc. ACM-SIGIR, 1997.
13. List, J., Mihazjlovic , V., de Vries A.P., Ramirez, G., Hiemstra, D. : The TIJAH XML-IR system at INEX 03. . In Proceedings of INEX 2003 Workshop, 2003.
14. Mass, Y., Mandelbrod, M. : Retrieving the most relevant XML component. . In Proceedings of INEX 2003 Workshop, 2003.
15. Ogilvie, P., Callan, J. : Using Language Models for Flat Text Queries in XML Retrieval. In Proceedings of INEX 2003 Workshop, 2003.
16. Pehcevski, J., Thom, J., Vercoustre, A-M. : RMIT experiments : XML retrieval using Lucy/eXist. . In Proceedings of INEX 2003 Workshop, 2003.
17. Piwowarski, B., Faure, G-E., Gallinari, P. : Bayesian networks and INEX. In Proceedings in the First Annual Workshop for the Evaluation of XML Retrieval (INEX), 2002.
18. Robertson, S.E., Walker, S., Hancock-Beaulieu, M.M. : Okapi at TREC 3. In Proceedings TREC 3, 1994.
19. Sauvagnat, K. , "XFIRM, un modèle flexible de Recherche d'Information pour le stockage et l'interrogation de documents XML", *CORIA'04*, Toulouse, France, 2004.

20. Sauvagnat, K., Boughanem, M. : Le langage de requête XFIRM pour les documents XML: De la recherche par simples mots-clés à l'utilisation de la structure des documents. Inforsid 2004, Biarritz, France .
21. Sauvagnat, K., Hubert, G., Boughanem, M., Mothe, J. : IRIT at INEX 03. In Proceedings of INEX 2003 Workshop, 2003.
22. Schlieder, T., Meuss, H. , "Querying and ranking XML documents". *Journal of the American Society for Information Science and Technology*, 53(6) : 489-503, 2002.
23. Sigurbjörnsson, B., Kaamps, J., de Rijke, M. : An element-based approach to XML retrieval. . In Proceedings of INEX 2003 Workshop, 2003.
24. J.E. Wolff, H. Flörke, A.B. Cremers : Searching and browsing collections of structural information. In Proc of IEEE advances in digital libraries, Washington, 2000.
25. W3C. XQuery 1.0 : an XML query language. W3C Working Draft, 2003.
26. W3C. Xquery and Xpath Full-Text Use Cases. W3C Working draft, 2003 .
27. W3C. M Fernandez et al. : XQuery 1.0 and XPath 2.0 Data Model. Working Draft, 2003.

Dealing with Syntactic Variation Through a Locality-Based Approach

Jesús Vilares and Miguel A. Alonso

Departamento de Computación, Universidade da Coruña
Campus de Elviña s/n, 15071 A Coruña, Spain
{jvilares,alonso}@udc.es
http://www.grupocole.org/

Abstract. To date, attempts for applying syntactic information in the document-based retrieval model dominant have led to little practical improvement, mainly due to the problems associated with the integration of this kind of information into the model. In this article we propose the use of a locality-based retrieval model for reranking, which deals with syntactic linguistic variation through similarity measures based on the distance between words. We study two approaches whose effectiveness has been evaluated on the CLEF corpus of Spanish documents.

1 Introduction

Syntactic processing has been applied repeatedly in the field of Information Retrieval (IR) for dealing with the syntactic variation present in natural language texts [14, 8, 11], although its use in languages other than English has not as yet been studied in depth. In order to apply these kind of techniques, it is necessary to perform some kind of parsing process, which itself requires the definition of a suitable grammar. For languages lacking advanced linguistics resources, such as wide-coverage grammars or treebanks, the application of these techniques is a real challenge. In the case of Spanish, for example, only a few IR experiments involving syntax have been performed [1, 18, 20, 19]. Even when reliable syntactic information can be extracted from texts, the issue that arises is how to integrate it into an IR system. The prevalent approaches consist of a weighted combination of multi-word terms – in the form of head-modifier pairs – and single-word terms – in the form of word stems. Unfortunately, the use of multi-word terms has not proven to be effective enough, regardless of whether they have been obtained by means of syntactic or statistical methods, mainly due to the difficulty of solving the overweighting of complex terms with respect to simple terms [13].

In this context, pseudo-syntactic approaches based on the distance between terms arise as a practical alternative that avoids the problems listed above as a result of not needing any grammar or parser, and because the information about the occurrence of individual words can be integrated in a consistent way with the information about proximity to other terms, which in turn is often related with the existence of syntactic relations between such terms.

A. Apostolico and M. Melucci (Eds.): SPIRE 2004, LNCS 3246, pp. 255–266, 2004.

In this work we propose the use of a *locality-based retrieval model*, based on a similarity measure computed as a function of the distance between terms, as a complement to classic IR techniques based on indexing single-word terms, with the aim of increasing the precision of the documents retrieved by the system in the case of Spanish.

The rest of the article is organized as follows. Section 2 introduces the locality-based retrieval model and our first approach for integrating it into our system; the experimental results of this first proposal are shown in Section 3. A second approach, based on data fusion, is described in Section 4, and its results are discussed in Section 5. Finally, our conclusions and future work are presented in Section 6.

2 Locality-Based IR

2.1 The Retrieval Model

In the *document-based* retrieval model prevalent nowadays, an IR system retrieves a list of documents ranked according to their degree of relevance with respect to the information need of the user. In contrast, a *locality-based* IR system goes one step further, and looks for the concrete *locations* in the documents which are relevant to such a need. *Passage retrieval* [10] could be considered as an intermediate point between these two models, since its aim is to retrieve portions of documents (called *passages*) relevant to the user. However, passage retrieval is closer to document-based than to locality-based retrieval: once the original documents have been split into passages they are ranked using traditional similarity measures. In this case, the main difficulty comes from specifying what a passage is, including considerations about size and overlapping factors, and how they can be identified.

In contrast, the locality-based model considers the collection to be indexed not as a set of documents, but as a sequence of words where each occurrence of a query term has an influence on the surrounding terms. Such influences are additive, thus, the contributions of different occurrences of query terms are summed, yielding a similarity measure. As a result, those areas of the texts with a higher density of query terms, or with important query terms, show peaks in the resulting graph, highlighting those positions of the text which are potentially relevant with respect to the query. A graphical representation of this process is shown in Fig. 1. It is worth noting that relevant portions are identified without the need to perform any kind of splitting in the documents, as is done in passage retrieval.

Next, we describe the original proposal of de Kretser and Moffat for the locality-based model [5, 6].

2.2 Computing the Similarity Measure

In the locality-based model the similarity measure only needs to be computed for those positions of the text in which query terms occur, a characteristic which

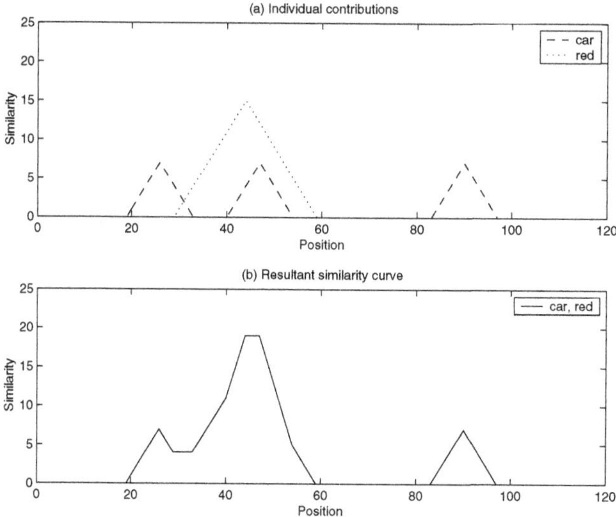

Fig. 1. Computing the similarity measure in a locality-based model: (a) positions where query terms occur and their regions of influence; (b) the resultant similarity curve

makes its application possible in practical environments due to its computational cost being relatively low.

The contribution to the similarity graph of a given query term is determined by a *similarity contribution function* c_t defined according to the following parameters [5]:

- The *shape* of the function, which is the same for all terms.
- The maximum *height* h_t of the function, which occurs in the position of the query term.
- The *spread* s_t of the function, that is, the scope of its influence.
- The distance, in words, with respect to other surrounding words, $d = |x - l|$, where l is the position of the query term and x is the position of the word in the text where we want to compute the similarity score.

Several function shapes are described in [5], but we only show here those with which we obtained better results in Spanish. They are the triangle (*tri*) and the circle (*cir*) function, defined by equations 1 and 2, respectively, and whose graphical representation is shown in Fig. 2:

$$c_t(x, l) = h_t(1 - d/s_t) \ . \tag{1}$$

$$c_t(x, l) = h_t\sqrt{1 - (d/s_t)^2} \ . \tag{2}$$

with $c_t(x, l) = 0$ when $|x - l| > s_t$.

The height h_t of a query term t is defined as an inverse function of its frequency in the collection:

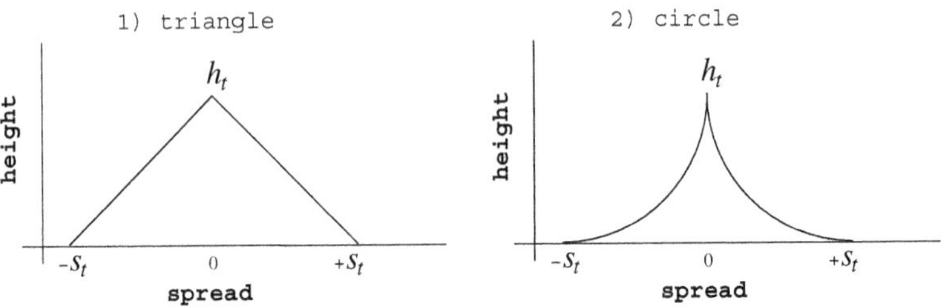

Fig. 2. Shapes of the similarity contribution function c_t

$$h_t = f_{q,t} \, log_e(N/f_t) \; . \tag{3}$$

where N is the total number of terms in the collection, f_t is the number of times term t appears in the collection, and $f_{q,t}$ is the within-query frequency of the term.

On the other hand, the spread s_t of the influence of a term t is also defined as an inverse function of its frequency in the collection, but normalized according to the average term frequency:

$$s_t = \frac{n}{N}\frac{N}{f_t} = \frac{n}{f_t} \; . \tag{4}$$

where n is the number of unique terms in the collection, that is, the size of the vocabulary.

Once these parameters have been fixed, the similarity score assigned to a location x of the document in which a term of the query Q can be found is calculated as:

$$C_Q(x) = \sum_{t \in Q} \sum_{\substack{l \in I_t \\ |l-x| \leq s_t \\ term(x) \neq term(l)}} c_t(x, l) \; . \tag{5}$$

where I_t is the set of word locations at which a term t of the query Q occurs, and where $term(w)$ represents the term associated to the location w. In other words, the degree of similarity or relevance associated with a given location is the sum of all the influences exerted by the rest of query terms within whose spread the term is located, excepting other occurrences of the same term that exist at the location examined [6].

Finally, the relevance score assigned to a document D is given in function of the similarities corresponding to occurrences of query terms that this document contains. This point is discussed in detail below.

2.3 Adaptations of the Model

The locality-based model not only identifies the relevant documents but also the relevant locations they contain, allowing us to work at a more detailed level than classical IR techniques. Thus, we have opted for using this model in our experiments. Nevertheless, before doing so, the model had to be adapted to our needs, which makes our approach different from the original proposal of the model [5, 6].

The approach we have chosen for integrating distance-based similarity in our IR system consists of postprocessing the documents obtained by a document-based retrieval system. This initial set of documents is obtained through a base IR system – we name it *lem* – which employs *content-word* lemmas (nouns, adjectives and verbs) as index terms. This list of documents returned by *lem* is then processed using the locality-based model, taking the final ranking obtained using distance-based similarity as the final output to be returned to the user.

It should be pointed out that the parameters of height, h_t, and spread, s_t, employed for the reranking are calculated according to the global parameters of the collection, not according to the parameters which are local to the subset of documents returned, in order to avoid the correlation-derived problems it would introduce[1].

Another aspect in which our approach differs from the original model is the employment of lemmatization, instead of *stemming*, for conflating queries and documents. We have made this choice due to the encouraging results previously obtained with such an approach, with respect to *stemming*, in the case of Spanish [20].

The third point of difference corresponds to the algorithm for calculating the relevance of a document, obtained from the similarity scores of its query term occurrences. Instead of the original iterative algorithm [5], our approach defines the similarity score $sim(D, Q)$ of a document D with respect to a query Q as the sum of all the similarity scores of the query term occurrences it contains:

$$sim(D, Q) = \sum_{\substack{x \in D \\ term(x) \in Q}} C_Q(x) \; . \qquad (6)$$

3 Experimental Results Using Distances

Our approach has been tested using the Spanish monolingual corpus of the 2001 and 2002 CLEF editions [15], composed of 215,738 news reports provided by EFE, a Spanish news agency. The 100 queries employed, from 41 to 140, consist of three fields: a brief *title* statement, a one-sentence *description*, and a more complex *narrative* specifying the relevance assessment criteria.

As mentioned in Sect. 2.3, the initial set of documents to be reranked is obtained through the indexing of *content word lemmas* (*lem*). For this purpose, the documents were indexed with the vector-based engine SMART [3], using the `atn·ntc` weighting scheme. In order to improve the performance of the whole system, we have tried to obtain the best possible starting set of documents by applying pseudo-relevance feedback (blind-query expansion) adopting Rocchio's approach [16]:

---

[1] For example, the parameter f_t, corresponding to the number of occurrences of a term t, is the number of occurrences of t in the entire collection, not the number of occurrences of t in the set of documents to be reranked.

Table 1. Reranking based on distances

	short queries				long queries			
	stm	*lem*	*tri*	*cir*	*stm*	*lem*	*tri*	*cir*
Documents	99k	99k	99k	99k	99k	99k	99k	99k
Relevant (5548 expected)	5086	5207	5207	5207	5208	5234	5234	5234
Non-interpolated precision	.5210	.5235	.4473	.4464	.5638	.5648	.4802	.4703
Document precision	.5502	.5814	.5154	.5188	.5925	.6038	.5366	.5376
R-precision	.4952	.4978	.4438	.4453	.5316	.5335	.4574	.4490
Precision at .00 recall	.8426	.8260	**.8402**	**.8394**	.9028	.8788	.8771	.8639
Precision at .10 recall	.7294	.7431	**.7551**	**.7533**	.7910	.7989	**.8167**	**.8022**
Precision at .20 recall	.6746	.6936	.6550	.6624	.7326	.7420	.7070	.6909
Precision at .30 recall	.6135	.6380	.5764	.5806	.6763	.6887	.6066	.5996
Precision at .40 recall	.5812	.5900	.5045	.5052	.6401	.6499	.5417	.5314
Precision at .50 recall	.5470	.5520	.4496	.4515	.5975	.6058	.4894	.4819
Precision at .60 recall	.5078	.5099	.3882	.3850	.5452	.5502	.4184	.4045
Precision at .70 recall	.4518	.4498	.3360	.3340	.4816	.4816	.3654	.3547
Precision at .80 recall	.3882	.3796	.2750	.2692	.4056	.4022	.3042	.2929
Precision at .90 recall	.3044	.2923	.1933	.1917	.3356	.3150	.2023	.1944
Precision at 1.0 recall	.1897	.1756	.1031	.1014	.2054	.1918	.1062	.1000
Precision at 5 docs	.6182	.6182	.6141	.6121	.6808	.6747	.6667	.6606
Precision at 10 docs	.5717	.5758	.5596	.5596	.6182	.6202	.5929	.5869
Precision at 15 docs	.5279	.5380	.5111	.5192	.5670	.5798	.5441	.5394
Precision at 20 docs	.4965	.5071	.4803	.4818	.5338	.5556	.5081	.5056
Precision at 30 docs	.4434	.4582	.4259	.4229	.4822	.5030	.4545	.4566
Precision at 100 docs	.2935	.3016	.2691	.2696	.3119	.3171	.2811	.2812
Precision at 200 docs	.1937	.2002	.1863	.1875	.2053	.2060	.1926	.1932
Precision at 500 docs	.0945	.0981	.0964	.0964	.0981	.0985	.0979	.0982
Precision at 1000 docs	.0514	.0526	.0526	.0526	.0526	.0529	.0529	.0529

$$Q_1 = \alpha Q_0 + \beta \sum_{k=1}^{n_1} \frac{R_k}{n_1} - \gamma \sum_{k=1}^{n_2} \frac{S_k}{n_2} . \tag{7}$$

where Q_1 is the new query vector, Q_0 is the vector of the initial query, R_k is the vector of relevant document k, S_k is the vector of non-relevant document k, n_1 is the number of relevant documents, n_2 is the number of non-relevant documents, and α, β and γ are, respectively, the parameters that control the relative contributions of the original query, relevant documents, and non-relevant documents. Our system expands the initial query automatically with the best 10 terms of the 5 top ranked documents, and using $\alpha = 1.40$, $\beta = 0.10$ and $\gamma = 0$.

It should be pointed out that the distance-based reranking process is performed according to the terms of the original query, without taking into account the terms added during the feedback. This is because there is no guarentee that these terms were syntactically related with the original query terms, since they only co-occur in the documents with such terms.

Two series of experiments have been carried out. Firstly, employing queries obtained from the title and description fields – *short queries* – and, secondly, employing queries obtained from the three fields, that is title, description and narrative – *long queries*. It should be noticed that in the case of long queries, the terms extracted from the title field are given double relevance with respect to description and narrative, since the former summarizes the basic semantics of the query.

The results obtained are shown in Table 1. The first column of each group shows the results obtained through a standard approach based on stemming (*stm*), also using pseudo-relevance feedback; the second column contains the results of the indexing of lemmas (*lem*) before the reranking, our baseline; the two other columns show the results obtained after reranking *lem* by means of distances employing a triangle (*tri*) and circle (*cir*) function.

The performance of the system is measured using the parameters contained in each row: number of documents retrieved, number of relevant documents retrieved (5548 expected), average precision (non-interpolated) for all relevant documents (averaged over queries), average document precision for all relevant documents (averaged over relevant documents), R-precision, precision at 11 standard levels of recall, and precision at N documents retrieved. For each parameter we have marked in boldface those values where there is an improvement with respect to the baseline *lem*.

As these results show, reranking through distances has caused a general drop in performance, except for low recall levels, where results are similar or sometimes even better. We can therefore conclude that this first approach is of little practical interest.

4 Data Fusion Through Intersection

4.1 Analysis of Results

Since the set of documents retrieved by the system is the same, the drop in performance in this first approach can only be caused by a worse ranking of the results because of the application of the distance-based model, and for this reason we decided to analyze the changes in the distribution of relevant and non-relevant documents in the K top retrieved documents. The results obtained in the case of using short queries and the triangle function (*tri*) are shown in Table 2. Changes in the type of query, short or long, or in the shape of the function, triangle or circle, has little effect on these results and the conclusions that can be inferred from them.

Each row contains the results obtained when comparing the K top documents retrieved by *lem* (set of results L), with those K top documents retrieved after their reranking using distances (set of results D). The columns show the results obtained for each of the parameters considered: average number of new relevant documents obtained through distances ($D \setminus L$), average number of relevant documents lost using distances ($L \setminus D$), average number of relevant documents preserved ($L \cap D$), overlap coefficient for relevant documents (R_{over}), precision of *lem* at K top documents ($Pr(L)$), precision at K top documents after reranking through distances ($Pr(D)$), precision for the documents common to both approaches in their K top documents ($Pr(L \cap D)$). The right-hand side of the table shows their equivalents for the case of non-relevant documents: average number of non-relevant documents added, lost and preserved, together with their degree of overlap.

Table 2. Document distribution (short queries - triangle function)

	relevant docs.							non-relevant docs.			
K	$D \setminus L$	$L \setminus D$	$L \cap D$	R_{over}	$Pr(L)$	$Pr(D)$	$Pr(L \cap D)$	$D \setminus L$	$L \setminus D$	$L \cap D$	N_{over}
5	1.60	1.62	1.44	0.47	**0.61**	**0.61**	*0.77*	1.54	1.52	0.42	0.22
10	2.73	2.89	2.81	0.50	**0.57**	**0.55**	*0.68*	3.14	2.98	1.32	0.30
15	3.37	3.77	4.22	0.54	**0.53**	**0.51**	*0.65*	5.13	4.73	2.28	0.32
20	3.92	4.44	5.59	0.57	**0.50**	**0.48**	*0.63*	7.24	6.72	3.25	0.32
30	4.66	5.62	7.99	0.61	**0.45**	**0.42**	*0.59*	11.84	10.88	5.51	0.33
50	5.95	9.16	20.69	0.73	**0.60**	**0.53**	*0.42*	45.04	41.83	28.32	0.39
100	5.10	7.84	31.78	0.83	**0.40**	**0.37**	*0.30*	88.13	85.39	74.99	0.46
200	1.99	2.82	45.72	0.95	**0.24**	**0.24**	*0.14*	164.28	163.45	288.01	0.64

Several important facts can be observed in these figures. Firstly, that the number of relevant documents retrieved by both approaches in their K top documents is very similar – a little smaller for distances – , as can be inferred from the number of incoming and outgoing relevant documents, and from the precisions at the top K documents of both approaches. This confirms that the problem has its origin in a bad reranking of the results.

The second point we need to point out refers to the overlap coefficients of both relevant (R_{over}) and non-relevant (N_{over}) documents. These coefficients, defined by Lee in [12], show the degree of overlap among relevant and non-relevant documents in two retrieval results. For two runs run_1 and run_2, they are defined as follows:

$$R_{over} = \frac{2\,|Rel(run_1) \cap Rel(run_2)|}{|Rel(run_1)| + |Rel(run_2)|} \ . \tag{8}$$

$$N_{over} = \frac{2\,|Nonrel(run_1) \cap Nonrel(run_2)|}{|Nonrel(run_1)| + |Nonrel(run_2)|} \ . \tag{9}$$

where $Rel(X)$ and $Nonrel(X)$ represent, respectively, the set of relevant and non-relevant documents retrieved by the run X.

It can be seen in Table 2 that the overlap factor among relevant documents is much higher than among non-relevant documents. Therefore, it obeys the *unequal overlap property* [12], since both approaches return a similar set on relevant documents, but a different set on non-relevant documents. This is a good indicator of the effectiveness of fusion of both runs.

Finally, and also related with the previous point, the figures show that the precision for the documents common to both approaches in their K top documents ($Pr(L \cap D)$) is higher than the corresponding precisions for lemmas ($Pr(L)$) and distances ($Pr(D)$); that is, the probability of a document being relevant is higher when it is retrieved by both approaches. In other words, the more runs a document is retrieved by, the higher the rank that should be assigned to the document [17].

According to these observations, we decided to take a new approach for reranking, this time through data fusion, by combining the results obtained initially with the indexing of lemmas with the results obtained when they are reranked through distances. Next, we describe this approach.

4.2 Description of the Algorithm

Data fusion is a technique of combination of evidences that consists of combining the results retrieved by different representations of queries or documents, or by different retrieval techniques [7, 12, 4].

In our data fusion approach, we have opted for using a boolean criterion instead of combining scores based on similarities [7, 12] or ranks [12].

Once the value K is set, the documents are retrieved in the following order:

1. First, the documents contained in the intersection of the top K documents retrieved by both approaches: $L_K \cap D_K$. Our aim is to increase the precision of the top documents retrieved.
2. Next, the documents retrieved in the top K documents by only one of the approaches: $(L_K \cup D_K) \setminus (L_K \cap D_K)$. Our aim is to add to the top of the ranking those relevant documents retrieved only by the distance-based approach at its top, but without harming the ranking of the relevant documents retrieved by the indexing of lemmas.
3. Finally, the rest of documents retrieved using *lem*: $L \setminus (L_K \cup D_K)$.

where L is the set of documents retrieved by *lem*, L_K is the set of the top K documents retrieved by *lem*, and D_K is the set of the top K documents retrieved by applying distances.

With respect to the internal ranking of the results, we will take the ranking obtained with *lem* as reference, because of its better behavior. In this way, when a subset S of results is retrieved, they will be retrieved in the same relative order they had when they were retrieved by *lem*[2].

5 Experimental Results with Data Fusion

After a previous phase of tuning of K, in which different values of K were tested[3], a value $K = 30$ was chosen as the best compromise, since although lower values of K showed peaks of precision in the top documents retrieved, their global behavior was worse.

Table 3 shows the results obtained with this new approach. Column *tri* shows the results obtained by means of the fusion through intersection of the set of documents initially retrieved with *lem* with the documents retrieved by applying reranking through distances using a triangle function. The results corresponding to the circle function are showed in *cir*.

The improvements attained with this new approach – in boldface – are general, particularly in the case of the precision at N documents retrieved. Moreover, there are no penalizations for non-interpolated precision and R-precision.

[2] That is, if the original sequence in *lem* was *d2-d3-d1* and a subset {*d1*,*d3*} is going to be returned, the documents should be obtained in the same relative order as in the original results: *d3-d1*.

[3] $K \in \{5, 10, 15, 20, 30, 50, 75, 100, 200, 500\}$.

Table 3. Reranking through data fusion; K=30

	short queries				long queries			
	stm	*lem*	*tri*	*cir*	*stm*	*lem*	*tri*	*cir*
Documents	99k	99k	99k	99k	99k	99k	99k	99k
Relevant (5548 expected)	5086	5207	5207	5207	5208	5234	5234	5234
Non-interpolated precision	.5210	.5235	.5204	.5206	.5638	.5648	**.5654**	.5647
Document precision	.5502	.5814	**.5829**	**.5836**	.5925	.6038	**.6083**	**.6094**
R-precision	.4952	.4978	.4911	.4911	.5316	.5335	.5311	.5306
Precision at .00 recall	.8426	.8260	**.8424**	**.8428**	.9028	.8788	**.8871**	**.8901**
Precision at .10 recall	.7294	.7431	**.7520**	**.7522**	.7910	.7989	**.8052**	**.8075**
Precision at .20 recall	.6746	.6936	**.7043**	**.7059**	.7326	.7420	**.7501**	**.7496**
Precision at .30 recall	.6135	.6380	**.6434**	**.6447**	.6763	.6887	**.6975**	**.6983**
Precision at .40 recall	.5812	.5900	**.5967**	**.5965**	.6401	.6499	**.6577**	**.6595**
Precision at .50 recall	.5470	.5520	.5447	.5454	.5975	.6058	**.6092**	**.6141**
Precision at .60 recall	.5078	.5099	.4997	.4999	.5452	.5502	.5443	.5362
Precision at .70 recall	.4518	.4498	.4325	.4282	.4816	.4816	.4729	.4644
Precision at .80 recall	.3882	.3796	.3665	.3653	.4056	.4022	.3929	.3885
Precision at .90 recall	.3044	.2923	.2846	.2857	.3356	.3150	.3045	.3036
Precision at 1.0 recall	.1897	.1756	.1687	.1684	.2054	.1918	.1862	.1857
Precision at 5 docs	.6182	.6182	**.6303**	**.6343**	.6808	.6747	**.6929**	**.6949**
Precision at 10 docs	.5717	.5758	**.5929**	**.5970**	.6182	.6202	**.6525**	**.6495**
Precision at 15 docs	.5279	.5380	**.5522**	**.5542**	.5670	.5798	**.5993**	**.5980**
Precision at 20 docs	.4965	.5071	**.5217**	**.5207**	.5338	.5556	**.5672**	**.5646**
Precision at 30 docs	.4434	.4582	.4582	.4582	.4822	.5030	.5030	.5030
Precision at 100 docs	.2935	.3016	**.3040**	**.3044**	.3119	.3171	**.3182**	**.3193**
Precision at 200 docs	.1937	.2002	**.2006**	**.2008**	.2053	.2060	**.2064**	**.2064**
Precision at 500 docs	.0945	.0981	**.0982**	**.0982**	.0981	.0985	**.0987**	**.0987**
Precision at 1000 docs	.0514	.0526	.0526	.0526	.0526	.0529	.0529	.0529

6 Conclusions and Future Work

In this article we have proposed the use of a distance-based retrieval model, also called locality-based, which allows us to face the problem of syntactic linguistic variation in text conflation employing a pseudo-syntactic approach.

Two approaches were proposed for this purpose, both based on reranking the results obtained by indexing content word lemmas. The first approach, where the ranking obtained by means of the application of the locality-based model is the final ranking to be retrieved, did not get, in general, good results. After analyzing the behavior of the system, a new approach was taken, this time based on data fusion, which employs the intersection of the sets of documents retrieved by both approaches as reference for the reranking. This second approach was fruitful, since it obtained consistent improvements in the ranking at all levels, without harming other aspects.

With respect to future work, several aspects should be studied. Firstly, we intend to extend our experiments to other retrieval models apart from the vector model, in order to test its generality. Secondly, we aim to improve the system by managing not only syntactic variants but also morphosyntactic variants [9].

Two new applications of this locality-based approach are also being considered. Firstly, in Query Answering, where it will in all probability prove most useful, since this distance-based model allows us to identify the relevant locations of a document, which probably contain the answer, with respect to the query. Once the relevant locations are identified, the answer would be extracted through further in-depth linguistic processing. Secondly, its possible application in query expansion through *local clustering based on distances* [2] is also being studied.

Acknowledgements

The research reported in this article has been partially supported by Ministerio de Ciencia y Tecnología (HF2002-81), FPU grants of Secretaría de Estado de Educación y Universidades (AP2001-2545), Xunta de Galicia (PGIDIT02PXIB30501PR, PGIDIT02SIN01E and PGIDIT03SIN30501PR) and Universidade da Coruña.

References

1. M. A. Alonso, J. Vilares, and V. M. Darriba. On the usefulness of extracting syntactic dependencies for text indexing. In M. O'Neill, F. F. E. Sutcliffe, C. Ryan, and M. Eaton, editors, *Artificial Intelligence and Cognitive Science*, volume 2464 of *Lecture Notes in Artificial Intelligence*, pages 3–11. Springer-Verlag, Berlin-Heidelberg-New York, 2002.
2. R. Attar and A.S. Fraenkel. Local feedback in full-text retrieval systems. *Journal of the ACM*, 24(3):397–417, July 1977.
3. C. Buckley. Implementation of the SMART information retrieval system. Technical report, Department of Computer Science, Cornell University, 1985. Sources available in `ftp://ftp.cs.cornell.edu/pub/smart`.
4. W. B. Croft. Combining approaches to information retrieval. In W. B. Croft, editor, *Advances in Information Retrieval. Recent Research from the Center for Intelligent Information Retrieval*, volume 7 of *The Kluwer International Series on Information Retrieval*, chapter 1, pages 1–36. Kluwer Academic Publishers, Boston/Dordrecht/London, 2000.
5. O. de Kretser and A. Moffat. Effective document presentation with a locality-based similarity heuristic. In *Proc. of the 22nd annual international ACM SIGIR conference on Research and Development in Information Retrieval*, pages 113–120, Berkeley, California, USA, 1999. ACM Press, New York.
6. O. de Kretser and A. Moffat. Locality-based information retrieval. In J. F. Roddick, editor, *Proc. of 10th Australasian Database Conference (ADC '99), 18-21 January, Auckland, New Zealand*, volume 21 of *Australian Computer Science Communications*, pages 177–188, Singapore, 1999. Springer-Verlag.
7. E. Fox and J. Shaw. Combination of multiple searches. In D. K. Harman, editor, *NIST Special Publication 500-215: The Second Text REtrieval Conference (TREC-2)*, pages 243–252, Gaithersburg, MD, USA, 1994. Department of Commerce, National Institute of Standards and Technology.
8. D. A. Hull, G. Grefenstette, B. M. Schulze, E. Gaussier, H. Schütze, and J. O. Pedersen. Xerox TREC-5 site report: Routing, filtering, NLP, and Spanish tracks. In E. M. Voorhees and D. K. Harman, editors, *NIST Special Publication 500-238: The Fifth Text REtrieval Conference (TREC-5)*, pages 167–180, Gaithersburg, MD, USA, 1997. Department of Commerce, National Institute of Standards and Technology.

9. C. Jacquemin and E. Tzoukermann. NLP for term variant extraction: synergy between morphology, lexicon and syntax. In *Natural Language Information Retrieval*, volume 7 of *Text, Speech and Language Technology*, pages 25–74. Kluwer Academic Publishers, Dordrecht/Boston/London, 1999.
10. M. Kaszkiel and J. Zobel. Effective ranking with arbitrary passages. *Journal of the American Society of Information Science*, 52(4):344–364, 2001.
11. C. H. Koster. Head/modifier frames for information retrieval. In A. Gelbukh, editor, *Computational Linguistics and Intelligent Text Processing*, volume 2945 of *Lecture Notes in Computer Science*, pages 420–432. Springer-Verlag, Berlin-Heidelberg-New York, 2004.
12. J. Lee. Analyses of multiple evidence combination. In *Proc. of SIGIR '97, July 27-31, Philadelphia, PA, USA*, pages 267–276. ACM Press, 1997.
13. M. Mitra, C. Buckley, A. Singhal, and C. Cardie. An analysis of statistical and syntactic phrases. In L. Devroye and C. Chrisment, editors, *Proc. of Computer-Aided Information Searching on the Internet (RIAO'97)*, pages 200–214, Montreal, Canada, 1997.
14. J. Perez-Carballo and T. Strzalkowski. Natural language information retrieval: progress report. *Information Processing and Management*, 36(1):155–178, 2000.
15. C. Peters, editor. *Results of the CLEF 2002 Cross-Language System Evaluation Campaign, Working Notes for the CLEF 2002 Workshop*, Rome, Italy, Sept. 2002. CLEF official site: `http://www.clef-campaign.org`.
16. J. Rocchio. Relevance feedback in information retrieval. In G. Salton, editor, *The SMART Retrieval System - Experiments in Automatic Document Processing*, pages 313–323. Prentice-Hall, Englewood Cliffs, NJ, 1971.
17. T. Saracevic and P. Kantor. A study of information seeking and retrieving. III. Searchers, searches, overlap. *Journal of the American Society for Information Science*, 39(3):197–216, 1988.
18. J. Vilares and M. A. Alonso. A grammatical approach to the extraction of index terms. In G. Angelova, K. Bontcheva, R. Mitkov, N. Nicolov, and N. Nikolov, editors, *International Conference on Recent Advances in Natural Language Processing, Proceedings*, pages 500–504, Borovets, Bulgaria, Sept. 2003.
19. J. Vilares, M.A. Alonso, and F.J. Ribadas. COLE experiments at CLEF 2003 Spanish monolingual track. To be published in *Lecture Notes in Computer Science*. Springer-Verlag, Berlin-Heidelberg-New York, 2004.
20. J. Vilares, M.A. Alonso, F.J. Ribadas, and M. Vilares. COLE experiments at CLEF 2002 Spanish monolingual track. In C. Peters, M. Braschler, J. Gonzalo, and M. Kluck, editors, *Advances in Cross-Language Information Retrieval*, volume 2785 of *Lecture Notes in Computer Science*, pages 265–278. Springer-Verlag, Berlin-Heidelberg-New York, 2003.

Efficient Extraction of Structured Motifs Using Box-Links

Alexandra M. Carvalho[1], Ana T. Freitas[1], Arlindo L. Oliveira[1], and Marie-France Sagot[2]

[1] IST/INESC-ID, Rua Alves Redol, 9, 1000-029 Lisboa, Portugal
{asmc,atf,aml}@algos.inesc-id.pt
[2] Inria Rhône-Alpes, Université Claude Bernard, Lyon I
43 Bd du 11 Novembre 1918, 69622 Villeurbanne Cedex, France
Marie-France.Sagot@inria.fr

Abstract. In this paper we propose a new data structure for the efficient extraction of structured motifs from DNA sequences. A structured motif is defined as a collection of highly conserved motifs with pre-specified sizes and spacings between them. The new data structure, called box-link, stores the information on how to jump over the spacings which separate each motif in a structured motif. A factor tree, a variation of a suffix tree, endowed with box-links provide the means for the efficient extraction of structured motifs.

Structured motifs try to capture highly conserved complex regions in a set of DNA sequences which, in the case of sequences from co-regulated genes, model functional combinations of transcription factor binding sites [1–3]. Formally, a *motif* is a non-empty string over an alphabet Σ (e.g., Σ ={A,C,T,G} for DNA sequences). A *structured motif* [1] is a pair (m, d) where m is a p-tuple of motifs $(m_i)_{1\leq i\leq p}$, denoting p boxes, and d is a $(p-1)$-tuple of pairs $(d_{\min_i}, d_{\max_i})_{1\leq i<p}$, denoting $p-1$ intervals of distance. In the following, we consider that all p boxes of a structured motif have a fixed length k and a fixed distance between boxes d. The general case was studied but is out of the scope of this abstract. Algorithms and complexity results are easily adaptable to the more general case.

A *factor tree*, also called a *k-factor tree* [4], is a data structure that indexes the factors of a string whose length does not exceed k. In the following we define box-links, whose purpose is to store the information needed to jump from box to box in a structured motif, over a factor tree. Formally, let L be the set of leaves at depth k of a k-factor tree $\mathcal{T}$ for a string s of length n and L_k^i denote all possible i-tuples over L. A *box-link of size* i, with $1 \leq i < p$, is a $(i+1)$-tuple in L^{i+1} such that there is a substring s' of s where: (i) the length of s' is $ik+(i-1)d$; (ii) the k-length substring of s' ending at position $jk+(j-1)d$, with $1 \leq j \leq i$, is the path in $\mathcal{T}$ spelled from the root to the j-th leaf of the box-link tuple. Box-links can be used to extract structured motifs when built over a *generalized factor tree* (a factor tree for a set of N sequences). However, in this case, box-links have to be endowed with a $Colors$ Boolean array [1] in order to distinguish in which of the N input sequences the corresponding boxes are linked.

In the following, we present an algorithm to build box-links. The algorithm makes use of two variables. First, the variable $list_{leaf}$ has the list of all leaves inserted in the

A. Apostolico and M. Melucci (Eds.): SPIRE 2004, LNCS 3246, pp. 267–268, 2004.

factor tree, which can be easily obtained during the factor tree construction. In fact, for the sake of exposition, $list_{leaf}$ can be seen as a family of variables $(list_{leaf_i})_{1 \leq i \leq N}$, where each $list_{leaf_i}$ has average length n, the average length of an input sequence. Observe that the substring labeling the path from the root to the j-th leaf of $list_{leaf_i}$ corresponds to the j-th at most k-length substring of the i-th input string. Second, the variable b_j stores the j-size box-links being built. We now describe AddBoxLink function. AddBoxLink(b,v,i) adds a box-link between an existing $(j-1)$-size box-link b and a leaf v for the i-th input sequence. However, it only creates a new box-link if there is not already a box-link between box-link b and node v. In either way, creating or not a new box-link, the AddBoxLink function sets the Boolean array entry i to 1. The pseudo-code of the algorithm to build box-links is presented in Algorithm 1.

Algorithm 1 BoxLink(Boxes p, BoxSize k, BoxDistance d, ListLeaf $list_{leaf}$)

1. for i from 1 to N
2.   while size of $list_{leaf_i} \geq pk + (p-1)d$
3. $b_0 =$ AddBoxLink$(nil, list_{leaf_i}[0], i)$
4.   for j from 1 to $p-1$
5. $b_j =$ AddBoxLink$(b_{j-1}, list_{leaf_i}[jk + jd], i)$
6.   remove the first leaf of $list_{leaf_i}$

Next, we establish the complexity for Algorithm 1. Let n_l be the number of nodes at depth l of the generalized suffix tree for the same input sequences as the factor tree where the box-links are being constructed, and $b_p(k,d) = \min\{n_k^p, n_{pk+(p-1)d}\}$.

Proposition 1. Algorithm 1 takes $O(N^2np)$ time and $O(Nb_p(k,d))$ space.

Proof. Step 1, 2 and 4 require $O(N)$, $O(n)$ and $O(p)$ time, respectively. Step 5 requires $O(N)$ time, which corresponds to the creation or update of $Colors$ array. Hence, Algorithm 1 takes $O(N^2np)$ time. The space complexity is given by the number of box-links, which can be upper bounded by $b_p(k,d)$, times its size, which is N. □

The use of box-links achieves a time and space exponential gain, in the worst case analysis, over approaches in [1]. Time improvement is obtained because the information required to jump from box to box in a structured motif is memorized and accessed very rapidly with box-links. Moreover, it is only required to build a k-factor tree, instead of a full suffix tree, or a $pk + (p-1)d$-factor tree, which leads to important space savings.

References

1. Marsan, L., Sagot, M.F.: Algorithms for extracting structured motifs using a suffix tree with an application to promoter and regulatory site consensus identification. J. Comp. Bio. **7** (2000) 345–362
2. Sharan, R., Ovcharenko, I., Ben-Hur, A., Karp, R.M.: Creme: a framework for identifying cis-regulatory modules in human-mouse conserved segments. Bioinformatics **19** (2003) i283–i291
3. Segal, E., Barash, Y., Simon, I., Friedman, N., Koller, D.: A discriminative model for identifying spatial cis-regulatory modules. In: Proc. RECOMB'04. (2004) 141–149
4. Allali, J., Sagot, M.F.: The at most k-deep factor tree. Submitted for publication (2003)

Efficient Computation of Balancedness in Binary Sequence Generators*

Pedro García-Mochales[1] and Amparo Fúster-Sabater[2]

[1] Instituto de Ciencia de Materiales de Madrid, C.S.I.C.
Cantoblanco. 28049 Madrid, Spain
pedrog@icmm.csic.es
[2] Instituto de Física Aplicada, C.S.I.C.
Serrano 144, 28006 Madrid, Spain
amparo@iec.csic.es

Abstract. An algorithm to compute the exact degree of balancedness in the output sequence of a LFSR-based generator (either nonlinear filters or combination generators) has been developed.

Keywords: Balancedness, bit-string algorithm, computational logics

1 Introduction

Generators of binary sequences based on Linear Feedback Shift Registers (LFSRs) [1] are electronic devices widely used to generate pseudorandom sequences in many different applications. The pseudorandom sequence is generated as the image of a nonlinear Boolean function F in the LFSR's stages. Balancedness in the generated sequence is a necessary condition that every LFSR-based generator must satisfy. Roughly speaking, a periodic binary sequence is balanced when the number of $1's$ and the number of $0's$ in a period are as equal as possible. Due to the long period of the sequences produced by LFSR-based generators, it is not possible to generate the whole sequence and then to count the number of $1's$ and $0's$. Therefore, in practical design of binary generators, statistical tests are applied to segments of the output sequence just to obtain *probabilistic evidence* that a generator produces a balanced sequence. In the present work, balancedness of pseudorandom sequences has been treated in a *deterministic way*. In fact, an algorithm to compute the exact number of $1's$ and $0's$ in the output sequence of a LFSR-based generator has been developed. To our knowledge, this is the first algorithm to perform this task. The algorithm input is the particular form of the generating function F while the algorithm output is the number of $1's$ in the generated sequence (as the period is known so is the number of $0's$). In this way, the degree of balancedness of the output sequence can be perfectly checked. The algorithm that is based on a L-bit string representation has been mainly applied to nonlinear filters (high-order functions F with a large number of terms); its generalization to combination generators (low-order functions F with a short number of terms) is just the simplification of the process.

* Work supported by Ministerio de Ciencia y Tecnología (Spain) under grant TIC 2001-0586.

A. Apostolico and M. Melucci (Eds.): SPIRE 2004, LNCS 3246, pp. 269–270, 2004.

2 Efficient Computation of Balancedness

Let F be a Boolean function in Algebraic Normal Form whose input variables a_i $(i = 0, ..., L-1)$ are the binary contents of the L stages of a LFSR. The function $\Phi(F)$ is defined as a Boolean function that substitutes each term $a_i\, a_j\, ...\, a_m$ of F for its corresponding minterm $A_{ij...m}$. Each term of F is the logic product of LFSR stages $a_i\, a_j\, ...\, a_m = a_{ij...m} = a_\alpha$ as well as each term of $\Phi(F)$ is notated $A_{ij...m} = A_\alpha$. Thus, the nonlinear functions F and Φ can be written as $F = \sum_{\oplus} a_{\alpha_k}$ and $\Phi = \sum_{\oplus} A_{\alpha_k}$, respectively, where the symbol $\oplus$ represents the exclusive-OR sum. In addition, the minterm A_{α_k} has in total $2^{L-d(\alpha_k)}$ terms, $d\,(\alpha_k)$ being the number of indexes in α_k. In order to implement this algorithm, every minterm A_α is represented by a L-bit string numbered $0, 1, ..., L-1$ from right to left. If the n-th index is in the set α $(n \in \alpha)$, then the n-th bit of such a string takes the value 1; otherwise, the value will be 0. Thus, $d\,(\alpha)$ equals the number of $1's$ in the L-bit string that represents A_α. We call *maximum common development* of two minterms A_α and A_β, notated $MD\,(A_\alpha, A_\beta)$, to the minterm A_χ such that $\chi = \alpha \cup \beta$. Under the L-bit string representation of the minterms, MD can be realized by means of a bit-wise OR operation between the binary strings of both functions. MD represents all the terms that A_α and A_β have in common.

Let $F = \sum_{\oplus} a_{\alpha_k}$ $(k = 1, ..., N)$ be a nonlinear Boolean function of N terms applied to a L-stage LFSR. In order to compute the number of $1's$ (notated $\mathcal{U}_F$) in the generated sequence, the following algorithm is introduced:

- *Step 1:* Define the function Φ from the N terms a_{α_k} of F. Initialize the function H with a null value, $H_0 = \oslash$.
- *Step 2:* For $k = 1\, ...\, N$: $\quad H_k = H_{k-1} + A_{\alpha_k} - 2 \cdot MD\,(A_{\alpha_k}, H_{k-1})$.
- *Step 3:* From the final form of $H_N = \sum_j s_j A_{\beta_j}$, compute the number of $1's$ in the generated sequence by means of the expression $\mathcal{U}_F = \sum_j s_j \cdot 2^{L-d(\beta_j)}$.

The calculations were performed on a simple PC computer (CPU Intel Xeon 2.8 GHz, 1 Gb of RAM) working with a Linux operative system. More than 40 different nonlinear functions F, each of them including 50 terms generated at random, were applied to a LFSR of $L = 32$. Numerical results prove that high performance computers are not needed in order to run the algorithm. In fact, the worse execution time obtained from one of the tested functions was less than 11 hours. Based on these implementations, the algorithm is believed to be a useful tool to calculate the exact degree of balancedness in sequences produced by LFSR-based generators.

References

1. A.J. Menezes *et al.* Handbook of Applied Cryptography, CRC Press, NY, 1997

On Asymptotic Finite-State Error Repair*

Manuel Vilares[1], Juan Otero[1], and Jorge Graña[2]

[1] Department of Computer Science, University of Vigo
Campus As Lagoas s/n, 32004 Ourense, Spain
{vilares,jop}@uvigo.es

[2] Department of Computer Science, University of A Coruña
Campus de Elviña s/n, 15071 A Coruña, Spain
grana@udc.es

Abstract. A major issue when defining the efficiency of a spelling corrector is how far we need to examine the input string to validate the repairs. We claim that regional techniques provide a performance and quality comparable to that attained by global criteria, with a significant saving in time and space.

1 Introduction

Although a lot of effort has gone into the problem of spelling correction over the years, it remains a research challenge. In particular, we are talking about a critical task in natural language processing applications for which efficiency, safety and maintenance are properties that cannot be neglected.

Most correctors assist users by offering a set of candidate repairs. So, any technique that reduces the number of candidates for correction will show an improvement in efficiency that should not have side effects on safety. Towards this aim, we focus on limiting the size of the repair region [2], in contrast to previous global proposals [1]. Our goal now is to evaluate our proposal, examining the error context to later validate repairs by tentatively recognizing ahead, avoiding cascaded errors and corroborating previous theoretical results.

2 Asymptotic Behavior

We introduce some preliminary tests illustrating that our proposal provides a quality similar to that of global approaches with a significant reduction in cost, only equivalent to that provided by global approaches in the worst case. To do it, we choose to work with Spanish, a language with a highly complex conjugation paradigm, gender and number inflection. The lexicon has 514.781 words, recognized by a *finite automaton* (FA) containing 58.170 states connected by 153.599 transitions, from which we have selected a representative sample

* Research partially supported by the Spanish Government under projects TIC2000-0370-C02-01 and HP2002-0081, and the Autonomous Government of Galicia under projects PGIDIT03SIN30501PR and PGIDIT02SIN01E.

A. Apostolico and M. Melucci (Eds.): SPIRE 2004, LNCS 3246, pp. 271–272, 2004.

that follows the length distribution of the words in the lexicon. For each length-category, a random number of errors have been generated in random positions.

We compare our proposal with the Savary's global approach [1], to the best of our knowledge, the most efficient method of error-tolerant look-up in finite-state dictionaries. We consider the set of calculations associated to a transition in the FA, that we call *item*, as the unit to measure the computational effort. Finally, the *precision* will reflect when the correction attended by the user is provided.

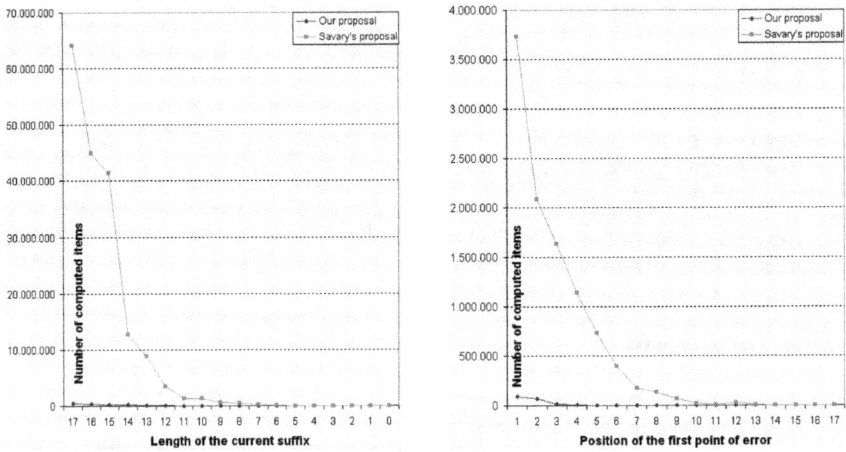

Fig. 1. Number of items generated in error mode.

Some preliminary results are compiled in Fig. 1. The graphic illustrates our contribution from two viewpoints. First, our proposal shows a linear-like behavior, in contrast to the Savary's approach that seems to be of exponential type, resulting in an essential property: the independence of the time of response on the initial conditions for the repair process. Second, the number of items is significantly reduced when we apply our regional criterion. These tests provided a precision of 77% (resp. 81%) for the regional (resp. global) approach. The integration of linguistic information should reduce this gap, less than 4%, or even eliminate it. In effect, our regional approach only takes now into account morphological information, which has an impact in the precision, while a global technique always provides all the repair alternatives without exclusion.

References

1. A. Savary. Typographical nearest-neighbor search in a finite-state lexicon and its application to spelling correction. *Lecture Notes in Computer Science*, 2494:251–260, 2001.
2. M. Vilares, J. Otero, and J. Graña. Regional finite-state error repair. In *Proc. of the Ninth Int. Conf. on Implementation and Application of Automata (CIAA'04)*, Kingston, Canada, 2004.

New Algorithms for Finding Monad Patterns in DNA Sequences*

Ravi Vijaya Satya and Amar Mukherjee

School of Computer Science, University of Central Florida
Orlando, FL USA 32816-2362
{rvijaya,amar}@cs.ucf.edu

Abstract. In this paper, we present two new algorithms for discovering monad patterns in DNA sequences. Monad patterns are of the form (l,d)-k, where l is the length of the pattern, d is the maximum number of mismatches allowed, and k is the minimum number of times the pattern is repeated in the given sample. The time-complexity of some of the best known algorithms to date is $O(nt^2l^d\sigma^d)$, where t is the number of input sequences, n is the length of each input sequence, and $\sigma = |\sum|$ is the size of the alphabet. The first algorithm that we present in this paper takes $O(n^2t^2l^{\frac{d}{2}})$ time and $O(ntl^{\frac{d}{2}}\sigma^{\frac{d}{2}})$ space, and the second algorithm takes $O(n^3t^3l^{\frac{d}{2}}\sigma^{\frac{d}{2}})$ time using $O(l^{\frac{d}{2}}\sigma^{\frac{d}{2}})$ space. In practice, our algorithms have much better performance provided the d/l ratio is small. The second algorithm performs very well even for large values l and d as long as the d/l ratio is small.

1 Introduction

Discovering regulatory patterns in DNA sequences is a well known problem in computational biology. Due to mutations and other errors, the actual occurrences of these regulatory patterns allow for a certain degree of error. There fore, the actual regulatory pattern (or the consensus pattern) may never appear in a gene upstream region, but d-mismatch occurrences of this pattern might appear. The general approach to this problem is to take a set of t DNA sequences each of length n, at least k of which are guaranteed to contain the desired binding site, and look for patterns of a certain length l that occur in at least k out of the t sequences with at most d mismatches at each occurrence. The values of l, d and k can be determined either from prior knowledge about the binding site, or by trial and error, trying different values of l and d. These single contiguous blocks of patterns are called *monad* patterns.

In general, many regulatory signals are made up of a group of monad patterns occurring within a certain distance form each other [EskKGP03, EskP02, GuhS01, vanRC00]. In such a case, the patterns are called dyad, triad, multi-ad, or in general as composite patterns. Finding the composite patterns by finding the component monad patterns individually is significantly more difficult, since

* This research was partially supported by NSF grant number: ITR-0312724.

A. Apostolico and M. Melucci (Eds.): SPIRE 2004, LNCS 3246, pp. 273–285, 2004.

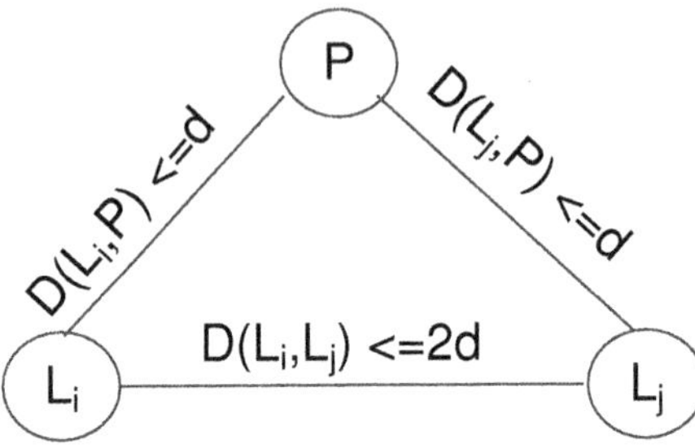

Fig. 1. A pattern P that is consistent with an l-gram pair (L_i, L_j)

the composite monad patterns might be too subtle to detect. Eskin and Pevzner [EskP02] present a simple transformation to convert a multi-ad problem into a slightly larger monad problem. In this paper, we present an algorithm to solve the monad-pattern finding problem. The same transformation as in [EskP02] can be applied to transform a multi-ad problem into a monad problem that is handled by our algorithm.

Pevzner and Sze [PevS00] have put forward a challenge problem: to find the signal in a sample of $t = 20$ sequences, each 600 nucleotides long, each containing an unknown pattern of length $l = 15$ with at most $d = 4$ mismatches. They presented the WINNOWER and SP-STAR algorithms that could solve this problem, which was not solvable by many of the earlier techniques. Many other approaches that can solve this problem have been proposed [Sag98, EskP02, Lia03, BuhT2001]. Time-complexity of the best known algorithms[Sag98, EskP02] is $O(nt^2l^d\sigma^d)$.

Many of the above algorithms search the d-mismatch neighborhood of each l-gram in the sample. The size of the d-mismatch neighborhood of an l-gram in $O(l^d\sigma^d)$. The main motivation for our algorithms is that in most practical scenarios, it might be possible to limit the search to a small portion of the d-mismatch neighborhood. We refer to the set of patterns that mismatch in at most d positions with two l-grams as the *consistent* patterns of the two l-grams. We denote the distance(the number of mismatches) between two l-grams L_i and L_j by $D(L_i, L_j)$. The distance relationships between two l-grams L_i and L_j and a pattern P that is consistent with both of them are shown in Figure 1. The following observations form the basis for our algorithm:

Observation 1: For each l-gram, it is sufficient to search the consistent patterns of the l-gram with respect to all other l-grams.

Observation 2: The number of other l-grams in the sample that are within h mismatches from the current l-gram reduces rapidly with decreasing h. This is illustrated in Figure 2-(a) for a random sample of 20 sequences of 600 nucleotides each. The size of the average $2d$-mismatch neighborhood is 571.395, where as the average size of the d-mismatch neighborhood is just 1.23.

Observation 3: The number of consistent patterns between two l-grams which mismatch in h positions decreases rapidly with increasing h. When h is greater

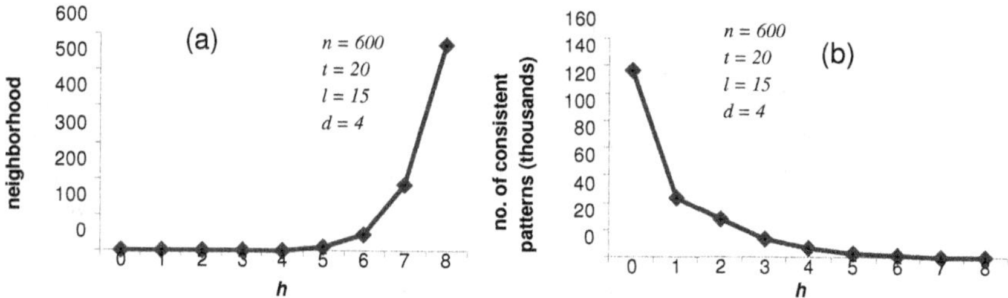

Fig. 2. Variation of: (a)h-mismatch neighborhood (b) consistent patterns with h

than $2d$, this number is zero, as two l-grams that mismatch in more than $2d$ positions can not have any patterns that mismatch with both of them in at most d positions.Therefore, as is illustrated in Figure 2-(b), the number of consistent patterns between two l-grams which mismatch in more than d positions is quite small.

2 Previous Approaches to Pattern Discovery

The pattern discovery problem can be formally stated as follows: Given a set of DNA sequences (also referred to as the sample) $S = \{S_1, S_2, ...S_t\}$, and a set of parameters l, d and k, the problem is to find all length-l patterns that occur with up to d mismatches in at least k different sequences in the sample.

One of the earliest techniques to solve this problem, as presented in [PevS00] is known as the pattern driven approach. The pattern driven approach searches all of the pattern space - it enumerates each possible pattern and checks if it meets the search criteria. If the pattern length is l, there are 4^l possible patterns, assuming a DNA alphabet. Pattern driven approaches take each one of these patterns and compare them with all the l-grams in the sample. This approach takes exponential time in terms of l, and the problem quickly becomes practically unsolvable even for moderate values of l.

A faster approach, termed by [EskP02] as the Sample Driven Approach (SDA), searches a reduced search space of only the l-grams that occur in the sample and their d-mismatch neighbors. The SDA algorithm trades in space for time: it maintains a table of size 4^l, each entry in the table corresponding to a pattern. For each l-gram in the input sample, the algorithm enumerates all the patterns that make up its d-mismatch neighbor hood. For each pattern in the neighborhood, the corresponding entry in the table is incremented. After all the l-grams have been processed, the patterns in the table that have a score greater than k are reported. The problem with the SDA approach is that the memory requirements are huge, and increase exponentially with l. Therefore the SDA approach, like the PDA approach, becomes quickly unmanageable, even for moderate values of l.

The WINNOWER algorithm [PevS00] and the cWINNOWER algorithm [Lia03] are based on graph theory. In these algorithms, a graph is constructed in which each vertex is an l-gram in the input sequence. Two l-grams are connected by an edge if they mismatch in at most $2d$ positions. Now, the problem is mapped to the problem of finding k-cliques in the graph. The problem of finding k-cliques in graph, when $k > 3$ is known to be np-complete. Therefore, WINNOWER and cWINNOWER try to apply some heuristics to arrive at a solution. In the first step, all the nodes that have a degree less than k-1 are removed. After that, different techniques are applied to try to remove the spurious edges in the graph that can not be part of a solution. The complexity of WINNOWER and cWINNOWER for the most sensitive versions of the algorithms are given by $O(t^3n^{2.66})$ and $O(t^4n^4)$, respectively. However, it is important to note that even though it is claimed that the most sensitive versions of these algorithms solve almost all practical problems, they are not guaranteed to solve a given problem.

Some of the other approaches include suffix tree -based approaches [Sag98, PavMP01]. The SPELLER algorithm presented in [Sag98] first builds a suffix tree for the input sequence. It then examines all possible patterns traversing through the suffix tree. If the paths to k different leaves of length l mismatch with the pattern in at most d positions, then the pattern is reported. Starting with zero characters at the root, the pattern is extended one character at a time. At any time if there are less than k different paths in the suffix tree that mismatch in at most d positions with the current pattern, the search is stopped and the (alphabetical) next pattern of the same length, or the next pattern of a shorter length is searched. The complexity of the algorithm is given as $O(nt^2l^d4^d)$.

In the sequence driven approach, each l-gram is searched separately. The Mitra-Count algorithm [EskP02] is based on the idea that if all the l-grams are searched concurrently, then only the information about those l-grams that meet the current search criteria need to be stored. This will reduce the memory requirements drastically. The MITRA algorithm searches the pattern search space in a depth first manner, abandoning the search whenever the search criterion is no longer met. For this it uses the mismatch tree data structure. The path from the root to a node at depth m in the mismatch tree represents a prefix of the pattern of length m. The list of l-grams from the sample whose m-length prefixes mismatch in at most d positions with the path label of the current node are stored at the node. The tree is built in a depth-first fashion. Whenever the size of the list of l-grams at a node falls below k, the node is discarded, and the sub tree of the node is never searched. Whenever the search reaches a depth l, the pattern corresponding to the path label is reported. The algorithm is memory efficient, since only the nodes that lie in the current path need to be stored at any time. An improved algorithm, Mitra-Graph, also presented in [EskP02] applies WINNOWER -like pair wise similarity information in order to maintain a graph at each node of the mismatch tree. If two l-grams L_1 & L_2 mismatch in d_1 & d_2 positions respectively with the node label, and if their suffixes beyond the current depth mismatch in q positions, then the two l-grams are connected by an edge if $d_1 + d_2 + q \geq 2d$. The nodes can be discarded if there is no possibility for a k-clique in the graph. Even though there is an extra overhead of maintaining the graph and extending the graph at each node, much smaller pattern sub-space needs to be searched in Mitra-Graph. The theoretical complexity of Mitra is claimed to be the same as that of the SPELLER algorithm.

3 The PRUNER Algorithm

3.1 Our Contributions

Our approach is based on the WINNOWER algorithm [PevS00, Lia03]. As in WINNOWER, we build a graph based on pair-wise similarity information, and prune the graph eliminating vertices that can not be part of a solution. However, after this point, we employ a different approach. The algorithms try to successively remove edges from the graph, after checking all the patterns that mismatch in at most d positions from both the l-grams that are connected by the edge. We categorize the edges into two groups. Group1 consists of edges that connect l-grams that differ in more than d positions, and Group2 consists of edges that connect l-grams that differ in less than or equal to d positions. In the following sections, we will show that there will be relatively fewer patterns that mismatch in at most d positions from both the l-grams that are connected by a Group1-edge. Precisely, we will show that there will be at most $O(l^{\frac{d}{2}}\sigma^{\frac{d}{2}})$ such patterns for every Group-1 edge. Each Group-2 edge, on the other hand, can have $O(l^d\sigma^d)$ such patterns. We present a technique which enumerates all the patterns corresponding to each Group1-edge, checks each one of them to see if they satisfy the search criteria, and removes the Group1-edge. We show that at least k monad patterns can be reported without enumerating the patterns corresponding to the Group-2 edges, there by avoiding the $O(l^d\sigma^d)$ complexity. Unlike WINNOWER and cWINNOWER[Lia03], our algorithm is guaranteed to find a solution in $O(n^2t^2l^{\frac{d}{2}}\sigma^{\frac{d}{2}})$ time using $O(ntl^{\frac{d}{2}}\sigma^{\frac{d}{2}})$ space.

3.2 Problem Statement

In the discussion that follows, for convenience in illustration, we treat the input sample as a single sequence of size n. The time and space complexities are not affected by this simplification. In section3.5, we explain the enhancements to handle t different sequences, instead of a single sequence. Therefore, the problem can be stated as follows: given a string S of length n over the alphabet $\sum = \{A, C, G, T\}$, the problem is to find a pattern P of length l that occurs at least k times in S with at most d mismatches in each occurrence.

3.3 Terms and Definitions

We denote a length-l substring(an l-gram) of S starting at position i in S by L_i. A score $h = D(L_i, L_j)$ indicates the number of positions in which the two l-grams L_i, L_j mismatch. We denote the set of patterns that mismatch with both L_i and L_j in at most d positions by $\rho(L_i, L_j)$. We refer to the set $\rho(L_i, L_j)$ also as the set of patterns that are consistent with L_i and L_j. We now describe,

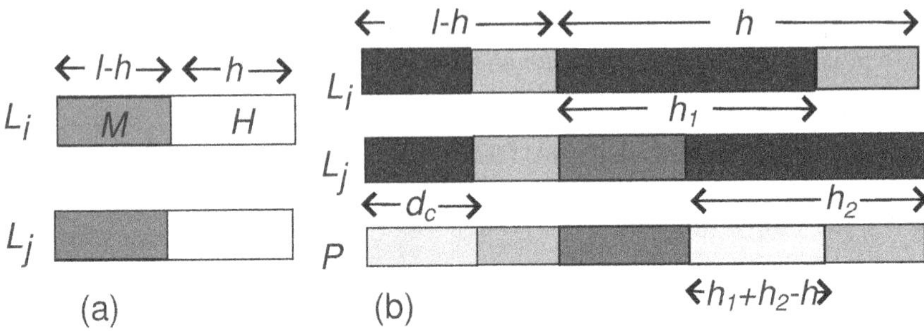

Fig. 3. (a) The matching(M) and mismatching(H) regions of L_i, L_j. (b) Different regions of the pattern P. The regions in black are the regions in which L_i, L_j mismatch with P

briefly, how to compute the size of the set $\rho(L_i, L_j)$. Let P be any pattern such that $P \in \rho(L_i, L_j)$. Now, it is important to note that $\rho(L_i, L_j) = \{\Phi\}$ if $h > 2d$. We have to enumerate all the different possibilities for P. Also, let us divide each l-gram into two regions: M-region, consisting of positions in which L_i and L_j match with each other, and the H-region, consisting positions in which L_i and L_j mismatch with each other, as shown in Figure 3-(a). Both the regions are shown to be contiguous for simplicity in illustration. In reality, these regions need not be contiguous. Now, let us assume patterns L_i and L_j mismatch with P in d_c positions within the M-region. Additionally, let L_i mismatch with P in h_1 positions, and let L_j mismatch with P in h_2 positions, as shown in Figure 3-(b). Again, none of these regions needs to be contiguous.

Now, d_c mismatch positions can be chosen from $l - h$ positions in $\binom{l-h}{d_c}$ ways. At each one of these positions, we have $\sigma - 1 = 3$ symbols to choose from. Similarly, h_1 positions in which L_i can mismatch with P can be selected from h positions in $\binom{h}{h_1}$ ways. The remaining $h - h_1$ positions in L_i have to match with P, and hence they mismatch with P in L_j (since we know that L_i mismatches with L_j in these positions). The remaining $(h_1 + h_2 - h)$ positions in which L_j mismatches with P can be selected from h_1 positions in $\binom{h_1}{h_1+h_2-h}$ ways. We have $\sigma - 2 = 2$ options at each one of these $(h_1 + h_2 - h)$ positions, since P mismatches with both L_i and L_j. Therefore, the total number of patterns in (L_i, L_j) is given by:

$$|\rho(L_i, L_j)| = \sum_{d_c=0}^{\lfloor \frac{2d-h}{2} \rfloor} \left[\binom{l-h}{d_c} 3^{d_c} \sum_{h_1=h-d+d_c}^{d-d_c} \sum_{h_2=h-h_1}^{d-d_c} \binom{h}{h_1} \binom{h_1}{h_1+h_2-h} 2^{h_1+h_2-h} \right], \text{ if } h \leq 2d$$
$$= 0 \text{ otherwise} \quad (1)$$

In the above expression, $|\rho(L_i, L_j)|$ increases when h decreases. When $d < h \leq 2d$, the maximum value of $|\rho(L_i, L_j)|$ occurs when $h = d+1$. When $h = d+1$, the maximum value that d_c can take is given by $d_c = \frac{d-1}{2}$ which is equal to $\frac{d}{2}$ when d is odd, and $\frac{d}{2} - 1$ when d is even. Now, $\binom{l-h}{d_c} 3^{d_c}$is in $O(l^{d_c} 3^{d_c})$. Therefore, on the whole, $|\rho(L_i, L_j)|$ is in $O(l^{\frac{d}{2}} 4^{\frac{d}{2}})$.

3.4 The PRUNER-I and PRUNER-II Algorithms

In both the algorithms, we construct a graph $G(L, E)$ where each vertex is an l-gram in the input sample, and there is an edge $(L_i, L_j, D(L_i, L_j))$ connecting two l-grams L_i and L_j if $D(L_i, L_j)$ is less than or equal to $2d$. We then successively remove vertices representing l-grams from the graph $G(L, E)$ that have a degree less than $k-1$, and remove the edges that are incident on these vertices. Until this point, our algorithms are no different from WINNOWER. However, they differ from WINNOWER in the following steps.

Both the PRUNER-I and the PRUNER-II algorithms process each vertex successively. The PRUNER-I algorithm enumerates the consistent patterns for every group1-edge (i.e., edges between l-grams which mismatch in more than d positions). It then computes how many times each pattern repeats. It does this by adding all the consistent patterns for each edge to a list, sorting and scanning the list. Each time a pattern appears, it means that the pattern is within d mismatches from another l-gram. Hence, if a pattern repeats $k-1$ times, it means that the pattern is within d mismatches from $k-1$ other l-grams. However, since we have not yet processed the Group2-edges(i.e., edges connecting l-grams that mismatch in d or fewer positions), we can not yet discard the patterns that repeat less than $k-1$ times. We do not want to evaluate all the consistent patterns for the Group2-edges, as there are too many ($O(l^d 4^d)$) such patterns. Therefore, we will have to take each pattern in the list, and compare it with each l-gram that is connected to the current vertex through a Group2-edge. Only then will we know how many times each one of those patterns has repeated. An efficient way of doing all this is presented below.

At each node L_i, we enumerate the consistent patterns $\rho(L_i, L_j)$ for all the Group1-edges, i.e., edges $(L_i, L_j, D(L_i, L_j))$, such that $d < D(L_i, L_j) \leq 2d$. We add these patterns to a list $\eta(i)$, and remove the edge $(L_i, L_j, D(L_i, L_j))$. Lemma 1 states that we can safely remove the edge $(L_i, L_j, D(L_i, L_j))$ after enumerating and adding $\rho(L_i, L_j)$ to $\eta(i)$.

Lemma 1. *After a vertex L_i in $(L_i, L_j, D(L_i, L_j))$ is processed, there can be no new patterns in $\rho(L_i, L_j)$ that were not reported while processing L_i, but will be reported while processing the vertex L_j.*

Proof. Let us assume that there is a pattern $P \in \rho(L_i, L_j)$ that was not reported while processing node L_i, but will be reported while processing node L_j. This means that there are a set of l-grams $\psi(P)$ other than L_i, such that for each $L_q \in \psi(P)$, there is an edge $(L_q, L_j, D(L_q, L_j))$ connecting L_q and L_j, and $D(L_q, P) \leq$

d. Additionally, since P will be reported while processing L_j, $|\psi(P)| \geq k-2$. Now, since for each $L_q \in \psi(P)$, $D(L_q, P) \leq d$ and $D(L_i, P) \leq d$ (as $P \in \rho(L_i, L_j)$ by definition), it implies that $D(L_i, L_q) \leq 2d$. Therefore, for each $L_q \in \psi(P)$ there is an edge $(L_i, L_q, D(L_i, L_q))$ connecting L_i and L_q. Since $|\psi(P)| \geq k-2$, and $P \in \rho(L_i, L_j)$, there are at least $k-1$ edges incident in L_i which contain P as one of their consistent patterns. Therefore, pattern P must have been reported while processing node L_i. Hence there can be no pattern $P \in \rho(L_i, L_j)$ that is not reported while processing L_i that can be reported while processing L_j. □

Now, we need to find out how many times each pattern is repeated in $\eta(i)$. An easy way of doing this will be to sort $\eta(i)$, and scan $\eta(i)$. As each pattern in $\eta(i)$ is a length-l string of a fixed alphabet, $\eta(i)$ can be sorted in linear time using radix sort. Let a pattern P repeat m times in $\eta(i)$. Let R be the degree of node L_i after processing and removing all Group1-edges. As explained in section1, R is expected to be very small. We do the following:

- If $m+R < k-1$, we discard P. The number of times P repeats can increase by at most R, by comparing P with each one of the Group2-edges. If $m < k-1-R$, there is no way that P can repeat $k-1$ times. So we can discard P.
- If $m \geq k-1$, report P, since it is clear that P has already occurred at least $k-1$ times.
- If $k-1 \leq m+R < k-1-R$, we compare P with all l-grams that are still connected to L_i. For each such l-gram that mismatches P in at most d locations, we increment the repeat count of P. If the repeat count reaches $k-1$, we report P. Other wise, we discard P.

Before we leave L_i and proceed to process the next vertex, we can do one more thing - we can remove the vertex L_i from the graph if $R < k-1$, without ever enumerating the consistent patterns for these edges. Lemma 2 proves this.

Lemma 2. *If the residual degree R of vertex L_i is less than $k-1$ after processing and removing all Group1-edges of L_i, there can be no new patterns that will be reported by processing the Group2-edges.*

Proof. Let us assume that there is a pattern P that was not reported while processing the Group1-edges, but will be reported while processing the Group2-edges. Since we will be reporting P, and since $R < k-1$, there should have been at least one Group1-edge $(L_i, L_q, D(L_i, L_q)$ such that $P \in \rho(L_i, L_q)$. Therefore, P was checked and reported while processing vertex L_q. Hence there can be no new patterns that will be reported by processing the Group2-edges. □

We are now left with a graph in which the score of each edge is at most d, and degree of each remaining vertex is at least $k-1$. Therefore, *if the graph has any vertices left, there will be at least* k *vertices left in each connected component of the graph.* In practice, we do not expect any vertices to remain at this stage, as our assumption is that there are not too many patterns that meet the search criteria. All the l-grams that do remain until this stage are themselves valid

```
ProcessLGram()
Inputs: G(L,E), i, l, d, k
Output: Reports patterns in the d-mismatch neighborhood of L_i that satisfy the search criteria
PatternList ← {φ}
for every j such that (L_i, L_j, D(L_i, L_j)) ∈ E do
        if D(L_i, L_j) > d /* checking if (L_i, L_j, D(L_i, L_j)) is a Group-1 edge*/
            PatternList ← PatternList ∪ ρ(L_i, L_j)
/* the set ρ(L_i, L_j) of consistent patterns is enumerated by a subroutine at this point*/
            E ← E − (L_i, L_j, D(L_i, L_j)) /* The Group-1 edge is immediately removed */
        end if
end for
RadixSort(PatternList)
Cnt ← 0 /* Cnt is the number of times the current pattern has repeated */
for j ← 1 to |PatternList| − 1
    if PatternList_j = PatternList_j-1
        Cnt ← Cnt + 1
    else if Cnt ≥ k − 1 − Degree(L_i) /*Degree(L_i) is the residual degree (the degree of
      Group-2 edges of L_i) , since all the Group-1 edges have been removed in step 6.*/
            for every r such that (L_i, L_r, D(L_i, L_r)) ∈ E do /* for each Group-2 edge */
                    ifD(PatternList_j, L_r) ≤ d
    /*check if the pattern PatternList_j is in the d-mismatch neighborhood of L_r*/
                        Cnt ← Cnt + 1
                    end if
            end for
            if Cnt > k − 1
                Report(PatternList_j) /*PatternList_j is an (l, d) − k pattern */
            end if
            Cnt ← 0
    end if
end for
```

Fig. 4. The routine that checks the d-mismatch neighborhood of each l-gram

solutions, since they mismatch in at most d positions with at least $k-1$ other l-grams. Hence, we report all the remaining l-grams. Beyond this, there might be other patterns in the graph that meet the search criteria, but in a general case, we assume that there are fewer than k distinct monad patterns in the given sample. In the almost impractical scenario that there are more than k distinct monad patterns, the algorithms we present report at least k of them. The PRUNER-I algorithm is presented in detail in figures 4 and 5.

The PRUNER-II algorithm is very similar to the PRUNER-I algorithm in concept. However, the PRUNER-II algorithm attempts to eliminate the potentially huge memory requirements of the PRUNER-I algorithm. While processing each node L_i, the PRUNER-I algorithm maintains a list $\eta(i)$ that contains all the patterns that are consistent with each one of the Group1-edges. When the number of such edges is huge, the amount of memory required for $\eta(i)$ may be too big. Especially, this might be the case when d is large and the d/l ratio is large, in which case the graph $G(L,E)$ will be highly connected.

At each vertex L_i, the PRUNER-II algorithm processes edges one by one. For each edge $(L_i, L_j, D(L_i, L_j))$, it enumerates the set of consistent patterns $\rho(L_i, L_j)$. For each consistent pattern $P \in \rho(Li, Lj)$, if we compare P with all the l-grams that are directly connected with vertex L_i, we can determine if P mismatches in at most d positions with at least $k-1$ of them. However, a deeper analysis reveals that it not necessary to compare P with all the l-grams that share an edge with L_i. For any l-gram L_q, if $D(L_q, P) \leq d$, then $D(L_q, L_j)$ will be less than or equal to $2d$. This means that the l-grams L_q and L_j will also be connected. Therefore, we only need to compare P with all vertices L_q such that the edge $(L_q, L_j, D(L_q, L_j)) \in E$. If at least $k-2$ of them mismatch with P in fewer than d positions, it reports P. Otherwise, P is discarded. As in the PRUNER-I algorithm, it removes the edge $(L_i, L_j, D(L_i, L_j))$ after checking all the patterns in $\rho(L_i, L_j)$.

```
SearchForPatterns()
Inputs: S, l, d, k, n
Buildgraph(S,l,d,k,n) /*The routine that builds the graph G(L,E)*/
PruneGraph(G(L,E),l,d,k,n) /* The pruning routine which removes
                              all the vertices with degree < k − 1*/
for i ← 0 to n − l + 1 do
    ProcessLGram(G(L,E),i,l,d,k,n)
    ifDegree(L_i) < k − 1
      RemoveLGram(G(L, E), i) /* remove the vertex L_i
    (and the edges incident on L_i) from the graph */
end for
PruneGraph(G(L,E), l, d, k, n) /* remove l-grams with degree < k − 1 */
for i ← 0 to n − l + 1 do /*check if any l-grams are still remaining*/
    if Degree(L_i) > k − 1
       Report(L_i) /* report all remaining l-grams*/
    end if
end for
```

Fig. 5. The PRUNER-I algorithm

3.5 Extending the Algorithm to Handle Multiple Sequences

When the input sample is made of t sequences of length n each, and the problem is to find an (l, d) motif that occurs in at least k of them, the graph $G(L, E)$ will be a t-partite graph. At each vertex in the graph, we need to maintain and update another variable, which we call t-degree. The variable t-degree stores the number of distinct sequences in t that the current vertex is connected to. In the algorithms that we discussed above, whenever we are referring to the degree of a vertex, we will be using t-degree instead of the actual degree of the vertex. Whenever we are checking for a pattern P, it is no longer sufficient to check if the pattern is within d mismatches from $k-1$ other l-grams. We need to make sure that the l-grams are derived from $k-1$ distinct sequences in the sample. The implementation typically involves maintaining a bit-vector of length t for the pattern that is being considered. Whenever the pattern is within d-mismatches from an l-gram, the bit corresponding to the sequence from which the l-gram is derived is set to 1. P satisfies the search criteria if at least $k-1$ (or whatever is necessary at that point in the algorithm) bits are set to 1.

3.6 Complexity Analysis

Building the graph involves calculating the mismatch count for each l-gram pair (L_i, L_j) such that L_i and L_j are derived from different input sequences. There are $(n-l+1)$ l-grams for each input sequence, and $n(t-1)$ other l-grams for each l-gram in the input sequence. Therefore, building the graph takes

Table 1. Performance of the algorithms

Test case (l, d)	d/l ratio	PRUNER-I		PRUNER-II		Test case (l, d)	d/l ratio	PRUNER-I		PRUNER-II	
		Time	Memory (MB)	Time	Memory (MB)			Time	Memory (MB)	Time	Memory (MB)
13,3	0.23	0.17	43	0.14	43	13,4	0.31	12.26	166	29.58	278
14,4	0.28	5.35	198	7.09	178	15,4	0.27	2.28	122	1.34	91
16,4	0.25	0.56	51	0.56	43	16,5	0.31	69.00	540	284.59	247
17,5	0.29	29.54	315	36.58	161	18,5	0.28	13.19	174	13.19	92
19,5	0.263	6.02	101	0.54	48	20,5	0.25	2.16	65	0.13	21
21,5	0.238	0.13	10	0.13	11	22,5	0.227	0.17	56	0.13	7
22,6	0.273		649	3.16	83	23,6	0.261	18.57	525	0.13	64
24,6	0.25	1.12	720	0.16	11	25,6	0.24	1.17	592	0.18	60
26,6	0.231	1.08	613	0.16	62	27,7	0.259	out of memory		2.27	614
28,7	0.25	out of memory		0.36	640	29,7	0.241	0.38	749	1.41	640

$O(n^2t^2)$. Pruning the graph involves removing all the edges incident on each vertex whose degree is less than $k-1$. In the worst case, we might have to delete all the nodes, so the maximum number of edges that need to be removed is $((k-1)nt-1)$, which is $O(ntk)$. This time is common for both PRUNER-I and PRUNER-II. In the PRUNER-I algorithm, each l-gram can have up to $n(t-1)$ $2d$-mismatch neighbors. Therefore, at each l-gram, we might have to enumerate the consistent patterns with $n(t-1)$ other l-grams. The maximum number of these consistent patterns as discussed in section 3.3, is $O(l^{\frac{d}{2}}4^{\frac{d}{2}})$. Hence the worst-case time complexity at each node is given by $O(ntl^{\frac{d}{2}}4^{\frac{d}{2}})$. We need to store all these patterns in a list, so we need $O(ntl^{\frac{d}{2}}4^{\frac{d}{2}})$ space. In the worst case, we will have to process $(t-k+1)n$ l-grams, since no new patterns can be discovered after removing all the vertices corresponding to $(t-k+1)$ sequences in the sample. Therefore, the overall complexity is given by $O(n^2t(t-k+1)l^{\frac{d}{2}}4^{\frac{d}{2}})$. If k is small w.r.t. t, this will be $O(n^2t^2l^{\frac{d}{2}}4^{\frac{d}{2}})$. When $k=t$, the complexity of the PRUNER-I algorithm is $O(n^2tl^{\frac{d}{2}}4^{\frac{d}{2}})$. In case of the PRUNER-II algorithm, each edge is processed separately. All the patterns consistent with each edge (L_i, L_j) have to be compared with all the l-grams that are connected to both L_i and L_j. In the worst case, there can be $n(t-2)$ vertices that are connected to both L_i and L_j. The total number of the edges could be $n^2t(t-1)$ in the worst case. The edge can have $O(l^{\frac{d}{2}}4^{\frac{d}{2}})$ patterns that are consistent with it, so the total time taken will be $O(n^3t^3l^{\frac{d}{2}}4^{\frac{d}{2}})$. Each pattern could be compared separately; therefore the space needed is approximately the same as that necessary for the graph.

4 Results

The algorithms were tested on generated samples containing 20 sequences of 600 nucleotides each. The sequences are implanted with randomly mutated patterns at randomly chosen positions. Each occurrence of the pattern is allowed to have up to d mismatches. The tests were carried out on a Pentium-4 3.2 GHz PC with 2GB of memory, running Redhat Linux 9.0. The time/memory results are presented in Table 1. The PRUNER-I algorithm ran out of memory for the (27,7) and the (28,7) cases. The implanted pattern was detected in all the remaining test cases.

5 Conclusion

We have presented two new algorithms for finding the monad patterns. Both the algorithms perform extremely well on the challenge problem of (15,4) on 20 input sequences of 600 nucleotides. As d increases in comparison to l, i.e., when the d/l ratio increases, the PRUNER-I algorithm takes a longer time and a larger memory. The PRUNER-I algorithm runs out of memory for large values of l and d. The PRUNER-II algorithm, on the other hand, can handle large values of l and d, but reacts very sharply to the d/l ratio. As long as the d/l ratio is around 0.25, the PRUNER-II algorithm performs very well, independent of the actual values of l and d. Unlike Winnower and cWinnower, the algorithms we presented here are not sensitive to k. Our algorithms will be able to detect patterns even for very small values of k. The only concern when dealing with very small values of k is that there could be random signals in the input sample that meet the search criteria. An interesting observation from the test cases is that the graph itself starts consuming more and more space as the d/l ratio gets bigger. This is because there are more and more edges in the graph, as there are a larger number of l-gram pairs that mismatch in less than $2d$ positions. In the future, we plan to investigate compact representations for the graph. Another approach may involve using a two-pass algorithm. WINNOWER or cWINNOWER can be used initially in order to remove some spurious edges. Our algorithms can be applied in the second pass. As the graph has much fewer edges now, PRUNER-I or PRUNER-II may have very good performance. For the first pass, we can use a low sensitivity version of WINNOWER or cWINNOWER in order to maximize the speed.

References

[BuhT2001] Buhler J. and Tompa B.: Finding motifs using random projections *Proc. of the Fifth Annual International Conference on Computational Molecular Biology (RECOMB01)* (2001) 69–76

[EskKGP03] Eskin E., Keich U., Gelfand M.S., Pevzner P.A.: Genome-wide analysis of bacterial promoter regions. *Proc. of the Pacific Symposium on Biocomputing PSB* – 2003 (2003) Kau'i, Hawaii, January 3-7, 2003

[EskP02] Eskin E. and Pevzner P.A.: Finding composite regulatory patterns in DNA sequences. *Proc. of the Tenth International Conference on Intelligent Systems for Molecular Biology (ISMB-2002)* (2002) Edmonton, Canada, August 3-7

[GuhS01] Guha Thakurtha D. and Stormo G.D.: Identifying target sites for cooperatively binding factors. *Bioinformatics* **15** (2001) 563–577

[HerS99] Hertz G.Z. and Stormo G.D.: Identifying DNA and protein patterns with statistically significant alignments of multiple sequences. *Bioinformatics* **10**, (1999) 1205–1214

[Lia03] Liang S.: cWINNOWER Algorithm for finding fuzzy DNA motifs. *Proc. of the 2003 IEEE Computational Systems Bioinformatics conference (CSB 2003)* (2003) 260–265

[MarS00] Marsan L. and Sagot M.: Algorithms for extracting structured motifs using suffix tree with applications to promoter and regulatory site consensus identification. *Journal of Computational Biology* **7**, (2000) 345–360

[PavMP01] Pavesi G., Mauri G. and Pesole G.: An algorithm for finding signals of unknown length in DNA sequences. *Proc. of the Ninth International Conference on Intelligent Systems for Molecular Biology* (2001)

[PevS00] Pevzner P.A. and Sze S.: Combinatorial approaches to finding subtle motifs in DNA sequences. *Proc. of the Eighth International Conference on Intelligent Systems for Molecular Biology* (2000) 269–278

[PriRP03] Price A., Ramabhadran S. and Pevzner A.: Finding subtle motifs by branching from sample strings. *Bioinformatics* **19**, (2003) 149–155

[Sag98] Sagot M.: Spelling approximate or repeated motifs using a suffix tree. *Lecture notes in computer science* **1380**, (1998) 111-127

[vanRC00] van Helden J., Rios A.F., and Collado-Vides J.: Discovering regulatory elements in non-coding sequences by analysis of spaced dyads. *Nucleic Acids Research* **28**, (2000) 1808–1818

Motif Extraction from Weighted Sequences

Costas S. Iliopoulos[1], Katerina Perdikuri[2,3], Evangelos Theodoridis[2,3,⋆], Athanasios Tsakalidis[2,3], and Kostas Tsichlas[1]

[1] Department of Computer Science, King's College London
London WC2R 2LS, England
{csi,kostas}@dcs.kcl.ac.uk

[2] Computer Engineering & Informatics Dept. of University of Patras
26500 Patras, Greece
{perdikur,theodori}@ceid.upatras.gr

[3] Research Academic Computer Technology Institute (RACTI)
61 Riga Feraiou St., 26221 Patras, Greece
tsak@cti.gr

Abstract. We present in this paper three algorithms. The first extracts repeated motifs from a weighted sequence. The motifs correspond to words which occur at least q times and with hamming distance e in a weighted sequence with probability $\geq 1/k$ each time, where k is a small constant. The second algorithm extracts common motifs from a set of $N \geq 2$ weighted sequences with hamming distance e. In the second case, the motifs must occur twice with probability $\geq 1/k$, in $1 \leq q \leq N$ distinct sequences of the set. The third algorithm extracts maximal pairs from a weighted sequence. A pair in a sequence is the occurrence of the same substring twice. In addition, the algorithms presented in this paper improve slightly on previous work on these problems.

1 Introduction

DNA and protein sequences can be seen as long texts over specific alphabets encoding the genetic information of living beings. Searching specific sub-sequences over these texts is a fundamental operation for problems such as assembling the DNA chain from pieces obtained by experiments, looking for given DNA chains or determining how different two genetic sequences are. However, exact searching is of little use since the patterns rarely match the text exactly. The experimental measurements have various errors and even correct chains may have small differences, some of which are significant due to mutations and evolutionary changes.

Finding approximate repetitions or signals arise in several applications in molecular biology. Moreover, establishing how different two sequences are is important to reconstruct the tree of the evolution (phylogenetic trees). All these problems require a concept of similarity, or in other words a distance metric between two sequences. Additionally, many problems in Computational Biology involve searching for unknown repeated patterns, often called motifs and

⋆ Partially supported by the National Ministry of Education under the program Pythagoras(EPEAEK).

A. Apostolico and M. Melucci (Eds.): SPIRE 2004, LNCS 3246, pp. 286–297, 2004.

identifying regularities in nucleic or protein sequences. Both imply inferring patterns, of unknown content at first, from one or more sequences. Regularities in a sequence may come under many guises. They may correspond to approximate repetitions randomly dispersed along the sequence, or to repetitions that occur in a periodic or approximately periodic fashion. The length and number of repeated elements one wishes to be able to identify may be highly variable.

In the study of gene expression and regulation, it is important to be able to infer repeated motifs or structured patterns and answer various biological questions, such as what elements in sequence and structure are involved in the regulation and expression of genes through their recognition. The analysis of the distribution of repeated patterns permits biologists to determine whether there exists an underlying structure and correlation at a local or global genomic level. These correspond to an ordered collection of p boxes (always of initially unknown content) and $p-1$ intervals of distances (one between each pair of successive boxes in the collection). Structured patterns allow to identify conserved elements recognized by different parts of a same protein or macromolecular complex, or by various complexes that then interact with one another.

In this work, we examine various instances of the *Motif Identification Problem* in weighted sequences. In particular, we are given a set of weighted sequences $S = \{S_1, S_2, \ldots, S_k\}, S_i \in \Sigma^*$ and we are asked to extract interesting motifs such that each motif occurs in at least q sequences.

Generally speaking, a weighted sequence could be defined as a *sequence of (symbol, weight) pairs*, $S = \langle (s_1, w_1), (s_2, w_2), \cdots (s_n, w_n) \rangle$, where w_i is the weight of symbol s_i in position i (occurrence probability of s_i at position i).

Biological weighted sequences can model important biological processes, such as the DNA-Protein Binding Process or Assembled DNA Chains. Thus, motif extraction from biological weighted sequences is a very important procedure in the translation of gene expression and regulation. In more detail, the extracted motifs from weighted sequences correspond in general to binding sites. These are sites in a biological molecule that will come into contact with a site in another molecule permitting the initiation of some biological process (for instance, transcription or translation). In addition, these weighted sequences may correspond to complete chromosome sequences that have been obtained using a whole-genome shotgun strategy [10]. By keeping all the information the whole-genome shotgun produces, we would like to dig out information that has being previously undetected after being faded during the consensus step. Finally, protein families can also be represented by weighted sequences ([4], in 14.3.1).

A weighted biological sequence is often represented as a $d \times n$ matrix, which is termed *weighted matrix*, where d is the size of the respective alphabet (in the case of DNA weighted sequences $d = 4$) and n is the length of the sequence. Each cell of the weighted matrix p_{ij} stores the probability of appearance of symbol i in the jth position of the input sequence. An instance of a weighted (sub)sequence p is a (sub)sequence of p where a symbol has been chosen for each position. The probability of occurrence of this instance is the product of the probabilities of the symbols of all positions of the instance. For example, for the instance

$$\begin{pmatrix} p_{A1} & p_{A2} & p_{A3} & \cdots & p_{An} \\ p_{C1} & p_{C2} & p_{C3} & \cdots & p_{Cn} \\ p_{G1} & p_{G2} & p_{G3} & \cdots & p_{Gn} \\ p_{T1} & p_{T2} & p_{T3} & \cdots & p_{Tn} \end{pmatrix}$$

Fig. 1. The Weight Matrix representation for a weighted DNA sequence

$A_1, A_2 \ldots, A_n$ of the weighted sequence shown in Figure 1, the probability of occurrence is $\prod_{i=1}^{n} p_{A_i}$.

A great number of algorithms has been proposed in the relative literature for inferring motifs in biological sequences (e.g. regulatory sequences, protein coding genes). The majority of algorithms relies on either statistical or machine learning approaches for solving the inference problem. In [11] authors defined a notion of maximality and redundancy for motifs, based on the idea that some motifs could be enough to build all the others. These motifs are termed *tiling motifs*. The goal is to define a basis of motifs, in other words a set of irredundant motifs that can generate all maximal motifs by simple mechanical rules.

Other approaches build all possible motifs by increasing length. These solutions have a high time and space complexity and cannot be applied in the case of weighted sequences, due to their combinatorial complexity. Finally, in [12, 8] authors use the suffix tree to spell all valid models (exact or approximate).

In addition, finding maximal pairs in ordinary sequences was firstly described by Gusfield in [4]. This algorithm uses a suffix tree to report all maximal pairs in a string of length n in time $O(n + \alpha)$ and space $O(n)$, where α is the number of reported pairs. In [1] authors presented methods for finding all maximal pairs under various constraints on the gap between the two substrings of the pair. In a string of length n, they find all maximal pairs with gap in an upper and lower bounded interval in time $O(n \log n + \alpha)$. If the upper bound is removed the time is reduced to $O(n + z)$.

The structure of the paper is as follows. In Section 2 we give some basic definitions on weighted sequences to be used in the rest of the paper. In Section 3 we address the problem of extracting simple models, while in Section 4 we address the problem of Motif Extraction in weighted sequences. Finally, in Section 5 we conclude and discuss open problems in the area.

2 Preliminaries

In this section we provide formal definitions of the problems we tackle, we give some basic definitions and finally we describe briefly the best known algorithms on these problems in the case of solid sequences (sequences that are not weighted). The first problem we wish to solve is the repeated motifs problem.

Problem 1 *Given a weighted sequence s and three integers $0 \le k < c$, $e \ge 0$ and $q \ge 2$, for some small constant c, find all models m with probability of occurrence $\ge \frac{1}{k}$ such that m is present at least q times in s and the Hamming distance between all occurrences is $\le e$. All these occurrences must not overlap.*

The non-overlapping restriction is added because when two models a and b of s overlap, then it may be the case that a cancels b. More specifically, assume that a and b overlap at position i. Then, it may be the case that a uses symbol $\sigma_1 \in \Sigma$ with probability $\pi_i(\sigma_1)$ while b uses symbol $\sigma_2 \in \Sigma$ with probability $\pi_i(\sigma_2)$, which is not correct. To overcome this difficulty we do not allow the occurrences of models to overlap. The second problem we wish to solve is the common motifs problem.

Problem 2 *Given a set of N weighted sequences $S = s_i$ $(1 \leq i \leq N)$ and three integers $0 \leq k < c$, $e \geq 0$ and $2 \leq q \leq N$, for some small constant c, find all models m with probability of occurrence $\geq \frac{1}{k}$ such that m is present in at least q distinct sequences of the set and the Hamming distance between them is $\leq e$.*

When a model satisfies the restrictions posed by each of the above problems, it is called *valid*. For the above two problems the spelling of models is done using the Weighted Suffix Tree (WST). The WST of a weighted sequence s, $WST(s)$, is the compressed trie of all valid weighted subwords, starting within each suffix s_i of $s\$$, $\$ \notin \Sigma$. A weighted subword is valid if its occurrence probability is $\geq 1/k$. The WST is built in linear time and space when k is a small constant. The WST was firstly presented in [5] as an elegant data structure for reporting the repetitions within a weighted biological sequence. In [6] authors presented an efficient algorithm for constructing the WST.

Finally, the third problem we wish to solve is the following.

Problem 3 *Given a set of N weighted sequences $S = s_1, s_2, \cdots s_n$, an integer $0 \leq k < c$ and a quorum $q \leq N$, for some small constant c, find all maximal pairs m such that m is valid, that is, it appears with probability greater than $\frac{1}{k}$ in at least q sequences of the set S.*

A pair in a string is the occurrence of the same substring twice. A pair is maximal if the occurrences of the substring cannot be extended to the left or to the right without making them different. The gap of a pair is the number of characters between the two occurrences of the substring. A pair is valid if each substring appears with probability $\geq \frac{1}{k}$.

2.1 Basic Definitions

Let Σ be an alphabet of cardinality $\sigma = \Sigma$. A sequence s of length n is represented by $s[1..n] = s[1]s[2] \cdots s[n]$, where $s[i] \in \Sigma$ for $1 \leq i \leq n$, and $n = |s|$ is the length of s. An empty sequence is denoted by ε; we write $\Sigma^* = \Sigma^+ \cup \{\varepsilon\}$. A weighted sequence is defined as follows.

Definition 1. *A weighted sequence $s = s_1 s_2 \cdots s_n$ is a set of couples $(s, \pi_i(s))$, where $\pi_i(s)$ is the occurrence probability of character s at position i. For every position $1 \leq i \leq n$, $\Sigma \pi_i(s) = 1$.*

Valid motifs in weighted sequences correspond to words that occur at least q times in the weighted sequence with probability of appearance $\geq \frac{1}{k}$. If we consider approximate motifs, then the distance of a valid motif should be $\leq e$.

Definition 2. *A set S_l of positions inside a weighted sequence s, represents a set of weighted factors of length l, that are similar, if and only if, there exists, (at least) a motif $m \in \Sigma^l$, such that for all elements i in S_l, $dist_l(m, s_i) \leq e$.*

In other words, the set S_l contains all motifs of length l with at most e mismatches. The size of S_l is represented by $V(e, l)$. We report the valid motifs using the WST. $V(e, l)$ is an upper bound for the number of motifs that correspond to the maximum size of the output.

Definition 3. *The WST of a weighted sequence S, denoted as $WST(S)$, is the compressed trie of all possible subwords made up from the weighted subwords starting within each suffix s_i of $S\$$, $\$ \notin \Sigma$, and having an occurrence probability $\geq \frac{1}{k}$, where k is a small constant. Let $L(v)$ denote the path-label of node v in $WST(S)$, which is the catenation of edge labels in the path from root to v. Leaf v of $WST(S)$ is labeled with index i if $\exists j > 0$ such that $L(v) = S_{i,j}[i..n]$ and $\pi(S_{i,j}[i \cdots n]) \geq 1/k$, where $j > 0$ denotes the j-th weighted subword starting at position i. The leaf-list $LL(v)$, is the list of the leaf-labels in the subtree of v.*

2.2 Previous Work

In the following, we sketch the algorithms proposed by Sagot [12] and Iliopoulos et al. [7], on which our solutions are based. The common characteristic of both papers is that the proposed algorithms make heavy use of suffix trees. In a nutshell, the suffix tree is an indexing structure for all suffixes of a string s and it is well known that it can be constructed in linear time and linear space [9]. The generalized suffix tree is a suffix tree for more than one strings. Since suffix trees is a well known indexing structure for strings, we will assume that the reader is familiar with its basic properties and characteristics. In the discussion to follow, for reasons of clarity we discuss the algorithm on the uncompressed suffix tree (a sequence of nodes with just one child is not collapsing into a single edge).

The repeated and common motifs problems are handled in [12]. For the first problem the input is a string s with length n over an alphabet Σ and two integers $q \geq 2$ (the quorum) and $e \geq 0$ (the maximum number of mismatches). In addition, the algorithm is given the length l of the wanted model. Consequently, if we want to find all possible models we have to apply the algorithm for each possible length (the same is applied also to the second problem). Finally, for both problems, the output of the algorithms is only the models and not the exact position of their appearance.

Assuming that $e = 0$, the algorithm for the common motifs problem locates each node v_i that corresponds to a model m_i of length l and then checks if this model is valid, that is if it satisfies the quorum constraint. This is easy to do, by checking whether the number of leaves of each node v_i is larger than q. If we allow for errors, then a model m_i corresponds to many nodes $v_{i_1}, v_{i_2}, \ldots, v_{i_j}$ on the suffix tree. Apparently, this model is valid if the sum of leaves of all these nodes is larger than q. By a simple linear-time preprocessing it is very easy to compute the number of leaves for each node of the suffix tree. Note that occurrences of models may overlap. The space used by the algorithm is linear while the time complexity for a specific length l is $O(nV(e,l))$.

For the common motifs problem, the input is a set of strings $S = s_1, s_2, \ldots, s_N$ and two integers $q \geq 2$ and $e \geq 0$. First, a generalized suffix tree is constructed for S in time $O(nN)$. Then, the mechanism to check the quorum constrained is implemented. For each node v in the suffix tree, a bit vector b_v of N positions is constructed such that $b_v[i] = 0$ when in the subtree of v there is no leaf with label i, that is there is no occurrence of a suffix of string s_i in the subtree of v (otherwise $b_v[i] = 1$). Then, the procedure is exactly the same as in the repeated motifs algorithm with the exception that we use the bit vectors to check whether the quorum constraint is satisfied. The space requirements of this algorithm is $O(n\frac{N^2}{w})$, where w is the word length of the machine. The time complexity is $O(nN^2V(e,l))$, for a specified length l.

Finally, we come to the solution described in Iliopoulos et al. [7]. In this work all maximal pairs which occur in each string of a set of strings without any restrictions on the gaps are reported in $O(n+\alpha)$, where α is the size of the output, and linear space. In addition, it reports all maximal pairs which occur in each string of a set of strings with the same gap that is upper bounded by a constant. This is achieved in $O(n\log^2 n + \alpha N \log n)$ time, where N is the number of strings and n is the total length of the strings, using linear space.

We supply in this paper methods that encounter the above problems on weighted sequences. For simple motifs we propose an algorithm that works in $O(nNqV(e,l))$ time and $O(nNq)$ space and for maximal pairs an $O(Nn\log(Nn) + \alpha)$ algorithm using linear space.

3 Extracting Simple Models

In this section we supply an algorithm for reporting all maximal pairs in a set of weighted sequences. More specifically, given a set of N weighted sequences $S = s_1, s_2, \cdots s_N$, a small integer $k \geq 0$ and a quorum $q \leq N$, we report all maximal pairs, whose components appear with probability greater than $1/k$ in at least q sequences of the set S. We have considered two variations of this problem depending on the restrictions on the gaps. In the first version we assume that there is no restriction on the gaps of the pairs, thus one pair may appear in different sequencs with different gaps. In the second version of the problem one pair has to come along with approximately the same gap, which is upper bounded by a constant value b. For solving these problems we suggest two methods that are extensions of the algorithms that are provided in [7] for these problems on plain sequences. Our solutions encounter these problems on weighted sequences in a more simple and efficient way.

Initially, a generalized weighted suffix tree $gWST(S)$ is constructed. A generalized weighted suffix tree is similar to the generalized suffix tree and is built upon all the weighted sequences of S. For the construction of $gWST(S)$ the algorithm of [6] is used for each of the weighted sequences in S and all the produced factors are superimposed in the same compacted trie. The total time for this operation is linear to the sum of length of each of the weighted sequences ($O(\sum_{i=1}^{n}|s_i|)$). The construction method is invoked for each of the weighted sequences starting from the root of the same compacted trie. The suffix links are preserved so it is like building a generalized suffix tree from a set of regular sequences using the same auxiliary suffix tree. Thus, the space of the $gWST(S)$ is linear to the total length of the weighted sequences. The $gWST(S)$ is a compacted trie with out-degree of internal nodes at least 2 and at most most $\sigma = |\Sigma|$. The first step, as mentioned and in [4], [1] and [7] is to binarize $gWST(S)$. Each node u with out-degree $|u| \geq 2$ is replaced by a binary tree with $|u|$ leaves and $|u| - 1$ internal nodes. Each edge is labeled with the empty string ϵ so that all new nodes have the same path-label as node u, which they replace. Assuming that the alphabet size σ is constant, the whole procedure needs linear time and the final data structure has linear space.

The indexes of the factors at the leaves of the $gWST(S)$ are organized in special leaf-lists according to the weighted sequence s_i that belong and the character to their left (left-character). The left-character of an index i is the character that exists at position $i - 1$. In weighted sequences for an index i, there may be more than one choices for left-character. For that cases we introduce a new class called $'lc'_*$ that keeps all the indexes with more than one left-character. This new class guarantees the left maximality, as for any left-character of one index x in that class there is at least one index y with a different one. Thus, a leaf-list is a set of N vectors, one for each of the weighted sequences, where each vector contains $\sigma + 1$ lists, one for each of the $\sigma + 1$ choices for left-character (Fig. 2).

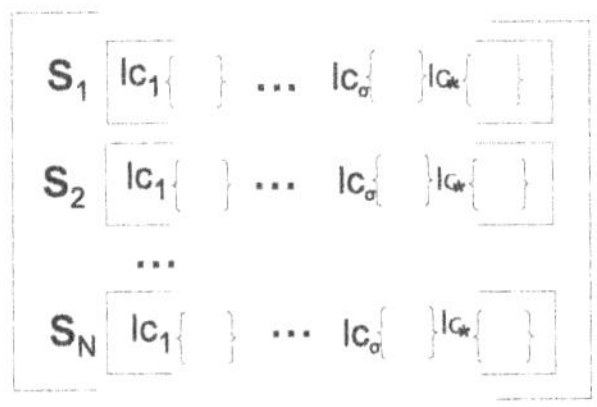

Fig. 2. The leaf-lists where the indexes are organized

When the construction of the $gWST(S)$ is completed, a bottom-up process is initiated. Let L_l and L_r be the leaf-lists of the left and right descendant of a node v. The candidate maximal pairs, defined by the path label of node u, for each of the sequences s_i can be found by combining $\forall j$ the indexes of list $L_l.s_i.lc_j$ (the list for symbol c_j in weighted sequence s_i) with the lists $L_r.s_i.lc_l, \forall l \neq j$. If we do not allow overlaps on the components of a pair we don't have to combine all the indexes of lists $L_l.s_i.lc_j$ and $L_r.s_i.lc_l$ but we want $\forall x \in L_l.s_i.lc_j$ to find all $y \in L_r.s_i.lc_l$ for which it holds that $x - (y + |path\_label(u)|) \geq 0$ or $y - (x + |path\_label(u)|) \geq 0$. In order to achieve that efficiently the lists are organized as AVL trees, and merging virtually the one list with the other. More specifically, we find the position where the items of the one list increased and decreased by $|path\_length(u)|$ will be placed if we really merge the two lists, and then by going rightwards and leftwards respectively. If we choose the smaller list and virtually merge it with the other, the following three lemmas guarantee that in total $O(Nn\log(Nn) + \alpha)$ time is needed.

Lemma 1. *The sum over all nodes u of an arbitrary tree of size n of terms that that are* $O(n_1)$*, where* $n_1 \leq n_2$ *are the weights (number of leaves)of the subtrees rooted at the two children of u, is* $O(n \log n)$

Proof. See [7].

Lemma 2. *Two AVL trees of size* n_1 *and* n_2*, where* $n_1 \leq n_2$*, can be merged in time* $O(\log \binom{n_1+n_2}{n_1})$

Proof. See [2].

Lemma 3. *Let T be an arbitrary binary tree with n leaves. The sum over all internal nodes* $u \in T$ *of terms* $\binom{n_1+n_2}{n_1}$*, where* $n_1 \leq n_2$ *are the weights of the subtrees rooted at the two children of u, is* $O(n \log n)$.

Proof. See [1].

Before we retrieve the output for this step, we have to check if at least q of the weighted sequences s_i report at least one pair. This can be accomplished during the virtual merging of the lists. We apply the virtual merge to all possible combination of lists but we spend two more operation for each of the items of the smaller list to check if there is at least one candidate pair for the corresponding sequence. If at least q sequences have at least one maximal pair we retrieve the rest of the answer. This additional step adds n_1 (the smaller half) more operations so according to Lemma 1 the overall cost is $O(n \log n)$. After the reporting step, the leaflists L_l and L_r are merged, merging each list $L_l.s_i.lc_j$ with the $L_r.s_i.lc_j$ $\forall i, j$. This step according to Lemma 3 costs $O(Nn\log(Nn))$ in total. The result is summarized in the following theorem.

Theorem 1. *Given a set of N weighted sequences* $S = s_1, s_2, \cdots s_n$*, a small integer* $k \geq 0$ *and a quorum* $q \leq N$*, we can find in time* $O(Nn\log(Nn) + \alpha)$ *all maximal pairs m such that each component of m appears with probability* $\geq \frac{1}{k}$ *and with no overlaps in at least q sequences of the set S, where* α *is the size of the size of the answer.*

When the overlap constraint is removed the query becomes more time consuming. The output has to be filtered and checked if the the overlap of the components of a pair is the same substring. This is the crucial step because at each position of overlap there must be the same choices of symbols from the two components. This can be accomplished by pre-processing of the $gWST(S)$ to answer nearest ancestor queries in constant time [13]. When a candidate pair of indexes x, y has an overlap ($y \leq x + |path\_label(u)|$) then the $nca(x, y)$ query upon the $gWST(S)$ dictates the longest common extension of these two sub-factors from positions x, y. If the answer of this query is greater than the positions of the overlap it means that the portion of the overlap is the same sub-string in the two factor. In this case the time complexity becomes $O((Nn)^2)$.

In the second version of the problem one pair has to come along with approximately the same gap, that is upper bounded by a constant value b, in at least q weighted sequences. We can extend the previous method in order to solve this variation of the problem. At each internal node u during the reporting step we apply a virtual merge and for each index from the smaller list we retrieve as described above at most $2b$ indexes for candidate pairs. The indexes that overlap with the former index are validated with nca queries and some are rejected. To check if a maximal pair with approximately the same gap occurs in at least q weighted sequences we apply the following bucketing scheme. We have b buckets, each for one of the permitted values of the gap. Each candidate pair is placed to one bucket according to the gap. At the end of the reporting step we scan all the buckets and we report the ones that have size at least q. The buckets can be implemented as linear lists and this checking can be done in constant time by storing the size of the lists. Then, the reporting step is invoked which is the same as in the case of unrestricted gaps. The running time of this method is determined by the actual and virtual merging step that as before is $O(n \log n)$ as well as a constant number of operations in every internal node. The following theorem summarizes the result:

Theorem 2. *Given a set of N weighted sequences $S = s_1, s_2, \cdots s_n$, a small integer $k \geq 0$ and a quorum $q \leq N$, we can find in time $O(Nn \log(Nn) + \alpha)$ all maximal pairs m such that each component of m appears with probability $\geq \frac{1}{k}$ and the gap is bounded by the constant b, in at least q sequences of the set S, where α is the size of the output.*

4 Extracting Simple Motifs

In this section we present algorithms for the repeated and common motifs problems on weighted sequences. Our algorithms are based on the algorithms of Sagot [12] with the exception that for the repeated motifs problem we add the restriction that the models must be non-overlapping while for the common motifs problem we slightly improve the time and space complexity.

4.1 The Repeated Motifs Problem

We are given a weighted sequence s and four integers $0 < k \leq c$, $e \geq 0$, $l \geq 2$ and $q \geq 2$, for some constant c, and we want to find all models m of length l with probability of occurrence $\geq \frac{1}{k}$ such that m is present at least q times in s and the Hamming distance between all occurrences of m is $\leq e$. The occurrences must not overlap.

First the weighted suffix tree of s is constructed given that the minimum probability of occurrence is $\frac{1}{k}$. This construction is accomplished in linear time and space. Then, we spell all models of length l on the tree. We do this in the same way as Sagot [12], so we are not going to elaborate on this procedure. The idea is that each time we extend a model m' of length $< l$ by one character either with a match or with a mismatch if the total number of errors in m' is $\leq e$. This procedure continues until we reach length l or the number of errors becomes larger than e.

The main problem to tackle is the non-overlapping constraint. We accomplish this by filtering the output of the algorithm on the WST. Since we only consider Hamming distance and no insertions or deletions are allowed, for the specific problem only nodes with path labels of length l will be considered.

Assume that the nodes with path label of length l constitute a set $L = v_1, v_2, \ldots, v_{|L|}$. For each $v \in L$, the leaves of its subtree are put in a sorted list v^l. These lists are implemented as van Emde Boad trees [14]. Since the numbers sorted are in the range $[1, n]$, we can sort them in linear time. As a result, the time complexity for this step will be $\sum_{i=1}^{|L|} O(|v_i^l|)$. Since all lists are disjoint, this sum is bounded by $O(n)$.

Assume that $L' = v_{i_1}, v_{i_2}, \ldots, v_{i_j} \in L$ are the nodes of path label with length l that constitute a candidate model m. First we check whether the sum of their leaves is larger than q. If it is not, then the model is not valid since the quorum constraint is not satisfied. If there are at least q leaves, then we have to check whether the non-overlapping constraint is also satisfied.

The naive solution would be to merge all lists $v_{i_1}^l, v_{i_2}^l, \ldots, v_{i_j}^l$ and perform q queries. In this case, the time complexity for q queries would be $O(q \log\log n)$ (the $\log\log n$ factor is by the van Emde Boas trees) but the merge step requires $O(n)$ time, which is very inefficient. We do this as follows:

We check among all nodes in L' to find the one with the minimum position of occurrence. This can be easily implemented in $O(|L'|)$ time, since the lists for each node are sorted and we check only the first element. Assume that this element is position x_1 on the string s. Then, among all lists we check to find the successor of value $x_2 = x_1 + |m| + 1$ and we keep doing this until the quorum constraint is satisfied (the final query will be of the form $\geq x_{q-1} + |m| + 1$). This solution has $O(q|L| \log\log |n|)$ time complexity which leads to an $O(nV^2(e, l) q \log\log n)$ time solution for the repeated motifs problem, for length l using linear space.

This problem, can be seen as a static data structure problem, which we call the *multiset dictionary problem.*

Definition 4. *Given a superset* $S = \{S_1, S_2, \ldots, S_x\}$*, of sets* $S_i \subseteq \{1, 2, \ldots, n\}$*, we want to answer* q *successor queries on the subset* $S' = \{S_{i_1}, S_{i_2}, \ldots, S_{i_y}\} \in S$*, where* $n = \sum_{i=1}^{x} |S_i|$.

This problem can be seen as a generalization of the iterative search problem [3]. In this problem, we are given a set of N catalogs and we are asked to answer N queries, one on each catalog. The straightforward solution is to search in each catalog, which means that the time complexity will be $O(N \log n)$, if each catalog has size n. If we apply the fractional cascading technique [3], then the time complexity will become $O(N + \log n)$. Unfortunately, we cannot do the same in the multiset dictionary problem, since we do not know in advance which catalogs we are going to use, while at the same time the queries are not confined to a single catalog but to their union. This problem is an interesting data structure problem and it would be nice to see solutions with better complexity than the rather trivial $O(qx \log \log n)$.

4.2 A Note on the Common Motifs Problem

We are given a set of N weighted sequences $S = s_i$ $(1 \leq i \leq N)$ and four integers $0 < k \leq c$, $e \geq 0$, $l \geq 2$ and $q \geq 2$, for some constant c, and we want to find all models m of length l with probability of occurrence larger than $\frac{1}{k}$ such that m is present at least in q strings in S and the Hamming distance between all occurrences of m is $\leq e$.

First, the generalized weighted suffix tree of S is constructed given that the minimum probability of occurrence is $\frac{1}{k}$. This construction is accomplished in linear time and space for a small constant k. Then, we spell all models of length l on the tree. We do this in the same way as Sagot [12], so we are not going to elaborate on this procedure. The idea is that each time we extend a model m' of length $< l$ by one character either with a match or with a mismatch if the total number of errors in m' is $\leq e$. This procedure continues until we reach length l or the number of errors becomes larger than e or the quorum constraint is violated. We sketched in 2.2 a solution with $O(nN^2V(e,l))$ time complexity using $O(n\frac{N^2}{w})$ space. We sketch an algorithm that reduces a factor N to q.

This additional N factor in the space and time complexity comes from the check of the quorum constraint. Sagot uses a bit vector of length N to do that. However, note that if a node has q different strings then all its ancestors will certainly contain q strings. In addition, we do not care for the exact number of strings in the subtree as far as this number is larger than q. In this way we attach an array of integers of length q to each internal node. If this array gets full, then the quorum constraint is satisfied for all its ancestors and we do not need to keep track of other strings.

We fill these arrays by traversing the suffix tree in a post-order manner. Assume the $|\Sigma|$ at most children of a node v. Assume that their arrays are sorted. If one of the children of v has a full array then v will also have a full array. In the other case, we merge all these arrays without keeping repetitions. This can be easily accomplished in $O(|\Sigma|q)$ time. Since the number of internal nodes will be $O(nN)$ then the pre-processing time is $O(nNq)$ while the space complexity of the suffix tree will be $O(nNq)$ (less than $O(nN^2)$ of [12]). Finally, the time complexity of the algorithm will be $O(nNqV(e,l))$, which is better than [12] since q is at most equal to N.

5 Discussion and Further Work

The algorithms we have presented in this paper solve various instances of the *motif identification problem* in weighted sequences, which is very important in the area of protein sequence analysis.

Our future research is to tackle the *structured motifs identification problem* in weighted sequences. In this paper we described an algorithm to compute the maximal pairs in weighted sequences. We would like to extend this algorithm for the extraction of general structured motifs composed of $p > 2$ parts.

References

1. G. Brodal, R. Lyngso, Ch. Pedersen, J. Stoye. Finding Maximal Pairs with Bounded Gap. *Journal of Discrete Algorithms*, 1:134-149, 2000.
2. M.R. Brown, R.E. Tarjan. A Fast Merging Algorithm. *J. ACM*, 26(2):211-226, 1979.
3. B. Chazelle and L.J. Guibas. Fractional Cascading: I. A data structuring technique. *Algorithmica*, 1:133-162, 1986.
4. D. Gusfield. Algorithms on Strings, Trees, and Sequences: Computer Science and Computational Biology. Cambridge University Press, New York, 1997.
5. C. Iliopoulos, Ch. Makris, I. Panagis, K. Perdikuri, E. Theodoridis, A. Tsakalidis. Computing the Repetitions in a Weighted Sequence using Weighted Suffix Trees. *In Proc. of the European Conference On Computational Biology (ECCB)*, 2003.
6. C. Iliopoulos, Ch. Makris, I. Panagis, K. Perdikuri, E. Theodoridis, A. Tsakalidis. Efficient Algorithms for Handling Molecular Weighted Sequences. *Accepted for presentation in IFIP TCS*, 2004.
7. C. Iliopoulos, C. Makris, S. Sioutas, A. Tsakalidis, K. Tsichlas. Identifying occurrences of maximal pairs in multiple strings. *In Proc. of the 13th Ann. Symp. on Combinatorial Pattern Matching (CPM)*, pp.133-143, 2002.
8. L. Marsan and M.-F. Sagot. Algorithms for extracting structured motifs using a suffix tree with application to promoter and regulatory site consensus identification. *Journal of Computational Biology*, 7:345-360, 2000.
9. E.M. McCreight. A Space-Economical Suffix Tree Construction Algorithm. *Journal of the ACM*, 23:262-272, 1976.
10. E.W. Myers and Celera Genomics Corporation. The whole-genome assembly of drosophila. *Science*, 287:2196–2204, 2000.
11. N. Pisanti, M. Crochemore, R. Grossi and M.-F. Sagot. A basis of tiling motifs for generating repeated patterns and its complexity for higher quorum. *In Proc. of the 28th MFCS*, LNCS vol.2747, pp.622-632, 2003.
12. M.F. Sagot. Spelling approximate repeated or common motifs using a suffix tree.*In Proc. of the 3rd LATIN Symp.*, LNCS vol.1380, pp.111-127, 1998.
13. B. Schieber and U. Vishkin. On Finding lowest common ancestors:simplifications and parallelization. *SIAM Journal on Computing*, 17:1253-62, 1988.
14. P. van Emde Boas. Preserving order in a forest in less than logarithmic time and linear space. *Information Processing Letters*, 6(3):80-82, 1977.

Longest Motifs with a Functionally Equivalent Central Block

Maxime Crochemore[1,2,⋆], Raffaele Giancarlo[3,⋆⋆], and Marie-France Sagot[4,2,⋆⋆⋆]

[1] Institut Gaspard-Monge, University of Marne-la-Vallée
77454 Marne-la-Vallée CEDEX 2, France
maxime.crochemore@univ-mlv.fr

[2] Department of Computer Science, King's College London
London WC2R 2LS, UK

[3] Dipartimento di Matematica ed Applicazioni, Universitá di Palermo
Via Archirafi 34, 90123 Palermo, Italy
raffaele@math.unipa.it

[4] Inria Rhône-Alpes, Laboratoire de Biométrie et Biologie Évolutive
Université Claude Bernard, 69622 Villeurbanne cedex, France
Marie-France.Sagot@inria.fr

Abstract. This paper presents a generalization of the notion of longest repeats with a block of k don't care symbols introduced by [8] (for k fixed) to longest motifs composed of three parts: a first and last that parameterize match (that is, match via some symbol renaming, initially unknown), and a functionally equivalent central block. Such three-part motifs are called *longest block motifs*. Different types of functional equivalence, and thus of matching criteria for the central block are considered, which include as a subcase the one treated in [8] and extend to the case of regular expressions with no Kleene closure or complement operation. We show that a single general algorithmic tool that is a non-trivial extension of the ideas introduced in [8] can handle all the various kinds of longest block motifs defined in this paper. The algorithm complexity is, in all cases, in $O(n \log n)$.

1 Introduction

Crochemore *et al.* [8] have recently introduced and studied the notion of longest repeats with a block of k don't care symbols, where k is fixed. These are words

⋆ Partially supported by CNRS, France, the French Ministry of Research through ACI NIM, and by Wellcome Foundation and NATO Grants.

⋆⋆ Partially supported by Italian MIUR grants PRIN "Metodi Combinatori ed Algoritmici per la Scoperta di Patterns in Biosequenze" and FIRB "Bioinformatica per la Genomica e La Proteomica". Additional support provided by CNRS, France, by means of a Visiting Fellowship to Institut Gaspard-Monge and by the French Ministritry of Research through ACI NIM.

⋆⋆⋆ Partially supported by French Ministry of Research Programs BioInformatique Inter EPST and ACI NIM and by Wellcome Foundation, Royal Society and Nato Grants.

A. Apostolico and M. Melucci (Eds.): SPIRE 2004, LNCS 3246, pp. 298–309, 2004.

of the form $V \diamond^k W$ that appear repeated in a string X, where $\diamond^k$ is a region of length k with an arbitrary content. Their work has some relation with previous work on repeats with bounded gaps [5, 12]. In general, the term *motif* [9] is used in biology to describe similar functional components that several biological sequences may have in common. It can also be used to describe any collection of similar words of a longer sequence. In nature, many motifs are *composite*, *i.e.*, they are composed of conserved parts separated by random regions of variable lengths. By now, the literature on motif discovery is very rich [4], although a completely satisfactory algorithmic solution has not been reached yet.

Even richer (see [15–17]) is the literature on the characterization and detection of regularities in strings, where the object of study ranges from identification of periodic parts to identification of parts that simply appear more than once. Baker [2, 3] has contributed to the notion of parameterized strings and has given several algorithms that find maximal repeated words in a string that p-match, *i.e.*, that are identical up to a renaming (initially unknown) of the symbols. Parameterized strings are a successful tool for the identification of duplicated parts of code in large software systems. These are pieces of code that are identical, except for a consistent renaming of variables. Motivated by practical as well as theoretical considerations, Amir *et al.* [1] have investigated the notion of function matching that incorporates parameterized strings as a special case. Such investigations of words that are "similar" according to a well defined correspondence hint at the existence of meaningful regularities in strings, such as motifs, that may not be captured by standard notions of equality.

In this paper, we make a first step in studying a new notion of motifs, where equality of strings is replaced by more general "equivalence" rules. We consider the simplest of such motifs, *i.e.*, motifs of the form $V \diamond^k W$, with k fixed, which we refer to as *block motifs*. One important point in this study is that the notation $\diamond^k$, which usually indicates a don't care block of length k, assumes in the case of the present paper a new meaning. Indeed, $\diamond^k$ is now a place holder stating that, for two strings described by the motif, the portion of each string going from position $|V| + 1$ to $|V| + k - 1$, referred to as the *central block*, must match according to a specified set of rules. To illustrate this notion, consider $ab \diamond^2 ab$ and the rule stating that any two strings described by the motif must have their central block identical, up to a renaming of symbols. For instance, $abxyab$ and $ababab$ are both described by $ab \diamond^2 ab$ and the given rule, since there is a one-to-one correspondence between $\{x, y\}$ and $\{a, b\}$. Notions associated with the example and the intuition just given are formalized in Section 3, where the central block $\diamond^k$ is specified by a set of matching criteria, all related to parameterized strings and function matching. Moreover, our approach can be extended to the case where such central block is a fixed regular expression, containing no Kleene closure or complement operation. Our main contribution for this part is a formal treatment of this extended type of motifs, resulting in conditions under which their definition is sound.

At the algorithmic level, our main contribution is to provide a general algorithm that extracts all longest block motifs, occurring in a string of length n, in $O(n \log n)$ time. Indeed, for each of the matching criteria for the central part presented in Section 3 the general algorithm specializes to find that type of motif by simply defining a new lexicographic order relation on strings. We also show that the techniques in [8], in conjunction with some additional ideas presented here, can be naturally extended to yield a general algorithmic tool to discover even subtler repeated patterns in a string.

Due to space limitations, proofs will either be omitted or simply outlined. Moreover, we shall discuss only some of the block motifs that can be identified by our algorithm.

2 Preliminaries

2.1 Parameterized Strings

We start by recalling some basic definitions from the work by Brenda Baker on parameterized strings [2, 3]. Let Σ and Π be two alphabets, referred to as *constant* and *parameter*, respectively. A *p-string* X is a string over the union of these two alphabets. A p-string is therefore just like any string, except that some symbols are parameters. In what follows, for illustrative purposes, let $\Sigma = \{a, b\}$ and $\Pi = \{u, v, x, y\}$. Baker gave a definition of matching for p-strings, which reduces to the following:

Definition 1. *Two p-strings X and Y of equal length p-match if and only if there exists a bijective morphism $G : \Sigma \cup \Pi \rightarrow \Sigma \cup \Pi$ such that $G(\alpha) = \alpha$ for $\alpha \in \Sigma$ and $Y_i = G(X_i)$, $\forall i \in [1..|X|]$.*

For instance, $X = abuvabuvu$ and $Y = abxyabxyx$ p-match, with G such that $G(u) = x$ and $G(v) = y$.

For ease of reference, let $\Sigma_1 = \Sigma \cup \Pi$. From now on, we refer to p-strings simply as strings over the alphabet Σ_1 and, except otherwise stated, we assume that the notion of match coincides with that of p-match. We refer to the usual notion of match for strings as exact match. In that case, Σ_1 is treated as a set of constants. Moreover, we refer to bijective morphims over Σ_1 as *renaming functions*. We also use the term prefix, suffix and word in the usual way, *i.e.*, the i-th suffix of X is $x_i x_{i+1} \cdots x_n$, where n is the length of the string. In what follows, let $\overline{X}$ denote its reverse, *i.e.*, $x_n \cdots x_1$.

We need to recall the definition of parameterized suffix tree, denoted by p-suffix tree, also due to Baker [2, 3]. Its definition is based, among other things, on a transformation of suffixes and prefixes of a string such that, when they match, they can share a path in a lexicographic tree. Indeed, consider the string $Y = uuuvvv$, made only of the parameters u and v. Notice that uuu and vvv p-match, and therefore they should share a path when the suffixes of the string are "stored" in a (compacted or not) lexicographic tree. That would not be possible if the lexicographic tree were over the alphabet Σ_1. We now briefly discuss the ideas behind this transformation. Consider a new alphabet $\Sigma_2 = \Sigma \bigcup N$, where N is the set of nonnegative integers.

Let *prev* be a *transformation function* on strings operating as follows on a string X. For each parameter, its first occurrence in X is replaced by 0, and each successive occurrence is represented by its distance, along the string, to the previous occurrence. Constants are left unchanged. We denote by $prev(X)$ the *prev representation* of X over the alphabet Σ_2.

The *prev* function basically substitutes parameters with integers, leaving the constants unchanged, *i.e.*, it transforms strings over Σ_1 into strings over Σ_2. For example, $prev(abxyxzzaaya) = ab0020aa5a$.

The notion of match on strings corresponds to equality in their *prev* representation [2, 3]:

Lemma 2. *Two strings X and Y p-match if and only if $prev(X) = prev(Y)$. Moreover, these two strings are a match if and only if $\overline{X}$ and $\overline{Y}$ are.*

Notice that the *prev* representation of two strings tells us nothing about which words, in each string, are a p-match. For instance, consider *abxyxzzaaya* and *zzzztzwaata*. Words *xyxzzaaya* and *ztzwaata* match, but that cannot be directly inferred from the *prev* representation of the two full strings.

Let X be a string that ends with a unique endmarker symbol. A *parameterized suffix tree* for X (p-suffix tree for short) is a compacted lexicographic tree storing the *prev* representation of all suffixes of X.

The above definition is sound in the sense that all factors of X are represented in the p-suffix tree (that follows from the fact that each such word is prefix of some suffix). Even more importantly, matching factors share a path in the tree. Indeed, consider two factors that match. Assume that they are of length m. Certainly they are prefixes of two suffixes of X. When represented via the *prev* function, these two suffixes must have equal prefixes of length at least m (by Fact 2). Therefore, the two words must share a path in the p-suffix tree. Consider again $Y = uuuvvv$. Notice that $prev(uuuvvv) = 012012$ and that $prev(vvv) = 012$, so *uuu* and *vvv* can share a path in the p-suffix tree.

For later use, we also need to define a lexicographic order relation on the prev representation of strings. It reduces to the usual definition when the string has no parameters. Consider the alphabet Σ_2 and let $\leq_2$ denote the standard lexicographic order relation for strings over a fixed alphabet: the subscript indicates to which alphabet the relation refers to.

Definition 3. *Let X and Y be two strings. We say that X is lexicographically smaller than Y if and only if $prev(X) \leq_2 prev(Y)$. We indicate such a relation via $\leq_2$.*

2.2 Matching via Functions

In what follows, we need another type of relation that, for now, we define as a *Table*. A *Table* T has domain Σ_1 and ranges over the power set of Σ_1.

Definition 4. *Given two tables T and T' and two strings X and Y of length n, we say that X table matches Y via the two tables T and T', or, for short, that X and Y t-match, if and only if $y_i \in T(x_i)$ and $x_i \in T'(y_i)$, for all $1 \leq i \leq n$.*

For instance, let $T(a) = \{a, u\}$, $T(b) = \{x, v, y\}$, $T'(a) = T'(u) = \{a\}$ and $T'(x) = T'(v) = T'(y) = \{b\}$. Then $X = aaabbb$ and $Y = auaxvy$ t-match.

A first difference between table and parameterized matches is that in the first case, all symbols in Σ_1 are treated as parameters and the correspondence is fixed once and for all.

A more substantial difference between table and parameterized matches is that tables may not be functions (as in the example above). For arbitrary tables, t-matching is also in general not an equivalence relation. Indeed, although symmetry is implied by the definition, neither reflexivity nor transitivity are. Notice also that t-matching incorporates the notion of match with don't care. In this latter case, both tables assign to each symbol the don't care symbol. We call this table the *don't care* table.

3 Functions and Block Motifs

We now investigate the notion of block motif, which was termed repeat with a block of don't cares in [8], in conjunction with that of parameterized and table match.

Let $\mathcal{T}$ be a family of tables and k an integer, with $0 \leq k \leq n$, where n is the length of a string X. Consider also a family of renaming functions.

Definition 5. *Let Y be a factor of X. Y is a general k-repeat if and only if the following conditions hold: (a) Y can be written as VQW, V and W both non-empty and $|Q| = k$; (b) there exists another word Z of X, two renaming functions F and G and two tables in $\mathcal{T}$, such that $Z = F(V)Q'G(W)$ and Q and Q' t-match, via the two tables.*

Definition 6. *Let $R(k, i, j)$ be the following binary relation on strings of length m, with $1 < i \leq j + 1$, $j < m$ and $k = j - i + 1$: $Z\ R(k, i, j)\ Y$ if and only if $(z_1 z_2 \cdots z_{i-1})$, $(z_{j+1} \cdots z_m)$ and $(y_1 y_2 \cdots y_{i-1})$, $(y_{j+1} \cdots y_m)$ match, respectively, while $(z_i \cdots z_j)$ and $(y_i \cdots y_j)$ t-match via two not necessarily distinct tables in $\mathcal{T}$.*

We now give a formal definition of motif. Intuitively, it is a representative string that describes multiple occurrences of "equivalent" strings.

Definition 7. *Given a string X, consider a factor Y of X, of length m, and assume that it is a general k-repeat. Let i and j be as in Definition 6 and consider all factors Z of X such that $Y\ R(k, i, j)\ Z$. Assume that $R(k, i, j)$ is an equivalence relation. Then, for each class with at least two elements, a block motif is any arbitrarily chosen word in that class, say Y. As for standard strings, the block motif can be written as $y_1 y_2 \cdots y_{i-1} \diamond^k y_{j+1} \cdots y_m$, once it is understood that $\diamond^k$ is a place holder specifying a central part of the motif and that the matching criterion for that part is given by the family of tables.*

For instance, restrict the family of tables to be the don't care table only. Let $Z = abvvva$ and $Y = abxxya$; then we have $Z\ R(2, 3, 4)\ Y$ with the identity function for the prefix ab and $G(v) = y$ and $G(a) = a$ for the suffix of length

2. Moreover, consider $X = YZ$. Then, $ab \diamond^2 va$ is a block motif. Also $ab \diamond^2 ya$ is a block motif, but it is equivalent to the other one, given the choices made about the family of tables and the fact that we are using a notion of match via renaming.

We now investigate the types of table families that allow us to properly define block motifs. As it should be clear from the example discussed earlier, the notion of block motifs, as defined in [8], is a special case of the ones defined here. It is also clear that the family of all tables yields the same notion of block motif as the one with the don't care table only. However, it can be shown that exclusion of the don't care table is not enough to obtain a proper definition of block motifs. Fortunately, there are easily checkable sufficient conditions ensuring that the family of tables guarantees R to be an equivalence relation, as we outline next.

Definition 8. *Consider two tables T and T'. Let their composition, denoted by $\circ$, be defined by $T \circ T'(a) = \bigcup_{c \in T'(a)} T(c)$, for each symbol a in the alphabet. Tha family $\mathcal{T}$ is closed under composition if and only if, for any two tables in the family, their composition is a table in the family.*

Definition 9. *A table T contains a table T' if and only if $T'(a) \subseteq T(a)$, for each symbol a in the alphabet.*

Lemma 10. *Assume that $\mathcal{T}$ is closed under composition and that there exists a table in $\mathcal{T}$ containing the identity table. Then R is an equivalence relation.*

We now consider some interesting special classes of table functions, in particular four of them, for which we can define block motifs. Let $\mathcal{T}_\diamond$ consist only of the don't care table. Let $\mathcal{T}_r$ and $\mathcal{T}_m$ consist of renaming functions and many-to-one functions, respectively. In order to define the fourth family, we need some remarks.

The use of tables for the middle part of a block motif allows us to specify simple substitution rules a bit more relaxed than renaming functions. We discuss one of them. Let us partition the alphabet into classes and let $\mathcal{P}$ denote the corresponding partition. We then define a *partition table* $\mathcal{T}_\mathcal{P}$ that assigns to each symbol the class it belongs to. For instance, fix two characters in the alphabet, say a and b. Consider the table, denoted for short $T_{a,b}$, that assigns $\{a, b\}$ to both a and b and the symbol itself to the remaining characters. In a sense, $\mathcal{T}_\mathcal{P}$ formalizes the notion of groups of characters being interchangeable, or equivalent. Such situations arise in practice (see for instance [6, 11, 13, 14, 19, 21, 22]), in particular in the study of protein folding.

Let the fourth family of tables consist of only $\mathcal{T}_\mathcal{P}$, for some given partition $\mathcal{P}$ of the alphabet Σ_1.

Lemma 11. *Pick any one of $\mathcal{T}_\diamond, \mathcal{T}_r, \mathcal{T}_m$ or $\mathcal{T}_\mathcal{P}$ and consider the relation R in Definition 6 for the chosen family. R is an equivalence relation. In particular, when the chosen family is $\mathcal{T}_m$, R is the same relation as that for $\mathcal{T}_r$. Therefore, for all those tables one can properly define block motifs.*

Let the family of tables be one-to-one functions. Consider $X = YZ$, where $Y = abxxya$ and $Z = abvvva$. Then, $ab \diamond^2 va$ and $ab \diamond^2 ya$ are block motifs representing the same class, the one consisting of Y and Z. We can pick any one of the two, since they are equivalent. Notice that the rule for the central part states that the corresponding region for two strings described by the motifs must be each a renaming of the other.

Let the family of tables be $T_{a,b}$, defined earlier. Let $Z = cdccdacdc$ and $Y = cdccdbcdc$. Let $X = ZY$. Then $cdc \diamond^3 cdc$ is a block motif, representing both Y and Z. Again, the rule for the central part states that the corresponding region for two strings described by the motif must be identical, except that a and b can be treated as the same character.

4 Longest Block Motifs with a Fixed Partition Table

We now give an algorithm that finds all longest block motifs in a string, when we use a partition table, known and fixed once and for all. The algorithm is a non-trivial generalization of the one introduced in [8]. In fact, we show that the main techniques used there, and that we nickname as *the two-tree trick*, represent a powerful tool to extract longest block motifs in various settings, when used in conjunction with the algorithmic ideas presented in this section.

Indeed, a verbatim application of the two-tree trick would work on the p-suffix trees for the string and its reverse. Unfortunately, that turns out to be not enough in our setting. We need to construct a tree somewhat different from a p-suffix tree, which we refer to as a p-suffix tree on a mixed alphabet. Using this latter tree, the techniques in [8] can be extended. Moreover, due to the generality of the algorithm constructing this novel version of the p-suffix tree, all the techniques we discuss in this section extend to the other three types of block motifs defined in section 3, as it is briefly outlined in section 5.

For each class in $\mathcal{P}$, select a representative. The representatives give a reduced alphabet Σ_3. For any string Y, let $\hat{Y}$ be its corresponding string on the new alphabet, obtained by replacing each symbol in Y with its representative. In what follows, for our examples, we choose $T_{a,b}$, with a as representative. Consider a string X and assume that it has block motif $V \diamond^k W$, with respect to table $\mathcal{T}_{\mathcal{P}}$. We recall that $V \diamond^k W$ is a shorthand notation for the fact that strings in the class (a) t-match in the positions corresponding to the central part and, (b) they (parameterize) match in the positions corresponding to V and W. We are interested in finding all longest block motifs.

Consider a lexicographic tree T, storing a set of strings. Let Y be a string. The locus u of Y in T, if it exists, is the node such that Y matches the string corresponding to the path from the root of T to u. Notice that when T is a p-suffix tree, then $prev(Y)$ must be the string on the path from the root to u. For standard strings, the definition of locus reduces to the usual one. With those differences in mind, one can also define in the usual way the notion of contracted and extended locus of a string. Moreover, given a node u, let $d(u)$ be the length of the string of which u is locus.

4.1 A p-Suffix Tree on a Mixed Alphabet

Definition 12. *The modified prev representation of a string Y, $mprev(Y)$, is defined as follows. If $|Y| \leq k$, then it is $\hat{Y}$. Else, it is $\hat{W} prev(Z)$, where $Y = WZ$ and $|W| = k$.*

For instance, let $Y = abauuxx$, and $k = 3$. Then, its modified *prev* representation is $mprev(Y) = aaa0101$.

Definition 13. *Let X be a string with a unique endmarker. Let T'_X be a lexicographic tree storing each suffix of X in lexicographic order, via its mprev representation. That is, T'_X is like a p-suffix tree, but the initial part of each suffix is represented on the reduced alphabet.*

For instance, let $X = abbabbb$ and $k = 2$, the first suffix of X is stored as $aababbb$.

Notice that T'_X has $O(n)$ nodes, since it has n leaves and each node has outdegree at least two. We anticipate that we only need to build and use the topology of T'_X, since we do not use it for pattern matching and indexing, as it is costumary for those data structures.

We now show how to build T'_X in $O(n \log n)$ time. Let `BuildTree` be a procedure that takes as input the n suffixes of X and returns as output T'_X. The only primitive that the procedure needs to use is the check, in constant time, for the lexicographic order of two suffixes, according to a new order relation that we define. The check should also return the longest prefix the two suffixes have in common, and which suffix is smaller than the other.

Definition 14. *Let Y and Z be two strings. Let $\leq_3$ be a lexicographic order relation over Σ_3. We define a new order relation $Y \leq_m Z$ as follows. When $|Y| \leq k$, it must be $\hat{Y} \leq_3 \hat{U}$, where U is a prefix of Z and $|U| = |Y|$. Assume that $|Y| > k$, and let $Z = US$ and $Y = RP$, with $|R| = |U| = k$. Then, it must be $\hat{R} <_3 \hat{U}$ or $\hat{R} = \hat{U}$ but $prev(P) \leq_2 prev(S)$. Abusing notation, we can write that $mprev(Y) \leq_m mprev(Z)$, when $Y \leq_m Z$.*

Let T be a tree and consider two nodes u and v. Let $LCA(u, v)$ denote the lowest common ancestor of u and v. Given the suffix tree $T_{\hat{X}}$ [18] and the p-suffix tree T_X, assume that they have been processed to answer LCA queries in constant time [10, 20]. Then, it is easy to check, in constant time, the $\leq_m$ order of two suffixes of X, via two LCA queries in those trees. Moreover, that also gives us the length of the matching prefix. The details are omitted. We refer to such an operation as `compare(i, j)`, where i and j are the suffix positions. It returns which one is smaller and the length of their common prefix.

Now, `BuildTree` works as follows. It simply builds the tree, without any labelling of the edges, as it is usual in lexicographic trees.

ALGORITHM BuildTree

1. Using compare and the $\leq_m$ relation, sort the suffixes of X with, say, Heapsort [7].
2. Process the sorted list $i_1, \cdots, i_n$ of suffixes in increasing order as follows:
   2.1 When the first suffix is processed, create a root and a leaf, push them in a stack in the order they are created. Label the leaf with i_1.
   2.2 Assume that we have processed the list up to i_g and that we are now processing i_{g+1}. Assume that on the stack we have the path from the root to leaf labeled i_g in the tree built so far, from bottom to top. Let it be $u_1, u_2, \cdots, u_s$.
      2.2.1 Using compare and the $\leq_m$ relation, find the longest prefix that i_g and i_{g+1} have in common. Let Z denote that prefix and d be its length.
      2.2.2 Pop elements from the stack until one finds two such that $d(u_i) \leq d < d(u_{i+1})$. Pop u_{i+1} from the stack. If $d(u_i) = d$, then u_i is the locus of Z in the tree built so far. Else, u_i and u_{i+1} are its contracted and extended locus, respectively. If u_i is the locus of Z, add a new leaf labeled i_{g+1} as offspring of u_i and push it on the stack. Else, create a new internal node u, as locus of Z, add it as offspring of u_i and make u_{i+1} an offspring of u. Moreover, add a new leaf labeled i_{g+1} as offspring of u and push the new created nodes on the stack, in the order in which they were created. We now have on the stack the path from the root to the leaf labeled i_{g+1}.

Lemma 15. *Tree T'_X can be correctly built in $O(n \log n)$ time.*

4.2 The Algorithm

Consider the trees T'_X and $T_{\overline{X}}$, where the latter one is a p-suffix tree. For each leaf labeled i in $T_{\overline{X}}$, change its label to be $n+2-i$, so that whenever the left part of a block motif starts at i in $\overline{X}$, we have the position in X where the right part starts, including the central part. We refer to those positions as *twins*. Visit T'_X in preorder. Consider the two leaves $\ell_1 \in T'_X$ and $\ell_2 \in T_{\overline{X}}$, corresponding to a pair of twins. Assign to ℓ_2 the same preorder number as that of ℓ_1. Let $V \diamond^k W$ be a block motif and let i be one of its occurrences in X, *i.e.*, where it starts. In order to simplify our notation, we refer to such an occurrence via the preorder number of the leaf assigned to $i+|V|+1$ in T'_X. From now on, we shall simply be working with those preorder numbers. Indeed, given the tree we are in, we can recover the positions in X or $\overline{X}$ corresponding to the label at a leaf in constant time, by suitably keeping a set of tables. The details are as in [8]. Moreover, we can also recover the position where a block motif occurs, given the block motif and the preorder number assigned to the position. Given a tree T, let $L(v)$ be the list of labels assigned to the leaves in the subtree rooted at v. For the trees we are working with, those would be preorder numbers.

Definition 16. *We say that $V \diamond^k W$ is maximal if and only if extending any word in the class, both to the left and to the right, results in the loss of at least one element in the class. That is, by extending the strings in the class, we can possibly get a new block motif, but its class does not contain that of $V \diamond^k W$.*

For instance, let $X = aabbaxxbxabababyyayabbbuu$. Block motif $ab\diamond^2 xx$ is maximal. Indeed, it represents the class of words $\{abbaxx, ababyy, abbbuu\}$. However, extending any of those words either to the right and to the left results in a smaller class.

Lemma 17. *Consider a string X, its reverse $\overline{X}$, the trees $T_{\overline{X}}$ and T'_X. Assume that $V \diamond^k W$ is maximal. Pick any representative in the class, say VQW. Then $\overline{V}$ and $mprev(QW)$ have a locus u in $T_{\overline{X}}$ and v in T'_X, respectively. Moreover, all the occurrences of $V \diamond^k W$ are in $L(u) \bigcap L(v)$. Conversely, pick two nodes u' and v', in $T_{\overline{X}}$ and T'_X, respectively. Assume that there are at least two labels i and j in $L(u') \bigcap L(v')$ such that $LCA(i,j) = u'$ and $LCA(i,j) = v'$, in $T_{\overline{X}}$ and T'_X, respectively. Assume also that $d(v') > k$. Then, they are occurrences of a maximal block motif.*

We also need the following:

Lemma 18. *Consider an internal node v in $T_{\overline{X}}$ and two of its offsprings, say, v_1 and v_2. Let $j_1, j_2, \cdots, j_m$ be the sorted list of labels assigned to the leaves in the subtree rooted at v_1 and let i be a label assigned to any leaf in v_2. Let g be the first index such that $j_g \le i$. Similarly, let c be the first index such that $i \le j_c$. The maximal block motif of maximum length that i forms with $j_1, j_2, \cdots, j_m$ is either with j_g, if it exists, or with j_c, if it exists, provided that either $d(LCA(i, j_g)) > k$ or $d(LCA(i, j_c)) > k$ and the LCA is computed on T'_X.*

We now present the algorithm.

`ALGORITHM LM`

1. Build $T_{\overline{X}}$ and T'_X. Visit T'_X in preorder and establish a correspondence between the preorder numbers of the leaves in T'_X and the leaves in $T_{\overline{X}}$. Transform $T_{\overline{X}}$ into a binary suffix tree $\mathcal{B}$ (see [8]);
2. Visit $\mathcal{B}$ bottom up and, at each node, merge the sorted lists of the labels (preorder numbers in T'_X) associated to the leaves in the subtrees rooted at the children. Let these lists be $\mathcal{A}_1$ and $\mathcal{A}_2$ and assume that $|\mathcal{A}_1| \le |\mathcal{A}_2|$. Merge $\mathcal{A}_1$ into $\mathcal{A}_2$. Any time an element i of the first list is inserted in the proper place in the other, *e.g.*, j_g and j_c in Lemma 18 are identified, we only need to check for two possibly new longest maximal block motifs that i can generate. While processing the nodes in the tree, we keep track of the longest maximal block motifs found.

Theorem 19. `ALGORITHM LM` *correctly identifies all longest block motifs in a string X, when the matching rule for the central part is given by a partition table. It can be implemented to run in $O(n \log n)$ time.*

Proof. The proof of correctness comes from Lemma 18. The details of the analysis are as in [8] with the addition that we need to build both $T_{\overline{X}}$ and T'_X, which can be done in $O(n \log n)$ time ([3, 18] and Lemma 15). □

5 Extensions

In this Section we show how to specialize the algorithm in Section 4 when the central part is specified by $\mathcal{T}_\diamond$. All we need to do is to define a lexicographic order relation, analogous to the one in Definition 14. In turn, that will enable us to define a variant of the tree T'_X, which can still be built in $O(n \log n)$ time with `Algorithm BuildTree` and used in `Algorithm LM` to identify block motifs with the don't care symbol. We limit ourselves to define the new tree. An analogous reasoning will yield algorithms dealing with a central part defined by either renaming functions or by regular expressions with no Kleene Closure or Complement operation. The details are omitted. For the new objects we define, we keep the same notation as for their analogous in Section 4.

Let $*$ be a symbol not belonging to the alphabet and not matching any other symbol of the alphabet. Consider Definition 12 and change it as follows:

Definition 20. *The modified prev representation of a string Y, $mprev(Y)$, is defined as follows. If $|Y| = m \leq k$, then it is $*^m$. Else, it is $*^k prev(Z)$, where $Y = WZ$ and $|W| = k$.*

For instance, let $Y = abauuxx$, and $k = 3$. Then, its modified *prev* representation is $mprev(Y) = ***0101$.

We now define another lexicographic tree, still denoted by T'_X. Consider Definition 13 and change it as follows:

Definition 21. *Let X be a string with a unique endmarker. Let T'_X be a lexicographic tree storing each suffix of X, via their mprev representation according to Definition 20. That is, T'_X is like a p-suffix tree, but the initial part of each suffix is represented with $*$'s.*

For instance, let $X = abbabbb$ and $k = 2$, the first suffix of X is stored as $**babbb$.

Finally, consider Definition 14 and change it as follows:

Definition 22. *Let Y and Z be two strings. We define a new order relation $Y \leq_m Z$ as follows. When $|Y| \leq k$, it must be $|Y| \leq |Z|$. Assume that $|Y| > k$, and let $Z = US$ and $Y = RP$, with $|R| = |U| = k$. Then, it must be $prev(P) \leq_2 prev(S)$. With a little abuse of notation, we can write $mprev(Y) \leq_m mprev(Z)$.*

Observe that `Algorithm BuildTree` will work correctly with this new definition of lexicographic order, except that now, in order to compare suffixes, we need only the p-suffix tree $T_{\hat{X}}$. Finally, the results in Section 4.2 hold verbatim:

Theorem 23. `ALGORITHM LM` *correctly identifies all longest block motifs in a string X, when the matching rule for the central part is given by the don't care table. It can be implemented to run in $O(n \log n)$ time.*

References

1. A. Amir, Y. Aumann, R. Cole, M. Lewenstein, and Ely Porat. Function matching: Algorithms, applications, and a lower bound. In *Proc. of ICALP 03, Lecture Notes in Computer Science*, pages 929–942, 2003.
2. B. S. Baker. Parameterized pattern matching: Algorithms and applications. *J. Comput. Syst. Sci.*, 52(1):28–42, February 1996.
3. B. S. Baker. Parameterized duplication in strings: Algorithms and an application to software maintenance. *SIAM J. Computing*, 26(5):1343–1362, October 1997.
4. A. Brazma, I. Jonassen, I. Eidhammer, and D. Gilbert. Approaches to the automatic discovery of patterns in biosequences. *J. of Computational Biology*, 5:277–304, 1997.
5. G.S. Brodal, R.B. Lyngsø, C.N.S. Pederson, and J. Stoye. Finding maximal pairs with bounded gaps. *J. of Discrete Algorithms*, 1(1):1–27, 2000.
6. H.S. Chan and K.A. Dill. Compact polymers. *Macromolecules*, 22:4559–4573, 1989.
7. T.H. Cormen, C.E. Leiserson, R.L. Rivest, and C. Stein. *Introduction to Algorithms – Second Edition.* MIT Press, Cambridge, MA, 1998.
8. Maxime Crochemore, Costas S. Iliopoulos, Manal Mohamed, and Marie-France Sagot. Longest repeated motif with a block of don't cares. In M. Farach-Colton, editor, *Latin American Theoretical INformatics (LATIN)*, number 2976 in LNCS, pages 271–278. Springer-Verlag, 2004.
9. D. Gusfield. *Algorithms on Strings, Trees and Sequences: Computer Science and Computational Biology.* Cambridge University Press, 1997.
10. D. Harel and R.E. Tarjan. Fast algorithms for finding nearest common ancestors. *SIAM J. on Computing*, 13:338–355, 1984.
11. S. Karlin and G. Ghandour. Multiple-alphabet amino acid sequence comparisons of the immunoglobulin kappa-chain constant domain. *Proc. Natl. Acad. Sci. USA*, 82(24):8597–8601, December 1985.
12. R. Kolpakov and G. Kucherov. Finding repeats with fixed gaps. In *Proc. of SPIRE 02,*, pages 162–168, 2002.
13. T. Li, K. Fan, J. Wang, and W. Wang. Reduction of protein sequence complexity by residue grouping. *Protein Eng.*, (5):323–330, 2003.
14. X. Liu, D. Liu, J. Qi, and W.M. Zheng. Simplified amino acid alphabets based on deviation of conditional probability from random background. *Phys. Rev E*, 66:1–9, 2002.
15. M. Lothaire. *Combinatorics on Words.* Cambridge University Press, 1997.
16. M. Lothaire. *Algebraic Combinatorics on Words.* Cambridge University Press, 2002.
17. M. Lothaire. *Applied Combinatorics on Words.* in preparation, 2004. http://igm.univ-mlv.fr/~berstel/Lothaire/index.html.
18. E.M. McCreight. A space economical suffix tree construction algorithm. *J. of ACM*, 23:262–272, 1976.
19. L.R. Murphy, A. Wallqvist, and R.M. Levy. Simplified amino acid alphabets for protein fold recognition and implications for folding. *Protein. Eng.*, 13:149–152, 2000.
20. B. Schieber and U. Vishkin. On finding lowest common ancestors: Simplification and parallelization. *Siam J. on Computing*, 17:1253–1262, 1988.
21. M. Spitzer, G. Fuellen, P. Cullen, and S. Lorkowsk. Viscose: Visualisation and comparison of consensus sequences. *Bioinformatics, to appear*, 2004.
22. J. Wang and W. Wang. A computational approach to simplifying the protein folding alphabet. *Nat. Struct. Biol.*, 11:1033–1038, 1999.

On the Transformation Distance Problem

Behshad Behzadi and Jean-Marc Steyaert

LIX, Ecole Polytechnique, Palaiseau cedex 91128, France
{Behzadi,Steyaert}@lix.polytechnique.fr

Abstract. Evolution acts in several ways on biological sequences: either by mutating an element, or by inserting, deleting or copying a segment of the sequence. Varré et al. [12] defined a transformation distance for the sequences, in which the evolutionary operations are copy, reverse copy and insertion of a segment. They also proposed an algorithm to calculate the transformation distance. This algorithm is $O(n^4)$ in time and $O(n^4)$ in space, where n is the size of the sequences. In this paper, we propose an improved algorithm which costs $O(n^2)$ in time and $O(n)$ in space. Furthermore, we extend the operation set by adding deletions. We present an algorithm which is $O(n^3)$ in time and $O(n)$ in space for this more general model.

1 Introduction

Building models and tools to quantify evolution is an important domain of biology. Evolutionary trees or diagrams are based on statistical methods which exploit comparison methods between genomic sequences. Many comparison models have been proposed according to the type of physico-chemical phenomena that underly the evolutionary process [5]. Different evolutionary operation sets are studied. Mutation, deletion and insertion were the first operations dealt with [7]. Duplication and contraction were then added to the operation set [2, 1]. All these operations were acting on single letters, representing bases, aminoacids or more complex sequences: they are called point transformations. Segment operations are also very important to study. In a number of papers [13, 12, 11], Varré et al. have studied an evolutionary distance based on the amount of segment moves that Nature needed (or is supposed to have needed) to transfer a sequence from one species to the equivalent sequence in another one. Their model is concerned with segments copy with or without reversal and on segment insertion: it is thus a very simple and robust model which can easily be explained from biological mechanisms (similar or simpler models had been previously discussed by Schöniger and Waterman [8] and Morgenstern et al. [6]). They developed this study on DNA sequences, but the basic concepts and algorithms apply as well to other biological sequences like proteins or satellites.

The algorithm they propose to compute the minimal transformation sequence is based on an encoding into a graph formalism, from which one can get the solution by computing shortest paths. This gives an $O(n^4)$ answer both in space

A. Apostolico and M. Melucci (Eds.): SPIRE 2004, LNCS 3246, pp. 310–320, 2004.

and time. In fact it is possible to give a direct solution based on dynamic programming which costs only $O(n^2)$ in time and and $O(n)$ in space[1]. This solution is obviously more efficient for long sequences and makes the problem tractable even for very long sequences.

In the second section we describe the model and the problem description.

In the third section our algorithm for calculating the transformation distance is presented. Our algorithm is a based on dynamic programming algorithm.

In section 4, we introduce the deletions in our model and we give an algorithm to solve the *extended* transformation distance problem in presence of deletions: this algorithm runs in time $O(n^3)$ and space $O(n)$.

In section 5, by using the biological sequences we justify the concept of extended transformation distance problem.

Finally, section 6 is dedicated to conclusion and remarks.

2 Model and Problem Description

The symbols are elements from an alphabet Σ. The set of all finite-length strings formed using symbols from alphabet Σ is denoted by Σ^*. In this paper, we use the letters x, y, z,... for the symbols in Σ and S, T, P, R, ... for strings over Σ^*. The empty string is denoted by ϵ. The length of a string S is denoted by $|S|$. The *concatenation* of a string P and R, denoted PR, has length $|P| + |R|$ and consists of the symbols from P followed by the symbols from R.

We will denote by $S[i]$ the symbol in position i of the string S (the first symbol of a string S is $S[1]$). The substring of S starting at position i and ending at position j is denoted by $S[i..j] = S[i]S[i+1]\dots S[j]$. The *reverse* of a string S is denoted by S^{-1}. Thus, if n is the length of S, $S^{-1}[i..j] = S[(n-j+1)..(n-i+1)]^{-1}$ and $S[i..j]^{-1} = S^{-1}[(n-j+1)..(n-i+1)]$. R is a substring of S if and only if R^{-1} is a substring of S^{-1}. We say that a string P is a *prefix* of a string S, denoted $P \sqsubseteq S$, if $S = PR$ for some string $R \in \Sigma^*$. Similarly, we say that a string P is a *suffix* of a string S, denoted by $P \sqsupseteq S$, if $S = RP$ for some $R \in \Sigma^*$. Note that P is a prefix of S if and only if P^{-1} is a suffix of S^{-1}. For brevity of notation, we denote the k-symbol prefix $P[1..k]$ of a string pattern $P[1..m]$ by P_k. Thus, $P_0 = \epsilon$ and $P_m = P = P[1..m]$. We recall the definition of a *subsequence*: Given a string $S[1..n]$, another string $R[1..k]$ is a *subsequence* of S, denoted by $R \prec S$, if there exists a strictly increasing sequence $< i_1, i_2, \dots, i_k >$ of indices of S such that for all $j = 1, 2, \dots, k$, we have $S[i_j] = R[j]$. For example, if $S = xxyzyyzx$, $R = zzxx$ and $P = xxzz$, then P is a subsequence of S, while R is not a subsequence of S. When a string S is a subsequence of a string T, T is called a *supersequence* of S, denoted by $T \succ S$. In the last example, S is a supersequence of P.

Varré et al. [12, 11] propose a new measure which evaluates segment-based dissimilarity between two strings: the source string S and the target string T. This measure is related to the process of constructing the target string T with

[1] In this paper, n is the maximum size of the sequences.

segment operations[2]. The construction starts with the empty string ϵ and proceeds from left to right by adding segments (concatenation), one segment per operation. The left-to-right generation is not a restriction if the costs of operations are independent of the time (which is the case in this problem). A list of operations is called a *script*. Three types of segment operations are considered: the *copy* adds segments that are contained in the source string S, the *reverse copy* adds the segments that are contained in S in reverse order, and the *insertion* adds segments that are not necessarily contained in S. The measure depends on a parameter that is the *Minimum Factor Length (MFL)*; it is the minimum length of the segments that can be copied or reverse copied.

Depending on the number of common segments between S and T, there exist several scripts for constructing the target T. Among these scripts, some are more likely; in order to identify them, we introduce a cost function for each operation. *InsertCost*($T[i..j]$) is the cost of insertion of substring $T[i..j]$. *CopyCost*($T[i..j]$) is the cost of copying the segment $T[i..j]$ from S if it is contained in S. Finally *RevCopyCost*($T[i..j]$) is the cost of copying substring $T[i..j]$ from S if the reverse of this substring is contained in the source S (which means this string is contained in S^{-1}). The cost of a script is the sum of the costs of its operations. The *minimal scripts* are all scripts of minimum cost and the *transformation distance*[3] *(TD)* is the cost of a minimal script. The problem which we solve in this paper is the computation of the transformation distance. It is clear that it is also possible to get a minimal script.

3 Algorithm

In this section we describe the algorithm to determine the transformation distance between two strings. As the scripts construct the target string T from left to right by adding segments, dynamic programming is an ideal tool for computing the transformation distance. Each added segment is a result of a copy, reverse copy or an insertion. Algorithm 1, determines the transformation distance between S and T by a dynamic programming algorithm (figure 1). Let $C[k]$ be the minimum production cost of $T[1..k]$ using the segments of S. We make use of generic functions *CopyCost*, *RevCopyCost* and *InsertCost* as defined at the end of section 2. In order to fix ideas, one can consider that these costs are proportional to the length of the searched segment (and ∞ if this segment does not occur in S). In fact any sub-additive function would be convenient.

Deciding whether a given substring of T exists in S or not, and finding its position in the case of presence, needs to apply a *string matching* algorithm. The design of string matching part of algorithm 1 is based on KMP (Knutt-Moris-Pratt) string matching algorithm with some changes. We need to recall the definition of *prefix function* π (adapted from the original KMP one), which is computed in **ComputePrefixFunction** (called in line 7). Given a pattern $P[1..m]$, the prefix function for pattern P is the function $\pi : \{1, 2, \ldots, m\} \rightarrow$

[2] In this paper we use segment as an equivalent word for substring.

[3] Although this measure is not a mathematical distance but we will use the term transformation distance which was introduced by Varré et al. [12, 11].

$\{0, 1, \ldots, m-1\}$ such that $\pi[q] = \max\{k : k < q \text{ and } P_k \sqsupset P_q\}$. That is, π_q is the length of the longest prefix of P that is a proper suffix of P_q. We have the following lemma for the prefix functions.

Lemma 1. *The prefix function of P_k is a restriction of prefix function of P to the set $\{1, 2, \ldots, k\}$.*

Proof: The proof is immediate by the definition of the prefix function because $\pi[i]$ for a given i can be obtained only from $P_{i-1} = P[1..(i-1)]$ and $P[i]$. □

Although simple, this lemma is a corner-stone of the algorithm. It shows that, one can search for the presence of the prefixes of a pattern string in the source string, in the same time of searching for the complete pattern, without increasing the complexity of the search. The lines 8-13 of the algorithm determine the existence of the prefixes of pattern P in S^{-1}. While S is scanned from right-to-left (loop line 9), q is the length of longest prefix of P which is a suffix of $S^{-1}[1..n-i+1]$ in line 14. Note that when we are searching for existences of prefixes of P in S^{-1}, in fact we are searching for the existence of suffixes of $T[1..k]$ in S.

The complexity of these lines 8-14 is $O(n)$ in time and space. Computation of π needs $O(n)$ in time and space (line 7). For the proof of the complexity and correctness of lines 6-13, see chapter 34.4 of [3].

Algorithm 1 TransformationDistance(S, T)

```
1.   C[0] ← 0
2.   for k ← 1 to |T| do
3.     C[k] ← ∞
4.     for i ← 1 to k do
5.       C[k] ← min{C[k], C[i − 1] + InsertCost(T[i..k])}
6.     P ← T[1..k]^{-1}
7.     ComputePrefixFunction(P, π)
8.     q ← 0
9.     for i ← |S| downto 1 do
10.        while q > 0 and P[q + 1] ≠ S[i] do
11.          q ← π[q]
12.        if q < |P| and P[q + 1] = S[i] then
13.          q ← q + 1
14.        C[k] ← min{C[k], C[k − q] + CopyCost(T[(k − q + 1)..k])}
15.        repeat lines 8..14 replacing S and CopyCost by S^{-1} and RevCopyCost respectively
16.  return C[n]
```

Fig. 1. Transformation Distance: a dynamic programming solution

Proposition 1 *Algorithm 1 correctly determines the transformation distance of S and T.*

Proof: We prove by induction on k that after the algorithm execution, $C[k]$ contains the minimum production cost of target $T[1..k]$ with the source string S. $C[0]$ is initialized to 0, because the cost of production of ϵ from S is zero.

Now, we suppose that $C[i]$ is determined correctly for all $i < k$ for some positive value of k. Let us consider the calculation of $C[k]$. The last operation in a minimal script which generates $T[1..k]$, creates a suffix of $T[1..k]$. Let this suffix be $T[i..k]$ (See figure 2). As the script is minimal, the script without its last operation is a minimal script for $T[1..(i-1)]$. The minimum cost of the script for $T[1..(i-1)]$ is $C[i-1]$ by induction hypothesis. If $T[i..k]$ exists in S, then q will be equal to $k-i+1$ in some moment during the algorithm execution in line 14 ($|T[i..k]| = k - i + 1$). If $T[i..k]$ exists in S and the last operation of the minimal script is a copy operation, the minimal cost of the script is $C[i-1] + CopyCost(T[i..k])$ (note that $q = k-i+1$ amounts to $i-1 = k-q$ in line 14). Similarly, if the last operation in the minimal script of $T[1..k]$ is a reverse copy operation, the minimal cost of the script is $C[i-1] + RevCopyCost(T[i..k])$ (line 15). Finally, if the last operation in the minimal script of $T[1..k]$ is an insertion, the minimal cost of the script is $C[i-1] + InsertCost(T[i..k])$ (lines 4-5). Thus, $C[n]$ is the minimum cost of production of $T = T[1..n]$ and the algorithm determines correctly the transformation distance of S and T. □

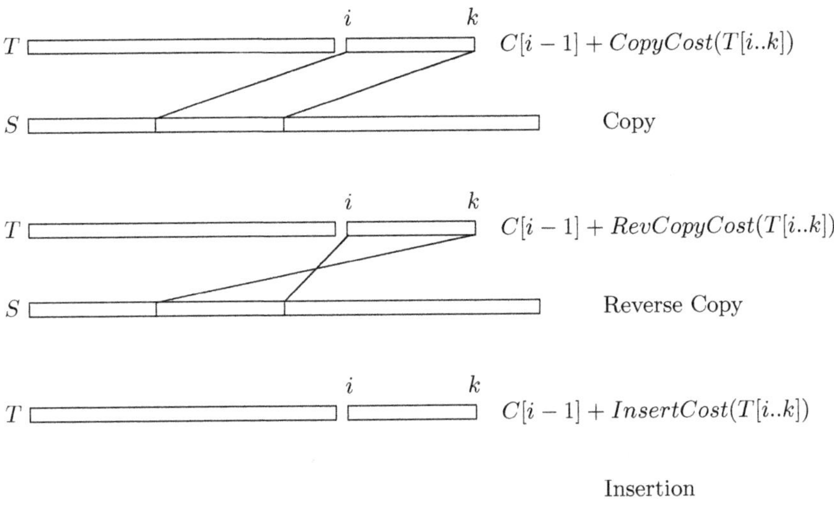

$$C[k] = \min_i\{C[i\text{-}1] + \min\{InsertCost(T[i..k]), CopyCost(T[i..k]), RevCopyCost(T[i..k])\}\}$$

Fig. 2. The three different possibilities for generation of a suffix of $T[1..k]$

Note that when the length of the substring $T[i..k]$ is smaller than MFL, *CopyCost*($T[i..k]$) and *RevCopyCost*($T[i..k]$) are equal to ∞.

The complexity of lines 6-13 is $O(n)$ in time and space. So the whole algorithm for calculation of transformation distance costs $O(n^2)$ in time and $O(n)$ in space.

4 An Additional Operation: Deletions

In this section, we extend the set of evolutionary operations by adding the *deletion* operation. During a deletion operation, one or more symbols of the string which is under evolution are eliminated. This is an important operation from the biological point of view; in the real evolution of biological sequences, in several cases after or during the copy operations some bases (symbols) are eliminated. We define a function *DelCost* for the cost of deletions; $DelCost(x)$ is the cost of deletion of a symbol x. For simplicity, we suppose that the deletion cost of a segment (substring) is equal to the sum of deletion costs of its symbols. Thus we have $DelCost(P[1..k]) = \sum_{i=1}^{k} Delcost(P[i])$.

As before, our objective is to find the minimum cost for a script generating a target string T, with the help of segments of a source string S. As the costs are independent of time and deletion cost of a segment is the sum of deletion costs of its symbols, we can consider that the deletions are applied only in the latest added segment (rightmost one), at any moment during the evolution. It should be clear that in an optimal transformation, deletions are not applied into an inserted substring (a substring which is the result of an insertion operation). Depending on the assigned costs, deletions can be used after the copy or reverse copy operations. We consider a copy operation together with all deletions which are applied to that copied segment as a unit operation. So we have a new operation called *NewCopy* which is a copy operation followed by zero or more deletions on the copied segment. In figure 3 a schema of a NewCopy operation is illustrated. Similarly, *NewRevCopy* is a reverse copy operation followed by zero or more deletions.

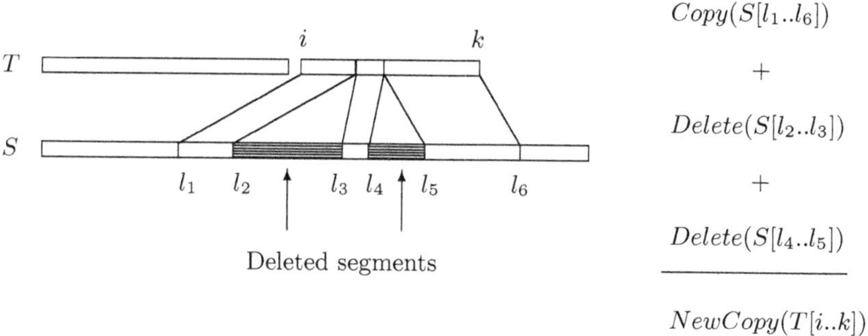

Fig. 3. The illustration of NewCopy operation: A copy operation + zero or more deletions

Solving the extended transformation distance with the deletions, amounts to solving the transformation distance with the following 3 operations: Insertion, NewCopy and NewRevCopy. A substring $T[i..j]$ of the target string can be produced by a unique NewCopy operation if and only if $T[i..j]$ is a subsequence string of source S. Conversely, $T[i..j]$ can be produced by a unique

NewRevCopy operation if and only if $T[i..j]^{-1}$ is a subsequence string of the source S. During the algorithm, we will need to the minimum generation cost by a NewCopy or NewRevCopy operation, for any substring of the target string T. This could be done as a preprocessing part, but for decreasing the space complexity we integrate this part in the core of the algorithm without increasing the total time complexity. For this aim, first we design a function called **ComputeNewCopyCost**(P, S) which fills a table $Cost$, with the following definition: $Cost[i]$ is the minimum cost of generating $P[1..i]$ by a NewCopy operation using a source string S, if $P[1..i]$ is a subsequence of S and ∞ otherwise (see figure 4).

We denote by *optimal supersequence* of $P[1..i]$, any substring of S which is (a) a supersequence of $P[1..i]$ and (b) has the minimum deletion cost among all these supersequences. If $S[l..k]$ is a supersequence for $P[1..i]$, the cost of generating $P[1..i]$ from $S[l..k]$ by a NewCopy operation is $CopyCost(S[l..k]) + DelCost(S[l..k]) - DelCost(P[1..i])$. The difference between the last two terms of this expression is the deletion cost of useless (extra) symbols. A necessary condition for optimality is $S[l] = P[1]$ and $S[k] = P[i]$. Before giving a proof of correctness of Algorithm 2, we state the following lemma.

Lemma 2. *If $S[l..k]$ is the optimal supersequence for $P[1..i]$ over $S[1..N]$, then it is the rightmost supersequence for $P[1..i]$ on $S[1..k]$.*

Proof: $S[l..k]$ is the optimal supersequence for $T[i..j]$ over $S[1..k]$ then it has smaller deletion cost than all $S[l'..k]$ for $l' < l$ and no $S[l''..k]$ can be a supersequence for $l'' < l$. □

Algorithm 2 ComputeNewCopyCost(P, S)

FillArray$(Cost, \infty)$
FillArray$(LastOcc, \infty)$
$Cost[0] \leftarrow 0$
for $k \leftarrow 1$ **to** $|S|$
    for each $i \leftarrow |P|$ **downto** 2
        if $S[k] = P[i]$ **and** $LastOcc[i-1] < \infty$ **then**
            $LastOcc[i] \leftarrow LastOcc[i-1]$
            $DifDel \leftarrow DelCost(S[LastOcc[i]..k]) - DelCost(P[1..i])$
            $Cost[i] \leftarrow \min\{Cost[i], CopyCost(S[LastOcc[i]..k]) + DifDel\}$
    if $S[k] = P[1]$ **then**
        $LastOcc[1] \leftarrow k$
        $Cost[1] \leftarrow CopyCost(P[1])$

Fig. 4. ComputeNewCopyCost

Proposition 2 *ComputeNewCopyCost(P,S) (given in figure 4) determines correctly in Cost[i], the minimum generation cost of $P[1..i]$ by a NewCopy operation from a source S, for all $i \leq |P|$.*

Rather than giving a formal proof for proposition 2, we will explain how the pseudocode of figure 4 works. The tables *Cost* and *LastOcc* are initialized by ∞ (lines 1-2). The algorithm scans the source from left to right to find the optimal supersequence for each prefix of P. The algorithm uses the auxiliary table *LastOcc* for this aim.

After the k-th letter of S is processed (loop of line 4), the following is true: $LastOcc[i]$ is the largest $l \leq k$ such that $S[l..k]$ is a supersequence of $P[1..i]$ or ∞ if no such l exists. The loop on P (line 5) is processed with decreasing indices for memory optimization. Whenever the letter $S[k]$ occurs in i-th position in P and $LastOcc[i-1] < \infty$ which means $P[1..i-1]$ has a supersequence in $S[1..k-1]$ (line 6), then there is an opportunity of obtaining a better supersequence for $P[1..i]$. $LastOcc[i]$ takes the value of $LastOcc[i-1]$ (computed for $k-1$) since $S[LastOcc[i-1]..k]$ is now the rightmost supersequence for $P[1..i]$ (line 7). Its cost is compared to the best previous one; if better, the new cost is stored in $Cost[i]$ (lines 8-9). One should observe that the rightmost supersequences are updated only when a new common letter is scanned. This is necessary and sufficient as stated in the lemma 2. Note that the process of $i = 1$ is done separately (lines 10-12).

Generating the target string T from left to right, the rightmost added segment is a result of an insertion, NewCopy or NewRevCopy operation. The following algorithm determines the extended transformation distance of target T from source S by a dynamic programming algorithm. $C[k]$ is by definition the ex-

Algorithm 3 ExtendedTransformationDistance(S, T)

```
1.  C[0] ← 0
2.  for k ← 1 to |T| do
3.     C[k] ← ∞
4.     for i ← 1 to k do
5.        C[k] ← min{C[k], C[i − 1] + InsertCost(T[i..k]}
6.     P ← T[1..k]^{-1}
7.     ComputeNewCopyCost(P, S^{-1})
8.     for i ← 1 to k do
9.        C[k] ← min{C[k], C[i − 1] + Cost[k − i + 1]}
10.    ComputeNewRevCopyCost(P, S)
11.    for i ← 1 to k do
12.       C[k] ← min{C[k], C[i − 1] + Cost[k − i + 1]}
13.  return C[n]
```

Fig. 5. Extended Transformation Distance: a dynamic programming solution

tended transformation distance of target string $T[1..k]$ from source string S. The different possibilities for generation of the rightmost added segment of $T[1..k]$ are considered at lines 4-12. **ComputeNewRevCopyCost** is very similar to ComputeNewCopyCost. For a NewCopy operation, as P is the reverse of $T[1..k]$, we need to search in S^{-1} (and not in S) for optimal supersequences (line 7). The proof of correctness of Algorithm 3, can be done by induction very similar to the proof of proposition 1.

The complexity of ComputeNewCopyCost is $O(n^2)$ in time and $O(n)$ in space. So, the total complexity of determination of the extended transformation distance is $O(n^3)$ in time and $O(n)$ in space.

5 Biological Justification

In this section, we show by using biological sequences that the extended transformation distance can be more realistic distance than transformation distance on the real biological sequences. For this aim, the data we use consists of partial DNA sequences which participate in coding of RNA 16s. These sequences are known to be good phylogenetic markers, because they evolve very slowly in general. Here we consider only three sequences of the data which correspond to three species: *Trichoniscus pusillus*, *Haplaphtalmus mengei* and *Aselles aquaticus*. The two first are from the same family (Trichoniscoidea) while the third is from the *Aselidea* family. The first family is a terrestrial family and the last family is an aquatic family. Although one expects that the sequences of *T.pusillus* should be more similar to *H.mengei* than to *A.aquaticus*, the transformation distance is unable to capture this relative similarity. In the other terms, the transformation distance from *A.aquaticus* into *T.pusillus* is smaller than the transformation distance from *H.mengei* into *T.pusillus* for the different choices of parameters for MFL and cost functions (This is confirmed in [10]). The extended transformation distance solves this problem. The following table shows the corresponding transformation and extended transformation distances. The MFL is 9 in this example. This shows us that deletions make the model more robust on the real data.

Table 1. Transformation and extended transformation distance from *A.aquati* and *H.mengei* into *T.pusillus*

	Transformation Distance	Extended Transformation Distance
H.mengei	1322	516
A.aquaticus	1189	522

Remarks and Conclusion

In this paper, we presented a new improved algorithm for calculation of the transformation distance problem. This question is central in the study of genome evolution. We largely improve the running time complexity (from $O(n^4)$ to $O(n^2)$) thus allowing to treat much longer sequences (typically 10000 symbols instead of 100) in the same time, while using only linear space. We also gave an algorithm for the transformation distance problem in presence of the deletion operations which gives to the model its full generality. In this version, costs have been given a special additive form for clarity. In fact a number of variations are possible within our framework: the main property needed on costs seems to be their subadditivity in which case our algorithms are correct.

If the *DelCost* function is a constant function over different symbols, which means that the deletions of any two symbols have the same cost, the optimal super-sequence problem becomes the *shortest supersequence* problem. This problem called *Episode Matching* is studied in several papers [9, 4]. For our particular purpose, the complexity we obtained by Algorithm 2 is better than the one that could achieved by algorithms using the best known episode matching algorithms.

In this paper, we state that Algorithm 2 complexity is $O(n^2)$; this stands for the worst case complexity; in fact only a small proportion of pairs $(S[k], T[j])$ imply running the inner loop. Under certain additional statistical hypotheses the average complexity could be less than $O(n^2)$: in particular if the alphabet size is of the order of the string lengths, the average cost falls down to $O(n)$ for Algorithm 2 and thus $O(n^2)$ for Algorithm 3.

Different implementations of our algorithms can be considered. In Algorithm 2, if for each symbol in string P we store the last occurrence of this symbol in the string (for example by adding a pre-processing part), the loop of lines 5-6 can pass only on these symbols, which yields a better experimental complexity. In Algorithm 1, one can use (generalized) suffix trees for the purpose of substrings searching, but the theoretical complexity is not improved.

In some variants of the transformation distance problem the offsets (indices) of copied segments in one or both of the source and target strings participate in the computation of the operation cost. Our algorithm can be adapted easily to solve these variants as well, because the substring (and subsequence) existence testings are realized in the core of algorithm (and not in the preprocessing). So one can search the indices minimizing the cost function. In some cases for general cost functions an additional $O(n)$ time is necessary but the space complexity remains linear. We will not enter in the details here.

Different directions can be considered for the future works on this problem. Different evolutionary operation sets, Different cost functions and considering some limits on the number of times that a source segment can be copied are some of the interesting ones.

References

1. Behzadi B. and Steyaert J.-M.: An Improved Algorithm for Generalized Comparison of Minisatellites. Lecture Notes in Computer Science, Proceeding of CPM 2003.
2. Bérard, S. and Rivals, E.: Comparison of Minisatellites. Proceedings of the 6th Annual International Conference on Research in Computational Molecular Biology. ACM Press, 2002.
3. Cormen, T.H., Leiserson, C.E., Rivest R.L.: Introduction to Algorithms. MIT Press, 1990.
4. Das, G., Fleischer, R., Gasieniec L., Gunopolus, D., Kärkkäinen, J.: Episode Matching. Lecture notes in Computer Science, Proceeding of CPM 1997.

5. Doolittle, R.F.: Similar amino acid sequences: chance or common ancestry?, Science,214,149-159, 1981.
6. Morgenstern, B., Dress, A. and Warner, T.: Multiple DNA and protein sequence alignment based one segment-to-segment comparison. Proc. Natl. Acad. Sci.USA, 93, pp 12098-12103.
7. Sankoff, D. and Kruskal, J.B: Time Warps, String Edits and Macromolecules: The Theory and Practice of Sequence Comparison. Addison-Wesley, 1983.
8. Schöniger, M. and Waterman, M.S: A local algorithm for DNA sequence alignment with inversions. Bull. Math. Biol. 54, pp 521-536, 1992.
9. Troníček Z.: Searching Subsequences. PhD thesis, 2001.
10. Varré, J.S.: Concepts et algorithmes pour la comparaison de séquences génétiques: une approche informationnelle. PhD thesis, 2000.
11. Varré, J.S., Delahaye, J.P., Rivals, E.: Transformation Distances: a family of dissimilarity measures based on movements of segments. Bioinformatics, vol. 15, no. 3, pp 194-202, 1999.
12. Varré, J.S., Delahaye, J.P., Rivals, E.: The Transformation Distance : A Dissimilarity Measure Based On Movements Of Segments,German Conference on Bioinformatics, Koel - Germany, 1998.
13. Varré, J.S., Delahaye, J.P., Rivals, E.: The Transformation Distance. Genome Informatics Workshop, Tokyo, Japan, 1997.

On Classification of Strings

Eljas Soisalon-Soininen[1] and Tatu Ylönen[2]

[1] Department of Computer Science and Engineering
Helsinki University of Technology, P.O.Box 5400, FIN-02015 HUT, Finland
ess@cs.hut.fi
[2] SSH Communications Security
ylo@ssh.com

Abstract. In document filtering and content-based routing the aim is to transmit to the user only those documents that match the user's interests or profile. As filtering systems are deployed on the Internet, the number of users can become large. In this paper we focus on the question of how a large set of user profiles can be quickly searched in order to find those that are relevant to the document. In the abstract setting we assume that each profile is given as a regular expression, and, given a set of regular languages (the set of profiles), we want to determine for a given input string (the document) all those languages the input string belongs to. We analyze this problem, called the classification problem for a set of regular languages, and we show that in various important cases the problem can be solved by a small single deterministic finite automaton extended by conditional transitions.

1 Introduction

In document filtering and content-based routing (e.g. [3–5, 7, 9–11, 13, 15]) the aim is to transmit to the user only those documents that match the user's interests or profile. For XML documents the profiles are defined by the XPath language based on a restricted form of regular expressions. (XPath also contains irregular parts that require other analysis methods than those for regular languages.) XML routers in a network forward XML packets continuously from data producers to consumers. Each packet obtained by a router will be forwarded to a subset of its neighboring nodes in the network, and the forwarding decisions will be made according to the subscriptions of the clients given by XPath expressions. The number of the clients' subscriptions, and thus the set of XPath expressions to be evaluated can be large; therefore it is important that the evaluation is efficient and scalable.

Apart from XML routing, regular expressions are important in other routing environments (see [5]). For example, in the BGP4 Internet routing protocol [19] routers transmit to neighboring routers advertisements of how they could transmit packets to various IP addresses. The router that receives advertisements is allowed to define regular expressions with priorities on routing system sequences. The priority of an advertisement is obtained by matching it with the given set of regular expressions.

A. Apostolico and M. Melucci (Eds.): SPIRE 2004, LNCS 3246, pp. 321–330, 2004.

Finite automata are a natural and efficient way to represent and process XPath expressions (see e.g. [3, 10]). Deterministic finite automata (DFAs) are of course more efficient that the nondeterministic ones (NFAs), because in DFAs there is only one possible next state. In [10] it is reported that for a large number of XPath expressions (up to 1,000,000 in the tests of [10]), processing using DFAs was many orders of magnitude faster than using NFAs.

The difficulty in using DFAs is their size, which can be exponential in the size of the NFA or the regular expression. In other words, NFAs and regular expressions are exponentially more succinct representations of regular languages than DFAs. Formally, there exists an infinite sequence of regular languages $L_1, L_2, \ldots$, such that each L_n is described by a regular expression (or nondeterministic automaton) of size $O(n)$, but any DFA that accepts L_n must have size exponential in n [14, 18]. It should be noted that NFAs seem to be the most succinct representation, because NFAs are also exponentially more succinct than regular expressions [8], but any regular expression can easily be transformed into an NFA in linear time (e.g. [12]).

In the context of applying regular expressions to routing problems, the question is not only to check whether or not an input string belongs to a single language, but to report for a (possibly large) set of languages all those languages the given string belongs to. This problem, called the classification problem for a set of languages, is reminiscent to the lexical analysis of programming languages, where a single DFA is constructed that extract the lexical items from the program text (see e.g. [2, 17]). Solving the classification problem of n regular languages by constructing a single DFA can result in the number of states that is exponential in n, even though the total number of states in the DFAs that correspond to the n languages is $O(n)$ [10].

The problem of the exponential size of a single DFA constructed for a set of XPath expressions is addressed in [10] by using a "lazy" DFA; that is, the complete "eager" DFA is not constructed before processing a string, but the usual subset construction in determinizing a NFA is applied when needed. In [10] an NFA from each XPath expression is constructed, and at run time, the processing of the NFAs is simulated by constructing those parts of the DFA that are reachable by the given input string. In [10] it is also demonstrated that this lazy evaluation can be efficient in the sense that the number of generated states remains small. The lazy DFA approach is further optimized in [6]. However, in [16] it is demonstrated that even a lazy DFA can become large when processing complex XML documents.

Even though the lazy evaluation is often efficient, it is certainly of interest to try to avoid the construction of DFA states altogether during the analysis of the input string. In this paper we consider the question of how the classification problem for a set of regular languages can be solved by an eager DFA. We show that in many interesting cases related to XPath expressions, a solution based on a complete DFA can be made efficient, although the direct construction of the DFA leads to an exponential number of states. In our solution the underlying DFA is generalized by allowing conditional transitions.

2 Problem Statement

Given a set of n regular languages, we consider the classification problem, when for $i = 1, \ldots, n$ language i is defined by a regular expression E_i of the form

$$E_i = Y_{i_0} \Sigma^* Y_{i_1} \Sigma^* Y_{i_2} \cdots \Sigma^* Y_{i_{m_i}} \Sigma^* Y_{i_{m_i+1}},$$

where Σ denotes the whole alphabet and each Y_{i_j} is a set of strings formed by concatenation from individual letters in Σ. For $j = 1, \ldots, m$, we require that Y_{i_j} does not contain the empty string ϵ. For Y_{i_0} and $Y_{i_{m_i+1}}$ we require that each of them is either $\{\epsilon\}$ or does not contain ϵ.

For solving the classification problem, given an input string w in Σ^*, we have to determine all languages $L(E_1), \ldots, L(E_n)$ which x belongs to. Our goal is to automatically generate in time $O(|E_1| + \cdots + |E_n|)$ an algorithm that has time complexity $O(|w|)$, where $|E_i|$ denotes the size of expression E_i and $|w|$ denotes the length of w. In order to achieve this we need to place some restrictions on the sets Y_{i_j}, as will be defined in further sections.

We will first consider our classification problem in the case in which for $i = 1, \ldots, n$ language i is defined by a regular expression E_i of the form

$$E_i = x_{i_0} \Sigma^* a_{i_1} \Sigma^* a_{i_2} \cdots \Sigma^* a_{i_{m_i}} \Sigma^* x_{i_{m_i+1}},$$

where all a_{i_j} are pairwise different symbols in Σ and each of x_{i_0} and $x_{i_{m_i+1}}$ is either the empty string ϵ or a single symbol in Σ. Neither x_{i_0} nor $x_{i_{m_i+1}}$ is allowed to be equal to any a_{j_k}.

The above simple form of language description may cause an exponential size in a DFA that solves the classification problem. As an example, consider the following three XPath expressions ([10]):

```
$X1 IN $R//book//figure
$X2 IN $R//chapter//figure
$X3 IN $R//table//figure
```

If an XML stream is processed against this set of XPath expressions using a single DFA (as defined e.g. in [10]), then this DFA recognizes the three regular languages defined by the following regular expressions (`book`, `chapter`, `table`, and `figure` are denoted by a_1, a_2, a_3, and b, respectively):

$$\Sigma^* a_1 \Sigma^* b, \quad \Sigma^* a_2 \Sigma^* b, \quad \text{and} \quad \Sigma^* a_3 \Sigma^* b,$$

where Σ denotes an alphabet containing, among other symbols, a_1, a_2, a_3, and b. The states and part of the transitions of this DFA, denoted D_3, is given in Figure 1. In D_3 self-loops occur in all states except the final ones on all other symbols than shown. The loops and backward transitions from the final states are not shown. The DFA D_3 is obtained by the usual subset construction from the nondeterministic automata corresponding to the regular expressions, and it cannot be further minimized, because the final states all accept different subsets of the three languages. There is a separate final state for all distinct subsets

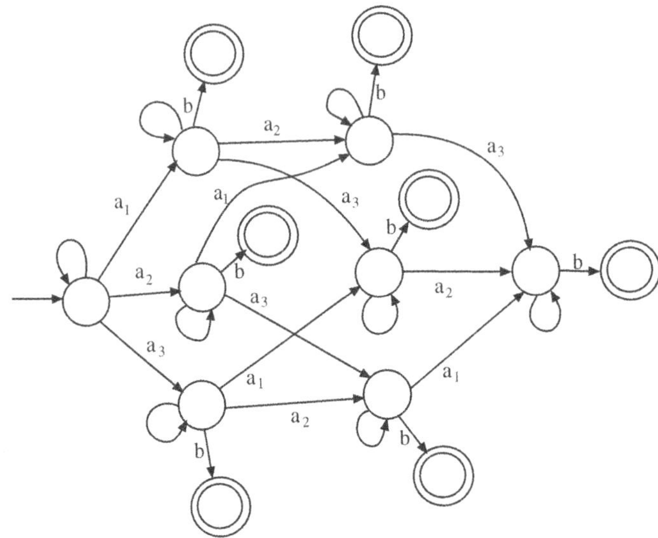

Fig. 1. Part of the transitions of the DFA that recognizes the languages $L(\Sigma^* a_1 \Sigma^* b), L(\Sigma^* a_2 \Sigma^* b)$, and $L(\Sigma^* a_3 \Sigma^* b)$. Transitions without an attached symbol are due for all other symbols than those that have a marked transition. The transitions from the final states are not shown.

of $\{a_1, a_2, a_3\}$. That is, in a final state the DFA must remember which of the symbols a_1, a_2, and a_3 it has seen. In general, the minimal DFA D_n that classifies the n languages $L(\Sigma^* a_1 \Sigma^* b), L(\Sigma^* a_2 \Sigma^* b), \ldots, L(\Sigma^* a_n \Sigma^* b)$, has $\Theta(2^n)$ states.

Based on this observation, it is clear that the classification of languages $L(E_1), \ldots, L(E_n)$, where E_i is a regular expression given as above, using a usual DFA is unfeasible, if n is large. Notice that the classification by final states means that no two final states that accept strings belonging to different subsets of $L(E_1), \ldots, L(E_n)$ cannot be combined as equivalent states. The exponential lower bound also holds, of course, if for all E_i the symbol after the last Σ^* is missing and $m_i > 1$.

It should be noted that the languages $L(\Sigma^* a_1 \Sigma^* b), \ldots, L(\Sigma^* a_n \Sigma^* b)$ can be classified by a small deterministic automaton, if we relax the requirement that classification is performed by final states only. We may fuse all states with input symbol a_i as a single state and all final states as a single state, and classify a string to belong to language $L(\Sigma^* a_i \Sigma^* b)$, if it has arrived at a final state and passed the unique state with input symbol a_i. In Figure 3, this DFA is shown for $n = 3$.

3 DFAs with Conditional Transitions

In the previous section we were able to find a small deterministic automaton that classifies strings to languages $L(\Sigma^* a_i \Sigma^* b)$. This was done simply by allowing the

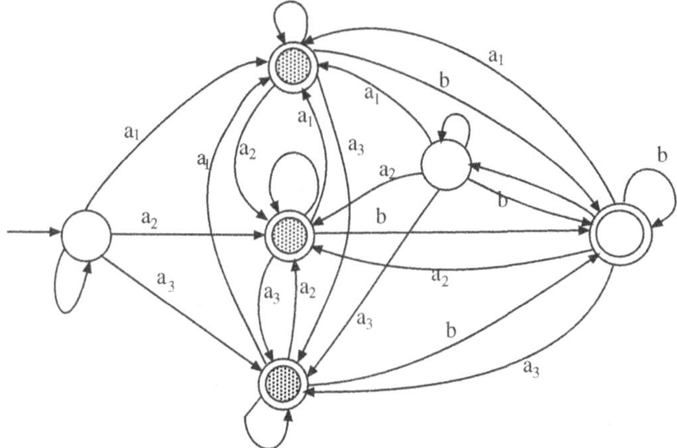

Fig. 2. DFA that can be used to classify the languages $L(\Sigma^* a_1 \Sigma^* b)$, $L(\Sigma^* a_2 \Sigma^* b)$, and $L(\Sigma^* a_3 \Sigma^* b)$. String w is in $L(\Sigma^* a_i \Sigma^* b)$ if it has passed a shaded final state with incoming edges labelled by a_i and the computation ends at the non-shaded final state. Edges with no attached label denote transitions on all other symbols than the explicitly given.

DFA to check whether or not a certain state has been visited after processing the input string. Such a test can be done efficiently by using, for example, a bit vector indexed by state number.

In the more general case when the expressions are of the form of our problem statement it is not enough to introduce such a classifying strategy.

Our solution is to introduce conditional transitions into DFAs such that the required conditions can be tested efficiently. A *DFA with conditional transitions*, denoted cDFA, has a set of states and a set transitions as usual DFAs, but a transition can be conditional such that it is allowed to be performed only when a certain condition is met. This condition is usually some simple property of the underlying cDFA.

Let $E_1, \ldots, E_n$ be regular expressions such that each E_i is of the form

$$E_i = x_{i_0} \Sigma^* a_{i_1} \Sigma^* a_{i_2} \cdots \Sigma^* a_{i_{m_i}} \Sigma^* x_{i_{m_i+1}}, \tag{1}$$

where Σ is the set of all those symbols that appear in some E_i, all symbols a_{i_j} are pairwise different, and x_{i_0} and $x_{i_{m_i+1}}$ both are either ϵ or a single symbol different from any a_{i_j}.

We consider the classification problem for $L(E_1), \ldots, L(E_n)$. In other words, given an input string w in Σ^*, we have to determine all languages $L(E_1), \ldots, L(E_n)$ which w belongs to. We construct a DFA with conditional transitions, denoted M_c, as follows. For simplicity, we assume here that each E_i is of the form $\Sigma^* a_{i_1} \Sigma^* a_{i_2} \cdots \Sigma^* a_{i_{m_i}} \Sigma^*$.

(i) There is a unique initial state, denoted q_0, in M_c.

(ii) The set Q of states of M_c is

$$\{q_0, q_{1_1}, \ldots, q_{1_{m_1}}, q_{2_1}, \ldots, q_{2_{m_2}}, \ldots, q_{n_1}, \ldots, q_{n_{m_n}}\}.$$

(iii) *Case 1.* Let q be any state in Q that is not the initial state q_0. There is a transition $qa_{i_j} \to q_{i_j}$ for all combinations of i and j, but these transitions are conditional in the following way. For $j > 1$, transition $qa_{i_j} \to q_{i_j}$ is to be performed, if in processing the current input string state $q_{i_{j-1}}$ has already been visited but state q_{i_j} has not been visited yet. For $j = 1$, transition $qa_{i_j} \to q_{i_j}$ is to be performed, if in processing the current input string state q_{i_j} has not been visited yet. *Case 2.* If at state q no transition as defined in Case 1 applies for the next input symbol a, then transition $qa \to q$ is applied.

(iv) For the initial state q_0 there are transitions $q_0a_{i_1} \to q_{i_1}$ for all $i = 1, \ldots n$, and transitions $q_0a \to q_0$ for all other input symbols a in Σ.

(v) M_c contains *classification* states, which are used in the following way. Assume that input string w has been fed to M_c and the process has ended after consuming the whole string. If q is a classifying state and it has been visited during the process of w, then M_c *classifies* w into the language containing all strings in Σ^* that pass q when feeding them to M_c. The states

$$q_{i_{m_i}},$$

for $i = 1, \ldots, n$, are chosen as classifying states in M_c.

Observe that by (iii) and (iv) M_c is deterministic, that is, there is always exactly one next state, because $a_{i_j} \neq a_{l_k}$ always when $i \neq l$ or $j \neq k$. Notice that the size of M_c would be $|Q|^2$, if the conditional transitions were explicitly stored. But it is not necessary to store the transitions, because they can be directly concluded from the current state and input symbol.

Example. Consider the regular expressions $E_1 = \Sigma^* a_{1_1} \Sigma^* a_{1_2} \Sigma^*$ and $E_2 = \Sigma^* a_{2_1} \Sigma^* a_{2_2} \Sigma^*$, and the classification problem for the languages $L(E_1)$ and $L(E_2)$. The corresponding cDFA has the set of states $\{q_0, q_{1_1}, q_{1_2}, q_{2_1}, q_{2_2}\}$. The transitions from the initial state q_0 are $q_0a_{1_1} \to q_{1_1}$, $q_0a_{2_1} \to q_{2_1}$, $q_0a_{1_2} \to q_0$, and $q_0a_{2_2} \to q_0$. The conditional transitions are $q_{1_1}a_{1_1} \to q_{1_1}$, $q_{1_1}a_{2_1} \to q_{2_1}$, $q_{1_1}a_{2_1} \to q_{1_1}$, $q_{1_1}a_{1_2} \to q_{1_2}$, $q_{1_1}a_{1_2} \to q_{1_1}$, $q_{1_1}a_{2_2} \to q_{2_2}$, $q_{1_1}a_{2_2} \to q_{1_1}$, $q_{2_1}a_{1_1} \to q_{1_1}$, $q_{2_1}a_{1_1} \to q_{2_1}$, $q_{2_1}a_{1_2} \to q_{1_2}$, $q_{2_1}a_{1_2} \to q_{2_1}$, $q_{2_1}a_{2_1} \to q_{2_1}$, $q_{2_1}a_{2_2} \to q_{2_2}$, $q_{2_1}a_{2_2} \to q_{2_1}$, $q_{1_2}a_{1_1} \to q_{1_1}$, $q_{1_2}a_{1_1} \to q_{1_2}$, $q_{1_2}a_{1_2} \to q_{1_2}$, $q_{1_2}a_{2_1} \to q_{2_1}$, $q_{1_2}a_{2_1} \to q_{1_2}$, $q_{1_2}a_{2_2} \to q_{2_2}$, $q_{1_2}a_{2_2} \to q_{1_2}$, $q_{2_2}a_{1_1} \to q_{1_1}$, $q_{2_2}a_{1_1} \to q_{2_2}$, $q_{2_2}a_{1_2} \to q_{1_2}$, $q_{2_2}a_{1_2} \to q_{2_2}$, $q_{2_2}a_{2_1} \to q_{2_1}$, $q_{2_2}a_{2_1} \to q_{2_2}$, $q_{2_2}a_{2_2} \to q_{2_2}$.

Recall that the conditional transitions need not be stored, because the possible transitions are always implied by the state and input symbol. The unique applicable transition is implied by the passed states, as explained in rule (iii) of the construction of M_c.

An example computation: $q_0a_{1_1}a_{1_1}a_{2_2}a_{2_2}a_{1_2}a_{2_1} \Rightarrow q_{1_1}a_{1_1}a_{2_2}a_{2_2}a_{1_2}a_{2_1}$ $\Rightarrow q_{1_1}a_{2_2}a_{2_2}a_{1_2}a_{2_1} \Rightarrow q_{1_1}a_{2_2}a_{1_2}a_{2_1} \Rightarrow q_{1_1}a_{1_2}a_{2_1} \Rightarrow q_{1_2}a_{2_1} \Rightarrow q_{2_1}$.

In this computation the state q_{1_2} is visited, and thus $a_{1_1}a_{1_1}a_{2_2}a_{2_2}a_{1_2}a_{2_1}$ is classified to belong to the language $L(\Sigma^* a_{1_1} \Sigma^* a_{1_2} \Sigma^*)$.

Let w be a string in language $L(E_i) = \Sigma^* a_{i_1} \cdots \Sigma^* a_{i_{m_i}} \Sigma^*$. Then w is of the form $w_1 a_{i_1} w_2 a_{i_2} ... w_{m_i} a_{i_{m_i+1}} w_{m_i+1}$, where w_i is in Σ^*. It is seen by a simple induction that this string is classified by M_c to the language containing those strings that pass the classification state $q_{i_{m_i}}$. On the other hand, any string classified by $q_{i_{m_i}}$ must be of the form $w_1 a_{i_1} w_2 a_{i_2} ... w_{m_i} a_{i_{m_i+1}} w_{m_i+1}$, where w_i is in Σ^*. Thus, the languages classified by $q_{i_{m_i}}$ are exactly the languages $L(E_i) = \Sigma^* a_{i_1} \cdots \Sigma^* a_{i_{m_i}} \Sigma^*$, for $i = 1, \ldots, n$.

If expression E_i has a leading symbol a_{i_0}, then the above construction must be changed such that there is a state q_{i_0} with input symbol a_{i_0} between the initial state and state q_{i_1}. If E_i has a last symbol $a_{i_{m_i+1}}$, then a *final* state $q_{i_{m_i+1}}$ must be introduced to M_c. Classification must also be changed to: string w is classified to language $L(E_i)$ if and only if string w passes classifying state $q_{i_{m_i}}$ and ends at the final state $q_{i_{m_i+1}}$.

We have:

Theorem 1. Let M_c be a cDFA constructed from regular expressions $E_1, \ldots, E_n$ of the form (1). Then M_c is constructed in time $O(|E_1| + \ldots + |E_n|)$, and M_c classifies all strings in Σ^* into languages with respect to $L(E_1), \ldots, L(E_n)$. The time complexity of classifying string w into all languages it belongs to is $O(|w|)$.

4 Classification of Strings for an Ordered Set of Patterns

In the previous section we considered the classification problem for a rather restricted class of regular languages. In this section we extend the result to the case in which the expressions can have a much more general form.

Let $E_1, \ldots, E_n$ be regular expressions defined on alphabet Σ such that each E_i is of the form:

$$Y_{i0} \Sigma^* Y_{i_1} \Sigma^* Y_{i_2} \cdots \Sigma^* Y_{i_{m_i}} \Sigma^* Y_{i_{m_i+1}}, \tag{2}$$

where each Y_{i_j} is a non-empty set of strings in Σ^*. For $j = 1, \ldots, m$, we require that Y_{i_j} does not contain the empty string ϵ. For Y_{i0} and $Y_{i_{m_i+1}}$ we require that they are either $\{\epsilon\}$ or do not contain ϵ.

In solving this classification problem efficiently, we apply the construction of the previous section, and the construction of Aho and Corasick [1] for recognizing regular languages defined by regular expressions of the form

$$\Sigma^* Y \Sigma^*,$$

where Y is a set of strings not containing the empty string. The method of [1] constructs a DFA in linear time from the expression. Given a set of n regular expressions $E_1, \ldots, E_n$ such that each E_i is of the form (2), we apply the construction of [1] to the expression

$$\Sigma^*(Y'_{10} \#_{10} \cup Y_{1_1} \#_{1_1} \cup \ldots \cup Y_{1_{m_1}} \#_{1_{m_1}} \cup Y'_{1_{m_1+1}} \#_{1_{m_1+1}} \cup \ldots \tag{3}$$

$$\cup Y'_{n0} \#_{n0} \cup Y_{n_1} \#_{n_1} \cup \ldots \cup Y_{n_{m_n}} \#_{n_{m_n}} \cup Y'_{n_{m_n+1}} \#_{n_{m_n+1}}) \Sigma^*,$$

where all $\#_{i_j}$ are new symbols and Y'_{i0} (resp. $Y'_{i_{m_i+1}}$) is the empty set, if $Y_{i0} = \{\epsilon\}$ (resp. $Y_{i_{m_i+1}} = \{\epsilon\}$), and otherwise Y_{i0} (resp. $Y_{i_{m_i+1}}$).

That is, we construct a deterministic automaton, denoted M_a, that recognizes the language defined by this expression. This automaton is used as follows: An input string in Σ^* not containing any symbol $\#_{i_j}$ is fed to the automaton, and whenever a state is reached from which there are transitions by symbols $\#_{i_j}$, all these symbols will be output (in any order). The output sequence obtained for an input string w in Σ^* is then used as an input string for a cDFA constructed from the expressions $E'_1, \ldots, E'_n$, where E'_i is

$$E'_i = y_{i0} \Sigma^* \#_{i_1} \Sigma^* \#_{i_2} \cdots \Sigma^* \#_{i_m} \Sigma^* y_{i_m+1}.$$

Here y_{i_0} (resp. y_{i_m+1}) is ϵ, if Y'_{i_0} (resp. Y'_{i_m+1}) is the empty set, and otherwise $\#_{i_0}$.

This cDFA performs the final classification. The construction works correctly, if and only if no non-empty suffix of a string in Y_{i_j} is a non-empty prefix of $Y_{i_{j+1}}$, for $j = 0, \ldots m_i + 1$.

We have:

Theorem 2. Let $E_1, \ldots, E_n$ be regular expressions of the form (2) such that for all E_i no non-empty suffix of a string in Y_{i_j} is a non-empty prefix of a string in $Y_{i_{j+1}}$. Moreover, assume that for no string w in $L(E_1) \cup \ldots \cup L(E_n)$ the deterministic automaton M_a constructed from the expression (3) does not output more than $c|w|$ symbols, where c is a constant. Then it is possible to construct in time $O(|E_1| + \cdots + |E_n|)$ a deterministic program that solves the classification problem in linear time. That is, for all w in Σ^* this program classifies w in time $O(|w|)$ with respect to the languages $L(E_1), \ldots, L(E_n)$.

5 Conclusions

Content-based classification is based on the information in the document itself and not on the information in the headers of the packets to be routed. Users' interests and subscriptions are typically given by regular expressions based on structure defining elements in the documents. The number of such expressions can become very large, and the classification problem cannot be solved by simply constructing by standard methods a single deterministic automaton, which decides for input strings all matching expressions. One possibility is to resort to using nondeterministic machines, but then for all input at least $O(nk)$ time is needed, where n is number expressions and k denotes the length of the input string.

In this paper, we defined a new class of regular expressions with the property that for sets of expressions in this class a deterministic program can be constructed in linear time, such that the program classifies input strings in linear time with respect to the expressions.

In further work we plan to define more new classes of regular expressions for which the classification problem can be solved efficiently. Specifically, it seems that some of the restrictions we now placed on the expressions can be considerably relaxed.

References

1. A.V.Aho and M.J.Corasick. Efficient string matching: An aid to bibliographic search. *Communications of the ACM* **18**:6 (1975), 333–340.
2. A.V.Aho, R.Sethi, and J.D.Ullman. *Compilers: Principles, Techniques, and Tools.* Addison-Wesley, Reading, Mass., 1986.
3. M.Altinel and M.J.Franklin. Efficient filtering of XML documents for selective dissemination of information. In: *Proceedings of the VLDB*, Cairo, Egypt, 2000, pp. 53–64.
4. C.-Y.Chan, P.Felber, M.Garofalakis, and R.Rastogi. Efficient filtering of XML documents with XPath expressions. In: *Proc. of the 18th International Conference on Data Engineering*, San Jose, California, February 2002. IEEE Computer Society, 2002, pp. 235–244.
5. C.-Y.Chan, M.Garofalakis, and R.Rastogi. RE-tree: An efficient index structure for regular expressions. In: *Proceedings of the 28th VLDB Conference*, Hong Kong, China, 2002.
6. D.Chen and R.K.Wong. Optimizing the lazy DFA approach for XML stream processing. In: *The Fifteenth Australasian Database Conference (ADC2004)*, Dunedin, New Zealand. Australian Computer Society, Inc., 2004.
7. Y.Diao, M.Altinel, P.Fischer, M.J.Franklin, and R.To. Path sharing and predicate evaluation for high-performance XML filtering. *ACM Trans. Database Systems* **28**:4 (2003), 467–516.
8. A.Ehrenfeucht and P.Zeiger. Complexity measures for regular languages. *J. Comput. Syst. Sci.* **12** (1976), 134–146.
9. M.Fisk and G.Varghese. An analysis of fast string matching applied to content-based forwarding and intrusion detection. Technical Report CS2001-0670 (updated version), University of California, San Diego, 2002.
10. T.J.Green, G.Miklau, M.Onizuka, and D.Suciu. Processing XML streams with deterministic automata. In: *Proceedings of the 9th International Conference on Database Theory*, Siena, Italy, January 2003. Lecture Notes in Computer Science 2572, Springer-Verlag, 2002, pp. 173–189.
11. P.Gupta and N.McKeown. Packet classification on multiple fields. In: *Proceedings of the ACM SIGCOMM Conference on Applications, Technologies, Architectures, and Protocol for Computer Communication.* ACM Press, 1999, pp. 147–160.
12. J.E.Hopcroft and J.D.Ullman. *Introduction to Automata Theory, Languages, and Computation.* Addison-Wesley, Reading, Mass., 1979.
13. T.V.Lakshman and D.Stiliadis. High-speed policy-based packet forwarding using efficient multi-dimensional range-matching. In: *Proceedings of ACM SIGCOMM Conference on Applications, Technolgies, Architectures, and Protoccols for Computer Communication.* ACM Press, 1998, pp. 203–214.
14. A.R.Meyer and M.J.Fischer. Economy of description by automata, grammars and formal systems. In: Proceedings of 12th Annual IEEE Symposium on Switching and Automata Theory, October 1972, IEEE Computer Society, New York, 1971, pp. 188–190.
15. B.Nguyen, S.Abiteboul, G.Cobena, and M.Preda. Monitoring XML data on the web. In: *Proceedings of the ACM SIGMOD Conference on Management of Data*, Santa Barbara, California, 2001. ACM Press, New York, 2001, pp. 437–448.
16. M.Onizuka. Light-weight XPath processing of XML stream with deterministic automata. In: *Proceedings of the 2003 CIKM International Conference on Information and Knowledge Management*, New Orleans, Louisiana, USA, November 3–8, 2003. ACM Press, New York, 2003.

17. S.Sippu and E.Soisalon-Soininen. *Parsing Theory. Vol I: Languages and Parsing.* Springer-Verlag, Berlin, 1988.
18. R.E.Stearns and H.B.Hunt. On the equivalence and containment problems for unambiguous regular expressions, grammars, and automata. In: *Proceedings of the 22nd Annual Symposium on Foundations of Computer Science*, October 1981. IEEE Computer Society, New York, 1981, pp. 74–81.
19. J.W.Stewart. *BGP4, Inter-Domain Routing in the Internet.* Addison-Wesley, Reading, Mass., 1998.

Author Index